ASSESSMENT IN
SPECIAL AND
REMEDIAL EDUCATION

ASSESSMENT

11, 15, 17

ASSESSMENT IN SPECIAL AND REMEDIAL EDUCATION

John Salvia
The Pennsylvania State University

James E. Ysseldyke
The University of Minnesota

HOUGHTON MIFFLIN COMPANY   BOSTON
Dallas   Geneva, Illinois   Hopewell, New Jersey   Palo Alto   London

TO: Jane and Faye
   Mary Kate, Amy, and Heather

Quotations from *Standards for Educational and Psychological Tests,* by the American Psychological Association, the American Educational Research Association, and the National Council on Measurement in Education, are copyright 1974 by the American Psychological Association. Reprinted by permission.

PRINTED IN THE U.S.A.

Library of Congress Catalog Card Number: 77-72891

ISBN: 0-395-25073-0

Contents

Preface

Children have the right to an appropriate education in the least restrictive educational environment. Decisions regarding the most appropriate environment and the most appropriate program for an individual should be data-based decisions. Assessment is one part of the process of collecting the data necessary for educational decision making, and the administration of tests is one part of assessment. To date, unfortunately, tests have sometimes been used to restrict educational opportunities; many assessment practices have not been in the best interests of students. Those who assess have a tremendous responsibility; assessment results are used to make decisions that directly and significantly affect students' lives. Those who assess are responsible for knowing the devices they use and for understanding the limitations of those devices and of the procedures they call for.

Teachers are confronted with the results of tests, checklists, scales, and batteries on an almost daily basis. This information is intended to be useful to them in understanding and making educational plans for the students they are working with. But the intended use and actual use of assessment information have often differed. However good the intentions of those who design tests, misuse and misunderstanding of tests may well occur unless teachers are informed consumers and users of tests. To be an informed consumer and user of tests, a teacher must bring to the task certain domains of knowledge, including a knowledge of the basic uses of tests, the important attributes of good tests, and the kinds of behaviors sampled by particular tests. This text aims at helping teachers to acquire that knowledge.

Assessment in Special and Remedial Education is intended as a first course in assessment for those whose careers require understanding and informed use of assessment data. The primary audience is those who are or will be teachers in special and remedial education at the primary or secondary level. The secondary audience is the large support system for students in special and remedial education: child development specialists, counselors, educational administrators, nurses, preschool educators, reading specialists, school psychologists, social workers, speech and language specialists, and specialists in therapeutic recreation. Writing for those who are taking their first course in assessment, we have assumed no prior knowledge of measurement and statistical concepts.

The text, in four parts, is an introduction to psychoeducational assessment in special and remedial education. Parts 1 and 2 provide a general overview of and orientation to assessment. Part 1 places testing in the broader context of assessment, describes assessment as a multifaceted process, delineates the fundamental purposes for assessment and the assumptions underlying it, and introduces basic terminology and concepts. Part 2 provides descriptions and examples of the basic measurement concepts and principles necessary for adequate understanding and use of test information.

Part 3 provides detailed discussions of assessment of achievement, intelligence, perceptual-motor skills, sensory functioning, language, personality and adaptive behavior, and readiness. Chapters 10 and 11 are detailed discussions of diagnostic testing in reading and mathematics. Chapter 12 differs from others in Part 3; it is a theoretical overview of the assessment of intelligence. With the exception of Chapter 12, each chapter in Part 3 follows a similar format. Initially, the kinds of behaviors generally sampled by tests within each domain are described. Representative tests are then reviewed. For each test, we describe its general format, the kinds of behaviors it samples, the kinds of scores it provides, the nature of the sample on whom it was standardized, and evidence for its reliability and validity. The technical adequacy of the tests is evaluated in light of the principles set forth in Part 2.

Part 4 is integrative and deals with the application of assessment practices in special and remedial education. Chapter 20 provides detailed examples of how assessment information of various kinds and from various sources should be integrated and interpreted. Chapters 21 and 22 describe ethical and legal principles involved in the collection, maintenance, and dissemination of assessment information. Chapter 23 could be considered both the first and last chapter of the book. It describes the state of the art in assessment—the extent to which the right tests are used for the right purposes, the extent to which fundamental assumptions are met in practice, and the extent to which currently used tests have the necessary technical adequacy to be used in making important educational decisions.

Throughout the text additional readings, problems, and study questions are provided to help readers expand and apply the fundamental concepts developed. Statistical and locating appendixes facilitate use of the text as a basic reference in assessment.

Assessment is a controversial topic; we have attempted to be objective and even-handed in our review and portrayal of current assessment practices.

Many people have been of assistance in our efforts. We wish to express our sincere appreciation to the following individuals who have provided constructive criticism and helpful suggestions during the development of this text: Bob Algozzine; Darwin Chapman; Gary M. Clark of the University of Kansas at Lawrence; Richard LeVan; Joe Muia; T. Ernest Newland;

Tom Oakland of the University of Texas at Austin; Dan Reschley of Iowa State University; Marjorie Ward; James Wardrop of the University of Illinois, Urbana–Champaign; Richard Weinberg; and Art Willans of the University of Wisconsin at Milwaukee. We especially appreciate the contribution of Tom Frank in writing the section describing the assessment of auditory acuity in Chapter 16. We thank Diane Bloom and Eleanore Miekam for their cheerful, rapid, and accurate assistance in the typing of the manuscript.

We thank the numerous publishers and authors who granted permission to reproduce material from their original sources. In particular, we are grateful to the Literary Executor of the late Sir Ronald A. Fisher, F.R.S., to Dr. Frank Yates, F.R.S., and to Longman Group Ltd., London, for permission to reprint the tables of Appendixes 1–3 from their book *Statistical Tables for Biological, Agricultural and Medical Research* (6th edition, 1974).

This text represents a collaborative effort of the authors in the best sense. We have contributed equally in the writing of the text, challenged one another's ideas, picked at each other's prose, and in this way produced what we believe is an integrated text that speaks for both of us.

J.S. J.Y.

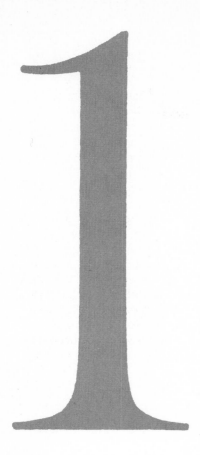

Part 1

Assessment: An Overview

Assessment data are used on a routine basis to make educational decisions about students. Part 1 describes assessment and is designed to provide an overview of assessment and its role in educational settings.

Chapter 1 is a description of assessment as an integral component in the educational enterprise and a delineation of the kinds of data used in making decisions. Chapter 2 describes the kinds of decisions that assessment data can indicate and discusses the basic assumptions underlying assessment. Chapter 3 presents basic considerations in the selection and administration of tests. The concepts and principles that are introduced throughout Part 1 constitute a foundation for informed and critical use of tests and of the information they provide.

Chapter 1
The Assessment of Children

All of us have taken tests during our lives. In elementary and secondary school, tests were administered to measure our scholastic aptitude or intelligence or to evaluate the extent to which we had profited from instruction. We may have taken personality tests, interest tests, or tests that would assist us in vocational selection and planning. As part of applying for a job, we may have taken civil service examinations or tests of specific skills like typing or manual dexterity. Enlisting in the Armed Forces meant taking a number of tests. Enrolling in college meant undergoing entrance examinations. Those of us who decided to go on to graduate school usually had to take an aptitude test; many of those who became teachers had to take a national teacher examination. Physicians, lawyers, psychologists, real estate agents, and many others were required to take tests to demonstrate their competence before being licensed to practice their profession or trade.

Throughout their professional careers, teachers, guidance counselors, school social workers, school psychologists, and school administrators will be required to give, score, and interpret a wide variety of tests. Because professional school personnel routinely receive test information from their colleagues within the schools and from a variety of community agencies outside the schools, they need a working knowledge of important facets of testing.

According to the joint committee of the American Psychological Association (APA), the American Educational Research Association (AERA), and the National Council on Measurement in Education (NCME), a test "may be thought of as a set of tasks or questions intended to elicit particular types of behaviors when presented under standardized conditions and to yield scores that have desirable psychometric properties . . ." (1974, p. 2). *Testing*, then, means exposing a person to a particular set of questions in order to obtain a score. That score is the end product of testing.

Testing may be part of a larger process known as *assessment*; however, testing and assessment are not synonymous. Assessment in educational settings is a multifaceted process that involves far more than the administration of a test. When we assess students, we consider the way they perform a variety of tasks in a variety of settings or contexts, the meaning of their performances in terms of the total functioning of the individual, and likely explanations for those performances. Good assessment procedures take into consideration the fact that anyone's performance on any task is influenced not only by the demands of the task itself but also by the history and characteristics the individual brings to the task and by factors inherent in the setting in which the assessment is carried out. Assessment is the process of understanding the performance of students *in their current ecology*. In fact, much assessment takes place apart from formal testing activity; parents' and teachers' observations may be considered part of assessment. Assessment is always an evaluative, interpretative appraisal of performance. Its goal is simple in one sense, tremendously difficult in another. Briefly, it provides information that can enable teachers and other school personnel to make decisions regarding the children they serve. Yet if the information it offers is misused or misinterpreted, these decisions can adversely affect children and limit their life opportunities.

FACTORS CONSIDERED IN ASSESSMENT

CURRENT LIFE CIRCUMSTANCES

An individual's performance on any task must be understood in light of that individual's current circumstances. We must understand current circumstances to be aware of what a person brings to a task.

In educational assessment, health is a significant current life circumstance. Health and nutritional status can play an important role in children's performances on a wide variety of tasks. Sick or malnourished children are apt to be lethargic, inattentive, perhaps irritable.

Children's attitudes and values also should contribute to our evaluation of their performance. Willingness to cooperate with a relatively unfamiliar adult, willingness to give substantial effort to tasks, and belief in the worth of the task or of schooling have their influence on performance.

Finally, the level of acculturation children bring to a task is of utmost importance. A child's knowledge and acceptance of societally sanctioned mores and values, use of standard English, and fund of general and specific cultural information all influence performance on school-related tasks.

DEVELOPMENTAL HISTORY

A person's current life circumstances are shaped by the events that make up his or her history of development. Deleterious events in particular may have profound effects on physical and psychological development. Physical and sensory limitations may systematically restrict a child's opportunity to acquire various skills and abilities. A history of poor health or poor nutrition may result in missed opportunities to acquire various skills and abilities. A child's history of reinforcement and punishment shapes what a child will achieve and how that child will react to others. In short, it is not enough to assess a child's current level of performance; diagnosticians must also understand what has shaped that current performance.

EXTRAPERSONAL FACTORS

In addition to the skills, characteristics, and abilities a pupil brings to any task, other factors affect the assessment process. How another person interprets or reacts to various behaviors or characteristics can even determine whether an individual will be assessed. For example, some teachers do not understand that a certain amount of physical aggression is typical of young children or that verbal aggression is typical of older students. Such teachers may refer "normally" aggressive children for assessment because they have interpreted aggression as a symptom of some pathology.

The theoretical orientation of the diagnostician (the person responsible for performing the assessment) also plays an important part in the assessment process. Diagnosticians' backgrounds and training may predispose them to look for certain types of pathologies. Just as Freudians may look for unresolved conflicts while behaviorists may look for antecedents and consequences of particular behaviors, diagnosticians may let their theoretical orientation influence their interpretation of particular information.

Finally, the conditions under which a child is observed or the conditions under which particular behaviors are elicited can influence that child's performance. For example, the level of language used in a question or the presence of competing stimuli in the immediate environment can affect a child's responses.

INTERPRETATION OF PERFORMANCE

After an individual's behavior and characteristics have been considered in light of current life circumstances, developmental history, and extrapersonal factors that may influence performance, the information is summarized. This often results in classification and labeling of the individual being assessed. The assessor arrives at the judgment that when all things are considered, the child "fits" a particular category. For example, a child may be judged mentally retarded, emotionally disturbed, learning disabled, educationally handicapped, culturally or socially disadvantaged, backward, normal, gifted, or a member of the Red Birds reading group.

Assessors, especially when they have assigned negative labels, often attempt to impute a cause for an individual's status. Classification according to cause (*etiology*) is common in medicine but less common in education and psychology. In some cases the cause of the condition is highly probable. For example, Kevin may be developing quite normally until he sustains a severe head injury, after which his performance and development are measurably retarded. However, in most instances, the causes are elusive and speculative.

PROGNOSIS

All assessments and classifications of children contain an explicit or implicit *prognosis*, a prediction of future performance. A prognosis may be offered for children both in their current environment and life circumstances and in some therapeutic, ameliorative, or remedial environment. For example: "If Rachel is left in her current educational placement, she can be expected to fall further and further behind the other children and to develop problem behaviors. If she is placed in an environment where she will receive more individual attention, she should make more progress academically and socially." Such prognoses are made, it is hoped, on the basis of empirical research rather than speculation.

KINDS OF ASSESSMENT INFORMATION

Although this book is concerned primarily with tests and testing, it is well to remember that a test is only one of several assessment techniques or procedures available to a diagnostician for gathering information. Figure 1.1 shows that there are six general classes of diagnostic-information sources; the classification shown in the figure depends on the time at which the information is collected (current or historical) and how the information is collected (from observation, tests, or judgments).

CURRENT VS. HISTORICAL INFORMATION

Diagnostic information can be categorized according to the currentness of the information: information that describes how a person is functioning now and information that describes how that person has functioned in the past. Obviously, the demarcation between current and historical information blurs, and the point at which current information becomes historical information depends in part on the particular fact or bit of information. For example, if Johnny had his appendix removed *three years ago*, we know he currently has no appendix. On the other hand, if 9-year-old Jane weighed fifty-six pounds *three years ago*, we could not conclude that she weighs the same today.

TIME AT WHICH INFORMATION IS GATHERED

		Current	Historical
TYPE OF INFORMATION	Observations	Frequency counts of occurrence of a particular behavior Antecedents of behavior Critical incidents	Birth weight Anecdotal records Observations by last year's teacher
	Tests	Results of an intelligence test administered during the assessment Results of this week's spelling test given by the teacher	Results of a standardized achievement-test battery given at the end of last year
	Judgments	Parents' evaluations of how well the child gets along in family, neighborhood, etc. Rating scales completed by teachers, social workers, etc. Teacher's reason for referral	Previous medical, psychological, or educational diagnoses Previous report cards Parents' recall of developmental history, of undiagnosed childhood illnesses, etc.

Figure **1.1**   Sources of diagnostic information, classified according to type of information and time at which the information is collected

There are several advantages in having and using current information. The first is the most obvious. Current information describes a person's current behavior and characteristics. It offers two more subtle advantages as well: (1) the diagnostician can select the information to be collected, and (2) the information can be verified. However, current information alone cannot provide a complete picture of a person's present level of functioning, because it does not consider the antecedents of this functioning. This is the advantage of historical information. School diagnosticians cannot go back in time to observe previous characteristics, behaviors, and situations. A diagnostician who wishes to incorporate a student's history into the assessment procedure must rely on previously collected information or the memory of individuals who knew the student.

Historical information has four limitations of which diagnosticians must be aware. First, a diagnostician cannot control what information was collected in the past; crucial bits of information may never have been collected. Second, past information is difficult and sometimes impossible to verify. Third, the conditions under which the information was collected are often difficult to evaluate. Fourth, remembered observations may not be as reliable as current observations.

TYPES OF INFORMATION

Diagnostic information can also be categorized according to the type of information: observations, tests, and judgments. Each of the three types of information has advantages as well as disadvantages. Each type can be collected by a diagnostician (in which case the data become *direct information*) or by another person (*indirect information*). Diagnosticians do not have the time, competence, or opportunity to collect all possible types of information. In cases where specialized information is needed, they must rely on the observations, tests, and judgments of others. If a behavior occurs infrequently or is demonstrated only outside of school, the diagnostician may have to rely on the observations and judgments of others who have more opportunity to collect the information — parents, perhaps, or ward attendants in institutional settings. For example, bed wetting does not occur at school, but few diagnosticians would question the accuracy of parents' reports of enuresis. Moreover, if a child is an intermittent bed wetter, a diagnostician might have to spend several nights at the child's home in order to observe the behavior directly. In such cases indirect information is usually adequate.

Observations can provide highly accurate, detailed, verifiable information not only about the person being assessed but also about the contexts in which the observations are being made. There are two types of observation: systematic and nonsystematic. In *nonsystematic observation*, the observer simply watches an individual in his or her environment and takes note of the behaviors, characteristics, and personal interactions that seem of significance. Nonsystematic observation tends to be anecdotal and subjective. In *systematic observation*, the observer sets out to observe one or more behaviors. The observer specifies or defines the behaviors to be observed and then typically counts or otherwise measures the frequency, duration, magnitude, or latency of the behaviors. The major disadvantage of systematic observation is that it may allow other important behaviors and characteristics to be ignored.

There are two major difficulties in collecting systematic and nonsystematic observational data. The first is that observation is very time-consuming; a diagnostician pays for the highly accurate, specific information that observation provides by not being able to collect other information. The second problem is that the very presence of an observer may distort or otherwise alter the situation to such a degree that the behavior of the individual being observed also is altered.

Tests are a predetermined collection of questions or tasks to which predetermined types of behavioral responses are sought. Tests are particularly useful because they permit tasks and questions to be presented in exactly the same way to each person tested. Because a tester elicits and scores behavior in a predetermined and consistent manner, the performances of several different test takers can be compared no matter who does the testing. Hence, tests tend to make many extrapersonal factors in assessment consistent for all those tested. Basically, two types of information, quantitative and qualitative, result from the administration of a test. *Quantitative* data refer to the actual scores achieved on the test. Examples of quantitative data include such statements as "Lee earned a score of 80 on her math test," or "Henry scored at the eighty-third percentile on a measure of scholastic aptitude." *Qualitative* information consists of nonsystematic observations made while a child is tested and tells us how the child achieved the score. For example, in earning a score of 80 on her math test, Lee may have solved all of the addition and subtraction problems with the exception of those that required regrouping. Henry may have performed best on measures of his ability to define words, while demonstrating a weakness in comprehending verbal statements. When tests are used in assessment, it is not enough to know simply the scores a student earned on a given test; it is important to know how the student earned those scores.

The *judgments* and assessments made by others can play an important role in assessment. In instances where a diagnostician lacks competence to render a judgment, the judgments of those who possess the necessary competence are essential. Diagnosticians seek out other professionals to complement their own skills and background. Thus, referring a student to various specialists (audiologists, ophthalmologists, reading teachers, and so on) is a common and desirable practice in assessment. Judgments by teachers, counselors, psychologists, and practically any other school employees may be useful in particular circumstances. Expertise in making judgments is often a function of familiarity with the student being assessed. Teachers regularly express professional judgments; for example, report-card grades represent the teacher's judgment of a student's academic progress during the marking period; referrals for psychological evaluation represent a different type of judgment based on experience with many students and observations of the particular student. Judgments represent both the best and the worst of assessment data. Judgments made by conscientious, capable, and objective individuals can be an invaluable aid in the assessment process. Inaccurate, biased, subjective judgments can be misleading at best and harmful at worst. Finally, all assessment ultimately requires judgment.

INTEGRATION OF ASSESSMENT INFORMATION

To see how the various types of information can come into play in an assessment, consider the following example. Mary, who is 6 years old, is falling behind in reading, her teacher reports (a current judgment). The teacher also reports that Mary does not listen or pay attention and doesn't associate sounds with letters (current observations). An inspection of Mary's kindergarten records indicates that she was absent thirty-one days in January and February (past observation). Mary's scores on the reading-readiness test administered in June of her kindergarten year were sufficiently high that her teacher recommended her promotion to the first grade (past judgment). An interview with Mary's parents revealed that Mary has a history of treated middle-ear infections (past observations and judgments) during the winters. According to her parents, she currently has an ear infection that is being treated by the family doctor (current observation). Pulling together all this information, the school authorities hypothesize that Mary is having hearing difficulties. They obtain a hearing examination (current test), which indicates that Mary is currently suffering from a moderate hearing loss of sufficient magnitude to affect her progress in phonics adversely (current judgment). With background and current information, it is now possible to assess (understand and interpret) Mary's classroom behavior. With medical treatment for her ear problem and some classroom intervention by the teacher, Mary can be expected to do better in school.

THE PROCESS OF ASSESSMENT

In selection of the kinds of information to collect, three facts are important:

1. Information differs in specificity.
2. General information is more rapidly collected than specific information.
3. The amount of time available to assess any particular individual is finite.

In assessment, the ease or efficiency of information gathering is usually balanced against the precision of the information gathered. For example, a teacher's judgment about a student's general academic progress is more readily obtained than a detailed analysis of that student's knowledge of phoneme-grapheme (sound-letter) correspondences; a teacher's judgment about the relative frequency of a student's displays of physical aggression is more readily obtained than a tally of the number of times in a week that the student hits someone. Both general information and highly specific information (as well as information of intermediate specificity) are valuable, but they are valuable for different purposes. Generally, greater faith is placed in more specific information. Judgments are more susceptible to biasing by extraneous factors such as a student's appearance than behavior counts are.

Given a finite amount of time in which to assess an individual, diagnosticians must select assessment procedures carefully. There is never enough time to amass highly specific information on every aspect of every individual requiring assessment. Consequently, the more specific the information gathered, the fewer the total behaviors and characteristics that can be assessed. Diagnosticians could probably gather very broad information about all major areas of functioning, but if they did so they would have little precise information upon which to build an assessment. Therefore, a careful balance must be struck between general and specific assessment procedures.

Diagnosticians have three choices in the assessment of any aspect of an individual: assess specifically; assess generally; do not assess. The choice is facilitated by the general information (a student's cumulative records, the reason for referral, and so on) a diagnostician has available. When available information indicates normal or adequate progress and development in a particular area (for example, reading), a diagnostician probably would not perform further assessment in that area, assuming that any "problems" in that area are not sufficiently severe to warrant the expenditure of time. When a student is not making adequate progress in a particular area, the student *may* have a problem. (Lack of progress does not necessarily imply the student is at fault; there may have been no opportunity for progress.) Inadequate progress in an important area of development is a warning signal that information should be collected. In the initial stage of assessment, general, relatively imprecise information is gathered in areas where there is no available information. General procedures are also used in areas of potential difficulty to confirm the existence of a problem. This is a crucial stage in assessment, because at this point entire areas of inquiry are dismissed as irrelevant — or at least, as of limited importance — and other areas are considered for further inquiry. If a diagnostician errs at this point, problems can go unevaluated.

Having identified one or more areas of potential weakness, the diagnostician then selects more precise assessment techniques to *confirm* the existence of a problem. Certain tests, direct observations, and current indirect expert judgments are particularly useful at this stage. Depending on what a diagnostician finds and how these findings are interpreted, assessment in a particular area may become more precise or may be abandoned.

Once problem areas have been delineated and specified, the diagnostician begins to interpret the problem. The type of interpretation often depends on the particular diagnostician's theoretical orientation as well as on the information already amassed. At this stage in the assessment process, an attempt usually is made to classify the individual or the problem (mental retardation, emotional disturbance, educational handicap, cultural or social deprivation, and so on). To make such a classification, additional information often is required. Such information is collected to confirm or disconfirm the tentative classification. At some point in the assessment process, the diagnostician must make a firm classification.

The final step in the assessment process is a prognosis for the individual's development. The prognosis is a prediction of the course of development with and without intervention. Statements of prognosis should include specific interventions (including their duration) and anticipated outcomes. If an intervention is actually used, it should be evaluated.

STUDY QUESTIONS

1. Identify and briefly describe three factors other than an obtained score that a diagnostician needs to take into consideration when interpreting a child's performance on a test.

2. List and explain four limitations of historical information used in assessment.

3. Differentiate between testing and assessment.

4. Differentiate between quantitative and qualitative information and give two examples of each.

5. Read the Eaves and McLaughlin paper listed in Additional Reading and identify the three levels of assessment the authors describe.

ADDITIONAL READING

American Psychological Association, American Educational Research Association, and National Council on Measurement in Education. *Standards for educational and psychological tests.* Washington, D.C.: American Psychological Association, 1974.

Baldwin, C. P. Naturalistic studies of classroom learning. *Review of Educational Research*, 1965, *35*, 107–113.

Eaves, R., & McLaughlin, P. A systems approach to the assessment of the child and his environment: Getting back to basics. *Journal of Special Education*, 1977, *11*, 99–111.

Gagné, R. M. Observations of school learning. *Educational Psychologist*, 1973, *10*, 112–116.

Goslin, D. A. *Teachers and testing.* New York: Russell Sage Foundation, 1967.

Himmelweit, B., & Swift, B. A model for the understanding of school as a socializing agent. In P. Mussen, J. Langer, & M. Covington (eds.), *Trends and issues in developmental psychology.* New York: Holt, Rinehart and Winston, 1969.

Medley, D. M., & Mitzel, H. E. Measuring classroom behavior by systematic observation. In N. L. Gage (ed.), *Handbook of research on teaching.* Chicago: Rand McNally, 1963. (Chapter 6, pp. 247–328.)

Weinberg, R. A., & Wood, F. H. (eds.). *Observation of pupils and teachers in mainstream and special education settings: Alternative strategies.* Minneapolis: Leadership Training Institute/Special Education, 1975.

Werry, J. S., & Quay, H. C. Observing the classroom behavior of elementary school children. *Exceptional Children*, 1969, *35*, 461–469.

Chapter 2

Purposes of and Assumptions in Assessment

When we select assessment techniques for use in educational settings, we must carefully consider the reasons for using those techniques. We must also be aware of certain assumptions inherent in assessment, and of ways in which failure to meet these assumptions affects directly the validity of obtained results. We use assessment data in making many different kinds of educational decisions, and each kind may require different information. If we fail to consider the purpose for which a test was administered, we may use that test inappropriately. Similarly, failure to take into account the assumptions inherent in assessment can lead to overgeneralization and abuse. This chapter describes both the different purposes for collecting assessment data and the assumptions inherent in collecting the data.

PURPOSES OF ASSESSMENT

Tests are administered in educational settings for a variety of purposes. In general, their purpose is to provide children, parents, teachers, school psychologists, and other professionals with information to assist them in making decisions that will enhance students' educational development. There are, however, at least five specific reasons for giving tests to students; these are screening, placement, program planning, program evaluation, and assessment of individual progress. Some tests can serve several of these purposes, while others are used primarily for one specific purpose.

SCREENING

Tests may be administered to identify students who are sufficiently different (in either a positive or negative sense) from their age-mates that they require special attention. Screening is usually accomplished by teacher administration of a test to a group of students. Just as vision tests and hearing tests are routinely given to identify students with visual or auditory acuity problems, intelligence tests are administered to identify students who require special attention, either because of limited intellectual capability or because of highly superior intellectual capability. Achievement tests, measures of what has been learned, are routinely administered to identify students experiencing academic difficulty for whom further diagnostic assessment may be appropriate.

PLACEMENT

Most state laws require that students be evaluated by a certified diagnostic specialist before they may enter or leave special educational programs. Furthermore, most state laws specify the criteria, in terms of test scores, necessary for placement of a student in a special educational program. Criteria vary from state to state, but in general a student must earn an IQ of 70 or below on an individually administered intelligence test to be considered for placement in a class for the mentally retarded. To be considered gifted, a student must typically earn an IQ above 130 on an individually administered test.

For placement in most classes for the learning disabled or brain injured, a student must demonstrate a current functioning (an achievement level) one and a half to two years below the level where he or she is capable of functioning (the intellectual level). In addition, the student must demonstrate a perceptual or language handicap. Intellectual level, achievement level, and the extent of perceptual or language handicap are identified by testing.

While there are many problems apparent in the use of tests to make placement decisions, most state regulations require that decisions be test-based. This requirement exists primarily for the protection of students. If teachers and administrators were allowed to make placement decisions on the basis of subjective impressions, placement could be haphazard and capricious.

PROGRAM PLANNING

Tests are often administered in an effort to assist teachers and administrators in the planning of educational programs for individuals or groups of students. Test information is used to decide placement in reading groups or to assign students to specific compensatory or remedial programs. Test results are also used in deciding what to teach and how to teach individuals as well as groups.

With the increase in the attention given to learning disabilities and with the efforts to develop individualized programs for handicapped youngsters, we have witnessed an expansion of the use of diagnostic profiles in planning instructional efforts. The merits and limitations in the use of tests in planning specific educational programs are discussed in several of the later chapters of this book.

PROGRAM EVALUATION

Evaluation differs from other purposes of testing in the sense that the educational program rather than the student is being evaluated. Tests are used in today's schools to evaluate the effectiveness of Head Start programs, specific preschool programs, transitional classes, specific curricula, and a variety of pupil-support services. Suppose, for example, that Briarcliff School District decides to implement an experimental program on a one-year trial basis in two of its elementary buildings. In most cases, tests would be administered both at the beginning and at the end of the trial year so that pupils' progress could be measured. Typically, a comparison would be made of progress both in the traditional and in the experimental programs in an effort to evaluate relative effectiveness.

ASSESSMENT OF INDIVIDUAL PROGRESS

A fifth reason for administering tests to students is to monitor their progress through the grades. Tests are used to tell teachers, parents, and students the extent of that progress. Grades on teacher-constructed tests and scores on standardized tests are usual indicators of academic progress. Some newer tests tell teachers and parents what specific educational objectives have or have not been achieved.

ASSUMPTIONS UNDERLYING PSYCHOEDUCATIONAL ASSESSMENT

A number of assumptions underlie the valid psychoeducational assessment of students. To the extent that these assumptions are not met, test results and interpretations lack validity. Newland (1971) has identified and discussed the following five assumptions underlying assessment.

THE PERSON GIVING THE TEST IS SKILLED

When children are tested, we assume that the person doing the testing has adequate training for the purpose of testing. We also assume that the tester knows how to — and indeed does — establish rapport with children; children generally perform best in an atmosphere of trust and security. We further assume that the tester knows how to administer the test correctly. Testing consists of a standardized presentation of stimuli. To the extent that the person giving the test does not correctly present the questions or materials, the obtained scores lose validity.

We also assume that the person who administers a test knows how to score the test. Correct scoring is a prerequisite to the attainment of a meaningful picture of a student. Finally, we assume that accurate interpretation can and will be made.

Test administration, scoring, and interpretation require different degrees of training and expertise depending on the kind of test being administered and the degree of interpretation required to draw meaning from the test taker's performance. While most teachers can readily administer or learn to administer group intelligence and achievement tests, a person must have considerable training to score and interpret most individual intelligence and personality tests. Most states now require that a person be certified or licensed as a psychologist in order to administer these types of tests. Licensing or certification, in turn, is often contingent on the demonstration of competence.

Obviously, a terribly important point is implicit in this first assumption. Professionals should administer only the tests they are qualified to administer. Too often, unfortunately, we hear of people with no training in individual intelligence testing who nonetheless administer individual intelligence tests; or we see people with no formal training in personality test administration or interpretation giving personality tests. Such tests may *look* easy enough to give; however, the correct administration, scoring, and interpretation are complex. Because tests are so often used to make decisions that will affect a child's future, this assumption of a skilled observer or tester is especially important.

ERROR WILL BE PRESENT

No psychological or educational measurement is free from error. A certain amount of error is always present when we test. Although measurement error is dealt with extensively in Chapter 6, a few points are appropriate here. Nunnally (1967) differentiates between two kinds of error in any measurement effort: *systematic error*, or bias, and *random error*. He illustrates systematic error by the example of a chemist who uses an inaccurate thermometer, one that always reads two degrees higher than the actual temperature of a liquid. All of the readings the chemist takes will be biased, but they will be biased systematically; that is, all readings will be in error by two degrees.

In the measurement process, random error occurs in two ways. First, the measurer may be inconsistent. Nunnally's illustration of this is a near-sighted chemist who reads an accurate thermometer inaccurately. The readings will be in error, but the amount and direction of error will be random. In some cases, the chemist may read the thermometer five degrees high, in others four degrees low. An indeterminate amount of error, then, affects obtained measurements. Second, measurement devices may produce inconsistent results. For example, an elastic rubber ruler produces inconsistent measures of length.

Reliability concerns the extent to which a measurement device is free from random error. A test with very little random error, an accurate test, is said to be reliable, while one with considerable random error, an inaccurate test, is said to be unreliable. Tests used to assess students differ considerably in degree of reliability. To the extent that unreliable devices (devices with considerable random error) are used to make decisions about students, those decisions may, in fact, be erroneous. Factors that contribute to lack of reliability in testing are discussed in Chapter 6.

ACCULTURATION IS COMPARABLE

Every schoolchild has a particular set of background experiences in educational, social, and cultural environments. When we test students using a standardized device and compare them to a set of norms to gain an index of their relative standing, we assume that the students we test are similar to those on whom the test was standardized; that is, we assume their acculturation is comparable, but not necessarily identical, to that of the students who made up the normative sample for the test.

When a child's general background experiences differ from those of the children on whom a test was standardized, then the use of the norms of that test as an index for evaluating that child's current performance or for predicting future performances may be inappropriate. Incorrect educational decisions may well be made. It must be pointed out that acculturation is a matter of experiential background rather than of skin color, race, or ethnic background. When we say that a child's acculturation differs from that of the group used as a norm, we are saying that the *experiential background* differs, not simply that the child is of different ethnic origin, for example, than the children on whom the test was standardized.

Unfortunately, many psychologists, counselors, remedial specialists, and others who select tests to be administered to students often do so with little regard to the characteristics of the students who constitute the normative samples. Many school administrators routinely purchase tests with more concern for price than for the technical adequacy and appropriateness of those tests.

The Peabody Picture Vocabulary Test, for example, was standardized on white children in Nashville, Tennessee; yet it is used daily to measure the "intelligence" of black ghetto children, children whose educational, social, and cultural background *may* differ extensively from that of the children on whom the test was standardized.

The performance section of the Wechsler Intelligence Scale for Children — Revised (WISC–R) consists of a variety of tests (mostly manipulative, like putting puzzle pieces together to form objects) that require no verbal response by the child. The fact that the child does not have to speak has encouraged psychologists to use the test in an effort to test deaf children. Levine (1974), in a survey of testing practices used by psychologists who work with the deaf, reported that the test most frequently used to measure the intelligence of deaf children is the WISC performance section: norms based entirely on the performance of youngsters who can hear are used to interpret the performances of deaf children! Appropriate application of the norms presumes that the child evaluated can *hear* the directions and has had acculturation comparable to that of the children on whom the test was standardized. Several nonverbal subtests of the Wechsler Scales (for example, Picture Completion and Picture Arrangement) require verbal competence.

BEHAVIOR SAMPLING IS ADEQUATE

A fourth assumption underlying psychoeducational assessment is that the behavior sampling is adequate in amount and representative in area. Any test is a sample of behavior. If we want information about a student's math skills, we give the student a sample of math problems to solve. Similarly, if we want to know about spelling skills, we ask the student to spell a representative number of words. When we administer a math or spelling test, we assume that we have a large enough sample of items to enable us to make statements regarding a student's overall skill development in that area. Few teachers would ask a student to solve only two arithmetic problems and presume that the results would tell much at all about that student's skill development in arithmetic. Testing requires an adequate sampling of behavior to assist in decision-making processes.

Not only do we assume that the behavior sampling is adequate in amount, but we assume that the test measures what its authors claim it measures. We assume that an intelligence test measures intelligence and that a spelling test measures spelling skills. A test of addition would be a poor measure of overall skill in math, because math entails much more than addition. Similarly, a measure of a student's skill in addition of single-digit numbers provides only one part of a test of that student's skill in addition. We cannot rely on a test's name in attempting to define the behaviors sampled by the test. Many tests, for example, are called "reading" tests. Yet reading has several subcomponents, such as recognition, comprehension, and phonetic analysis. As we shall show in Chapter 10, no reading test samples reading per se. Each test samples one or more reading behaviors. The user of reading tests — or any tests, for that matter — must go beyond test names in an effort to ascertain the behaviors the tests measure.

To the extent that tests used to measure students' performances are incomplete or fail to measure what they claim to measure, decisions based on scores made on those tests may well be wrong decisions.

PRESENT BEHAVIOR IS OBSERVED; FUTURE BEHAVIOR IS INFERRED

When we give a test, we observe only the test taker's performance on one sampling of behavior, at a particular time, under particular testing conditions, and in a particular situation. We observe what a person *does*; we may or may not observe what that person is capable of doing. We sample a limited number of behaviors and generalize the individual's performance to other, similar behaviors. For example, because Heathcote correctly works ten of ten problems in single-digit addition, we infer that he could add any two single digits correctly. Moreover, judgments or predictions about an individual's behavior at some future time may be made. These predictions are inferences in which we may place varying degrees of confidence. We may better trust the inferences we make about future performance if we have seen to it that the other assumptions about assessment have been satisfied. If we have administered a test that is adequate in its behavior sampling and representative in area, that is relatively free from error, and that was accurately administered, scored, and interpreted, using as norms students of background comparable to the background of those we tested, then we may put a reasonable amount of faith in the adequacy of observed data. Data obtained from such an administration may be used with greater assurance in making predictions than data obtained under conditions in which any of the assumptions were not met. Human behavior is extremely complex, and we must remember that any prediction about future behavior is an inference.

SUMMARY

Testing, while it appears simple, is a complex process. A test is administered to a person or group of persons, and a score or scores are obtained. The particular use to which the score is put largely depends on the reason the test was administered. We have seen that, in actual practice, tests are administered for the purposes of screening, placement, program planning, program evaluation, and assessment of individual progress. Tests are devices that assist us in decision making.

Educational decisions based on the results of testing have differing degrees of appropriateness, depending on the extent to which certain assumptions have been met. Failure to meet any of five specific assumptions underlying psychoeducational assessment adversely affects the decision-making process.

Knowledge of the purposes and assumptions discussed in this chapter will facilitate understanding of fundamental points that will be made in later references to specific tests and testing practices.

STUDY QUESTIONS

1. Why should individually administered tests, rather than group tests, be used to make placement decisions regarding students?

2. Examine your state's criteria for placement of children in special-education classes or programs. What kinds of assessment data are required to support decisions to place children in classes for the mentally retarded?

3. Aside from subject-matter grades, how is pupil progress evaluated in a representative school or school district in your area?

4. Examine the catalogues of any two test publishers. What restrictions, if any, are listed about who may *purchase* tests?

5. When we test students, we assume that their acculturation has been comparable to that of the test's norm group. Differentiate between identical acculturation and comparable acculturation.

6. Test A is more reliable than test B. If other factors are comparable, why would it be better to use test A than test B?

7. Ms. Henry wants to divide her class into reading groups for instructional purposes. She tests the students by asking each of them to read the words *cat*, *riches*, and *rhythm*. Performance on this task serves as the basis for assigning students to the different reading groups. What assumption has Ms. Henry probably violated?

8. When we test students, we assume they have been exposed to acculturation comparable to that of the test's norm group. What is the effect of violating this assumption?

9. Jimmy Becker correctly solves one of twenty single-digit arithmetic problems. His teacher concludes that Jimmy cannot solve math problems and will have difficulty learning to add and subtract. What basic assumption has the teacher violated?

ADDITIONAL READING

Anastasi, A. *Psychological testing*. New York: Macmillan, 1976. (Chapter 2: Nature and uses of psychological tests, pp. 23–44.)

Cronbach, L. J. *Essentials of psychological testing*. Englewood Cliffs, NJ: Prentice-Hall, 1970. (Chapter 2: Purposes and types of tests, pp. 22–43.)

Lawson, D. E. Need for safe-guarding the field of intelligence testing. *Journal of Educational Psychology*, 1944, *35*, 240–247.

Newland, T. E. Psychological assessment of exceptional children and youth. In W. Cruickshank (ed.), *Psychology of Exceptional Children and Youth*, 1971, pp. 115–174.

Newland, T. E. Assumptions underlying psychological testing. *Journal of School Psychology*, 1973, *11*, 316–322.

Chapter 3

Considerations in Test Selection and Administration

Before we can select an appropriate test, we must determine exactly what kinds of information we want and how we will be using the information we obtain. The process of test selection is analogous to the preparation of behavioral objectives; there must be a very clear idea of what is to be tested, how it is to be tested, and under what conditions it will be tested. In Figure 3.1 four major questions are presented. The order in which the questions are asked is less important than the nature of the questions. Each question has at least two subquestions. Once we have a purpose for testing, we must ask who is to be tested, what behaviors are to be tested, what interpretative data are desired, and whether a commercially prepared test will be used.

WHO IS TO BE TESTED?

In answering the question "Who is to be tested?" we must address two issues. First, we must decide whether we want to test a single student or a group of students. Second, we must determine to what extent the single student (or any student in the group) demonstrates special limitations that must be taken into account in testing.

GROUP VS. INDIVIDUAL TESTS

The distinction between a group test and an individual test is both obvious and subtle. Group tests can be given to one person or to several people simultaneously; individual tests must be administered to only one person at a time. Any group test can be administered to an individual; no individual test should be administered to more than one person at the same time. This is the obvious distinction. There are several subtle distinctions, however.

In an individual test, the questions and demands usually are given orally by a tester who also observes the individual's responses directly and in many cases records these responses. The tester is able to control the tempo

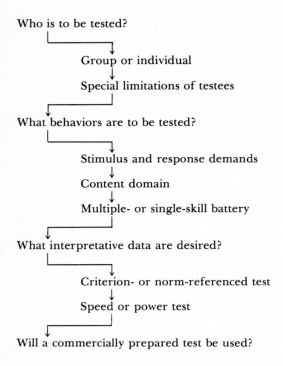

Figure **3.1**   Basic questions in test selection

and pace of the testing and often can rephrase or clarify questions as well as probe responses to elicit the best performance. If a child undergoing testing becomes fatigued, the tester can interrupt or terminate the test. If a child loses his or her place on the test, the tester can help; if the child dawdles, the tester can urge; if the child lacks confidence, the tester can reinforce effort. Individual tests usually allow the tester to encourage a test taker's best efforts and to gather a considerable amount of qualitative information. Thus, the examiner can infer strengths and weaknesses in terms of both quantitative *and* qualitative information.

With a group test, the examiner may provide oral directions for younger children, but for children beyond the fourth grade, the directions usually are written. The children write or mark their own responses, and the examiner must monitor the progress of several test takers simultaneously. The examiner typically cannot rephrase, probe, or prompt responses. Even when a group test is given to a single student, qualitative information is very difficult, if not impossible, to obtain.

The choice between an individual or a group test is determined in part by the purpose of testing and the efficiency with which that purpose can be achieved. Basically, when we test for program evaluation, screening, and some types of program planning (for example, tracking students into ability groups), group tests can be appropriately used. Individual tests *could* be used, but the time and expense would not be justified in terms of the information desired. When we plan individual programs, individual tests are more appropriate. Typically, when a student is to be placed in a special-education program, an individually administered test is required by law.

SPECIAL LIMITATIONS AND CONSIDERATIONS

A particular student may have special limitations that make a group test inappropriate. As previously discussed, most group-administered tests are limited in their applicability because of the way the questions are presented (that is, they require that test takers be able to read) and the way responses are to be made (generally, by writing or marking). Common sense tells us that if a student cannot read the directions or write the responses, a test requiring these abilities is inappropriate. In such cases, the test measures inability in reading directions or writing answers rather than skill or ability in the content of the test. A child without arms may know the content of the test but cannot answer any questions correctly because she cannot write. Similarly, children without speech or with severe speech impediments may know the answers to the questions a test asks but be unable (or unwilling) to respond to *even* the most sensitively administered individual test that requires oral answers. Children with physical or sensory handicaps may perform more slowly than nonhandicapped children simply because of their handicaps. A test that awards "points" for the speed as well as the accuracy of response would not be a valid test of such children's mastery of content.

A related concern is the relationship between a person's functional level and social maturity. Often, older individuals with relatively low levels of skill development are assessed. In such cases, the tester must be careful to select test materials that reflect the test taker's social maturity. An adolescent who is just learning to read may well resent test materials geared to 6-year-old children. The use of test materials that are inappropriate in terms of the older individual's social maturity may reduce or eliminate rapport and thereby jeopardize the accuracy of the test results.

WHAT BEHAVIORS ARE TO BE TESTED?

In deciding what behaviors to test, an examiner must take into account three subquestions: What stimulus and response demands will be made?

What domain (content) will be measured? How many domains will be tested?

STIMULUS AND RESPONSE DEMANDS

A test or an individual test item measures an individual's ability to receive a stimulus and then express a response. These demands are present in *all* tests. Skill in the content of a test cannot be measured accurately if the stimulus and response demands of a question are beyond the capabilities of the test taker. As noted earlier, tests can be administered orally or visually: an examiner can show written materials to a student while simultaneously reading them. There is little reason why a test could not be tactilely administered, too, so that specially limited students could understand its basic stimulus demands.

Response demands can also vary. Test instructions may call for an oral *yes* or *no* response or for oral definition or elaboration. Tests may also require written responses that can range from a simple yes-no, true-false, or multiple-choice response to an elaborate, written essay.

A tester should be sensitive to any limitations a student may have. Such limitations are especially important in relation to the stimulus and response demands of testing. The tester should also have quite specific intentions to measure a particular skill or trait. How to measure should be considered as well as what to measure. For example, all spelling tests are not the same. Writing words from dictation is a different kind of spelling test than recognizing a correctly or incorrectly spelled word in a multiple-choice format.

THE DOMAIN

The content domain that is tested is generally what we think of as the "kind" of test. There are many kinds of tests, many traits or characteristics that can be measured: intelligence, personality, aptitude, interest, perceptual-motor development, linguistic ability, and so on. Most general traits or characteristics can be further subdivided. For example, intelligence can be divided into performance abilities and verbal abilities or fractionated into as many as 120 separate abilities (Guilford, 1967). There are also many skills and knowledge areas that can be measured: reading, mathematics, social studies, and anatomy are only a few. Some tests are designed to measure skill development in one specific content area (for example, reading) whereas other tests measure skill development in several different areas. The former are known as *single-skill tests* while the latter are *multiple-skill batteries.*

Oftentimes, a test item readily lends itself to only one domain. We'd have trouble using the question "Do you like yourself?" on other than a personality test. Generally, however, particular test items are identified with particular domains as a function of a student's age or experience. For instance, the question "What is 3 and 5?" can be used to measure several different domains, depending on the particular student. If a child has just received systematic instruction in the addition of single-digit numbers, the question would be appropriate in an achievement test. If the question were asked of a child who had not received formal instruction in addition (a 4-year-old, for instance), the question would be appropriate in an intelligence test. If the same question were given to a child who had received several years of systematic instruction, it would be appropriate in a math aptitude test. In short, the type of test in which an item is placed depends more on the characteristics of the person to be tested or on the intended use of the test than on content of the particular item.

WHAT INTERPRETATIVE DATA ARE DESIRED?

The process of deciding what interpretative data the examiner wants to obtain necessarily includes answering several subquestions: (1) Is the examiner interested in the student's actual level of mastery or in an index of the student's relative standing? In other words, will the examiner use criterion-referenced or norm-referenced assessment? (2) Is the examiner interested in the student's maximum performance or in the level of performance the student can attain in a given amount of time? In other words, will the examiner use *power tests* (untimed tests) or *speed tests* (timed tests)?

NORM-REFERENCED VS. CRITERION-REFERENCED TESTS

Most noneducational tests are *norm-referenced devices*, which compare an individual's performance to the performance of his or her peers. In norm-referenced assessment, learning of particular content or skills is important only to the extent that differential learning allows the tester to rank individuals in order, from those who have learned many skills to those who have learned few. The emphasis is on the relative standing of individuals rather than on absolute mastery of content.

Norm-referenced tests are of two types: point scales and age scales. These differ in their construction. Age scales are less common today than in the past because of both statistical and conceptual limitations. Age scales are developed by scaling test items in terms of the percentages of children of different ages responding correctly to each test item. For example, an item would be placed at the 6-year level if 25 percent of 5-year-olds responded to it correctly, 50 percent of the 6-year-olds responded to it correctly, and 75 percent of 7-year-olds responded to it correctly. When a test question is correctly placed in an age scale, younger children fail the item while older children pass it. The statistical and conceptual limitations of age scales are discussed in Chapter 5 in the sections dealing with developmental scores and quotients. The reader is cautioned that some tests, such as the 1972 revision of the Stanford-Binet, appear to be age scales but are more correctly considered point scales (compare Salvia, Ysseldyke, & Lee, 1975).

A point scale is constructed by selecting and ordering items of different levels of difficulty. The levels of difficulty are not associated with ages. In point scales, the correct responses (that is, points) are summed, and the total raw score is transformed to various derived scales (see Chapter 5).

Norm-referenced devices typically are designed to do only one thing: to separate the performances of individuals so that there is a distribution of scores. They allow the tester to discriminate among the performances of a number of individuals and to interpret how one person's performance compares to that of other individuals with similar characteristics. In norm-referenced testing, a person's performance on a test is measured relative to or in reference to the performances of others who are presumably like that person. Norm-referenced tests are standardized on groups of individuals, and typical performances for students of certain ages or in certain grades are obtained. The raw score an individual student earns on a test is compared to the scores earned by other students, and a transformed score (for example, a percentile rank) is used to express the given student's standing in the group.

All norm-referenced and criterion-referenced tests are objective. Objective tests are tests that have predetermined answers and standards for scoring a response. They are objective in the sense that attitudes, opinions, and idiosyncrasies of the examiner do not affect scoring; any two examiners would score a response in the same way.[1] Objective scoring does not imply "fair" or justifiable scoring; it implies only predetermined criteria and standardized scoring procedures. Suppose a tester shows a child pictures of a ship, an automobile, the car of a passenger train, and a bus and then asks the child, "Which one is different?" The keyed response (the objective answer) is *ship*; the ship is the only water transport. If the child reasons that only an automobile is private transportation and gives the response *car*, the response would be scored as an incorrect answer. Similarly, if the child reasons that the car on the passenger train is the only

---

1. A subjective test, by contrast, is a test for which a predetermined answer does not exist. Therefore, the examiner's subjective judgments, attitudes, and opinions can affect the scoring. Many people erroneously define an essay test as a subjective test. Such a test would be objective if there were predetermined, explicit criteria for correct responses; then the "same" response would be assigned the same score by two or more examiners.

vehicle that is not self-propelled — or the only one that requires tracks — and responds accordingly, the response is scored incorrect. "Being fair" has nothing to do with scoring objectively.

Norm-referenced devices have an advantage over criterion-referenced devices when the purpose of testing is screening or program evaluation: they provide a means of comparing a student's performance to the performance typically expected of others. Placement decisions, too, are most often made following the administration of norm-referenced devices, which enable the school psychologist to see where a student stands relative to other students. In fact, in most states evaluation with norm-referenced tests *must* play a part in any placement decision. In addition, norm-referenced tests are helpful in screening entire classes of students to identify those who demonstrate particular kinds of difficulties. Yet norm-referenced tests have many limitations.

Criterion-referenced tests are a recent development in education and behavioral psychology. Rather than indicating a person's relative standing in skill development, criterion-referenced tests measure a person's development of particular skills in terms of absolute levels of mastery. Thus, criterion-referenced tests provide answers to specific questions such as, "Does Maureen spell the word *dog* correctly?"

When tests are administered for the purpose of assisting the classroom teacher in planning appropriate programs for children, criterion-referenced devices are recommended. When planning a program for an individual student, a teacher obviously should be more concerned with identifying the specific skills the student does or does not have than with knowing how the student compares to others. In criterion-referenced measurement the emphasis is on assessing specific and relevant behaviors that have been mastered. Criterion-referenced tests treat the student as an individual rather than simply providing numerical indexes of where the student stands on a variety of subtest continua.

Items on criterion-referenced tests are often linked directly to specific instructional objectives and therefore facilitate the writing of objectives. Test items sample sequential skills, enabling a teacher not only to know the specific point at which to begin instruction but also to plan those instructional aspects that follow directly in the curricular sequence.

WILL A COMMERCIALLY PREPARED TEST BE USED?

The preceding three sections can be applied to teacher-made and commercially prepared tests. Teacher-made tests are often termed "informal" tests. Yet teachers can prepare group or individually administered tests that measure single or multiple skills and that require speed or power.

Such tests can be criterion-referenced or, if the teacher has a little statistical background, norm-referenced.[2] The only type of informal test your authors have not seen is an age scale.

Commercially prepared, or formal, tests may offer several advantages. They are often carefully constructed. The procedures for administering and scoring are standardized so that the test can be administered in a variety of settings. A description of the technical characteristics of the test (reliability, validity, norms) is often available. Finally, commercially prepared tests save the tester the time and effort required to develop a test.

In deciding whether to use a commercially prepared test as opposed to a homemade device, the domain of behaviors to be sampled is of prime concern. Informal achievement tests have one major advantage over commercially prepared achievement tests: teacher-made tests can correspond very closely to the content being taught and may therefore be superior for measuring the content of specific classroom experiences. Commercially prepared achievement tests are useful in screening, program evaluation, and individual program planning. Moreover, because most people within the profession are familiar with standardized achievement tests, the results based on such tests are readily communicated to other professionals. In personality assessment, in cases when the test materials are used mainly as a device for eliciting a person's responses, either informal or standardized procedures can probably be used with equal effectiveness.

In areas other than achievement and personality testing, commercially prepared devices are usually superior to informal tests. In these areas (intelligence, readiness, and so on), a great deal of experimental work is necessary in order to develop accurate tests, and this is better done by the professional test maker.

SELECTING A TEST

The focus of this book is commercially prepared, standardized tests. There are literally thousands of such tests available. Selecting an appropriate test for a particular purpose can be time-consuming and difficult, but it is tremendously important. Tests should not be given purposelessly.

After determining the purpose of testing and answering the questions posed in this chapter, the tester must select the test. The questioning process seldom narrows the choice to only one test. Given the choice among several devices, the tester must look to the technical characteristics

---

2. Such norm-referenced devices would employ local norms. See Chapter 8.

of the test. Tests differ dramatically in terms of technical characteristics. We have often heard it said that there are no bad tests, only incompetent testers. We would argue that some tests are *so* defective technically that they should not be marketed. However, there is no Food and Drug Administration for tests; the consumers must protect themselves. Consequently, those charged with test selection must be knowledgeable about the psychometric characteristics of tests in order to select adequate instruments. There are good tests; there are also terrible tests.

SUGGESTIONS FOR TEACHER ADMINISTRATION OF STANDARDIZED TESTS

When administering standardized tests to children, teachers must take a number of factors into consideration.

GROUP SIZE

Generally, when group tests are administered, the smaller the group the better. The optimal group size depends on the ages or grades of the test takers. For young children (kindergarten through grade 3) group size should not exceed fifteen. Young handicapped children should be tested in even smaller groups. When as many as fifteen children are tested at one time, it is advisable to have a monitor (another teacher, a teacher's aide, or some other informed adult) present to insure that directions are followed, broken pencils are replaced, and children do not dawdle or lose their place. Group size may be increased for older students, but, again, the presence of at least one additional monitor is advised. When handicapped children are tested, group size should probably not exceed five.

ADHERENCE TO STANDARDIZED PROCEDURES

The examiner must at all times administer tests *exactly* according to directions. Standardized tests were meant to be given in exactly the same way each time. Departure from standardized procedures destroys the meaning of test scores by rendering the norms useless. Test users must not coach children on test items before administering the test; they must not alter time limits.

LENGTH OF SITTINGS

The length of testing sessions will vary with the age of the test takers and the extent of their handicaps. As a general rule, a testing session should not exceed thirty minutes in the primary grades, forty to sixty minutes in the intermediate grades, and ninety minutes in junior and senior high school. However, the tester must exercise common sense. If children become restless, unruly, distracted, or distinterested, testing can be interrupted, the children given a brief break, and the testing resumed. If the test is timed, administration should be interrupted only *between* subtests and never during a subtest.

ELIMINATION OF DISTRACTIONS

Tests should not be administered at times when children are regularly engaged in particularly pleasurable activities. Tests should not be administered at times when children regularly go to assembly, recess, gym, lunch, or art class. Care should be taken to avoid testing at times when other classes are having lunch, recess, and so on. Furthermore, it is usually not advisable to administer tests just before or after a long vacation, a special event, or a holiday.

While administering a group test, the tester should be as unobtrusive as possible. The tester should not move around the room and ask children how they are doing or make small talk. Likewise, conversations between the tester and the monitors should be minimized. Finally, the teacher should avoid publicly preparing an interesting activity to follow the test. Children will attend to the movie projector that's being set up, the novel apparatus for a lab experiment, the elephant that has just been brought into the classroom.

PROVIDING OF ENCOURAGEMENT

Testers can use discretion in encouraging children taking tests. If a tester sees a child watching a bird building a nest outside the window, the child can be encouraged to pay attention to the test now and watch the bird later; the tester can also draw the window shades. The tester must use common sense so that the standard administration procedures are not violated.

KNOWLEDGE OF THE TESTS

The tester should carefully study the manuals provided with the tests. The joint committee of the American Psychological Association, the American Educational Research Association, and the National Council on Measurement in Education stated that "it is appropriate to ask that any test manual provide the information necessary for a test user to decide whether the consistency, relevance, or standardization of a test makes it suitable for [the user's] purpose" (1974, p. 5). Users must study the actual content of a test carefully to make sure that the test adequately assesses the curricular content being taught and that the child has the skills necessary to take the test.

In addition to inspecting test manuals, all test users should be familiar with O. K. Buros's *Mental Measurements Yearbooks*, available in the reference departments of most libraries. The yearbooks provide reviews of tests by individuals prominent in the field of assessment.

SUMMARY

In selecting a test, one must consider who will be tested. Of special importance are limitations a child or a group of children bring to the testing situation. The tester must consider the stimulus and response demands of the test as well as the domain or content to be tested. It is also important to consider the types of interpretative data available. Will students' performances be compared to the performances of other students (norm-referenced testing) or to curriculum content (criterion-referenced testing)? The tester must then decide to construct a device or to use a commercially prepared test. After selecting a test, the user must then administer it correctly.

STUDY QUESTIONS

1. Differentiate between norm-referenced and criterion-referenced tests, and give an advantage of each type.

2. Identify three ways in which individually administered tests are superior to group-administered tests.

3. Identify at least three characteristics students may have (for example, blindness) that require special kinds of tests or adaptations in test administration.

4. Identify three disadvantages of informal (teacher-made) tests.

5. In using a standardized test, why should one follow standardized procedures?

ADDITIONAL READING

Proger, B., & Mann, L. Criterion-referenced measurement: The world of gray versus black and white. *Journal of Learning Disabilities*, 1973, *6*, 72–84.

Part 2

Basic Concepts of Measurement

Part 2 begins with a chapter on basic measurement concepts. Chapter 4, designed for the person who has no background in descriptive statistics, presents the major concepts necessary for understanding the remaining chapters in this part and later parts of the book. Throughout Part 2 the emphasis is on the basic technical information a consumer needs to understand and interpret tests adequately. Many nuances and niceties are not dealt with. No derivations or proofs are presented. We *do* include equations and computational examples to show how particular numbers are obtained as well as to provide material for the logical understanding of basic measurement concepts that is crucial to an understanding of tests and testing.

Basic statistics form the foundation of tests. The use of tests by those who do not understand basic statistics has caused considerable misuse and misinterpretation of tests in educational settings. The rationale of Part 2 is based on this fact. An individual who uses tests simply must understand basic statistics to use the tests intelligently. We realize that numbers often scare both beginning students and seasoned veterans. Yet the heart of testing is the quantification of behavior.

Chapter 4

Descriptive Statistics

Descriptive statistics summarize data (information) for a particular group of people (a sample). This chapter deals with the basic concepts needed for an understanding of descriptive statistics. Specifically, it discusses scales of measurement, distributions, measures of central tendency, measures of dispersion, and measures of relationship.

SCALES OF MEASUREMENT

There are four scales of measurement: nominal, ordinal, equal interval, and ratio.[1] Ordinal and equal-interval scales are the most frequently used scales in norm-referenced measurement in education and psychology. Nominal and ratio scales are seldom used. The distinction among the four scales is made primarily on the basis of the relationship between adjacent values on the measurement continuum. An *adjacent value* in this case means a potential or possible rather than an obtained or measured value. In Figure 4.1, which depicts a portion of a yardstick, the possible values are any points between 2 inches and 6 inches, measured in intervals of eighths of an inch. Any two consecutive points (for instance, $3\frac{1}{8}$ inches and $3\frac{1}{4}$ inches) are adjacent values. Any two points on the scale that have intervening values (for instance, $3\frac{1}{8}$ inches and $4\frac{1}{4}$ inches) are *not* adjacent points. We could, of course, think of adjacent intervals larger than $\frac{1}{8}$ inch. For example, adjacent 1-inch intervals could be considered, and the adjacent "points" would then be 1 inch, 2 inches, and so on.

NOMINAL SCALES

When numbers are used to designate people or objects and when these numbers have no inherent relationship to one another in terms of their adjacent values, the scale of measurement is a *nominal scale*. An obvious

---

1. For a more complete discussion, see S. S. Stevens, Mathematics, measurement, and psychophysics. In S. S. Stevens (ed.), *Handbook of experimental psychology*. New York: Wiley, 1951, p. 23.

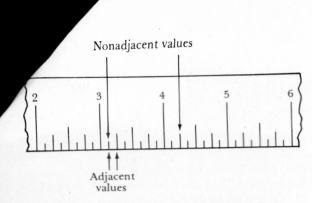

Figure **4.1** Adjacent and nonadjacent values

illustration of a nominal scale is the assignment of numbers to football players. A number is used simply to identify an individual player. The player who wears the number 80 is not necessarily a better player than 70 or 77; 80 is just a different player. Numbers 68 and 69, which are typically thought of as adjacent values, have no relationship to each other on a nominal scale; there is no implied rank ordering in the numbers worn on the jerseys. Furthermore, it would make no sense mathematically to add all the numbers worn by one team and compare the sum to the sum of the numbers on the jerseys of the opposing team. Sets of telephone numbers, course numbers, social security numbers, and disability labels (such as mentally retarded and learning disabled) are further examples of nominal scales.

ORDINAL SCALES

Ordinal scales order or rank information or scores on some continuum. Adjacent numbers on an ordinal scale indicate higher or lower value. A simple example of an ordinal scale is a ranking of persons from first to last for some trait or characteristic, such as weights or test scores. Suppose Ms. Smith administers a test to her arithmetic class, which has twenty-five students enrolled. The test results are reported in Table 4.1. Column 1 gives the name of each student, while column 2 contains each child's raw score. Column 3 contains the ranking of the twenty-five students; the children are listed in decreasing rank order from the student with the "best" performance to the student with the "worst" performance. It is important to note that the difference in raw-score points between adjacent ranks is not the same at each point on the rank (or order) continuum. For example, the difference between the "best" student and the next best

Table **4.1**   Ranking of Students in Ms. Smith's Arithmetic Class

STUDENT	RAW-SCORE TOTAL	RANK	DIFFERENCE BETWEEN SCORE AND NEXT HIGHER SCORE
Bob	27	1	0
Lucy	26	2	1
Sam	22	3	4
Mary	20	4	2
Albert	18	5	2
Barbara	17	6	1
Carmen	16		
Jane	16	8	1
Charles J.	16		
Hector	14		
Virginia	14		
Charlotte	14		
Sean	14	13	2
Joanne	14		
Jim	14		
John	14		
Charles B.	12		
Dave	12	18	2
Ron	12		
Carole	11	20	1
Bernice	10	21	1
Hugh	8	22	2
Lance	6	23	2
Ludwig	2	24	4
Harpo	1	25	1

student is not the same as the difference between the second-best and the third-best students. Column 4 contains the difference between each student's raw score and the raw score of the immediately preceding student. From this column, it is apparent that differences in adjacent *ranks* do not reflect the magnitude of differences in raw scores. The difficult concept to keep in mind is that while the difference between rank scores (first, second,

third, and so on) is 1 everywhere on the scale, the differences between the
raw scores that correspond to the ranks are not equal.

EQUAL-INTERVAL SCALES

Equal-interval scales have all the characteristics of ordinal scales, but in
addition the *magnitude* of the difference between any two adjacent points
on the scale is the same. For example, length in inches or centimeters is
measured with an equal-interval scale. The difference between 1 and 2
inches is the same as the difference between 15 and 16 inches or any other
pair of adjacent (1-inch-interval) values. In Table 4.1, if we *assume* that
each raw-score point that makes up the student's total score is of the same
value, then the test total is an equal-interval scale. This assumption requires that we accept the notion that the difference between 18 and 17
correct is the same as the difference between 11 and 10 correct (or between
any other pair of adjacent scores).

One important shortcoming of equal-interval scales must be noted.
Equal-interval scales do not have a rational or logical zero point. Only ratio
scales have logical zero points. Temperature measurement on the Kelvin
scale has an absolute zero, and the Kelvin is therefore a ratio scale. Temperature measurement on the Fahrenheit and centigrade scales does not
have an absolute or logical zero; these scales are equal-interval (not ratio)
scales. Weight and length scales may be ratio scales since they have logical
zero points. However, if measurement is not begun at the zero point, the
scale is an equal-interval scale.

With equal-interval scales, differences between scores are measured in
equal intervals, but the measurement does not start from a logical or
absolute zero point. In Figure 4.2, the differences among lines A, B, C,
and D are readily measured. We can start measuring from any point, for
example, point S. Measured from point S, line A is $\frac{1}{2}$ inch long; line B is 1
inch long; line C is $1\frac{1}{4}$ inches long; and line D is $1\frac{3}{4}$ inches long. The lines
are measured on an equal-interval scale (inches), and the *differences* among
the lines would be the same no matter where the starting point S was
located. However, because S is not the logical zero point from which to
begin measuring, we cannot make ratio comparisons. Although we have
begun measuring from point S and found line A to measure $\frac{1}{2}$ inch and line
B to measure 1 inch, the whole line B is obviously not twice as long as line
A. Without an absolute and logical zero point, we cannot make ratio
comparisons. Just as line B is not twice as long as line A, an IQ of 100 is not
twice as large as an IQ of 50. IQ is not measured on a ratio scale.[2]

---

2. The scale used to measure IQ is at least an ordinal scale, and some consider it to be an
equal-interval scale.

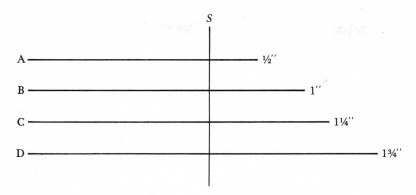

Figure **4.2** The measurement of lines as a function of the starting point

DISTRIBUTIONS

Setting up a *distribution* is a way of summarizing a group or a set of scores. Distributions may be graphed to demonstrate visually the relations among the scores in the group or set. In such graphs, the horizontal axis (*abscissa*) is the continuum on which the individuals are measured; the vertical axis (*ordinate*) is the frequency (or the number) of individuals earning any given score shown on the abscissa.   Three types of graphs of distributions are common in education and psychology: *histograms*, *polygrams*, and *curves*.   To illustrate these, let us graph the examination scores already presented in Table 4.1.   The scores earned on Ms. Smith's arithmetic examination can be grouped in three-point intervals (that is, 1 to 3, 4 to 6, . . . , 25 to 27). The grouped scores are presented as a histogram in the first part of Figure 4.3.   In the second part of that figure, the same data are presented as a polygram; note that the midpoints of the intervals used in the histogram are connected in constructing the polygram.   The third part of Figure 4.3 contains a smoothed curve.

Distributions are defined by four characteristics: mean, variance, skew, and kurtosis.   The *mean* is the arithmetic average of the scores and is the balance point of the distribution.   The *variance* describes the "spread" or clustering of scores in a distribution.   Both of these characteristics are discussed in greater detail in later sections.

Skew refers to the symmetry of a distribution.   The distribution of scores from Ms. Smith's exam is not skewed; the distribution is *symmetrical*.   However, if Ms. Smith had given a very easy test on which many students earned very high scores while only a few students earned fairly low scores, the distribution would have been skewed.   In such a case, the distribution would have "tailed off" to the low end and would be called a *negatively*

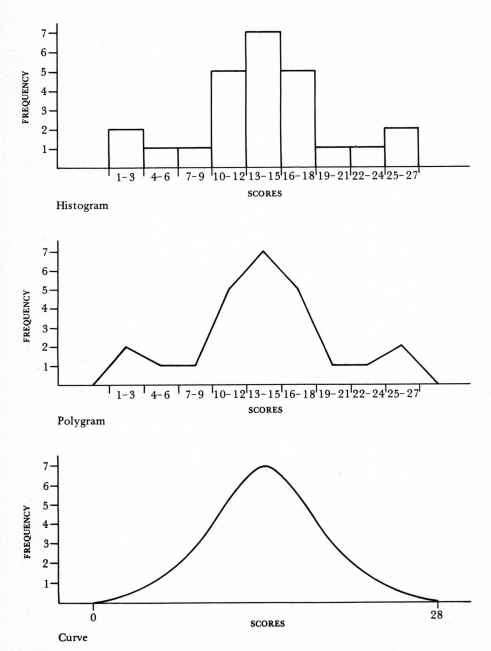

Figure **4.3**   Distribution of Ms. Smith's pupils on a histogram, polygram, and curve

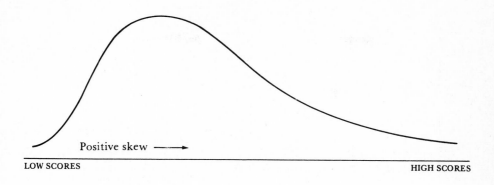

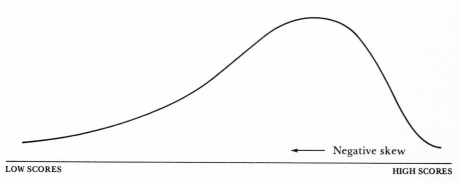

Figure **4.4**   Positive and negative skew

skewed distribution. On the other hand, if she had given a very hard test on which most of her students earned low scores and relatively few earned high scores, the distribution of scores would have tailed off to the higher end of the continuum. Such a distribution is called a *positively skewed* distribution. Figure 4.4 contains an example of a positively skewed curve and a negatively skewed curve. The label assigned to a skewed distribution is determined by the direction of the tail of the distribution. Skewed distributions in which the tail is in the upper (higher-score) end are positively skewed, while those in which the tail slopes toward the lower end are negatively skewed.

Kurtosis, the fourth characteristic of curves, describes the "peakedness" of a curve or the rate at which a curve rises. Distributions that are flat and slow rising, such as the distribution formed by the scores on Ms. Smith's test, are called *platykurtic curves*. (*Platy*kurtic curves are flat, just as a plate

Platykurtic curve

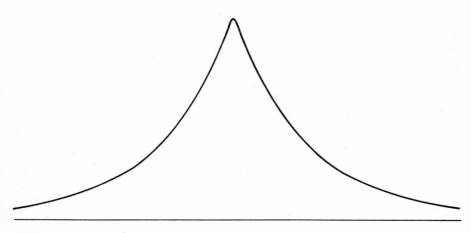

Leptokurtic curve

Figure **4.5**   A platykurtic and a leptokurtic curve

or a plateau is flat.) Fast-rising curves are called *leptokurtic curves*. Tests that do not "spread out" (or discriminate among) those taking the test are typically leptokurtic. Figure 4.5 provides an example of both a platykurtic and a leptokurtic curve.

The normal curve is a particular symmetrical curve. Many variables are distributed normally in nature; many are not. The *only* value of the normal curve lies in the fact that it is known exactly how many cases fall between any two points (ordinates) on the curve.

BASIC NOTATION

A number of symbols are used in statistics; these symbols are presented in Table 4.2. The summation sign Σ means "add the following," while X denotes any score. The number of scores in a distribution is symbolized by N, while f is used to denote the frequency of occurrence of a particular

Table **4.2**   Commonly Used Statistical Symbols

SYMBOL	MEANING
Σ	Summation sign
X	Any score
N	Number of cases
f	Frequency
$\bar{X}$	Mean
S^2	Variance
S	Standard deviation

score. The arithmetic average (*mean*) of a distribution is denoted by $\bar{X}$. The variance of a distribution is symbolized by S^2; the standard deviation, by S.

MEASURES OF CENTRAL TENDENCY

Three measures of central tendency are used: mode, median, and mean. The *mode* is defined as the score most frequently obtained. A mode (if there is one) can be computed for data on a nominal, ordinal, equal-interval, or ratio scale. Distributions may have two modes (if they do, they're *bimodal* distributions) or more than two. The mode of the distribution of raw scores obtained by Ms. Smith's class on the arithmetic test is readily apparent from an inspection of the data in Table 4.1 and the graphs in Figure 4.3. The mode of this distribution is 14; seven children earned this score.

A *median* is the score that divides the top 50 percent from the bottom 50 percent. It is that point on a scale above which 50 percent of the cases occur and below which 50 percent of the cases occur. Medians can be computed for ordinal, equal-interval, and ratio scales. Every distribution has a median. The median score may or may not be actually earned by a student. In Ms. Smith's arithmetic-test distribution, the median is 14. Seven children earned the median score.

The *mean* is the arithmetic average of the scores in a distribution. It is the sum of the scores divided by the number of scores. The formula for computing the mean, using statistical notation, is given in equation 4.1. Using the scores obtained from Ms. Smith's arithmetic examination (Table 4.1), we find that the sum of the scores is 350 and that the number of scores is 25. The mean (average) score, then, is 14. The mean score was earned by seven children in the class. The mean, like the median, may or may not be earned by a child in the distribution.

$$\bar{X} = \frac{\Sigma X}{N}$$

(4.1)

The mode, median, and mean have particular relationships depending on the symmetry (skew) of a distribution. As Figure 4.6 shows, in symmetrical unimodal distributions the mode, median, and mean are at the same point. In positively skewed distributions, the median and mean are displaced toward the positive tail of the curve; the mode is a lower value than the median, and the median is a lower value than the mean. In negatively skewed distributions, the median and mean are displaced toward the negative tail of the curve; the mode is a higher value than the median, and the median is a higher value than the mean.

MEASURES OF DISPERSION

Four measures of dispersion are commonly computed: range, semi-interquartile range, variance, and standard deviation. The *range* is the distance between the extremes of a distribution, including those extremes; it is the highest score less the lowest score plus one. On Ms. Smith's test (Table 4.1), it is 27 ($27 = 27 - 1 + 1$). The range is a relatively crude measure of dispersion since it summarizes only two bits of information.

The *semi-interquartile range* is a more useful indication of the amount of dispersion in a distribution. It is one-half the distance between the top 25 percent of the scores and the bottom 25 percent of the scores.[3]

The variance and the standard deviation are of primary concern. The *variance* is a numerical index describing the dispersion of a set of scores around the mean of the distribution. Specifically, the variance (S^2) is the average squared-distance of the scores from the mean. Since the variance is an average, it is not related to the number of cases in the set or distribution. Large sets of scores may have large or small variances; small sets of scores may have large or small variances. Also, since the variance is measured in terms of distance from the mean, it is not related to the actual value of the mean. Distributions with large means may have large or small variances; distributions with small means may have large or small variances. The variance of a distribution may be computed with equation 4.2. The

---

3. Technically, it is the average distance between the median and the score at the twenty-fifth percentile and the median and the score at the seventy-fifth percentile.

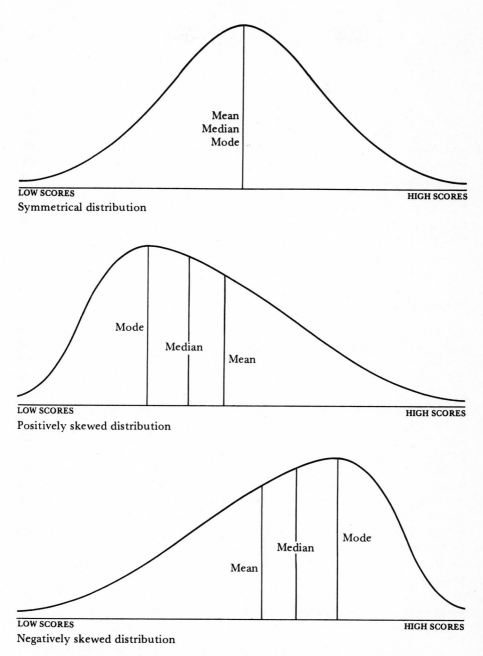

Symmetrical distribution

Positively skewed distribution

Negatively skewed distribution

Figure **4.6**   Relationships among mode, median, and mean for symmetrical and asymmetrical distributions

variance (S^2) equals the sum (Σ) of the square of each score less the mean $[(X - \bar{X})^2]$, divided by the number of scores (N).

$$S^2 = \frac{\Sigma(X - \bar{X})^2}{N} \tag{4.2}$$

The scores from Ms. Smith's arithmetic test are reproduced in Table 4.3. The second column contains the score earned by each student. The first step in computing the variance is to find the mean. Therefore, the scores are added and the sum is divided by the number of scores. The mean in this example is 14. The next step is to subtract the mean from each score; this is done in column 3 of Table 4.3, which is labeled $X - \bar{X}$. Note that the scores above the mean are positive, the scores at the mean are zero, and the scores below the mean are negative. The differences (column 3) are then squared (multiplied by themselves); the squared differences are in column 4, labeled $(X - \bar{X})^2$. Note that all numbers in this column are positive. The squared differences are then summed; in this example, the sum of all the squared distances of scores from the mean of the distribution is 900. The variance equals the sum of all the squared distances of scores from the mean divided by the number of scores; in this case, the variance equals 900/25, or 36.

The variance is of little direct importance in measurement. Its calculation is necessary for the computation of the standard deviation (S), which is *very* important. The standard deviation is the positive square root ($\sqrt{}$) of the variance.[4] Thus, in our example, since the variance is 36, the standard deviation is 6. In later chapters, the standard deviation will be used in other computations such as standard scores and the standard error of measurement. It is also very important in the interpretation of test scores.

The standard deviation is used as a *unit of measurement* in a similar way as an inch or ton is used as a unit of measurement. With *normal* distributions, scores can be measured in terms of standard deviation units from the mean; we know exactly how many cases occur between the mean and the particular standard deviation. As shown in Figure 4.7, approximately 34 percent of the cases always occur between the mean and one standard deviation (S) either above or below the mean. Thus, approximately 68 percent of all cases occur between one standard deviation below and one standard deviation above the mean (34% + 34% = 68%). Approximately 14 percent of the cases occur between one and two standard deviations below the mean *or* between one and two standard deviations above the mean. Thus, about 48 percent of all cases occur between the mean and two

---

4. The square root of a particular number is the number that when multiplied by itself produces the particular number. For example: $\sqrt{144} = 12$, $\sqrt{25} = 5$, $\sqrt{4} = 2$. Appendix 1 contains a table of square roots for numbers between 1 and 100.

Table **4.3** Computation of the Variance of Ms. Smith's Arithmetic Test

STUDENT	TEST SCORE	$X - \bar{X}$	$(X - \bar{X})^2$
Bob	27	13	169
Lucy	26	12	144
Sam	22	8	64
Mary	20	6	36
Albert	18	4	16
Barbara	17	3	9
Carmen	16	2	4
Jane	16	2	4
Charles J.	16	2	4
Hector	14	0	0
Virginia	14	0	0
Charlotte	14	0	0
Sean	14	0	0
Joanne	14	0	0
Jim	14	0	0
John	14	0	0
Charles B.	12	−2	4
Dave	12	−2	4
Ron	12	−2	4
Carole	11	−3	9
Bernice	10	−4	16
Hugh	8	−6	36
Lance	6	−8	64
Ludwig	2	−12	144
Harpo	1	−13	169
SUM	350	0	900

standard deviations either above or below the mean (34% + 14% = 48%). About 96 percent of all cases occur between two standard deviations above and two standard deviations below the mean. Appendix 2 lists the proportion of cases in a normal distribution occurring between the mean and any standard deviation above or below the mean.

As shown by the positions and values for scales A, B, and C in Figure 4.7, it does not matter what the values of the mean or standard deviation are. The relationship holds for various obtained values of the mean and the standard deviation. For scale A, where the mean is 25 and the standard deviation is 5, 34 percent of the scores occur between the mean (25) and

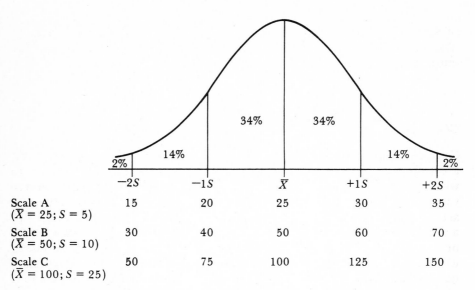

	−2S	−1S	$\overline{X}$	+1S	+2S
Scale A ($\overline{X} = 25; S = 5$)	15	20	25	30	35
Scale B ($\overline{X} = 50; S = 10$)	30	40	50	60	70
Scale C ($\overline{X} = 100; S = 25$)	50	75	100	125	150

Figure **4.7**   Scores on three scales, expressed in standard-deviation units

one standard deviation below the mean (20) *or* between the mean and one standard deviation above the mean (30). Similarly, for scale B, where the mean is 50 and the standard deviation is 10, 34 percent of the cases occur between the mean (50) and one standard deviation below the mean (40) *or* one standard deviation above the mean (60).

It is extremely important that those who use tests to make decisions about students be aware of the means and standard deviations of the tests they use. The Stanford-Binet Intelligence Scale, for example, has a mean of 100 and a standard deviation of 16. If scores on the Stanford-Binet are normally distributed, we would expect approximately 68 percent of the school population to have IQs between 84 and 116. The Slosson Intelligence Test, on the other hand, has a mean of 100 and a standard deviation of approximately 24 (Slosson, 1963, p. v). We would expect approximately 68 percent of the school population to have IQs between 76 and 124 if scores on the Slosson are normally distributed. The meaning of a score in a distribution depends on the mean, the standard deviation, and the shape of that distribution. This is an obvious point, yet it is often overlooked. For example, some states use an absolute score in the school code for the placement and retention of mentally retarded children in special educational programs; Pennsylvania uses a score of 75 (±5) for maintaining eligibility for placement. On the Stanford-Binet, a score of 80 is 1.25 standard deviations below the mean [(100 − 80)/16]; on the Slosson, a score of 80 is .83 standard deviation below the mean [(100 − 80)/24]. If a single absolute score is specified, two *different* levels of eligibility for special-education classes are written into the school code.

CORRELATION

Correlations quantify relationships between variables. *Correlation coefficients* are numerical indices of these relationships. They tell us the extent to which any two variables go together, the extent to which changes in one variable are reflected by changes in the second variable. These coefficients are used in measurement to estimate both the reliability and the validity of a test. Correlation coefficients can range in value from .00 to *either* +1.00 or −1.00. The sign (+ or −) indicates the direction of the relationship while the number indicates the magnitude of the relationship. A correlation coefficient of .00 between two variables means that there is no relationship between the variables. The variables are independent; changes in one variable are not related to changes in the second variable. A correlation coefficient of either +1.00 or −1.00 indicates a perfect relationship between two variables. Thus, if you know a person's score on one variable, you can know that person's score on the second variable.

THE PEARSON PRODUCT-MOMENT CORRELATION COEFFICIENT

The most commonly used correlation coefficient is the Pearson product-moment correlation coefficient (r). This is an index of the straight-line (*linear*) relationship between two variables measured on an equal-interval scale. Suppose Ms. Smith administered a second exam to her arithmetic class. The results of the first exam (the data from Table 4.1) are represented in column 2 of Table 4.4, while the results of the second exam are presented in column 3. (For the sake of simplicity, the example has been constructed so that the second test has the same mean and the same standard deviation — that is, 14 and 6 — as the first test.) The two scores for each student are plotted on a graph (called a *scattergram* or *scatterplot*) in Figure 4.8. The scatterplot contains twenty-five points — one for each child. Inspection of the figure indicates that there is a pronounced tendency for high scores on the first test to be associated with high scores on the second test. There is a *positive* relationship (correlation) between the first and second tests. The line drawn through the scatterplot in Figure 4.8 is called a *regression line*. When the points corresponding to each pair of scores cluster closely around the regression line, there is a high degree of relationship. The points from Table 4.4 do cluster closely around the

Table **4.4**   Scores Earned on Two Tests Administered by Ms. Smith
to Her Arithmetic Class

STUDENT	RAW SCORE, TEST 1	RAW SCORE, TEST 2
Bob	27	26
Lucy	26	22
Sam	22	20
Mary	20	27
Albert	18	14
Barbara	17	18
Carmen	16	16
Jane	16	17
Charles J.	16	16
Hector	14	14
Virginia	14	14
Charlotte	14	16
Sean	14	14
Joanne	14	12
Jim	14	14
John	14	12
Charles B.	12	14
Dave	12	11
Ron	12	12
Carole	11	10
Bernice	10	14
Hugh	8	6
Lance	6	1
Ludwig	2	2
Harpo	1	8

regression line; there is a high correlation (specifically, .89) between the
first and second tests.[5] If all the points fell on the regression line, there
would be a perfect correlation (1.00).

Figure 4.9 contains six scatterplots of different degrees of relationship.
In parts a and b all points fall on the regression line so that the correlation

---

5. The correlation coefficient can be computed with the following formula:

$$r = \frac{N\Sigma XY - (\Sigma X)(\Sigma Y)}{\sqrt{N\Sigma X^2 - (\Sigma X)^2}\ \sqrt{N\Sigma Y^2 - (\Sigma Y)^2}}$$

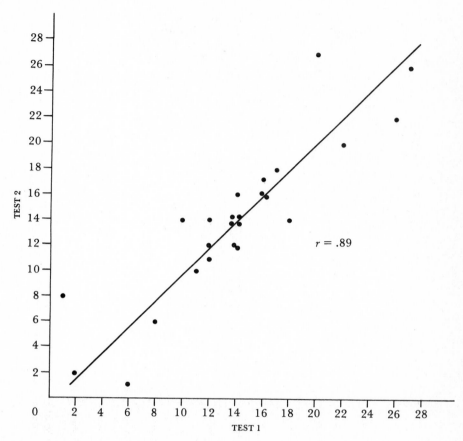

Figure **4.8** Scatterplot of the two tests administered by Ms. Smith

between the variables is perfect. Part a has a correlation coefficient of +1.00; high scores on one test are associated with high scores on the other test. Part b has a correlation of −1.00; high scores on one test are associated with low scores on the other test (this negative correlation is called an *inverse* relationship). Parts c and d show a high degree of positive and negative relationship, respectively. Note that the departures from the regression lines are associated with lower degrees of relationship. Parts e and f show scatterplots with a low degree of relationship. Note the wide departures from the regression lines.

Zero correlations can occur in three ways, as shown in Figure 4.10. First, if the scatterplot is essentially circular (part a), the correlation is approximately .00. Second, if either or both variables are constant (part b), the

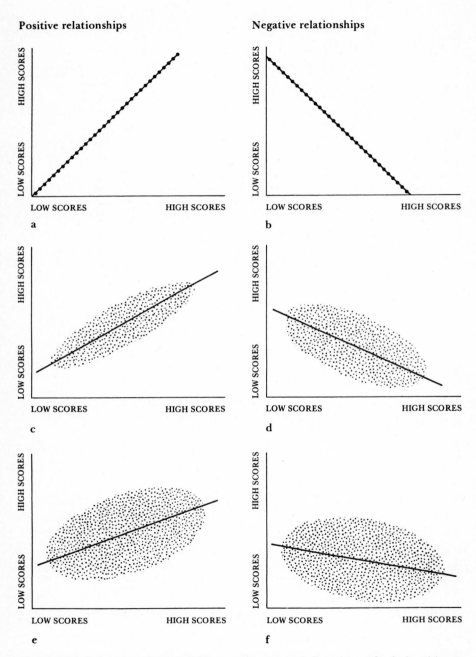

Figure **4.9** Six scatterplots of different degrees and directions of relationship

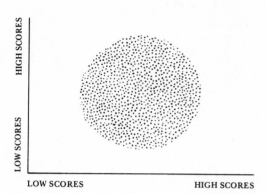

a. No relationship

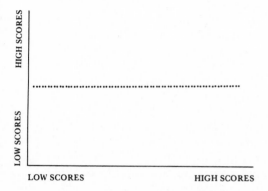

b. No relationship; one variable is constant

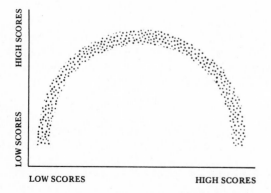

c. No linear relationship; relationship is curvilinear

Figure **4.10**   Three zero-order, linear correlations

correlation is .00. And third, if the two variables are related in a nonlinear way, the correlation is .00. In part c, for example, there is a very strong curvilinear relationship where all points fall close to a curved line, but the *linear* regression line would parallel one of the axes. Thus, while there is a curvilinear relationship, the coefficient of linear correlation is approximately .00.

VARIANT CORRELATION COEFFICIENTS

Six variations of linear correlation are commonly found in test manuals and research literature dealing with reliability and validity. Four are members of the Pearson family of correlation coefficients and are computed by the same or by computationally equivalent formulas (see footnote, p. 52). Two are not members of the Pearson family of coefficients and are calculated differently.

Pearson-Family Coefficients

Different names are typically given to the Pearson product-moment correlation coefficient depending on the scale of measurement used. The first member of the family of correlation coefficients is called the *Pearson product-moment* correlation coefficient and is symbolized by the letter r. This name or symbol is used when the variables to be correlated are measured on an equal-interval (or ratio) scale. The second member of the Pearson family is called the Spearman rho (ρ). This coefficient is used when both variables are measured on an ordinal scale. The third and fourth members of the Pearson family are used when either or both of the variables to be correlated are naturally occurring dichotomous variables (for example, male/female). When a naturally occurring dichotomous variable such as sex is correlated with a continuous, equal-interval variable (height measured in inches for example), the correlation coefficient is called a *point biserial* correlation coefficient ($r_{pt\ bis}$). When two sets of naturally occurring dichotomous variables (for example, male/female and dead/alive) are correlated, the correlation coefficient is called a *phi* coefficient (ϕ).

Non-Pearson-Family Coefficients

A continuous variable can be forced into a dichotomy. For example, the entire range of intelligence can be dichotomized into smart and dull at some arbitrary point on the continuum. If a variable that has been forced into an arbitrary dichotomy (for example, smart/dull) is correlated with a continuous equal-interval variable (for example, grade-point average), the resulting coefficient is called a *biserial* correlation coefficient (r_{bis}). If two arbitrarily dichotomized variables (for example, tall/short, smart/dull) are correlated, the coefficient is called a *tetrachoric* correlation coefficient (r_{tet}).

These two correlation coefficients are computed differently than the Pearson-family coefficients are.

Figure 4.11 illustrates the different correlation coefficients commonly used in measurement that we have discussed.

In test manuals you'll often see correlations between individual test items or between each test item and the total test score. Test authors typically report phi and point biserial correlation coefficients rather than tetrachoric and biserial coefficients in such cases. In selecting particular coefficients, an author assumes the nature of correct or incorrect response. An author who selects phi and point biserial correlations assumes that each response is either correct or incorrect; there are no "in-betweens." The author who reports tetrachoric and biserial correlations assumes that each test item represents a continuum ranging from totally correct to totally incorrect, even though the individual items are scored only as right or wrong. The differences between Pearson-family and non-Pearson-family coefficients should not cause a test administrator any difficulty. Modern tests rely almost exclusively on Pearson-family coefficients. But occasionally one sees r_{tet} or r_{bis}.

CAUSALITY

No discussion of correlation is complete without mentioning causality. Correlation is a necessary but insufficient condition for determining causality. Two variables cannot be causally related unless they are correlated. However, the mere presence of a correlation does not imply causality. For any correlation between two variables (A and B), *three* causal interpretations are possible: A causes B; B causes A; or a third variable, C, causes both A and B. For example, firemen (A) are often present at fires (B). Firemen do not cause fires (A doesn't cause B).[6] Fires cause firemen to be present (B causes A). As a second example, in a sample of children ranging from 6 months to 8 years of age, we might find a positive relationship between shoe size and mental age. Big feet do not cause intelligence (A does not cause B). Moreover, intelligence does not cause big feet (B does not cause A). More likely, as children grow older (C) they tend to increase in both shoe size and mental age; C causes both A and B.

While the above examples illustrate fairly obvious instances of inappropriate reasoning, in testing situations the errors or potential errors are not

---

6. Exceptions have been reported by Bradbury (1953).

CHARACTERISTICS OF VARIABLE 1

		Pearson family			Non-Pearson family
		Ordinal	Equal interval	Natural dichotomy	Forced dichotomy
C H A R A C T E R I S T I C S O F V A R I A B L E 2	Ordinal	Spearman's rho (ρ)			
	Equal interval		Pearson product-moment (r)	Point biserial ($r_{pt\ bis}$)	Biserial (r_{bis})
	Natural dichotomy			Phi (ϕ)	
	Forced dichotomy				Tetrachoric (r_{tet})

Figure **4.11** Different kinds of correlation coefficients are used, depending on the scales of measurement for each variable. There are coefficients for some of the blanks in this figure (for example, biserial phi and rank biserial). Test users are not likely to encounter these in test manuals.

so clear. Since there are at least three possible interpretations of correlational data — and since correlational data do not tell us which interpretation is true — we must never draw causal conclusions from such data.

SUMMARY

Descriptive statistics provide summary information about groups of individuals. Data can be obtained on one of four scales of measurement: *nominal*, *ordinal*, *equal-interval*, and *ratio* scales. Collections of scores are called *distributions*. Distributions are defined by four characteristics: *mean*, *variance*, *skew*, and *kurtosis*. Depending on the scale of measurement, three indices may be used to indicate a distribution's central tendency: the *mode* (the most frequent score), the *median* (the score that separates the top 50 percent from the bottom 50 percent), and the *mean* (the arithmetic average). Depending on the scale of measurement, the dispersion of a distribution can be described by several indices: the *range* of scores, the *semi-interquartile range*, the *variance*, and the *standard deviation*. The quantification of the relationship between two variables is called *correlation*. When there is no relation between variables, the correlation is zero. When there is a perfect relationship between variables, the correlation is one. A plus or a minus sign indicates the type of relationship, not the magnitude of relationship. A positive correlation indicates that high scores on one variable are associated with high scores on the second variable. A negative correlation indicates an inverse relationship: high scores on one variable are associated with low scores on the other variable. There are several types of correlations that are often used in tests.

STUDY QUESTIONS

1. All third-grade pupils in a particular state took an achievement test. The superintendent of public instruction reviewed the test results and in a news conference reported concern for the quality of education in the state. The superintendent reported, "Half the third-grade children in this state performed below average." What is foolish about that?

2. What is the relationship among the mode, median, and mean in a normal distribution?

3. The following statements about test A and test B are known to be true:

Tests A and B measure the same behavior.

Tests A and B have means of 100.

Test A has a standard deviation of 15.

Test B has a standard deviation of 5.

    a. Following classroom instruction, the pupils in Mr. Radley's room earn an average score of 130 on test A. Pupils in Ms. Purple's room earn an average score on test B of 110. On this basis, the local principal concludes that Mr. Radley is a better teacher than Ms. Purple. Why is this inappropriate?

    b. Assuming the pupils were equal prior to instruction, what conclusions could the principal legitimately make?

4. On the Stanford-Binet Intelligence Scale, Harry earns an IQ of 52 and Ralph earns an IQ of 104. Their teacher concludes that Ralph is twice as smart as Harry. To what extent is this conclusion warranted?

PROBLEMS

1. Ms. Robbins administers a test to ten children in her class. The children earn the following scores: 14, 28, 49, 49, 49, 77, 84, 84, 91, 105. For this distribution of scores, find the
  a. Mode
  b. Mean
  c. Range
  d. Variance and standard deviation

2. Mr. Garcia administers the same test to six children in his class. The children earn the following scores: 21, 27, 30, 54, 39, and 63. For these scores, find the
  a. Mean
  b. Range
  c. Variance and standard deviation

3. Ms. Shumway administers a test to six children in her nursery school program. The children earn the following scores: 23, 33, 38, 53, 78, and 93. Find the mean and standard deviation of these six scores.

ANSWERS

1. (a) 49; (b) 63; (c) 92; (d) 784 and 28.

2. (a) 39; (b) 43; (c) 225 and 15.

3. Mean = 53; standard deviation = 25.

ADDITIONAL READING

McCollough, C., & VanAtta, L. *Introduction to descriptive statistics and correlation*. New York: McGraw-Hill, 1965.

Chapter 5
Quantification of Test Performance

Most behaviors occur without systematic observation, quantification, and evaluation; the vast majority of behaviors do not occur in situations specifically structured to quantify and evaluate them. A test is an exception. A test is a structured, standardized situation in which standardized materials are presented to an individual in a predetermined manner in order to evaluate that individual's responses.

How the individual's responses are quantified depends on the test materials, the intent of the test author, and our intent in choosing the test. If we were interested only in a particular question and the response to it (that is, can our student perform one particular task correctly?), we could simply classify the response as right or wrong. Essentially, we'd have no need to quantify the test results. If the task were sufficiently complex, we could expand the classification of the response further (for example, correct, mostly correct, somewhat correct, totally wrong), but still there would be no need for quantification.

More often, though, we are interested in a particular item or question as a representative of a larger population of items, an item domain. For example, we might want to give a test that requires a child to add two single-digit numbers (including zero) whose sum was 10 or less. Since this is a very small domain, our test could well include all fifty-five possible problems. With larger domains of items, it is seldom either practical or desirable to select all the items in the domain. When we sample, particular items are important as representatives of the domain and tend to lose their individual importance. Consequently, we are more likely to be concerned with total scores, either the number correct or the number of partial-credit and full-credit points. We assume that a student's performance on all the items in the domain can be accurately inferred from the performance on the sample of items.

A score on a test that samples a domain of items is difficult to interpret. For example, if Carol earns a raw score of 17 on her spelling test, how good was her performance? Generally, we would first attempt to understand her performance by expressing her raw score as a percentage correct. If there were 50 spelling words, Carol spelled 34 percent of the words correctly. Typically, we would then evaluate Carol's performance by comparing it to the performances of her classmates on the same test. If the raw scores in

Carol's class ranged from 17 to 3, we would conclude that Carol's performance was a good one.

A test performance is typically interpreted by comparing it to the performances of a group of subjects of known demographic characteristics
(age, sex, grade in school, and so on). This group is called a *normative
sample* or *norm group*. These comparison scores are called *derived scores* and
are of two types: developmental scores and scores of relative standing.

Not only are derived scores useful in interpreting the score earned by an
individual, they allow comparisons of several scores earned by one individual or one or more scores earned by several individuals. For example, it
is not terribly helpful to know that George is 70 inches tall; Bill is 6 feet, 3
inches tall; Bruce is 1.93 meters tall; and Alan is 177.8 centimeters tall. To
compare the heights, it is necessary to transform the heights into comparable units. In feet and inches, the four heights are: George, 5 feet, 10
inches; Bill, 6 feet, 3 inches; Bruce, 6 feet, 4 inches; and Alan, 5 feet, 10
inches. Derived scores put raw scores into approximately comparable
units.

DEVELOPMENTAL SCORES

DEVELOPMENTAL LEVELS

Developmental scores are one method of transforming raw scores. The most
common types of developmental scores are age equivalents (mental ages,
for example) and grade equivalents. Suppose the average performance of
10-year-old children on an intelligence test was twenty-seven correct answers. Further, suppose that Horace answered twenty-seven questions
correctly. Horace would have answered as many questions correctly as the
average of 10-year-old children. He would have earned a mental age of 10
years. An *age equivalent* means that a child's raw score is the average (the
median or mean) performance for that age group. Age equivalents are
expressed in years and months; a hyphen is used in age scores (for example, 7-1). A *grade equivalent* means that a child's raw score is the average
(the median or mean) performance for that grade. Grade equivalents are
expressed in grades and tenths of grades; a decimal point is used in grade
scores (for example, 7.1). Age-equivalent and grade-equivalent scores are
interpreted as a performance equal to the average X-year-old's and average
Xth grader's performance, respectively.

Suppose we gave a test to 1,000 children, 100 at each age (within two
weeks of their birthdays) from 5 to 14 years. For each 100 children at each
age, there is a distribution with a mean. These hypothetical means are
connected in Figure 5.1. As the figure shows, a raw score of 16 corre-

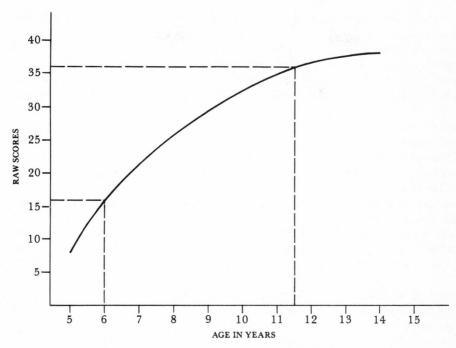

Figure **5.1** Mean number correct for eleven age groups: an example of arriving at age-equivalent scores

sponds exactly to the average score earned by children in the 6-year-old distribution. Thus, the child who earns a score of 16 has an age equivalent of 6 years, 0 months, or 6-0. A score of 36, by contrast, falls *between* the average of the 11-year-old distribution and the average of the 12-year-old distribution. A raw score of 36 would be estimated (*interpolated*) as an age score of 11-6; it would be awarded a score between 11 and 12, despite the fact that no children between 11 and 12 years of age were tested. A score of 4 would fall below the average of the lowest age group, the 5-year-olds. If a child earned a raw score of 4, that child's age equivalent would be estimated (*extrapolated*) by continuing the curve in Figure 5.1. A raw score of 4 could be extrapolated to be the equivalent of an age score of 3-6 although *no* children that young are included in the sample. Similarly, a score greater than the average performance of the oldest children could also be extrapolated.

The interpretation of age and grade equivalents must be done with care. Four problems occur in the use of developmental scores. The first problem is that a child who earns an age equivalent of 12-0 has merely answered

correctly as many questions as the average of children 12 years of age. He
has not necessarily "performed as" a 12-year-old child in the sense that he
may well have attacked the problems in a different way or demonstrated a
different performance pattern than many 12-year-old children. Similarly,
a second grader and a ninth grader may both earn grade equivalents of 4.0.
They have probably not performed identically. Thorndike and Hagen
(1961) have suggested that it is more likely that the younger child has
performed lower-level work with greater accuracy (for instance, successfully answered thirty-eight of the forty-five problems attempted) while the
older child has attempted more problems (for instance, successfully answered thirty-eight of the seventy-eight problems attempted).

The second problem inherent in the use of development scores is interpolation and extrapolation. Average age and grade scores are estimated
for groups of children who are never tested. Consequently, a child can
earn a grade equivalent of 3.2 when only children in the first and last tenth
of third grade have ever been tested; or a child can earn a grade equivalent
of 8.0 even though no children above the sixth grade have been tested.

The third problem is that the use of developmental scores promotes
typological thinking. The average 12-0 child does not exist. The child is a
composite of all 12-0 children. Average 12-0 children more accurately
represent a range of performances, typically the median 90 percent. If we
think of the average performance as only the median value, we are in the
awkward position of having 50 percent of the population performing *below*
average.

The fourth problem with developmental scores is that such scales tend to
be ordinal, not equal interval. The line relating the number correct to the
various ages is typically curved, with a flattening of the curve at higher ages
or grades. Figure 5.1 is a typical developmental curve.

DEVELOPMENTAL QUOTIENTS

Before we try to interpret a developmental score, we must know the age of
the person being evaluated. Knowing developmental age as well as
chronological age (CA) allows a judgment about an individual's relative
performance. Suppose Horace earns a mental age (MA) of 120 months. If
Horace is 8 years (96 months) old, his performance is above average. If
he's 35 years old, however, it's below average. The relationship between
developmental age and chronological age is often quantified as a developmental quotient. For example:

$$IQ = \frac{MA \text{ (in months)}}{CA \text{ (in months)}} \times 100$$

All the problems that apply to developmental levels also apply to developmental quotients. There is one additional problem that is particularly

bothersome. The variance of age scores within various chronological age groups is not constant. As a result, the same quotient may mean different things at different ages. Also, different quotients may mean the same thing at different ages.

RELATIONSHIP BETWEEN DEVELOPMENTAL AGES AND QUOTIENTS

The developmental age is often interpreted as the level of functioning while the quotient is interpreted as the rate of development. In any such scheme, a third variable, chronological age, is always involved. Of the three variables, only chronological age and the developmental quotient are independent of each other (that is, uncorrelated). The developmental age is related to both of the other two variables. In the case of intelligence, the developmental age is far more closely associated with chronological age than it is with the quotient (see Kappauf, 1973). Developmental levels do not provide independent information. They only summarize data for age (or grade) and relative standing.

SCORES OF RELATIVE STANDING

PERCENTILE FAMILY

Percentile ranks (%iles) are useful for both ordinal and equal-interval scales. They are derived scores that indicate the percentage of people or scores that occur *at or below* a given raw score. The percentage correct is *not* the same as the percentage of people scoring below. Percentiles corresponding to particular scores can be computed by a four-step sequence.

1. Arrange the scores from the highest to the lowest (that is, best to worst).

2. Compute the percentage of cases occurring *below* the score to which you wish to assign a percentile rank.

3. Compute the percentage of cases occurring *at* the score to which you wish to assign a percentile rank.

4. Add the percentage of cases occurring below the score to one-half the percentage of cases occurring at the score to obtain the percentile rank.

In Table 5.1, a numerical example is provided. Mr. Greenberg gave a test to his developmental-reading class, which has an enrollment of twenty-five children. The scores are presented in column 1, and the number of children obtaining each score (the *frequency*) is in column 2. Column 3 gives the percentage of all twenty-five scores that each score obtained represents. Column 4 contains the percentage of all twenty-five scores that occurred below that particular score. In the last group of columns, the percentile rank is computed. Only one child scored 24; the one score is 1/25, or 4 percent. No one scored lower than 24 so there is 0 percent (0/25) below 24. The child who scored 24 received a percentile rank of 2 — that is, 0 plus one-half of 4. The next score obtained is 38, and again only one child received this score. Four percent of the total (1/25) scored at 38, and 4 percent of the total scored below 38. Therefore, the percentile rank corresponding to a score of 38 is 6 — that is, $4 + (\frac{1}{2})(4)$. Two children earned a score of 40, and two children have scored below 40. Therefore, the percentile rank for a score of 40 is 12 — that is, $8 + (\frac{1}{2})(8)$. The same procedure is followed for every score a child obtains. The best score in the class, 50, was obtained by two students. The percentile rank corresponding to the highest score in the class is 96.

The interpretation of percentile ranks is straightforward. The data from Table 5.1 provide a specific example. *All* students who score 48 on the test have a percentile rank of 84. These four students have *scored as well as or better than* 84 percent of their classmates on the test. Similarly, an individual who obtains a percentile rank of 21 on an intelligence test has scored as well as or better than 21 percent of the people in the norm sample.

Since the percentile rank is computed using one-half of the percentage of those obtaining a particular score, it is not possible to have percentile ranks of either 0 or 100. Generally, percentile ranks may contain decimals, so it is possible for a score to receive a percentile rank of 99.9 or .1. The fiftieth percentile rank is the median.

Deciles are bands of percentiles that are 10 percentile ranks in width; each decile contains 10 percent of the norm group. The first decile contains percentile ranks from .1 to 9.9; the second decile contains percentile ranks from 10 to 19.9; the tenth decile contains percentile ranks from 90 to 99.9.

Quartiles are bands of percentiles that are 25 percentile ranks in width; each quartile contains 25 percent of the norm group. The first quartile contains percentile ranks from .1 to 24.9; the fourth quartile contains the ranks 75 to 99.9.

STANDARD SCORES

Standard scores are derived scores that transform raw scores in such a way that the set of scores always has the same mean and the same standard deviation. They are used appropriately only with equal-interval (or ratio) scales.

z-Scores

A *z-score* is defined as a standard score with a mean of 0 and a standard deviation of 1. A raw score is converted to a z-score by equation 5.1.

$$z = \frac{X - \bar{X}}{S}$$

$$(5.1)$$

Table **5.1** Computing Percentile Ranks for a Hypothetical Class of Twenty-five

SCORE	FREQUENCY	PERCENT AT THE SCORE	PERCENT BELOW THE SCORE	PERCENTILE RANK				
				PERCENT BELOW THE SCORE	+	$\frac{1}{2}$ OF PERCENT AT THE SCORE	=	PERCENTILE
50	2	8	92	92	+	$(\frac{1}{2})(\,8)$	=	96
49	0							
48	4	16	76	76	+	$(\frac{1}{2})(16)$	=	84
47	0							
46	5	20	56	56	+	$(\frac{1}{2})(20)$	=	66
45	5	20	36	36	+	$(\frac{1}{2})(20)$	=	46
44	3	12	24	24	+	$(\frac{1}{2})(12)$	=	30
43	2	8	16	16	+	$(\frac{1}{2})(\,8)$	=	20
42	0	—	—					
41	0	—	—					
40	2	8	8	8	+	$(\frac{1}{2})(\,8)$	=	12
39	0	—	—					
38	1	4	4	4	+	$(\frac{1}{2})(\,4)$	=	6
.								
.								
.								
24	1	4	0	0	+	$(\frac{1}{2})(\,4)$	=	2

A z-score equals the difference between the raw score less the mean of the distribution, divided by the standard deviation of the distribution. The z-scores are interpreted as standard deviation units. Thus, a z-score of +1.5 means that the score is 1.5 standard deviations *above* the mean of the group. A z-score of −.6 means that the score is .6 standard deviation *below* the mean. A z-score of 0 is the mean performance.

Since + and − signs have a tendency to "get lost" and decimals may be awkward to work with, z-scores often are transformed to other standard scores. The general formula for changing a z-score into a different standard score is given by equation 5.2. In the equation, SS stands for any standard score, as does the subscript ss. Thus, any standard score equals the mean of the distribution of standard scores ($\bar{X}_{ss}$) plus the product of the standard deviation of the distribution of standard scores (S_{ss}) multiplied by the z-score.

$$SS = \bar{X}_{ss} + (S_{ss})(z) \tag{5.2}$$

T-Scores

A *T-score* is a standard score with a mean of 50 and a standard deviation of 10. In Table 5.2, five z-scores are converted to *T*-scores. A *T*-score of 60 is

Table **5.2**   Converting z-Scores to T-Scores

T-SCORE $= 50 + (10)(z)$	
$z = +1.0$	$60 = 50 + (10)(+1.0)$
$z = -1.5$	$35 = 50 + (10)(-1.5)$
$z = -2.1$	$29 = 50 + (10)(-2.1)$
$z = +3.6$	$86 = 50 + (10)(+3.6)$
$z = \quad .0$	$50 = 50 + (10)(\quad .0)$

10 points above the mean (50). Since the standard deviation is 10, a T-score of 60 is one standard deviation above the mean.

Deviation IQs

When the IQ was first introduced, it was defined as the ratio of mental age (*MA*) divided by chronological age (*CA*) multiplied by 100. Soon enough, statisticians found that MA has different variances and standard deviations at different chronological ages. Consequently, the same IQ has different meanings at different ages; the same IQ corresponds to different z-scores at different ages. To remedy that situation, MAs are converted to z-scores for each age group, and z-scores are converted to deviation IQs. *Deviation IQs* are standard scores with a mean of 100 and a standard deviation of 15 or 16 (depending on the test). A z-score can be converted to a deviation IQ by equation 5.2. In Table 5.3, five z-scores are converted to deviation IQs with standard deviations of 15 (column 2) and 16 (column 3).

Stanines

Stanines are standard-score bands that divide a distribution into nine parts. The first stanine includes all scores that are 1.75 standard deviations or more below the mean, and the ninth stanine includes all scores 1.75 or more standard deviations above the mean. The second through eighth stanines are each .5 standard deviation in width with the fifth stanine ranging from .25 standard deviation below the mean to .25 standard deviation above the mean.

COMPARING DERIVED SCORES

Developmental scores, percentiles, and standard scores are interchangeable only under very restricted conditions. Typically, if one wishes to go from one derived score, such as deviation IQ, to another, such as mental

Table **5.3**   Converting z-Scores to Deviation IQs ($\overline{X} = 100$)

z-SCORE	IQ ($S = 15$)	IQ ($S = 16$)
−2.00	70	68
−1.00	85	84
.00	100	100
+1.00	115	116
+2.00	130	132

age, one must go to the raw score and then convert the raw score to the desired derived score. There is an exception to this generalization. If the distribution of raw scores is normal or if the scores have been normalized, there is a direct relationship between percentiles and standard scores. The relationships between developmental scores and both percentiles and standard scores vary with the ages of test takers and the particular tests being used. Figure 5.2 compares various types of scores when the distribution of raw scores is normal.

The selection of the particular type of score to use and to report depends on the purpose of testing and the sophistication of the consumer. In our opinion, developmental scores have little to offer except as extremely vague indications of developmental level. They are readily misinterpreted by both lay and professional people. In order to understand a test performance that is reported in developmental scores, the consumer must generally *convert* developmental scores to other derived scores.

Standard scores are convenient for test authors. Their use allows the author to give equal weight to various test components or subtests. Their utility for the consumer is twofold. First, *if* the score distribution is normal, the consumer can readily *convert* standard scores to percentile ranks. Second, standard scores are very useful in profile analysis.

We favor the use of percentiles. These unpretentious scores require the fewest assumptions for accurate interpretation. The scale of measurement need only be ordinal, although it is very appropriate to compute percentiles on equal-interval or ratio data. The distribution of scores need not be normal; percentiles can be computed for any shape of distribution. They are readily understood by professionals, parents, and children. Most important, however, is the fact that percentiles tell us nothing more than what any norm-referenced derived score can tell us — namely, an individual's relative standing in a group. Reporting scores in percentiles may remove some of the aura surrounding test scores, but it permits test results to be presented in terms users can understand.

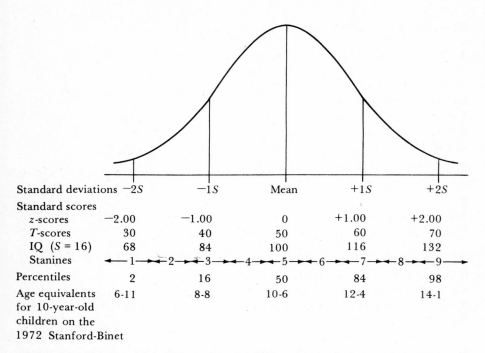

Standard deviations	−2S	−1S	Mean	+1S	+2S
Standard scores					
z-scores	−2.00	−1.00	0	+1.00	+2.00
T-scores	30	40	50	60	70
IQ (S = 16)	68	84	100	116	132
Stanines	←—1—►◄—2—►◄—3—►	◄—4—►◄—5—►◄—6—►	◄—7—►◄—8—►◄—9—►		
Percentiles	2	16	50	84	98
Age equivalents for 10-year-old children on the 1972 Stanford-Binet	6-11	8-8	10-6	12-4	14-1

Figure **5.2** Relationship among selected standard scores, percentiles, and *one* age score and the normal curve

SUMMARY

The number of correct answers or the number of errors a student makes on a test provides the examiner with relatively little information. One method of interpreting such raw scores is to compare them to the raw scores of a group of students of known characteristics called a norm group.

   Two types of comparisons can be made — across ages and within ages. *Developmental scores* (that is, age and grade equivalents) compare students' performances across age or grade groups. Within a group, comparisons can be made using several different types of scores that have different characteristics. A *developmental quotient* (an age or grade equivalent divided by chronological age or actual grade placement, respectively) is the least desirable within-age comparison. Of greater value are *standard scores* (for example, z-scores, T-scores, and deviation IQs). Such scores have a predetermined mean and standard deviation that define them. The best derived scores for general use are percentile ranks.

STUDY QUESTIONS

1. Eleanore and Audrey take an intelligence test. Eleanore obtains an MA of 3-5 and Audrey obtains an MA of 12-2. The test had been standardized on fifty boys and girls at each of the following ages: 3-0 to 3-1, 4-0 to 4-1, 5-0 to 5-1, 6-0 to 6-1, and 7-0 to 7-1. The psychologist reports that Eleanore functions like a child aged 3 years and 5 months, while Audrey has the mental age of a 12-year-old child. Identify five problems inherent in these interpretations.

2. Differentiate between a *ratio IQ* and a *deviation IQ*. Why is a deviation IQ preferable?

3. Sam earned a percentile rank of 83 on a kindergarten admission test. What is the statistical meaning of his score? To what *decile* does the score correspond? To what *quartile* does the score correspond?

4. Marietta takes a battery of standardized tests. The results are as follows:

Test A: Mental age = 8-6
Test B: Reading grade equivalent = 3.1
Test C: Developmental age = 8-4
Test D: Developmental quotient = 103
Test E: Percentile rank = 56

What must the teacher do in order to interpret Marietta's performances on these five scales and compare the performances to each other?

5. Andrew earns a stanine of 1 on an intelligence test. To what *z-scores*, *percentile ranks*, and *T-scores* does his stanine score correspond?

PROBLEMS

Turn back to Table 4.4, which shows the results of the two tests Ms. Smith gave to her arithmetic class. For test 1, make the following computations.

1. Compute the percentile rank for each student.

2. Compute each student's z-score.

3. Convert Bob's, Sam's, Sean's, and Carole's z-scores to T-scores.

4. Convert Lucy's, Carmen's, John's, and Ludwig's z-scores to deviation IQs with a mean of 100 and a standard deviation of 15.

ANSWERS

1. 98, 94, 90, 86, 82, 78, 70, 70, 70, 50, 50, 50, 50, 50, 50, 50, 30, 30, 30, 22, 18, 14, 10, 6, 2

2. 2.17, 2.00, 1.33, 1.00, .67, .5, .33, .33, .33, 0, 0, 0, 0, 0, 0, 0, −.33, −.33, −.33, −.5, −.67, −1.00, −1.33, −2.00, −2.17

3. 72, 63, 50, 45

4. 130, 105, 100, 70

Chapter 6
Reliability

Reliability is a major consideration in evaluating the psychometric characteristics of a test or scale. If a test is reliable and the tested trait or behavior is stable, a person will receive the same score on repeated testings. To the extent that a person's score fluctuates randomly, the test lacks reliability. In education and psychology, we want reliable tests.

Consider the data that are shown in columns 1 and 2 of Table 6.1. A piece of wood was measured with a stretchable rubber ruler ten times on the same morning between 9:00 and 9:02. The measured length varied from 42 inches to 53 inches. The real length — the true length — did not vary; wood cannot expand and contract several inches in a period of two minutes. Length is a stable characteristic, at least over a period of minutes. Therefore, something must be wrong with the ruler. The ruler is an unreliable device, a device that does not produce consistent lengths with repeated measurements.

An easy way to think of reliability is to think of any measurement (any *obtained score*) as consisting of two parts: *true score* and *error*. Error is uncorrelated with the true score and is random. It can as often inflate a score as deflate it; the mean of the error, in the long run, is equal to zero. Since error has a long-term mean of zero, the long-term mean of the obtained scores must equal the true score. In Table 6.1 (columns 3 and 4), it can be seen that each obtained length is the sum of the true length (47 inches) and some amount of error.

Now suppose we measured the length a second time — with a steel ruler. The results of the second set of recordings are in Table 6.2. Note that there is still some variation in length (from $46\frac{3}{4}$ to $47\frac{1}{4}$), but it is considerably less than in the first measurement, with the rubber ruler. The second set of measurements are *more reliable* than the first because they are *less variable*. Since the true score does not fluctuate, variability in the obtained scores is due to error. The greater the error, the greater the variability of obtained (measured) scores. The more variation in an individual's scores from one occasion to another, the lower the reliability of those scores.

The measurement of skills, abilities, characteristics, and traits is analogous to the measurement of length. When psychologists, teachers, and diagnosticians administer tests to children, they would like to assume that those children would earn the same scores if tested again. Test results

Table **6.1**   The Effect of Error on Obtained Length Measured by a
Rubber Ruler

MEASUREMENT TRIAL	OBTAINED LENGTH	=	TRUE LENGTH	+	ERROR
1	48	=	47	+	(1)
2	42	=	47	+	(−5)
3	46	=	47	+	(−1)
4	43	=	47	+	(−4)
5	47	=	47	+	(0)
6	45	=	47	+	(−2)
7	52	=	47	+	(5)
8	50	=	47	+	(3)
9	44	=	47	+	(−3)
10	53	=	47	+	(6)
SUM	470		470	+	0
MEAN	47		47	+	0

would have little meaning if they fluctuated wildly from one occasion to the next. There would be no point in administering an intelligence test if we could not assume that the person tested would earn a similar score tomorrow, next week, or next month. We would not administer an achievement test to a child if we had to assume that the child, without additional instruction, might earn a score 20 percent lower or 20 percent higher if retested with the same test. For an educational or psychological test to be useful, it must be reliable.

As you may recall from the discussion of the assumptions underlying psychological assessment, error of measurement is always present. The important question is, How much error is attached to a particular score? Unfortunately, a direct answer to this question is not readily available. To estimate both the amount of error attached to a particular test score and a person's true score, two statistics are needed: (1) a reliability coefficient of the particular test, and (2) the standard deviation of the test.

THE RELIABILITY COEFFICIENT

The symbol used to denote a reliability coefficient is r with two identical subscripts (for example, r_{xx} or r_{aa}). The *reliability coefficient* is generally defined as the square of the correlation between obtained scores and true scores on a measure (r_{xt}^2). As it turns out, this quantity is identical to the

Table **6.2** Relationship of Obtained Scores (Length) and True Scores Plus Error, for Measurement by a Steel Ruler

MEASUREMENT TRIAL	OBTAINED LENGTH	=	TRUE LENGTH	+	ERROR
1	$47\frac{3}{4}$	=	47	+	$(+\frac{1}{4})$
2	$46\frac{15}{16}$	=	47	+	$(-\frac{1}{16})$
3	$46\frac{15}{16}$	=	47	+	$(-\frac{1}{16})$
4	$47\frac{1}{8}$	=	47	+	$(+\frac{1}{8})$
5	$47\frac{1}{16}$	=	47	+	$(+\frac{1}{16})$
6	$46\frac{3}{4}$	=	47	+	$(-\frac{1}{4})$
7	$46\frac{7}{8}$	=	47	+	$(-\frac{1}{8})$
8	$46\frac{3}{4}$	=	47	+	$(-\frac{1}{4})$
9	$47\frac{1}{16}$	=	47	+	$(+\frac{1}{16})$
10	$47\frac{1}{4}$	=	47	+	$(+\frac{1}{4})$
SUM	470	=	470	+	0
MEAN	47	=	47	+	0

ratio of the variance of true scores to the variance of obtained scores for a distribution. Accordingly, a reliability coefficient indicates the *proportion* of variability in a set of scores that reflects true differences among individuals. In the special case where two parallel forms of a test exist, the Pearson product-moment correlation coefficient between scores from the two forms is equal to the reliability coefficient for either form. These relationships are summarized in equation 6.1, where x and x' are parallel measures, and S^2 is, of course, the variance.

$$r_{xx'} = r_{xt}^2 = \frac{S^2_{\text{true scores}}}{S^2_{\text{obtained scores}}} = r_{xx'} \tag{6.1}$$

If there is relatively little error, the ratio of true-score variance to obtained-score variance approaches a reliability index of 1.00 (*perfect reliability*); if there is a relatively large amount of error, the ratio of true-score variance to obtained-score variance approaches .00 (*total unreliability*).[1] Thus, a test with a reliability coefficient of .90 has relatively less error of measurement and is more reliable than a test with a reliability coefficient of .50.

There are three methods of estimating a reliability coefficient. Depending on the particular test and the preferences of the test authors, the

---

1. Although it is mathematically possible to obtain a negative reliability estimate, such an obtained coefficient is theoretically meaningless.

coefficient may be obtained by test-retest, alternate-form, or internal-consistency methods. Test authors should report their test's estimated reliability and the method (or methods) used to obtain the estimate. Test users should look for reliability information in test manuals in order to evaluate the adequacy of the device.

TEST-RETEST RELIABILITY

Test-retest reliability is an index of *stability*. Educators are interested in many human traits and characteristics that, theoretically, change very little over time. For example, children diagnosed as colorblind at age five are expected to be diagnosed as colorblind at any time in their lives. Colorblindness is an inherited trait that cannot be corrected. Consequently, the trait should be perfectly stable. When a test identifies a child as colorblind on one occasion and not colorblind on a later occasion, the test is unreliable.

Other traits are less stable than color vision over a long period of time; they are developmental. A person's height will increase from birth through adulthood. The increase is relatively slow and predictable. Consequently, measurement with a reliable ruler should indicate little change in height over a one-month period. Radical changes in height (especially decreases!) over short periods of time would cause us to question the reliability of the measurement device. Most educational and psychological characteristics are conceptualized much as height is. For example, we expect reading achievement to increase with length of schooling but to be relatively stable over short periods of time, like two weeks. Devices used to assess traits and characteristics must produce sufficiently consistent and stable results if those results are to have practical meaning in the making of educational decisions.

The procedure for obtaining a stability coefficient is fairly simple. A large number of students are tested. A short time later (preferably two weeks, but the time interval can vary from one day to several months) they are retested with the same device. The students' scores from the two administrations are then correlated. The obtained correlation coefficient is the *stability coefficient*.

Estimates of the amount of error derived from stability coefficients tend to be inflated. Any change in the students' true scores attributable to maturation or learning is added to the error variance unless every student in the sample changes in the same way. Thus, if there is a "maturational spurt" between the two test administrations for only a few students, the change in the true score is incorporated into the error term. Similarly, if some of the students cannot answer some of the questions on the first administration of the test but learn the answers by the second administration, the learning (change in true score) is interpreted as error. The experience of taking the test once may also make answering the same questions the second time easier; the first test may sensitize the student to the second administration of the test. Generally, the closer together in time the test and retest are, the higher the reliability is, since within a shorter time span there is less chance of true scores changing.

ALTERNATE-FORM RELIABILITY

Alternate forms of a test are defined as two tests that measure the same trait or skill to the same extent and are standardized on the same population. Alternate forms offer essentially equivalent tests; sometimes, in fact, they're called *equivalent forms*. Let us look at a nonpsychometric example. At a local variety store counter, where several 12-inch rulers are sold, any ruler is thought to be the equivalent (or alternate form) of any other ruler. If a red ruler and a green ruler are bought and if several objects are measured with both, we would expect a high correlation between the green measurements and the red measurements. The red ruler and green ruler example is analogous to alternate-form reliability. There is one important difference, however. Alternate forms of tests do not contain the same items. Still, while the items are different, the means and variances for the two tests are assumed to be (or should be) the same. In the absence of error of measurement, any subject would be expected to earn the same score on both forms.

To estimate the reliability coefficient by two alternate forms (A and B), a large sample of students is tested with both forms. Half the subjects receive form A, then form B; the other half receive form B, then form A. Scores from the two forms are correlated. The correlation coefficient is a reliability coefficient.

Estimates of reliability based on alternate forms are subject to one of the same constraints as stability coefficients: the more time between the administration of the two (or more) forms, the greater the likelihood of change in true scores. Unlike stability coefficients, alternate-form reliability estimates are not subject to a sensitization effect since the subjects are not tested with the same items twice.

INTERNAL-CONSISTENCY RELIABILITY

The third method of estimating a test's reliability, *internal consistency*, is a little different from the preceding two. Suppose we construct a test containing ten items and administer the test to twenty children. The results of this hypothetical test are presented in Table 6.3. If the ten individual test items all measure the same trait or characteristic, we can divide the test into two five-item tests, each measuring the same trait or characteristic. Thus,

Table **6.3**   Hypothetical Performance of Twenty Children on a Ten-Item Test

| | ITEMS | | | | | | | | | | TOTALS | | |
CHILD	1	2	3	4	5	6	7	8	9	10	TOTAL TEST	EVENS CORRECT	ODDS CORRECT
1	+	+	+	−	+	−	−	−	+	−	5	1	4
2	+	+	+	+	−	+	+	+	−	+	8	5	3
3	+	+	−	+	+	+	+	−	+	+	8	4	4
4	+	+	+	+	+	+	+	+	−	+	9	5	4
5	+	+	+	+	+	+	+	+	+	−	9	4	5
6	+	+	−	+	−	+	+	+	+	+	8	5	3
7	+	+	+	+	+	−	+	−	+	+	8	3	5
8	+	+	+	−	+	+	+	+	+	+	9	4	5
9	+	+	+	−	+	+	−	+	+	+	9	5	4
10	+	+	+	+	+	−	+	+	+	+	9	4	5
11	+	+	+	+	+	−	+	−	−	−	6	2	4
12	+	+	−	+	+	+	+	+	+	+	9	5	4
13	+	+	+	−	−	+	−	+	−	−	5	3	2
14	+	+	+	+	+	+	+	−	+	+	9	4	5
15	+	+	−	+	+	−	−	−	−	−	4	2	2
16	+	+	+	+	+	+	+	+	+	+	10	5	5
17	+	−	+	−	−	−	−	−	−	−	2	0	2
18	+	−	+	+	+	+	+	+	+	+	9	4	5
19	+	+	+	+	−	+	+	+	+	+	9	5	4
20	+	−	−	−	−	+	−	+	−	−	3	2	1

after the test is administered, we can create two alternate forms of the test, each containing one-half of the total number of test items, or five items. We can then correlate the two sets of scores and obtain an estimate of the reliability of each of the two halves in the same way we would estimate the reliability of two alternate forms of a test. This procedure for estimating a test's reliability is called a *split-half reliability estimate*.

It should be apparent that there are many ways to divide a test into two equal-length tests. The ten-item test in Table 6.3 can be divided into 126 different pairs of five-item tests.[2] If the ten items in our full test are arranged in order of increasing difficulty, both halves must contain items from the beginning of the test (that is, easier items) and items from the end of the test (harder items). There are many ways of dividing such a test (for example 1, 4, 5, 8, 9, and 2, 3, 6, 7, 10). The most common way to divide a test is by odd-numbered and even-numbered items (see the columns labeled "evens correct" and "odds correct" in Table 6.3).

2. $126 = 10!/(5!5!)$

While odd-even divisions and subsequent correlation of the two halves of a test are a common method for estimating a test's internal-consistency reliability, they do not necessarily offer the best method. In fact, depending on how the test is divided into two parts, the estimated reliability will vary. A more generalizable method of estimating internal consistency has been developed by Cronbach (1951) and is called *coefficient alpha*. Coefficient alpha is the average split-half correlation based on all possible divisions of a test into two parts. In practice there is no need to compute all possible correlation coefficients; coefficient alpha can be computed from the variances of individual test items and the variance of the total test score as shown in equation 6.2, where k is the number of items in the test.

$$r_{aa} = \frac{k}{k-1} \left(1 - \frac{\Sigma S^2_{\text{items}}}{S^2_{\text{test}}} \right)$$

(6.2)

Coefficient alpha can be used when test items are scored pass-fail or when more than one point of credit is awarded for a correct response. An earlier, more restrictive method of estimating a test's reliability, a method based on the average correlation between all possible split halves, was developed by Kuder and Richardson. This procedure is called *KR-20* and *is* coefficient alpha for dichotomously scored test items (that is, those that can be scored only right or wrong). Equation 6.2 can be used with dichotomous data; however, in this case the resulting estimate of reliability is usually called a KR-20 estimate rather than coefficient alpha.

There are two major considerations in the use of internal-consistency estimates. First, this method should not be used for timed tests or tests that are not completed by all those being tested. Second, it provides no estimate of stability over time.

WHAT METHOD SHOULD BE USED?

The particular trait or skill being assessed has a great deal to do with the best choice of a method for computing the reliability coefficient. But in general, for educational and psychological tests, we subscribe to Nunnally's (1967, p. 217) hierarchy for estimating reliability:

1. Use alternate-form reliability with a two-week interval.

2. If alternate forms are not available, divide the test into equivalent halves and administer the halves with a two-week interval between, correcting the correlation coefficient by the Spearman-Brown formula, equation 6.3 below.

3. When alternate forms are not available and subjects cannot be tested more than one time, use coefficient alpha.

FACTORS AFFECTING RELIABILITY

Several factors affect a test's reliability, and these factors can inflate or deflate reliability estimates.

TEST LENGTH

As a general rule, the more items on a homogeneous test, the more reliable the test. Thus, long tests tend to be more reliable than short tests. This fact is especially important in an internal-consistency estimate of reliability, because in this kind of estimate the number of test items is reduced by 50 percent. Internal-consistency estimates of reliability actually estimate the reliability of half the test. Therefore, such estimates are often corrected by a formula developed by Spearman and Brown. As shown in equation 6.3, the reliability of the total test is equal to twice the reliability as estimated by internal consistency divided by the sum of one plus the reliability estimate.

$$r_{xx} = \frac{2r_{(1/2)(1/2)}}{1 + r_{(1/2)(1/2)}} \tag{6.3}$$

For example, if coefficient alpha were computed on a test and found to be .80, the corrected estimated reliability would be .89:

$$.89 = \frac{(2)(.80)}{1 + .80} = \frac{1.60}{1.80}$$

TEST-RETEST INTERVAL

A person's true abilities can and do change between two administrations of a test. The greater the amount of time between the two administrations, the more likely the possibility that true scores will change. Thus, when employing stability or alternate-form estimates of reliability, one must pay close attention to the interval between tests. Generally, the shorter the interval, the higher the estimated reliability.

CONSTRICTION OF RANGE

The reliability coefficient is directly related to the variability of the test.[3] The greater the variance of a test, the greater its reliability estimate. When samples with relatively small variances are used to estimate reliability, the resulting estimates will be lower.

---

3. The relationship is shown in the formula $r_{xx} = 1 - SEM^2/S_{test}^2$. The SEM (standard error of measurement) is discussed in a later section of this chapter.

GUESSING

Guessing is responding randomly to items. Even if a guess results in a correct response, it introduces error into a test score and into our interpretation of that score.

VARIATION WITHIN THE TESTING SITUATION

The amount of error that variation in the testing situation introduces into the results of testing can vary considerably. Children can misread or misunderstand the directions for a test, get a headache halfway through testing, lose their place on the answer sheet, break the point on their pencil, or choose to watch a squirrel eat nuts on the windowsill of the classroom rather than taking the test. All such situational variations introduce an indeterminate amount of error in testing and, in doing so, lower reliability.

STANDARD ERROR OF MEASUREMENT

One of the primary reasons for obtaining a reliability coefficient is to be able to estimate the amount of error usually "attached" to a subject's true score. The standard error of measurement (SEM) allows the test user to do this.

In the first part of this chapter, the difficulties stemming from measuring with a rubber ruler were presented. If we measured a 47-inch piece of wood a large number of times (say, twenty-five times) with the rubber ruler, we might get a normal distribution of lengths centered at 47 (the "true score" in Figure 6.1). Departures from 47 inches represent the addition of error to the true length; the distribution is an error distribution around the true length. The standard deviation of this error distribution around a true score is called the *standard error of measurement* (SEM).

When we test a student, we typically test only once. Therefore, we cannot generate a distribution similar to the one depicted in Figure 6.1. Consequently, we do not know the test taker's true score or the variability of the measurement error that forms a distribution around that true score. However, we can use what we know about the test's reliability and standard deviation to estimate what that distribution would be. Equation 6.4 is the formula for finding the standard error of measurement of a test. The standard error of measurement (SEM) equals the standard deviation of the obtained scores (S) multiplied by the square root of one minus the reliability coefficient. The type of unit (IQ, raw score, or whatever) in which the SEM

$$\text{SEM} = S\sqrt{1 - r_{xx}} \qquad (6.4)$$

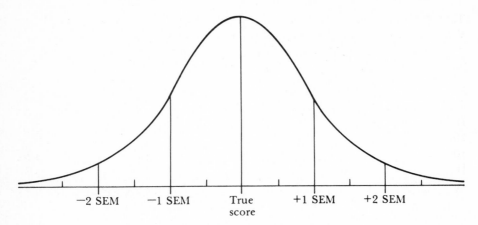

Figure **6.1**   The standard error of measurement is the standard deviation of the error distribution around a true score for one subject

is expressed is the type of unit in which the standard deviation is expressed. From equation 6.4 it is apparent that as the standard deviation increases, the SEM increases; and as the reliability coefficient decreases, the SEM increases. In part a of Table 6.4 the same standard deviation (10) is used with different reliability coefficients. As reliability coefficients decrease, SEMs increase. When the reliability coefficient is .96, the SEM is 2; when the reliability is .64, the SEM is 6. In part b of Table 6.4, different standard deviations are used with the same reliability coefficient ($r_{xx} = .91$). As the standard deviation increases, the SEM increases.

Because of the presence of measurement error, there is always some uncertainty about an individual's true score. The standard error of measurement provides information about the certainty or confidence with which a test score can be interpreted. When the SEM is relatively large, the uncertainty is large; we cannot be very sure of the individual's score. When the SEM is relatively small, the uncertainty is small; we can be more sure of the score.

ESTIMATED TRUE SCORES

Unfortunately, we never know a subject's true score. Moreover, the obtained score on a test is not the best estimate of the true score. As mentioned in the previous discussion, true scores and errors are uncorrelated. However, obtained scores and errors *are* correlated. Scores above the test mean have more "lucky" error (error that raises the obtained score above the true score), while scores below the mean have more "unlucky" error

Table **6.4** Relationship Between Reliability Coefficient and SEM (part a) and Relationship Between Standard Deviation and SEM (part b)

PART a			PART b		
S	r_{xx}	SEM	S	r_{xx}	SEM
10	.96	2	5	.91	1.5
10	.84	4	10	.91	3.0
10	.75	5	15	.91	4.5
10	.64	6	20	.91	6.0
10	.36	8	25	.91	7.5

(error that lowers the obtained score below the true score). Thus, obtained scores above or below the mean are often more discrepant than true scores. As can be seen from Figure 6.2, the less reliable the test, the greater the discrepancy between obtained scores and true scores. Nunnally (1967, p. 220) has provided an equation (equation 6.5) for determining the estimated true score (X'). The estimated true score equals the test mean plus the product of the reliability coefficient and the difference between the obtained score and the group mean. The discrepancy between obtained

$$X' = \overline{X} + (r_{xx})(X - \overline{X}) \tag{6.5}$$

scores and estimated true scores is a function of both the reliability of the obtained score and the difference between the obtained score and the mean. In Table 6.5, the mean in each example is 100; the obtained scores are 90, 75, and 50. The reliability coefficients are .90, .70, and .50. When the obtained score is 90 and the estimated reliability is .90, the estimated true score is 91 [91 = 100 + (.90)(90 − 100)]. However, when the obtained score is 50 and the reliability coefficient is .90, the estimated true score is 55 [100 + (.90)(50 − 100)]. Even when the reliability coefficient is constant, the farther an obtained score is from the mean, the greater will be the discrepancy between the obtained score and the estimated true score.

When the obtained score is 75 and the reliability coefficient is .90, the estimated true score is 77.5 [100 + (.90)(75 − 100)]. However, when the reliability coefficient drops to .50 and the obtained score doesn't change, the estimated true score rises to 87 [100 + (.50)(75 − 100)].

When the obtained score is below the test mean and the reliability coefficient is less than 1.00, the estimated true score is *always* higher than the obtained score. Conversely, when the obtained score is above the test mean and the reliability coefficient is less than 1.00, the estimated true score is *always* less than the obtained score. Note that the equation does not give the *true score*, only the *estimated true score*.

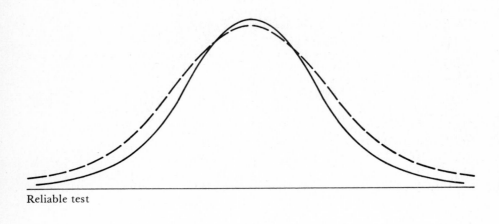

Reliable test

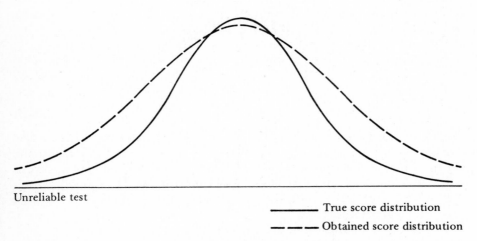

Unreliable test

————— True score distribution

— — — Obtained score distribution

Figure **6.2**   Relationship between true-score distribution and obtained-score distribution for reliable and unreliable tests

CONFIDENCE INTERVALS

Although we can never know a person's true score, measurement is not a hopeless activity. We can estimate a true score, and we can estimate the standard deviation of the error of measurement about the true score. With these two bits of information, we can construct a range within which we know the exact probability of including a person's true score. This range is

Table **6.5** Estimated True Scores for Different Obtained Scores on Tests with Different Reliability Coefficients

TEST MEAN ($\overline{X}$)	RELIABILITY COEFFICIENT (r_{xx})	OBTAINED SCORE (X)	ESTIMATED TRUE SCORE (X')	DIFFERENCE BETWEEN OBTAINED SCORE AND ESTIMATED TRUE SCORE
100	.90	90	91.0	1.0
100	.90	75	77.5	2.5
100	.90	50	55.0	5.0
100	.70	90	93.0	3.0
100	.70	75	82.5	7.5
100	.70	50	65.0	15.0
100	.50	90	95.0	5.0
100	.50	75	87.5	12.5
100	.50	50	75.0	25.0

called a *confidence interval*. A 50 percent confidence interval is a range of values within which the true score will be found 50 percent of the time. Of course, 50 percent of the time the true score will be outside the interval. A larger range — a greater confidence interval — could make us feel more confident that we have included the true score within the range. But it is impossible to construct an interval in which the true score will always be contained. However, if we construct 95 percent or 99 percent confidence intervals, then the chances are only 5 percent and 1 percent, respectively, that the true score will fall outside the confidence interval.

ESTABLISHING SYMMETRICAL CONFIDENCE INTERVALS
FOR TRUE SCORES

The characteristics of a normal curve have already been discussed. We can apply the relationship between z-scores and areas under the normal curve to the normal distribution of error around a true score. We can use equation 6.5 to estimate the mean of the distribution (the true score) and equation 6.4 to estimate the standard deviation of the distribution (the standard error of measurement). With these two estimates, we can construct a confidence interval for the *true score*. Since 68 percent of all elements in a normal distribution fall within one standard deviation of the mean, there is a 68 percent chance that the true score is within one SEM of the estimated true score. We can construct an interval with almost any

Table **6.6** Commonly Used z-Scores, Extreme Areas, and Area
Included Between + and − z-Score Values

Z-SCORE	EXTREME AREA	AREA BETWEEN + AND −
.67	25.0%	50%
1.00	16.0%	68%
1.64	5.0%	90%
1.96	2.5%	95%
2.33	1.0%	98%
2.57	.5%	99%

degree of confidence except 100 percent confidence. Table 6.6 contains the extreme area for the z-scores most commonly used in constructing confidence intervals. The general formula for a confidence interval is given in equation 6.6. The lower limit of the confidence interval equals the estimated true score less the product of the z-score associated with that level of confidence and the standard error of measurement. The upper limit of the confidence interval is the estimated true score plus the product of the z-score and the SEM.

Lower limit of c.i. $= X' - (z\text{-score})(\text{SEM})$
Upper limit of c.i. $= X' + (z\text{-score})(\text{SEM})$ (6.6)

To construct a symmetrical confidence interval for a true score, a simple procedure is followed.

1. Select the degree of confidence, for example, 95 percent.

2. Find the z-score associated with that degree of confidence. (For example, a 95 percent confidence interval is between z-scores of −1.96 and +1.96.)

3. Multiply each z-score associated with the confidence interval (for example, 1.96 for 95 percent confidence) by the SEM.

4. Find the estimated true score.

5. Take the product of the z-score and the SEM, and both add it to and subtract it from the estimated true score.

For example, assume that a person's estimated true score is 75 and that the SEM is 5. Further assume that you wish to be 68 percent sure of constructing an interval that will contain the true score. Sixty-eight percent of the time, the true score will be contained in the interval of 70 to 80

[75 − (1)(5) to 75 + (1)(5)]; there is a 16 percent chance that the true score is less than 70 and a 16 percent chance that the true score is greater than 80. If you are unwilling to be wrong 32 percent of the time, you must increase the width of the confidence interval. Thus, with the same true score (75) and SEM (5), if you wish 95 percent confidence, the size of the interval must be increased; it would have to range from 65 to 85 [75 − (1.96)(5) to 75 + (1.96)(5)]. Ninety-five percent of the time the true score will be contained within that interval; there is a 2.5 percent chance that the true score is less than 65, and there is a 2.5 percent chance that it is greater than 85.

ESTABLISHING ASYMMETRICAL CONFIDENCE INTERVALS
FOR TRUE SCORES

Although symmetrical confidence intervals are the rule rather than the exception when confidence intervals are used, it is also possible to establish asymmetrical confidence intervals for true scores. Massing extreme areas puts more uncertainty in one direction than in the other; all the uncertainty can even be put in one tail of the error distribution. As part a of Figure 6.3 shows, we can be 95 percent sure that the true score is equal to or *less* than 1.64 SEMs *above* the estimated true score. As part b shows, we can just as easily be 95 percent sure that the true score is equal to or *higher* than 1.64 SEMs *below* the estimated true score.

Whether it is better to distribute the extreme area symmetrically or mass it in one tail depends on the use to which test information is to be put and the consequences of that use. For example, if the results of a standardized achievement battery for an "average" third grader are reported to a parent, a 50 percent symmetrical confidence interval is probably adequate. If the results of an individually administered intelligence test are used to recommend placement in a special class for the educable mentally retarded, we would want greater confidence and a massed extreme area. For example, if a state requires an IQ of 75 for special class placement[4] and if a child earns an IQ of 60 on an intelligence test ($\bar{X} = 100, S = 15, r_{xx} = .91$), how sure can we be that the child is eligible for placement? The child's estimated true IQ is 64, and the SEM is 4.5.[5] Let us mass the extreme area at the upper end of the error distribution and select the 95 percent level of confidence. Ninety-five percent of the time the child's true score would be equal to or less than 71.[6] Thus, we can be sure the child is eligible for placement.

---

4. IQs necessary for special educational placement vary from state to state.
5. Estimated true score = 100 + (60 − 100)(.91) = 63.6; SEM = $15\sqrt{1 − .91}$ = 4.5.
6. Upper limit of the massed 95 percent confidence interval = 64 + (1.64)(4.5) = 71.38.

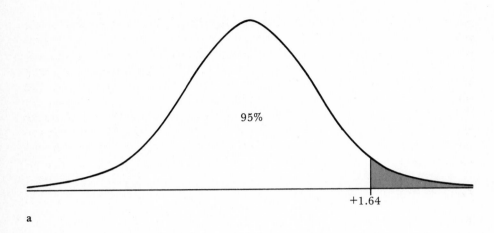

a

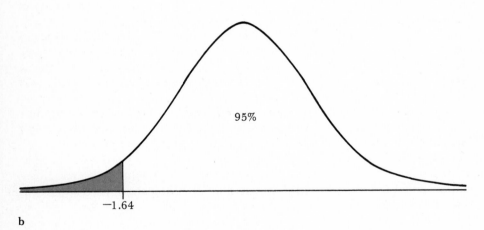

b

Figure **6.3** Massed extreme areas (one tail) for 95 percent confidence interval

DIFFERENCE SCORES

In many applied settings, we are interested in discrepancies (differences) between two scores. For example, we might wish to know if a child's achievement age or her perceptual age is commensurate with her mental age. In many definitions of educational disorders (for example, learning disabilities), a "significant" discrepancy is specified. There is one major difficulty in the use of difference or discrepancy scores. *If the two tests on*

*which the discrepancy is based are correlated, the discrepancy score may be less
reliable than either score.*

The reliability of a difference between two scores (A and B) is a function
of four things: (1) the reliability of test A, (2) the reliability of test B, (3) the
correlation between test A and test B, and (4) differences in norm groups.
The formula for the reliability of a difference is given in equation 6.7
(Thorndike & Hagen, 1961, p. 192). The reliability of a difference equals
the average reliability of the two tests $[\frac{1}{2}(r_{aa} + r_{bb})]$ less the correlation
between the two tests $(-r_{ab})$; this difference is divided by one minus the
correlation between the two tests $(1 - r_{ab})$. This formula does *not* account

$$r_{xx(\text{dif})} = \frac{\frac{1}{2}(r_{aa} + r_{bb}) - r_{ab}}{1 - r_{ab}} \tag{6.7}$$

for differences in norm populations. Table 6.7 demonstrates how quickly
differences between tests become unreliable as a function of the correlation
between tests A and B and their average reliability. As the correlation
between the two tests approaches the average reliability, the reliability of
the difference between scores on the two tests approaches zero.

As for single scores, a standard deviation for difference scores can be
computed. The formula for the standard deviation of a difference is given
in equation 6.8. The standard deviation of a difference is equal to the
square root of the sum of the variances of tests A and B less twice the
product of the correlation of A and B multiplied by the standard deviations
of A and B. The reliability of a difference and the standard deviation of a
difference are combined in the same manner for a difference as for a single
score. Substituting in equation 6.4, equation 6.9 is generated.

$$S_{\text{dif}} = \sqrt{S_a^2 + S_b^2 - 2r_{ab}S_aS_b} \tag{6.8}$$

$$\text{SEM}_{\text{dif}} = \sqrt{S_a^2 + S_b^2 - 2r_{ab}S_aS_b} \sqrt{1 - \frac{\frac{1}{2}(r_{aa} + r_{bb}) - r_{ab}}{1 - r_{ab}}} \tag{6.9}$$

The standard error of measurement of a difference describes the distribution of differences between *obtained* scores. To evaluate difference
scores, the simplest method is to establish a level of confidence (for example, 95%) and find the z-score associated with that level of confidence
(1.96). We then divide the obtained difference by the SEM of difference.
If the quotient exceeds the z-score associated with the level of confidence
selected (1.96), the obtained difference is reliable. When a difference is
assumed reliable at a particular level of confidence, we can estimate the
true difference in the same manner as we estimate a true score on one test.
In general, we assume that the group mean difference is .00. Thus, the
formula for estimating the true difference for a particular student sim-
plifies to equation 6.10.

Estimated true difference = (obtained difference)$(r_{xx(\text{dif})})$ \hfill (6.10)

Table **6.7**   The Reliability of a Difference Score Is a Function of the
Average Reliability and Intercorrelation of the Two Tests

AVERAGE RELIABILITY	CORRELATION BETWEEN A AND B	RELIABILITY OF THE DIFFERENCE BETWEEN A AND B
.90	.80	.50
.90	.60	.75
.90	.40	.83
.70	.60	.25
.70	.40	.50
.50	.40	.50

As an illustration of the procedure for evaluating a difference, consider
the following data for a child from tests having the psychometric characteristics shown in Table 6.8. The mental-ability test and the reading test
are fairly reliable (.90 and .86). The two tests are correlated (.75). The
reliability of the difference between scores on these two tests is poor (.52),
and the SEM of the difference (.5 year) is larger than the SEM of either test
taken alone. The hypothetical child's obtained difference (−3 years) shows
a large discrepancy. To be 95 percent sure that the observed discrepancy
represents a reliable difference, we divide the obtained difference (−3
years) by the SEM of the difference (.5 year). The obtained quotient (−6.0)
exceeds 1.96. We can be 95 percent sure that the child's mental ability and
reading performance are not equal. To estimate the extent of the discrepancy, we can compute the estimated true difference. Using equation 6.10,
we find the hypothetical child's estimated true difference to be about −1.5
years.

Educators and psychologists routinely make decisions about placement
and programs for children on the basis of differences between scores the
children earn on various tests. They typically do so without examining
carefully the reliability of the tests used and, more important, without
considering the reliability of difference scores. In view of what Part 3 of
this book will have to say about the relatively low reliability of many tests
used with children, it should be clear that failure to consider the lowered
reliability of differences and to estimate true differences not only can but
does lead to haphazard programming and placement.

We realize that computing estimated true scores, standard errors of
measurement, and confidence levels for both single scores and difference
scores can be very time-consuming. However, we believe that a little more

Table **6.8**   Reliability of a Difference Between Mental Age and Reading Age for a Hypothetical Child, Where Mental Age and Reading Age Are Correlated (.75)

SCORE	$\bar{X}$ YEARS	S YEARS	r_{xx}	SEM	CHILD'S SCORE	ESTIMATED TRUE SCORE
Reading age	9.0	1.0	.86	.38[c]	5.5	6.0[e]
Mental age	9.0	1.0	.90	.32[c]	8.5	8.55[e]
Difference	.0	.71[a]	.52[b]	.50[d]	3.0	−1.5[f]

[a] From equation 6.9.   [d] From equation 6.10.
[b] From equation 6.7.   [e] From equation 6.5.
[c] From equation 6.4.   [f] From equation 6.10.

time devoted to making decisions about a child's future is time wisely spent if it results in *appropriate* placement for the child. Almost everyone believes that placement should not be left to chance. It is time to put this belief into operation. Chapter 20 provides several detailed examples of the computation of estimated true scores, standard errors of measurement, and confidence intervals.

DESIRABLE STANDARDS

It is important that test authors present sufficient information in test manuals for the test user to interpret test results accurately. A test must consistently measure something before we can say it measures anything. However, we cannot assume that because a test measures some trait or skill consistently (reliably), it consistently measures what we want to measure. Whether a test measures what it purports to measure is a question of validity, which is the topic of the next chapter. However, for a test to be valid (to measure what its authors claim it measures), it must be reliable. Although not the only condition that must be met, reliability is a necessary condition for validity. No test can measure what it purports to measure unless it's reliable. No score is interpretable unless it's reliable. Therefore, test authors and publishers must present sufficient reliability data to allow the user to interpret test results accurately. Reliability indexes for each type of score (for example, raw scores, grade equivalents, and standard scores) must be reported. These should be reported for each age and grade. Furthermore, these should be presented clearly in tabular form in one place. Test authors should not play "hide and seek" with reliability data. Test authors who recommend computing difference scores should provide, whenever possible, the reliability of the difference and the SEM of the difference. Once test users have access to reliability data, they must judge the adequacy of the test.

When a test score is reported, we strongly recommend that the estimated true score and a 68 percent confidence interval for that true score also be reported. How high must a reliability coefficient be before it can be used in applied settings? It depends on the use to which test data are put. A simple answer is to use the most reliable test available. However, such a response is misleading, for the "best" test may have a reliability coefficient too low for any application (for example, .12). We recommend that two standards of reliability be used in applied settings.

1. *Group data.* If test scores are to be used for administrative purposes and are reported for groups, a reliability of .60 should probably be the minimum.

2. *Individual data.* If a test score is used to make a decision for one student, a much higher standard of reliability is demanded. When important educational decisions, such as tracking and placement in a special class, are to be made for a student, the minimum standard should be .90. When the decision being made is a screening decision, such as a recommendation that a child receive further assessment, there is still need for high reliability. For screening devices, we recommend a .80 standard.

SUMMARY

Reliability refers to the absence of error in measurement. Three methods of computing a *reliability coefficient* are commonly used: *test-retest*, *alternate-form*, and *internal-consistency*. Reliability coefficients may range from .00 (total lack of reliability) to 1.00 (total reliability); .90 is recommended as the minimum standard for tests used to make important educational decisions for children. In diagnostic work with children the reliability coefficient has three major uses: It allows the user (1) to estimate the test's relative freedom from measurement error, (2) to estimate an individual subject's true score, and (3) to find the standard error of measurement. Knowledge of the standard error of measurement and the estimated true score allows the test user to construct confidence intervals for a subject's true score.

The discussion of estimated true scores, standard error of measurement, and confidence intervals can be extended to difference or discrepancy scores. The reliability of a difference score is affected by the reliability of the tests and by the correlation between the tests on which the difference is based. Differences in norm samples also affect difference scores, but this effect cannot be evaluated. Provided the two tests are correlated, difference scores are less reliable than the average of the reliabilities of the tests on which the difference is based.

There are several factors that affect reliability: the method used to calculate the reliability coefficient, test length, the test-retest interval, constriction of range, guessing, and variation within the testing situation.

STUDY QUESTIONS

1. Why is it necessary that a test be reliable?

2. Test A and test B have identical means and standard deviations. Test A has a standard error of measurement of 4.8; test B has a standard error of measurement of 16.3. Which test is more reliable, and why?

3. What is the greatest limitation of reliability estimates based on test-retest correlation?

4. List and explain five factors that affect the estimated reliability of a test.

5. The standard error of measurement is the standard deviation of what? Illustrate your answer with a drawing.

PROBLEMS

1. Mr. Treacher administers an intelligence test ($\bar{X} = 100$, $S = 16$, $r_{xx} = .75$) to his class. Five children earn the following scores: 68, 124, 84, 100, and 148. What are the estimated true scores for these children?

2. What is the standard error of measurement for the intelligence test in problem 1?

3. What are the upper and lower boundaries of a symmetrical confidence interval of 95 percent for the first child?

4. What are the upper and lower boundaries of a symmetrical confidence interval of 50 percent for the child who earns a score of 100?

5. Test A and test B have reliabilities of .90 and .80; the correlation between tests A and B is .50. What is the reliability of a difference between a score on test A and test B?

ANSWERS

1. 76, 118, 88, 100, 136
2. 8
3. 92, 60
4. 105, 95
5. .70

ADDITIONAL READING

American Psychological Association, American Educational Research Association, & National Council on Measurement in Education. *Standards for educational and psychological tests*. Washington, DC: American Psychological Association, 1974, pp. 48–55.

Ghiselli, E. E. *Theory of psychological measurement*. New York: McGraw-Hill, 1964. (Chapter 8, pp. 207–253.)

Chapter 7
Validity

Validity refers to the extent to which a test measures what its authors or users claim it measures. Specifically, test validity concerns the appropriateness of the inferences that can be made on the basis of test results. A test's validity is not measured; rather, a test's validity for various uses is judged on the basis of a wide array of information. The process of gathering information about the appropriateness of test-based inferences is called *validation*. Three interrelated types of validity are usually considered in the validation of tests: content validity, criterion-related validity, and construct validity.

The valid use of tests is the responsibility of both the test author and the test user. A test author

should present the evidence of validity for each type of inference for which use of the test is recommended. (APA et al., 1974, p. 31)

If a user wants to use a test in a situation for which the use of the test has not been previously validated, or for which there is no supported claim for validity, he is responsible for validation. . . . He who makes the claim for validity is responsible for providing the evidence. (APA et al., 1974, p. 33)

To evaluate a test's validity, test users must have a clear understanding of what is to be measured. The definition of what is to be measured precedes the decision about how the measuring is to be done. Test authors should not start with a series of test items and then decide what those items might measure. Rather, they should first define what a trait (or characteristic or skill) is and what it is not and then select items to measure it. Selection of test items depends on a test author's own definition of and assumptions about the domain to be measured.

METHODS OF TEST VALIDATION

This section treats content, criterion-related, and construct validity separately. However, it is important to note that these three aspects of validity are not separable in the real world; they are interdependent.

CONTENT VALIDITY

Content validity is evaluated by a careful examination of the content of a test. Such an examination is judgmental in nature and requires a clear definition of what the content should be. Content validity is established by examining three factors: the appropriateness of the types of items included, the completeness of the item sample, and the way in which the items assess the content.

The first factor to examine in determining content validity is the appropriateness of the items included in the test. We must ask, "Is this an appropriate test question?" and "Does this test item really measure the domain?" Consider the four test items from a hypothetical elementary (kindergarten through grade 3) arithmetic achievement test presented in Figure 7.1. The first item requires the student to read and add two single-digit numbers whose sum is less than 10. This seems to be an appropriate item for an elementary arithmetic achievement test. The second item requires the student to complete a geometric progression. While this item is mathematical, the skills and knowledge required to complete the question correctly have not typically been taught by the time a child is in third grade. Therefore, one should question the validity of the test item. The third item also requires the student to read and add two single-digit numbers whose sum is less than 10. However, the question is written in Spanish. While the content of the question is suitable (this is an elementary addition problem), the methods of presentation require other skills. Failure to complete the item correctly could be attributed to the fact that the child does not know Spanish and/or to the fact that the child does not know "2 + 3 = 5." One should conclude that the item is not valid for an arithmetic test for children who do not read Spanish. The fourth item requires that the student select the correct form of the Latin verb *amare* ("to love"). Clearly, this is an inappropriate item for an elementary arithmetic test and should be rejected as invalid.

The second factor to examine in determining content validity is the completeness of the item sample. The validity of any elementary arithmetic test would be questioned if it included *only* problems requiring the addition of single-digit numbers whose sum was less than 10. One would reasonably expect an arithmetic test to include a far broader sample of tasks (for example, addition of two- and three-digit numbers, subtraction, and so forth).

The third factor to examine is how the test items assess the content — that is, the level of mastery at which the content is assessed. In the previous example, the child was expected to add two single-digit numbers whose sum was less than 10. However, one could evaluate a child's arithmetic skills in a variety of ways. The child might be required to recognize the

1. Three and six are _____.
   a. 4
   b. 7
   c. 8
   d. 9
2. What number follows in this series? 1, 2.5, 6.25, _____
   a. 10
   b. 12.5
   c. 15.625
   d. 18.50
3. ¿Cuántos son tres y dos?
   a. 3
   b. 4
   c. 5
   d. 6
4. Ille puer puellas _____.
   a. amo
   b. amat
   c. amamus
   d. amant

Figure **7.1**   Sample multiple-choice questions for an elementary-level (K–3) arithmetic achievement test

correct answer in a multiple-choice array, supply the correct answer, apply the proper addition facts in a word problem, or analyze the condition under which the mathematical relationship obtains.

One way to insure content validity of a test is to construct a test that measures the desired content in the desired way. Bloom, Hastings, and Madaus (1971) have devoted several hundred pages to this topic in their book *Handbook of formative and summative evaluation of student learning*. They have recommended that authors of achievement tests develop a *table of specifications* for the content to be tested. Such a table can be readily generalized to other types of tests. A table of specifications formally enumerates the particular contents of a test and the processes (or behaviors) it assesses. Content refers to the particular domains or subdomains the test author wishes to assess. The task of the test author is to specify the content as precisely as possible in order to convey clearly to both test author and test user what is being measured. The next step is to specify how the particular content objectives will be measured (the process by which the measurement will occur). Several levels of measurement are possible; they range from knowledge objectives to evaluation objectives. The definitions used by Bloom (1956) and Bloom, Hastings, and Madaus (1971) follow.

1. *Knowledge* is the "recall or recognition of specific elements in a subject area" (Bloom et al., p. 41).

2. *Comprehension* consists of three types of measurement: translation, interpretation, and extrapolation. Translation refers to rewording information or putting it into one's own words. Interpretation is evidenced "when a student can go beyond recognizing the separate parts of a communication . . . and can see the interrelationships among the parts" (Bloom et al., p. 149). Interpretation also is evidenced when a student can differentiate the essentials of a message from unimportant elements. Extrapolation refers to the student's ability to go beyond literal comprehension and to make inferences about what the anticipated outcome of an action is or what will happen next.

3. *Application* is "the use of abstractions in particular and concrete situations. The abstractions may be in the form of general ideas, rules of procedures, or generalized methods. The abstractions may also be technical principles, ideas, and theories which must be remembered and applied" (Bloom, 1956, p. 205).

4. *Analysis* is "the breakdown of a communication into its constituent elements or parts such that the relative hierarchy of ideas is made clear and/or the relations between ideas expressed are made explicit. Such analyses are intended to clarify the communication, to indicate how the communication is organized, and the way in which it manages to convey its effects, as well as its basis and arrangements" (Bloom, 1956, p. 205).

5. *Synthesis* refers to "the putting together of elements and parts so as to form a whole. This involves the process of working with pieces, parts, elements, etc., and arranging and combining them in such a way as to constitute a pattern or structure not clearly there before" (Bloom, 1956, p. 206).

6. *Evaluation* means "the making of judgments about the value, for some purpose, of ideas, works, solutions, methods, material, etc. It involves the use of criteria as well as standards for appraising the extent to which particulars are accurate, effective, economical, or satisfying. The judgments may be quantitative or qualitative, and the criteria may be either those determined by the student or those which are given to him" (Bloom, 1956, p. 185).

To illustrate how a table of specifications can be used, let us assume that we wish to develop a test to assess the understanding of reliability demonstrated by beginning students of psychoeducational assessment. The first step is to enumerate the *content areas* of the domain. Using Chapter 6 as a guide, we could assess the following areas: the reliability coefficient (meaning, methods of estimating it, and factors affecting it), standard error of measurement (meaning and computation), estimated true scores, confidence intervals (meaning, computation, and symmetrical and asymmetrical intervals), and difference scores. One might reasonably expect a test user to have a better understanding of the meaning of the reliability coefficient and the construction and interpretation of confidence intervals. Therefore, these content areas could be stressed. The next step is to specify the *processes* by which the content areas are to be measured. One might expect beginning students to demonstrate understanding at the *knowledge*, *comprehension*, and *application* levels only. Therefore, the test might not contain items assessing analysis, synthesis, or evaluation. A table of specifications for this hypothetical test would resemble Table 7.1.

The number of questions used to assess each cell also is given in the table. The table of specifications shows that, of the twenty-eight questions in the test, eight deal with the reliability coefficient and nine deal with confidence intervals; eight questions assess knowledge, twelve questions assess comprehension, and eight assess application. Thus, while the hypothetical test assesses a student's understanding of reliability, it does so by emphasizing comprehension of the reliability coefficient and applications of confidence intervals.

Content validity is a major component of the validation process for any educational and psychological test. It is hard to imagine a valid test that lacks content validity. The best way for a test author and test user to establish a test's content validity is to examine the relationship among the test items, the domain of test content, and the methods of measuring that content.

The definition of the universe of tasks represented by the test scores should include the identification of that part of the content universe represented by each item. The definition should be operational rather than theoretical, containing specifications regarding classes of stimuli, tasks to be performed and observations to be scored. The definition should not involve assumptions regarding the psychological processes employed since these would be matters of construct rather than of content validity. (APA et al., 1974, p. 45)

CRITERION-RELATED VALIDITY

A test's *criterion-related validity* refers to the extent to which a person's score on a criterion measure can be estimated from that person's test score. This is usually expressed as a correlation between the test and the criterion. The correlation coefficient is called a *validity coefficient*. Concurrent validity and predictive validity denote the time when a person's score on the criterion measure is obtained. *Concurrent* criterion-related validity refers to how accurately a person's current test score can be used to estimate the *current* criterion score. *Predictive* criterion-related validity refers to how accurately

Table **7.1** Table of Specifications for a Hypothetical Reliability Test

PROCESSES	CONTENTS				
	RELIABILITY COEFFICIENT	STANDARD ERROR OF MEASUREMENT	ESTIMATED TRUE SCORES	CONFIDENCE INTERVALS	DIFFERENCE SCORES
KNOWLEDGE	3 questions	2 questions	1 question	1 question	1 question
COMPREHENSION	5 questions	2 questions	1 question	3 questions	1 question
APPLICATION	Not tested	2 questions	1 question	5 questions	Not tested
ANALYSIS	Not tested	Not tested	Not tested	Not tested	Not tested
SYNTHESIS	Not tested	Not tested	Not tested	Not tested	Not tested
EVALUATION	Not tested	Not tested	Not tested	Not tested	Not tested

a person's current test score can be used to estimate what the criterion score will be *at a later time*. Thus, concurrent and predictive criterion-related validity of a test refer to the temporal sequence by which a person's score on some criterion measure is estimated on the basis of that person's current test score; concurrent and predictive validity differ as a function of the time at which scores on the criterion measure are obtained.

The nature of the criterion measure is extremely important. The criterion itself must be valid if it is to be used to establish the validity of another measure. Let's investigate this point by looking briefly at two examples of criterion-related validation, the first concurrent and the second predictive.

Concurrent Criterion-related Validity

The basic concurrent criterion-related validity question is, "Does knowledge of a person's test score allow the accurate estimation of that person's performance on a criterion measure?" For example, if the Acme Ruler Company manufactures yardsticks, how do we know that a person's height as measured by the yardstick is that person's true height? How do we know that the "Acme foot" is really a foot? The first step is to find a valid criterion measure. The National Bureau of Standards maintains *the* foot (.3048 meter), and *the* foot is the logical choice for a criterion measure. We can take the Acme foot to the Bureau and compare Acme measurements with measurements made with *the* foot. If the two sets of measurements correspond closely (that is, are highly correlated and have very similar means and standard deviations), we can conclude that the Acme foot is a valid measure of length.

Similarly, if we are developing a test of achievement, we can ask, "How does knowledge of a person's score on our achievement test allow the estimation of that person's score on a criterion measure?" How do we know that our new test really measures achievement? Again, the first step is to find a valid criterion measure. However, there is no National Bureau of Standards for Educational Tests. Therefore, we must turn to a less-than-perfect criterion. There are two basic choices: other achievement tests that are presumed to be valid and teacher judgments of achievement. We can, of course, use both. If our new test presents evidence of content validity and elicits test scores corresponding closely (correlating significantly) to teacher judgments and scores from other achievement tests presumed to be valid, we can conclude that our new test is a valid measure of achievement.

Predictive Criterion-related Validity

The basic predictive criterion-related validity question is, Does knowledge of a person's test score allow an accurate estimation of that person's score on a criterion measure administered some time in the future? For example, if Acme Ruler Company decides to diversify and manufacture tests of color vision, how do we know that a diagnosis of colorblindness made on the basis of the Acme test is accurate? How do we know that the Acme-based diagnosis will correspond to next month's diagnosis made by an ophthalmologist? We can test several children with the Acme test, schedule an appointment with an ophthalmologist, and compare the Acme-based diagnosis with the ophthalmologist's diagnosis. If the Acme test accurately predicts the ophthalmologist's diagnosis, we can conclude that the Acme test is a valid measure of color vision.

Similarly, if we are developing a test to assess reading readiness, we can ask, "How does knowledge of a child's score on our reading readiness test allow an accurate estimation of the child's actual readiness for subsequent instruction?" How do we know that our test really predicts reading readiness? Again, the first step is to find a valid criterion measure. In this case, the child's initial progress in reading can be used. Reading progress can be assessed by a reading achievement test (presumed to be valid) or by teacher judgments of reading ability or reading readiness at the time reading instruction was actually begun. If our reading readiness test has content validity and corresponds closely with either later teacher judgments of readiness or validly assessed reading skill, we can conclude that ours is a valid test of reading readiness.

Three aspects of criterion-related validity are extremely important. First, *"All measures of criteria should be described completely and accurately"* (APA et al., 1974, p. 33). Obviously, since the validity of the test is established by its relationship to a criterion, the criterion itself must be valid. The test author should present sufficient information to allow the test user to judge the adequacy of the criterion. *"A criterion measure should itself be studied for evidence of validity and that evidence should be presented in the* [test] *manual or report"* (APA et al., 1974, p. 34). Second, "The sample employed in a validity study and the conditions under which testing is done should be consistent with the recommended test use . . ." (APA et al., 1974, p. 36). The test authors must demonstrate that their test is valid not only for the recommended purposes of the test but also for the people who will be tested. Third, *"The* [test] *manual or research report should provide information on the appropriateness of or limits to the generalizability of validity information"* (APA et al., 1974, p. 35).

CONSTRUCT VALIDITY

To validate a test of a construct, the test author must rely on indirect evidence and inference. The definition of the construct, the theory from which the construct is derived, and empirical research form the basis of a series of directional hypotheses about various test performances. These hypotheses are then tested. If the test results confirm the hypotheses, some claim to construct validity can be made.

For example, learning ability is inferred from the differences in performance observed in individuals of the same age on a variety of learning tasks when they are presumed to have had equal opportunity to learn. One can predict, therefore, that the individuals who learn more in a given amount of time have more learning ability; that is, they would have higher scores on a measure of learning ability. This is a testable prediction. If children with IQs of 125 on test X learn more material in one week than do children with IQs of 100 on test X, there would be some evidence that test X measures learning ability. In a similar vein, one would expect scores from a test that measures learning ability to correlate substantially (.40 to .70) with school achievement, since learning ability is thought *in part* to determine differences in school success. However, if the correlation is sufficiently large, there is a rival interpretation of the relationship: the test may measure school achievement.

NONVALIDITY DATA

Information intended to document validity is often presented in test manuals and advertisements, but some of these data are not appropriate criteria for determining validity. The following are examples of "nonvalidity" data — data that may sound impressive but are not true indications of validity.

1. *Cash Validity.* Just because a test is a "big seller" does not imply that it is also valid. The only thing that large sales guarantee is cash for the authors and publishers. Good tests may or may not sell well; poor tests may or may not sell well.

2. *Clinical Utility.* Unevaluated, uncontrolled clinical reports are simply testimonials. Testimonials about the practical utility of a test are not validity data. Only controlled experiments and evaluated investigations should be considered potentially useful in assessing a test's validity.

3. *Internal Consistency.* The internal consistency of a test (inter-item or item-total correlations) is reliability information, not validity data. A high degree of internal consistency insures only that the test items are drawn from the same domain. That domain may or may not be the one the test is intended to measure. A reliable test may or may not be valid.

FACTORS AFFECTING VALIDITY

Whenever a test fails to measure what it purports to measure, validity is threatened. Consequently, any factor that results in measuring "something else" affects a test's validity. Unsystematic error (unreliability) and systematic error (bias) threaten validity.

RELIABILITY

Reliability is a necessary but not a sufficient condition for valid measurement. The relationship between reliability and validity is expressed in equation 7.1. The empirically determined validity coefficient (r_{xy}) equals the correlation between true scores on the two variables $(r_{x(t)y(t)})$ multiplied by the square root of the product of the reliability coefficients of test X and test Y $(\sqrt{r_{xx}r_{yy}})$. Hence, the reliability of the test limits its potential validity.

$$r_{xy} = r_{x(t)y(t)}\sqrt{r_{xx}r_{yy}} \tag{7.1}$$

All valid tests are reliable; no unreliable tests may be valid; reliable tests may or may not be valid. In Chapter 6, the examples of a rubber and a steel ruler were used to explain reliability. With the rubber ruler, length varied considerably over repeated measurement; there was no way that *each* measurement could be correct. On the other hand, a steel ruler that gives consistent measurements does not necessarily give accurate measurements. A steel ruler can consistently measure a line as $3\frac{1}{2}$ inches long. Unfortunately, the line may be 5 inches long. The measurement is consistent (reliable) but not correct (valid). Only when the "true" length and the obtained length are the same can there be valid measurement.

Finally, the validity of a particular test can never exceed the reliability of that test. Unreliable tests measure error; valid tests measure the traits they are designed to measure.

SYSTEMATIC BIAS
Method of Measurement

The method used to measure a skill or trait often determines what score a child will receive. A true score can be considered a composite of trait variance and method-of-measurement variance (Campbell & Fiske, 1959). To take just one example: Werner and Strauss (1941) conducted a series of experiments to study the figure-background perception of brain-injured and non-brain-injured retarded persons. They presented stimulus items tachistoscopically for a fraction of a second and asked their subjects to name what they saw. They found that brain-injured retarded persons responded more often to the background stimuli than did the non-brain-injured retarded persons. They concluded that brain injury results in figure-ground dysfunction. However, the method of testing (tachisto-scopic presentation) and the trait to be tested (figure-ground perception) were confounded by the testing procedure. Rubin (1969) later demon-strated that under different testing procedures there were no differences between brain-injured and non-brain-injured retarded persons in figure-background responses. The differences between the findings of Strauss and Rubin are attributable to *how* figure-background perception was meas-ured. It seems likely that Strauss was measuring perceptual speed because of his method of measurement. To the extent that trait or skill scores include variance attributable to method of measurement, these scores may lack validity.

Enabling Behaviors

Several behaviors are assumed in any testing situation. We must assume that the subject is fluent in the language in which the test is prepared and administered if there are any verbal components to the test directions or test responses. Yet in many Western states with substantial Spanish-speaking populations, students whose primary language is not English are tested in English. Intelligence testing in English of non-English-speaking children was sufficiently commonplace that a group of parents brought suit against a school district (*Diana* v. *State Board of Education*). Deaf children are routinely given the Performance subtests of the Wechsler intelligence scales (Levine, 1974) even though they cannot *hear* the directions. Children with extreme communication problems (speech impediments, for example) often are required to respond orally to test questions. Such obvious limita-tions or absences of enabling behaviors frequently are overlooked in testing situations even though they invalidate the test results.

Item Selection

Test items often presume that the subjects taking the test have had ex-posure to concepts and skills measured by the test. For example, standardized achievement tests presume that the students taking the tests have been exposed to similar curricula. If a teacher has not taught the content being tested, the results of the achievement test are invalid.

Administration Errors

Unless a test is administered according to the standardized procedures, the results are invalid. Suppose a teacher wished to demonstrate how effective her teaching was by administering an intelligence test and an achievement test to her class. She allows the children five minutes less than the stan-dardized time limits on the intelligence test and five minutes more on the standardized achievement test. The result is that the children earn scores lower than their true intelligence (since they did not have enough time) and scores higher than their true achievement (since they had too much time). The apparent results, that slow children had learned more than anticipated, would not be valid.

SUMMARY

Validity is the only technical characteristic of a test in which we are interested. All other technical considerations, such as reliability, are subsumed under the issue of validity and are separated to simplify the issue of validity. We must know if a test measures what it purports to measure and if scores derived from the test are accurate. Adequate norms, reliability, and lack of bias are all necessary conditions for validity. None — separately or in total — is sufficient to guarantee validity.

When the necessary conditions for validity are met, systematic validation can proceed. The content may be inspected to see if each item is valid and to insure that all aspects of the content are represented. If a standard or criterion of known validity is available, the test should be compared to that standard. In the absence of a known standard, construct validation should proceed. In this case, directional predictions are made based on the constructed trait; these predictions are empirically tested.

STUDY QUESTIONS

1. Why is it necessary that test authors demonstrate validity for their tests?

2. What is the relationship between reliability and validity?

3. Identify three factors that must be considered in the establishment of content validity.

4. Ms. Wilson uses a new math curriculum to teach her class of third graders. She uses a traditional math test to assess pupil progress. All pupils score in the bottom quartile according to the test norms. What can Ms. Wilson legitimately conclude?

5. There are many tests whose manuals include absolutely no evidence as to validity. These tests are used in schools to make important educational decisions about children. Under what circumstances could such tests be used?

6. Test author G presents interitem correlation coefficients as evidence for the validity of his scale. To what extent are these coefficients evidence of validity?

7. Kim Ngo, a recent arrival from a Vietnamese orphanage, speaks no English. When she enrolls in a U.S. school, her intelligence is assessed by means of a verbal test that has English directions and requires English responses. Kim performs poorly on the test, earning an IQ of 37. The tester concludes that Kim is a trainable mentally retarded child and recommends placement in a special class. Identify two major errors in the interpretation of the test results.

8. Professor Johnson develops a test that he claims can be used to identify learning-disabled children who will profit from perceptual-motor training. What must he do to demonstrate that his test is valid?

ADDITIONAL READING

American Psychological Association, American Educational Research Association, & National Council on Measurement in Education. *Standards for educational and psychological tests.* Washington, DC: American Psychological Association, 1974, pp. 25–48.

Ghiselli, E. E. *Theory of psychological measurement.* New York: McGraw-Hill, 1964. (Chapter 11, pp. 335–369.)

Chapter 8
Norms

It is seldom possible to test everyone in a particular population, since the membership of the population is constantly changing. Some children who are in the 6-year-old population today will be 7 years old tomorrow. Grade populations change at least once a year. However, testing an entire population is not only virtually impossible but also unnecessary. The characteristics of a population can be accurately estimated from the characteristics of a representative subset of the population (called a *sample*); inferences based on what one has learned from a sample can be extended to a population at large. Thus, the normative samples used in norm-referenced assessment are intended to allow inferences to be made about a population.

In norm-referenced assessment, norms are important for two reasons. First, the normative sample is often used to obtain the various statistics on which the final selection of test items is based. For example, Wechsler (1974, p. iii) states that "the final selection of test items and scoring procedures was fixed only after all the standardization data had been analyzed and evaluated." Consequently, measures of internal consistency, item-total correlations, and indices of item difficulties (p-values), as well as item selection and item scoring procedures, are all affected by the adequacy of the standardization sample.

The second reason that norms are important is the more obvious. An individual's performance is evaluated in terms of other people's performances. Even if a test is reliable and otherwise valid, test scores may be misleading if the norms are inadequate. The adequacy of a test's norms depends on three factors: the representativeness of the norm sample, the number of cases in the norm sample, and the relevance of the norms in terms of the purpose of testing.

REPRESENTATIVENESS

In evaluation of representativeness, particular attention is paid to demographic variables because of their relationship — either theoretical or empirical — to what the test is intended to measure. Which demographic variables are significant for a particular test depends on the content of the test and/or the construct being measured. Representativeness hinges on two questions. The first is, Does the norm sample contain the same *kinds* of people as the population that the norms are intended to represent? "Kinds" of people usually refers to relative levels of maturation, levels of skill development, and degrees of acculturation. The second question of representativeness is, Are the various kinds of people present in the same proportion in the sample as they are in the population of reference?

When we compare a child's performance to a norm sample in order to predict future behavior, we assume that the child has had an opportunity to acquire skills, concepts, or experiences comparable to the opportunities of the children in the norm sample. When we compare a child's performance to a norm sample in order to understand better that child's current level of functioning, we need assume only that the norm sample is representative of the population. The distinction between understanding current level of functioning and predicting future behavior is part of the culture-free (or culture-fair) testing controversy. If a 10-year-old child has had no opportunity to learn to read (and consequently has not acquired the skills), the tester who notes that the child *currently* lacks skill is not being unfair or biased. On the other hand, if the child being tested and the children in the normative sample have not had comparable opportunities to acquire the behaviors sampled in the test, it may be misleading to use the child's test score to predict *future* behavior. When we predict future behavior, we assume that children have learned what they *can* learn. Children who have had no chance to learn have not been able to demonstrate what they *can* learn. Not knowing how well such children *will* learn given the opportunity, we cannot use their test scores to make predictions.

KINDS OF PEOPLE

Several factors are usually considered in the development of norms for psychoeducational tests. Following is a brief discussion of the most commonly considered factors together with a rationale for the importance of each.

Age

A child's age is an excellent general indicator of several important factors. Physiological maturation is an important variable in motor and perceptual-motor tests, and age is directly related to maturation. It would be foolish to say that a 6-year-old child lacks physical stamina because that child can run for only as long a period of time as 2 percent of all 10-year-olds. Six-year-old children are not as big and strong as 10-year-old children. Consequently, we would not want to compare children of different ages on tests where there are physical, developmental effects.

A child's amount of experience with practically everything is a function of age. Indeed, age is an excellent indicator of the opportunity to acquire skills, information, and concepts. Mental growth (as measured by mental ages) and chronological ages are very highly correlated; Kappauf (1973) has empirically estimated the correlation to be in excess of .90. Again, it would usually be inappropriate to compare a 6-year-old's fund of general information with that of a 12-year-old. The 6-year-old simply has not been around as long and therefore has not had the opportunity to acquire as much information.

There is a tendency for test authors to assume some psychological traits stop developing after 16 or 18 years of age — and many traits do. In such instances, all individuals over a given age are treated as adults. For example, Slosson (1963, p. 17) directs the users of his test never to use more than 16 years in computation of the ratio IQ. The assumption of no growth after 16 may be tenable with supporting data, but Slosson does not present any. On the other hand, Wechsler (1955) provides adult norms that clearly indicate age is an important variable in interpreting IQ beyond 16. As shown in Figure 8.1, verbal ability continues to grow until 25 to 34 years of age; after 35 it slowly declines. Scores on the performance scale, however, peak between 20 and 24 years and then rapidly decline. Different abilities may be expected to have different growth curves (see Guilford, 1967, pp. 417–426).

Grade

All achievement tests and most intelligence tests measure the results of systematic academic instruction. Children of different ages are present in most grades. Consequently, grade norms are more appropriate than age norms for such tests when used with children of school age. Grade in school bears a more direct relationship to what is taught in school than does age. Some 7-year-old children may not be enrolled in school; some may be in kindergarten, some in first grade, some in second grade, and some even in third grade. The academic proficiency of 7-year-olds can be expected to be more closely related to what they have been taught than to what age they are.

Sex

Gender also plays an important role in a child's development. There are pronounced differences in typical patterns of physical development around puberty (Tanner, 1970). Personality differences have also been observed; boys tend to be more aggressive than girls, while girls tend to be more dependent and socially passive (Mischel, 1970).

Sex differences have also been reported in intellectual development. For example, Roberts (1971) reported that boys scored higher than girls on the Vocabulary and Block Design subtests of the Wechsler Intelligence Scale

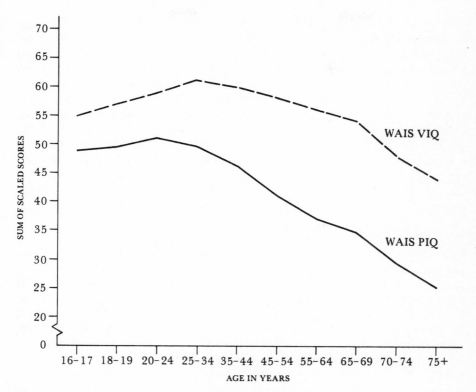

Figure **8.1**   Sums of scaled scores on the WAIS for performance IQs and verbal IQs of 100, by ages

for Children. But the magnitude of sex differences on ability, achievement, and aptitude measures is nearly always very small; the male and female distributions overlap a great deal.

Although sex-role expectations seem to be changing, gender still may systematically limit the types of activities in which a child engages. This may result from such influences as modeling, peer pressure, or responsiveness to the attitudes of significant adults. For whatever reasons boys and girls differ systematically on tests, children of both sexes should be represented in the norm sample. Appropriate representation is especially important for behaviors on which there are known sex differences.

Acculturation of Parents

The level of acculturation of a child's parents or guardians has a direct impact on the child's performance on intellectual and academic tests. One can consider the academic or occupational attainment (*socioeconomic status*) of the parents as an indication of the child's acculturation as well as the level of acculturation in the home. There is a consistent relationship between these indices of acculturation and the performance of the child on various psychoeducational measures. Parental occupation and income have been consistently reported to be related to school achievement (for example, Schaie & Roberts, 1971) and intelligence (for example, Burt, 1959; Roberts, 1971). The causes of these consistent social class differences have been debated for years, and the debate continues today (see Gottesman, 1968). However, the causes of such differences are beyond the scope of this text. Whether one subscribes to a genetic interpretation, an environmentalist interpretation, or an interactionist interpretation, the fact of social class differences is undeniable. For this reason, test standardizations should include children of all social classes.

Geographic Factors

Different geographic regions of the United States differ in values and mores, and various psychoeducational tests reflect these regional differences. Children in the Midwest typically score better than children in the South on achievement tests (for example, Schaie & Roberts, 1971). During World War II rates of rejection for military service because of mental deficiency varied according to geographic region (Ginzberg & Bray, 1953); these differences reflected both intellectual and achievement differences. Community size is also related to academic and intellectual development; urban children typically score higher on achievement tests than rural children do (Schaie & Roberts, 1971).

Race

Race is a particularly sensitive issue, especially since the scientific community has often been insensitive to the issue and has even on occasion been blatantly racist (for example, Down, 1866). With few exceptions children of minority races score lower than white children on intellectual measures (for example, Roberts, 1971) and academic achievement (for example, Coleman et al., 1966).

Most explanations for racial differences are beyond the scope of this text. Two are not. First, there has been a tendency to systematically *exclude* nonwhite children from standardization samples. For example, the 1972 edition of the Stanford-Binet Intelligence Test included nonwhite children in the norms, but as late as 1960 the test excluded Blacks from the standardization sample. To the extent that children of different races undergo cultural experiences that differ even within social class and geographic region, norm samples that exclude them are biased. Also, to the extent that nonwhite children score lower than white children of equal social standing and from the same geographic region, test-score distributions that exclude nonwhites are unrepresentative of the total population.

The second argument deals with item selection. If nonwhites differ in acculturation and are excluded from the field tests of the test items, item difficulty estimates (p-values) and point biserial (item-total) correlations may be inaccurate. Hence, the test scaling may be in error. We believe that both these arguments have merit. It is important to include children of all racial and ethnic groups in both field tests of items and in the standardization of a test.

Intelligence

A representative sample of individuals, in terms of their level of intellectual functioning, is essential for standardizing an intelligence test — or any other kind of test. Intelligence is related to a number of variables that are considered in psychoeducational assessment. It is certainly related to achievement, since most intelligence tests were actually developed to predict school success. Correlations ranging between .60 and .80 are typical (for example, Tiegs & Clark, 1970). Since language development and facility are often considered an indication of intellectual development, intelligence tests are often verbally oriented. Consequently, one would also expect to find substantial correlations between scores on tests of intelligence and scores on tests of linguistic or psycholinguistic ability, as did Mueller (1965). Items thought to reflect perceptual ability appear on intelligence tests, and Thurstone (1944) found various perceptual tasks to be a factor in intelligence. Koppitz (1975) reports substantial correlations between scores on the Bender Visual Motor Gestalt Test and scores on intelligence tests. Thus, intelligence should be considered in the development of norms for perceptual and perceptual-motor tests.

In the development of norms for intelligence tests per se, it is essential to test the full range of intellectual ability. Restriction of the sample to children enrolled in and attending school (usually regular classes) restricts the norms. Failure to consider the mentally retarded in standardization procedures introduces systematic bias into test norms. It has been estimated that 3 percent of the school-age population may be mentally retarded (Robinson & Robinson, 1976; Farber, 1968, pp. 46, 58). Dingman and Tarjan (1960) estimated that there is an excess frequency at the lower end of the intelligence distribution, probably as a result of pathological genetic conditions. They estimated that the mean IQ of this group was approximately 32, with a standard deviation approximately the same as that in the intellectually normal population. Exclusion of such a large portion of the school-age population seriously biases the estimate of the population mean and standard deviation. For example, let us assume that a test is standardized excluding mentally retarded children and that the scores of the children in the normative sample are converted to deviation IQs with a mean of 100 and a standard deviation of 16. Increasing the sample by including 3 percent more subjects whose scores have a mean IQ of 32 and a standard deviation of 16 would have the same effect as including the mentally retarded children who were excluded. The mean would be lowered from 100 to 98.[1] The standard deviation would be increased from 16 to 19.7.[2] A score that fell two standard deviations below the mean would be 68 without the retarded; it would be 59 if the retarded were included. Representative sampling would substantially reduce the ranks of the mentally retarded.

Date of Norms

An often overlooked consideration in assuring representativeness is the date the norms were collected. We live in an age of rapidly expanding knowledge and rapidly expanding communication of knowledge. Children of today know more than did the children of the 1930s or the 1940s. Children of today probably know less than will the children of tomorrow. For a norm sample to be representative it must be *current*.

Special Population Characteristics

Some characteristics of the sample and of the population are important only for particular types of tests. For example, test authors often caution test users to make sure the content of achievement tests reflects the content of the test user's classroom curriculum. However, the test author must also make sure that the content is appropriate for the norm sample. Thus, for reading diagnostic tests, which often measure specific skills such as syllabi-

---

1. If the number of subjects in the norm group is 1,000 and the mean is 100, the sum of all scores is 100,000. If 30 children (3 percent of 1,000) whose mean is 32 are added to the 1,000 children, the sum of all scores is increased by 960 (30 × 32). The mean of the 1,030 children is 98 (100,960/1,030).
2. The variance is computationally equal to $\Sigma X^2/N - (\Sigma X/N)^2$. If the number of subjects (N) is 1,000 and the mean is 100, the sum of all scores is 100,000; if the standard deviation is 16, the variance is 256. By substituting these figures into the preceding formula, we obtain the sum of the squared scores, which is 10,256,000:

$$256 = \frac{\Sigma X^2}{1,000} - \left(\frac{100,000}{1,000}\right)^2$$

If we increase the sample by 30 children whose scores have a mean of 32 and standard deviation of 16, we increase the sum of the squared scores by 38,400:

$$256 = \frac{\Sigma X^2}{30} - \left(\frac{960}{30}\right)^2$$

The variance of the 1,030 children is 386.76:

$$386.76 = \frac{10,256,000 + 38,400}{1,030} - \left(\frac{100,000 + 960}{1,030}\right)^2$$

The standard deviation (the square root of the variance) is 19.67.

cation and sound blending, the author must specify the curriculum followed by the children in the norm sample. If a visual, sight-vocabulary orientation is used by children in the norm sample, the derived scores of children taught by a phonics method may be inflated; the children taught by the phonics method may earn relatively high scores when compared to the less skilled children in the norm group.

Tests used to identify children with particular problems should include such children in their standardization sample. For example, the Illinois Test of Psycholinguistic Abilities is often used to identify children with psycholinguistic dysfunctions that presumably underlie academic difficulties. Yet the norm sample included "only those children demonstrating average intellectual functioning, average school achievement, average characteristics of personal-social adjustment, sensory-motor integrity, and coming from predominantly English-speaking families" (Paraskevopoulos & Kirk, 1969, pp. 51–52). How can a test be used to identify children whose academic difficulties are caused by psycholinguistic dysfunction when such children are *excluded* from the normative sample? A child who earns the same score as any child in the norm sample has earned a score associated with school success!

PROPORTION OF THE KINDS OF PEOPLE

Implicit in the foregoing discussion of characteristics of the representative normative sample was the notion that the various kinds of people should be included in the *same proportion* in the sample as in the population. The development of systematic norms requires systematic data collection, which is both time-consuming and expensive. It is incumbent on the author of a test to demonstrate that its norms are in fact representative. Samples that are convenient, such as samples consisting of volunteers, are not necessarily representative; in fact, they are probably unrepresentative. Large numbers of subjects do not guarantee a representative sample. Roosevelt was re-elected President of the United States, even though predictions based on a large sample had proclaimed that Alf Landon would be the next president; the sample had been unrepresentative.

A test author demonstrates that a test is representative by presenting data to that effect. For example, French (1964) presented data to show that his stratification procedure was effective. He compared his norm sample to the 1960 census in order to ascertain the discrepancy between the population at large and his sample. As French's table (Table 8.1) shows, there was close agreement in the occupational strata. The norms of the Pictorial Test of Intelligence (French, 1964) are credible on all stratification variables (occupation of father, geographic region, and community size).

Table **8.1** Sample by Occupational Level

OCCUPATIONAL CLASS	PERCENT 1960 CENSUS	PERCENT TESTED	PERCENT DISCREPANCY
Professional and technical	16	16	0
Proprietary, manager, and officials	13	15	+2
Clerks and sales	15	15	0
Foremen and skilled	19	16	−3
Operatives and semiskilled	22	20	−2
Laborers, service workers, and unskilled	15	18	+3
	100%	100%	

SOURCE: J. L. French, *Manual for the Pictorial Test of Intelligence* (Boston: Houghton Mifflin, 1964), p. 11. Copyright © 1964 by Houghton Mifflin Company and reprinted with their permission.

CONCLUDING COMMENT: CAVEAT EMPTOR

If the test author recognizes that the test norms are inadequate, the test user should be explicitly cautioned (APA et al., 1974). The inadequacies do not, however, disappear on the inclusion of a cautionary note; the test is still inadequate. It is occasionally argued that inadequate norms are better than no norms at all. This argument is analogous to the argument that even a broken clock is correct twice a day. With 86,400 seconds in a day, remarking that a clock is right twice a day is an overly optimistic way of saying that the clock is wrong 99.99 percent of the time. Inadequate norms do not allow meaningful and accurate inferences about the population. If poor norms are used, misinterpretations follow. The difficulty is that the test user seldom knows whether a particular test has an inflated or deflated mean or variance.

A joint committee of the American Psychological Association, the American Education Research Association, and the National Council on Measurement in Education (1974) have prepared a pamphlet, *Standards for Educational and Psychological Tests and Manuals*, which outlines the standards to which test authors should adhere: *"Norms presented in the test manual should refer to defined and clearly described populations. These populations should be the groups with whom users of the test will ordinarily wish to compare the persons tested"* (p. 20). The pamphlet states that the test author should report how the sample was selected and whether any bias was present in the sample. The author should also describe the sampling techniques and the resultant sample in sufficient detail that the test user can judge the utility of the norms. "The description should include number of cases, classified by one or more of such relevant variables as ethnic mix, socioeconomic level, age, sex, locale, and educational status" (p. 21).

In the marketplace of testing, let the buyer beware.

NUMBER OF SUBJECTS

The number of subjects in a norm sample is important for several reasons. First, the number of subjects should be large enough to guarantee stability. "If the number of cases is small we cannot put much dependence on the norms, since another group consisting of the same number of persons might give quite different results. The larger the number of cases the more stable will be the norms" (Ghiselli, 1964, p. 49). Next, the number of cases should be large enough so that infrequent elements in the population can be represented. Finally, there should be enough subjects that the sizes of interpolations and extrapolations are relatively small. In a normally distributed array of scores, one hundred subjects are the minimum number for which a full range of percentiles can be computed and for which standard scores between ±2.3 standard deviations can be computed without extrapolation. Consequently, we believe that one hundred should be the minimum number of persons in any norm sample. If the test spans a number of ages or grades, the norm sample should contain at least one hundred subjects per age or grade.

RELEVANCE OF THE NORMS

The major question regarding relevance of norms concerns the extent to which people in the norm sample will provide comparisons that are relevant in terms of the purpose for which the test was administered. For some purposes national norms are the most appropriate. If we are interested in knowing how a particular child is developing intellectually, perceptually, linguistically, or physically, national norms would be the most appropriate.

In other circumstances norms developed on a particular portion of the population may be meaningful. For example, if we wished to ascertain the degree to which a student had profited from his twelve years of schooling, norms developed for the particular school district he had been served by might be appropriate. Suppose the school district is providing such poor educational services that, as a district, it falls well below the national average. If this is the case, our twelfth grader could earn a percentile rank of 75 based on district norms and a percentile rank of only 35 based on representative national norms. Still, despite the fact that his score looks low in comparison to scores made nationwide, it's clear that our student has made comparatively good use of the inadequate services he has been getting. The same relationship between scores based on national and scores based on local norms might also be obtained if the school district were teaching materials not covered by the achievement test.

Local norms may be more useful in retrospective interpretations of a student's performance than in predictive interpretations. Thus, in the preceding example, if the content of the achievement test was appropriate in terms of what the schools were actually attempting to teach, we could conclude that the student had profited from instruction but nonetheless would likely be at a disadvantage if he entered college.

In addition, norms based on particular groups may be more relevant than those based on the population as a whole. Some devices are standardized on unusual populations: the Nebraska Test of Learning Aptitude is standardized on the deaf, the AAMD Adaptive Behavior Scale on institutionalized retardates, and the Blind Learning Aptitude Test on blind children. Aptitude tests are often standardized on individuals in specific trades or professions. The utility of special population norms is similar to the utility of local norms: they are likely to be more useful in retrospective comparisons than in future predictions. Without knowing how the special population corresponds to the general population, inferences may not be appropriate. Suppose a deaf child earns a learning quotient of 115 derived from norms based on deaf children. One knows only that the child scored better than the average deaf child. The basic question that must be addressed is, Does the score based on special population norms lead to correct interpretations? Thus, the test user must know how the change in norms affects predictive validity.

There are, however, specific instances in which special population norms have been misused. When a person's performance is similar to that of a special population, it does *not* mean the person belongs to or should belong to that population. Because Mary earns the same score as a typical lawyer on a test of legal aptitude does not mean Mary is or should become a lawyer. The argument that she should contains a logical fallacy, an undistributed middle term. (Clearly, if dogs eat meat and university professors eat meat, dogs are not university professors.)

Reasoning of this sort is often inferred when criterion groups are used in test standardization. Such inferences are valid if it can be demonstrated that *only* members of a particular group score in a particular manner. If some people who are *not* members of the particular group earn the same scores as members of that group, the relationship between group membership and scores should be quantified. For example, let us assume that 90 percent of brain-injured children make unusual — perhaps rotated, distorted, or simplified — reproductions of geometric designs. Let us also assume that 3 percent of the population is brain injured. If *only* non-brain-injured children made normal drawings, we could say with certainty that any child who makes normal drawings is not brain injured. However, since 10 percent of brain-injured children make normal reproductions, we cannot be so sure: .31 percent of the children who make normal drawings *are* brain injured.

In some instances, the "normal" population makes deviant responses. Assume that 20 percent of the normal population and all brain-injured children make unusual drawings. If 3 percent of the population is brain injured, 22.4 percent of the population will perform as brain injured (100% of 3% + 20% of 97% = 22.4%). A deviant performance on the test would mean only a 13 percent (.03/.224) chance that the child is brain injured.

USING NORMS CORRECTLY

The manuals accompanying commercially prepared tests usually contain a table that allows a tester to convert raw scores to various derived scores, such as percentile ranks, without laborious calculations. Occasionally, the tester is even confronted with several tables for converting raw scores. For example, it is not uncommon for the same manual to contain one set of tables for converting raw scores to percentile ranks on the basis of the age of the person tested and another set of tables for converting raw scores to percentile ranks on the basis of the school grade of the person tested. The tester must select tables based either on age or on grade. To select the appropriate table, the tester must determine the population to which the performance of the sample is inferred. This can be learned by examining how the norm group was selected. If the test author sampled by grades in school, then the population of reference is students in a particular grade; consequently, the grade tables should be used for converting raw scores to derived scores. Conversely, if the test author sampled by age, the age tables should be used, since the population of reference is a particular age group.

A problem arises when especially advanced or backward individuals undergo testing. Tests often lose their power to discriminate near the extremes of the distribution. For example, an intelligence test might be constructed in such a way that even if a person failed every item it might not be possible for that person to earn an IQ of less than 50. Since complete failure on a test provides little or no information about what a person *can* do, testers often administer tests based on a norm sample of people younger than the test taker. While such a procedure may provide useful *qualitative* information, norm-referenced interpretations are unjustified because the ages of the individuals in the norm group and the age of the person being tested are not the same. Another serious error is committed when the tester uses a person's mental age to obtain derived scores from conversion tables set up on the basis of chronological age. The reasoning behind such practices, we suppose, is that if the person functions as an 8-year-old child intellectually, the use of conversion tables based on the performances of 8-year-old children is appropriate. Such practices are incorrect, since the norms were not established by sampling persons of a particular mental age. When assessing the reading skill of an adolescent or adult who performs below the first percentile, a tester has little need for further or more precise norm-referenced comparisons. The tester already knows the person is not a good reader. If the examiner wants to ascertain which reading skills a person has or lacks, a criterion-referenced (norm-free) device would be more suitable. Sometimes the most appropriate use of norms is no use at all.

To use norms effectively, the tester must be sure that the norm sample is appropriate both for the purpose of testing and for the person being tested.

SUMMARY

The normative sample is important because it is the group of individuals with whom a tested person is compared. Norms should be representative of the population to which comparisons are made. A number of variables typically considered important have been discussed: age, grade, sex, acculturation of the persons tested and of their parents, geographic factors, race, intelligence, the date of the norms, and special population characteristics. The norm sample should contain the same types of people in the same proportion as the population of reference contains. The norm sample should be large enough to be stable and to provide a full range of derived scores. The norms should be relevant in terms of the purposes of testing, and they should be used correctly.

STUDY QUESTIONS

1. Identify two fundamental reasons why norms are important.

2. Willy Smith has only one leg. His teacher concludes that he cannot be tested in reading because no test demonstrates inclusion of one-legged children in its normative group. To what extent is the teacher's conclusion warranted?

3. Test X is standardized on fifty boys and fifty girls at each grade level from kindergarten through sixth grade. The children who made up the norm group were white, middle-class children living in Mount Pleasant, Michigan. Separate norm tables are provided for boys and girls in each grade. Danny, a third-grade black child residing in Oakland, California, is tested with test X, and the norm tables are used to interpret his score.

    a. To how many children is Danny being compared?

    b. To whose performance is Danny's performance being compared?

    c. What assumptions are being made about the relationship between Danny's acculturation and the acculturation of the normative sample?

4. There are many tests that were initially developed to discriminate between brain-injured and non-brain-injured adults. These same tests are now used to identify brain-injured children. Why is such a use inappropriate?

5. Under what conditions are local norms useful?

6. How might the author of a test demonstrate that its normative sample is representative of the population of children attending school in the United States?

ADDITIONAL READING

American Psychological Association, American Educational Research Association, National Council on Measurement in Education. *Standards for educational and psychological tests*. Washington, DC: American Psychological Association, 1974, pp. 9–24.

Part 3

Testing: Domains Sampled and Representative Tests

Part 3 is a description of the most common domains in which assessment of children is carried out. Each chapter in Part 3 focuses on a different domain, and each chapter follows a similar format. We first describe the kinds of behaviors within a given domain, and we then discuss the most commonly used tests within that domain.

For each of the tests described in Part 3 we examine five factors. First, we describe the general format of each device and the specific behaviors the test is designed to sample. The descriptions allow the reader to evaluate the extent to which specific tests sample the behaviors in the domain. Second, we describe the kinds of scores each device provides for the educational practitioner. This gives information about the meaning and interpretation of those scores. Third, we examine the standardization population for each test. This enables the reader to judge — recalling the discussion in Chapter 8 — the adequacy of the norm group and to evaluate the appropriateness of each of the tests for use with specific populations of children. Fourth, we evaluate evidence of the reliability of each of the tests using the standards set forth in Chapter 6. Finally, for each device, we examine evidence of its validity and evaluate the adequacy of the evidence in light of the standards set forth in Chapter 7. Each chapter concludes with a chapter summary.

Two principles guided our development of Part 3. First, we did not try to include all the available measures for each of the domains. We selected representative and commonly used tests in each area. We suggest that readers who want information about additional devices examine all the tests available in each of the domains in Buros's *Mental Measurements Yearbooks*. This series of yearbooks includes critical reviews by noted authorities of all currently available psychometric tests.

Second, in evaluating the technical adequacy of each of the specific tests described, we restricted our evaluation to information included in the test manuals rather than attempting exhaustive reviews of research in the professional literature. There were two reasons for this decision. First, as stated in the *Standards for Educational and Psychological Tests*, test authors are responsible for providing all necessary technical information in their test manuals, so we searched the manuals for the information. Second, an attempt to include the vast body of research on commonly used tests would have been beyond the scope of this book.

Chapter 9

Assessment of Academic Achievement: Screening Devices

Achievement tests are devices that directly assess students' skill development in academic content areas. In contrast to aptitude tests, which are intended to assess a student's potential to profit from instruction in specific areas, achievement tests sample the products of past formal and informal educational experiences. They measure the extent to which a student has profited from schooling and/or life experiences compared to others of the same age or grade.

Various kinds of tests were described in Chapter 3. Figure 9.1 shows the different categories of achievement tests. Any achievement test is first of all either a screening or a diagnostic device. Screening devices are used to ascertain, in a global fashion, current level of functioning and to assess the extent to which a student has acquired those skills that most others of the same age have acquired. Diagnostic achievement tests are designed to pinpoint, in a diagnostic sense, skill-development strengths and weaknesses.

Achievement tests can be further categorized as either group-administered or individually administered devices. While group tests can be given to entire classes at a time, individual tests require a one-to-one student-examiner relationship. A group test may also be appropriately administered to one student at a time.

Achievement tests must reflect the content of the curriculum. If they do not, they provide misleading information. Most achievement tests are norm-referenced, while some more recent devices are criterion-referenced. The former are designed by subject-matter experts, are thought to reflect national curricular trends, and are standardized on national samples. Criterion-referenced achievement tests, on the other hand, are designed to reflect the objectives of specific academic content areas and to assess the extent to which students have attained very specific skills.

Achievement tests assess skill development either in many areas or in single subject-matter areas. Some devices are multiple-skill batteries, while others are specific to single content areas, such as reading, spelling, or math.

Figure 9.1 illustrates that the Stanford Achievement Test is, for example,

Figure **9.1**   Categories of achievement tests

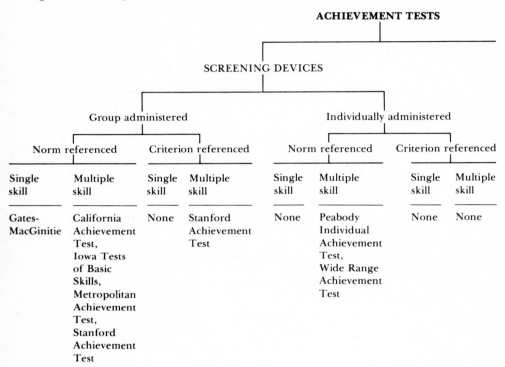

both a norm-referenced and a criterion-referenced (objective-referenced) group-administered screening test that samples skill development in many content areas. The Stanford Diagnostic Reading Test is both a norm-referenced, group-administered and a criterion-referenced, individually administered diagnostic test that samples skill-development strengths and weaknesses in the single skill of reading. The SDRT provides the classroom teacher with a more detailed analysis of the student's strengths and weaknesses in reading and greater assistance in program planning.

This chapter is addressed specifically to screening devices, while Chapter 10 is a detailed discussion of diagnostic achievement testing.

The very term *screening device* reflects the major purpose of these tests. Achievement tests are used most often to screen students in an effort to identify those who demonstrate relatively low-level, average, or high-level skills in comparison to their peers. Achievement tests provide a global

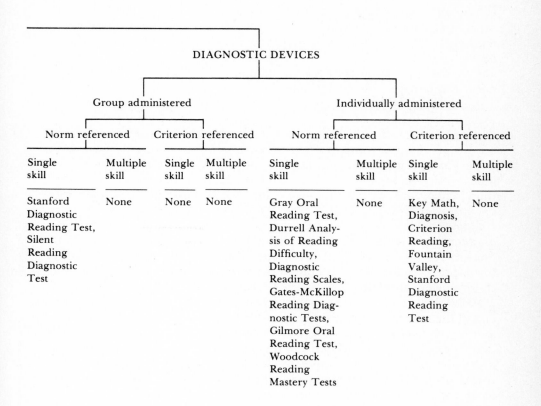

	DIAGNOSTIC DEVICES						
Group administered				**Individually administered**			
Norm referenced		Criterion referenced		Norm referenced		Criterion referenced	
Single skill	Multiple skill	Single skill	Multiple skill	Single skill	Multiple skill	Single skill	Multiple skill
Stanford Diagnostic Reading Test, Silent Reading Diagnostic Test	None	None	None	Gray Oral Reading Test, Durrell Analysis of Reading Difficulty, Diagnostic Reading Scales, Gates-McKillop Reading Diagnostic Tests, Gilmore Oral Reading Test, Woodcock Reading Mastery Tests	None	Key Math, Diagnosis, Criterion Reading, Fountain Valley, Stanford Diagnostic Reading Test	None

index of academic skill development and may be used to identify individual students for whom educational intervention is necessary — either in the form of remediation for those who demonstrate relatively low-level skill development, or in the form of academic enrichment for those who exhibit exceptionally high-level skill development.

Although individually administered achievement tests should be used in making placement decisions, screening tests are often used. Such a use is inappropriate. Students are placed in programs for the "gifted" if they demonstrate superior intelligence *and* superior academic achievement. Students labeled "mentally retarded" usually demonstrate developmental retardation in both capability and academic skill development. That standardized achievement testing plays a major role in identifying children as "learning disabled" is evidenced by the traditionally accepted definition of a learning-disabled child as one who is achieving one and a half to two years below her or his capability and who, in addition, demonstrates a specific perceptual and/or language handicap. Students' scores on group achievement tests may be used inappropriately as indexes of skill development for placement decisions; they are often used inappropriately by teachers to plan instructional programs. Teachers often use achievement tests to group children within regular classroom programs. Group-administered achievement tests are designed to be used as *screening* tests, not to support placement decisions.[1]

A third use of achievement testing, after screening and placement, is progress evaluation. Most school districts use routine testing programs at various grade levels to evaluate the extent to which pupils in their schools are progressing in comparison with some national standard. Scores on achievement tests provide communities, school boards, and parents with an index of the quality of schooling. Schools and, indeed, the teachers within those schools are often subject to question when pupils fail to demonstrate expected progress.

Finally, achievement tests are used to evaluate the relative effectiveness of alternative curricula. Brown School may choose to use the Scott-Foresman Reading Series in third grade, while Green School decides to use the Lippincott Reading Program. If school personnel can assume that children were at relatively comparable reading levels on entering the third grade of the two schools, then achievement tests may be administered at the end of the year to ascertain the relative effectiveness of the Scott-Foresman and Lippincott programs. There are, of course, many assumptions in such evaluations (for example, that the quality of individual teachers and the instructional environment are comparable in the two schools) and many research pitfalls that must be avoided if comparative evaluation is to have meaning.

The most obvious merit of achievement tests is the fact that they can provide teachers with data that show the extent to which their pupils have profited from instruction. By using group-administered multiple-skill batteries, teachers can obtain a considerable amount of information in a relatively short time. Use of norm-referenced devices allows teachers to evaluate pupil progress relative to a national sample of the same age or grade level.

---

1. A careful distinction must be made. We note that performance on group-administered achievement tests should not be used to support placement decisions. The important consideration is the *way* in which the test was administered. Considerably more qualitative information is obtained in individual testing than in group testing. Group tests, of course, can be individually administered. When this occurs and when the examiner is willing to go beyond scores earned to examine pupil performance on specific items, the use of group tests to support placement decisions may be appropriate.

limitations

Two limitations affect the use of achievement tests as screening devices. ①
As was noted earlier, unless the content of an achievement test reflects the
content of the curriculum, the obtained results are meaningless. If students are instructed in new math but tested with traditional math achievement tests, they may well perform poorly. Yet the obtained results cannot
be said to reflect accurately and validly a student's level of skill development
in math.

② A second limitation is inherent in the way most achievement tests are
administered. Most achievement tests are group administered, and
teachers giving a group-administered test are unable to observe individual
pupil performance. They may lose valuable information about how a
student goes about solving problems, analyzing words, and spelling, because they cannot observe individual behavior directly. And then, because
most screening devices provide global scores by content areas, teachers
must actually return to a student's test blank or answer sheet to investigate
the kinds of errors made. Otherwise, teachers are left with a score but little
information about how the score was obtained and no systematic analysis of
skill-development strengths and weaknesses.

OBTAINED SCORES

As in any form of norm-referenced testing, the raw scores obtained on
achievement tests are of no direct value in interpretation. Scores must be
transformed. All norm-referenced achievement tests provide the teacher
with transformed scores of some kind. Most provide age- or grade-
equivalent scores, percentile ranks within grades, and standard scores
and/or stanines. In all cases, scores are reported by subtest, and the
teacher is usually given a total achievement score. Procedures for and
problems in the interpretation of the scores obtained from achievement
tests used for screening purposes are discussed later in this chapter.

SPECIFIC TESTS OF ACADEMIC ACHIEVEMENT

The remainder of this chapter examines four very popular group-
administered multiple-skill batteries (the California Achievement Test, the
Iowa Tests of Basic Skills, the Metropolitan Achievement Test, and the
Stanford Achievement Test), one group-administered reading test (the
Gates-MacGinitie), and two individually administered multiple-skill bat-
teries (the Peabody Individual Achievement Test and the Wide Range
Achievement Test).

In selecting an achievement test to be used in screening, teachers must consider several factors. First, they must evaluate the extent to which tests sample behaviors relevant to the content of the school's curriculum. Second, teachers must evaluate the adequacy of each test's norms, asking whether the normative group is composed of the kinds of individuals to whom they wish to compare their students. Third, for the tests reported in this chapter, teachers must examine the extent to which a total test and its subtests have the reliability necessary for use in screening. Finally, teachers must evaluate evidence for content validity, the most important kind of validity for achievement tests.

✓ CALIFORNIA ACHIEVEMENT TEST

The California Achievement Test (CAT) (Tiegs & Clark, 1970) is a group-administered, norm-referenced, multiple-skill assessment battery measuring skill development in several areas, from grades 1.5 to 12. There are two forms of the test at each of five educational levels. The levels and the grades for which they are appropriate are as follows: level 1, grades 1.5 to 2; level 2, grades 2 to 4; level 3, grades 4 to 6; level 4, grades 6 to 9; and level 5, grades 9 to 12.

The CAT assesses skill development in three academic content areas: reading, math, and language. Specific subtests in each area, the number of items, and the time required to administer the test are summarized in Table 9.1.

The specific subtests sample the following behaviors.

Vocabulary   The student is required to select from four alternative response words the word with the same meaning as a stimulus word used in context. In addition, some items at levels 1 and 2 assess word skills such as sentence-picture association, beginning sounds, ending sounds, and word recognition.

Comprehension   The student must read sentences or passages and indicate comprehension of the material by answering multiple-choice questions.

Mathematics Computation   The student must solve computational problems of increasing difficulty.

Mathematics Concepts   The student must demonstrate knowledge and use of such concepts as forms of measurement, sequences, money, time, geometry, and place values.

Table **9.1** Skills Areas and Normed Sections with Numbers of Items and Time Limits (in Minutes) for Five Levels of the CAT, Form A

SKILLS AREA AND NORMED SECTION	LEVEL 1		LEVEL 2		LEVEL 3		LEVEL 4		LEVEL 5	
	ITEMS	TIME	ITEMS	TIME	ITEMS	TIME	ITEMS	TIME	ITEMS	TIME
Reading										
Vocabulary	92	30	40	13	40	10	40	10	40	10
Comprehension	24	16	45	27	42	35	45	40	45	40
Mathematics										
Computation	40	14	72	26	68	46	48	28	48	33
Concepts and Problems	47	17	45	22	40	18	50	23	50	23
Language										
Auding	15	6	—	—	—	—	—	—	—	—
Mechanics	38	10	66	22	80	24	72	21	80	25
Usage and Structure	20	11	25	6	41	11	50	14	54	14
Spelling	20	10	25	7	32	8	32	8	32	8
TOTAL BATTERY	296	114	318	123	343	152	337	144	349	153

SOURCE: From *Test Coordinators Handbook, California Achievement Tests*, devised by Ernest W. Tiegs and Willis W. Clark. Copyright © 1970 by McGraw-Hill, Inc. Reprinted by permission of the publisher, CTB/McGraw-Hill, Monterey, CA 93940. All rights reserved.

Mathematics Problems   The student must comprehend and answer correctly a variety of word problems ranging from those involving basic one-step operations to those requiring two-step and three-step operations.

Language Mechanics   The student must capitalize and punctuate sentences and paragraphs.

Language Usage and Structure   The student must select which of four response possibilities best fits a blank in a sentence, thereby demonstrating knowledge of grammatical usage and structure.

Language Spelling   The student must select which of four response possibilities best fits a blank in a sentence, thereby demonstrating spelling knowledge.

Scores

Five different scores can be calculated on the basis of obtained raw scores on the CAT: (1) percentile ranks, (2) stanines, (3) grade equivalents, (4) achievement-development scaled scores, and (5) anticipated achievement scores. The latter two types of scores are highly unconventional and of limited use. Achievement-development scaled scores, having an approximate range of from 100 to 900, a mean of 600, and a standard deviation of 100 at grade 10, are a unique means of comparing student performance on different forms and levels and of looking at gain from grades 1.5 to 12. They are of use to guidance counselors and program evaluators but of limited use to the classroom teacher.

Anticipated achievement scores are computed by comparison of a student's performances on the CAT and the Short Form Test of Academic Aptitude administered at the same time. The amount of gain in achievement one can expect from a student is estimated by means of multiple-regression formulas that use several predictors. Student records are submitted to the publishers' scoring service for scoring.

Norms

A nationwide sample of approximately 203,700 students enrolled in public and Catholic schools participated in standardization of both the CAT and the California Test of Mental Maturity. The standardization sample was selected on the basis of geographic region, average enrollment per grade, and type of community (urban, rural, town). After stratifying school districts on the basis of the above three variables, entire districts were randomly selected to participate in standardization.

Of all districts initially invited to participate, only 60.1 percent of the public school districts and 90 percent of the Catholic school districts were willing to participate. This fact probably introduced some bias into the normative sampling. Data regarding the race, sex, and socioeconomic status of the normative sample are reported in the Technical Bulletin that accompanies the test. Tiegs and Clark (1970, p. 40) state that "the ratio of each minority in the sample to the total sample can be expected to approximate the ratio of the total number of minority group students to the total school population."

Reliability

Kuder-Richardson-20 subtest reliabilities for the five levels of the CAT are presented in Table 9.2. For specific reliabilities at each grade level, pages 78–83 in the Technical Bulletin should be consulted. Reported reliabilities range from a low of .69 for the Language Usage and Structure subtest at level 3 to a high of .98 for the total battery at levels 1–4. The Language Usage and Structure and the Spelling subtests, in comparison to other CAT subtests, demonstrate consistently lower reliability. The reliabilities for the Language Usage and Structure subtest are considerably lower than the desired reliability of .90 for tests that are to be used in making important decisions about children.

Validity

Thirty-three pages in the Technical Bulletin for the CAT are devoted to a discussion of validity and a presentation of evidence about the validity of the scale. However, neither the discussion nor the reported data support the notion that the CAT measures what it purports to measure. The discussion about content validity describes steps in the development of the test and procedures used in item selection. A review of currently used textbooks and curriculum objectives serves as the source of item content.

Data regarding validity consist of tables of subtest intercorrelations and a breakdown of the percentage of pupils in the normative sample who responded correctly on each item. These data are valuable for evaluating the extent to which subtests overlap and items are arranged in order of difficulty; they do not necessarily support the validity of the test.

Summary

The California Achievement Test is a norm-referenced, group-administered achievement test assessing skill development in many academic content areas. The adequacy of the normative sample for the CAT is difficult to evaluate because the selected sample was solicited by invitation and only 60 percent of those school districts selected agreed to participate in the standardization. Reliability of the CAT is generally good, although two subtests fail to meet desirable standards for educational

Table **9.2** Subtest Reliabilities (KR-20) for the Five Levels of the CAT

| | LEVEL | | | | |
SUBTEST	1	2	3	4	5
Reading	.97	.96	.95	.94	.93
Vocabulary	.96	.92	.92	.91	.88
Comprehension	.91	.93	.89	.89	.87
Mathematics	.95	.95	.95	.95	.96
Computation	.95	.92	.92	.92	.92
Concepts and Problems	.90	.90	.90	.90	.92
Language	.94	.95	.95	.95	.94
Mechanics	.94	.95	.95	.95	.94
Usage and Structure	.78	.83	.69	.73	.76
Spelling	.86	.86	.89	.89	.88
BATTERY	.98	.98	.98	.98	.97

SOURCE: Table 9.2 is a compilation of figures reported in various sections of the Test Coordinator's Handbook for the CAT.

decision making. The materials accompanying the test provide no specific data regarding its validity.

IOWA TESTS OF BASIC SKILLS

The Iowa Tests of Basic Skills (ITBS) (Hieronymus & Lindquist, 1974) are designed to assess "generalized intellectual skills and abilities" as opposed to specific content skills. The authors state that

the Iowa Tests of Basic Skills differ from most other elementary achievement test batteries in that they are concerned only with generalized intellectual skills and abilities and do not provide separate measures of achievement in the content subjects, such as the social studies, literature, general science, and descriptive geography. (p. 6)

The authors' stated reason for this different approach to the assessment of academic achievement is based upon their belief that the heterogeneity of classroom instruction renders specific skill assessment nearly impossible.

There are seven levels of the ITBS. Levels 7 and 8 are the primary battery, while levels 9 through 14 are used in grades 3 through 8. The ITBS assesses five major content areas: vocabulary, reading, language, work study, and mathematics.

Vocabulary This subtest assesses knowledge of the meanings of words by requiring children to identify which of four response words is a synonym of a stimulus word, which they must read. At lower levels of the test, children demonstrate knowledge of word meanings by associating words with pictures.

Reading Lower levels of the ITBS assess word-analysis skills and require children to associate pictures with sentences or stories they read. Upper levels of the test sample skill development in both literal and inferential reading comprehension by requiring students to read paragraphs and then answer specific questions about the content of the paragraphs.

Language This subtest assesses skills in four subareas: spelling, capitalization, punctuation, and usage. The spelling subtest is a measure of recognition in which children identify one of four words as the correct spelling of a word read by the teacher. Capitalization requires children to identify words that should be capitalized in sentences or paragraphs. The punctuation subtest, on the other hand, requires children to identify those places in sentences that need specific punctuation marks. The usage subtest assesses knowledge of grammatical rules by requiring children to identify which of three alternative sentences employs correct usage.

Work Study This subtest assesses generalized skill development in three areas: map reading, reading graphs and tables, and knowledge and uses of references. The map-reading section requires children to answer specific questions by reading maps, while the second section assesses similar skills, requiring children to answer specific questions by reading graphs and tables. The section on use of references requires children to demonstrate knowledge of how to alphabetize, read tables of contents, use a dictionary, classify information, and indicate reference sources for specific material.

Mathematics Two kinds of math tests are included in the ITBS. The first assesses knowledge of mathematical concepts while the second requires children to solve computational problems and written problems. At lower levels of the test, the directions are read to the children, while at upper levels, children must read the directions themselves.

There are no grade-level editions of the ITBS per se. Rather, each test (such as Vocabulary) is continuous. The authors designed the test in this way to reflect overlap of content and objectives across grade levels. There is no reference to grade levels on the test booklets and answer sheets. Instead, test levels are referred to. For purposes of simplification, the number assigned to a test level is simply the grade level plus 6. Level 9, therefore, is the level of the test appropriate to the third grade. The ITBS can be purchased in a multilevel edition or separately by level.

Numbers assigned to levels, of course, also match the ages of children in specific grades. Level 10 is at the fourth-grade level; most fourth graders are 10 years old. The authors recommend "individualized testing" of certain youngsters, stating that under such a plan "each pupil takes the level which corresponds most closely to the instructional objectives *for him* and to *his* level of skills development" (p. 4). Selection of appropriate levels is based on subjective opinion.

Specific skills assessed by the various subtests and, for the most part, by each item are listed along with suggestions for remedial activities in the Teacher's Guide for Administration, Interpretation, and Use (Hieronymus & Lindquist, 1971). Many of the suggestions are overgeneralized and nonspecific. In taking levels 9 through 14 of the ITBS, the pupil marks responses on a machine-scored answer sheet; for levels 7 and 8, the pupil responds directly on the test booklet.

Scores

Five different derived scores are obtained for the ITBS: grade equivalents, age equivalents, percentile ranks, stanines, and standard scores ($\bar{X} = 80$, $S = 20$). Grade equivalents are obtained for subareas, such as reading graphs and tables; for areas, such as work study skills; and for the composite of all the areas. Grade equivalents for areas are obtained by averaging the scores in subareas, while grade equivalents for the composite are obtained by averaging area scores. Averaging different behavior samplings to get totals is, as we have stated before, a very haphazard practice.

Norms

The standardization of the ITBS was completed simultaneously with standardization of the Cognitive Abilities Test and the Tests of Academic Progress. Levels 9 to 14 of the ITBS were standardized on 124,259 children in grades 3 to 8, while levels 7 and 8 were standardized on 35,824 children in grades 1 and 2. Several different normative comparisons can be made using the ITBS. There are separate norms for pupil scores, school averages, and item performance. National norms for fall, midyear, and spring are available as are special norms for geographic regions, for large cities, and for Catholic schools.

The normative sample for the ITBS was stratified on the basis of community size and socioeconomic status (based on median years of education for those over 25 years of age, and median family income). The sample was not stratified on the basis of geographic region or racial and ethnic factors. The authors do, however, include comparative tables in the manual reporting differences between proportions in the ITBS sample and proportions in the 1970 census. Norms for item performance are reportedly available from the publisher (p. 20).

Reliability

Two kinds of reliability data are reported in the ITBS manual. Split-half reliabilities are reported by subtest for each level of the test, based on the performance of 12.5 percent of the children in the standardization populations. Split-half reliability coefficients ranged from .70 for Reading Graphs and Tables at level 12 to .98 for the Composite at levels 9, 10, 11, 12, and 13. While the reliabilities were computed on the basis of the performance of a proportion of children in the national standardization sample, standard errors of measurement are reported for a "weighted national standardization sample."

Equivalent-forms reliabilities are reported only for the old edition of the ITBS. The authors state that

Equivalent forms reliability data were secured from a special study in Iowa schools involving Forms 3 and 4. In view of the similarity of the content and difficulty specifications of Forms 5 and 6 to those of previous forms, the reliabilities of the current forms are probably not greatly different. (p. 60)

No test-retest reliability data for the 1974 ITBS are reported in the manual. Instead, the authors report the results of three studies designed to ascertain the stability of scores on the 1965 ITBS.

Validity

Content validity of the ITBS, as for most achievement tests, is largely a matter of expert opinion. The authors of the ITBS went through a number of procedures in selecting content for the test. Criteria used in item selection included (1) the use of material in current curricula and the emphasis placed on that material, (2) recommendations by experts in methods and by national curriculum committees, (3) studies of the frequency of certain kinds of errors made by pupils, (4) importance of content, (5) technical characteristics of various kinds of items, and (6) feedback from users of earlier editions of the test. Individual teachers must still, as is the case with any achievement test, judge the usefulness and appropriateness of the test for their own purposes.

The authors do present evidence for the predictive validity of the ITBS. The data are, however, based on a 1962 study of freshmen entering the University of Iowa and a 1958 study of "pupils entering one of the two state universities in Iowa during a four-year period" (p. 55). The data are based on earlier editions of the ITBS.

Summary

The Iowa Tests of Basic Skills are a comprehensive achievement battery designed to assess "generalized intellectual skills and abilities" in pupils in grades 3 through 8. While construction and standardization of the scale appear, for the most part, to be adequate, technical adequacy is relatively limited. With the exception of split-half reliabilities on the 1974 ITBS, all reliability data are on earlier editions of the ITBS. Content validity, as is the case for the other screening batteries discussed in this chapter, is a matter of expert opinion.

METROPOLITAN ACHIEVEMENT TEST   K - 9

The Metropolitan Achievement Test (MAT) (Durost, Bixler, Wrightstone, Prescott, & Balow, 1971) is a norm-referenced group-administered achievement test appropriate for use with students in kindergarten through ninth grade. There are six levels of the test, and three forms at each level except Primer, where there are two forms. While each level except Primer can be machine scored, scoring stencils are provided for hand scoring at all levels. There is a separate teacher's handbook for each level of the test. The authors do provide in each teacher's handbook a description of the content sampled by the subtests, but there is no listing of specific behaviors sampled. Table 9.3 is a summary of levels, subtests, and times required for administration. The test requires from one to four and one-half hours to administer depending on the grade level at which it is used.

According to the test's authors, the following specific contents are sampled by the subtests of the MAT:

Word Knowledge Items require the student to match pictures to words at the primary levels and later to identify synonyms and antonyms. This subtest assesses reading vocabulary.

Word Analysis This subtest occurs only at the Primary levels of the test. The items measure decoding skills or knowledge of sound-letter relationships.

Reading This subtest assesses skill in comprehending the material read. At the primary levels, the student selects sentences to describe pictures. At higher levels, the student reads a paragraph and is asked to answer questions about it.

Language This subtest assesses knowledge of basic conventions (rules of punctuation, capitalization, or usage) in standard written English.

Table **9.3** Levels and Subtests of the MAT: Summary of Levels and Tests

TESTS	PRIMER (K.7–1.4)		PRIMARY I (1.5–2.4)		PRIMARY II (2.5–3.4)		ELEMENTARY (3.5–4.9)		INTERMEDIATE (5.0–6.9)		ADVANCED (7.0–9.5)	
	ITEMS	TIME[b]	ITEMS	TIME	ITEMS	TIME	ITEMS	TIME	ITEMS	TIME	ITEMS	TIME
Word Knowledge	39	20	35	15	40	18	50	15	50	15	50	15
Word Analysis[c]	33	20	40	15	35	15	45	25	45	25	45	25
Reading			42	30	44	30	50	30	103	50	90	45
Language							40	20	50	15	50	15
Spelling					30	10	40	35	40	35	50	15
Math. Computation					33	18	40	25	40	25	40	25
Math. Concepts[d]	34	20	62	30	40	20	35	30	40	25	40	25
Math. Problem Solving					35	25			35	25	35	25
Science									78	35	80	35
Social Studies									93	45	94	45

[a] Indicates grades for which each battery is primarily intended.

[b] Time in minutes.

[c] Referred to as "Listening for Sounds" at Primer level.

[d] At Primer and Primary levels, only a Total Mathematics score, based on both concepts and computation, is reported. At the Primer level, Mathematics is referred to simply as "Numbers."

Spelling   The student is required to write words dictated by the teacher.

Mathematics Computation   This subtest assesses basic computation skills ranging from simple addition of single-digit numbers to complex multiplication and division.

Mathematics Concepts   This subtest assesses understanding of basic mathematical principles and relationships including laws and properties of number systems, measurement, place value, sets, and geometry.

Mathematics Problem Solving   The problem-solving subtest assesses ability to apply knowledge in solving numerical problems.

Science   This subtest assesses knowledge and use of scientific concepts, facts, and skills. Items assess knowledge of plant and animal biology, human health and safety, chemistry, magnetism and electricity, energy and machines, sound, light, heat, weather and climate, earth science, astronomy, and the history and methodology of science.

Social Studies   This subtest measures both the content and the skills of social studies (knowledge of important concepts, names, and facts; skill in using maps and charts to get specific information and to make generalizations).

Scores

Four different scores can be calculated on the basis of obtained raw scores on the MAT: (1) percentile ranks, (2) stanines, (3) grade equivalents, and (4) standard scores. The standard scores are not well explained or readily interpreted. "Within a single subtest area, standard scores are directly comparable from battery to battery and form to form" (Durost et al., 1971, p. 4). However, standard scores are *not* comparable between subtest areas; standard scores correspond to different percentile ranks depending on the particular area being assessed.

Norms

The standardization sample for the MAT was chosen by dividing the country into eight census districts and inviting samples of each census group to participate in the standardization. A total of twenty-nine school systems in nineteen states accepted the invitation. The actual size of the standardization sample is not specified in the teacher's handbook that serves as a manual for the test. Data were reportedly analyzed using a "special socioeconomic index" based on median family income and median

Table **9.4** Split-half Reliabilities for Subtests of the Metropolitan Achievement Test

SUBTEST	PRIMARY I	PRIMARY II	ELEMENTARY	INTERMEDIATE	ADVANCED
Word Knowledge	.88	.93	.94	.92	.93
Word Analysis	.90	.90			
Reading	.95	.93	.92	.93	.92
Language			.93	.95	.96
Spelling		.94	.96	.90	.91
Math Computation		.86	.88	.84	.91
Math Concepts		.85	.90	.88	.90
Math Problem Solving		.88	.91	.89	.90
Total Math	.93	.95	.96	.95	.96
Science				.94	.94
Social Studies				.95	.95

years of schooling for adults in the standardization communities. These data were reportedly used to select the MAT standardization sample, but the data do not appear in the manual.

Reliability

Split-half reliabilities for the six levels of the test are reported in Table 9.4. Reliabilities are adequate in most cases, ranging from .84 to .96.

Validity

Data regarding test validity are not included in the materials accompanying the test but are reportedly available in a series of technical supplements. The authors of the test state that because each school has different curricula, content validity of the tests will have to be judged by the individual schools.

Summary

The Metropolitan Achievement Test is a norm-referenced, group-administered screening test assessing academic skill development in multiple areas. The normative sample for the test is inadequate, based on assessment of students in only twenty-nine school systems in nineteen states; the number of students in the sample is not specified. The normative sample was obtained by invitation. Reliabilities for the MAT appear adequate, but there are no data in the test manual regarding the validity of the scale.

Table **9.5**   Subtests of the SAT According to Battery Level, Number of Items,

| | BATTERY LEVEL | | | | | |
| | PRIMARY LEVEL I Gr. 1.5–2.4 16 pages | | PRIMARY LEVEL II Gr. 2.5–3.4 24 pages | | PRIMARY LEVEL III Gr. 3.5–4.4 32 pages | |
TEST	ITEMS	TIME[a]	ITEMS	TIME[a]	ITEMS	TIME[a]
Vocabulary	37	20	37	20	45	25
Reading Comprehension[b]	87	45	93	45	70	35
Word Study Skills	60	25	65	25	55	25
Mathematics Concepts	32	25	35	20	32	20
Mathematics Computation	32	30	37	30	36	30
Mathematics Applications	—	—	28	20	28	25
Spelling	30	20	43	25	47	15
Language	—	—	—	—	55	35
Social Science	—	—	27	20	44	25
Science	—	—	27	20	42	25
Listening Comprehension	26	25	50	35	50	35
STANFORD TOTAL	304	190	442	260	504	295

[a] In minutes.
[b] At Primary Level I and Primary Level II in two parts which may be administered separately.

STANFORD ACHIEVEMENT TEST   1.5-9.5

The Stanford Achievement Test (SAT) (Madden, Gardner, Rudman, Karlsen, & Merwin, 1973) is both a norm-referenced and "objective-referenced" test designed to assess skill development in several academic content areas. Three forms of the test, A, B, and C, are available at six levels from grades 1.5 to 9.5. A lower level of the test, the Stanford Early School Achievement Test, is appropriate for children in kindergarten and first grade. An upward extension of the SAT, the Stanford Test of Academic Skills (TASK) is used to assess the preparation of high school students in the basic skill areas of reading, English, and math. TASK level II is a special edition available for use in community colleges.

The SAT is comprehensive in nature, measuring important knowledge, skills, and understandings believed to be the goals of an elementary school curriculum. The subtests included in the various levels of the SAT and the administration time for the test are reported in Table 9.5. As the table

and Administration Time per Test

BATTERY LEVEL (cont.)

INTERMEDIATE LEVEL I Gr. 4.5–5.4 32 pages		INTERMEDIATE LEVEL II Gr. 5.5–6.9 32 pages		ADVANCED LEVEL Gr. 7–9.5 32 pages		TASK LEVEL I Gr. 9–10 16 pages		TASK LEVEL II Gr. 11–12 16 pages	
ITEMS	TIME[a]	ITEMS	TIME[a]	ITEMS	TIME[a]	ITEMS	TIME[a]	ITEMS	TIME[a]
50	25	50	25	50	20	—	—	—	—
72	35	71	35	74	35	78	40	78	40
55	25	50	20	—	—	—	—	—	—
32	20	35	20	35	20	48	40	48	40
40	35	45	35	45	35	—	—	—	—
40	35	40	35	40	35	—	—	—	—
50	15	60	20	60	20	—	—	—	—
79	35	80	35	79	35	69	40	69	40
60	30	54	30	60	30	—	—	—	—
60	30	60	30	60	30	—	—	—	—
50	35	50	35	—	—	—	—	—	—
588	320	595	320	503	260	195	120	195	120

SOURCE: Reproduced by permission from the promotional brochure for the Stanford Achievement Test (1973 edition). Published by Harcourt Brace Jovanovich, Inc., New York, N.Y. All rights reserved.

shows, some subtests occur at all levels, others at only some of the levels. The behaviors assessed by each subtest are different at each level of the test. Table 9.6 is the authors' statement of the behaviors sampled by each subtest. In addition to a general description of the behaviors, the authors have published two separate manuals. One manual groups items by major instructional objectives; the other manual describes the behaviors sampled by every item on every subtest at every level of the SAT, as well as providing instructional objectives and suggestions regarding ways to teach to those objectives.

The manual for the SAT is actually a five-part manual. Part 1, unique to each level of the test, contains the Teacher's Directions for Administering the Test; part 2, also unique to each level of the test, consists of the Norms Booklet. The remaining three parts are: Teacher's Guide for Interpreting the Test, Administrator's Guide for Interpreting, and the Technical Data Report. The manual is both clear and comprehensive.

Table 9.6 Behaviors Sampled by the Stanford Achievement Test

	VOCABULARY	READING COMPREHENSION	WORD STUDY SKILLS	LANGUAGE ARTS
PRIMARY I	**Primary I** Teacher dictated measure of pupils' verbal competence independent of their reading ability. Test basically measures the verbal competence the child brings to school.	**Primary I** Two part test. Part A: Word Reading tests words that are generally in the average child's speaking and listening vocabulary. It is essentially a decoding test. Part B: Reading Comprehension, using very simple paragraphs, measures pupils' ability to recall and identify facts stated in the text.	**Primary I** Sixty dictated items selected on the basis of curriculum content in reading and phonics programs. Seven item groupings provide complete and detailed coverage of letter-sound combinations such as initial single consonant sounds, blends, digraphs, and simple and complex vowels.	
PRIMARY II	**Primary II** Dictated test measures verbal competence independent of reading ability. Half of the words are content-dependent, words child encounters in school textbooks in mathematics, science, social studies; the other half are general words frequently encountered in language arts.	**Primary II** Two part test essentially same as Primary I.	**Primary II** Sixty-five item test presented in two parts. Part A (dictated) measures pupils' ability to discriminate letter sounds, blends, digraphs. Part B (not dictated) measures pupils' knowledge of the major variant spellings (graphemes) of sounds (phonemes). Items tested cover consonant blends, consonant digraphs, simple vowel sounds, long vowel sounds, vowel digraphs, and uncommon vowels.	
PRIMARY III	**Primary III** Dictated test similar in design to Primary II. Words increase in difficulty reflecting the growth of the child in age and school situation.	**Primary III** Test has 14 reading paragraphs and one poem, arranged in order of difficulty, which measure pupils' comprehension of connected discourse. Content of paragraph is designed to appeal to pupils of diverse backgrounds.	**Primary III** Three part test. Parts A & B (dictated) measure knowledge of beginning and ending sounds such as single consonant sounds, consonant blends, consonant digraphs, long vowel sounds, variant vowel sounds, common affixes. Part C emphasizes decoding effectiveness with variant spellings of the sounds. About two thirds of Part C deals with vowel phonemes.	**Primary III** Part A written in continued discourse style deals with capitalization, punctuation and usage. Part B tests syntactical matters such as interrelationships of parts of sentences. All of these areas are tested functionally so items do not represent a nomenclature test.

SAT

	Vocabulary	Reading	Word Analysis	English
INTERMEDIATE I	**Intermediate I** Dictated test similar in design to vocabulary test at other levels. Test is included in battery because of its usefulness in educational planning for pupils and in making more meaningful, interpretation of scores on the other tests.	**Intermediate I** Similar to Primary III. Paragraphs sample a wide variety of content that pupils in the intermediate grades are likely to encounter and pupils of diverse backgrounds would enjoy reading.	**Intermediate I** Two parts. Part A. Phonetic Analysis measures pupils' knowledge of variant spellings of the sounds. Part B. Measures knowledge and blending of word parts. Five specific rules of word division are sampled. Each word used to measure the objectives is a word that the students should be able to decode if they have learned the skill measured by that word.	**Intermediate I** Four part test dealing with the conventions of punctuation, capitalization, and usage, language sensitivity, and dictionary skills. Standard usage is emphasized when pupil is asked to select best form to use in writing a school paper. All of these areas are tested functionally.
INTER II	**Intermediate II** Same as above.	**Intermediate II** Essentially same as Intermediate I. Paragraphs increase in difficulty.	**Intermediate II** Essentially same content as Intermediate I. Items increase in difficulty.	**Intermediate II** Similar to above yet reflecting curriculum of grade levels for which this test is designed.
ADVANCED	**Advanced** Vocabulary at this level must be read by the pupil. The design of test remains the same. Half of the words are content oriented; half of the words are general in nature. The reading level of the words is lower than the grade levels for which this battery is designed.	**Advanced** Same as Intermediate II — From Primary Level III items designed to sample pupils' knowledge of these objectives of reading instruction: global meaning, meaning of explicit detail, meaning of implied detail, meaning from context, and inferential meaning.		**Advanced** Four part test covering the conventions of capitalization, punctuation, and usage; language sensitivity, dictionary skills, English learning skills. Part D measures additional English learning skills such as use of different types of reference books, literary concepts, knowledge of morphemes, grammatical concepts, etc.
TASK	**Task Levels I & II** Part of the Reading test. Twenty-seven words that students at high school level are likely to encounter in their school texts and life situations. Students show knowledge of meaning of word by indicating one of five categories to which the word has some relation.	**Task — Levels I & II** Test contains a wide variety of paragraphs and one poem designed to appeal to students at the high school and community college level.		**Task — Levels I & II English** Five part test that measures students' mastery of learning skills including appropriateness of speech, using reference sources, word formation, grammar; of usage conventions such as punctuation, capitalization and usage; spelling; sentence sensitivity; paragraph arrangement.

(continued)

Table 9.6 (Continued)

	SPELLING	MATHEMATICS CONCEPTS	MATHEMATICS COMPUTATION	MATHEMATICS APPLICATIONS
PRIMARY I	**Primary I** Optional Spelling Test of 30 dictated words.	**Primary I** Dictated test — no reading ability required. Measures pupils' knowledge of meaning of number, reading and writing numerals, symbols of operations, measurement, and geometric figures.	**Primary I** No reading ability required. This is a combination mathematics computation and applications test. Items 1–14, dictated by the teacher, measure pupils' ability to understand the language of mathematical problem situations and to solve problems by the choice of mathematical operations. Items 15–32 are traditional computation problems.	**Primary I** Combined into one test with Mathematics Computation.
PRIMARY II	**Primary II** Machine scorable test — 43 words spelled correctly or incorrectly in the booklet which the pupil has to identify as such. Pupils' misspellings of 32 of the words are usually related to sound-letter correspondence (phonics). Errors in the remaining words usually result from changing the meaning, adding a prefix, converting to plural tense (morphemes and "rules").	**Primary II** Dictated test. Four item groupings place greater emphasis on competence with number and notation, as well as operations, geometry, measurement, concepts of sets and logical thinking.	**Primary II** Test measures pupils' knowledge of 34 addition and subtraction facts and includes three multiplication comparisons. Twenty-nine items are presented in traditional computation form. Eight items are presented as incomplete mathematical sentences which require determination of two basic facts and a comparison of the values determined in order to complete the sentence.	**Primary II** Items cover processes directly concerned with problem solving, measure, graphs or charts, rate problems, language that signals addition, subtraction, multiplication and simple division.
PRIMARY III	**Primary III** 47 multiple choice items. Each item consists of four words, one of which is misspelled. Misspellings to be detected consist of consonant errors (phonology), and errors resulting from adding suffixes (morphology). Some of the errors may be due to poor perception of the written word or faulty pronunciation. Errors used are those most commonly made by pupils in their writing.	**Primary III** Dictated test reflects integration of "modern" and "traditional" mathematics as now taught in current textbooks. Item content measures pupils' competence with numbers, fractions, notation, operations, geometry and measurement.	**Primary III** Test measures pupils' knowledge of 36 fundamental facts in addition, multiplication and division. The first twenty-four items are presented as incomplete mathematical sentences as in Primary Level II. The remaining 12 items are presented in traditional computation form.	**Primary Level III** Designed to use pupils' knowledge of concepts and computational ability to solve problems that occur in life situations. Topics covered are selection of solution model to solve problem, graphs, advertising displays, rate problems, measurement, buying and selling, and language which commonly signals a specific operation.

INTERMEDIATE I	**Intermediate I** 50 multiple choice items. Misspellings to be detected consist of using the wrong homophone (meaning), errors in vowels and consonants (phonology), and errors encountered when adding prefixes and suffixes (morphology). Basic causes of misspellings same as outlined above.	**Intermediate I** Involves some reading ability. Measures pupils' knowledge of number, notation, operations, with some items on measurement, geometry, sets, the "clock" module, function and average or "middle."	**Intermediate I** Similar in format to Primary III, eighteen items are presented as incomplete mathematical sentences and the remaining items are traditional computation problems. Items increase in difficulty to include the addition of four-digit addends, difficult subtraction, multiplication and division.	**Intermediate I** Covers above topics at a more advanced level. The pupils are required to analyze the problem and to use their mathematical knowledge appropriately.
INTER II	**Intermediate II** 60 multiple choice items. Same format as Intermediate I. Words, however, reflect the spelling curriculum of grade levels for which test is designed.	**Intermediate II** Similar to above. Increased emphasis is placed on geometry. Also included are items on fractions, easy percent-idea and logical thinking.	**Intermediate II** Same as above with the addition of items involving common fractions.	**Intermediate II** Same design as above. Problems cover a wide range of situations, including the interpretation of data presented in graphs and tables. Some of the problems require the identification of missing data or the conversion of a problem into a mathematical sentence rather than determining a numerical answer. A few easy common fractions are used.
ADVANCED	**Advanced** 60 multiple choice items. Same format as Intermediate I and II again designed to reflect common misspellings found at this grade level.	**Advanced** Similar to above in content. The range of difficulty of items is wide, from matching an Arabic numeral with equivalent English words to determining simple probability.	**Advanced** Similar format to Intermediate II. Common and decimal fractions, percent, average, estimation, exponents, graphing of a solution set, and simplification of sentence integers are all introduced at this level.	**Advanced** As in Intermediate II, covers a wide range of situations including English and metric measures, map scales, averages and probability, graphing solution sets.
TASK	**Task Levels I & II** Fifteen items of four words each spelled correctly or incorrectly. Student asked to indicate number of correctly spelled words one, two, three, four or none. Words chosen reflect those errors most commonly found in the writings of high school students.	**Task — Levels I & II** Both levels measure students' knowledge of concepts of number properties and operations, common and decimal fractions, integers and exponents, mathematical sentences, geometry and measurement, graphs, probability and statistics (Level II) and mathematical reasoning (Level II).	**Task — Levels I & II** Computation strand of the Mathematics Test has items covering number properties and operations, common and decimal fractions, integers and exponents, mathematical sentences, ratio and percent.	**Task — Levels I & II** Problems presented test common and decimal fractions, mathematical sentences, mathematical reasoning, graphs, probability and statistics.

(continued)

Table 9.6 (Continued)

	SCIENCE	SOCIAL SCIENCE	LISTENING COMPREHENSION
			For levels Primary I through Intermediate II An auditory test designed to measure pupils' progress in comprehension through listening, the most commonly used mode of communication, and to use the listening test results to assist in the interpretation of reading comprehension. Test consists of dictated passages of wide variety of content designed to complement the reading test. It requires pupils to show competence in recognizing the central focus of the passage, specific meanings, implied meanings, perception of concepts and relations, and identification of inferences.
PRIMARY II	**Primary II** No reading required. Options presented pictorially. Test measures pupils' ability to understand basic concepts reflecting the natural and physical sciences. Pupils are called upon to make estimates, to measure and to draw inferences from data given.	**Primary Level II** No reading ability required. Options are presented pictorially. Test samples broadly among six social science disciplines of Geography, History, Economics, Political Science, Anthropology and Sociology. In recognition of the conceptual approach to teaching of social science, two-thirds of items are concepts-process type, one-third factual type.	
PRIMARY III	**Primary III** The following concepts of science are measured: matter, energy, change in the physical universe, the environmental interaction of living objects, the effect of heredity and environment upon living things, the basic processes of science and the ability to test hypotheses.	**Primary Level III** Test requires some reading ability. Covers same six social science disciplines outlined above. Test designed to reflect contemporary social science programs which feature an emphasis upon the structure of the social sciences and a conceptual approach which relies heavily on inquiry skills.	

Intermediate I All of the above concepts are tested with the addition of the concept of the functional skills of science, i.e. making a probability statement. Level of difficulty is in keeping with grade level of pupils.

Intermediate Level I Test covers the same social disciplines as above. Test measures higher-order reasoning skills as well as facts which require recall. The ability to infer, to reason, to predict and to conclude is measured through reading of maps and globes, political posters, pictographs, charts, as well as questions which call directly for the display of these inquiry skills.

Intermediate II Same as above; items suited to science curriculum for these grade levels.

Intermediate Level II Same as above. Items designed for appropriate grade level. Test reflects that the social sciences at this level encourage the child to apply concepts to different social situations.

Advanced Same as above.

Advanced Same as above with the addition of items concerned with interrelated maps, demographic data, political posters and organizational charts. Inference skills are measured through questions that call for display of problem solving skills.

INTERMEDIATE I

INTER II

ADVANCED

SOURCE: Reproduced by permission from the promotional brochure for the Stanford Achievement Test (1973 edition). Published by Harcourt Brace Jovanovich, Inc., New York, N.Y. All rights reserved.

There are eleven separately available research reports on the SAT. These describe development of the test and its standardization, provide equivalency tables for transforming SAT scores to scores on the 1970 Metropolitan Achievement Test, report middle-of-year norms for upper levels of the test, and so on.

A number of materials accompany the SAT. The authors have prepared a multimedia presentation, *Stanford Strategies*, to describe the administration, interpretation, and uses of the SAT. The presentation describes the rationale for achievement testing and the reasons for using the SAT, illustrates administration of the test in two classes, and describes interpretation of scores and uses of the test.

There are two special editions of the SAT: one for assessing the blind or partially sighted and one for assessing the deaf. The edition for use with blind or partially sighted students can be obtained in either braille or large print from the American Printing House for the Blind, while the edition for hearing-impaired students may be obtained from Gallaudet College. Both special editions were standardized on the respective handicapped populations.

Practice tests are available for use with the Primary-I through Intermediate-II levels of the test. They are administered two days before administration of the tests and insure that students understand how to take the tests.

Scores

A variety of transformed scores are obtained for the SAT: stanines, grade-equivalent scores, percentiles, age scores, and various standard scores. The tests may be scored by hand or submitted to the publisher for machine scoring. By submitting the protocols to the publisher's scoring service, it is possible to obtain record sheets for individual students, forms for reporting test results to parents, item analyses, class profiles, profiles comparing individual achievement with individual capability, analyses of each student's performance in attainment of specific objectives, local norms, and so forth.

Norms

In the preparation of this book, the authors reviewed numerous test manuals. In no other case did we find test standardization done so adequately and described so completely. The standardization of the SAT is a model of how tests ought to be standardized. The authors describe the steps in standardization of the test. We are reporting the standardization in detail because it does serve as a model.

The first step in standardization of the SAT was a decision to standardize the test during both May and October. The authors selected these months as appropriate times of the year for standardization because schools typically administer tests at the beginning and the end of the school year. For younger students (those for whom the Primary I and Primary II levels would be appropriate) standardization data were also collected in the middle of the year.

The second step in standardization was a decision by the authors to standardize the three forms simultaneously. Typically, alternate forms of a test are developed by standardizing one form and then developing equivalent forms. The equivalent forms are not standardized, but their adequacy is judged on the basis of their correlations with the one standardized form. By simultaneous standardization of the three forms, the authors provide actual norms specific to each form rather than merely providing derived norms.

The third step was a decision to administer the Otis-Lennon Mental Ability Test as a control measure. Selection of a standardization sample representative in terms of intellectual ability is a problem inherent in the development of an achievement test. If, for example, the average intellectual quotient of the normative sample was 108 (but erroneously assumed to be 100), students assessed later would be compared to a nonrepresentative group of students. By administering an intellectual measure concurrent with the standardization of the SAT, the authors evaluated empirically the assumption of average intellectual ability in the normative sample and were able to adjust scores earned so as to produce results consistent with this assumption.

The fourth step was a decision about the specifications of the normative sample. Selection was based on several variables, including geographic region, community size, median years of schooling for persons over 25 years old in the community, types of school systems (public, private, parochial), number of pupils per grade, and the extent of cooperation on the part of the schools.

The sampling procedure for standardization of the SAT involved development of thirty-eight cells of students broken down on the basis of four geographic regions, school-system size, and community socioeconomic status (based on the income and median years of schooling for individuals over 25 years old).

Before inviting schools to participate in standardization, the authors constructed three comparable samples (lists) of schools. If a school system originally invited to participate declined, it could be replaced in the sample by one with comparable characteristics. The authors mailed questionnaires to each school that agreed to participate, seeking demographic data such as average class size, average teachers' salaries, and the number of kindergarten pupils.

Following administration of the SAT and the Otis-Lennon Mental Ability

Test, the SAT data were adjusted to fit an IQ distribution with a mean of 100 and a standard deviation of 16.

Reliability

Reliability data for the SAT consist of split-half estimates and KR-20 coefficients. The authors used the KR-20 coefficients to compute standard errors of measurement for all subtests at all levels and on all forms of the SAT. Six pages of reliability data and standard errors of measurement are reported in part 5 of the manual. Reliabilities ranged from .65 to .97 with the majority between .85 and .95.

Validity

As for any achievement test, the validity of the SAT rests primarily on its content validity. Items for the SAT were originally written by the test authors and submitted to a group of subject-matter experts to establish the content accuracy. Several measurement experts edited the items for technical item-writing adequacy, and the items were then reviewed by general editors for writing clarity. The test items were submitted to a group of minority-group persons who screened the items in terms of the appropriateness of content for various cultural groups. Finally, a group of teachers were asked to evaluate the clarity of both the instructions and the items.

Empirical validity was established on the basis of two factors: an increasing difficulty of items with higher grade levels, and a moderate to high relationship with previous SATs and with the current and previous Metropolitan Achievement Tests. The authors state that three other factors were used to establish validity: (1) internal consistency, (2) correlation of obtained scores with scores expected on the basis of performance on the Otis-Lennon, and (3) "continuing reviews by representatives of minority and other groups." The first two are not necessarily validity data; the third we have previously discussed under content validity.

Summary

The Stanford Achievement Test is a model of what adequately developed achievement tests should be. Its development, standardization, and technical characteristics are exemplary. The description of item-by-item behavior samplings and the provision of specific instructional objectives make it one of the most useful tests available to the classroom teacher.

GATES-MACGINITIE READING TESTS

The Gates-MacGinitie Reading Tests (Gates & MacGinitie, 1972) are a series of norm-referenced screening tests assessing skill development in reading from kindergarten through twelfth grade. There are two or three forms of the test at each of eight educational levels.

The specific subtests of the Gates-MacGinitie Reading Tests and the behaviors they sample follow:

Vocabulary   This subtest assesses reading vocabulary. The actual demand of the task varies with grade level. The Vocabulary subtest at grades 1, 2, and 3, for example, presents the child with four printed words and a picture illustrating one of the words. The child must circle the word that best corresponds to the picture. From grade level 4 and through grade level 12, the student is presented with a stimulus word and five additional words. The student must identify the response word that has the same meaning as the stimulus word.

Comprehension   This subtest assesses ability to read and understand whole sentences and paragraphs. In grades 1 and 2 the child must read a selection and choose the picture that best describes its content. In grade 3, the child reads a paragraph and then selects, from among four response choices, the best answer to specific questions about the paragraph. In grades 4 through 12 the student is presented with paragraphs in which there are a number of blank spaces. The student must select from five response alternatives the word or phrase that best fits in the blank.

Speed and Accuracy   This subtest is available in a separate booklet, Form CS, for grades 2 and 3 and is included in all the forms of the test beyond grade 4. It assesses how rapidly a student can read with understanding. The subtest consists of a series of short paragraphs, each ending in questions or incomplete sentences with four response choices. The time limit for the test (five minutes) is short enough that not all students complete it.

Scores

The scores for Vocabulary and Comprehension are simply the number of items for which the student selects the correct answer. Two scores are obtained for the Speed and Accuracy subtest. The first score, a measure of speed, is the number of items answered, either correctly or incorrectly. The second score, a measure of accuracy, is the number of items answered correctly. All scores can be transformed to grade equivalents, percentile scores, or standard scores (T-scores with a mean of 50 and a standard deviation of 10). Machine-scored versions of the test provide average reading scores for each pupil, obtained by averaging scores earned on the Vocabulary and Comprehension subtests. The authors rightfully caution against the use of such scores, stating that in cases where a large difference exists between scores on the two subtests, considerable error is introduced by averaging them. Averaging obtained scores on Vocabulary and Comprehension is, in our opinion, inappropriate. The two subtests sample different behaviors; combining them simply ignores this fact.

Norms

The Gates-MacGinitie Reading Tests were standardized on a nationwide sample of 40,000 students in thirty-seven communities. Communities were selected by the test authors on the basis of size, geographic location, educational level, and family income. In each community, testing was carried out in schools "judged by the school officials" to be representative of the community. There are no data in the tests' technical manual reporting the actual composition of the normative group by race, socioeconomic status, geographic location, parental education, and so on.

Reliability

Reliability data are based on "separate reliability testing of four to six communities" (Gates & MacGinitie, 1972, p. 3). Reliability coefficients consist of alternate-form coefficients, and in all cases the test authors report *median* coefficients obtained. In other words, data were analyzed *by classes* and the median reliability at each grade level was reported. Hypothetically, then, if reliability data were available for five classes and the alternate-form reliabilities were .36, .46, .61, .72, and .98, the reliability would be reported as .61. Alternate-form and split-half reliabilities are reported in Table 9.7.

Alternate-form median reliabilities range from .67 to .89 while median split-half reliabilities range from .88 to .96.

Validity

Few specific data regarding validity are reported in the technical manual accompanying the tests. The test authors state that content validity for any achievement test depends on the extent to which the test assesses skills taught in any particular curriculum, and they encourage teachers to examine the test. The authors do report the results of an unpublished doctoral dissertation by Davis (1968) in which subtests of the Gates-MacGinitie were found to correlate in the .70 to .85 range with four other standardized reading tests.

Summary

The Gates-MacGinitie Reading Tests are a series of norm-referenced, group-administered tests that provide the classroom teacher with an assessment of skill development in reading. While there are some questions regarding the adequacy of the normative sample for the test, reliability does, in most cases, appear adequate for screening purposes, but not for

Table **9.7**   Reliability Coefficients for the Gates-MacGinitie Reading Tests

TEST	GRADE	SUBTEST	ALTERNATE-FORM RELIABILITY	SPLIT-HALF RELIABILITY
Primary A	1	Vocabulary	.86	.91
		Comprehension	.83	.94
Primary B	2	Vocabulary	.87	.93
		Comprehension	.81	.93
Primary C	3	Vocabulary	.85	.89
		Comprehension	.87	.91
Primary CS	3	Number attempted	.72	—
		Number correct	.86	—
Survey D	4	Vocabulary	.85	.88
		Comprehension	.83	.94
		SA number attempted	.67	—
		SA number correct	.80	—
	5	Vocabulary	.87	.92
		Comprehension	.89	.96
		SA number attempted	.75	—
		SA number correct	.76	—
	6	Vocabulary	.85	.89
		Comprehension	.87	.95
		SA number attempted	.72	—
		SA number correct	.78	—
Survey E	7	Vocabulary	.78	.88
		Comprehension	.81	.94
		SA number attempted	.69	—
		SA number correct	.70	—
	8	Vocabulary	.80	.89
		Comprehension	.81	.93
		SA number attempted	.72	—
		SA number correct	.76	—
	9	Vocabulary	.83	.88
		Comprehension	.80	.89
		SA number attempted	.68	—
		SA number correct	.77	—

NOTE: 1964–1965 reliability data.

making educational decisions about individual children. Data regarding validity are very limited.

K-12

PEABODY INDIVIDUAL ACHIEVEMENT TEST

The Peabody Individual Achievement Test (PIAT) (Dunn & Markwardt, 1970) is a norm-referenced, individually administered test designed to provide a wide-range screening measure of academic achievement in five content areas. The test can be used with students in kindergarten through twelfth grade. PIAT test materials are contained in two easel kits — one for each volume of the test. Easel-kit volumes present stimulus materials to the student at eye level; the examiner's instructions are placed on the reverse side (see Figure 9.2). The student can see one side of the response plate, while the examiner can see both sides.

Behaviors sampled by the five subtests of the PIAT follow.

Mathematics   This subtest contains eighty-four multiple-choice items ranging from items that assess such early skills as matching, discriminating, and recognizing numerals, to items that assess advanced concepts in geometry and trigonometry.

Reading Recognition   This subtest also contains eighty-four items ranging in difficulty from preschool level through high school level. Items assess skill development in matching letters, naming capital and lower-case letters, and recognizing words in isolation.

Reading Comprehension   This subtest contains sixty-six multiple-choice items assessing skill development in understanding what is read. After reading a sentence the student must indicate comprehension by choosing the correct picture out of a group of four.

Spelling   This subtest consists of eighty-four items sampling behaviors from kindergarten level through high school level. Initial items assess the student's ability to distinguish a printed letter of the alphabet from pictured objects and to associate letter symbols with speech sounds. Items 15 to 84 assess the student's ability to identify, from a response bank of four words, the correct spelling of a word read aloud by the examiner.

General Information   This subtest consists of eighty-four orally presented questions that the student must answer verbally. Items assess the extent to which the student has learned facts in social studies, science, sports, and the fine arts.

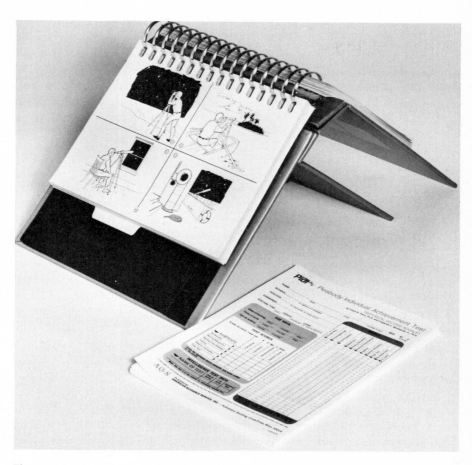

Figure **9.2** Easel kit for the Peabody Individual Achievement Test. (Test by L. M. Dunn and F. C. Markwardt. Photo courtesy American Guidance Service, Inc.)

Scores

Four kinds of scores are obtained for each subtest of the PIAT and for the test as a whole: age equivalents, grade equivalents, percentile ranks, and standard scores. The standard scores are based on a distribution with a mean of 100 and a standard deviation of 15.

Norms

The population from which the standardization sample was drawn consisted of students enrolled in the "mainstream of education," attending regular classes in public day schools. The standardization sample was selected on the basis of geographic region and community size. Twenty-nine school districts participated in the standardization. A total of 2,899 children, at least two hundred at each of thirteen grade levels, made up the normative sample. Approximately half the subjects were boys; 11.3 percent of the sample were Blacks; and the percentages of the subjects' parents in various occupations were comparable to the percentages in the general U.S. population, as reported in the 1967 census.

Reliability

Reliability evidence for the PIAT consists of test-retest reliability on fifty to seventy-five subjects at selected grade levels (specifically, kindergarten and grades 1, 3, 5, 8, and 12). Table 9.8 contains test-retest reliability coefficients for raw scores by selected grade levels. Median reliabilities for the subtests range from .64 for Reading Comprehension to .89 for Reading Recognition. The authors included no data regarding internal consistency in the test manual, because they believed attempts to evaluate internal consistency would have resulted in spuriously high coefficients.

Validity

Two kinds of validity information, content validity and concurrent validity, are reported in the manual. Content validity is largely a matter of expert opinion and is based on "extensive reviews of curriculum materials used at each grade level" (p. 50).

Concurrent validity was said to be established by correlating scores on the PIAT, an achievement test, with scores on the Peabody Picture Vocabulary Test, an intelligence test. Obviously, the data cannot be considered a full and completely relevant estimate of the test's validity.

The authors of the PIAT essentially argue that because the correlations between the PIAT and the PPVT are similar to those between the PPVT and other achievement tests, the PIAT measures achievement. The logic of this argument contains an illicit step (the PPVT is a correlate of achievement; the PPVT is a correlate of the PIAT; therefore, the PIAT is a correlate of achievement). While the conclusion *could* be correct, it cannot logically be derived from the premises. One other validity investigation (Sitlington, 1970) is reported in the manual. Sitlington compared scores earned by forty-five educable mentally retarded children on the PIAT and the Wide Range Achievement Test (WRAT) (Jastak & Jastak, 1965). Correlations were .58 between PIAT Mathematics and WRAT Arithmetic, .95 between PIAT Reading Recognition and WRAT Reading, and .85 between PIAT Spelling and WRAT Spelling.

Table **9.8** Test-Retest Reliability Coefficients for PIAT Raw Scores by Selected Grade Levels

GRADE	N	MATHE-MATICS	READING RECOG-NITION	READING COMPRE-HENSION[a]	SPELL-ING	GENERAL INFOR-MATION	TOTAL TEST	MEDIAN
K	75	.52	.81	—	.42	.74	.82	.74
1	60	.83	.89	.78	.55	.70	.89	.80
3	54	.68	.94	.73	.78	.77	.91	.77
5	51	.73	.89	.64	.53	.88	.89	.80
8	68	.76	.87	.61	.75	.83	.89	.80
12	60	.84	.86	.63	.75	.73	.92	.79
MEDIAN		.74	.89	.64	.65	.76	.89	.78

[a] Kindergarten-level subjects did not take Reading Comprehension subtest.

SOURCE: L. M. Dunn & F. C. Markwardt, *Manual for the Peabody Individual Achievement Test* (Circle Pines, Minn.: American Guidance Service, 1970), p. 44. Reprinted by permission of American Guidance Service, Inc.

Summary

The Peabody Individual Achievement Test is designed to provide screening information on development of skills in five academic areas. Its standardization seems superior to that of most other individually administered achievement tests. While the reliabilities of the PIAT subtests are too low for use in making important educational decisions, the reliabilities of some subtests are adequate for screening purposes. Validity of the PIAT rests on its content validity. Teachers need to assess its appropriateness for the curricula they use.

WIDE RANGE ACHIEVEMENT TEST

The Wide Range Achievement Test (WRAT) (Jastak & Jastak, 1965) is an individually administered, norm-referenced, paper-and-pencil test that assesses performance in reading, spelling, and arithmetic. There are two levels of the test: level 1 for students younger than 12, and level 2 for those over 12. Three subtests at each level assess reading, spelling, and arithmetic.

Reading This subtest assesses skills in recognizing capital letters, naming capital letters, and recognizing words in isolation.

Spelling This subtest assesses skills in copying marks on paper, writing one's name, and writing single words from dictation.

Arithmetic   This subtest assesses skills in counting, reading numerals, solving orally presented problems, and performing written computation of arithmetic problems.

The major criticism of the test is that it provides relatively few behavior samples of a student's skills in specific content areas. The level-I Arithmetic subtest, for example, has only three items, one oral and two written, that assess skill in adding single-digit numbers.

Scores

Three types of scores are obtained for each of the subtests of the WRAT: grade equivalents, percentile ranks within grades, and standard scores with a mean of 100 and a standard deviation of 15.

Norms

The authors of the WRAT state that no attempt was made to obtain a representative national sample of students for the standardization of the test. Each level of the test was standardized on at least 150 males and 150 females at each of nineteen age levels, producing a total standardization population of 5,868 persons for level I and 5,933 persons for level II. Norms were not stratified on the basis of race, ethnic-group membership, socioeconomic level, or geographic region. Schools in only seven states were included in the standardization sample. No handicapped children were included.

Reliability

The only reliability coefficients reported in the manual are split-half reliabilities for each of the subtests by grade level. All reliability coefficients exceed .90. The authors do not report test-retest reliabilities for the WRAT.

Validity

As discussed earlier, the most important kind of validity for an achievement test is content validity. If the test does not assess the content of the curriculum, then interpretations based on obtained results may be very misleading. Although the subtests of the WRAT sample only very limited aspects of reading, spelling, and arithmetic curricula, the authors never question its content validity. A teacher who adjusted a student's reading curriculum on the basis of scores obtained on the Reading subtest of the WRAT would be on shaky ground indeed. The subtest assesses only skill in decoding isolated words, with no consideration of the student's skill in deriving meaning from those words, reading phrases and sentences, or comprehending what is read. Similarly, the Spelling subtest assesses only skill in writing dictated words, while the Arithmetic subtest is simply a measure of the student's computational skills.

Several intended uses of the WRAT are listed in the test manual (for instance, "the accurate diagnosis of reading, spelling, and arithmetic disabilities in persons of all ages"), but few of these proposed uses are validated.

Summary

The Wide Range Achievement Test is one of two currently available individually administered devices used to assess academic achievement. The most serious criticisms of the WRAT are its limited and questionable normative population and its limited behavior sampling. The test manual states that the test may be used for many purposes, but few of these proposed uses are validated. Teachers of regular or special classes can use the WRAT to obtain a global picture of achievement, but they should make actual curricular decisions on the basis of tests that provide more extensive samples of behavior.

GETTING THE MOST MILEAGE OUT OF AN ACHIEVEMENT TEST

The achievement tests described in this chapter provide the teacher with global scores in areas such as word meaning and map-reading skills. While global scores can help us in screening children, they generally lack the specificity to help us in planning individualized instructional programs. Merely knowing that Emily earned a grade-equivalent score of 3.5 on the Mathematics Computation subtest of the Metropolitan Achievement Test does not tell us what math skills Emily has. In addition, a teacher cannot rely on test names as an indication of what is measured by a specific test.

A teacher must look at any screening test — and *any* test for that matter — in terms of the *behaviors* sampled by that test. Let's take a case in point. Suppose Richard earned a grade score of 3.2 on a spelling subtest. What do we know about Richard?

We know Richard earned the same raw score on the test as the average of children in the second month of third grade. That is *all* we know without going beyond the score and looking at the kinds of behaviors sampled by the test. The test title tells us only that the test measures skill development in spelling. But we still do not know *what* Richard did to earn a grade score of 3.2.

First, we need to ask, "What is the nature of the behaviors sampled by the test?" Spelling tests can be of several kinds. Richard may have been asked to write a word read by his teacher, as is the case in the spelling subtest of the Wide Range Achievement Test. Such a behavior sampling demands that he recall the correct spelling of a word and actually produce that correct spelling in writing. On the other hand, Richard's grade score of 3.2 may have been earned on a spelling test that asked him to recognize the correct spelling of a word. For example, the spelling subtest of the Peabody Individual Achievement Test presents the child with four alternative spellings of a word (like *empti, empty, impty, emity*), and the teacher asks a child to point to the word *empty*. Such an item demands recognition and pointing rather than recall and production. We need to look first at the nature of the behaviors sampled by the test.

Second, a teacher must look at these specific items a student passes or fails. This requires actually going back to the original test protocol to analyze the specific nature of skill development in a given area. We need to ask, "What kinds of items did the child fail?" and to look for consistent patterns among the failures. In trying to identify the nature of spelling errors, the teacher needs to ask such questions as, "Does the child consistently demonstrate errors in spelling words with long vowels? with silent *e*'s? with specific consonant blends?" and so on. The search is for specific patterns of errors, and the teacher tries to ascertain the relative degree of consistency in making certain errors.

Similar procedures are followed with any screening device. Quite obviously, the information achieved is not nearly as specific as the information we get from diagnostic tests. Administration of an achievement test that is a screening test gives the classroom teacher a general idea of where to start with any additional diagnostic assessment.

SUMMARY

This chapter has provided an intense look at screening devices used to assess academic achievement. Such devices provide a global picture of a student's skill development in academic content areas. The most commonly used screening tests have been discussed with an emphasis on the kinds of behavior each test samples, the adequacy of its norms, its reliability, and its validity. When selecting an achievement test or when evaluating the results of a student's performance on an achievement test, the classroom teacher needs to take into careful consideration not only the technical characteristics of the test but also the extent to which the behaviors sampled represent the goals and objectives of the student's curriculum. Our discussion also included suggestions for the teacher for administering group tests and for getting the most mileage out of the results of group tests.

STUDY QUESTIONS

1. Give at least three reasons for using the tests described in this chapter.

2. Differentiate between screening tests and diagnostic tests.

3. Why is it important that teachers select achievement tests that sample content comparable to the content taught in their own classrooms?

4. There are four important considerations in selecting achievement tests. Briefly describe them.

5. Identify similarities and differences in the domains of behavior sampled by the California Achievement Test, the Iowa Tests of Basic Skills, the Metropolitan Achievement Test, and the Stanford Achievement Test.

6. Mr. Wright decides to assess the achievement of his fifth-grade pupils. He believes his pupils are unusually "slow" and estimates that, in general, they are functioning on about a third-grade level. Mr. Wright decides to administer Primary Level III of the SAT. What difficulties will he face in doing so?

7. Ms. Spencer, a fourth-grade teacher in Mayberry, Kansas, wants to group students in her class for reading instruction. She administers the Reading Recognition subtest of the Wide Range Achievement Test and assigns students to groups on the basis of the grade scores they earn on the test. Which of the basic assumptions underlying psychoeducational assessment has Ms. Spencer violated?

ADDITIONAL READING

Buros, O. K. *Seventh mental measurements yearbook.* Highland Park, NJ: Gryphon Press, 1972. (Pp. 2–68, reviews of achievement batteries.)

Gronlund, N. E. *Preparing criterion-referenced tests for classroom instruction.* New York: Macmillan, 1973.

Gronlund, N. E. *Constructing achievement tests.* Englewood Cliffs, NJ: Prentice-Hall, 1968.

LaManna, J., & Ysseldyke, J. Reliability of the Peabody Individual Achievement Test with first grade children. *Psychology in the Schools,* 1973, *10*, 437–439.

Chapter 10

Diagnostic Testing in Reading

In Chapter 9 we discussed achievement tests used for screening purposes, to provide us with relatively global information about students' skill development. The primary use of diagnostic tests, on the other hand, is to obtain data that will help teachers pinpoint skill-development strengths and weaknesses and thereby plan appropriate educational programs for students. Diagnostic reading tests fulfill this purpose to a varying degree, depending largely on the technical adequacy of the testing devices and the relative skill and experience of the person using them.

This chapter includes a detailed description of the kinds of behaviors sampled by diagnostic reading tests and describes the most commonly used norm-referenced and criterion-referenced reading tests.

Reading is a complex behavior composed of numerous skills. No diagnostic reading test assesses all aspects of reading completely. Rather, the test samples specific reading or reading-related behaviors. The particular behaviors assessed by any one test are those that the test authors believed most important to assess. Whereas some of the more recent tests are criterion-referenced, most diagnostic reading tests are norm-referenced devices and are designed to compare a student's skill development to the skill development of his or her peers.

Diagnostic reading tests provide the classroom teacher with a systematic analysis of strengths and weaknesses in reading. It is extremely important, however, to look at an individual pupil's performance in light of the behaviors sampled by such tests. Grade scores, stanines, and percentiles earned on norm-referenced diagnostic reading tests are of little importance in program planning. Diagnostic testing is individual; our interest is to gain information about an individual's reading strengths and weaknesses, so there often is little need to conduct norm-referenced interpretations on diagnostic reading tests. For instance, knowing where Felicia stands in reference to her peers does not help her teacher plan a reading program for her. On the other hand, careful analysis of Felicia's performance on individual items of a norm-referenced device or on a criterion-referenced diagnostic reading test can help her teacher to plan the best instruction for Felicia.

One of the major limitations of diagnostic reading tests is their relative lack of reliability and the absence of empirical evidence for their validity.

Thus, it is imperative that the diagnostic assessment of reading skills consist of repeated measures of those skills. By repeated observations, which confirm initial impressions or call them into question, examiners can cut down on the amount of error involved and increase the reliability of their diagnostic decisions.

In a broad sense, several different categories of behaviors are sampled by diagnostic reading tests. Specific tests or subtests assess oral reading skills, comprehension skills, word-attack skills, and rate of reading. A variety of supplementary subtests are included in a number of diagnostic reading tests.

THE SKILLS ASSESSED BY DIAGNOSTIC READING TESTS

ASSESSMENT OF ORAL READING SKILLS

A number of tests or parts of tests are designed to assess the accuracy and fluency of a student's oral reading. Oral reading tests consist of series of paragraphs arranged sequentially from very easy paragraphs to relatively difficult ones. The student reads aloud while the examiner notes both the kinds of errors made and the behaviors that characterize the student's oral reading. Two commonly used tests, the Gray Oral Reading Test and the Gilmore Oral Reading Test, are designed specifically to assess skill development in oral reading, while two other commonly used tests, the Gates-McKillop Reading Diagnostic Tests and the Durrell Analysis of Reading Difficulty, include oral reading subtests.

Different oral reading tests record different behaviors as errors in oral reading. The kinds of errors recorded on the different tests and subtests are summarized in Table 10.1. A description follows of the behaviors demonstrated as each specific kind of error takes place.

Aid

If a student either hesitates for a time without making an audible effort to pronounce a word or appears to be attempting for 10 seconds to pronounce the word, the examiner pronounces the word and records an error. The error is recorded by an underlined bracket.

Gross Mispronunciation of a Word

"A gross mispronunciation is one in which the pupil's pronunciation of a word bears so little resemblance to the proper pronunciation that the examiner must be looking at the word to recognize it" (Gray & Robinson, 1967, p. 5). An example of a gross mispronunciation is one in which the

Table **10.1**   Kinds of Behaviors Recorded as Errors on Specific Oral Reading Tests or Subtests

	GRAY ORAL READING TEST	GILMORE ORAL READING TEST	GATES-MCKILLOP READING DIAGNOSTIC TEST	DURRELL ANALYSIS OF READING DIFFICULTY
Aid	X	X		X
Gross mispronunciation	X	X	X	X
Omission	X	X	X	X
Insertion	X	X	X	X
Substitution	X	X		
Repetition	X	X	X	X
Inversion	X		X	
Partial mispronunciation	X			
Disregard of punctuation		X		X
Hesitation		X		X

pupil reads the word *encounters* as "acors." The examiner records the error phonetically above the mispronounced word.

3. Omission of a Word or Group of Words

Omissions consist of skipping individual words or groups of words. The examiner simply circles the word or group of words omitted.

4. Insertion of a Word or Group of Words

Insertions consist of the student's putting one or more words into the sentence being read. The student may, for example, read *the dog* as "the mean dog." Insertions are recorded by placing a carat (^) in the sentence and writing in the word or words inserted.

5. Substitution of One Meaningful Word for Another

Substitutions consist of the actual replacement of one or more words in the passage by one or more meaningful words. The student might read *is* as "it" or *dense* as "depress." Children often replace entire sequences of words with others as illustrated in the reading of *he is his own mechanic* as "he sat on his own machine." The examiner records substitutions by underlining the word or words substituted and writing in the substitutions.

6. Repetition

Repetition consists of repeating words or groups of words while attempting to read sentences or paragraphs. In some cases if a student repeats a group of words to correct an error, the original error is struck but a repetition error is recorded. In other cases such behaviors are recorded simply as spontaneous corrections. Repetitions are recorded by underlining the repeated word or words with a wavy line. Errors due to stuttering are not recorded as repetition errors.

7. Inversion, or Changing of Word Order

Errors of inversion are recorded when the child changes the order of words appearing in a sentence. Inversions are indicated as follows: the house.

8. Partial Mispronunciation

A partial mispronunciation can be one of several different kinds of errors. The examiner may have to pronounce *part* of a word for a student (an aid); the student may phonetically mispronounce specific letters by reading words like *red* as "reed"; the student may omit part of a word, insert elements of words, make errors in syllabication, accent, or inversion. Such errors are recorded phonetically and scored as partial mispronunciations.

9. Disregard of Punctuation

The student may fail to observe punctuation — that is, may not pause for a comma, stop for a period, or indicate by vocal inflection a question mark or exclamation point. These errors of disregard of punctuation are recorded by circling the punctuation mark.

10. Hesitation

The student hesitates for two or more seconds before pronouncing a word. The error is recorded as a check (√) over the word. If the examiner then pronounces the word, it is recorded √p.

In addition to making a systematic analysis of oral reading errors, the examiner can note the behaviors that characterize a student's oral reading. Although, certainly, any characteristics may be observed, the indicators of difficulty more frequently looked for include head movement, finger pointing, loss of place, word-by-word reading, poor phrasing, lack of expression, reading in a monotonous tone, and reading in a strained voice.

B. ASSESSMENT OF COMPREHENSION SKILLS

Diagnostic reading tests assess three kinds of comprehension skills: literal comprehension, inferential comprehension, and listening comprehension. Assessment of *literal comprehension* is usually accomplished by asking a number of factual questions based directly on the content of a paragraph or story the student has read. The answers to such questions appear directly in the story or paragraph. Such comprehension tests require specific recall of material read and for that reason are sometimes characterized as memory tests — appropriately, unless, of course, the passage is available for the student to refer to when responding to the questions.

Inferential comprehension tests require interpretation and extension of what has been read. The student must demonstrate an ability to derive meaning from printed paragraphs or stories.

Assessment of *listening comprehension* is accomplished by reading a story or paragraph to a student and then asking questions based on recall or understanding of the material read. Listening comprehension tests can measure both literal and inferential comprehension.

In the process of assessing the development of comprehension skills, it is absolutely necessary for the teacher or diagnostic specialist to examine critically how those skills are assessed. The method by which comprehension skills are assessed may muddy the waters, in that pupil performance may depend more on other traits or skills than on comprehension of what is read. When literal comprehension is assessed by asking the student to read a passage and recall, without observing the passage, what has been read, performance may depend more on memory than on reading comprehension. Similarly, asking students to infer meaning on the basis of what they have read probably requires as much cognition as comprehension. In our opinion, the best way to assess comprehension is to ask students to state or paraphrase what they have read.

ASSESSMENT OF WORD-ATTACK SKILLS

Word-attack or word-analysis skills are those used "to derive the meaning and/or pronunciation of a word through phonics, structural analysis, or context clues" (Ekwall, 1970, p. 4). Children must decode words before they can gain meaning from the printed page. Since word-analysis difficulties are among the principal reasons why children have trouble reading, a variety of subtests of commonly used diagnostic reading tests specifically assess word-analysis skills.

Subtests assessing skill in word analysis range from such basic assessments as analysis of a student's skill in associating letters with sounds to tests of blending and syllabication. Subtests that assess skill in associating letters with sounds are generally of a format in which the examiner reads a word aloud and the child must identify the consonant, vowel, consonant cluster, or digraph that has the same sound as the beginning, middle, or ending letter in the words. Syllabication subtests present polysyllabic words, and the child must either divide the word into syllables or circle specific syllables. Blending subtests, on the other hand, are of three types. First, the examiner may read syllables out loud ("wa - ter - mel - on," for

Figure **10.1** An item that assesses blending skill

example) and ask the child to pronounce the word. Second, the child may be asked to read word parts and pronounce whole words. Third, the child may be presented with alternative beginning, middle, and ending sounds and asked to produce a word. Figure 10.1 illustrates the third method as employed on the Stanford Diagnostic Reading Test.

D. ASSESSMENT OF WORD-RECOGNITION SKILLS

Subtests of diagnostic reading tests that assess a pupil's word-recognition skills are designed to ascertain what many call *sight vocabulary*. A person learns the correct pronunciation of letters and words through a variety of experiences. The more exposure a person has to specific words and the more familiar those words become, the more readily the person recognizes those words and pronounces them. Well-known words require very little reliance on word-attack skills. Most readers of this book immediately recognize the word *hemorrhage* and do not have to employ phonetic skills to pronounce it. On the other hand, words like *nephrocystanastomosis* are not a part of the sight vocabulary of most of us. The word slows us down, and we have to use phonetics to analyze it.

Word-recognition subtests form a major part of most diagnostic reading tests. Some tests use paper tachistoscopes to expose words for brief periods of time (usually one-half second). Students who recognize many words are said to have good sight vocabularies or good word-recognition skills. Other subtests assess letter recognition, recognition of words in isolation, and recognition of words in context.

E. ASSESSMENT OF RATE OF READING

Reading rate is generally played down in the diagnostic assessment of reading difficulties. There are, however, some exceptions. Level II of the Stanford Diagnostic Reading Test has a specific subtest to assess rate of reading. On the other hand, tests such as the Gray Oral Reading Test are timed, with time affecting the score a pupil receives. A pupil who reads a passage on the Gray Oral slowly but makes no errors in reading can earn a lower score than a rapid reader who makes one or two errors in reading.

F. ASSESSMENT OF OTHER READING AND
READING-RELATED BEHAVIORS

A variety of subtests that fit none of the above categories are included in diagnostic reading tests as either major or supplementary subtests. Examples of such tests include oral vocabulary, spelling, handwriting, and auditory discrimination. In most cases such subtests are included simply to provide the examiner with additional diagnostic information.

ORAL READING TESTS

GRAY ORAL READING TEST

The Gray Oral Reading Test (Gray & Robinson, 1967) is designed to provide an objective measure of skill development in oral reading from early first grade through college. The test was specifically designed to facilitate the diagnosis of oral reading difficulties. The Gray Oral Reading Test (Gray) is available in forms A, B, C, and D. All forms are similar in organization, length, and difficulty level; this enables periodic retesting with comparable but nonidentical forms of the test.

The Gray consists of a series of graded reading passages in a spiral-bound booklet. The student reads the passages aloud while the examiner records errors and notes reading characteristics on a separate student record booklet. Following the reading of each passage, the materials are removed and the examiner asks a series of questions designed to assess the student's literal comprehension of material contained in the passage.

The Gray Oral Reading Tests provide the teacher, reading specialist, or psychologist with an assessment of both the speed and accuracy of oral reading. The examiner records the length of time it takes a student to read each individual passage. Starting points differ for individual students. The test manual provides general guidelines, based on a student's grade level, about the point where the test should be started. Each form contains thirteen reading passages of increasing difficulty. Students begin with an easy passage that they can read without error and read to the point where they make seven or more errors in two consecutive passages. For each reading passage the examiner records the number and kinds of errors in oral reading, along with the time it took a student to read the passage.

Actual administration of the device is simple, but recording and scoring are so difficult that a tape recorder should be used regularly. Considerable training and practice must precede the use of this device in the making of diagnostic decisions, and those decisions must take note of the fact that speed affects the scores earned. Errors recorded for the Gray include aids, partial mispronunciations, gross mispronunciations, omissions, insertions,

All of us admire the great skill of a good truck driver. He hauls many tons of things almost daily, including dangerous explosives. On mountain roads and in other isolated places he faces real dangers alone. He is his own mechanic. Sturdy and dependable, he will interrupt his schedule to help anyone who encounters real difficulty on a highway.

Figure **10.2** An illustration of errors on the Gray Oral Reading Test. (Redrawn from the booklet of reading passages for W. S. Gray and H. M. Robinson's *Gray Oral Reading Test*. Copyright 1967 by the Bobbs-Merrill Company, Inc. Used by permission.)

inversions, substitutions, and repetitions. The test has a convenient list of reading characteristics enabling examiners to check those they observe.

Figure 10.2 is an illustration of the kinds of errors made by Marjorie in the oral reading of a passage from the Gray. Marjorie made fifteen errors in reading the passage. The examiner had to pronounce four words (*admire*, *explosives*, *sturdy*, and *encounter*) for her. One gross mispronunciation ("dipiple" for *dependable*) and one omission (*a*) occurred. Marjorie inserted one word (*good*) and made three substitution errors ("his" for *he*, "machine" for *mechanic,* and "study" for *schedule).* On two occasions she repeated what she had read, as evidenced by the underlining of groups of words with wavy lines. Marjorie made three partial mispronunciation errors, one a phonetic mispronunciation (*isolated*) and two items consisting of partial insertions ("drivers" for *driver* and "another" for *other*).

Figure 10.2 illustrates Marjorie's reading of only one passage. From an analysis of errors made in all passages read, the examiner can get a picture of the kinds of difficulties Marjorie has in oral reading. Both the rate of reading and the number of errors affect the score a child earns. The characteristics observed do not enter into scoring of the test as such, but they provide additional qualitative information to assist in planning developmental, corrective, or remedial strategies.

Scores

Two kinds of information are obtained from the Gray. The student earns a grade score that reflects in a global sense the speed and accuracy of oral reading. The most useful information, however, is the error analysis resulting from the administration of the Gray. Given a pattern of the kinds of errors individuals most frequently make, the teacher can at least begin to attempt differentiated instruction.

Norms

The Gray norms are described as "tentative" because they are based on the testing of only 502 children (256 boys and 246 girls), 40 at each grade, from schools in Florida and in Chicago and its suburbs. The test provides separate normative tables for boys and girls. The only information provided about the nature of the standardization population is information on sex, geographic location, and types of students excluded from the sample; students with speech problems, serious health problems, emotional problems, or students who had been held back or double promoted were excluded from the normative population. They do not identify the reading curriculum in which the students were enrolled.

It is important to note that since separate norms are provided for boys and girls and since normative data are based on forty children per grade, the population against whom we compare the performance of a specific boy or girl is twenty children at his or her grade level. While this normative sample is limited, the user of the Gray should remember that the test's real benefit is in systematic analysis of oral reading errors rather than in obtaining a grade score.

Reliability

Reliability data for the Gray consist of intercorrelations among grade scores on each of the four forms. Alternate-form reliability coefficients range from .97 to .98 for girls, and from .96 to .98 for boys. The standard error of measurement for the test is four raw-score points for the total score. No rest-retest reliability data are reported.

Validity

The test authors devote two sentences in the manual to the issue of the validity of the test. They state that the tests are valid primarily because of the procedures used in constructing them and because of the test's discrimination between students at different grade levels. Test construction was a matter of expert opinion based on data from a 1915 version of the test and a search of contemporary basal readers.

Summary

The Gray Oral Reading Test consists of series of passages the student reads aloud to the examiner. The examiner records both the kinds of errors the student makes and the student's oral reading characteristics. The test provides grade scores that indicate in a global sense the level at which a student is reading. The most useful information to a teacher, however, is the systematic analysis of oral reading errors.

Norms for the Gray are at this time both "tentative" and limited. The authors do not state whether more permanent norms will ever be provided. Original standardization occurred during 1959–1960. If more complete norms were to be provided, one would expect them to have appeared by now.

Reliability data presented in the manual are limited. Validity is based on expert opinion. The Gray will provide the teacher with estimates of the student's speed and accuracy in oral reading and will enable tentative hypotheses to be made about the nature of oral reading difficulties.

GILMORE ORAL READING TEST

The Gilmore Oral Reading Test (Gilmore & Gilmore, 1968) is an individually administered test designed to assess skill development in oral reading from grades 1 through 8. The test consists of two forms, C and D, that assess the accuracy of oral reading, reading comprehension, and rate of reading. Each form of the test contains ten paragraphs of increasing difficulty. These ten paragraphs form a continuous story. Administration of the test generally takes 15 to 20 minutes.

The Gilmore is very much like the Gray Oral Reading Test with one major exception. A score earned on the Gray is a function of both the number of errors in oral reading and the rate of reading. The grade scores on the Gilmore are a function only of the errors made. Although the test is timed, rate is not used in arriving at the grade score.

The Gilmore provides a systematic analysis of the kinds of errors the child makes in oral reading. The kinds of errors recorded for the Gilmore include (1) substitutions, (2) mispronunciations, (3) words pronounced by the examiner (aids), (4) disregard of punctuation, (5) insertions, (6) hesitations, (7) repetitions, and (8) omissions. Substitution errors, aids, insertions, repetitions, and omissions are errors we discussed earlier and are scored identically to the errors of the same name on the Gray Oral Reading Test. Errors counted as gross mispronunciations and partial mispronunciations in the Gray are grouped into the category of "mispronunciations" on the Gilmore.

Errors scored as disregard of punctuation on the Gilmore consist of failures to observe punctuation, while a hesitation error is scored each time the child hesitates for at least two seconds before pronouncing a word. Whereas repetitions of words or phrases to correct other kinds of errors were counted as repetition errors in the Gray Oral, they do not count as repetition errors in the Gilmore. According to the Gilmore manual, a child

Table **10.2** Performance Ratings for Accuracy and Comprehension on the
Gilmore Oral Reading Test

RATING	STANINE	PERCENTILE BAND	PERCENTAGE OF PUPILS
Superior	9	Above 95	4
Above average	7, 8	77–95	19
Average	4, 5, 6	23–76	54
Below average	2, 3	4–22	19
Poor	1	Below 4	4

who immediately corrects an error does not erase the error. The error is still counted.

There are quite obvious differences in the kinds of errors scored on the Gray and the Gilmore. It is imperative, therefore, that in using and interpreting the two tests the teacher look beyond the grade scores earned to note the kinds of errors the child has made.

Scores

Two kinds of scores, grade scores and performance ratings, are provided by the Gilmore. The child earns both grade scores and performance ratings (poor, below average, average, above average, and superior) for accuracy and comprehension. Performance ratings for accuracy and comprehension are based on stanines as shown in Table 10.2. Rate of reading is scored as slow, average, or fast. Within each grade, those whose rate of reading is within the top quartile are designated as fast readers, those in the bottom quartile as slow readers, and those in the two middle quartiles as average.

As in the Gray Oral Reading Test, grade scores — and in this case performance ratings, too — are global scores. The information of most use in designing programs of instruction is provided by the systematic analysis of errors in oral reading.

Norms

Standardization of the Gilmore was completed in 1967 in eighteen schools in six school systems selected to include children from a variety of socioeconomic backgrounds. The total normative sample included 4,455 children in grades 1 through 8. Form C was administered to 2,246 children, while form D was given to 2,209 children. There are no data in the test manual on the sex, ethnic background, or reading curriculum of the children in the normative sample.

Table **10.3** Alternate-Form Reliability Data for the Gilmore Oral Reading Test

GRADE	N	ACCURACY	COMPREHENSION	RATE
3	51	.94	.60	.70
6	55	.84	.53	.54

Reliability

The only reliability data reported in the test manual are alternate-form reliabilities for fifty-one children in grade 3 and fifty-five children in grade 6. Reliabilities are reported in Table 10.3. There are no data on test-retest reliability for the Gilmore Oral Reading Test.

Validity

No validity was established for the current Gilmore. There are validity data in the manual, but these data are for an earlier edition (Form A) of the test.

Summary

The Gilmore Oral Reading Test is an individually administered test designed to assess oral reading skills, reading comprehension, and rate of reading. The child earns grade scores for accuracy and comprehension as well as performance ratings on all three scales.

The test was standardized on 4,455 children, who are inadequately described in the manual. Reliability data consist of alternate-form coefficients, all but one of which are considerably lower than the .90 standard. There are no data reported in the manual regarding the validity of forms C and D. The Gilmore Oral Reading Test may provide the experienced examiner with diagnostic information with which to construct instructional hypotheses. Its technical characteristics are such that one must use it with caution.

DIAGNOSTIC READING TESTS

GATES-MCKILLOP READING DIAGNOSTIC TESTS   grades 2-6

The Gates-McKillop Reading Diagnostic Tests (Gates & McKillop, 1962) consist of a battery of seventeen individually administered subtests and parts of subtests designed to assess skill development in reading. The tests are designed for use with children in grades 2 through 6. The two forms of the test, form I and form II, are reported to be of equivalent difficulty and to contain comparable material. Only certain subtests are administered to each test taker. Those chosen depend on the child's age and level of skill development.

The manual for the Gates-McKillop states no qualifications as necessary for administering the test other than familiarity with the test and the contents of the manual. Most subtests are easy enough for a classroom teacher with little testing experience to administer. Scoring and interpretation, are, however, complex and difficult for even the most experienced examiner. In general, administration time ranges from 30 to 60 minutes.

Behaviors sampled by the test follow.

Oral Reading   The Oral Reading subtest of the Gates-McKillop is similar to the Gray and the Gilmore oral reading tests. The errors recorded for this subtest include omissions, additions, repetitions, reversals, and mispronunciations. Mispronunciations are scored in terms of the kind of error made, including words with wrong beginnings, wrong middles, or wrong endings, and words wrong in several parts.

Words: Flash Presentation   This subtest purports to assess sight vocabulary. A cardboard tachistoscope is provided for the examiner to use to expose single words for one-half second. The child reads the words aloud.

Words: Untimed Presentation   This subtest purports to assess word-attack skills. The child is required to read words without time restriction.

Phrases: Flash Presentation   This subtest purports to assess sight vocabulary. It is similar to the Words: Flash Presentation subtest. The child is required to read phrases exposed by a cardboard tachistoscope for one-half second.

Knowledge of Words Parts: Word Attack   This subtest has four parts, all assessing skill development in word attack.

1. *Recognizing and Blending Common Word Parts*. This part of the subtest is complex, both in administration and scoring. The examiner asks the child to read nonsense words like *drack* and *glebe*. When the child reads a nonsense word incorrectly, the word is presented in two parts ("dr - ack") and the child is requested to blend the parts.

2. *Giving Letter Sounds*. The child is shown letters and asked to give their sounds.

3. *Naming Capital Letters*. The child is shown capital letters and asked to name them.

4. *Naming Lower-Case Letters.* The child is shown lower-case letters and asked to name them.

Recognizing the Visual Form or Word Equivalents of Sounds This subtest has four parts.

1. *Nonsense Words.* The examiner reads a nonsense word, and the child identifies which of four printed words matches it.

2. *Initial Letters.* The examiner reads a word; the child listens to the beginning sound and then identifies which of four letters has the same sound as the beginning sound of the word read.

3. *Final Letters.* The examiner reads a word; the child listens to the ending sound and then identifies which of four letters has the same sound as the ending sound of the word read.

4. *Vowels.* The child is shown the five vowels (*a, e, i, o,* and *u*). The examiner reads a nonsense word, and the child identifies the vowel corresponding to the middle sound of the word read.

Auditory Blending The examiner pronounces words part by part: "z - ip." The child must blend the parts to pronounce the word.

Spelling The child writes words read aloud by the examiner.

Oral Vocabulary This subtest assesses ability to define words.

Syllabication This subtest assesses ability to divide words into syllables.

Auditory Discrimination This subtest assesses ability to discriminate among common English phonemes.

Scores and Norms

A number of normative tables appear in the Gates-McKillop manual, but there is no information about the population or populations on which the norms are based. Two kinds of conversion tables are provided, grade-score tables and interpretation tables. Grade-score tables enable the examiner to convert raw scores to grade scores, which in turn are rated high, medium, low, or very low, in relation to the child's actual grade placement. Interpretation tables are used to compare performance on the Oral Reading subtest with each of the subtests assessing specific skills. Specific skills are rated as indicative of either normal, low, or very low development. Ratings for grade scores are based on the authors' opinion, and the authors specifically state that such ratings must be interpreted with caution.

Ratings for other subtests are such that a rating of "normal progress" means a child's score was in the middle 50 percent of scores earned by children at that child's oral reading level.

We commented earlier on the relative educational meaninglessness of scores that compare children to one another; transformed scores earned on the Gates-McKillop have little meaning. Normative comparisons provide very limited help in the teacher's attempts to differentiate instruction. The value of the Gates-McKillop is in its clinical use; it can provide the skilled examiner with relatively specific data regarding reading strengths and weaknesses, provided the examiner goes beyond scores to look at performance on particular kinds of items.

Reliability

The provision of systematic data regarding learner strengths and weaknesses is helpful only if we can measure those strengths and weaknesses consistently. A major weakness of the Gates-McKillop is the absence of data regarding its reliability. There are no data in the manual regarding the reliability of this test.

Validity

No data are reported in the test manual regarding the test's validity, so the examiner and consumer must judge its validity for their own purposes.

Summary

The Gates-McKillop Reading Diagnostic Tests are a widely used diagnostic instrument in spite of significant limitations. The manual provides numerous, relatively difficult-to-use normative tables without including information about the population on whom the test was normed. The many scores obtained on the Gates-McKillop are subject to serious misinterpretation. Data regarding reliability and validity are simply absent.

The test battery requires very little experience to administer correctly but considerable sophistication to interpret. The Gates-McKillop can be a useful diagnostic device only if its limitations are kept in mind.

DURRELL ANALYSIS OF READING DIFFICULTY   PP - 6th grade

The Durrell Analysis of Reading Difficulty (Durrell, 1955) is designed "to discover weaknesses and faulty habits in reading which may be corrected through a remedial program" (p. 3). The test covers a wide range of reading ability from the nonreader or preprimer level to the sixth-grade level.

The Durrell is administered individually, and the test manual states that although anyone with training in understanding reading problems can give the test, it is preferable that an experienced reading teacher do the administering. Materials include a booklet of reading paragraphs to be used in the major subtests, a manual of directions for the examiner, a twelve-page individual record booklet, and a cardboard tachistoscope with accompanying test cards and word lists. Test administration takes 30 to 90 minutes.

The Durrell samples several different reading and reading-related behaviors. The major subtests follow.

Oral Reading   This subtest consists of eight paragraphs of increasing difficulty that the child is required to read aloud. The subtest is scored similarly to the Gray, Gilmore, and the Oral Reading subtest of the Gates-McKillop. The child responds to literal comprehension questions following the reading of each paragraph.

Silent Reading   The Silent Reading subtest contains eight paragraphs of comparable difficulty to those in the Oral Reading subtest. The examiner tests and records voluntary memory (simple recall), prompted memory (responses to specific questions), and eye movement.

Listening Comprehension   The examiner reads the seven paragraphs of this subtest aloud and asks specific comprehension questions. The most difficult paragraph in which the child misses no more than one comprehension question is identified, by grade and score, as the child's listening comprehension level.

Word Recognition and Word Analysis   This subtest contains several parts. The examiner uses a cardboard tachistoscope, exposing words for one-half second, to assess word recognition skills. When the child reads a word unsuccessfully, the same word is presented in an untimed format. The child is then asked to name the letters seen and is given an opportunity to sound out the word.

The Durrell Analysis of Reading Difficulty includes a number of supplementary subtests designed either to assess very-low-level reading skills or to provide the examiner with additional diagnostic information on the following reading-related behaviors.

Naming letters

Identifying letters named

Matching letters

Visual memory for words

Hearing sounds in words

Learning to hear sounds in words

Sounds of letters

Learning rate

Phonic spelling of words

Spelling

Handwriting

Scores

Most subtests of the Durrell Analysis of Reading Difficulty provide raw scores that can be converted to grade scores. However, the greatest emphasis in the interpretation and use of the test results is placed on the Checklist of Reading Difficulties that follows most of the subtests. The checklists are comprehensive and are completed by the examiner after the administration of each subtest.

After scoring the Durrell, the examiner constructs a profile of the child's scores. A representative profile is illustrated in Figure 10.3.

Norms

In a seven-line statement at the end of the manual, the author states that "wherever norm tables are presented the norms are based on no fewer than a thousand children for each test. In the extensive use of these tests, the norms have been found to check satisfactorily against other measures of reading ability" (p. 32). The only other reference to norms is the author's statement that the 1937 edition of the test was administered to hundreds of thousands of children by several thousand examiners and that their suggestions have resulted in "change and improvement."

In short, there simply are no reported data on the nature of the population on whom the Durrell Analysis of Reading Difficulty was standardized. On the other hand, this fact must be tempered by the consideration that the really useful information obtained from the Durrell Analysis consists of a systematic analysis of reading difficulties.

Reliability and Validity

There is no evidence of either reliability or validity in the Durrell manual. One searches in vain for the use of *reliable* or *valid* even as generic adjectives.

Summary

The Durrell Analysis of Reading Difficulty is designed to assist classroom teachers in the delineation of specific skill-development strengths and

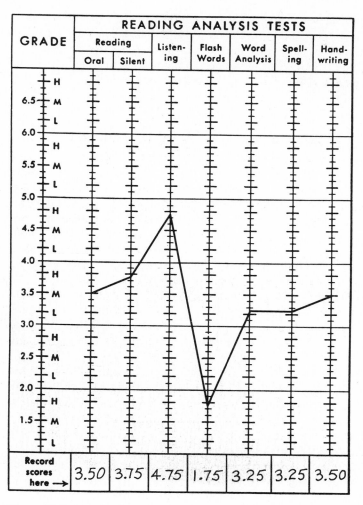

GRADE	READING ANALYSIS TESTS						
	Reading		Listen-ing	Flash Words	Word Analysis	Spell-ing	Hand-writing
	Oral	Silent					
Record scores here →	3.50	3.75	4.75	1.75	3.25	3.25	3.50

Figure **10.3**   Profile of scores earned on the Durrell Analysis of Reading Difficulty. (Reproduced from the Durrell Analysis of Reading Difficulty, copyright © 1937, 1955, by Harcourt Brace Jovanovich, Inc. Reproduced by special permission from the publisher.)

weaknesses in reading. As long as the examiner and user of the test data place little emphasis on scores obtained and look instead at the qualitative information afforded by the test, the results may be useful in reaching tentative hypotheses regarding the nature of a child's reading difficulties. The fact that no data appear in the manual about either the normative population, reliability, or validity renders the norms useless.

STANFORD DIAGNOSTIC READING TEST

The Stanford Diagnostic Reading Test (SDRT) (Karlsen, Madden, & Gardner, 1976) consists of a series of measures of specific reading skills. There are four overlapping levels of the test, with two parallel forms (A and B) at each level. Levels of the test are identified by color. The Red level is designed to be used at the end of grade 1, in grade 2, and with low-achieving pupils in grade 3 and succeeding grades, while the Green level is intended for use in grades 3 and 4 and with low-achieving pupils in grade 5 and succeeding grades. Children in grades 5 through 8 and low achievers in higher grades are assessed using the Brown level. The Blue level, also known as the SDRT III, was published before the other three (Karlsen, Madden, & Gardner, 1974) and is intended for use in grades 9 through 12. Whereas the diagnostic reading tests described thus far must be individually administered, the SDRT can be group administered by classroom teachers.

Four skill domains are sampled by the SDRT, though not all domains are sampled at all levels. Subtests and skill domains sampled are reported in Figure 10.4. Behaviors sampled by the subtests of the SDRT are as follows.

Auditory Vocabulary   This subtest assesses skill in identifying synonyms of words read by the examiner. Initial items in the Red level require the child simply to associate words with pictures. The subtest is included at the Red, Green, and Brown levels of the SDRT.

Auditory Discrimination   This subtest assesses skill in hearing similar and different sounds in words. At the Red level, the pupil must identify whether two words begin with or end with the same sound. The Green level assesses identification of similar and different beginning, middle, and ending sounds. The subtest is not included at the Brown and Blue levels.

Phonetic Analysis   The Phonetic Analysis subtest assesses skill in identifying letter-sound relationships. Easier items assess skill in identifying letters that represent the beginning or ending sounds in words. More difficult items assess similar behaviors using both common and variant spellings of sounds. The subtest is included at all four levels.

Subtests and skill domains of the Stanford Diagnostic Reading Test.

(handwritten annotations:) domains — g.1–2 — 3–4 — Decoding — 5–8 & low achievers — 9.–12 grade

Decoding

RED LEVEL	GREEN LEVEL	BROWN LEVEL	BLUE LEVEL (SDRT III)
TEST 2: Auditory Discrimination Consonant Sounds (24 items) Vowel Sounds (16 items)	TEST 2: Auditory Discrimination Consonant Sounds (18 items) Vowel Sounds (18 items)		
TEST 3: Phonetic Analysis Consonant Sounds (24 items) Vowel Sounds (16 items)	TEST 3: Phonetic Analysis Consonant Sounds (18 items) Vowel Sounds (18 items)	TEST 3: Phonetic Analysis Consonant Sounds (18 items) Vowel Sounds (18 items)	TEST 3: Phonetic Analysis Consonant Sounds (15 items) Vowel Sounds (15 items)
	TEST 4: Structural Analysis Word Division (30 items) Blending (30 items)	TEST 4: Structural Analysis Word Division (48 items) Blending (30 items)	TEST 5: Structural Analysis Blending (24 items)

Vocabulary

RED LEVEL	GREEN LEVEL	BROWN LEVEL	BLUE LEVEL (SDRT III)
TEST 1: Auditory Vocabulary (36 items)	TEST 1: Auditory Vocabulary (40 items)	TEST 1: Auditory Vocabulary (40 items)	
			TEST 2: Word Meaning (30 items)
			TEST 3: Word Parts (30 items)

Comprehension

RED LEVEL	GREEN LEVEL	BROWN LEVEL	BLUE LEVEL (SDRT III)
TEST 4: Word Reading (42 items)			
TEST 5: Reading Comprehension Sentence Reading (32 items) Paragraph Comprehension (16 items)	TEST 5: Reading Comprehension Literal Comprehension (30 items) Inferential Comprehension (30 items)	TEST 2: Reading Comprehension Literal Comprehension (30 items) Inferential Comprehension (30 items)	TEST 1: Reading Comprehension Literal Comprehension (30 items) Inferential Comprehension (30 items)

Rate

RED LEVEL	GREEN LEVEL	BROWN LEVEL	BLUE LEVEL (SDRT III)
		TEST 5: Reading Rate (34 items)	TEST 7: Fast Reading (30 items) TEST 6: Scanning and Skimming (32 items)

Figure 10.4 Subtests and skill domains of the Stanford Diagnostic Reading Test. (Reproduced from the Stanford Diagnostic Reading Test, copyright © 1973, 1976, by Harcourt Brace Jovanovich, Inc. Reproduced by special permission from the publisher.)

Structural Analysis   The Structural Analysis subtest is included only in the Green, Brown, and Blue levels. Behaviors sampled include the use of syllables, prefixes, root words, and blends. This subtest replaces the Syllabication and Blending subtests of the previous edition of the SDRT.

Word Reading   The Red level of the SDRT includes a Word Reading subtest, which measures skill in word recognition. The child must identify which of several response words most closely represents a picture.

Reading Comprehension   Behaviors sampled by this subtest vary at the different levels. At the Red level, the children must read sentences and identify the pictures that best represent what they have read; they must also complete sentences and paragraphs that use a modified cloze format.[1] At the Green level, two formats are used to assess comprehension: the modified cloze format and a paragraph-comprehension format requiring literal comprehension of what has been read. The Brown and Blue levels assess both literal and inferential comprehension using a paragraph-reading format.

Rate   The subtest on rate of reading is included only at the Brown and Blue levels. It assesses skill in reading easy material quickly.

Scores

The SDRT is both norm-referenced and criterion-referenced. It can be used to assess a pupil's performance relative to the performance of others, and it can be used to pinpoint individual pupils' strengths and weaknesses in specific reading skills.

Students respond either directly in the test booklets or on machine-readable answer sheets. The test can, therefore, be either hand scored or machine scored. Six kinds of scores can be obtained; which scores are useful depends on the purpose for which the test has been administered.

Raw scores are obtained for each subtest and can be transformed to "Progress Indicators," percentile ranks, stanines, grade equivalents, and scaled scores. Progress Indicators are criterion-referenced scores, while

---

1. The "cloze" procedure is a technique in which words are omitted from a sentence. To close the sentence correctly, the student must comprehend the story. Many programmed texts, for example, use a cloze format. The modified cloze format used in the SDRT gives the student a choice of several words. The following is an illustration:

Elephants are well known as animals that never forget. But Henry was a strange elephant who, unlike other elephants, always _____ things.
(a) wanted   (b) forgot   (c) remembered   (d) liked

the other four scores are norm-referenced. Progress Indicators are "+" or "−" indications as to whether a pupil achieved a predetermined cutoff score in a specific skill domain; they show whether a pupil demonstrates mastery of specific skills important to the various stages in the process of learning to read effectively. It is reported that

in setting the Progress Indicator cutoff scores, the SDRT authors were guided by the relative importance of the skills to the reading process, by the location of these skills in the developmental sequence of the reading process, and by the performance of pupils at different achievement levels on the items measuring these skills. (Karlsen, Madden, & Gardner, 1976, p. 33)

The manual for each level of the SDRT includes an appendix that lists specific instructional objectives assessed by each level of the test.

The norm-referenced scores obtained by administering the SDRT can be used for a variety of purposes. The authors suggest that comparisons to national norms be made using percentile ranks, stanines, or grade equivalents. Detailed procedures for the use of stanines to group students for instructional purposes are included in the manuals. Scaled scores, because they are comparable across both grades and levels, are most useful in evaluating pupil growth and in interpreting the performance of pupils who are tested out of level (for example, the scores of a fifth grader who has taken the Red level).

Norms

In selecting the standardization sample for the SDRT, the authors used a stratified random-sampling technique. Socioeconomic status, school-system enrollment, and geographic region were the stratification variables. School-system data were obtained from the United States Office of Education's 1970 census tapes. The tapes were used to generate a random sample of 3,000 school districts. A composite socioeconomic-status index for each system was determined by weighting family income twice and averaging it with the median years of parental schooling. Age and sex were not controlled in standardizing the SDRT.

Within each of the stratified cells, school districts were invited to participate in standardization of the test. A random sample of consenting districts within each cell was selected. The test was standardized in 55 school districts; approximately 31,000 pupils participated in the standardization. The manual includes detailed tables illustrating that the demographic characteristics of the school districts sampled closely parallel those indicated in the 1970 census.

Reliability

Two types of reliability information are available for the SDRT: reliability of raw scores and reliability of Progress Indicators. Reliability of raw scores earned on the test was ascertained by assessing both internal-consistency and alternate-form reliability. Internal-consistency coefficients for all sub-tests at all levels exceed .90 with the exception of coefficients for Auditory Vocabulary (these consistently range from .85 to .90). Alternate-form reliability coefficients range from .75 to .94. Standard errors of measurement in both raw-score and scaled-score units are tabled in the manuals.

The reliability of the Progress Indicators was determined by administering both forms to the same pupils and establishing each pupil's Progress Indicator on each form. Contingency tables provided in the manual enable the user to estimate the probability that a student would obtain a different Progress Indicator if she or he took the alternate form of the test. Data reported in the manuals indicate that the SDRT is a reliable measure of specific reading skills.

Validity

Limited space in the SDRT manuals is devoted to the issues of content validity and criterion-related validity. The authors state that the test's content validity, like the content validity of any other measure of academic achievement, must be based on an evaluation of the extent to which test content reflects local curricular content. Criterion-related validity was established by correlating performance on each of the SDRT subtests with performance on the reading subtests of the Stanford Achievement Test. These correlations range from .61 to .98 for the Red and Green levels, and from .39 to .94 for the Brown level.

Summary

The Stanford Diagnostic Reading Test is a group-administered device that is both norm-referenced and criterion-referenced. The device was exceptionally well standardized and is reliable enough to be used in pinpointing specific domains of reading in which pupils demonstrate skill-development strengths and weaknesses. Validity for the SDRT, as for any achievement measure, must be judged relative to the content of local curricula.

SILENT READING DIAGNOSTIC TESTS

The Silent Reading Diagnostic Tests (SRDT) (Bond, Balow, & Hoyt, 1970) are a series of group-administered tests designed to assess silent reading abilities. According to the authors, the tests may be administered to individuals of any age who are reading at a second-grade through a sixth-grade level. Eight subtests comprise the test battery and assess the following skills:

Recognition of words in isolation
Recognition of words in context
Identification of root words
Skill in separating words into syllables
Application of the common rules of syllabication
Skill in synthesizing or blending words
Skill in distinguishing beginning sounds
Skill in distinguishing ending sounds
Skill in distinguishing vowel and consonant sounds

As is apparent in the above list, the behaviors assessed include only word-recognition and word-attack skills. The SRDT does not assess comprehension skills. Instructions for administering the test are straightforward, and the classroom teacher, with some study and practice, should be able to administer this test with little difficulty. The authors suggest that the test be given in three separate periods of about 30 to 45 minutes each. Scoring keys for individual hand scoring are included with each set of teachers' materials.

Scores

By using hand-scoring keys, the examiner can obtain both raw scores and, to a certain extent, information about the specific kinds of errors the pupil has made. Raw scores are plotted on a pupil profile (see Figure 10.5) and may be converted to grade equivalents, percentile ranks, and stanines. The pupil profile has a place to plot vocabulary and comprehension scores, but these scores must be obtained from other reading tests. The test authors recommend the computing of an "average reading" score based on an average of the scores a pupil earns on measures of vocabulary and comprehension. Averaging scores for tests that sample different behaviors is, as we have stated before, a haphazard practice.

Norms

The Silent Reading Diagnostic Tests were standardized on 2,500 children in ten cities in three states. The authors state that the normative sample was selected from a representative distribution of socioeconomic strata but provide no data regarding any of the demographic characteristics of the sample.

Grade Equivalent

BASIC DATA	Pupil Score	1.5	2.0	2.5	3.0	3.5	4.0	4.5	5.0	5.5	6.0	6.5	7.0	7.5	8.0
Grade in School															
Chronological Grade															
Reading Expectancy															
READING ABILITIES															
Vocabulary															
Literal Comprehension															
Creative Comprehension															
Average Reading															
WORD-RECOGNITION SKILL (Tests 1 and 2)															
Total Right (1 + 2)		11	21	29	38	49	60	65	70	75	77	80	82	84	
Words in Isolation (1)		12	17	23	29	37	42	45	47	49	51	52	53	54	
Words in Context (2)		1	5	7	10	15	18	21	23	25	26	28	30		
ERROR PATTERN (1 + 2)															
Total Omitted (1 + 2)		37	29	17	7	4	1								
Total Errors (1 + 2)		31	29	28	27	22	17	15	13	10	7	4	2	1	
Error Type (1 + 2) Initial		9	8	7	6	5	4	3	3	2	2	1	1	0	
Error Type (1 + 2) Middle		10	9	7	6	5	4	3	2	1	1	0			
Error Type (1 + 2) Ending		8	7	7	6	6	5	5	4	3	2	2	1	0	
Error Type (1 + 2) Orientation		8	7	7	6	6	5	4	3	2	2	1	0		
RECOGNITION TECHNIQUES (Tests 3, 4, and 5)															
Total Right (3 + 4 + 5)		19	23	27	32	38	44	50	55	58	60	69	78	83	85
Visual-Structural Analysis (3)		3	6	7	8	9	10	12	13	14	16	20	26	28	30
Syllabication (4)		8	11	13	15	17	19	20	21	22	23	25	26	28	30
Word Synthesis (5)		4	6	7	9	12	14	17	19	20	22	25	28	30	
PHONIC KNOWLEDGE (Tests 6, 7, and 8)															
Total Right (6 + 7 + 8)		39	45	51	58	63	66	68	71	73	75	78	83	85	88
Beginning Sounds (6)		9	14	17	20	22	23	23	24	25	26	27	28	29	30
Ending Sounds (7)		8	10	12	15	17	19	20	21	22	23	25	27	28	30
Vowel and Consonant Sounds (8)		16	20	22	23	24	24	25	25	26	26	27	28	29	30
		1.5	2.0	2.5	3.0	3.5	4.0	4.5	5.0	5.5	6.0	6.5	7.0	7.5	8.0

Grade Equivalent

Figure **10.5**   Profile of scores on the Silent Reading Diagnostic Test. (Reprinted with permission of the publisher from *Silent Reading Diagnostic Tests*, Bond et al., developed by Lyons & Carnahan, copyright © 1970 by Rand McNally & Company.)

Reliability

Reliability data consist of split-half reliability coefficients for the scores of two randomly selected classrooms of third-grade pupils for five subtests. Reliability data for the three other subtests are based on the performance of two randomly selected fourth-grade classes. Reliability coefficients range from .85 to .97 with reported reliabilities of all but two subtests exceeding .90. It is unfortunate that reliabilities are not reported for each grade in the standardization sample, since the authors obviously had the data. No test-retest reliabilities are reported.

Validity

The authors present considerable information in the test manual to support their belief that the SRDT has good content validity. They describe procedures used in constructing the tests and present a table of moderate subtest intercorrelations (reliability information), stating that the intercorrelations vary according to subtest and grade level in a manner that would be predicted by reading experts.

Summary

The Silent Reading Diagnostic Tests contain eight subtests designed to assess skill-development strengths and weaknesses in reading. The tests are group administered and assess silent reading skills. The tests were normed on 2,500 children in grades 2 through 6 and appear to have adequate reliability. Evidence of validity must be judged in relation to the goals and objectives of specific developmental, corrective, or remedial reading programs. The scores obtained on the SRDT must be interpreted as global scores, and program planning for individual children must be based on close inspection of how they earned the scores.

DIAGNOSTIC READING SCALES

The Diagnostic Reading Scales (Spache, 1963) are a series of individually administered tests designed to provide standardized evaluations of oral and silent reading skills and of auditory comprehension. The tests consist of three lists of words to be recognized, twenty-two reading passages of graduated difficulty, and six supplementary phonics tests. The Diagnostic Reading Scales can be used with children in grades 1 through 6.

The word lists are administered as an assessment of a child's skill in pronouncing words in isolation. According to the author, the word lists serve three purposes: to estimate the instructional level of reading, to reveal the child's methods of word attack and analysis, and to evaluate sight vocabulary. The reading passages are used to assess literal and inferential comprehension of material read by the child orally or silently and material read to the child. The six supplementary phonics tests are designed to assess specific phonics skills: (1) consonant sounds, (2) vowel sounds, (3) consonant blends, (4) common syllables, (5) blends, and (6) letter sounds.

Scores

The word lists are administered to determine which of the several reading passages should be used as a starting point for the assessment of oral, silent, and auditory comprehension skills. The author states that on the basis of a child's score in oral reading the teacher can ascertain the child's instructional level, that is, the level at which instruction in reading should be given. Performance in comprehension of passages read silently is used to ascertain the child's independent level, the grade level at which the child can read recreational and supplementary reading materials. Performance in auditory comprehension is used as an assessment of the child's "potential reading level."

As is the case with most diagnostic reading tests, the most valuable information is obtained by careful analysis of the kinds of errors the child makes in oral reading and on the six supplementary subtests.

Norms

Although tables for interpreting scores on the Diagnostic Reading Scales are included in the manual, there are no data about the nature of the standardization sample. This is obviously a very serious limitation.

Reliability

Test-retest reliability for the instructional and independent levels of the Diagnostic Reading Scales was established by administering the test to groups of children over intervals varying from four to ten weeks. Reliability for the instructional level was .84 and for the independent level, .88. The author does report the number of children on whom the reliability data are based but does not describe them in terms of grade level, sex, socioeconomic status, and so on. Internal consistency of the word lists was reported as ranging from .87 to .96 on three unspecified samples of fifty children each. Data regarding reliability are insufficient.

Validity

The author states that "validity of the Diagnostic Reading Scales was established through careful test construction and numerous studies conducted during eight years of development and research" (p. 8). Content validity is reportedly adequate based upon "careful selection" of words for the word lists and of reading passages. The author reports that construct validity (criterion validity is more likely) was established by comparing performance on the Diagnostic Reading Scales with performance on a "similar test." The test is not specified, and the results are not reported.

Concurrent validity of the Diagnostic Reading Scales was established in a number of studies by the author and others. Correlations between performance on the Diagnostic Reading Scales and performance on the California Reading Test ranged from .63 to .92 for whole classes in grades 2 through 6. In a second study, forty-two children earned comparable mean scores on the reading passages of the Diagnostic Reading Scales and on the Paragraph Meaning subtest of the Stanford Achievement Test. The correlation, however, was reported as .49 for the independent level and .30 for the instructional level. The author additionally reports a study illustrating that performance on the Diagnostic Reading Scales was more closely related to teacher judgment than was performance on the Metropolitan Reading Test.

Summary

The Diagnostic Reading Scales are an individually administered series of scales designed to assess oral and silent reading skills and auditory comprehension. The manual includes normative tables but no data about the group on whom the scales were standardized. Reliability and validity are questionable.

WOODCOCK READING MASTERY TESTS

The Woodcock Reading Mastery Tests (Woodcock, 1973) are a battery of five individually administered tests used to assess skill development in reading with students in kindergarten through grade 12. The complete materials for the test are contained in an easel kit similar to the easel kit illustrated earlier for the Peabody Individual Achievement Test (Figure 9.2). There are two alternate forms of the battery, each of which can be administered in 20 to 30 minutes. The five subtests and the behaviors they sample follow.

Letter Identification This subtest assesses skill in naming letters of the alphabet. Identification of both manuscript and cursive letters is assessed.

Word Identification This subtest assesses ability to pronounce words in isolation.

Word Attack This subtest assesses ability to use phonic and structural analysis skills in the identification of nonsense words.

Word Comprehension This subtest assesses knowledge of word meaning.

Passage Comprehension This subtest uses a modified cloze procedure in which the student's task is to read silently a passage that has a word missing and then tell the examiner an appropriate word to fill the blank space.

Scores

Raw scores for subtests of the Woodcock Reading Mastery Tests can be converted to grade scores, age scores, percentile ranks, and standard

scores. Separate scores are earned in each of the subtests, and the test also
provides a total score for reading based on a combination of the performances on the five subtests. Although the author states that the total score is
the most reliable index of skill development in reading, it must be remembered that the total score is a global, undifferentiated score based on an
average of several different kinds of behavior samplings.

In addition to the more traditional scores, the Woodcock provides "mastery scores." The author states that

the Mastery Scale is an equal interval scale that directly reflects changes in an
individual's proficiency with a task. Any given difference between two points on
the Mastery Scale has the same meaning at any level and in any of the five skill
areas measured by the test.   (p. 28)

Tables in the test manual facilitate conversion of raw scores to mastery
scores. Essentially, the purpose of the mastery score is to provide an index
of a student's reading proficiency at different levels of difficulty. A student
may be reading at a fourth-grade level with 75 percent accuracy while
reading third-grade material with 96 percent accuracy.

By using a Mastery Scale, the examiner can chart an individual's range of
reading behaviors, from the level at which the student reads with ease to
the level at which he or she fails to read.

Norms

The standardization of the Woodcock took place over a two-year period in
fifty school districts throughout the United States. A total of 5,252 subjects
in kindergarten through grade 12 were tested. The manual includes a
detailed description of the normative sample in terms of community size,
race, years of schooling, occupation, and income. The sample appears to
be representative of the U.S. population, and in those cases where it is not,
the author clearly says so. The normative sample and its description in the
test manual are superior to those of other norm-referenced diagnostic
reading tests.

Reliability

Two kinds of reliability data are included in the Woodcock manual. The
author reports split-half reliabilities for forms A and B for second-grade
and seventh-grade populations. Alternate-form test-retest data are reported for three second-grade and three seventh-grade classes. Split-half
reliability coefficients are reported for a prepublication form of the test,
but because this form differs from either form A or B, the data have
limited meaning. Split-half reliability coefficients for forms A and B are
summarized in Table 10.4, while alternate-form test-retest reliability coefficients are reported in Table 10.5. Reliability for the test is lower in grade

Table **10.4** Split-half Reliabilities for Subtests of the Woodcock Reading Mastery Tests

	GRADE LEVEL (TEST FORM)			
	2.9 (A)	2.9 (B)	7.9 (A)	7.9 (B)
Letter Identification	.79	.86	.02	.20
Word Identification	.99	.98	.96	.97
Word Attack	.97	.98	.94	.94
Word Comprehension	.88	.93	.86	.83
Passage Comprehension	.95	.93	.93	.93
Total Reading	.99	.99	.98	.98

SOURCE: Adapted from table 7 in R. W. Woodcock, *Woodcock Reading Mastery Test* (Circle Pines, Minn.: American Guidance Service, 1973), p. 57, with permission of American Guidance Service, Inc.

7 than in grade 2. The extremely low reliabilities reported for the Letter Identification subtest at grade 7 are the result of most students' correctly identifying all letters.

In view of the reliability standards suggested in Chapter 6, some subtests of the Woodcock Reading Mastery Tests must be used with a degree of caution.

Validity

Data regarding content validity, construct validity, and predictive validity are reported in the Woodcock manual. Evidence for content validity, as in most diagnostic tests, is based on the procedures used to select test items. The author states that items were selected to assess identification, word attack, and comprehension.

The test author uses a sophisticated statistical procedure for establishing construct validity, the multitrait-multimethod matrix (Campbell & Fiske, 1959). Not only was this method overly sophisticated for the purpose of establishing validity, but, as the author states, the use of the procedure may well overestimate the validity of the separate tests.

Intercorrelations between subtests of the Woodcock range from −.04 to .92 depending on both the subtests considered and the grade level of the population of concern.[2] The intercorrelations are highly variant, but this is

2. Subtest intercorrelations, in general, range from .35 to .92. The lower intercorrelations all include the Letter Identification subtest at grade 7, a grade at which most students demonstrate 100 percent mastery of the task.

Table **10.5**   Alternate-Form Test-Retest Reliabilities for the
Woodcock Reading Mastery Tests

	GRADE LEVEL (TEST SAMPLE SIZE)	
	2.9 (103)	7.9 (102)
Letter Identification	.84	.16
Word Identification	.94	.93
Word Attack	.90	.85
Word Comprehension	.90	.68
Passage Comprehension	.88	.78
Total Reading	.87	.83

SOURCE: Reprinted from p. 58 of R. W. Woodcock, *Woodcock Reading Mastery Test* (Circle Pines, Minn.: American Guidance Service, 1973), with permission of American Guidance Service, Inc.

expected, given the hierarchical nature of the development of reading skills.

Predictive validity for the Woodcock was established by predicting performance on an alternate form of the test from scores on the first form. Using test-retest data on 205 subjects, the author was able to predict with from 30 to 80 percent accuracy the scores on an alternate form of the test. These are reliability, not validity, data.

Summary

The Woodcock Reading Mastery Tests are an individually administered battery of tests used to assess skill development in five areas. The author states that the tests can be used in either a norm-referenced or a criterion-referenced manner. The test was adequately standardized and provides both traditional scores and mastery ratings. The Mastery Scale, a unique feature of the Woodcock, provides an index of a student's reading proficiency at different levels of difficulty. For instance, a student may show 75 percent mastery of fourth-grade material and 96 percent mastery of third-grade material.

Reliability data are limited, and the reliability of specific subtests is below desirable standards. The author has gone to great lengths to demonstrate the validity of the tests.

The Woodcock Reading Mastery Tests provide diagnostic data that may help a classroom teacher pinpoint skill-development strengths and weaknesses in order to plan remedial programs. How much the test can help in doing so depends largely on the interpretative skill of the individual classroom teacher.

CRITERION-REFERENCED DIAGNOSTIC TESTING IN READING

The tests we have discussed to this point are norm-referenced tests, which are designed to provide diagnostic data and compare individuals to their peers. Criterion-referenced diagnostic testing in reading is a relatively new practice, dating from the late 1960s. Criterion-referenced diagnostic reading tests are designed to analyze systematically an individual's strengths and weaknesses without comparing that individual to others. The principle objective of criterion-referenced tests is to assess the specific skills a pupil does and does not have and to relate the assessment to curricular content. Criterion-referenced assessment is tied to instructional objectives, and individual items are designed to assess mastery of specific objectives.

While all criterion-referenced reading tests are based on task analyses of reading, the particular skills assessed and their sequences differ from test to test. This is because different authors view reading in different ways and see the sequence of development of reading skills differently. For this reason, it is especially important with criterion-referenced tests that, as with norm-referenced tests, teachers pay special attention to the behaviors and sequences of behaviors sampled by the tests.

Because normative comparisons are not made in criterion-referenced assessment, no derived scores are calculated. For that reason, many authors of criterion-referenced tests downplay the importance of reliability for their scales. But reliable assessment *is* important in criterion-referenced assessment. For criterion-referenced tests we are concerned not with the consistency of derived scores but with the consistency of responses to items. If a different pattern of item scores is obtained each time an individual takes the test, we begin to question the reliability of the device. Because criterion-referenced devices generally contain relatively limited samples of behavior, it is important that test authors report the consistency with which their tests assess each specific behavior. Test authors *can* and should report test-retest reliabilities for each item. When alternate forms of a criterion-referenced test are available, the authors should report correlations between performances on the two forms.

Most currently available criterion-referenced reading tests are part of entire reading systems. The remainder of this chapter looks at three criterion-referenced reading systems: Diagnosis, Criterion Reading, and the Fountain Valley Teacher Support System in Reading.

K – 3 gr
4 – 6 gr

DIAGNOSIS: AN INSTRUCTIONAL AID

Diagnosis: An Instructional Aid (Shub, Carlin, Friedman, Kaplan, & Katien, 1973) is designed both to assess specific reading skills and to assist the classroom teacher in the systematic planning of appropriate instruction. There are two levels of Diagnosis: level A, which is appropriate for those whose reading skills are at a kindergarten to third-grade level, and level B, which is appropriate for those whose skill development in reading is at a fourth- to sixth-grade level. Each level contains a number of specific components including survey tests, probes, cassettes, a prescription guide, and a class progress chart. Each level is called a classroom laboratory. The heart of the diagnostic-instructional system is the set of thirty-four probes, each a criterion-referenced diagnostic test. Each of the items in the probes is related specifically to instructional objectives. The thirty-four probes measure skill in phonetic analysis (letter recognition, consonant identification, blends and vowels), structural analysis (compound words, contractions, prefixes, suffixes, and so on), comprehension, vocabulary, and use of sources (alphabetizing, dictionary use, and so on). Each area assessed is subdivided into specific skills.

The procedures employed in using Diagnosis are illustrated in Figure 10.6. The teacher begins systematic instructional planning for an individual student by administering a survey test, which assesses, in a limited fashion, the development of specific reading skills. The survey test is scored by a key in the teacher's handbook, and the results provide a global overview of strengths and weaknesses in reading. From results of the survey test the teacher or other examiner determines which of the thirty-four probes should be administered. The probes are self-scoring, and each item administered is paired with a specific instructional objective. Once the particular pattern of a child's performance is known, instructional objectives appropriate for the child are provided.

The program does not quit at this point. Teachers frequently complain that even when they have written or have been provided with an instructional objective, they do not know what materials to use or how to teach to the objective. Diagnosis provides a prescription guide with each of the specific objectives cross-referenced to six basal reading programs: Ginn, Harper and Row, Houghton Mifflin, Scott-Foresman (the New Basic Reading Program and the Open Highways Program), Macmillan, and Science Research Associates. The prescription guide identifies the pages in the teacher's manual for a given series that tell how to teach to a particular objective, the specific pages in the series that teach to that objective, and appropriate spirit masters to use (see Figure 10.7).

The classroom teacher (or other examiner, for that matter) administers a survey test to learn what skills need to be further assessed by the use of

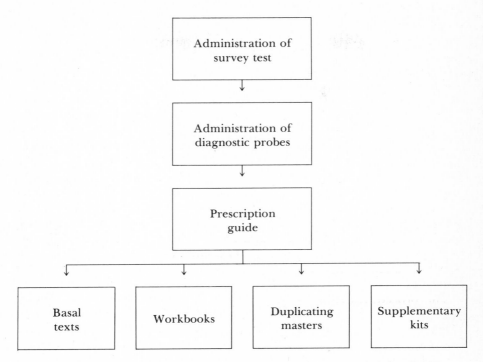

Figure **10.6** Flowchart of activities in using Diagnosis: An Instructional Aid. (From Diagnosis: An Instructional Aid — Reading Level A, Teacher's Handbook. © 1973, Science Research Associates, Inc. Reprinted by permission of the publisher.)

probes. One or more probes are given, and the child's performance enables the teacher to pinpoint skill-development strengths and weaknesses and to specify instructional objectives relevant to skill development. The teacher uses the prescription guide to suggest appropriate materials and then, after teaching to a specific objective, readministers the probe to ascertain the extent to which the child has achieved the objective.

Scores and Norms

No norm-referenced scores are obtained by administering Diagnosis. The system is comprehensive, based on a task analysis of reading skills in kindergarten through grade 6. The child is not compared to others; the emphasis is on subject-matter content mastered. There are, for that reason, no norms for the test.

PHONETIC ANALYSIS
Initial Consonants

Index Code	Teaching Guide	Workbook	Spirit Masters
2-Q	A: 25-41, 50-57, 74-102 B: 16-66	A: 6-17, 24-30, 45-72 B: 1-62	A: 3-8, 12-15, 24-43 B: 1-32
Medial Consonants			
3-A	E: 16-33	E: 1-10	E: 1-6
3-B			
3-C	E: 16-33	E: 1-10	E: 1-6
3-D	E: 16-33	E: 1-10	E: 1-6
3-E	E: 16-33	E: 1-10	E: 1-6
3-F	E: 16-33	E: 1-10	E: 1-6
3-G	E: 16-33	E: 1-10	E: 1-6
3-H	E: 16-33	E: 1-10	E: 1-6
3-I	E: 16-33	E: 1-10	E: 1-6
3-J	E: 16-33	E: 1-10	E: 1-6
3-K	E: 16-33	E: 1-10	E: 1-6
Final Consonants and Blends			
4-A	A: 58-65, 117-121 B: 54-66	A: 31-37, 87-94 B: 47-62	A: 16-19, 53-56 B: 25-32
4-B	B: 83-96	B: 79-94	B: 41-48
4-C			
4-D	A: 15-32, 88-95 B: 40-53	A: 1-11, 59-65 B: 31-46	A: 1-5, 34-38 B: 17-24
4-E	A: 74-80 B: 67-82	A: 45-51 B: 63-78	A: 24-28 B: 33-40
4-F	A: 50-57, 81-87 B: 16-28	A: 24-30, 52-58 B: 1-15	A: 12-15, 29-33 B: 1-8
4-G			
4-H	A: 66-73, 110-116 B: 67-82	A: 38-44, 80-86 B: 63-78	A: 20-23, 48-52 B: 33-40

PHONETIC ANALYSIS
Final Consonants and Blends

Index Code	Teaching Guide	Workbook	Spirit Masters
4-I	A: 33-41, 103-109 B: 54-66	A: 12-17, 73-79 B: 47-62	A: 6-8, 44-47 B: 25-32
4-J	A: 74-80	A: 45-51	A: 24-28
4-K	C: 61-70	C: 42-51	C: 29-35
4-L	C: 49-60	C: 32-41	C: 22-28
4-M	C: 38-48	C: 22-31	C: 15-21
4-N	C: 38-48	C: 22-31	C: 15-21
4-O	C: 40-61	C: 17-31	C: 12-21
4-P	C: 49-60	C: 32-41	C: 22-28
Consonant Blends I			
5-A	C: 71-84, 114-138	C: 52-61, 84-94	C: 36-42, 57-63
5-B	C: 71-84, 114-138	C: 52-61, 84-94	C: 36-42, 57-63
5-C	C: 71-84, 114-138	C: 52-61, 84-94	C: 36-42, 57-63
5-D	C: 71-84, 114-138	C: 52-61, 84-94	C: 36-42, 57-63
5-E	C: 71-84, 114-138	C: 52-61, 84-94	C: 36-42, 57-63
5-F	C: 71-84, 114-138	C: 52-61, 84-94	C: 36-42, 57-63
5-G	C: 97-138	C: 73-94	C: 50-63
5-H	C: 97-138	C: 73-94	C: 50-63
5-I	C: 97-138	C: 73-94	C: 50-63
5-J	C: 97-113	C: 73-83	C: 50-56
5-K	C: 97-138	C: 73-94	C: 50-63
5-L			
5-M	C: 97-138	C: 73-94	C: 50-63
Consonant Blends II			
6-A	C: 85-96, 114-138	C: 62-72, 84-94	C: 43-49, 57-63
6-B	C: 85-96, 114-138	C: 62-72, 84-94	C: 43-49, 57-63
6-C	C: 85-96, 114-138	C: 62-72, 84-94	C: 43-49, 57-63

Figure 10.7 Sample of prescription guide page correlating learning objective 5-A with the SRA Basic Reading Program. (From *Diagnosis: An Instructional Aid — Reading Level A, Teacher's Handbook.* © 1973, Science Research Associates, Inc. Reprinted by permission of the publisher.)

Reliability and Validity

No reliability data are reported for Diagnosis. There are two alternate forms of the survey test, both of which provide relatively limited samples of behavior. Alternate-form reliabilities are not reported. We advise that the examiner administer both forms of the survey test to increase reliability.

At the lower levels, the probes are pretty exhaustive, in many cases sampling the entire domain of behaviors. In assessing skill in naming lower-case letters, for example, skill in naming *all* lower-case letters is assessed. At the upper levels, behavior sampling is necessarily more limited.

Validity for Diagnosis is based on expert opinion. As is the case with any criterion-referenced system, the skills assessed and the sequence in which they are assessed depend on the authors' viewpoints about reading.

Summary

Diagnosis: An Instructional Aid is a criterion-referenced system used to assess skill-development strengths and weaknesses in reading. Use of the system allows teachers to assess specific skill-development weaknesses, the program provides instructional objectives, and the prescription guide can be used to select materials to teach to the objectives.

The use of criterion-referenced diagnostic devices such as Diagnosis enables the classroom teacher to go about individualized reading instruction in a very systematic manner. Much of the hit-or-miss of norm-referenced approaches is avoided, producing considerably more efficiency in assessment.

CRITERION READING

Criterion Reading (Hackett, 1971) is both a diagnostic system designed to assess skill-development strengths and weaknesses in reading and a learning-management system designed to facilitate systematic individualized instruction in reading. The system is criterion-referenced to a hierarchy of 450 reading skills that are divided into five levels and tied to eight areas of competence. The system is self-contained in that pupil workbooks are provided; it is not a system cross-referenced to basal readers.

Criterion Reading has its basis in a task analysis of reading, provides performance objectives for each specific reading skill, and provides tests to assess mastery of the performance objectives. The system is appropriate for use from kindergarten through junior high school and may be used in adult basic education courses.

Eight areas of competence are assessed in Criterion Reading. These are described by the author as follows.

8 areas of Competence

1. *Motor Skills* Skills in such motor activities as holding a pencil, tying a shoelace, and walking on a balance beam are assessed.

2. *Visual Input — Motor Response* Competence in matching symbols, objects, and colors is assessed.

3. *Auditory Input — Motor Response* Competence in such skills as matching beginning sounds and repeating initial consonants is assessed.

4. *Phonology* Skill development in identifying, classifying, using, and producing alphabet-letter names, consonants, vowels, and their combinations is assessed.

5. *Structural Analysis* Competence in such skills as classifying singular possessive nouns, using rules for forming singulars and plurals, and using rules to divide words into syllables is assessed.

6. *Verbal Information* Identification, classification, use, and production of concepts and facts are assessed.

7. *Syntax* Skill development in classification of verbs, subject-predicate function, and the use of rules for sentence punctuation is assessed.

8. *Comprehension* Competence in analyzing, synthesizing, and evaluating language is assessed.

The first three competence areas listed above are assessed only at level I of Criterion Reading and generally pertain only to children in kindergarten and grade 1.

The use of Criterion Reading involves several procedures. The examiner administers one or more of the major tests assessing diagnostic outcome skills. The examiner continues to administer diagnostic outcome tests until the student encounters difficulty. The student is assessed using measures of "process skills" related to the diagnostic outcome tests that she or he has failed. In this way, diagnosis of the nature of the student's skill development in reading becomes increasingly refined. Figure 10.8 illustrates the hierarchy of activities in Criterion Reading.

Figure 10.8 illustrates that reading is assessed and taught in terms of pupil mastery of certain motor, listening/speaking, reading, and writing skills. Areas of competence are spelled out and each student's competence is assessed using measures of diagnostic outcome skills. For each diagnostic outcome skill there are a number of process skills, essentially related to enabling objectives. Having assessed a student using measures of the enabling objectives, the teacher knows to what extent the student demonstrates specific skill competencies. The program provides specific instruc-

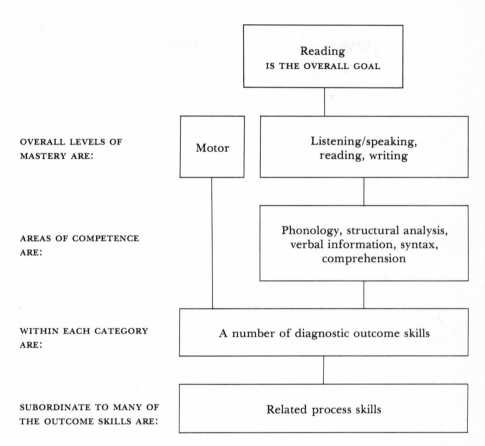

Figure **10.8**   The Criterion Reading hierarchy. (Redrawn from M. G. Hackett, *Criterion Reading teacher's guide*, p. 10. Copyright © 1971, Random House, Inc. Used by permission.)

tional objectives and includes workbooks designed to help the student achieve those objectives. Objectives are written in such a way that the behaviors can be observed. For example, the examiner can observe that, given rows of consonants, the student identifies initial single-consonant sounds with 95 percent accuracy.

The absence of a survey test for Criterion Reading means that teachers or other examiners have to spend considerable time assessing individual children. Teachers must use their own judgment in deciding where to start with a particular child. The administration of each diagnostic outcome test (there are a total of twenty-three) takes about 20 minutes. If teachers misjudge the starting point, then assessment can take an inordinately long time.

Scores and Norms

Diagnostic Outcome Assessments are scored by students for the most part. For very young children, the teacher must score the Diagnostic Outcome Assessments, but since 95 percent mastery is required and because most Diagnostic Outcome Assessments have twenty or fewer items, the scoring is pretty much pass-fail.

Criterion Reading is a criterion-referenced system and for that reason no traditional norm-referenced scores are obtained. The student is not compared to others in a normative sense.

Reliability and Validity

As is the case for most criterion-referenced devices and systems, there are no data regarding reliability and validity. There is an extensive listing of skills in the manual, and individual teachers will have to use their own judgment to decide whether the program is appropriate for specific uses.

Summary

Criterion Reading is an individualized, performance-based, criterion-referenced reading program designed to facilitate assessment of skill-development strengths and weaknesses in reading. The program is structured around 450 specific reading skills and includes a series of Diagnostic Outcome Assessments to assess mastery of the skills. While Criterion Reading has possibilities, and while the major objective of the program is a noble one, it is at this time probably too complex a program for the average school system to adopt.

Criterion Reading is a very expensive program. It is doubtful that a school system could afford to adopt the program on a mass basis without considerable expense in both materials and time necessary to conduct in-service training sessions for teachers.

Criterion Reading is a refreshing switch from the typical norm-referenced test. It provides specific direction as opposed to simple scores. The system appears to be embryonic; yet it should be of considerable use to remedial specialists.

FOUNTAIN VALLEY
TEACHER SUPPORT SYSTEM IN READING

The Fountain Valley Teacher Support System in Reading (Zweig Associates, 1971) consists of seventy-seven separate self-scoring criterion-referenced tests measuring 367 behavioral objectives in reading. Fountain Valley is more than a series of tests, however, as it includes continuous pupil profiles designed to keep a record of individual pupil achievement and a cross-referenced prescription guide designed to help the teacher locate the pages in specific basal reading series appropriate to teaching to the instructional objectives.

Reading skills are evaluated in five areas: phonetic analysis, structural analysis, vocabulary development, comprehension, and study skills. The tests are arranged in order of difficulty and are color coded. Students may take the tests independently, in small groups, or as total classes.

Scores and Norms

Because Fountain Valley is a criterion-referenced system, there are no scores and no norms. After taking the criterion-referenced tests, the student has either passed or failed items related to specific instructional objectives. Rather than providing the teacher with certain scores such as grade scores, age scores, or percentiles, the system facilitates delineation of specific skill-development strengths and weaknesses in reading.

Reliability and Validity

Since Fountain Valley is a criterion-referenced system, there are no data about reliability and validity in the test manual. The tests provide relatively limited samples of specific reading behaviors, so test results must be interpreted cautiously. Validity of the system is based largely on expert opinion, but the system is flexible enough that teachers can adjust the sequence of objectives to fit the idiosyncrasies of nearly any classroom arrangement or instructional system.

Summary

The Fountain Valley Teacher Support System in Reading is designed to provide teachers with more than test scores. By using the criterion-referenced tests, classroom teachers, school psychologists, resource teachers, and other examiners can pinpoint where a student stands in the developmental sequence of reading. It enables teachers to pinpoint appropriate instructional objectives and to select from a variety of sources the particular methods, materials, and teaching strategies they want to use. The pupil record form enables teachers to monitor individual pupil progress and thus to engage in systematic instruction. The system is both diagnostic and prescriptive.

SUMMARY

In this chapter we have reviewed the kinds of behaviors sampled by diagnostic reading tests. Several specific norm-referenced and criterion-referenced tests have been evaluated in terms of the kinds of behaviors they sample and their technical adequacy. Most of the norm-referenced devices clearly lack the technical characteristics necessary to be used in making specific instructional decisions. Many do not present evidence of reliability and validity. In fact, some tests (Gates-McKillop, Durrell, and Diagnostic Reading Scales) present the consumer with numerous normative tables for interpreting test data without even describing the nature of the normative population.

Criterion-referenced testing in reading is a relatively new practice that appears promising. The criterion-referenced tests described in this chapter are parts of comprehensive systems designed to pinpoint skill-development strengths and weaknesses, provide teachers with instructional objectives, and direct teachers to materials that help teach to those objectives. We do not yet have sufficient empirical evidence to judge the extent to which criterion-referenced tests meet their stated objectives. Teachers need to judge for their own purposes the adequacy of the behavior samplings and the sequences of behaviors sampled. The systems still contain many rough spots that must be smoothed out.

How, then, do teachers and diagnostic specialists assess skill development in reading and prescribe developmental, corrective, or remedial programs? Reliance on scores provided by diagnostic reading tests is indeed precarious. Teachers and diagnostic specialists must rely on the qualitative information obtained in testing. Some tests provide checklists of observed difficulties, and these may be of considerable help in identifying individual pupil's reading characteristics.

In assessing reading strengths and weaknesses, teachers must first ask themselves what kinds of behaviors they want to assess. Specific subtests of larger batteries may then be used to assess those behaviors. Teachers should choose the subtests that are technically most accurate. Interpretation must be in terms of behaviors sampled rather than in terms of subtest names.

STUDY QUESTIONS

1. For what purpose are diagnostic reading tests given?

2. What are the relative merits and limitations in using criterion-referenced and in using norm-referenced diagnostic reading tests?

3. Several shortcomings have been noted for each of the specific norm-referenced diagnostic reading tests described in this chapter. What shortcomings do most of the tests have in common?

4. Dierdre, a student in Mr. Albert's fifth-grade class, has considerable difficulty reading. Mr. Albert wants to know at what level to begin reading instruction. Given the state of the art in diagnostic testing in reading, what are some alternative ways for Mr. Albert to identify a starting point?

5. You are teaching reading to a third-grade class. The school psychologist assesses one of the children in your class and reports that the child earned a grade score of 1.6 in reading. What additional information would you ask the psychologist to give you?

6. When teachers use criterion-referenced reading tests, they often find that the sequence in which specific individuals learn reading skills differs from the sequence of skills assessed by the test. How might this be explained?

7. It has been argued that norms are more important for screening tests than for diagnostic tests. Why?

ADDITIONAL READING

Bond, G., & Tinker, M. A. *Reading difficulties: Their diagnosis and correction.* New York: Appleton-Century-Crofts, 1967.

Buros, O. K. (ed.). *Reading tests and reviews.* Highland Park, NJ: Gryphon Press, 1968.

Buros, O. K. (ed.). *Seventh mental measurements yearbook.* Highland Park, NJ: Gryphon Press, 1972. (Reviews of reading tests, pp. 1109–1131; pp. 1146–1148.)

Guthrie, J. T. Models of reading and reading disability. *Journal of Educational Psychology*, 1973, *65*, 9–18.

Chapter 11

Diagnostic Testing in Mathematics

Diagnostic testing in mathematics is designed to identify specific strengths and weaknesses in skill development. We have seen that all major achievement tests designed to assess multiple skills include subtests that measure mathematics skills. These tests are necessarily global and attempt to assess a wide range of skills. In most cases, the number of items assessing specific math skills is insufficient for diagnostic purposes. Diagnostic testing in mathematics is more specific, providing a detailed assessment of skill development within specific areas.

There are fewer diagnostic math tests than diagnostic reading tests, but math assessment is more clear-cut. Because the successful performance of some mathematical operations clearly depends on the successful performance of other operations (for instance, multiplication depends on addition), it is relatively easier to sequence skill development and assessment in math than in reading. Diagnostic math tests generally sample similar behaviors. They sample various contents or mathematical concepts, various operations, and various applications of mathematical facts and principles. A description of the kinds of behaviors sampled by diagnostic math tests follows.

BEHAVIORS SAMPLED BY DIAGNOSTIC MATHEMATICS TESTS

Behaviors sampled by diagnostic math tests have been classified by Connolly, Nachtman, and Pritchett (1971). A description of those behavior samples follows.

CONTENT

A number of content areas are assessed by diagnostic math tests. Facts, knowledge, and concepts necessary for the successful performance of mathematical operations and for meaningful applications of math are assessed in each of the following content areas.

Numeration

Diagnostic math tests include subtests designed to assess knowledge of the number system. Items include those that assess identification of quantities and set value, rounding, identification of missing numbers in sequences, and counting.

Fractions

In nearly all cases and especially in tests designed to be used with students who are beyond fourth grade, understanding of basic concepts about fractions, decimals, and percentages is assessed.

Algebra

Some diagnostic math tests include subtests or items designed to assess knowledge and understanding of principles involved in the solution of linear and quadratic equations.

Geometry

Items that assess knowledge of geometry typically measure skill in recognizing specific shapes and, in some cases, understanding of theorems.

OPERATIONS

Subtests and items designed to assess children's skill in carrying out fundamental arithmetic operations include measures of counting, computation, and arithmetic reasoning.

Counting

Items designed to assess skill in counting usually require the student to count dots or objects and to select or write numerals to represent the number of objects counted.

Computation

Items and subtests designed to assess computational skills range from those that sample the traditional arithmetic operations of addition, subtraction, multiplication, and division to those that require the student to complete as many as four computational operations in problem-solving tasks. Items designed to assess specific operations generally range from those that require performance of the operation in the form of word problems to those that require the written solution of relatively complex computational problems.

Arithmetic Reasoning

Arithmetic reasoning subtests require the solution of problems with missing number facts.

APPLICATIONS

Diagnostic math tests include assessment of students' skills in applying mathematical facts and concepts to the solution of problems. Tasks generally include the following kinds of behavior samplings.

Measurement

Items assessing measurement require the recognition and application of common measurement units and the practical application of length, weight, and temperature measures.

Problem Solving

Problem-solving tasks require students to solve "story problems" that are read to them or that they read themselves. Four kinds of problems are generally included: (1) those requiring only a one-step mathematical operation, (2) those requiring more than one computational operation, (3) those requiring that the student differentiate between essential and nonessential information in solving problems, and (4) those requiring that the student demonstrate logical thinking by solving problems with missing elements.

Reading Graphs and Tables

The application of mathematical skills and concepts may be assessed by requiring the student to read graphs and tables in the solution of problems.

Money and Budgeting

The application of mathematical skills and concepts may be assessed by requiring the student to solve money problems. Items include those that assess the extent to which the student can make value judgments about purchasing articles, can interpret budgets, and can comprehend checks and checking accounts.

Time

The application of mathematical facts and concepts to the solution of problems involving time includes test items requiring the student to read clocks and to identify time intervals, holidays, and seasons.

SPECIFIC DIAGNOSTIC MATHEMATICS TESTS

The remainder of this chapter reviews three diagnostic mathematics tests: the Key Math Diagnostic Arithmetic Test, the Stanford Diagnostic Mathematics Test, and Diagnosis: an Instructional Aid in Mathematics.

KEY MATH DIAGNOSTIC ARITHMETIC TEST

The Key Math Diagnostic Arithmetic Test (Connolly, Nachtman, & Pritchett, 1971) is an individually administered diagnostic test designed to assess math skill development in kindergarten through the eighth grade. The test, which is contained in an easel kit similar to those used with the Peabody Individual Achievement Test and the Woodcock Reading Mastery Test, includes fourteen subtests organized into three areas: content, operations, and applications. The test gives four levels of diagnostic information: total test performance, area performance, subtest performance, and item performance. Examiners can use differing degrees of specificity in interpreting children's performances. An appendix contains a description of the specific behaviors sampled by each item included in the test.

Administration of Key Math is relatively simple, and the authors state that no formal training is required to administer the test. The efficiency and meaningfulness with which the test is interpreted are a function of the expertise of the person who interprets a child's performance. According to the authors, maximum diagnostic meaningfulness will be achieved by those who have a background in teaching math. Each of the fourteen subtests is administered by assessing children's performances on a range of items. A basal (three consecutive correct responses) and a ceiling (three consecutive failures) are established for each subtest.

Subtests included in Key Math, grouped according to the three areas measured by the test, are reported in Table 11.1.

Scores

Detailed directions for computing raw scores are included in the Key Math manual. Four kinds of interpretation can be employed in evaluating a child's performance on the test. Total test performance can be evaluated by transforming raw scores to grade equivalents. A second way of interpreting a child's performance on Key Math is to look at the performance pattern across the three areas. Area scores provide some indication of relative strengths and weaknesses in content, operations, and application of mathematical knowledge.

Third, the user of Key Math can interpret a child's test performance by looking at relative performance on the fourteen subtests. The authors

Table **11.1** Subtests of Key Math

CONTENT	OPERATIONS	APPLICATIONS
Numeration	Addition	Word Problems
Fractions	Subtraction	Missing Elements
Geometry and Symbols	Multiplication	Money
	Division	Measurement
	Mental Computation	Time
	Numerical Reasoning	

suggest that a child who is performing at a lower grade level on one subtest than on the other thirteen is demonstrating a weakness in that area. No evidence is presented to support the contention that discrepant scores represent significant deficiencies. Errors in interpretation could well result from use of the suggested procedures for interpreting subtest scores.

The fourth way of interpreting performance on Key Math is, in our opinion, the real strength of this test. The authors have included a description of the specific behaviors sampled by each of the test items and have written behavioral objectives to correspond to each particular sampling. The classroom teacher or other diagnostic specialist interested in developing an educational program for children taking the test can analyze a child's performance on specific items. In this manner, the teacher receives specific information about the behaviors that individual children do and do not demonstrate. This fourth way of interpreting test performance is actually criterion-referenced. Although normative data are available for making both interindividual and intraindividual comparisons, these data have some real shortcomings, as we shall see. If interpreted by evaluation of individual children's performances on specified behavior samples, Key Math has the potential of providing excellent diagnostic information.

Norms

The original item pool for Key Math evolved from the doctoral dissertations of three authors. The studies were coordinated with each other and involved field testing of 1,400 educable mentally retarded children. Later, math curricula were searched, and additional items were written for inclusion in the test. The test was then administered to 950 children in kindergarten through grade 8 in four midwestern and one northwestern school districts in a "calibration study" designed to ascertain item difficulty and select final items for the scale. Actual standardization of the test was done by administering it to 1,222 children in kindergarten through grade 7 in forty-two school systems. On the basis of the calibration study conducted earlier, the authors stated that standardization could be completed by administering only *five items* to each child. Allegedly, the five would be representative of the total range of item difficulty. Nineteen items were selected as representative of the total 209 items included in this test. Each child in the standardization group took five of the nineteen items.

The description of the normative sample is post hoc and incomplete. Apparently, the normative sample was not systematically selected on the basis of traditional normative variables. The manual does report comparisons of community size and racial representation with census figures. No information is included regarding socioeconomic status, parental occupation, or parental education. More important, the authors do not report the kinds of math curricula in which the children were enrolled.

While standardization of Key Math was certainly less than desirable, it must be remembered that the real value of this test is in the specific diagnostic information it provides. If Key Math is used as a criterion-referenced test, normative comparisons are unnecessary.

Reliability

The authors report internal-consistency reliability coefficients for children included in the calibration study. Reliability coefficients, reported by subtest and grade level (kindergarten through grade 7), range from .39 to .90. Standard errors of measurement for each subtest are reported in both the record booklet and the manual. The inclusion of these data should help the test user to establish confidence intervals and to interpret pupil performance. The authors do not report test-retest reliability, a feature that would have been of considerable value in such a heterogeneous test. Also, they do not include data on significance of differences between subtest scores, data that are necessary if the use of the diagnostic profile is to be meaningful.

Validity

Because Key Math is most useful as a criterion-referenced device for very specific diagnosis, its ultimate utility must be judged on the basis of its content validity. Content for this test was carefully selected, based on the research findings of the three authors and the field testing of the scale with over 3,000 children. The fact that the authors have provided specific information about the behaviors sampled by each item in the scale should allow teachers to judge readily the usefulness of the test for their purposes and the relevance of the content to their instructional goals.

Concurrent validity was investigated by comparing the Key Math performance of twenty-eight "normal" fifth graders to their performance on the Iowa Tests of Basic Skills (ITBS) arithmetic subtests. A correlation of

.38 was obtained between Key Math performance and performance on the composite of arithmetic test scores. The authors admit that the data are inadequate for demonstrating concurrent validity.

Summary

Key Math is an individually administered test designed to provide diagnostic analysis of skill development in mathematics. The device can be used in either a norm-referenced or criterion-referenced manner. The real value of the test is in its use as a criterion-referenced device. The specific listing of behavioral objectives for every item of the test and the grouping of items into logical instructional clusters should facilitate both program planning and evaluation.

STANFORD DIAGNOSTIC MATHEMATICS TEST *g. 1. 5 – H.S.*

The Stanford Diagnostic Mathematics Test (SDMT) (Beatty, Madden, Gardner, & Karlsen, 1976) is a group-administered test designed to be both norm-referenced and criterion-referenced. The test measures competence in the basic mathematical concepts and skills that are important in daily affairs and prerequisite to the continued study of mathematics. The primary purpose of the SDMT is to identify specific areas in which a pupil is having difficulty. There are four levels of the test: the Red level (grades 1.5 to 4.5), the Green level (grades 3.5 to 6.5), the Brown level (grades 5.5 to 8.5), and the Blue level (grades 7.5 to high school). Each level consists of three subtests: Number System and Numeration, Computation, and Applications. A description of the kinds of behaviors sampled by each of the subtests follows.

Number System and Numeration   Items included in this subtest range from samples of skill in identifying numerals and comparing sets to samples of competence in fractions and the more complex arithmetic operations. The items are noncomputational and are designed to assess pupils' understanding of numbers and their properties.

Computation   The Computation subtest assesses knowledge of the primary facts and algorithms of addition, subtraction, multiplication, and division and the methods for solving simple and compound number sentences.

Applications   This subtest assesses skill in applying basic mathematical facts and principles. Items range in difficulty from those that require students to solve simple story problems and select correct models for solving one-step problems to those that require students to solve multiple-step problems and measurement problems and to read tables and graphs.

The SDMT is norm-referenced in the sense that it was standardized on a sample representative of the United States public school population. It is criterion-referenced in the sense that groups of items have been assigned a "passing" score, called by the authors a "Progress Indicator cutoff score." Pupils who reach or exceed the Progress Indicator cutoff on the group of items that measure a particular objective are said to be competent in that objective. The cutoffs were set by the authors of the test on the basis of a number of factors, including (1) the skills prerequisite to attaining the objective, and (2) the performance of pupils on the test items measuring the objective. The criteria were not set according to a strict norm-referenced procedure but are based primarily on expert opinion.

Item selection for the SDMT was based on a number of factors. Items initially were written to produce four complete test forms that would measure each of the objectives at the four levels of the test. Each item was reviewed and edited for content, style, and appropriateness in measuring a stated objective. A major concern in editing was, reportedly, the elimination of ethnic, cultural, racial, and sexual bias. The items were assembled into four forms and administered to a nationwide sample. Each level of the test was item analyzed in the grades for which the test was intended as well as in one grade lower and one grade higher. For each level, two forms (judged equivalent after content and item analysis) were assembled from the four experimental forms. Items were assigned to forms in such a way that the tasks required by the items, the statistical characteristics of the items, and the context of the items were balanced for each objective across the two forms.

Scores

The SDMT yields raw scores, scaled scores, grade equivalents, percentile ranks, stanines, and "Progress Indicators." The Progress Indicators are simply "+" or "−" indications as to whether the child reached or exceeded the predetermined Progress Indicator cutoff score for a specific skill domain. The derived scores (scaled scores, grade equivalents, percentile ranks, and stanines) are available on the subtests and the total.

Norms

The standardization sample for the SDMT was selected by means of a stratified random-sampling technique, with socioeconomic status, school-system enrollment, and geographic region as the stratification variables. School-system data were obtained from the United States Office of Education's 1970 census tapes. The tapes were used to generate a random sample of 3,000 school districts. A composite socioeconomic-status index for each system was determined by weighting family income twice in comparison to median years of schooling of parents. Age and sex were not controlled in the standardization of the SDMT.

Within stratified cells, school districts were invited to participate in standardization of the test. A random sample of consenting districts within each cell was selected. The test was standardized in 37 school districts on approximately 38,000 pupils. The manual includes detailed tables illustrating that the demographic characteristics of the school districts sampled closely parallel those indicated in the 1970 census.

Reliability

Two types of reliability information are available for the SDMT: reliability of test scores and reliability of the Progress Indicators. Reliability of the raw scores for the test was determined by assessing internal consistency (using Kuder-Richardson 20); alternate-form reliability was computed by correlating performance of the same pupils on both forms of the test. Internal-consistency coefficients range from .84 to .97 for the four levels of the test; alternate-form coefficients range from .64 to .94, with most exceeding .80. Standard errors of measurement in both raw-score and scaled-score units are tabled in the manuals.

The reliability of the Progress Indicators was determined by administering both forms to the same pupils and establishing each pupil's Progress Indicator on both forms. Contingency tables provided in the manual may be used to estimate the probability of a student's obtaining a different Progress Indicator on taking the alternate form of the test.

Validity

Limited space in the SDMT manual is devoted to the issue of content validity and criterion-related validity. The authors state that the content validity of the SDMT, like that of any other achievement test, must be based on an evaluation of the extent to which the content of the test reflects local curricular content. Criterion-related validity was established by correlating performance on the subtests of the SDMT with performance on the mathematics subtests of the Stanford Achievement Test. Correlations ranged from .64 to .94.

Summary

The Stanford Diagnostic Mathematics Test is a group-administered device that is both norm-referenced and criterion-referenced. The device was exceptionally well standardized and demonstrates enough reliability to be used in pinpointing specific domains of skill-development strengths and weaknesses in mathematics. Validity must be judged relative to the content of local curricula.

A K-3
B 3-6

√ DIAGNOSIS: AN INSTRUCTIONAL AID IN MATHEMATICS

Diagnosis: An Instructional Aid in Mathematics (Guzaitis, Carlin, & Juda, 1972) is a counterpart to Diagnosis: An Instructional Aid, which tests reading; it is designed both to assess specific mathematical skills and to help the classroom teacher in the systematic planning of appropriate instruction. There are two levels of the system, level A, for those whose math skills are at a kindergarten to third-grade level, and level B, for those whose math skills are at a third- to sixth-grade level. Each of the levels contains a number of specific components including survey tests, probes, a prescription guide, a teachers' handbook, and a class progress chart.

Diagnosis is not a self-contained instructional system; rather, it is cross-referenced to basic elementary school mathematics curricula. The system helps teachers pinpoint instructional weaknesses and teach to specific objectives using materials already available in their classrooms.

The heart of this diagnostic-instructional program is the set of thirty-two probes, each of which is a criterion-referenced diagnostic device. Each item in the probes is related specifically to an instructional objective. The thirty-two probes measure competence in whole-number computation (addition, subtraction, multiplication, and division), fractional computation, decimal computation, numeration, mathematical operations, problem solving, measurement, and geometry.

The teacher or diagnostic specialist begins systematic instructional planning by administering a survey test that assesses, in a limited manner, the development of specific math skills. The survey test is scored by use of a key included in the teachers' handbook to obtain a global assessment of strengths and weaknesses in math. The teacher or other examiner uses the results of the survey test to determine which of the specific probes should be administered.

The probes are self-scoring; by simply tearing off a face sheet, teachers can identify items answered correctly. Each item is matched to a specific instructional objective. Teachers can identify specific instructional weaknesses and specify instructional goals to alleviate each weakness. The prescription guide directs teachers to the sections of several basic math curricula where the instructional objective is taught and to appropriate instructional materials.

Scores and Norms

No norm-referenced scores are obtained for Diagnosis. The system is comprehensive, based on a task analysis of math skills in kindergarten through grade 6. The child is not compared to others; the emphasis is on subject-matter content mastered.

Reliability and Validity

No reliability data are reported for Diagnosis. There are two alternate forms of the survey test, both of which provide only very limited samples of each of the math skills assessed. Alternate-form reliabilities are not reported; we advise concurrent administration of both forms to insure reliability.

Validity for the system is based on expert opinion. As with any criterion-referenced system, the skills assessed and the sequence in which they occur depend on the authors' view of the development of math skills.

Summary

Diagnosis is a criterion-referenced system used to assess skill-development strengths and weaknesses in mathematics. The system allows teachers to assess specific skill-development weaknesses, to specify instructional goals, and to select materials to teach to those goals. The use of a system like this enables the teacher to individualize math instruction in a systematic manner. Much of the hit-or-miss of traditional diagnostic-instructional intervention is avoided, providing considerably more efficiency in instruction.

SUMMARY

In this chapter we have reviewed the kinds of behaviors sampled by diagnostic mathematics tests and have evaluated the most commonly used tests in terms of the kinds of behaviors they sample and their technical adequacy. The three tests reviewed in this chapter are designed essentially to provide teachers and diagnostic specialists with specified information on those math skills that pupils have and have not mastered. Compared to diagnostic testing in reading, diagnostic testing in math puts less emphasis on the provision of scores.

The tests described in this chapter differ in their technical adequacy for use in making instructional decisions for students. Knowledge of pupil mastery of specific math skills as gained from administration of one or more of the tests, along with knowledge of the general sequence of development of math skills, can help teachers design curricular content for individuals.

STUDY QUESTIONS

1. Identify four ways a teacher can interpret the performance of a pupil on the Key Math Diagnostic Test.

2. The Stanford Diagnostic Mathematics Test is both norm-referenced and criterion-referenced. Under what circumstances would a teacher want to use the norms for the SDMT?

3. Given the state of the art in diagnostic assessment in math, identify at least two ways a classroom teacher can pinpoint a starting place for teaching math to an individual pupil.

4. You are teaching arithmetic to a third-grade class. The local school psychologist assesses one of the children in your class and reports that the child earned a grade equivalent of 5.6 in arithmetic. What additional information would you ask the psychologist to give you?

ADDITIONAL READING

Brumfiel, C. F., & Krause, E. *Introduction to the theory of arithmetic.* Reading, MA.: Addison-Wesley, 1970.

Buros, O. K. (ed.) *Seventh mental measurements yearbook.* Highland Park, NJ: Gryphon Press, 1972. (Pp. 842–890, reviews of mathematics tests.)

Copeland, R. W. *How children learn mathematics: Implications of Piaget's research.* New York: Macmillan, 1970.

Chapter 12

Assessment of Intelligence: An Overview

No other area of assessment has generated as much attention, controversy, and debate as "intelligence" testing. For centuries philosophers, psychologists, educators, and laymen have debated the meaning of intelligence. Numerous definitions of the term *intelligence* have been proposed, each definition serving as a stimulus for counterdefinitions and counterproposals. Several theories have been advanced to describe and explain intelligence and its development. The extent to which intelligence is genetically or environmentally determined has been of special concern. Genetic determinists, environmental determinists, and interactionists have all observed differences in the intelligence-test performances of different populations of children. The interpretation of group differences in intelligence measurements and the practice of testing the intelligence of schoolchildren have been topics of recurrent controversy and debate, aired in professional journals, the popular press, and on television. In some instances the courts have acted to curtail or halt intelligence assessment in the public schools, while in other cases the courts have defined what intelligence assessment must consist of. Debate and controversy have flourished about whether intelligence tests should be given, what intelligence tests measure, and how different levels of performance attained by different populations of children are to be explained.

No one, however, has seen a thing called intelligence. Rather, we observe differences in the ways people behave — either differences in everyday behavior in a variety of situations or differences in responses to standard stimuli or sets of stimuli; then we *infer* a construct called *intelligence*. In this sense, intelligence is an inferred entity, a term or construct we use to explain differences in present behavior and to predict differences in future behavior.

We have repeatedly stressed the fact that any test is a sample of behavior. So, too, intelligence tests are samples of behavior. Regardless of how an individual's performance is viewed and interpreted, intelligence tests and items on those tests simply sample behaviors. A variety of different kinds of behavior samplings are used to assess intelligence; in most cases, the kinds of behaviors sampled reflect a test author's conception of intelligence.

This chapter reviews the kinds of behaviors sampled by intelligence tests with particular emphasis on the psychological demands of different test items as a function of pupil characteristics.

INTELLIGENCE TESTS AS SAMPLES OF BEHAVIOR

There is a hypothetical domain of items that could be used to assess intelligence. In practice, it is impossible to administer every item in the domain to a child whose intelligence we want to assess. The dots in Figure 12.1 represent different items in the domain of behaviors that could be used to assess intelligence. No two tests contain identical samples of behavior; some tests overlap in the kinds of behaviors they sample, while others do not. No test samples all possible behaviors in the domain. In Figure 12.1 we see that tests A and D sample different behaviors. Both tests assess some behaviors sampled by test E. None of the tests samples all the possible behaviors in the domain.

The characterization of behaviors sampled by intelligence tests is complex. Some persons have, for example, argued that intelligence tests assess a student's capacity to profit from instruction, while others argue that such tests assess merely what has been learned; some have characterized intelligence tests as either verbal or nonverbal; some characterize intelligence tests as either culturally biased or culture fair. In actuality, nearly any contention regarding what it is that intelligence tests measure can be supported. The relative merit of competing opinions, theories, and contentions is primarily a function of the interaction between the characteristics of an individual and the psychological demands of items in an intelligence test. It is also a function of the stimulus and response requirements of the items.

There are many kinds of "nonverbal" behavior samples. A test might require children to point to objects in response to directions read by the examiner, to build block towers, to manipulate colored blocks in order to reproduce a design, or to copy symbols or designs on paper. Similarly, there are many kinds of "verbal" behavior samples. We could, for example, ask children factual questions, like "Who wrote *Huckleberry Finn?*" We could ask them to define words or to identify similarities and differences in words or objects. We could ask children to state actions they would take in specific social situations or ask them to repeat sequences of digits. Test items may be presented orally, or the test takers may have to read the items themselves.

Similar behaviors may be assessed in different ways. In assessing vocabulary, for example, the examiner may ask children to define words, to name

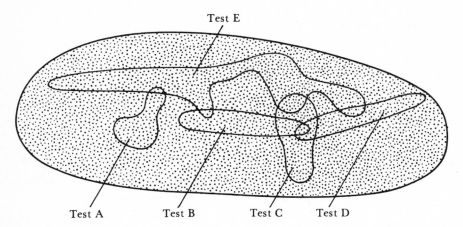

Figure **12.1**   Intelligence tests as samples of behavior from a larger domain of behaviors

pictures, to select a synonym of a stimulus word, or to point to pictures depicting words read by the examiner. All four kinds of assessments are called vocabulary tests, yet they sample *different* behaviors. The psychological demands of the items change with the ways the behavior is assessed.

In evaluating children's performances on intelligence tests, teachers, administrators, counselors, and diagnostic specialists must go beyond test names and scores to look at the kind or kinds of behaviors sampled on the test. They must be willing to question the ways test stimuli are presented to a child, to question the response requirements, and to evaluate the psychological demands placed on a child.

THE EFFECT OF PUPIL CHARACTERISTICS ON ASSESSMENT OF INTELLIGENCE

Acculturation is the most important characteristic in evaluating a child's performance on intelligence tests. *Acculturation,* as we have stated earlier, refers to a child's particular set of background experiences and opportunities to learn in both formal and informal educational settings. This, in turn, depends on the experiences available in the child's environment (that is, culture) and the length of time the child has had to assimilate those experiences. The culture in which a child lives and the length of time that child has lived in that culture effectively determine the psychological demands a test item presents. Simply knowing the kind of behavior sampled by a test is not enough, for the same test item may create different psychological demands for different children.

Suppose, for example, that we assess intelligence by asking children to tell how hail and sleet are alike. Children may fail the item for very different reasons. A child who does not know what hail and sleet are stands little chance of telling how hail and sleet are alike. He will fail the item simply because he does not know the meanings of the words. Another child may know what hail is and what sleet is but fail the item because she is unable to integrate these two words into a conceptual category (precipitation). The psychological demand of the item changes as a function of the children's acculturation. For the child who has not learned the meanings of the words, the item assesses vocabulary. For the child who knows the meanings of the words, the item is a generalization task.

In considering children's performance on intelligence tests, we need to know how acculturation affects test performance. Items on intelligence tests range along a continuum from items that sample fundamental psychological behaviors relatively unaffected by learning history to items that sample primarily learned behavior. To determine exactly what is being assessed, we need to know the essential background of the child. Consider for a moment the following item from the 11-year level of the 1972 Stanford-Binet Intelligence Scale:

Donald went walking in the woods. He saw a pretty little animal that he tried to take home for a pet. It got away from him, but when he got home his family immediately burned all his clothes. Why?[1]

For a student who knows what a skunk is and what a skunk does when approached by a person, the item can assess comprehension, abstract reasoning, and problem-solving skill. The student who does not know what a skunk is or what a skunk does may very well fail the item. In this case, failure is due not to an inability to comprehend or solve the problem but to a deficiency in background experience.

Similarly, we could ask a child to identify the seasons of the year. The experiences available in children's environments are reflected in the way they respond to this item. Children from central Illinois, who experience four discernibly different climatic conditions, may well respond, "Summer, fall, winter, and spring." Children from central Pennsylvania, who also experience four discernibly different climatic conditions but who live in an environment where hunting is prevalent, often respond, "Buck season, doe

1. From L. Terman and M. Merrill, *Stanford-Binet Intelligence Scale, 1972 norms edition* (Boston: Houghton Mifflin, 1973), pp. 98–99. Copyright © 1973 by Houghton Mifflin Company and reprinted with their permission.

season, rabbit season, and squirrel season." Response differences are a function of experiential differences. Within specific cultures, both responses are logical and appropriate; only one is *scored* as correct.

Intelligence-test items also sample different behaviors as a function of the age of the child assessed. Age and acculturation are positively related; older children in general have had more opportunities to acquire the skills assessed by intelligence tests. The performances of 5-year-old children on an item requiring them to tell how a cardinal, a bluejay, and a swallow are alike are almost entirely a function of their knowledge of the word meanings. Most college students know the meanings of the three words; for them the item assesses primarily their ability to identify similarities and integrate words or objects into a conceptual category. As children get older, they have increasing opportunity to acquire "the more abstruse elements of the collective intelligence of a culture" (Horn, 1965, p. 4).

The interaction between acculturation and the behavior sampled determines the psychological demands of an intelligence-test item. For this reason, it is impossible to define exactly what intelligence tests assess. *Identical test items actually place different psychological demands on different children.* Thirteen kinds of behaviors sampled by intelligence tests are described in the next section of this chapter. For the sake of illustration, let us assume that there are only three discrete sets of background experiences (this is a very conservative estimate; there are probably many times this number in the United States alone). To further simplify our example, let us consider only the thirteen kinds of behaviors sampled by intelligence tests rather than the millions of items that could be used to sample each of the thirteen kinds. With these very restrictive conditions, there are still $(mn)!/m!n!$ possible interactions between behavior samples and types of acculturation. This very restrictive estimate produces more than 1.35×10^{32} interactions! No wonder there is controversy about what intelligence tests measure. They measure more things than we can conceive of; they measure different things for different children.

BEHAVIORS SAMPLED BY INTELLIGENCE TESTS

Regardless of the interpretation of measured intelligence, it is a fact that intelligence tests simply sample behaviors. A description of the kinds of behaviors sampled follows.

DISCRIMINATION

Intelligence-test items that sample skill in discrimination usually present a variety of stimuli and ask the student to find the one that is different from all the others. Figural, symbolic, or semantic discrimination may be as-

Figural discrimination

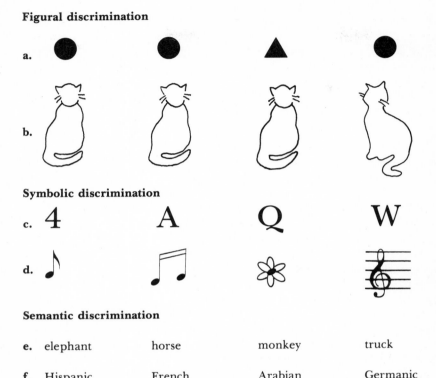

Symbolic discrimination

Semantic discrimination

e. elephant	horse	monkey	truck
f. Hispanic	French	Arabian	Germanic

Figure **12.2** Items that assess figural, symbolic, and semantic discrimination

sessed. Figure 12.2 illustrates items assessing discrimination: items a and b assess discrimination of figures; items c and d assess symbolic discrimination; items e and f assess semantic discrimination. In each case, the student must identify the item that is different from the others. The psychological demand of the items, however, differs depending on the student's age and particular set of background experiences.

GENERALIZATION

Items assessing generalization present a stimulus and ask the student to identify which of several response possibilities goes with the stimulus. Again, the content of the items may be figural, symbolic, or semantic, while the difficulty may range from simple matching to a more difficult type of classification. Figure 12.3 illustrates several items assessing generalization. In each case, the student is given a stimulus element and required to identify the one that is like it or that goes with it.

Figural generalization

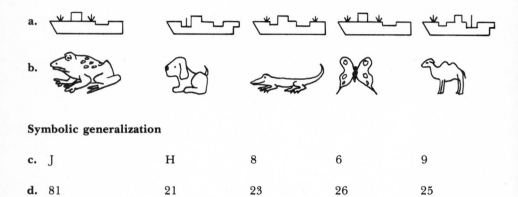

Symbolic generalization

c. J   H   8   6   9

d. 81   21   23   26   25

Semantic generalization

e. tree   car   man   house   walk

f. salvia   flashlight   frog   tulip   banana

Figure **12.3**   Items that assess figural, symbolic, and semantic generalization

MOTOR BEHAVIOR

Many items on intelligence tests require a motor response. The intellectual
level of very young children, for example, is often assessed by items requiring them to throw objects, walk, follow moving objects with their eyes,
demonstrate a pincer grasp in picking up objects, build block towers, and
place geometric forms in a recessed-form board. Most motor items at
higher age levels are actually visual-motor items. The student may be
required to copy geometric designs, trace paths through a maze, or recon-
struct designs from memory. Obviously, since motor responses can be
required for items assessing understanding and conceptualization, many
items assess motor behavior at the same time as they assess other behaviors.

GENERAL INFORMATION

Items on intelligence tests sometimes require a student to answer specific
factual questions, such as, "In what direction would you travel if you were
to go from Poland to Argentina?" and "What is the cube root of 8?"

Essentially, such items are like the kinds of items in achievement tests; they assess primarily what has been learned.

VOCABULARY

Many different kinds of test items are used to assess vocabulary. The student must name pictures in some cases and in others must point to objects in response to words read by the examiner. Some vocabulary items require the student to produce oral definitions of words, while others call for reading definitions and selecting one of several words to match the definition. Some tests score a student's definitions of words as simply pass or fail, while others use a weighted scoring system to reflect the degree of abstraction used in defining words. The Wechsler Intelligence Scale for Children—Revised, for example, assigns zero points to incorrect definitions, one point to definitions that are descriptive (an orange is round) or functional (an orange is to eat), and two points to more abstract definitions (an orange is a citrus fruit).

INDUCTION

Induction items present a series of examples and require the student to induce a governing principle. For example, the student is given a magnet and several different cloth, wooden, and metal objects and is asked to try to pick up the objects with the magnet. After several trials the student is asked to state a governing rule or principle about the kinds of objects magnets can pick up.

COMPREHENSION

There are three kinds of items used to assess comprehension. The student gives evidence of comprehension of directions, printed material, or societal customs and mores. In some instances, the examiner presents a specific situation and asks what actions the student would take (for example, "What would you do if you saw a train approaching a washed-out bridge?"). In other cases, the examiner reads paragraphs to a student and then asks specific questions about the content of the paragraphs. In still other instances, the student is asked specific questions like "Why should we keep promises?"

SEQUENCING

Items assessing sequencing consist of a series of stimuli that have a progressive relationship among them, and the student must identify a response

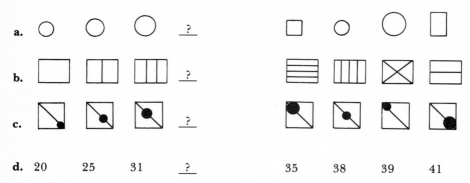

Figure 12.4   Items that assess sequencing skill

that continues the relationship. Four sequencing items are illustrated in Figure 12.4.

DETAIL RECOGNITION

In general, not many tests or test items assess detail recognition. Those that do evaluate the completeness and detail with which a student solves problems. For example, certain drawing tests, such as the Goodenough-Harris, evaluate a student's drawings of a person on the basis of inclusion of detail. The more details in a student's drawing, the more credit the student earns. In other instances, items require a student to count the blocks in pictured piles of blocks in which some of the blocks are not directly visible, to copy geometric designs, or to identify missing parts in pictures. To do so correctly, the student must attend to detail in the stimulus drawings and reflect this attention to detail in making responses.

ANALOGIES

"A is to B as C is to ___" is the usual form for analogies items. Element A is related to element B. The student must identify the response that has the same relationship to C as B has to A. Figure 12.5 illustrates several different analogies items.

ABSTRACT REASONING

A variety of items on intelligence tests sample abstract reasoning ability. The Stanford-Binet Intelligence Scale, for example, presents absurd verbal statements and pictures and asks the student to identify the absurdity. It also includes a series of proverbs whose essential meanings the student

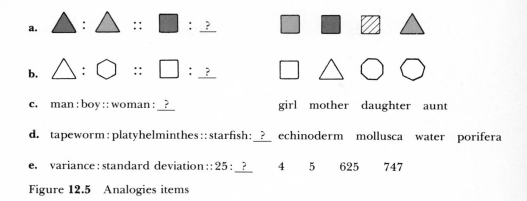

a. man : boy :: woman : _?_   girl   mother   daughter   aunt

d. tapeworm : platyhelminthes :: starfish: _?_ echinoderm   mollusca   water   porifera

e. variance : standard deviation :: 25 : _?_   4   5   625   747

Figure **12.5**   Analogies items

must state. In the Stanford-Binet and other scales, arithmetic-reasoning problems are often thought to assess abstract reasoning.

MEMORY

Several different kinds of tasks assess memory: repetition of sequences of orally presented digits, reproduction of geometric designs from memory, verbatim repetition of sentences, and reconstruction of the essential meaning of paragraphs or stories. Simply saying an item assesses memory is too simplistic. We need to ask, "Memory for what?" The psychological demand of a memory task changes in relation to both the method of assessment and the meaningfulness of the material to be recalled.

PATTERN COMPLETION

Some tests and test items require a student to select from several possibilities the one that supplies the missing part of a pattern or matrix. Figures 12.6 and 12.7 illustrate two different completion items. The item in Figure 12.6 requires identification of a missing part in a pattern. The item in Figure 12.7 calls for identification of the response that completes the matrix by continuing the horizontal, vertical, and diagonal sequences.

SUMMARY

The practice of intellectual assessment of children is currently marked with controversy. However, much of that controversy could be set aside if intelligence tests were viewed appropriately. Intelligence tests are simply samples of behavior. And different intelligence tests sample different

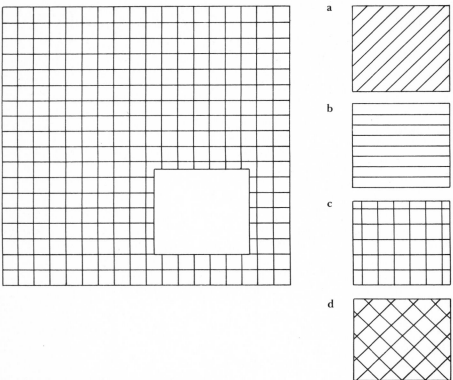

Figure 12.6 A pattern-completion item

behaviors. For that reason, it is wrong to speak of a person's IQ. Instead, we can refer only to a person's IQ on a specific test. An IQ on the Stanford-Binet Intelligence Scale is not derived from the same samples of behaviors as an IQ on any other intelligence test. Because the behavior samples are different for different tests, one must always ask, "IQ *on what test?*"

The same test may make different psychological demands on test takers, depending on their ages and acculturation. Test results mean different things for different students. It is imperative that we be especially aware of the relationship between a person's acculturation and the acculturation of the normative group to which that person is compared.

Used appropriately, intelligence tests can provide information that can lead to enhancement of individual opportunity and protection of the rights of students. Used inappropriately, they can restrict opportunity and rights. Chapter 23 includes a discussion of both abuses and appropriate uses of intelligence tests.

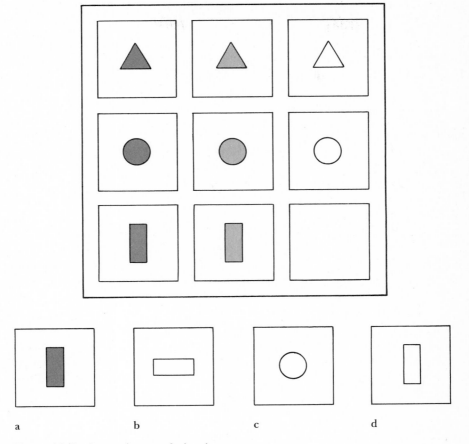

Figure **12.7** A matrix-completion item

The next two chapters review commonly used group-administered and individually administered intelligence tests, with particular reference to the kinds of behaviors sampled by those tests and their technical adequacy.

STUDY QUESTIONS

1. How would you demonstrate that a particular test item measured intelligence?

2. Describe at least three kinds of behaviors sampled by intelligence tests.

3. Bill Jones fails an item requiring him to state the difference between an optimist and a pessimist. Give two explanations for Bill's failure.

4. The school psychologist tells you that Emily Andrews has an IQ of 89. What additional information do you need before you are able to know the meaning of the score?

5. Using the categorization of behavior samplings described in this chapter, identify the kind or kinds of behaviors sampled by the following test items.

    a. How many legs does an octopus have?

    b. In what way are *first* and *last* alike?

    c. Find the one that is different:

       (1) table   (2) bed   (3) pillow   (4) chair

    d. Who wrote *Macbeth?*

    e. Window is to sill as door is to _____.

       (1) knob   (2) entrance   (3) threshold   (4) pane

    f. Define: *hieroglyphic.*

    g. Identify the one that comes next: 3, 6, 9, ___.

       (1) 12   (2) 11   (3) 18   (4) 15

6. Public Law 94-142 requires nondiscriminatory assessment of handicapped children. How can you demonstrate that a test is nondiscriminatory?

ADDITIONAL READING

Anastasi, A., & Cordova, F. A. Some effects of bilingualism upon the intelligence test performance of Puerto Rican children in New York City. *Journal of Educational Psychology,* 1953, *44*, 1–19.

Bersoff, D. N. Silk purses into sows' ears: The decline of psychological testing and a suggestion for its redemption. *American Psychologist,* 1973, *28*, 892–899.

Bouchard, T. Current conceptions of intelligence and their implications for assessment. In P. McReynolds (ed.), *Advances in Psychological Assessment,* vol. 1. Palo Alto: Science and Behavior Books, 1968, 14–33.

Cancro, R. (ed.) *Intelligence: Genetic and environmental contributions.* New York: Grune and Stratton, 1971.

Cronbach, L. J. Five decades of public controversy over mental testing. *American Psychologist,* 1975, *30*, 1–14.

Guilford, J. P. *The nature of human intelligence.* New York: McGraw-Hill, 1967.

Matarazzo, J. D. *Wechsler's measurement and appraisal of adult intelligence* (5th ed.). Baltimore: Williams and Wilkins, 1972.

McClelland, D. Testing for competence rather than for "intelligence." *American Psychologist,* 1973, 1–14.

Sattler, J. M. *Assessment of children's intelligence.* Philadelphia: W. B. Saunders, 1974. (Chapter 2: Historical survey and theories of intelligence, pp. 6–14. Chapter 2: Issues related to the measurement of intelligence, pp. 16–23.)

Chapter 13

Assessment of Intelligence: Individual Tests

In Chapter 12 we discussed the various kinds of behaviors sampled by intelligence tests, indicating that different tests sample different behaviors. In this chapter we will review the most commonly used individually administered intelligence tests with special reference to the kinds of behaviors they sample and their technical adequacy.

Few individual intelligence tests can or should be administered by classroom teachers. You will recall that one of the basic assumptions underlying psychoeducational assessment is that the person who uses tests is adequately trained to administer, score, and interpret them. The correct administration, scoring, and interpretation of individual intelligence tests is complex. Such tests should be used only by licensed or certified psychologists, who have specific training in their use.

Individually administered intelligence tests are most frequently used for making educational placement decisions. State special-education standards typically specify that the collection of data about intellectual functioning must be included in the decision-making process for placement decisions and that these data must come from individual intellectual evaluation by a certified psychologist.

Three kinds of individually administered intelligence tests are reviewed in this chapter. First, we review the most commonly used global measures of intelligence — the Stanford-Binet Intelligence Scale, the three Wechsler scales, the Slosson Intelligence Test, and the McCarthy Scales of Children's Abilities. In general, these tests sample the thirteen different kinds of behavior described in Chapter 12.

The second section of this chapter reviews the most commonly used picture vocabulary tests, instruments that assess receptive vocabulary but yield IQs.

Many children have handicaps (for example, blindness, deafness, and physical handicaps) that interfere with their capability to respond to traditional general intelligence tests. This fact has led several test authors to develop individually administered tests designed to assess the intelligence of blind, deaf, physically handicapped, and multiply handicapped persons. In a sense, the old adage "Necessity is the mother of invention" applies to these devices. The third section of this chapter reviews individually administered tests designed for use with special populations of children.

GENERAL INTELLIGENCE TESTS

STANFORD-BINET INTELLIGENCE SCALE

The Stanford-Binet Intelligence Scale is the grandfather of all intelligence tests. The original Binet scales were developed by Alfred Binet in 1905 following a request by the Minister of Public Instruction in Paris, France, to devise a method of differentiating between normal and mentally retarded children. Binet, in collaboration with Theodore Simon, constructed the Binet-Simon scale. In 1908 the scale was revised by grouping items according to age and the concept of *mental age* (MA) was introduced. The Binet-Simon scale was subsequently revised in 1911. In 1916 Louis Terman revised and extended the scale for use in the United States, entitling it the Stanford Revision and Extension of the Binet-Simon Intelligence Scale (Sattler, 1974).

The 1960 version of the Stanford-Binet Intelligence Scale was still an age scale; items were grouped according to age level (that is, an item at the 10-year level is typically answered correctly by the majority of 10-year-olds). The 1972 normative edition of the Stanford-Binet (Terman & Merrill, 1973) is the third revision of the test that was developed in 1916 and revised in 1937 and 1960. The current edition of the Stanford-Binet was developed by renorming the 1960 edition.

In the process of renorming, a chief characteristic of the 1960 scale, placement of items in terms of the age of children passing the items, was lost. In the 1960 edition and in earlier editions, an item was placed, for example, at the 8-year level because the majority of 8-year-old children responded correctly to the item. In renorming the test, the placement of items was not changed, but the proportion of children passing the items did change. Salvia, Ysseldyke, and Lee (1975) discussed the potential difficulties for interpretation resulting from norm changes without changing test content. They illustrated that an average 10-year, 11-month-old child earned a mental age of 10 years, 11 months, on the 1960 Binet; but the "average" 10-year, 11-month-old child earned a mental age of 11 years, 5 months on the 1974 edition. In other words, renorming has produced a test in which children must perform above age level to earn average IQs; the items are no longer appropriately "age-placed."

The Stanford-Binet includes items ranging in difficulty from the 2-year level to the superior-adult level, but characterization of the kinds of behaviors sampled is difficult. Behavior samples change as a function of age; a variety of behaviors are sampled at each age level, and some behaviors are sampled at several age levels. In general, the Stanford-Binet stresses verbal skills and responses, although items at the early age levels require predominantly motor responses. The Binet probably represents the best cross-section of the behavior samples described and discussed in Chapter 12. Except for very young children (those 2 to 5 years of age), all thirteen behaviors discussed in Chapter 12 are sampled either singly or in combination in the assessment of intelligence. Several systems have been developed to classify the kinds of behaviors sampled by the Stanford-Binet. Meeker (1969) used Guilford's (1967) "Structure of the Intellect" model to classify items on the Stanford-Binet. Sattler (1965) presented a classification system which identifies seven types of items: language, memory, conceptual thinking, reasoning, numerical reasoning, visual-motor, and social intelligence. Valett (1964) classified Stanford-Binet items into six categories: general comprehension, visual-motor ability, arithmetic reasoning, memory and concentration, vocabulary and verbal fluency, and judgment and reasoning. The three classification systems were developed in an effort to simplify interpretation of the Stanford-Binet. Similarly, although never formally done, items could be classified on the basis of the thirteen kinds of behavior samplings described in Chapter 12.

Scores

Two scores, an MA and a deviation IQ ($\overline{X} = 100$, $S = 16$), are obtained from the Stanford-Binet. Only those items between a basal and a ceiling are administered to each individual. A *basal* is defined as "that level at which all tests are passed which just precedes the level where the first failure occurs" (Terman & Merrill, 1973, p. 60). A *ceiling* is defined as the maximal level of the test, the lowest age level at which an individual fails all items. A specified number of months' credit is earned for each item passed. It is assumed that an individual passes all items below the basal and fails all items above the ceiling. The number of months' credit is added to get a mental age. Tables in the test manual are used to convert MAs to deviation IQs.

Norms

The 1972 normative edition of the Stanford-Binet was standardized on approximately 2,100 subjects. A "representative sample" of approximately one hundred individuals was tested at each Stanford-Binet age level. The publisher of the Stanford-Binet had previously standardized the Cognitive Abilities Test. The scores earned on the Cognitive Abilities Test were used as the principal stratifying variable in selection of the standardization sample for the Stanford-Binet. The Cognitive Abilities Test was originally standardized on 20,000 subjects per grade, selected on the basis of community size, geographic region, and socioeconomic status. The Cognitive Abilities Test, however, had been standardized only on subjects in grades 3 through 12. In order to get subjects younger than 8 and older than 17 for the Binet standardization, siblings of those in the larger standardization group were selected.

There are no data in the 1973 Stanford-Binet manual identifying the demographic characteristics of subjects in the new normative sample. The test was standardized in only seven communities.

Reliability

There are no data regarding the reliability of the 1972 Stanford-Binet. There is an implicit assumption that the 1972 normative edition is reliable because earlier editions of the test are reliable. Internal-consistency data are reported for the 1960 Stanford-Binet, a revision based on selection of items from the 1937 edition. Reliability of the Stanford-Binet is still based on the performances of individuals in 1937.

Validity

Validity data are also lacking for the 1972 normative edition. Once again, there is an assumption that the 1972 Stanford-Binet is valid because earlier editions were valid.

Summary

Although the Stanford-Binet has often been acclaimed as *the* intelligence test, the most recent edition of the test has questionable merit. The device has a long history and has been generally well accepted. However, the 1972 edition was standardized on subjects never adequately described in the manual. There are no reliability or validity data included in the manual for the 1972 normative edition. In our opinion, the authors of the Stanford-Binet need to provide sufficient data about the new edition in order to warrant the continued faith that professionals place in this device.

THE WECHSLER SCALES

Three different measures of intelligence have been constructed by David Wechsler. Wechsler summarized his views on the concept of intelligence by stating that "intelligence is the overall capacity of an individual to understand and cope with the world around him" (Wechsler, 1974, p. 5). Wechsler states that his definition of intelligence differs from the conceptions of others in two important respects:

(1) It conceives of intelligence as an overall or *global* entity; that is, a multidetermined and multifaceted entity rather than an independent, uniquely defined trait.
(2) It avoids singling out any ability (e.g., abstract reasoning), however esteemed as crucial or overwhelmingly important. In particular, it avoids equating general intelligence with intellectual ability.   (p. 5)

The original Wechsler scale, the Wechsler-Bellevue Intelligence Scale (1939), designed to assess the intelligence of adults, was revised in 1955 and called the Wechsler Adult Intelligence Scale (WAIS). In 1949, Wechsler developed the Wechsler Intelligence Scale for Children (WISC). This scale was revised and restandardized in 1974; its present form is called the Wechsler Intelligence Scale for Children—Revised (WISC–R). In 1967, Wechsler developed a downward extension of the WISC, the Wechsler Preschool and Primary Scale of Intelligence (WPPSI). Although the three scales are similar in form and content, they are distinct scales designed for use with persons at different age levels. The WAIS is designed to be used with individuals over 16 years of age; the WISC–R is designed to assess the intelligence of persons 6 through 16 years of age; the WPPSI is used with children ages 4 through 6½. All three scales are point scales; all three include both verbal and performance subtests. Subtests of the three Wechsler scales are summarized in Table 13.1.

Although the Wechsler scales differ in terms of age-level appropriateness, they sample similar behaviors. Descriptions of the behaviors sampled by each of the verbal and performance subtests follows; differences in format among the three scales are noted where appropriate.

Information   The Information subtest assesses ability to answer specific factual questions. The content is learned; it consists of information that a person is expected to have acquired in both formal and informal educational settings.

Comprehension   The Comprehension subtest assesses ability to comprehend verbal directions or to understand specific customs and mores.

Similarities   This subtest requires identification of similarities or commonalities in superficially unrelated verbal stimuli.

Arithmetic   This subtest assesses ability to solve problems requiring the application of arithmetic operations. Individual items range from relatively simple counting tasks on the WPPSI to more conceptually and computationally difficult problems on the WISC–R and the WAIS.

Vocabulary   Items on the vocabulary subtest assess ability to define words.

Digit Span   This subtest assesses immediate recall of orally presented digits.

Sentences   This subtest is included only in the WPPSI. It assesses ability to repeat sentences verbatim.

Picture Completion   This subtest assesses the ability to identify missing parts in pictures.

Table **13.1**   Subtests of the Three Wechsler Scales

	WAIS	WISC–R	WPPSI
Verbal subtests			
Information	X	X	X
Comprehension	X	X	X
Similarities	X	X	X
Arithmetic	X	X	X
Vocabulary	X	X	X
Digit Span	X	S[b]	
Sentences			S
Performance subtests			
Picture Completion	S	X	X
Picture Arrangement	X	X	
Block Design	X	X	X
Object Assembly	X	X	
Coding[a]	X	X	X
Mazes		S	X
Geometric Design			X

[a] Called Digit Symbol on the WAIS and Animal House on the WPPSI.
[b] S's in the table indicate that although the subtest is included in the scale, it is considered a supplementary subtest and was not used in establishing IQ tables.

Picture Arrangement   The Picture Arrangement subtest assesses comprehension, sequencing, and identification of relationships by requiring a person to place pictures in sequence to produce a logically correct story.

Block Design   This subtest assesses ability to manipulate blocks in order to reproduce a visually presented stimulus design.

Object Assembly   This subtest assesses ability to place disjointed puzzle pieces together to form complete objects.

Coding   This subtest assesses the ability to associate certain symbols with others and to copy them on paper. The WPPSI uses the Animal House subtest in place of the Coding subtest. Instead of copying symbols on paper, the child must associate certain colored cubes with specific animals and match them.

Mazes The Mazes subtest assesses ability to trace a path through progressively more difficult mazes.

Geometric Design This subtest assesses ability to copy geometric designs. It appears on only the WPPSI.

Scores

Raw scores obtained on the three Wechsler scales are transformed to scaled scores with a mean of 10 and a standard deviation of 3. The scaled scores for verbal subtests, performance subtests, and all subtests combined are added and then transformed to obtain verbal, performance, and full-scale IQs. IQs for the Wechsler scales are deviation IQs with a mean of 100 and a standard deviation of 15. For the WPPSI and the WISC-R, but not for the WAIS, raw scores may be transformed to test ages. Test ages represent the average performance on each of the subtests by individuals of specific ages.

The Wechsler intelligence scales employ a differential scoring system for some of the subtests. Responses for the Information, Digit Span, Sentences, Picture Completion, and Geometric Designs subtests are scored pass-fail. A weighted scoring system is used for the Comprehension, Similarities, and Vocabulary subtests. Incorrect responses receive a score of zero, lower-level or lower-quality responses a score of one, while more abstract responses are assigned a score of two. The remainder of the subtests are timed. Individuals who complete the tasks in relatively short periods of time receive more credit. These differential weightings of responses must be given special consideration, especially when the timed tests are used with children who demonstrate motoric impairments that interfere with the speed of response.

Norms

All three Wechsler intelligence scales were standardized by selecting stratified samples and having individual examiners around the country administer the tests to specified kinds of individuals. The standardization of the WAIS was "based on groups considered representative of United States adults" (Wechsler, 1955, p. 5). A stratified sampling plan based on age, sex, geographic region, urban-rural residence, race, occupation, and education was used. Proportions of specific kinds of individuals were included commensurate with their representation in the 1950 census. The WAIS was standardized on 1,700 adults, and extensive tables in the manual compare the percentage of the U.S. population to the percentage of specific kinds of individuals in the norms.

The WISC-R was standardized on 2,200 children of ages $6\frac{1}{2}$ to $16\frac{1}{2}$. The standardization group was stratified on the basis of age, sex, race, geographic region, occupation of head of household, and urban-rural residence according to 1970 U.S. census information.

The WPPSI was standardized on 1,200 children stratified according to the 1960 census on the basis of age, sex, geographic region, urban-rural residence, "color," and father's occupation.

Reliability

Internal-consistency reliability is reported for the WAIS, WISC–R, and WPPSI in the forms of split-half reliability coefficients. The reliabilities differ for the specific subtests and the age levels on which the coefficients are based. Ranges of reliability are reported for the three scales in Table 13.2. Reliabilities for the separate subtests are reliabilities of scaled scores while reliabilities for verbal, performance, and full-scale IQs are reliabilities for the IQs. Reliabilities for the Digit Symbol (coding) subtest on the WAIS are alternate-form reliabilities, while those for the Digit Span and Coding subtest of the WISC–R and the Coding subtest (Animal House) of the WPPSI are test-retest reliabilities. Test-retest reliabilities are reported for all subtests of the WISC–R in the test manual and range from .63 to .95.

Validity

The validity of the WAIS was established by correlating the scores earned by fifty-two white male adult residents of a New Jersey Reformatory with their scores on the Stanford-Binet Intelligence Scale. Correlations of the verbal, performance, and full-scale IQs with performance on the Stanford-Binet were .86, .69, and .85 respectively. In all cases the mean IQs earned on the WAIS were lower than the mean IQ earned on the Stanford-Binet.

Three concurrent validity studies were used to ascertain the relationship between performance on the WISC–R and on other measures of intelligence. In the first study, fifty 6-year-old children were administered both the WISC–R and the WPPSI. The WISC–R full-scale IQ and the WPPSI full-scale IQ had a .82 correlation. Individual verbal subtests correlated more highly with the WPPSI verbal IQ than with the WPPSI performance IQ. Similarly, individual performance subtests correlated more highly with the WPPSI performance IQ than with the WPPSI verbal IQ. In a second study, forty children aged 16 years, 11 months, were given the WISC–R and the WAIS; the full-scale IQs on the two devices had a .95 correlation. Verbal IQs on the two devices were intercorrelated .96; performance IQs, .83. A third study was conducted to compare performance on the WISC–R with performance on the Stanford-Binet Intelligence Scale. Small samples of children (twenty-seven to thirty-three) at four ages were given both tests.

Table **13.2** Split-half Reliabilities for Subtests of the Three
Wechsler Scales

	WAIS	WISC–R	WPPSI
Verbal subtests			
Information	.91–.92	.67–.90	.77–.84
Comprehension	.77–.79	.69–.87	.78–.84
Similarities	.85–.87	.74–.87	.82–.85
Arithmetic	.79–.86	.69–.81	.78–.86
Vocabulary	.94–.96	.70–.92	.72–.87
Digit Span	.66–.71	.71–.84[b]	—
Sentences	—	—	.81–.88
Verbal IQ	.96	.91–.96	.93–.95
Performance subtests			
Picture Completion	.82–.85	.68–.85	.81–.86
Picture Arrangement	.60–.74	.69–.78	—
Block Design	.82–.86	.80–.90	.76–.88
Object Assembly	.65–.71	.63–.76	—
Coding	.92[a]	.63–.80[b]	.62–.84[b]
Mazes	—	.62–.82	.82–.91
Geometric Design	—	—	.77–.87
Performance IQ	.93–.94	.89–.91	.91–.95
Full-scale IQ	.97	.95–.96	.96–.97

[a] Alternate-form reliability.
[b] Test-retest reliability.

Average correlations between Stanford-Binet IQs and WISC–R verbal, performance, and full-scale IQs were .71, .60, and .73 respectively.

Summary

The three Wechsler intelligence scales are widely used individually administered intelligence tests. Although they are designed for different age levels, the three scales are similar in content and format. For the most part, the devices are technically adequate. Evidence for reliability is good, while the limited evidence available indicates that the devices have satisfactory validity. Examiners who want to assess the intellectual capability of children and adults must be willing to go beyond the more global verbal, performance, and full-scale scores provided to look at individual performances on the specific subtests.

SLOSSON INTELLIGENCE TEST

The Slosson Intelligence Test (SIT) (Slosson, 1971) is a relatively short screening test designed to evaluate mental ability. The test is a Binet-type scale and actually includes many items that appear in the Stanford-Binet Intelligence Scale. The test is designed to be administered by teachers, guidance counselors, principals, psychologists, school nurses, and "other responsible persons who, in their professional work, often need to evaluate an individual's mental ability" (p. iii). The author does not report an age range for individuals who may be tested with the Slosson. Items range from the .5-month level to the 27-year level. Apparently, the author believes the test is appropriate for nearly anyone, as there are directions in the manual about testing infants, those who have "reading handicaps" or "language handicaps," the blind, the hard of hearing, those with organic brain damage, the emotionally disturbed, and the "deprived."

Behaviors sampled by the Slosson include most of the behaviors described and discussed in Chapter 12.

Scores

The raw score on the SIT is an age score. As on the Stanford-Binet, an individual earns a specific number of months' credit for each item answered correctly. Only those items between a basal and a ceiling are administered. The age score can be transformed into a ratio IQ. Data for validity indicate that the SIT has different means and standard deviations at different age levels. Means for the test range from 91.7 at age 15 to 114.6 at age 4. Standard deviations range from 16.7 at age 17 to 31.2 at age 18 and older. Data about the reliability of the scale indicate that across ages the mean IQs for two administrations of the SIT were 99.0 and 101.3, while standard deviations were 24.7 and 25.1.

Norms

The normative sample for the SIT consisted of a potpourri of individuals who are described by Slosson (1971) as follows:

The children and adults used in obtaining comparative results came from both urban and rural populations in New York State. The referrals came from cooperative nursery schools, public, parochial and private schools, from junior and senior high school. They came from gifted as well as retarded classes — white, negro, and some American Indian. Some came from a city Youth Bureau, some from a Home for Boys. The very young children resided in an infant home. The adults came from the general population, from various professional groups, from a university graduate school, from a state school for the retarded and from a county jail.

Many of these individuals were difficult to test as they were disturbed, negativistic, withdrawn, and many had reading difficulties. Some suffered from neurological disorders or other defects. The only cases which were excluded from this study were individuals who could not speak English. (p. iv)

The description of the normative sample is as inadequate as was the sample. Given the author's information, users of the test have no idea to whom they are comparing those they test.

Reliability

The author reports that a test-retest reliability coefficient of .97 was obtained over a two-month interval on 139 individuals ranging in age from 4 to 50 years. This sampling procedure allows true-score variance and chronological-age variance to be confounded. Thus, the reliability coefficient may be spuriously high. No other reliability data are reported.

Validity

Validity data for the SIT consist of correlations of scores earned on the test with scores earned on the Stanford-Binet. The correlations are high (ranging from .90 to .98), but this is really to be expected since the two tests contain so many items in common. Moreover, since the means and standard deviations vary so greatly at different ages, the SIT cannot be used interchangeably with the Stanford-Binet, even though they are highly correlated.

Summary

The Slosson Intelligence Test is an individually administered device designed to serve as a screening instrument in the assessment of mental ability. It is a widely used device and is permitted by some states to be used in making placement decisions for exceptional children. The test was standardized on an unspecified sample, and information about its technical adequacy is limited. The test provides a broad sample of behaviors, but those who use it are cautioned to be particularly aware of its large and variable standard deviation.

MCCARTHY SCALES OF CHILDREN'S ABILITIES

The McCarthy Scales of Children's Abilities (MSCA) (McCarthy, 1972) were designed to evaluate children's (ages 2½ to 8½) general intellectual level as well as their strengths and weaknesses in a number of ability areas. The test consists of eighteen subtests that make up six scales: Verbal, Perceptual-Performance, Quantitative, Memory, Motor, and General Cognitive. The General Cognitive scale is a composite of the Verbal, Perceptual-Performance, and Quantitative scales. The interrelationships among the eighteen separate subtests and the six scales are shown in Figure 13.1.

The behaviors sampled by the subtests are described by the author as follows.

Block Building Children copy four structures that the examiner has constructed. The author suggests that these items provide an opportunity to observe children's manipulative skills and perception of spatial relations.

Puzzle Solving In this subtest children are required to assemble puzzle pieces to form six common animals and foods. The items measure perceptual and motor skills as well as general cognition.

Pictorial Memory In this subtest children are shown a card with six pictured objects on it. The objects are named by the examiner, and children are then asked to recall what they saw. The test measures immediate memory, general cognition, and verbal ability.

Word Knowledge This subtest consists of two parts. In part 1 children are required to point to five common objects and name four additional objects shown to them on cards. Part 2 is an oral vocabulary test requiring children to define words.

Number Questions Children are given twelve questions requiring quantitative thinking and involving solution of addition, subtraction, multiplication, and division problems.

Tapping Sequence This subtest requires children to imitate the examiner's performance on a four-note xylophone. Memory, perceptual-motor coordination, and general cognition are said to be measured.

Verbal Memory This is a two-part test. Part 1 requires children to repeat words and sentences. Part 2 requires them to recall the highlights of a paragraph read by the examiner.

Right-Left Orientation Children are required to demonstrate knowledge of left and right with regard to their own bodies and then to demonstrate generalization of left and right to a picture of a boy. This subtest is not administered to children younger than 5.

Leg Coordination Items requiring children to engage in a variety of exercises, such as walking backwards and on tiptoe, are used to assess the maturity of leg coordination.

TEST	VERBAL	PERCEPTUAL-PERFORMANCE	QUANTI-TATIVE	GENERAL COGNITIVE	MEMORY	MOTOR

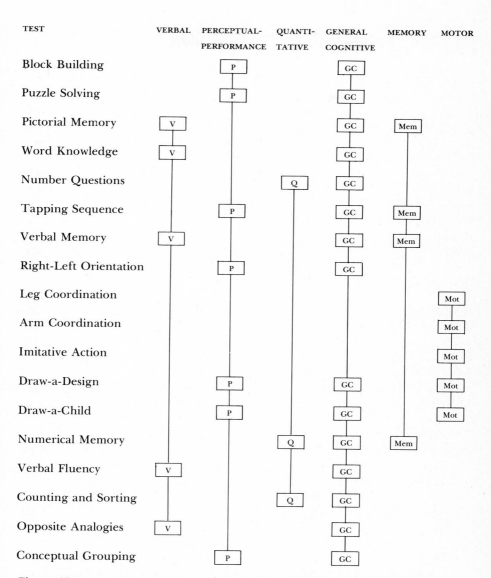

Figure **13.1** Interrelationship of the six scales and eighteen subtests of the MSCA. (Reproduced by permission from the Manual for the McCarthy Scales of Children's Abilities. Copyright © 1970, 1972 by The Psychological Corporation, New York, N.Y. All rights reserved.)

Arm Coordination   Development of the arms is assessed in a variety of gamelike activities.

Imitative Action   Eye preference is assessed by requiring children to sight through a plastic tube.

Draw-a-Design   Children are required to copy various geometric designs.

Draw-a-Child   This subtest requires males to draw a boy and females to draw a girl.

Numerical Memory   This subtest assesses immediate recall by requiring children to repeat sequences of digits both forward and backward.

Verbal Fluency   This subtest requires children to classify and think categorically. Children must name words that fall into each of four different categories within a time limit.

Counting and Sorting   Children are required to count blocks and to sort them into quantitative categories (for example, two piles with *the same* number).

Opposite Analogies   Children are required to provide opposites of key words in statements spoken by the examiner (for instance, "Milk is *cold,* but coffee is _____").

Conceptual Grouping   Children must manipulate from one to three variables to discover classification rules for problems.

All the directions for administering the test are extremely clear and specific. Procedures for scoring are clearly described; an eight-step procedure is outlined. Scores are described in language that teachers can easily understand.

Scores

Four kinds of scores are obtained on the MSCA: a general cognitive index, scale indexes, percentile ranks, and MA. The author states that the general cognitive index "is a scaled score; it is not a quotient" (p. 24). The score has a mean of 100 and a standard deviation of 16. Separate indexes are obtained for each of the other five major scales; they have a mean of 50 and a standard deviation of 10. Tables in the manual are used to transform scaled scores into percentile ranks and to provide estimated MAs for performance on the general cognitive scale.

Norms

The standardization of the MSCA was excellent. One hundred children at each of ten age levels participated in the standardization; the sample was stratified on the basis of sex, age, "color," geographic region, father's occupation, and urban-rural residence. Proportions in the normative sample approximate very closely the 1970 U.S. census data.

Reliability

Reliability data consist of internal-consistency coefficients for all but three subtests of the MSCA. For these three, internal-consistency estimates were viewed as inappropriate, and test-retest coefficients were computed. Reliability coefficients and standard errors of measurement for the six MSCA scales are reported in Table 13.3. Reliabilities for the Verbal and General Cognitive scales are excellent; coefficients for the other scales are lower.

Validity

Studies of both predictive and concurrent validity are reported in the manual. Thirty-one children were tested using the MSCA and then tested four months later using the Metropolitan Achievement Test. Correlations among the six scales of the MSCA and the six scales of the MAT were high for the Perceptual-Performance and Quantitative scales, mediocre for the General Cognitive Scale, and poor for the Verbal, Memory, and Motor scales. The last three MSCA scales had correlations averaging .15, .26, and .03 with the MAT. The author rightfully states that the results should be interpreted with caution because of the small size of the sample.

To establish concurrent validity, MSCA scores were correlated with scores obtained on the Stanford-Binet and the Wechsler Preschool and Primary Scale of Intelligence (WPPSI). The sample consisted of thirty-five white children (aged 6 to 6½) enrolled in a Catholic school in New York City. The obtained intercorrelations are reported in Table 13.4. The results lend some support to the concurrent validity of the MSCA.

Summary

In our opinion, it is only a matter of time before the MSCA becomes one of the most popular tests for assessing the abilities of preschool children. The tasks are interesting and enjoyable; the directions are clear; the standardization and reliability are excellent. Evidence about validity of the MSCA is still limited. Certain claims for the usefulness of the test with exceptional children appear unsubstantiated for two reasons: no exceptional children were included in the standardization, and there is no evidence for the validity of the scale with specific groups. The test does meet the majority of the standards of the American Psychological Association.

Table **13.3** Reliability Coefficients and Standard Errors of Measurement of the Six MSCA Scales, by Age, for the Standardization Sample

AGE IN YEARS	N	VERBAL		PERCEPTUAL-PERFORMANCE		QUANTI-TATIVE		GENERAL COGNITIVE		MEMORY		MOTOR	
		r	SEM	r	SEM	r	SEM	r	SEM	r	SEM	r	SEM
2½	102	.90	3.2	.76	4.8	.77	4.9	.93	4.2	.78	4.6	.84	4.0
3	104	.89	3.2	.87	3.6	.82	4.2	.94	3.8	.73	5.0	.82	4.2
3½	100	.92	2.8	.90	3.2	.83	4.2	.96	3.4	.83	4.1	.84	4.1
4	102	.90	3.2	.86	3.6	.78	5.3	.91	4.7	.83	4.0	.78	4.6
4½	104	.88	3.5	.89	3.3	.79	4.6	.94	3.8	.74	5.0	.84	4.1
5	102	.87	3.6	.87	3.7	.86	3.7	.94	3.9	.78	4.9	.82	4.3
5½	104	.87	3.5	.84	3.9	.86	3.7	.93	4.2	.72	5.3	.80	4.5
6½	104	.84	3.9	.77	4.7	.80	4.3	.90	5.0	.84	4.0	.69	5.5
7½	104	.90	3.3	.84	4.1	.82	4.1	.94	3.9	.83	4.0	.75	5.1
8½	106	.86	3.7	.75	5.0	.83	4.2	.92	4.5	.82	4.3	.60	6.2
AVERAGE AND SEM FOR THE 10 AGE GROUPS[a]		.88	3.4	.84	4.0	.81	4.3	.93	4.1	.79	4.5	.79	4.7

NOTE: The reliability coefficients presented here are based on split-half correlations corrected by the Spearman-Brown formula for the component tests, except for the Memory tests, Right-Left Orientation, and Draw-a-Child, for which that method was inappropriate. For these, test-retest correlations, based on smaller groups and corrected for restriction of range, were used in the computation of Scale reliability coefficients (Guilford, 1954, pp. 392–393).

The standard errors of measurement are in GCI units for the General Cognitive Scale, and in Scale Index units for the other five Scales. . . . Standard deviations . . . were used to compute the standard errors of measurement.

[a] The average coefficients were obtained by using Fisher's z transformation (Walker & Lev, 1953, p. 254).

SOURCE: Reproduced by permission from the Manual for the McCarthy Scales of Children's Abilities. Copyright © 1970, 1972 by The Psychological Corporation, New York, N.Y. All rights reserved.

Table **13.4**   Coefficients of Correlation Between MSCA Scale Indexes and IQs
Obtained on the Wechsler Preschool and Primary Scale of Intelligence (WPPSI)
and Stanford-Binet

MSCA SCALES	WPPSI IQ			STANFORD-BINET (FORM L-M) IQ	MSCA SCALE INDEX	
	VERBAL	PERFORM-ANCE	FULL-SCALE		MEAN	SD
Verbal	51	.43	.54	.66	52.5	8.2
Perceptual-Performance	.47	.59	.61	.70	53.4	10.3
Quantitative	.41	.27	.38	.41	50.0	8.4
General Cognitive	.63	.62	.71	.81	104.0	13.3
Memory	.42	.39	.46	.67	51.0	8.6
Motor	.02	.10	.07	.06	51.5	7.3
MEAN	106.7	104.6	106.3	115.5		
STANDARD DEVIATION	10.9	12.4	11.1	14.2		

NOTE: Intervals between the administration of the MSCA and each of the other tests ranged from three to twenty days. Testing order was counterbalanced. $N = 35$ first-grade children aged 6 to 6½.

SOURCE: Data reproduced by permission from the Manual for the McCarthy Scales of Children's Abilities. Copyright © 1970, 1972 by The Psychological Corporation, New York, N.Y. All rights reserved.

PICTURE VOCABULARY TESTS

A number of picture vocabulary tests are among the most widely used tests for assessment of children's intelligence. Before describing individual picture vocabulary tests, it is important to state what these devices measure. The tests are *not* measures of intelligence per se; rather, they measure only one aspect of intelligence, receptive vocabulary. Picture vocabulary tests present drawings to a child, who is asked to identify pictures corresponding to words read by the examiner. Some authors of picture vocabulary measures state that the tests measure receptive vocabulary; others equate receptive vocabulary with intelligence and claim that their tests assess intelligence. Because the tests measure only one aspect of intelligence, they should not be used to make placement decisions.

FULL-RANGE PICTURE VOCABULARY TEST

The Full-Range Picture Vocabulary Test (Ammons & Ammons, 1948) is designed to assess the "intelligence" of individuals from 2 years of age through adulthood. Materials for the test consist of thirteen plates with four pictures on each plate, a one-page manual, and an answer sheet with norms printed on the back. Directions for administering the test are complex. For each plate, there are words representing levels of performance. Point levels are assigned to each of the words on a given plate and "represent approximately the mental age at which fifty percent of a representative population would fail the word" (Ammons & Ammons, 1948, p. 1). Test takers are given words for individual cards until they pass three consecutive levels and fail three. However, three plates have only three words, while two plates have only two words. Administration is complicated; while there may be only three words for certain plates, the words may represent levels that are very disparate. The examiner must assume "hypothetical levels" for certain plates.

Scores

Although administration is based on levels completed, scoring is based on number of *items* answered correctly. A table of norms is used to transform raw scores to MAs. Interpolation is often necessary because MAs are not specified for all possible raw scores. The authors state that a Wechsler-like scale of IQs accompanies each test kit. The scale was not included in our specimen kit.

Norms

The authors of the FRPVT state that "the present norms are based on 589 representative cases from two years of age to adult level" (p. 1). There is no specification or description of the population on whom this test was standardized.

Reliability

The one-page manual for the FRPVT does not include reliability data. In the manual for the Quick Test (Ammons & Ammons, 1962), the authors of the FRPVT state that

critics of the FRPV not familiar with its widespread use and our extensive research program have implied or stated that the FRPV is "poorly standardized," etc. Actually, this is not at all the case. Rather, since shortly after the FRPV was made available for use, there has been so much research with it that we have not been able to keep up with the findings. One of the consequences of this widespread use has been that we have been unable to prepare a comprehensive manual, although many separate articles reporting various aspects of work with the FRPV have been published. In order to make sure that a QT manual would be published, we deliberately refrained from releasing the QT until this manual was ready, reporting all experience and known research to date. If our experience with the FRPV is any indication, we may never get caught up again. (p. i)

Validity

There is no evidence for the validity of the FRPVT.

Summary

The FRPVT and its accompanying manual violate the majority of the standards for educational and psychological tests published by the joint committee of the American Psychological Association, the American Educational Research Association, and the National Council on Measurement in Education.

QUICK TEST

The Quick Test (Ammons & Ammons, 1962) is described by its authors as the "little brother of the Full Range Picture Vocabulary Test (FRPV), one of the most widely used brief tests of intelligence" (p. i). There are three forms of the Quick Test, each consisting of one plate of four drawings and a series of words that the examiner reads. The child or adult taking the test is required to point to the picture that most nearly represents the meaning of the word read by the examiner. The authors state that the single forms of the Quick Test can be given in 2 minutes or less, that "it can be seen that the three forms of the QT are 'short forms' of the FRPV, which itself is a very brief, but highly reliable and valid, test of intelligence" (p. i).

Scores

Raw scores for the Quick Test consist of the number of correct responses between the basal and the ceiling. Raw scores may be transformed to MAs and ratio IQs for children and to deviation IQs ($\overline{X} = 100$, $S = 15$) for adults. Actually, seven MAs and seven IQs are obtained (for form 1, form 2, form 3, forms 1 and 2 combined, forms 1 and 3 combined, forms 2 and 3 combined, and forms 1, 2, and 3 combined).

Norms

The Quick Test was standardized on 458 white children and adults from geographically restricted areas (parts of Montana and Louisville, Kentucky). The authors state that they attempted to control for age, grade, occupation of parents, and sex. They state, "We did not attempt any geographical control for practical reasons and because previous work with the FRPV had indicated such control was very likely not important" (p. 121).

Reliability

Ten studies are cited in the Quick Test manual to support the contention that the test is reliable. All ten studies are equivalent-form reliability studies. There are no reported investigations of either internal-consistency or test-retest reliability. Equivalent-form reliabilities range from .60 to .96. Apparently, very disparate scores are often earned on the three forms of the Quick Test. The authors state:

From time to time, FRPV or QT users have written to us, quite disturbed to find a testee who has shown a difference of two or three years in mental age on different forms of the test. Relatively inexperienced testers are inclined to say that the test is at fault, which of course it may be. However, in most instances, these discrepancies are well within the range which would be expected from the standard error of a test score. The tester only notices the few very large discrepancies, disregarding the far more numerous times when performances have been very similar. The tester should note that almost never has a large discrepancy been found for a good-sized group. Discrepancies are usually due to peculiar performance on a few (one to three) items and may very well have clinical significance. (p. 137)

Since reliability and standard error of measurement are inversely related, we wonder how the authors can claim that the test is highly reliable and still dismiss large discrepancies as "within the range which would be expected from the standard error of a test score."

Validity

Validity data for the Quick Test consist of both concurrent and predictive data. Concurrent validity was studied by correlating performance on the Quick Test with performance on the FRPVT. Since the Quick Test is the "little brother" of the FRPVT, the reported correlations of .62 to .93 are not surprising.

Predictive validity was established by correlating performance on the Quick Test with school grades and scores on achievement tests. Intercorrelations with subtests of the Iowa Tests of Basic Skills ranged from .32 to .59.

Summary

The Quick Test is a very brief measure of verbal intelligence that may be appropriate as a screening device but has many limitations for use in decision making. Standardization was carried out in a geographically circumscribed area, evidence regarding reliability is limited to equivalent-form reliability, and validity evidence is still limited.

PEABODY PICTURE VOCABULARY TEST

The Peabody Picture Vocabulary Test (PPVT) (Dunn, 1965) is designed "to provide an estimate of a subject's *verbal intelligence* through measuring his hearing vocabulary" (p. 25). More correctly, it assesses receptive language. The test may be administered to persons between 2-6 and 18 years of age.

To administer the PPVT, the examiner shows a student a series of plates on which four pictures are drawn. The examiner then reads stimulus words, and the student points to the picture that best represents the stimulus word. The PPVT is available in forms A and B, which use the same plates but differ in the stimulus words and, therefore, the correct response. The PPVT is an untimed test and usually takes 10 to 15 minutes to administer.

Scores

The student's raw score is the number of correct pictures identified between the basal and ceiling items. Because the test employs a multiple-choice format, the basal is defined as the highest level at which the student makes eight consecutive correct responses, while a ceiling is defined as the point at which the student makes six errors in any eight consecutive items. Raw scores may be transformed to MAs, percentile ranks, and deviation IQs ($\overline{X} = 100$, $S = 15$).

Norms

The PPVT was standardized on 4,012 white people residing in or around Nashville, Tennessee. Several different procedures were used to select the normative sample. In selecting preschool children, the author examined scores earned by children in the Nashville Schools on the Kuhlmann-Finch Intelligence Tests (Finch, 1951). Four schools were identified; a composite of their scores produced a normal distribution. Preschool children in these four areas were then individually tested by four examiners.

The authors had data for 6-, 7-, and 8-year-old children who were attending four elementary schools. Metropolitan Readiness Test scores were available for children in grades 1 and 2, and Kuhlmann-Finch scores (Finch, 1951) were available for children in grade 3. Children were randomly selected until a normal distribution of scores on these other measures was attained. Children were individually tested.

Norms for students aged 9 through 18 were established by *group testing* all individuals. PPVT plates were projected on a screen, and an examiner read the words to the students.

The standardization of the PPVT has some serious limitations. Geographic and racial generalization are limited because of the restrictive nature of the sample. There are no data in the manual about other demographic characteristics of the sample. A test intended to be individually administered was standardized in part by group testing procedures. In essence, after a student's score on the PPVT is obtained and the test norms are used to transform that score to a standard score, the examiner is left with an interpretation of the student's performance relative to white children in Nashville, Tennessee.

Reliability

Alternate-form reliabilities for the PPVT were computed for each age level in the standardization sample and range from .67 to .84. The manual for the PPVT includes a summary of the findings of eleven separate reliability studies conducted between 1959 and 1964. Most were studies of alternate-form reliability, and the results were comparable to those obtained for the standardization sample. Four studies of test-retest reliability have produced mixed results. Reliabilities ranged from .54 to .88.

Validity

The author of the PPVT states that content validity of the test was insured by item selection. In the selection of items for the PPVT, *Webster's New Collegiate Dictionary* (Merriam, 1953) was searched for all words that could be represented by a picture. Dunn (1965) states that

since a good cross section was obtained of words in common use today in the United States, and since care was taken to keep the final selection of response and decoy items unbiased, the final product is assumed to meet adequate standards for a picture vocabulary test. (p. 32)

The results of thirty-three specific validity studies are reported in the manual. The results of those studies were mixed. Validity studies are reported for persons of average intellect, for institutionalized retardates, for the emotionally disturbed, for trainable retardates, and for speech-impaired, deaf, gifted, and visually limited persons. Dunn reports correlations of the PPVT with 1937 Stanford-Binet MAs ranging from .60 to .87 and with 1937 Stanford-Binet IQs ranging from .43 to .92. Correlations between the PPVT and WISC full-scale IQ scores ranged from .30 to .84.

The studies summarized in the PPVT manual reported concurrent-validity coefficients for the PPVT, as demonstrated by correlations with measures of academic achievement ranging from .04 to .91. Predictive-validity coefficients ranged from .22 to .43.

Summary

The PPVT is an individually administered test designed to measure verbal intelligence through receptive vocabulary. As such, it provides a measure of only one aspect of intelligence: receptive vocabulary. While the standardization of the PPVT was such that it has limited generalizability, overall its technical characteristics far surpass those of other picture vocabulary tests. Used properly and with awareness of its limitations, the PPVT can serve as an extremely useful screening device. Its danger is that inexperienced individuals may overgeneralize its utility.

SCALES FOR SPECIAL POPULATIONS

As noted in the introduction to this chapter, a variety of devices have been developed to assess the intellectual capability of people who have difficulty responding to traditional devices. Assessment of special populations is usually carried out by one of the three following practices.

1. *Adapting Test Items.*   In some cases, examiners change the procedures for administering an item to compensate for the handicaps of the person they are testing. Items normally timed are presented without time limits; verbal items are presented in pantomime; and so on. In such efforts, examiners often "forget" to consider the fact that the test is standardized using standardized procedures. If, as is usually the case, examiners use the published norms for the test, they may make inappropriate comparisons. The children on whom the test was standardized will have been tested using procedures *different* from those adapted procedures an examiner chooses to use.

2. *Using Response-fair Tests.*   In other cases, examiners select tests to which the person can respond with minimal difficulty. Some tests, for example, employ no verbal instructions and require no verbalized responses. Deaf persons *can* respond and items *can* be given to deaf persons. However, many of the tests that *can* be given are standardized on nonhandicapped persons. The acculturation of the handicapped differs from that of the nonhandicapped. In this instance the normative comparisons are unfair because the acculturation of those tested differs from the acculturation of those on whom the test is standardized.

3. *Using Tests Designed for and Standardized on Handicapped Populations.*   In still other cases, when examiners are required to test persons who demonstrate specific handicaps, they choose to use tests developed for use with and standardized on specific groups of handicapped individuals. A limited number of such devices are available, but they have the distinct advantages of appropriateness in both response requirements and normative comparisons.

In assessing special populations, examiners must be concerned with two restrictions. They must be sure that response requirements are fair and reasonable — that is, that the person being tested can reasonably be expected to be able to respond. They must be cautious also in the use of norms — in being reasonably certain that those they test have had comparable acculturation to those in the normative sample. The remainder of this chapter describes devices most often used with special populations.

THE NEBRASKA TEST OF LEARNING APTITUDE

The Nebraska Test of Learning Aptitude (NTLA) (Hiskey, 1966) is an individually administered test designed to assess the learning aptitude of deaf and hearing individuals between 3 and 16 years of age. The NTLA has twelve subtests with instructions for pantomime administration of the test to deaf persons and verbal directions for use with hearing children. To use the NTLA, the examiner must have considerable experience in individual intellectual assessment. To assess deaf children, the examiner should have specialized preparation and considerable experience working with the deaf. The manual for the NTLA includes suggestions about specific procedures to use in establishing rapport with deaf children, including suggested ways of correcting mistakes and of giving the child nonverbal reinforcement.

The NTLA may be administered either by pantomime or by verbal directions. The test was standardized using pantomime directions with deaf children and verbal directions with hearing children. For that reason, if pantomime directions are used, the scoring must be based on the norms for deaf children. If verbal directions are used, scoring must be based on the norms for hearing children.

Each of the twelve subtests is a power test beginning with very simple items designed to give the child practice in the kind of behavior being sampled. Response requirements in all subtests are nonverbal, requiring a choice (by pointing) of several alternatives or a motor response such as stringing beads or drawing parts of pictures. Some subtests are administered only to 3- to 10-year-olds; some are administered to all ages; others are given only to those 11 years old or older. A description of the twelve subtests follows.

Bead Patterns (ages 3 to 10)   This subtest assesses ability to string beads, copy bead patterns, and reproduce bead patterns from memory.

Memory for Color (ages 3 to 10)   This subtest assesses ability to remember a visually presented series of colors after a short delay.

Picture Identification (ages 3 to 10)   This subtest assesses ability to match identical pictures of increasing complexity.

Picture Association (ages 3 to 10)   This subtest assesses the ability to match pictures to other picture pairs on the basis of perceptual and conceptual relationships.

Paper Folding (ages 3 to 10)   This subtest assesses ability to fold pieces of paper to reproduce a sequence of folds previously made by the examiner.

Visual Attention Span (all ages)   This subtest assesses ability to remember sequences of pictures after a short delay.

Block Patterns (all ages)   This subtest assesses ability to build block patterns from pictorial representations including three-dimensional arrays. A person is allowed 2 minutes to build each pattern and receives bonus points for faster solutions.

Completion of Drawings (all ages)   This subtest assesses ability to isolate missing parts in line drawings and to draw in missing parts with a pencil.

Memory for Digits (11 and above; omitted if mental retardation is suspected)   This subtest assesses ability to reproduce sequences of visually presented digits. A sequence on a card is shown, the card is removed, and the person must reproduce the sequence using plastic digits.

Puzzle Blocks (ages 11 and above)   This subtest assesses ability to assemble disjointed cubes into a whole. It employs varying time limits, and bonus points are given for rapid solutions.

Picture Analogies (ages 11 and above)   This subtest assesses ability to solve visually presented analogies. Three pictures are shown and there is a relationship between the first two. The third picture bears the same relationship to a fourth picture that must be chosen from a response bank.

Spatial Reasoning (ages 11 and above)   This subtest presents a whole figure and several samples of disjointed parts. It requires identification of the samples that could be put together to form the whole objects.

The NTLA is a point scale; that is, the child earns points on the specific subtests that are administered. Different subtests employ different ceiling rules. Criteria for stopping each of the subtests are adequately described in the test manual.

Scores

The kinds of scores obtained for the NTLA depend on how the test is administered. As noted earlier, the NTLA may be administered either in pantomime or verbally. When the test is administered in pantomime, the norms for deaf children are used to obtain a learning age (LA) and a learning quotient (LQ). When the test is administered verbally, the norms for hearing children are used to obtain a mental age (MA) and an intelligence quotient (IQ). Both scores and quotients are based on the median subtest learning ages and mental ages. Hiskey recommends that in interpreting the test performance of hearing children, teachers and diagnostic specialists rely primarily on the MA. He advises that the learning age and learning quotient obtained for deaf children are not equivalent or comparable to MAs and IQs. He recommends that the learning age should be the only score used to interpret the performance of deaf children.

Norms

The NTLA was originally developed in 1941. Norms for hearing children were first published in 1957, and the revised edition of the test with norms for both deaf and hearing children was published in 1966 (Hiskey, 1966). The standardization sample for the 1941 edition included 466 children enrolled in state schools for the deaf in seven midwestern states and in one day school for the deaf in Lincoln, Nebraska.

In the revision and restandardization of the NTLA, Hiskey added one subtest (Spatial Relations) and many more difficult items. The revised NTLA was administered to 1,107 deaf children and 1,101 hearing children between the ages of 2-6 and 17-5 in ten "widely separate states." The deaf children were primarily from state schools for the deaf with no other data reported on the nature of the normative sample. The hearing children were selected on the basis of their parents' occupational levels with reference to the percentages found in the 1960 census. Hiskey states that "the samples included representatives from minority groups, although no effort was made to obtain a specified percentage of such children" (p. 10).

For the purpose of establishing age norms, the children from both samples were divided into fifteen age groups (all children between 2-6 and 3-5 were placed in the 3-year-old group, and so on). The number of children at each year level varied more for the deaf (25 to 106) than for the hearing (47 to 85). The 3- and 4-year-old samples of deaf children and the samples of older hearing children were limited in size. The final item placement was based on the performance of deaf children, and there are no comparisons reported in the manual between the performances of deaf children and hearing children. Thus, while evidence is reported on the increasing difficulty of items within subtests for deaf children, comparable data for hearing children are not reported.

The published norms are based on the performances of 1,079 deaf children and 1,074 hearing children. As noted earlier, both samples are inadequately described.

Reliability

The only reliability data presented in the manual for the NTLA are split-half reliabilities for the standardization groups. Hiskey reports split-half reliabilities of .95 for the 3- to 10-year-old deaf group, .92 for the 11-

to 17-year-old deaf group, .93 for 3- to 10-year-old hearing children, and .90 for 11- to 17-year-old hearing children. No data about the standard errors of measurement are included in the manual.

Hiskey does report data on the internal consistency of the test but does so in an effort to demonstrate validity for the measure. In citing evidence of content validity, Hiskey reports subtest intercorrelations and correlations of each subtest learning age with the median learning age for the entire test. There are no data on the reliabilities of the individual subtests. Hiskey states that "studies in the near future will provide additional evidence of reliability based on re-test results after varying periods of time have elapsed" (p. 16). We have searched the literature and have failed to find these studies.

Validity

Hiskey states that "the best evidence of the validity of a test is to be found in its successful use over a period of years. Research reported during the past twenty years indicates that the original scale has been a valid instrument" (p. 12). He provides very little empirical evidence to support his contention. Data on validity consist of reported concurrent validity and evidence about correlation of subtest learning ages with median learning ages for the total test.

Hiskey reports correlations between subtest learning ages and the median learning age for the total test ranging from .55 to .89 for 3- to 10-year-old deaf children, from .59 to .67 for 11- to 17-year-old deaf children, from .51 to .77 for 3- to 10-year-old hearing children, and from .54 to .67 for 11- to 17-year-old hearing children.

Most data about the concurrent validity of the NTLA are based on the earlier edition of the test. Hiskey does, however, report the following concurrent validity coefficients for the 1966 revision of the NTLA: .86 for 99 hearing children (ages 3 to 10) between NTLA and Stanford-Binet IQs; .78 between the NTLS and Stanford-Binet IQs for fifty hearing children between 11 and 17 years of age; .82 between WISC and NTLA IQs for fifty-two hearing children between 5 and 11 years of age.

Summary

The NTLA is an individually administered measure of learning aptitude standardized on both deaf and hearing children. The test is administered by pantomime procedures for deaf children and by verbal instructions for hearing children. When administering the test, the examiner must be especially careful to use the appropriate set of normative data. The test was standardized using pantomime procedures for deaf children and verbal instructions for hearing children. The standardization samples are not described fully enough.

Reliability data for the NTLA are limited. No subtest reliabilities are reported; only split-half reliabilities for the entire scale are included in the manual. Validity data consist of reported correlations between subtest learning ages and the median learning age for the total test, data on the earlier edition of the test, and concurrent correlations of the NTLA scores with scores of hearing children on the Stanford-Binet and the WISC.

The Nebraska Test of Learning Aptitude is the best available device for the assessment of the learning aptitude of deaf children between 5 and 12 years of age. Because of limited technical data, results on the test must be interpreted with considerable caution.

BLIND LEARNING APTITUDE TEST

The Blind Learning Aptitude Test (BLAT) (Newland, 1969)[1] was developed for assessing the learning aptitude of young blind children. Newland (1969) states that the BLAT was devised to give a clearer picture of the learning potential of young blind children than was possible using existent measures. He states:

While a certain amount and kind of light could be thrown on their basic learning capacities by means of more widely used individual tests, the kinds of behaviors sampled by such tests did not yield as full, and early, psychological information as is needed, particularly at the time such children entered upon formal educational programs — whether in residential or day schools. In a psychological sense, young blind children come into such programs from a much more diversified background of acculturation than do non-impaired children. (p. 1)

In developing materials for the BLAT, Newland states, he used five guiding principles:

(1) the test items were to be bas-relief form, consisting of dots and lines; (2) the spatial discriminations to be made by the child among these dots and lines were to be greater than those called for in the reading of Braille; (3) no stimulus materials, other than the directions, were to be verbal in nature, (4) verbalization of response was not to be required in solving the items or in specifying the solutions to items. Pointing behavior was to be accepted although accompanying verbalization could be accepted; (5) a variety of test-element patterns was to be developed, all of which would necessitate eduction of relationships and/or correlates by the child. (p. 1)

Newland designed the BLAT to sample "six discernibly different kinds of behavior." His descriptions of the kinds of behaviors sampled is compa-

---

1. All quotations from the *Manual for the Blind Learning Aptitude Test* used in this discussion are copyrighted by T. Ernest Newland and reprinted by his permission.

rable to our descriptions of items assessing discrimination, generalization, sequencing, analogies, and pattern or matrix completion.

The BLAT was standardized on individuals from 6 to 20 years of age, but it is intended primarily for children between 6 and 12 years of age. There is a unique feature in the administration of BLAT subtests: training items are presented before the actual administration of subtest items. This allows the examiner to be certain that a child understands the kind of behavior required before being asked to demonstrate the behavior for a scored test item.

Scores

Two scores, learning-aptitude test age and learning-aptitude test quotient, are obtained from the BLAT. Newland (1969) describes the test age by stating that

a child who earns a given score on BLAT can be regarded as having earned a BLAT test age which is the midpoint of an age range. This is indicative of the level of his learning capability as a blind child, as reflected by his performance on the kinds of behavior being sampled by BLAT.   (p. 19)

The learning quotient is a deviation score with a mean of 100 and a standard deviation of 15.

Norms

The BLAT was standardized on 961 blind students in both residential and day schools. The standardization sample was stratified on the basis of geographic region, age, sex, race, and socioeconomic status. Extensive tables comparing standardization data to U.S. census data appear in the manual. In most instances BLAT sample proportions are closely comparable to the census proportions.

Reliability

Two kinds of reliability were ascertained for the BLAT. Internal consistency of the test for all 961 children in the standardization sample was .93. Test-retest reliability was reported as .87 for a sample of 93 children ranging in age from 10 through 16 who were retested seven months after the original testing. There was a median gain of 5.8 points between the original testing and subsequent retesting.

Validity

Validity for the BLAT was demonstrated in three ways. Newland states that estimates of concurrent validity would have limited value because "the 'intelligence' tests generally used with young blind children were regarded as having limited value in sampling learning potential — due to the nature of behavior samplings made and the very widely differing kinds and amounts of acculturation among blind children" (p. 10).

To establish validity for the BLAT it was demonstrated that performance on BLAT

(1) progressively improves across random samples of increasing chronological age levels;
(2) correlates well enough with performances on the Hayes-Binet and the WISC Verbal to suggest that the measurements are in a comparable domain, yet low enough to suggest differences in the behavior samplings; and
(3) correlates promisingly with measured educational achievement as compared with correlations between performances on the Hayes-Binet and WISC Verbal and measured educational achievement.   (Newland, 1969, p. 10)

Summary

The Blind Learning Aptitude Test uses a bas-relief format and six different kinds of behavior samples to assess the intelligence of blind children between 6 and 12 years of age. The BLAT was standardized on blind children whose characteristics closely approximate census proportions. The test is sufficiently reliable to be used in making important decisions about children. Validity of the test is still based largely on theoretical postulates. The BLAT is currently the most adequate test for assessing the learning aptitude of young blind children.

ARTHUR ADAPTATION OF
THE LEITER INTERNATIONAL PERFORMANCE SCALE

The Leiter International Performance Scale was first constructed by Russell Leiter in 1929 for the purpose of assessing the intelligence of children who might experience difficulty responding to a verbal test: the deaf, the hard of hearing, those who demonstrate speech difficulties, the bilingual, and those who do not speak English. The 1929 scale was an experimental edition; subsequent revisions were published in 1934, 1936, 1938, 1940, and 1948. In 1950, Grace Arthur published an adaptation (AALIPS) of the Leiter International Performance Scale.

The AALIPS is an untimed, nonverbal age scale containing sixty items ranging from the 2-year to the 12-year level. The 1948 edition of the LIPS contains additional items and can be used to assess the intelligence of persons 2 through 18 years of age. The test materials for the LIPS and the AALIPS are identical through the 12-year level.

Materials for the AALIPS consist of a response frame with an adjustable

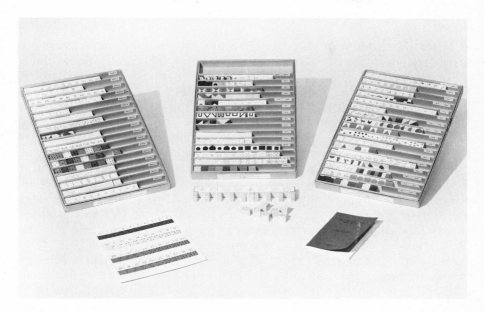

Figure **13.2**   An item from the Arthur Adaptation of the Leiter International Performance Scale. (Photo courtesy Stoelting Company)

card holder and two trays of response blocks with corresponding stimulus cards (see Figure 13.2). All tests are administered by placing a stimulus card on the response frame and pantomiming the directions. The child responds by placing blocks in the response frame. The actual tasks range from matching colors and forms to completion of patterns, analogous designs, and classification of objects. Behaviors predominantly sampled, therefore, include discrimination, generalization, sequencing, analogies, and pattern completion. Most items require considerable perceptual organization and discrimination.

The directions for administering the scale that are included in the manual are confusing. They're illustrated by black and white pictures that, unfortunately, are of little assistance with items in which color is the discriminative feature in both administration and solution. Colored pictures would facilitate ease of administration; the use of black and white pictures necessitates reading an entire page of instructions in order to ascertain proper alignment of stimulus cards and pictures and to insure correct standardized administration.

Scores

A major shortcoming of the AALIPS is the fact that the correct answers (arrangements of blocks) to test questions are not included in the manual. Examiners must judge the correctness of a child's response on the basis of what they believe the correct response should be. We suggest that examiners solve the problems themselves before giving the test to children, that they obtain the consensus of others (preferably, reasonably "bright" persons) about the correctness of their responses, and that they then mark the blocks using a coding system to avoid scoring errors.

Two scores, MA and a ratio IQ, are obtained by administering the AALIPS. There are four subtests at each age level of the test. The child earns a certain number of months' credit for each subtest passed and the number of months are summed to produce a mental age. Only items between the child's basal and ceiling are administered. A basal is located by identifying the level at which a child answers all items correctly. A double ceiling is attained; the child must fail all items at two consecutive year levels before testing is discontinued. Comparisons of the AALIPS with other intelligence tests (that is, the WISC and Stanford-Binet) have consistently shown that scores on the AALIPS tend to be about five points lower than those earned on other scales. Arthur devised a bonus system that raises the basal and increases credit for subtests passed at the various year levels, thus bringing scores on the AALIPS into line with those on other tests.

Norms

Normative data for the LIPS are not included in the AALIPS manual. The AALIPS, on the other hand, was standardized on only 289 children. All 289 came from a homogeneous middle-class, midwestern, metropolitan background. There were few children at either extreme of the socioeconomic scale and apparently few or none who were the kind of children for whom the scale was originally developed — that is, children who experience difficulty responding to a verbal scale.

Reliability and Validity

No reliability data are published in the manual for the AALIPS. Arthur reports a number of studies as evidence for the concurrent validity of the AALIPS. Correlations between performance on the AALIPS and on the Stanford-Binet Intelligence Scale for 4-, 5-, 7-, and 8-year-old children ranged from .69 to .93; for a sample of mentally retarded and brain-injured children these correlations were between .56 and .86. The AALIPS correlates more highly with the performance scale (from .79 to .80) than with the verbal scale (.40 to .78) of the WISC.

Summary

The AALIPS is, in theory and design, a test that holds considerable promise for the intellectual assessment of children who have difficulty responding verbally. It lacks the necessary technical characteristics to make it psychometrically adequate. The test is inadequately standardized, and few data about its reliability and validity are given in the manual. Until this test is made technically adequate, its use should be restricted to procurement of qualitative information by only the most experienced examiners.

PICTORIAL TEST OF INTELLIGENCE

The Pictorial Test of Intelligence (PTI) (French, 1964) was designed "to provide an easily administered, objectively scored individual testing instrument to be used in assessing the general intellectual level of both normal and handicapped children between the ages of three and eight" (p. 1). The test employs an objective, multiple-choice format and requires no verbal response; children respond either by pointing or, in the case of those who cannot point, by focusing their eyes on specific response items.

The PTI includes six subtests designed to assess general mental ability. All items are administered by showing the child a large picture card containing four response possibilities. The child points to or focuses on one of the four drawings in response to orally presented directions. According to the author, the six subtests sample the following behaviors.

Picture Vocabulary This subtest assesses verbal comprehension. The child must identify which response best fits the meaning of a stimulus word read by the examiner.

Form Discrimination This subtest assesses perceptual organization. The child is shown increasingly complex stimulus drawings on a second card and must match these to one of four response drawings.

Information and Comprehension The child must demonstrate a "range of knowledge, general understanding, and verbal comprehension" by pointing to pictures in response to verbal statements read by the examiner.

Similarities This subtest requires the child to identify which of four pictures does not belong in either a perceptual or conceptual category with the other three.

Size and Number This subtest assesses quantitative language (for example, *bigger*), enumeration, and word problems that require skills ranging from the addition of single-digit numbers to those needed to perform multiple arithmetic operations in the same problem.

Immediate Recall   This subtest assesses "ability to retain momentary perceptions of size, space, and form relationships." The examiner presents a stimulus card for five seconds, removes it, and then asks the child to identify the identical stimulus on the four-choice response card.

Scores

Raw scores for the PTI are obtained by objective scoring of the multiple-choice responses. Raw scores may be transformed to MAs, percentiles, and deviation IQs ($\bar{X} = 100$, $S = 16$). All children take every item of the test; there are no basal and ceiling rules. A short form of the test, which may be administered to 3- and 4-year-old children, provides the same kinds of scores as the long form.

Norms

As we mentioned in Chapter 8, the PTI is one of the most adequately standardized devices. The standardization sample consisted of 1,830 children selected as representative of the population of children ages 3 through 8 living in the United States. 1960 census data were used, and the sample was stratified on the basis of geographic region, community size, occupational level of head of household, and sex. Race was not employed as a specific stratification variable, since the author believed that "the most appropriate procedure would be to include all races with socioeconomic status as the prime control variable" (p. 12). Extensive tables in the manual compare proportions of individuals in the normative sample with proportions in the population of the United States. All children who participated in the normative sample were individually tested by experienced psychologists.

Reliability

Both internal-consistency and test-retest reliability data are reported in the PTI manual. Internal-consistency coefficients were computed separately for each age level and ranged from .87 to .93. Separate internal-consistency estimates for the short form were .86 at age 3 and .88 at age 4.

Five studies investigated the test-retest reliability of the PTI. The results of these studies, time intervals between testings, and the age levels of the children are reported in Table 13.5. The PTI has the necessary reliability to be used in making important educational decisions.

Validity

Content validity for the PTI was inferred on the basis of item selection and test development. Predictive validity for the test is based upon studies of its predecessor, the North Central Individual Test of Mental Ability

Table **13.5** Summary of Studies on Test-Retest Reliability for the PTI

AGE	TIME LAPSE	r	N
3, 4; 8, 9	54–56 mos.	.69[a]	49
3, 4, 5	3–6 wks.	.96	27
5	2–6 wks.	.91	31
6	2–4 wks.	.90	30
7	2–4 wks.	.94	25

[a] NCITMA (ages 3 and 4) vs. PTI (ages 8 and 9).

SOURCE: J. L. French, *Manual for the Pictorial Test of Intelligence* (Boston: Houghton Mifflin, 1964), p. 19. Copyright © 1964 by Houghton Mifflin Company and reprinted with their permission.

(NCITMA). Concurrent validity of the PTI was established by correlating performance on the scale with performance on the Stanford-Binet, WISC, and Columbia Mental Maturity Scale. Correlations obtained for a sample of thirty-two first graders are reported in Table 13.6. However, for this same sample the means and standard deviations differed considerably (PTI: $\bar{X} = 114.5, S = 8.2$; Stanford-Binet: $\bar{X} = 113.6, S = 17.6$; and WISC: $\bar{X} = 101.5, S = 10.1$).

The performance of thirty-two first graders on the PTI correlated .61 with their performance on the Lorge-Thorndike Intelligence Scale (now the Cognitive Abilities Test), while the PTI performance of thirty first graders correlated .62 with their earlier scores on the California Test of Mental Maturity.

Construct validity was established by demonstrating increasing scores with chronological ages and occupational level of children's parents.

Summary

The Pictorial Test of Intelligence is an individually administered device composed of six separate subtests designed to assess general mental ability. The test does not require the child to respond verbally and is thus suitable for administration to children who experience difficulty making verbal responses (young children with speech and language difficulties, with cerebral palsy, and so on). The test is adequately standardized and has the necessary reliability to be used in making important educational decisions.

COLUMBIA MENTAL MATURITY SCALE

The Columbia Mental Maturity Scale (CMMS) (Burgemeister, Blum, & Lorge, 1972) is an individually administered device that assesses general reasoning ability by requiring a child to make visual-perceptual discrimina-

Table **13.6**   Correlations of PTI Total Test and Subtests with Other Intelligence Tests (32 First Graders)

	STANFORD-BINET MA	WISC SCORES		PERFORM-ANCE	CMMS IQ	PTI TOTAL
		FULL-SCALE	VERBAL			
SUBTESTS						
Picture Vocabulary	.45	.38	.38	.33	.42	.55
Form Discrimination	.53	.56	.52	.49	.45	.68
Information and Comprehension	.41	.56	.23	.16	.22	.48
Similarities	.55	.25	.41	.23	.40	.63
Size and Number	.52	.50	.53	.42	.38	.74
Immediate Recall	.22	.14	.10	.14	.26	.38
Total raw scores	.77	.67	.71	.55	.61	—

SOURCE: J. L. French, *Manual for the Pictorial Test of Intelligence* (Boston: Houghton Mifflin, 1964), p. 21. Copyright © 1964 by Houghton Mifflin Company and reprinted with their permission.

tions in order to classify and relate series of pictures, colors, forms, and symbols. The ninety-two figural and pictorial classification items that make up the scale are arranged in eight overlapping levels and may be used with children between 3 years, 6 months, and 9 years, 11 months, of age. Children take the level of the test appropriate for their chronological age. The authors describe administration of the scale as follows.

Each item consists of a series of from three to five drawings printed on a 6-by-19-inch card. . . . The objects depicted are, in general, within the range of experience of most American children, even those whose environmental backgrounds have been limited. . . . For each item the child is asked to look at all the pictures on the card, select the one which is different from, or unrelated to, the others, and indicate his choice by pointing to it. In order to do this, he must formulate a rule for organizing the pictures so as to exclude just one. The bases for discrimination range from the perception of rather gross differences in color, size, or form, to recognition of very subtle relations in pairs of pictures so as to exclude one from the series of drawings.   (p. 7)

Administration of the CMMS takes from 15 to 20 minutes. The child is taught the task by three training items and then takes the appropriate age level of the test.

Scores

The raw score for the CMMS is simply the number of items answered correctly. Raw scores may be converted to age-deviation scores, percentile ranks, stanines, and a maturity index. The age-deviation score is a standard score with a mean of 100 and a standard deviation of 16. Maturity indexes are essentially comparable to MAs, although they are more global, encompassing ranges rather than being specific MAs. A maturity index of 4U, for example, indicates that the child earned the same score on the test as did those in the standardization group who were in the range from 4 years, 6 months, to 4 years, 11 months. The symbols U and L are used to depict upper and lower ranges of a given year level.

Norms

The CMMS was standardized on 2,600 children stratified on the basis of geographic region, race, parental occupation, age, and sex. Proportions of children in each of the demographic groups closely approximate 1960 U.S. census data, with one exception. Figures reported for community size indicate that a greater proportion of children in the normative sample were from large cities (43.74 percent) than is true of the general population (28.5 percent). The selection of the normative sample was in all other ways exemplary.

Reliability

Both internal-consistency (split-half) and test-retest reliability are reported in the CMMS manual. Internal-consistency coefficients ranged from .85 to .91. Test-retest reliability for three different age groups ranged from .84 to .86. Children gained an average of 4.6 age-deviation score points between administrations.

Validity

Validity for the CMMS is based on two kinds of data: data indicating that scores on the test correlate substantially with scores on the Stanford Achievement Test (.31 to .61) and with scores on other intelligence tests. The CMMS scores of 353 children in grades 1 through 3 in a single school system correlated .62 to .69 with their scores on the Otis-Lennon Mental Ability Test and .67 with their scores on the Stanford-Binet.

Summary

The CMMS is an easily administered individual intelligence test designed to assess children's "reasoning ability." The test is adequately standardized and appears technically adequate. The instrument may be used to assess children who have difficulty responding verbally. It does, however, sample only two kinds of intellectual behavior, discrimination and classification; users must be careful not to overgeneralize the test results.

SUMMARY

Many different individually administered tests are currently used to assess intelligence. The tests differ considerably in their basic design, the kinds of behaviors they sample, and their technical adequacy. In evaluating performance on intelligence tests, it is especially important that teachers and examiners go beyond obtained scores to consider the specific tests on which the scores were obtained and the kinds of behaviors sampled by those tests. The information in this chapter will facilitate that evaluation.

Special attention was given in this chapter to individually administered tests designed to assess the intelligence of special populations. Individual intellectual assessment of children with specific handicaps should be carried out using tests designed to minimize the effects of the handicaps on their performances.

STUDY QUESTIONS

1. The Stanford-Binet Intelligence Scale and the Wechsler Intelligence Scale for Children—Revised are the two intelligence tests most frequently used with school-age children. Identify similarities and differences in the domains of behavior sampled by these two tests.

2. Why is it inappropriate to use the same intelligence tests with sensorily or physically handicapped children as with children who do not have such handicaps?

3. Identify the major advantages of using the Stanford-Binet Intelligence Scale as opposed to the Slosson Intelligence Test.

4. In Chapter 12, we stated that IQs earned on different intelligence tests cannot be viewed as comparable. Using the Peabody Picture Vocabulary Test, the Quick Test, and the Wechsler Intelligence Scale for Children — Revised, support the statement.

5. The Performance sections of the Wechsler Scales are currently the tests most commonly used to assess the intelligence of deaf children. What are the major shortcomings in this current practice? What alternatives exist?

6. Using the manual for any of the individual tests described in this chapter, characterize the domain or domains of behaviors sampled by any ten *items*. Use the domains described in Chapter 12.

7. For what reasons would school personnel give individual intelligence tests?

ADDITIONAL READING

Buros, O. K. (ed.) *Seventh mental measurements yearbook*. Highland Park, NJ: Gryphon Press, 1972 (Reviews of individual intelligence tests, pp. 727–809.)

Gerweck, S., & Ysseldyke, J. E. Limitations of current psychological assessment practices with the deaf: A response to the Levine survey. *Volta Review*, 1974, *77*, 243–48.

Keogh, B. Psychological evaluation of exceptional children: Old hangups and new directions. *Journal of School Psychology*, 1972, *10*, 141–145.

Sattler, J., & Tozier, L. A review of intelligence test modifications used with the cerebral palsied and other handicapped groups. *Journal of Special Education*, 1971, *4*, 391–398.

Sattler, J. *Assessment of children's intelligence*. Philadelphia: W. B. Saunders, 1974. (Chapter 5: The role of the examiner in administering individual intelligence tests, pp. 53–64. Chapter 7: Suggestions for testing children with special problems, pp. 77–83. Appendix B: List of validity and reliability studies for the Stanford-Binet, WISC, WPPSI, PPVT, Quick Test, Leiter, and Slosson.)

Chapter 14

Assessment of Intelligence: Group Tests

Group intelligence tests typically are used for one of two purposes. Most often, they are routinely administered as screening devices to identify those who are different enough from average to warrant further assessment. Their merit, in this case, is that they can be administered relatively quickly by teachers to large numbers of students. Their drawback is that they suffer from the same limitations as any group test: they can be made to yield qualitative information only with difficulty, and they require that students can sit still for about twenty minutes, that they can mark with a pencil, and, often, that they can read. When used as screening devices, group intelligence tests must be followed by individual assessment or they do not meet this purpose.

Group intelligence tests are also used to provide descriptive information about the level of capability of students in a classroom, district, or even state. They are, on occasion, used in place of or in addition to achievement tests to track students. When used in this way, they set expectations; they are thought to indicate the level of achievement to be expected in individual classrooms or districts.

Group intelligence tests differ from one another in three ways. First, they differ in format. Whereas some group tests consist of a single battery to be administered in one sitting, others contain a number of subscales or subtests and are administered in two or more sittings. Second, they differ in the kinds of scores they provide. Some provide IQs and/or mental ages based on a global performance; others provide the same kinds of scores, but these are differentiated into subscale scores (for example, verbal, performance, and total; language, nonlanguage, and total). Third, some group intelligence tests are speed tests (timed), while others are power tests (untimed).

LIMITATIONS OF GROUP INTELLIGENCE TESTS

A number of specific limitations are inherent in the construction and use of group intelligence tests. The first limitation is that most tests have a number of levels designed for use in specific grades (for example, level A for kindergarten through third grade, level B for third through sixth grade). Tests are typically standardized by grade. Students of different ages are enrolled in the same grade; students of the same age are enrolled in different grades. Test authors use interpolation to compute mental ages for students based on grade sampling. In earlier discussions, an age score was defined as the average score earned by individuals of a given age. Let us now consider a problem.

Suppose that an intelligence test has a level Q, which is designed to measure the intelligence of students in grades 6 through 9. As is typical of group intelligence tests, the test is standardized on students in grades 6 through 9, students who range in age from approximately 10 to 15 or 16 years. Norms are based on this age range. The test is later administered to Stanley, age 10-8, who earns a mental age of 7-3. How can this be? Stanley, who is 10 years, 8 months, old, could not possibly earn the same score as is typically earned on the test by students who are 7 years, 3 months, old, since no 7-year, 3-month-old students were included in the normative sample. The score is based on an extrapolation.

The second limitation is that most group intelligence tests, while standardized on large numbers of students, often are not standardized on representative populations. Most are typically standardized on districts, not on individual students. An effort is made to select representative districts, but not necessarily a representative population of individuals. Yet, the normative tables for group intelligence tests typically provide scores for individuals, not for groups.

The third limitation is that most group intelligence tests are standardized on volunteer samples. In the process of standardizing the test, representative districts are selected and are asked to participate. Those districts refusing, for any number of reasons, are replaced by "comparable" districts. This process of replacement may introduce bias into the standardization.

Finally, it must be remembered that when tests are standardized in public schools, those students who are excluded from school are also excluded from the standardization population. Severely retarded students, severely disturbed students, and dropouts are excluded from the norms. Similarly, most authors of group intelligence tests do not describe the extent to which they included students enrolled in special-education classes in their standardization samples. Exclusion of students with low IQs biases the norms; the range of performance of the standardization group is reduced, and the standard deviation is decreased. It is extremely important for the authors of group tests to provide tables in test manuals illustrating the composition of the standardization sample. In doing so, it is preferable to include descriptions of the kinds of individuals on whom a test was standardized rather than descriptions of districts.

SPECIFIC GROUP TESTS OF INTELLIGENCE

CULTURE FAIR INTELLIGENCE TESTS

Three different scales comprise the Culture Fair Intelligence Tests. Scale 1 (Cattell, 1950) is used with students between 4 and 8 years of age. Scale 2 (Cattell & Cattell, 1960a) is used with those who are between 8 and 14 years of age; scale 3 (Cattell & Cattell, 1963) is used with those who are over 14 years of age. The Culture Fair Intelligence Tests are unique among group intelligence tests, and it is helpful to note the rationale for the tests and the theoretical orientation of their author.

According to Cattell (1962), the motivation for construction of the Culture Fair Intelligence Tests "was originally the need for a test which would fairly measure the intelligence of persons having different languages and cultures, or influenced by very different social status and education" (p. 5). Cattell (1973a) states that "the Culture Fair Intelligence Tests measure individual intelligence in a manner designed to reduce, as much as possible, the influence of verbal fluency, culture climate, and educational level" (p. 5).

Cattell believes culture-fair intelligence tests are more adequate measures of learning potential than are traditional intelligence tests. The latter, he argues, are contaminated by the effects of prior learning. Many have argued that scores on the Culture Fair Intelligence Tests do not effectively predict academic achievement. Cattell (1973b) states that the tests have been criticized because "within the same year and among students all in the same kind of school, the Culture Fair does not correlate with ('predict') achievement quite so highly as the traditional test" (p. 8). Cattell (1973b) states that

this is not only admitted, but treasured by the exponent of the newer tests. The reason that the traditional test gives a better immediate "prediction" is that it already contains an appreciable admixture of the school achievement it is supposed to predict. If all we want to do is predict, in March, children's school achievement in, say, July, we can do better than any intelligence test by predicting from their school achievement scores in March. The very object of an intelligence test, however, is to be *analytical*. As we study any individual child we are interested in the *discrepancy* between his native intelligence and his school achievement, and the more clearly and reliably this is brought out, the better the test. The claim of the Culture Fair Tests is that it will make a more fair selection for future performance when the passage of some years has given a chance for the present accidental inequalities of achievement opportunity to be ironed out. (p. 8)

The Culture Fair Intelligence Tests are designed to measure general mental ability and, with the exception of some parts of scale 1, consist

Table **14.1**   Subtests of the Three Scales of the Culture Fair
Intelligence Tests

SCALE 1	SCALES 2 AND 3
Substitution[a,b]	Series
Classification[b]	Classification
Mazes[a,b]	Matrices
Selecting Named Objects[a]	Conditions (Typology)
Following Directions	
Wrong Pictures	
Riddles	
Similarities[a,b]	

[a] Group-administered form.
[b] Fully culture-fair form.

entirely of figural analogies and figural reasoning items. Time limits are 22
minutes for scale 1 and $12\frac{1}{2}$ minutes each for scales 2 and 3. Only parts of
scale 1 can be group administered; the scale consists of eight different
subtests; some are individually administered, while others are group administered. Only four of the subtests make up the group test, while only
four are judged by the author to be culture fair. Subtests of scales 1, 2, and
3 are listed in Table 14.1. As we noted earlier, scale 1 contains eight
subtests. Four of these make up the group-administered version of the
scale; the behaviors they sample are as follows.

Substitution   This subtest is a coding task that requires the student to
associate symbols with pictures and to copy them on paper.

Mazes   The student is required to trace paths out of increasingly complex
mazes.

Selecting Named Objects   This subtest is essentially a picture vocabulary task
requiring the student to identify pictures of words read aloud by the
examiner. This is one of the subtests that, according to the author, is not
culture fair.

Similarities   The student is required to identify which of several response
pictures is just like a stimulus picture.

Scales 2 and 3 are made up of the same four subtests. Behaviors sampled
by these subtests are as follows.

Series   The student is given a sequence of figures having some progressive relationship to each other and is required to choose from four possible responses the figure that continues the progressive relationship. The first item in Figure 14.1 is a Series item.

Classification   The student is given five figures and is required to identify which picture is different from the other four. The second item in Figure 14.1 is a Classification item.

Matrices   The student is given a matrix and is required to identify the response that is the missing element in the matrix. The third item in Figure 14.1 is a matrix-completion item.

Conditions (Typology)   The student is given a stimulus figure in which a dot is placed in a certain relationship (that is, inside the circle, but outside the square). The student must identify that response element in which the dot is in the same relationship to the other elements as in the stimulus figure (that is, *inside* the circle, but *outside* the square). The fourth item in Figure 14.1 is a Conditions item.

Scores

In taking scale 1, students mark their responses in consumable test booklets, and the booklets are hand scored. Raw scores may be transformed to mental ages or to ratio IQs. The ratio IQs have a mean of 100, but a standard deviation of approximately 20. Cattell believes the higher standard deviations obtained from culture-fair tests are more nearly correct values than those obtained from traditional intelligence tests because "the reduced scatter in traditional intelligence tests is probably due to a contamination of intelligence with achievement" (1962, p. 14). One must remember, therefore, that an IQ of 120 on scale 1 is the standard-score equivalent of an IQ of 116 on the Stanford-Binet Intelligence Scale. Similarly, an IQ of 60 on scale 1 is the standard score equivalent of an IQ of 68 on the Stanford-Binet. Ratio IQs obtained for scale 1 may be transformed to percentiles on an IQ distribution with a standard deviation of 20.

On scales 2 and 3 of the Culture Fair Intelligence Tests, students respond on answer sheets that may be machine scored or scored by hand using a stencil. Raw scores on these scales may be transformed to mental ages and to three different IQs, each having a mean of 100 but standard deviations of 24.4, 24, or 16. The first two distributions are recommended for use when doing research on practical application of the tests and when one wishes to obtain the full spread of IQs typically obtained in administration of the device. The third distribution is a distribution of normalized standard scores with the standard deviation set at the standard deviation of

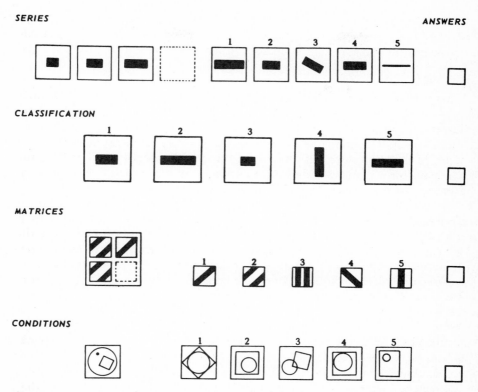

Figure 14.1   Items representative of those in the subtests of the Culture Fair Intelligence Tests. (Copyright 1949, 1957 by the Institute for Personality and Ability Testing. Reproduced by permission.)

"attainment-contaminated" tests. The distribution is used when one wishes to compare the results obtained on the Culture Fair Intelligence Tests with those obtained on more traditional intelligence tests.

Norms

The populations on whom the Culture Fair Intelligence Tests were standardized are inadequately described in the manuals. Cattell states that scale 1 was standardized on "more than 400 cases combining American and British samples" (1962, p. 12). He states that scale 2 was standardized on 4,328 boys and girls from varied regions of the United States and Great Britain. The sample was apparently not stratified on the basis of any population characteristics. Norms for scale 3 were based on "3,140 cases, consisting of American high school students equally divided among freshmen, sophomores, juniors, and seniors, and young adults in a stratified job sample" (Cattell, 1973a, p. 21). There are no data in the manuals regarding the specific characteristics of the standardization samples.

Reliability

Data about reliability and validity of the three scales are reported in a separate Technical Supplement for scales 2 and 3 (Cattell, 1973b). Both internal consistency and test-retest data are reported for scale 1 on the basis of the test performance of 113 elementary school children of unspecified ages. Test-retest reliability based on the performances of 57 Head Start children over an unspecified time interval was reported to be .80 for the total test and to range from .57 to .71 for the subtests.

Three kinds of reliability data — internal-consistency, equivalent-form, and test-retest — are reported for scale 2. Based on the performances of 102 female Job Corps applicants, internal consistency for scale 2 was reported to range from .77 to .81 for form A and from .71 to .76 for form B. Split-half reliability, ranging from .95 to .97, was computed from a sample of 200 Mexican and American subjects. Equivalent-form reliability for scale 2 ranged from .58 to .72 with individuals of various ages. Test-retest reliability over an unspecified time interval was .82 for 200 American high school students and .85 for 450 11-year-old British secondary school students. There are no reliability data for the use of scale 2 with those under 11 years of age.

Reliability for scale 3 is reported in terms of internal-consistency and equivalent-form reliability for 202 high school students. Internal-consistency coefficients ranged from .51 to .68 for form A and from .53 to .64 for form B. Equivalent-form reliability ranged from .32 to .68.

Reliability for the Culture Fair Intelligence Tests sometimes approaches the necessary values for use of the test in screening. However, reliability data are incomplete.

Validity

The majority of evidence for the validity of the scales rests on a series of factor-analytic studies conducted by Cattell. Essentially, Cattell extracted a general ability factor ("g") and then correlated performance on each of the subtests with that factor. According to Cattell and Cattell, "The real basis of validity of an intelligence test is its correlation with the 'construct' or concept of intelligence in the general ability factor" (1960b, p. 5). Cattell reports that correlations of the subtests with "g" range from .53 to .99.

Additional evidence for the validity of Scale 1 consists of reported correlations with the Stanford-Binet (r = .62 for 25 "underprivileged children") and the Goodenough-Harris (r = .46 for 72 unspecified children). Scale 2 has been correlated with a number of other tests, and the correlations are

Table **14.2** Correlations of Scores on Scale 2 of the Culture Fair
Intelligence Tests with Scores Earned on Other Intelligence Tests

TEST	CORRELATION WITH SCALE 2
Otis Beta	.49
Pintner General Ability	.69
WISC Verbal	.62
WISC Performance	.63
WISC Full Scale	.72

reported in Table 14.2. Samples ranged in size from 186 to 1,000 and
came from both the United States and Hong Kong. Validity for Scale 3 is
based on studies conducted with individuals in Taiwan and mainland
China. Cattell reports that the scale correlated .29 with a critical thinking
test, .22 with teacher ratings of intelligence, .23 with total grade average,
.32 with math test scores, and .31 with math grades.

In addition, a number of studies are cited in the manual for scale 2 of the
Culture Fair Tests that provide evidence, according to the author, of
immunity of the tests from specific cultural influences.

Summary

The Culture Fair Intelligence Tests provide the examiner with a nontradi-
tional approach to the assessment of intelligence. The tests assess intelligence with relatively little contamination by formal instruction. In evaluating how much meaningful information for one's own setting the tests
provide, one must examine both the kind of information sought and one's
own theoretical approach to intelligence testing. In interpreting the scores
students earn on the scales, one must be especially aware of the large
standard deviations of obtained scores. A major shortcoming of the Culture Fair Intelligence Tests is the inadequate description of the standardization group.

COGNITIVE ABILITIES TEST

The Cognitive Abilities Test (CAT) (Thorndike & Hagen, 1971) is a
further development of the Lorge-Thorndike Intelligence Tests, which
first appeared in 1954. There are ten levels of the CAT. Primary I is
appropriate for use in kindergarten and grade 1; Primary II is to be used in
grades 2 and 3. The multilevel edition of the CAT includes the remaining

eight levels of the test in a single booklet. Items in the multilevel edition range from easy third-grade items to very difficult items at the twelfth-grade level. Examinees start and stop at different points, depending on the level being administered. The inclusion of eight levels of the test in a single multilevel edition allows teachers to administer levels of difficulty appropriate to the ability of their students. The scales increase in difficulty in very small steps. For students who attain little more than chance-level performance, the next easier level of the scale may be administered; while for those who get nearly every item correct, the next more difficult level may be administered. Practice tests are available for all subtests in the scale.

According to the test authors, the CAT "provides a set of measures of the individual's ability to use and manipulate abstract and symbolic relationships" (Thorndike & Hagen, 1971, p. 3). Whereas the original Lorge-Thorndike Intelligence Test included a verbal and nonverbal scale, the CAT consists of three batteries: Verbal, Quantitative, and Nonverbal. Ten subtests comprise the entire battery. The authors simply list the subtests without specifically describing the behaviors sampled by each, but examination of the test shows what kinds of behaviors each battery samples.

The *Verbal* battery has four subtests:

Vocabulary   This subtest assesses skill in selecting synonyms of words read by the student.

Sentence Completion   The student reads a sentence with a missing word and must select the response word that most appropriately fills the blank.

Verbal Classification   The student is given three or four words that are members of a conceptual category and must identify which response word best fits into the same category as the stimulus words.

Verbal Analogies   The student must complete verbal analogies of the nature $A : B :: C : ?$.

The *Quantitative* battery is made up of three subtests:

Quantitative Relations   Given two quantities (one might be $2\sqrt{4}$ and the other $\sqrt{2 \times 4}$), the student must identify which one is greater.

Number Series   Given a series of numbers that have a progressive relationship to one another, the student must select that number that best completes the relationship.

Equation Building The student must use numbers and symbols for mathematical operations to construct correct equations.

A *Nonverbal* battery that requires no reading has three subtests:

Figure Analogies The student must complete figural analogies of the nature $\triangle : \blacktriangle :: \bigcirc : \underline{\quad}$.

Figure Classification Given three figures that are alike in some way, the student must identify the response that best fits into the same conceptual category.

Figure Synthesis The student is given parts of figures and must identify the whole figure that could be formed by placing the parts together.

Scores

Transformed scores obtained from the CAT include: standard scores by ages (IQs with a mean of 100 and a standard deviation of 16), percentiles by age, stanines by age, and percentiles and stanines by grade. Separate scores may be obtained for the Verbal, Quantitative, Non-Verbal and Total batteries.

Norms

The CAT was standardized along with the Iowa Tests of Basic Skills and the Tests of Academic Progress. The tests were standardized on approximately 20,000 pupils per grade. The only variable used to stratify the sampling population was community size; within given communities school personnel were asked to rank specific schools on the basis of estimated aptitude and achievement. The authors state that "when these were received, a plan for sampling attendance units was worked out for each system to obtain the necessary sampling fraction of pupils" (p. 11). The manual includes no specific descriptions of the normative sample, only tables of proportions based on geographic region and community size.

Reliability

To establish reliability for the scale, five hundred students were randomly selected from the standardization sample, and internal-consistency coefficients were computed for their performance on each of the eight levels in the multilevel edition. Obtained coefficients ranged from .91 to .95. No test-retest coefficients were reported. However, the authors do report data showing the practice effect of taking the test. When five hundred students per grade level were given the test and then retested one week later with the Lorge-Thorndike Intelligence Test (an earlier edition of this scale), they tended to gain about three IQ points on readministration.

Validity

Evidence for content validity is based on item selection. The authors state that they attempted to select items that measured the more "fluid" aspects of general ability, specifically designing the test to measure the reasoning process rather than facts and information that had been learned.

Criterion-related validity was established by concurrent administration of the CAT, the Iowa Tests of Basic Skills, and the Tests of Academic Progress. Correlations between performance on the three CAT batteries and subtests of the ITBS for students in grades 3 through 8 ranged from .52 to .84. Correlations between the three CAT subtests and subtests of the TAP for students in grades 9 through 12 ranged from .53 to .82. The complete listing of intercorrelations is reported on page 104 in the examiner's manual. On page 29 of the technical manual for the test, the authors report correlations between performance on the CAT and end-of-year grades.

Two procedures were used to establish the construct validity of the scale. A total of 554 children took the CAT in 1970 and the Stanford-Binet Intelligence Scale during the 1971–1972 school year. Correlations with the Binet ranged from .72 to .78 for the Verbal scale, .65 to .68 for the Quantitative scale, and .60 to .65 for the Nonverbal scale. The second validation procedure consisted of factor analysis of the performance of children in grades 3, 5, 7, 9, and 11. The factor analysis demonstrated that a general factor of abstract reasoning accounted for a majority of the variance measured by each of the subtests. In addition, it demonstrated that the verbal battery also measures a word-knowledge factor, that the Nonverbal battery measures a figural factor, and that while the Quantitative battery measures largely the general factor, each of its separate subtests measures a set of specific quantitative skills.

Summary

The CAT consists of three batteries designed to measure the intelligence of students in kindergarten through grade 12. For the most part, the test is a technically adequate device. Information about reliability indicates that the device is highly reliable. The adequacy of the standardization sample could well be challenged, while validity data are adequate.

GOODENOUGH-HARRIS DRAWING TEST

The Goodenough-Harris Drawing Test (G-H) (Harris, 1963) is designed to measure *intellectual maturity*, which, according to the author, consists of "the ability to form concepts of increasingly abstract character" (p. 5). Harris states that intellectual maturity requires the ability to perceive, to abstract, and to generalize. The student is required to complete three drawings: one of a man, one of a woman, and one of himself or herself. Drawings can be scored by two methods, qualitative or quantitative. In quantitative scoring, points are awarded on the basis of the amount of detail in the drawing. For example, a student receives points for including a neck, indicating fingers, styling hair, and so forth. Artistic merit does not earn points, but smooth and well-controlled lines do. Harris states that "the literature on children's drawings shows quite clearly that the nature and content of such drawings are dependent primarily upon intellectual development" (1963, p. 68). The device may be administered individually or to groups of students aged 3 through 15.

Scores

As noted above, scoring of the G-H is both quantitative and qualitative. A point scale is used to assign points for inclusion of specific features in drawings. A student's drawings of a man and of a woman are scored separately, but the self-drawing is never formally scored. Examples of criteria used in assigning points are illustrated in Figure 14.2.

The quality of the student's drawing is scored on a twelve-point scale. Figure 14.3 contains illustrations of drawings of a man that earn one, four, eight, and twelve points. The Quality scale was constructed and standardized for convenient and rapid scoring of the man and woman drawings. It was constructed on the basis of the opinions of a group of judges who were asked to sort 240 drawings (completed by twenty children at each age level) into twelve categories, with category 1 representing drawings of the "least excellence," category 6 those of "median excellence," and category 11 those of "greatest excellence." Categories 0 and 12 were included to sort out drawings that were outstandingly poor or outstandingly good. According to Harris (1963), "These scales are not as sensitive measures of development as the Point scales, especially after age eight or nine. Moreover, the Quality scales tend to magnify the sex differences observed on the Point scales" (p. 227).

Two kinds of scores are obtained for the G-H. Raw scores on the Point scale and on the Quality scale may be transformed to standard-score IQs (mean = 100, standard deviation = 15), which in turn may be transformed to percentile ranks. Scoring is in terms of whole-year intervals, so the same normative data are used for children who are 4 years, 1 month, and those who are 4 years, 11 months.

18. Hair I   Any indication of hair, however crude.

19. Hair II   Hair shown on more than circumference of head and more than a scribble. Nontransparent, unless it is clear that a bald-headed man is portrayed. A simple hairline across the skull on which no attempt has been made to shade in hair does *not* score. If any attempt has been made, even in outline or with a little shading, to portray hair as having substance or texture, the item scores.

Credit

No Credit

20. Hair III   Any clear attempt to show cut or styling by use of side burns, a forelock, or conformity of base line to a "style." When a hat is drawn, credit the point if hair is indicated in front as well as behind the ear, or if hairline at back of neck or across forehead suggests styling.

21. Hair IV   Hair shaded to show part, or to suggest having been combed, or brushed, by means of *directed* lines. Item 21 is never credited unless Item 20 is; it is thus a "high-grade" point.

Credit

No Credit

22. Ears present   Any indication of ears.

23. Ears present:
proportion and   The vertical measurement must be greater than the
position   horizontal measurement. The ears must be placed somewhere within the middle two-thirds of the head.

Full Face: The top of the ear must be separated from the head line, and *both* ears must extend from the head.

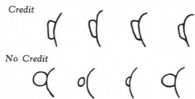

Credit

No Credit

Profile: Some detail, such as a dot, to represent the aural canal must be shown. The shell-like portion of the ear must extend toward the back of the head. (Some children, especially retarded boys, tend to reverse this position, making the ear extend toward the face. In such drawings this item is never credited.)

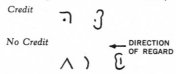

Credit

No Credit   DIRECTION
                   OF REGARD

Figure 14.2 Examples of scoring criteria for the Draw-a-Man scale of the Goodenough-Harris Drawing Test. (From *Children's Drawings as Measures of Intellectual Maturity* by Dale B. Harris, © 1963 by Harcourt Brace Jovanovich, Inc., and reproduced with their permission.)

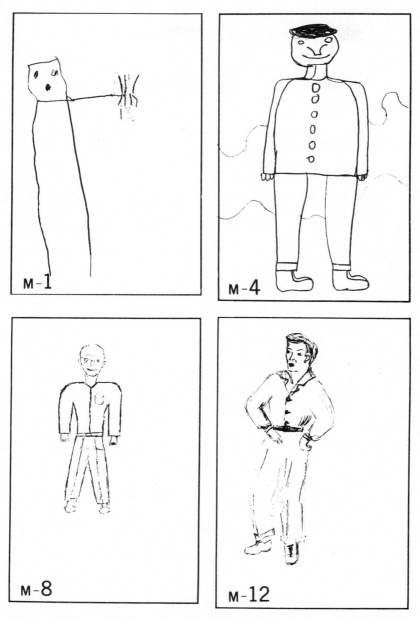

Figure **14.3** Examples of drawings that earn one, four, eight, and twelve points on the Goodenough-Harris Quality scale. The letter M indicates that the drawings are of males, and the numbers give the point values assigned. (From *Children's Drawings as Measures of Intellectual Maturity* by Dale B. Harris, © 1963 by Harcourt Brace Jovanovich, Inc., and reproduced with their permission.)

Norms

The G-H is a revision of the original Goodenough Draw-a-Man Test. In revising the scale, it was administered to "several thousand" children in four geographic areas. Harris reports that the final normative data were based on a selection of seventy-five children at each age level from this initial pool of subjects, stratified on the basis of the occupations of their parents. An equal number of boys and girls were selected at each age level. The manual does not include sufficient detail to demonstrate the extent to which the sample is adequate.

Reliability

Harris reports that studies of interscorer reliability have produced reliability coefficients ranging from the low .80s to as high as .96. Interscorer reliability for the Quality scale ranges from .71 to .91. Thus, the device can be scored with adequate reliability. Harris also summarizes several studies of the test-retest reliability of the scale, reporting that test-retest reliability coefficients are in the .60s to .70s over a time interval as long as three months.

Validity

Harris reports the results of a number of studies demonstrating indirect evidence for the validity of the G-H. In addition, he reports the results of twenty investigations correlating performance on the G-H with scores on other intellectual measures. The correlations range from .05 to .92, with the majority in a range from .50 to .80. Correlations of performance on the revised G-H and the original 1929 scale ranged from .91 to .98. To establish validity for the Quality scale, Harris reports that it correlates .76 to .91 with the Point scale.

Summary

The Goodenough-Harris Drawing Test is either a group-administered or individually administered scale designed to assess students' intellectual development on the basis of their drawings of men, women, and themselves. In using the scale, one must be careful to remember that the test measures only one aspect of intelligence, detail recognition. In addition, the scale was standardized and scoring criteria developed during the 1950s. To the extent that dress styles change, students may be at a disadvantage. This is especially evident in the scoring of the Draw-a-Woman scale. On this scale, students receive credit if they draw a "skirt modeled to indicate pleats or draping: an irregular hemline is not sufficient; lines, shading, or sketching must appear" (Harris, 1963, p. 228). With contemporary styles of dress, it is unlikely that students will draw a woman in a pleated skirt.

HENMON-NELSON TESTS OF MENTAL ABILITY

The Henmon-Nelson Tests of Mental Ability (Lamke, Nelson, & French, 1973; Nelson & French, 1974) are "designed to measure those aspects of mental ability which are important for success in school work" (p. 3). There are four levels of the test, designed for assessment of children in grades kindergarten through 2, 3 through 6, 6 through 9, and 9 through 12. The Primary form, for kindergarten through grade 2, contains eighty-six items and is published as a consumable test booklet in which pupils record their responses directly. The other three levels each contain ninety items and have an accompanying self-scoring answer sheet so that the test booklets may be reused. Each level takes approximately 30 minutes to administer. The Primary form (kindergarten through grade 2) includes three subtests: Listening, Vocabulary, and Size and Number. These are designed to measure the following behaviors.

Listening   This subtest assesses knowledge of factual information, reasoning ability, and understanding of logical relationships. In each case, information is read to the student, who is then required to identify pictures.

Vocabulary   This subtest assesses understanding of words by requiring the student to identify which of four pictures best matches a word read by the examiner.

Size and Number   This subtest assesses understanding of basic spatial and numerical concepts by measuring "perception and recognition of size, number comprehension, ability to count, and ability to solve simple arithmetic problems" (1974, p. 4).

The remainder of the Henmon-Nelson levels do not include subtests but sample several different behaviors that are combined in a global score. A description of the kinds of behaviors sampled follows.

Vocabulary   The student is required to identify synonyms for stimulus words.

Sentence Completion   The student is required to select which of five response choices best completes a sentence.

Opposites   The student is required to identify antonyms for stimulus words.

General Information   The student is required to answer specific factual questions.

Verbal Analogies   The student is required to complete verbal relationships of the nature A : B :: C : ?.

Verbal Classification   The student is required to identify which of five response possibilities does not belong with the other four.

Verbal Inference   The student is given verbal information and must solve problems by inference.

Number Series   The student is given a sequence of numbers having some relationship to one another and must identify the number or numbers that continue the relationship.

Arithmetic Reasoning   The student is required to solve arithmetic problems employing one or more computational operations.

Figure Analogies   The student is required to solve analogies that employ symbols as stimuli.

Scores

Raw scores that students earn on the Henmon-Nelson may be transformed to deviation IQs (mean = 100, standard deviation = 16), percentile ranks, and stanines.

Norms

The levels of the Henmon-Nelson for grades 3 through 12 were standardized on 48,000 pupils (4,000 from each grade plus an additional 4,000 per grade in grades 6 and 9). The Primary form was standardized on 5,000 children from the same schools as those used in the standardization of the other levels. The standardization was completed in regular classes, and the sample was stratified only on the basis of community size and geographic region. The authors provide descriptive tables for community size and geographic region, comparing sample proportions to U.S. population proportions. They do not provide descriptive data about individual students in the standardization sample.

Reliability

Reliability data for the Henmon-Nelson consist of internal-consistency coefficients (split-half reliability estimates corrected by the Spearman-Brown formula) for each of the levels by grade. These coefficients are reported in Table 14.3. The reported reliabilities are satisfactory for the use of the test as a screening instrument. No test-retest reliabilities are reported.

Table **14.3**   Odd-Even Reliability Coefficients for the
Henmon-Nelson Tests of Mental Ability

LEVEL	GRADE	r (CORRECTED)
Primary	K	.84
Primary	1	.89
Primary	2	.88
3–6	3	.95
3–6	4	.96
3–6	5	.96
3–6	6	.97
6–9	6	.95
6–9	7	.94
6–9	8	.95
6–9	9	.95
9–12	9	.93
9–12	10	.95
9–12	11	.95
9–12	12	.96

SOURCE: T. Lamke, M. Nelson, and J. French, *Examiner's manual for the Henmon-Nelson Tests of Mental Ability, 1973 revision* (Boston: Houghton Mifflin, 1973), p. 38, copyright © 1973 by Houghton Mifflin Company; and M. Nelson and J. French, *Examiner's manual for the Henmon-Nelson Tests of Mental Ability, Primary form 1* (Boston: Houghton Mifflin, 1974), p. 31, copyright © 1974 by Houghton Mifflin Company. Reprinted with permission of Houghton Mifflin Company.

Validity

Validity data are reported separately in the Primary manual and the manual for grades 3 through 12. The authors of the Henmon-Nelson report concurrent validity for the Primary form based on correlations of scores earned on the Henmon-Nelson and scores earned on the Metropolitan Achievement Test (MAT) by thirty disadvantaged children (the author's definition of *disadvantaged* is not given) and thirty nondisadvantaged children. For the combined groups, the total score on the Henmon-Nelson correlated .72 with the total score on the MAT, while subtest correlations ranged from .41 to .73.

Two sets of validity data are reported for the levels of the test for grades 3 through 12, but they cover specifically grades 3, 6, and 9 only. The Lorge-Thorndike Intelligence Test (grades 3 and 6), the Otis-Lennon

Mental Ability Test (grade 9), and the Iowa Tests of Basic Skills were administered to three hundred pupils "representative of those enrolled in grades 3, 6, and 9 in Clearfield, Pennsylvania," during the spring of the year. The following fall, the Henmon-Nelson was given. Correlations between the Henmon-Nelson and the Lorge-Thorndike ranged from .78 to .83; those between the Henmon-Nelson and the Otis-Lennon from .75 to .82. Correlations between scores earned on the Henmon-Nelson and scores earned on subtests of the ITBS ranged from .60 to .86. Predictive validity requires that the predictor test be given first. What the authors have done, in fact, is to establish predictive validity for the other tests using the Henmon-Nelson as a criterion. There are no validity data on other grades or samples of pupils. The authors state that "since the 1973 Revision retains the essential characteristics of the earlier Henmon-Nelson forms, it is reasonable to expect that Form I [for grades 3–6] will show similar patterns of relationships with achievement tests" (p. 41).

Summary

The Henmon-Nelson Tests of Mental Ability are quickly administered group tests of mental ability. Levels of the scale for grades 3 through 12 are revisions of the earlier forms of the test. The level appropriate for use in kindergarten through grade 2 is a new downward extension of the test. While data about the reliability of the scale indicate adequate reliability for use of the test in screening, there are some serious questions about the adequacy of standardization of the scale. Data regarding validity are inadequate.

KUHLMANN-ANDERSON INTELLIGENCE TESTS

The Kuhlmann-Anderson Intelligence Tests (KA) (Kuhlmann & Anderson, 1963) are now in their seventh edition. There are eight overlapping levels of the test designed to assess the learning aptitude of students in kindergarten through grade 12. Each test battery is untimed and consists of twelve subtests: twenty-four subtests are unique to specific levels, while twenty subtests appear in adjacent batteries. It is literally impossible to describe the behaviors sampled by the KA. The authors neither name the subtests nor describe the kinds of behaviors sampled. Like the Stanford-Binet Intelligence Scale, the KA is designed to assess "general mental ability." In doing so, it samples all of the kinds of behaviors described in Chapter 12. Not all behaviors are sampled at all levels. Levels of the test and grades for which they are used are listed in Table 14.4.

Table **14.4**   Levels of the Kuhlmann-Anderson Tests and Grades
for Which They Are Designed

LEVEL	GRADES	LEVEL	GRADES
K	K	D	4–5
A	1	EF	5–7
B	2	G	7–9
CD	3–4	H	9–12

Scores

Raw scores for performance on the KA can be transformed to mental ages,
deviation IQs ($\overline{X} = 100$, $S = 16$), and percentile ranks. The test is scored
by hand with scoring stencils, and directions for scoring are extremely
clear. Scores are obtained only for the total test, not for the subtests.

Norms

The KA was standardized on 27,853 students. The normative sample was
selected on the basis of community size, geographic location, and
socioeconomic level. At least 3,000 students per grade level and between
700 and 800 students per three-month interval made up the normative
sample. The authors list communities participating in standardization.
They provide no specific data about individual students.

Reliability

Three kinds of reliability data (internal-consistency, alternate-form, and
test-retest) are reported for the KA. Internal-consistency coefficients reported for the total battery for forms K, A, B, and CD range from .93 to
.95. Internal-consistency coefficients for subtest scores range from .51 to
.69 for the B battery, from .51 to .86 for CD, from .48 to .80 for D, and
from .71 to .81 for battery EF.

   Test-retest reliability data are reported in the manual for all batteries of
the KA. For levels K through EF, test-retest coefficients over two- to
four-month intervals are reported for deviation IQs. The coefficients
range from .83 to .90. For levels G and H, test-retest reliabilities are
reported for deviation IQs over periods of time ranging from one to two
years. The reliability coefficients range from .83 to .92.

   Sufficient evidence is reported in the manual to indicate that the KA is a
reliable group-intelligence test. Subtest reliabilities are not sufficient to
warrant comparisons among subtests.

Validity

The results of over 150 concurrent validity studies are reported in the KA manual. Most studies involved correlation of deviation IQs earned on the KA with scores earned on achievement and other intelligence tests. For the various levels, correlations were moderate.

Information about the predictive validity of the KA varies for each of the specific batteries of the test. The K, D, EF, G, and H batteries have adequate predictive validity. Evidence for the predictive validity of the A, B, and CD batteries is either insufficient or not reported in the manual for the test.

Summary

The seventh edition of the Kuhlmann-Anderson Intelligence Tests is one of the better group-administered devices for measuring learning aptitude. The only weakness that is readily apparent is the authors' failure to provide an adequate description of the content of the tests. The directions for administering, scoring, and interpretation are clear enough to be understood easily by classroom teachers. Internal-consistency and test-retest reliability are adequate for screening purposes. The tests have good concurrent validity and, more importantly, good predictive validity.

OTIS-LENNON MENTAL ABILITY TEST

The Otis-Lennon Mental Ability Test (Otis & Lennon, 1969) is the fourth edition of the Otis series. The original Otis test, the Otis Group Intelligence Scale, was the first group intelligence test designed for use in American schools. The test represented an effort to develop a paper-and-pencil test similar to the individually administered Stanford-Binet Intelligence Scale. The Otis Self-Administering Tests of Mental Ability were published between 1922 and 1929, while the Otis Quick Scoring Mental Ability Tests were developed later. The most recent edition is a revision of these earlier scales.

The Otis-Lennon is designed to measure general mental ability in the form of "verbal-educational" intelligence in kindergarten through grade 12. According to the authors, "The various items comprising the tests measure broad reasoning abilities involving the abstract manipulation of ideas expressed in verbal, figural or symbolic form" (p. 8). The authors carefully indicate that performance on the tests reflects a complex interaction of genetic and environmental factors, that the tests measure "learned or developed abilities in the broadest sense" (Otis & Lennon, 1969, p. 7).

There are six levels of the Otis-Lennon and two forms of the test at each level. The test contains no subtests, but a variety of behaviors are sampled at each level. The Primary I, Primary II, and Elementary I levels contain

Table **14.5** Grade Levels and Behaviors Sampled by the Six Levels of the Otis-Lennon Mental Ability Test

LEVEL	GRADES	BEHAVIORS SAMPLED
Primary I Primary II	K.5–K.9 1.0–1.5	Classification Following directions Quantitative reasoning Comprehension of verbal concepts
Elementary I	1.5–3.9	Classification Following directions Quantitative reasoning Comprehension of verbal concepts Reasoning by analogy

Elementary II
Intermediate
Advanced
	4.0–6.9
	7.0–9.9
	10.0–12.9
		Verbal comprehension
		  Synonyms
		  Opposites
		  Sentence completion
		  Scrambled sentences
		Verbal reasoning
		  Word-letter matrix
		  Verbal analogies
		  Verbal classification
		  Inference
		  Logical selection
		Figural reasoning
		  Figure analogies
		  Series completion
		  Pattern matrix
		Quantitative reasoning
		  Number series
		  Arithmetic reasoning

only pictorial and geometric content; they require no reading. Levels of the test, grades at which the levels are appropriate, and behaviors sampled at each level are illustrated in Table 14.5. The upper levels of the test sample fourteen different kinds of behavior by means of verbal, figural, and numerical stimuli. The tests are untimed, and administration time varies with the level of the test: the Primary forms require 25 to 30 minutes; Elementary I, 50 to 55 minutes; and the other forms, 40 to 50 minutes.

Scores

Three kinds of transformed scores may be obtained on the Otis-Lennon. Raw scores may be transformed to deviation IQs with a mean of 100 and a standard deviation of 16. They may also be transformed to percentile ranks and stanines for either age-level or grade-level comparisons.

Norms

The Otis-Lennon was standardized on approximately 12,000 pupils per grade in kindergarten through grade 12 (approximately 156,000 pupils). The standardization program was carried out in 103 public and parochial school systems, and the sample was chosen on the basis of system size, socioeconomic status, and geographic region. Within each school system, school personnel selected schools that demonstrated high, average, or low achievement; and these data were used to select the sample in such a way that it would represent the achievement level of the entire system. Several tables in the technical handbook compare Otis-Lennon sample proportions to proportions reported in the 1964–1965 *Education Dictionary*. For the most part, characteristics in the sample approximate characteristics of students attending U.S. public schools.

Reliability

Data derived by the most common ways of estimating reliability are reported in the technical handbook. Alternate-form reliabilities were computed by testing one thousand children at each grade level on both forms of the test. The tests were administered within a two-week interval. Thus, reliability estimates include both error of measurement associated with differences in item content and differences in test occasion. Alternate-form reliability coefficients ranged from .83 to .94.

Internal consistencies were computed using both split-half and Kuder-Richardson techniques. Reliability coefficients ranged from .88 to .96. Test-retest reliability over a one-year time interval ranged from .80 to .94.

Validity

Evidence about the content validity, criterion-related validity, and construct validity is reported in the technical handbook. Numerous tables are used to summarize the relationship between performance on the Otis-Lennon and performance on subtests of the California Achievement Test, the Ohio Survey Test, the Metropolitan Achievement Test, the Stanford Achievement Test, the Sequential Tests of Educational Progress, and the Iowa Tests of Educational Development. In general, the correlations are in the range from .50 to .80, indicating that although performance on the test is substantially related to academic achievement, the test measures behaviors other than achievement. Correlations between scores earned on the Otis-Lennon and end-of-year course grades are typically in a range from .45 to .70.

Construct validity for the Otis-Lennon was established by correlating performance on the test with performance on a number of readiness, intelligence, and aptitude measures. Again, extensive tables in the technical handbook report the results of these validity studies. Most of these studies indicate that the Otis-Lennon correlates in a range from about .70 to .85 with other measures of mental ability.

Summary

The Otis-Lennon Mental Ability Test is a group-administered test designed to assess verbal-educational intelligence by measuring the extent to which pupils can solve abstract reasoning problems in verbal, figural, and symbolic format. The tests were adequately standardized and demonstrate the necessary technical characteristics to be used as screening devices.

PRIMARY MENTAL ABILITIES TEST

The Primary Mental Abilities Test (PMA) (Thurstone & Thurstone, 1965) is designed to measure both general intelligence and five specific intellectual factors, called by the authors *primary mental abilities*. There are five levels of the PMA appropriate for grades kindergarten to 1, 2 to 4, 4 to 6, 6 to 9, and 9 to 12. Administration time varies from 34 to 52 minutes for upper levels of the test. For the first two levels, the teacher reads most of the directions, and there is, therefore, no formal time limit. A description of the behaviors sampled by the five subtests of the PMA follows.

Verbal Meaning This subtest assesses skill in deriving meaning from words. At the lower levels, the student must select from four response pictures the one that best represents the meaning of a word read by the examiner. At the upper levels, this subtest is a vocabulary test, requiring that the student read both the stimulus words and the response choices.

Number Facility This subtest assesses the "ability to work with numbers, to handle simple quantitative problems rapidly and accurately, and to understand and recognize quantitative differences" (Thurstone & Thurstone, 1965, p. 1). The battery for kindergarten and grade 1 uses pictures and requires no reading; all other batteries include computation and arithmetic reasoning problems.

Reasoning This subtest requires the student to solve logical problems. The subtest is not included in the first two levels.

Perceptual Speed   This subtest assesses skill in quick and accurate recognition of similarities and differences in pictured objects or symbols. This ability is tested only in the three batteries for kindergarten through sixth grade.

Spatial Relationships   This subtest assesses "ability to visualize how parts of objects or figures fit together, what their relationships are, and what they look like when rotated in space" (Thurstone & Thurstone, 1965, p. 1).

Scores

Different kinds of scores are provided by the different levels of the PMA. Therefore, some difficulty may be encountered in comparing a student's performance on one level of the test with an earlier or later performance on a different level. For the kindergarten and first-grade level of the test, mental ages and ratio IQs are obtained for both the subtests and the total. At the second- to fourth-grade level, deviation IQs (mean = 100, standard deviation = 16) and percentiles may be obtained for the subtests and the total, or mental ages and ratio IQs may be obtained for the subtests. For the fourth- to sixth-grade level and above, deviation IQs and percentiles for both subtests and the total score may be obtained.

Norms

The PMA was standardized on 32,393 children enrolled in seventy-three schools in thirty-nine school systems. Although the sample was stratified on the basis of geographic region, age, and grade, no attempt was made to stratify on the basis of other demographic variables, such as socioeconomic status or parental occupation. The authors include tables in the manual comparing standardization-sample proportions and U.S. population proportions based on geographic region. They do not otherwise describe the normative sample.

Reliability

The authors report the results of a test-retest study at each grade level from the second to twelfth at both one- and four-week intervals. The number of subjects per grade ranged from fourteen to thirty-four. Test-retest reliability coefficients ranged from .54 for Perceptual Speed at grade 1 to .95 for the total score at grade 5. The median reliability for the total score was .91, while the other median reliabilities were: Verbal Meaning = .89, Number Facility = .81, Reasoning = .83, Perceptual Speed = .67, and Spatial Relationships = .78. Subtest reliabilities are questionable for use in making important decisions for individual students but high enough for use in making group decisions. No reliability data are reported for the kindergarten and first-grade level of the test.

Validity

It is difficult to ascertain the validity of the PMA because unique procedures were used to validate the scale. To support the validity of the scale,
the authors report correlations between scores earned on the PMA and
end-of-year grades for 2,558 children in grades 1 through 8 and 824 high
school students. Reported correlations range from .03 for Spatial Relationships at grade 10 to .78 for the total score at grade 7.

In a second validation study, the PMA was administered to students in
grades 2 through 7, and their performance on the test was correlated with
scores earned on the Kuhlmann-Anderson administered in grade 3. In
some instances, then, performances on tests administered as many as four
years apart were compared. Correlations ranged from .23 to .80.

A third validation study consisted of correlating performance on the
PMA with performance on the Iowa Tests of Basic Skills. In some cases the
comparisons were concurrent; in others they were predictive. Correlations
between total score on the PMA and the composite score on the ITBS
ranged from .75 to .84.

Summary

The PMA is a group-administered intelligence test designed to measure
both general intelligence and five primary mental abilities. There are five
levels of the test designed for use in kindergarten through grade 12. The
test has several technical limitations. Standardization of the scale was based
only on geographic, age, and grade stratification; reliabilities of the subtests
are not included for kindergarten and grade 1 and are relatively low for
the other levels.

SHORT FORM TEST OF ACADEMIC APTITUDE

The Short Form Test of Academic Aptitude (SFTAA) (Sullivan, Clark, &
Tiegs, 1970) was derived from the earlier California Test of Mental Matur-
ity. Three different publications contain information regarding the
SFTAA: the technical report that contains research data for 1973, the Test
Coordinator's Handbook for the series of tests, and the examiner's manuals
that accompany each level of the test. The SFTAA, designed to assess the
intellectual maturity of students in grades 1 through 12, has five levels.
The levels and their corresponding grades are reported in Table 14.6.

Each level of the SFTAA contains two sections: language and nonlanguage. The language section includes two subtests, Vocabulary and Memory, while the nonlanguage section includes Analogies and Sequencing.
Behaviors sampled by the respective subtests are as follows.

Table **14.6**   Levels of the Short Form Test of Academic Aptitude

LEVEL	GRADES
1	1.5–3.4
2	3.5–4.9
3	5.0–6.9
4	7.0–9.9
5	9.0–12.9

Vocabulary   This subtest differs at each level of the test. Level 1 employs a picture-vocabulary format to assess the extent to which children are able to identify pictures of words read by the teacher. Levels 2 through 5 require students to identify synonyms of words they must first read.

Memory   This subtest assesses the recall of factual information as well as comprehension and interpretation of the content of stories. Levels 1 and 2 use pictured responses, while the other levels employ a printed-question format. The teacher reads the content of the stories, then administers the other subtests before administering the Memory subtest. In this way, there is a 30-minute delay with a considerable amount of interpolated material before the student is asked to recall information.

Analogies   Pictures are employed at all levels to assess the extent to which the student is able to solve analogies of an A : B :: C : ? format.

Sequencing   In this subtest the student looks at a sequence of stimuli having some progressive relationship to one another and then must identify a missing element in the sequence. Numerical and figural stimuli are employed at all levels.

Scores

Raw scores earned on the SFTAA are transformed to what the authors label *reference scale scores*, standard scores with a mean of 600 and a standard deviation of 100. These scores may be converted to deviation IQs with a mean of 100 and a standard deviation of 16. Deviation IQs may be transformed into either age percentile ranks, grade percentile ranks, or grade stanines. Mental ages may also be obtained for scores on the SFTAA. Separate scores are obtained for the language, nonlanguage, and total scores.

Norms

The SFTAA was standardized on a national sample of 197,912 students in first through twelfth grade; it was standardized jointly with the California Achievement Test. In the selection of students for the normative sample, the authors selected schools rather than individual students. A stratification based on "1967 census figures" for geographic region, community type (urban, suburban, and so on), and district size was used to select 108 school *districts*; 60.1 percent agreed to participate. Replacements were selected for those districts that did not wish to participate, and the final sample was made up of 397 public and 42 Catholic schools. Although these variables were not used to select the sample, the manual does include a description of the normative sample in terms of student mobility, PTA attendance of parents, employed mothers, racial characteristics, kindergarten attendance, number of students with only one parent, number of students for whom English was a second language, occupational level of parents, and characteristics of the physical plant and administration of the school.

Reliability

Internal-consistency and test-retest reliability coefficients are reported by grade and level of the test for a subsample of those who made up the standardization sample. Internal-consistency coefficients ranged from .70 to .91 for individual subtests, from .85 to .93 for the language section, from .84 to .92 for the nonlanguage section, and from .90 to .96 for the total test.

Test-retest reliabilities over a two-week interval ranged from .82 to .94 for the language section, from .83 to .94 for the nonlanguage section, and from .89 to .96 for the total test. Over a fourteen-week interval, test-retest coefficients ranged from .73 to .89 for the language section, from .49 to .83 for the nonlanguage section, and from .68 to .91 for the total test. In general, the test demonstrates adequate reliability for screening purposes.

Validity

Validity was established by means of three correlational studies. A concurrent validity study compared pupil performance on the SFTAA with performance on the Short Form of the California Test of Mental Maturity, its parent test. Correlations between the language sections of the two scales ranged from .64 to .86, between the two nonlanguage sections from .38 to .74, and between total scores on the two devices from .63 to .84.

A second concurrent validity study looked at the relationship between performances of pupils in grades 2, 4, 6, 8, and 10 on the SFTAA and their performances on a measure of academic achievement, the Comprehensive Test of Basic Skills. Correlations between language, nonlanguage, and total scores and area totals on the CTBS ranged from .40 to .86.

A third concurrent validity study was completed by ascertaining the degree of relationship between performances on the SFTAA and on the California Achievement Test for students at every grade level. Twelve tables reporting the results of this investigation are in the technical manual. Although these tables must be examined carefully to get a true picture of the kinds and degrees of relationships identified, in general the correlations are adequate.

Summary

The SFTAA is a group-administered device designed to provide an index of general mental ability. The test consists of both a language and a nonlanguage section. The standardization of this test was based on a stratification of school districts, with only 60.1 percent of the originally chosen sample participating. The reliability of the scale is adequate for use in screening. Reliabilities for the subsections of the test are lower than reliabilities for the total, as is usually the case. Validity information is, at this time, limited. The only evidence the authors report to support the contention that the test measures general mental ability or intellectual maturity is a comparison of scores on the SFTAA and its parent test, the Short Form of the California Test of Mental Maturity. The items for the two tests are different.

SUMMARY

Group intelligence tests are used primarily as screening devices; they are designed to identify those whose intellectual development deviates significantly enough from "normal" to warrant individual intellectual assessment. Many different group intelligence tests are currently used in the schools. This chapter reviewed the most commonly used group tests, to illustrate the many kinds of behaviors sampled in the assessment of intelligence. When teachers evaluate students' performances on group intelligence tests, they must go beyond obtained scores to look at the kinds of behaviors sampled by the tests. When selecting group intelligence tests, teachers must evaluate the extent to which specific tests are standardized on samples of students to whom they want to compare their pupils and the extent to which the tests are technically adequate for their own purposes.

STUDY QUESTIONS

1. A teacher goes to Harold's cumulative folder and finds the following listing of scores earned on group-administered and individually administered intelligence tests.

DATE	TEST	SCORE
9/71	Primary Mental Abilities Test	68
12/72	Cognitive Abilities Test	68
6/73	Slosson Intelligence Test	50
12/74	Culture Fair Intelligence Tests	52
12/75	Peabody Picture Vocabulary Test	68
12/76	Wechsler Intelligence Scale for Children — Revised	70

Identify two alternative explanations for the observed differences in obtained scores.

2. Get a copy of any group intelligence test and identify the domains of behaviors sampled by at least ten *items*. Use the domains described in Chapter 12.

3. Identify at least four major factors a teacher must consider when administering group intelligence tests to students.

4. For what reasons would school personnel give group intelligence tests to students?

5. Of what value to classroom teachers are scores from group-administered intelligence tests?

Chapter 15

Assessment of Perceptual-Motor Skills

Educators and psychologists have operated for quite some time under the assumption that adequate perceptual-motor development is important both in and of itself and as a prerequisite to the development of academic skills. A wide variety of devices designed to assess children's perceptual-motor functioning are in use in the public schools today. While many measures of learning aptitude include items designed to assess perceptual or motor skills and while many readiness tests assess aspects of perceptual-motor development, this chapter focuses on those devices designed specifically and exclusively to assess perceptual-motor skills.

Perceptual-motor assessment typically takes place for one of several purposes. In some cases, the perceptual-motor skills of entire classes of students are assessed in an effort to identify those with perceptual-motor difficulties so that training programs can be instituted to prevent incipient learning difficulties. Students who perform poorly on perceptual-motor devices are said to demonstrate perceptual-motor problems thought to contribute to or cause learning problems. In other cases, students having academic difficulties are assessed by means of perceptual-motor tests in an effort to identify the extent to which perceptual-motor difficulties may be causing the academic difficulties. In both instances, efforts are made to identify perceptual-motor problems so that training programs can be prescribed. Finally, perceptual-motor tests are widely used to diagnose brain injury.

THE INTERESTING PAST AND PROBLEMATICAL PRESENT OF PERCEPTUAL-MOTOR ASSESSMENT

The practice of perceptual-motor assessment, while relatively new, has an interesting history. In the early 1900s gestalt psychology was born with a paper by Max Wertheimer that reported the work of Wertheimer, Kurt Koffka, and Wolfgang Kohler on perceptual phenomena such as apparent movement and afterimages. In 1923 Wertheimer put together a set of empirical statements known as the *principles of perceptual organization*. Gestalt psychologists, while certainly concerned with other aspects of psychology, made perception their major study. The early work of Wertheimer and his associates is apparent even today in the assessment of perceptual-motor development.

More recently, Hallahan and Cruickshank (1973) traced the history of the study of perceptual-motor problems in mentally retarded, brain-injured, and learning-disabled children. According to Hallahan and Cruickshank, the historical roots of current practices in perceptual-motor assessment can be traced to the early work of Goldstein and of Werner and Strauss. Goldstein (1927, 1936, 1939) was engaged in the study of soldiers who had suffered traumatic head injuries during World War I. According to Hallahan and Cruickshank (1973), "Goldstein . . . found in his patients . . . the psychological characteristics of concrete behavior, meticulosity, perseveration, figure-background confusion, forced responsiveness to stimuli, and catastrophic reaction" (p. 59).

In the mid-1940s the two German psychologists Heinz Werner and Alfred Strauss began to study the behavioral pathology evidenced by brain-injured persons. In a series of studies at the Wayne County Training School in Detroit, Michigan, Werner and Strauss studied two kinds of brain-injured subjects: brain-injured retardates, and nonretardates who had experienced traumatic head injury from an automobile accident, a fall, a gunshot wound, or other similar incident. Their early research resulted in a list of behavioral characteristics said to differentiate brain-injured and non-brain-injured persons. The tests that were constructed to assess these behavioral chracteristics are used today for that purpose.

Hallahan and Cruickshank state that "for Werner and Strauss it became a major concern to learn whether the psychological manifestations of brain injury found in adults by Goldstein would also be observable in children" (p. 60). Despite this interest in children, it must be remembered that the subjects studied in early investigations and on whom early tests were developed differ significantly from the children we currently assess using perceptual-motor tests. Subjects in early investigations were primarily adults who exhibited focal brain injury in the form of tissue damage, lesions, or tumors. To generalize characteristics of such persons to children with "diffuse brain injury" ignores neurological differences as well as developmental differences between children and adults. Many current perceptual-motor tests were developed using a criterion-group approach; they were developed to differentiate between *groups* of persons known to have sustained brain injury and non-brain-injured persons. They are currently used to differentiate between *individuals* whose problems may or may not be due to brain injury and who usually have no proven injury to the central nervous system.

While perceptual-motor tests have been used for some time to diagnose brain injury, recently there has been a dramatic and significant increase in the use of various perceptual-motor devices to diagnose learning disabilities. According to Hallahan and Cruickshank (1973), those who are the contemporary leaders in the field of learning disabilities, who were responsible for its origin and development and for the development of the major perceptual-motor tests, were at one time associates or students of Werner and Strauss or were at least significantly influenced by their work. William Cruickshank, Samuel Kirk, and Newell Kephart were all associated with the Wayne County Training School at the time Werner and Strauss were engaged in their early investigations. Gerald Getman, an optometrist, later worked with Kephart at Purdue University, while Ray Barsch worked with both Getman and Strauss. Marianne Frostig, while not a direct associate of Werner and Strauss, has stated that she was significantly influenced by their early investigations (Hallahan & Cruickshank, 1973).

The associates of Werner and Strauss went on to apply their early work to the study of behavioral pathology in nonretarded children who were experiencing learning difficulty. While Kirk emphasized psycholinguistic disabilities and with his students constructed the Illinois Test of Psycholinguistic Abilities, the others stressed perceptual problems, Cruickshank focusing on brain-injured children and children with cerebral palsy, and Kephart, Getman, Barsch, and Frostig focusing on the academic correlates of perceptual-motor problems.

Out of the long history of interest in perception and perceptual problems among adults and brain-injured retardates has grown today a particular concern for the perceptual and motor problems of nonretarded children who fail academically. The thinking underlying this concern is illustrated by statements made by Frostig, Lefever, and Whittlesey (1966).

It is most important that a child's perceptual disabilities, if any exist, be discovered as early as possible. All research to date which has explored the child's general classroom behavior has confirmed the authors' original finding that kindergarten and first-grade children with visual perceptual disabilities are likely to be rated by their teachers as maladjusted in the classroom; not only do they frequently find academic learning difficult, but their ability to adjust to the social and emotional demands of classroom procedures is often impaired.

Identification and training of children with visual perceptual disabilities during the preschool years or at the time of school entrance would help prevent many instances of school failure and maladjustment *caused* [emphasis added] by visual perceptual difficulties. Although some children may overcome these difficulties at a later age, there is as yet no method to predict whether a child will be able to do so without help. . . . The authors' research has shown that visual perceptual difficulties, regardless of etiology, can be ameliorated by specific training. Pinpointing the areas of a child's visual perceptual difficulties and measuring their severity is helpful and is often necessary in designing the most efficient training program to aid in overcoming the disabilities. (p. 6)

The writers of the preceding paragraphs (they are also the authors of the Developmental Test of Visual Perception) do not cite empirical support for their contentions. We would argue that the claims made are unwarranted. The majority of the research does not support the contention that children with visual-perceptual disabilities are likely to be rated as maladjusted. At most, it can demonstrate simply that children who are rated as maladjusted also perform poorly on perceptual-motor tests. Furthermore, the authors recommend assessment of perceptual-motor difficulties under the assumption that remediation of identified disabilities will lead to greater academic success, and yet reviews of the efficacy of perceptual-motor training demonstrate that it is grossly ineffective in improving academic performance (Mann, 1971b; Hammill & Wiederholt, 1973; Ysseldyke, 1973).

What the majority of the research *has* shown is that most perceptual-motor tests are unreliable. We do not know what they measure, because they do not measure anything consistently. Unlike the majority of intelligence and achievement tests, the tests used to assess perceptual-motor skills in children are technically inadequate. And for the most part they are neither theoretically nor psychometrically sound. For example, they are designed to assess perceptual-motor abilities under the assumption that such abilities cause academic success or academic failure (see Ysseldyke & Salvia, 1974). Or they are designed to assess hypothetical constructs like figure-ground perception and body image and differentiation but do not do so with consistency (see Ysseldyke, 1973; Ysseldyke & Salvia, 1974). Or they may be based on criterion keying, an approach that can lead to logical fallacies of undistributed middle terms (all canaries eat birdseed; Esmeralda eats birdseed; therefore, Esmeralda is a canary).

In short, the devices currently used to assess children's perceptual-motor skills are extremely inadequate. The real danger is that reliance on such tests in planning interventions for children may actually lead to assigning children to activities that do them absolutely no good. While we believe that few currently available perceptual-motor devices approach either theoretical or psychometrical adequacy, we review those most often used.

SPECIFIC TESTS OF PERCEPTUAL-MOTOR SKILLS

BENDER VISUAL MOTOR GESTALT TEST

The Bender Visual Motor Gestalt Test (BVMGT), consisting of nine geometric designs to be copied on paper, was originally developed by Loretta Bender in 1938. The designs in the test were originally used by Wertheimer in 1923 to illustrate the perceptual principles of gestalt psychology. Bender used the designs in a test to differentiate brain-injured

from non-brain-injured adults and to detect signs of emotional disturbance. The test has gained widespread popularity among clinical psychologists and has become one of the most frequently administered psychometric devices.

Administration of the BVMGT consists simply of presenting nine
geometric designs, one at a time, to a subject who is asked to copy each of
them on a plain sheet of paper. Although Bender provided criteria for
scoring the test, a variety of other scoring systems have been developed, the
most common of which is the system developed by Elizabeth Koppitz in
1963. The impetus for Koppitz's work arose from her experience in a child
guidance clinic, where she was reportedly impressed with the frequency of
perceptual problems among children with learning or emotional difficulties.

The Koppitz scoring system, restricted to use with children between 5
and 11 years of age, is the system most often used by psychologists in school
settings. In 1963, Koppitz published a text describing the scoring system,
the various uses of the BVMGT with children, normative data for the
scoring system, and limited information about reliability and validity. In
1975, Koppitz published volume 2 of *The Bender Gestalt Test for Young
Children,* a compilation and synthesis of research on the BVMGT between
1963 and 1973. This latter text is a commendable effort that eliminates
having to search the literature for research on the test.

Our discussion of the BVMGT is based entirely on use of the Koppitz
scoring system with the test.

Scores

When scoring according to the Koppitz system, the examiner records the
number of errors on each of the nine separate geometric forms. Four
kinds of errors are recorded.

Distortion of Shape   Errors are scored as distortion of shape when a child's
reproduction of the stimulus design is so misshapen that the general
configuration is lost. If a child converts dots to circles, alters the relative
size of components of the stimulus drawing, or in other ways distorts the
design, errors are recorded.

Perseveration   Perseveration errors are recorded when a child fails to stop
after completing the required drawing — for example, a child is asked to
copy eleven dots in a row and then copies significantly more than eleven.

Integration   Integration errors consist of a failure to juxtapose correctly
parts of a design, as illustrated in Figure 15.1. In drawing a, the components of the design fail to meet. In drawing b, they overlap.

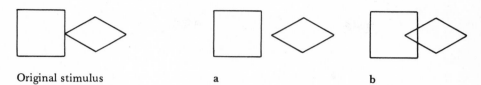

Original stimulus   a   b

Figure 15.1   Two integration errors in Koppitz's scoring of the Bender Visual Motor Gestalt Test

Rotation   Rotation errors are recorded when a child rotates a design by more than 45 degrees or rotates the stimulus card, even though the drawing is correctly copied. Reversals are 180-degree rotations and are scored as rotation errors.

More than one error can be scored on each drawing. The total number of possible errors is twenty-five. The examiner adds the number of errors to obtain a total raw score for the test. The higher the total raw score, the poorer the performance.

The Koppitz manual (1963) contains a normative table reporting means and standard deviations of error scores for specific age levels in half-year intervals. This normative table, based on the 1963 standardization of the test, is used to transform error scores to developmental ages. The 1975 publication reporting research on the BVMGT from 1963 to 1973 includes two features. A new set of examples for scoring individual items has been included to eliminate the scoring difficulties that examiners reported to the author. It also includes a new set of normative tables based on a 1974 renorming of the test. This set of tables can be used to convert error scores to age equivalents and to percentile ranks.

Norms

Two sets of norms are now available for the Koppitz scoring system. The test was originally standardized on 1,104 children from forty-six classes in twelve public schools. The schools were reportedly selected from rural, urban, and suburban areas in unspecified proportions. The original normative sample included 637 boys and 467 girls. There are no data in the 1963 manual on the geographic areas the sample was drawn from or their demographic characteristics. In volume 2 (1975), Koppitz reports that 98 percent of the original sample was white.

Koppitz renormed the test in 1974 in an effort to achieve a more representative sample of American schoolchildren. The 1974 normative sample included 975 children between the ages of 5 and 11. A geographic cross section was not attained: 15 percent of the children were from the

West, 2 percent were from the South, and 83 percent were from the Northeast. Racial balance is more nearly representative; 86 percent of the sample was white, 8.5 percent black, 4.5 percent were either Mexican-American or Puerto Rican, and 1 percent was Oriental. There is no indication of the socioeconomic level of the sample; Koppitz states that research has demonstrated that socioeconomic status is not an important variable in children's performance on the BVMGT. Community size is adequately described; 7 percent were from rural communities, 31 percent were from small towns, 36 percent from suburbs, and 26 percent were from large metropolitan areas.

The sample sizes for half-year-interval age groups in both the 1963 and 1974 norms are unevenly distributed. For the 1963 norms, the norm group ranged in size from 27 children at ages 10-0 to 10-5 to 180 children at ages 6-6 to 6-11. For the 1974 norms, the norm group ranges in size from 47 children (at ages 5-0 to 5-5, 7-6 to 7-11, and 9-6 to 9-11) to 175 children at ages 6-0 to 6-5. Another major difficulty was present in the 1963 standardization: after age 8-6 the standard deviations for raw scores exceeded the means. For the 1974 norms, the standard deviations after age 8-6 are about equal to the means.

Reliability

Two kinds of reliability data are reported for the BVMGT. Koppitz (1975) summarizes twenty-three studies of the interscorer reliability for her scoring system. Interscorer reliabilities ranged from .79 to .99, with 81 percent exceeding .89. The revised set of scoring examples that Koppitz published in 1975 after test users reported scoring difficulties will probably facilitate interscorer agreement in scoring a child's performance.

In her 1975 addition to the 1963 manual, Koppitz reports research on factors she believes may affect performance on the scale. Her review of research on the effects of motivation, task familiarization, verbal labeling, tracing and copying, and specific perceptual-motor training led to the conclusion that the BVMGT does indeed serve mainly as a measure of children's level of maturation in integration of perceptual and motor functions. Only secondarily does it reflect their various learning experiences with specific perceptual-motor tasks.

The 1975 manual also summarizes the results of nine test-retest reliability studies with normal elementary school children. Reliability coefficients ranged from .50 to .90 (mean = 71.48; mode = .76). On the basis of her review, Koppitz made a claim for the essential reliability of the BVMGT scores for normal children. Yet five of the nine reliability studies she reports are on kindergarten children only; and only one of twenty-five reported coefficients exceeds the standard of .90 recommended for tests used to make important decisions. As Koppitz valuably cautions: "Certainly no diagnosis or major decision should ever be made on the basis of a single scoring point, nor for that matter on the basis of a youngster's total Developmental Bender Test score" (p. 29).

Validity

The construct of *visual-motor perception* is never adequately defined in either Koppitz manual. There is no evidence about the extent to which the test assesses visual-motor perception; the copying of nine designs is believed to be a measure of visual perception because some experts say it is one.

Koppitz (1975) cites several uses for the BVMGT and reports research on each of the suggested uses. She reports correlations of performance on the BVMGT and performance on measures of intelligence, academic achievement, and visual perception. She also cites evidence for use of the test in diagnosing minimal brain dysfunction and emotional disturbance. The paragraphs that follow describe some of her findings and recommendations.

In her 1963 manual, Koppitz reported results of tests of the relationship between scores earned on the BVMGT and scores earned on intelligence tests. She concluded that the BVMGT may be substituted "with some confidence" for a screening test of intelligence. She stated:

In clinical and school settings psychologists are constantly faced with the problem of how to use their limited time most economically. A full scale intelligence test usually requires so much time that only a brief period is left for other tests or an interview. The author has used the Bender test frequently with young children of normal intelligence who primarily seemed to show emotional problems and revealed no learning difficulties. The Bender test not only gives the examiner a rough measure of the youngster's intellectual ability, but also serves as a nonthreatening introduction to the interview. Children tend to enjoy copying the Bender designs, and in some cases the Bender figures evoke associations and spontaneous comments which can lead to further discussions. In most cases the Bender Test will suffice to rule out mental retardation or serious perceptual problems associated with neurological impairment and the examiner can use most of his/her time for projective tests and an interview rather than spending it on a lengthy intelligence test which offers little insight into the dynamics of the child's emotional problems. (p. 51)

In the 1975 addition to the 1963 manual, Koppitz continues to support the use of the BVMGT as a rough test of intelligence.

The statement "The Bender Gestalt Test can be used with some degree of confidence as a short nonverbal intelligence test for young children, particularly for screening purposes" (Koppitz, 1963, p. 50) has been supported by a number of recent studies. But as I previously suggested, the Bender Test should if possible be combined with a brief verbal test. (p. 47)

The BVMGT is *not* an intelligence test but a measure of a child's skill in copying geometric designs. It provides a very limited sample of behavior; in fact, of the thirteen kinds of behaviors described in Chapter 12 as being regularly sampled in intelligence tests, the Bender samples only one. In our opinion, the BVMGT should never be used as, or substituted for, a measure of intellectual functioning.

Koppitz (1975) reviews numerous investigations of the relationship between children's performance on the BVMGT and their academic achievement. Good students and poor students, she concludes, tend as groups to make significantly different total scores on the test. Furthermore, the scores normal children earn show a positive correlation with their academic achievement. Koppitz uses observed differences to conclude that scores earned on the BVMGT

appear to be most successful in predicting overall school functioning and rate of progress in total achievement. A child with a marked discrepancy between IQ and Bender Test scores usually has specific learning difficulties. LD pupils and slow learners mature at a significantly slower rate in visual-motor integration, as measured on the Bender Test, than do well-functioning children. Scores from repeated administrations of the Bender Test are good indicators of progress a child is making, and they are helpful in planning an individualized educational program. (p. 70)

Children who perform well in school may well do better on the BVMGT than children who experience academic difficulty. But as Koppitz herself states, the test cannot be used to predict the academic performance of *individual* children (1975, p. 70). Moreover, Koppitz has not provided evidence to support the contention that the test facilitates individualization of instruction. To do so would require demonstration of an interaction between test performance and success under different forms (methods, techniques) of instruction — demonstration, in other words, of evidence for aptitude-treatment interactions.

Koppitz (1975) reviewed many studies of the use of the BVMGT to diagnose minimal brain dysfunction in schoolchildren. She concluded that the test is a valuable aid for this purpose but should never be used in isolation. Rather, she believes test results are valuable when combined with other medical and behavioral data.

Koppitz (1975) also claims that recent research gives additional validity to the ten indicators of emotional problems that she delineated in her 1963 text. Although she again provides notes of caution indicating that not all children with poor Bender protocols have emotional problems, she does state that "the presence of three or more emotional indicators on a Bender Test protocol tends to reflect emotional difficulties that warrant further investigation" (p. 92).

Koppitz (1975) provides evidence to support the contention that performance on the BVMGT is significantly related to performance on other visual-perceptual measures. She does not report the extent to which pupils who achieve low scores on the BVMGT perform well on these other tests or vice versa.

The BVMGT is, quite simply, a measure of skill development in copying geometric designs. It is *not* designed as a measure of intelligence, predictor of achievement, or measure of emotional disturbance or minimal brain dysfunction. Using it as any of these is risky.

Summary

The BVMGT is a test requiring the child to copy nine geometric designs. The test was originally developed by Bender who used designs developed earlier by Wertheimer. Koppitz has developed a scoring system for the test, and her system is designed for ages 5 to 11. The BVMGT is today one of the most widely used psychometric devices.

Reliability for the BVMGT is relatively low, at least too low for use in making placement decisions. Yet, performance on the test is used as a criterion in the differential identification of children as brain injured, perceptually handicapped, or emotionally disturbed. Validity for the BVMGT is currently not clearly established. The authors have not empirically demonstrated that the test measures visual-motor perception or that it discriminates *individual* cases of brain injury, perceptual handicap, or emotional disturbance. The test certainly provides a very limited sample of perceptual-motor behavior, and for this reason if none other, one would have to be extremely cautious in interpreting and using its results.

A statement by Koppitz is a fitting conclusion to our discussion of her test. "The very fact," she writes, "that the Bender Test is so appealing and is easy to administer presents a certain danger. Because it is so deceptively simple, it is probably one of the most overrated, most misunderstood, and most maligned tests currently in use" (1975, p. 2).

DEVELOPMENTAL TEST OF VISUAL PERCEPTION

The Developmental Test of Visual Perception (DTVP) (Frostig, Maslow, Lefever, & Whittlesey, 1964; Frostig, Lefever & Whittlesey, 1966) is designed to measure "five operationally-defined perceptual skills" (Frostig et al., 1966, p. 5): eye-hand coordination, figure-ground perception, form constancy, position in space, and spatial relations. The areas were selected for assessment, according to the authors, because (1) they are critical for the acquisition of academic skills; (2) they affect the total organism to a greater extent than other functions such as color vision or tone discrimination; (3) they develop relatively early in life; (4) they are frequently disturbed in children diagnosed as neurologically handicapped; and (5) they are suitable for group testing.

The DTVP consists of a thirty-five-page consumable pupil response booklet. There are two manuals for the test, a standardization manual (Frostig et al., 1966) and an administration and scoring manual (Frostig et al., 1964). The test can be individually or group administered; it takes about 40 minutes. Behaviors sampled by each of the five subtests are described by the authors.

Eye-Hand Coordination   This subtest assesses skill in drawing various kinds of continuous lines within boundaries and from point to point.

Figure-Ground Perception   This subtest assesses skill in identifying figures as distinct from increasingly complex backgrounds and in discriminating intersecting and hidden geometric figures.

Form Constancy   This subtest assesses skill in recognizing various geometric shapes regardless of size or orientation.

Position in Space   This subtest assesses skill in discriminating reversals and rotations of figures in a series.

Spatial Relations   This subtest assesses skill in copying patterns using dots as guide points. The child is shown a sample pattern and required to copy it by following the dots.

Scores

Scoring of the DTVP is objective. Ample scoring examples and in some cases scoring stencils are provided. Points earned depend on the quality of a child's responses to test items, and a raw score is earned for each of the subtests. Three kinds of derived scores are obtained for the DTVP: perceptual ages, scale scores, and perceptual quotients. Perceptual ages are age-equivalent scores and are derived separately for each subtest. The scale score is a ratio score obtained by dividing the perceptual age by the chronological age and multiplying by 10.[1] Thus, a child who is 6 years, 6 months, old who has a perceptual age on the DTVP of 5 years, 3 months, is given a scale score of 8.3. In the scoring procedures for the DTVP, the

---

1. The scale score obtained for the DTVP is *not* a scale score. Scaled scores are standard scores and have a predetermined mean and standard deviation (see also the scaled scores for the Wechsler Intelligence Scale for Children—Revised). The scale scores for the DTVP are ratios. These ratios have different means and different standard deviations for children of different ages.

scale score is rounded to the nearest whole number. The perceptual quotient is a deviation score obtained by adding the subtest scale scores and using a table in the manual. The perceptual quotients are constructed so that a perceptual quotient of 100 is always at the fiftieth percentile; one of 90 is always at the twenty-fifth percentile; one of 110 is always at the seventy-fifth percentile; and so on.

Procedures recommended in the manual for the DTVP for transforming raw scores to scale scores and perceptual quotients are unnecessarily complex. Without really giving a rationale for doing so, the authors employ four different scoring procedures depending on the age of the child assessed. For children between the ages of 3 and 4, a table is used to convert raw scores to perceptual ages. These perceptual ages are then divided by chronological age to obtain scale scores. However, in all cases, regardless of the raw score, a constant score of 10 is assigned to a child's performance on the Spatial Relations subtest. For children between 4 and 8 years of age, different tables for different chronological ages are used to convert raw scores to scale scores and to obtain perceptual quotients.

A child between 8 and 10 years of age who receives the maximum perceptual age for any subtest is credited with a scale score of 10. It is, however, possible for a child who does *not* earn the maximum perceptual age to earn a higher scale score, and thus a higher perceptual quotient, than a child who earns the maximum score. Let us assume that two children, Amy and Christopher, who are both 8 years, 1 month old, take the DTVP. On subtest 1, Eye-Hand Coordination, Amy earns a raw score of 19, while Christopher earns a raw score of 20. Using table 1 in the DTVP manual, Amy earns a perceptual age of 9-6, while Christopher earns a perceptual age of 10+. To obtain scale scores, the perceptual age is divided by the chronological age; the quotient is multiplied by 10; and the product is rounded to the nearest whole number. Amy earns a scale score of 12 ($114/9 \times 10 = 11.7$). Christopher, however, because he obtained the maximum perceptual age, is assigned a scale score of 10. A child who earns a maximum perceptual age on every subtest *cannot* earn a perceptual quotient greater than 100. Think for a moment what this must do to the reliability of the test. Raw scores and scale scores can actually be inversely related, and there is a ceiling effect.

Finally, the authors of the DTVP state that "any child of 10 years or more who does not receive the maximum Perceptual Age Equivalent for any subtest is presumed to have difficulty in the area measured" (1966, p. 31). *The transformed scores for the DTVP are not only confusing; they are questionably derived and therefore absolutely must not be used in making diagnostic decisions.*

The authors of the DTVP state that scale scores of less than 8 indicate perceptual-motor weaknesses that need to be remediated. They further state that "it has been found very helpful to use a perceptual quotient of 90 as the cut-off point in the scores of kindergarten children, below which a child should receive special training" (1964, p. 479). Such interpretations simply cannot be made when the scores obtained on the DTVP do not have consistent meaning.

Norms

The 1963 edition of the DTVP was standardized on 2,116 children, between 107 and 240 children at each half-year level between the ages of 3 and 9. The authors (1964) do state, though, that the test was designed primarily for use with young children. The entire sample was drawn from nursery schools and public elementary schools in southern California. The sample was selected on the basis of the following three considerations: (1) an attempt to get a stratified sample of children from different socioeconomic levels, (2) the willingness of schools to cooperate, and (3) the proximity to Frostig's research center. By Frostig's own admission the sample has some serious shortcomings. The sample was drawn from a geographically and socioeconomically restricted area. It was overwhelmingly middle class (93 percent), despite the reported attempt to obtain a stratified sample of children from different socioeconomic backgrounds, and it had little minority representation (a few Chicanos, fewer Orientals, and no Blacks). Nowhere in the manual is there a report of the sex, grade level, or occupation and education of the parents of those in the normative group.

In Chapter 3, on the administration of tests, we discussed optimal group size for testing. The standardization of the DTVP was completed by testing *no fewer* than fifteen kindergarten and first-grade children at one time. Nursery school children were tested in groups of two to eight.

Reliability

Frostig et al. (1964) report the results of three test-retest reliability studies carried out in 1960 with a small sample of fifty children who were experiencing learning difficulties. The test-retest reliability for the perceptual quotient was reported as .98 using the full range of ages. In a second study of two groups of thirty-five first graders and two groups of thirty-seven second graders a reliability of .80 was obtained. Test-retest reliability for subtest scale scores, however, ranged from .42 (Figure-Ground) to .80 (Form Constancy).

A third study was conducted in 1962 to ascertain test-retest reliability when the device was administered by trained personnel who were not psychologists or psychometricians. The test was given to three kindergarten and three first-grade classes with a fourteen-day interval between test and retest. Obtained reliability coefficients for subtest scale scores ranged from .29 (Eye-Hand Coordination) to .74 (Form Constancy) for kindergarten children and from .39 (Eye-Hand Coordination and Figure-Ground) to .68 (Form Constancy) for first graders. The reliability coefficient for the total scale score was .69.

Split-half reliabilities obtained for the total scale score for the various age levels were .89 (5 to 6 years) to .68 (6 to 7 years) to .82 (7 to 8 years) to .78 (8 to 9 years). Reliabilities decreased with increasing age.

The low reliabilities for individual subtests certainly raise serious questions about their use in differential diagnosis, the very procedure Frostig recommends. You will recall that tests should have reliabilities in excess of .90 to be used in differential diagnosis and in making instructional decisions. Reliabilities for subtests of the DTVP come nowhere near this figure.

Validity

Frostig et al. (1964) report two validity studies in the manual for the DTVP. Correlations between total scale scores on the DTVP and teacher ratings of classroom adjustment, motor coordination, and intellectual functioning were .44, .50, and .50 respectively. The authors state that "the correlation found between teacher ratings of classroom adjustment and scores on the Frostig Test (1961 standardization) suggests the correctness of the hypothesis that disturbances in visual perception during the early school years are likely to be reflected in disturbances in classroom behavior" (p. 492).

In showing a moderate correlation between scores on the DTVP and teacher ratings the authors have demonstrated only a relationship, not necessarily a cause-effect relationship. The study does not provide validity evidence for the scale. A test's measuring what it is designed to measure would be validity evidence. The DTVP was designed to assess visual-motor skills, not classroom adjustment or intellectual functioning.

The second validity study, based on the contention that the Goodenough-Harris Test is a measure of intellectual functioning, perceptual development, and personality, was designed to ascertain to what extent the DTVP and the Goodenough-Harris measured factors in common. Correlations between scores on the DTVP and the Goodenough-Harris were .46 for kindergarten, .32 for first-grade, and .36 for second-grade children.

As mentioned above, the test authors believe that for kindergarten children a perceptual quotient of 90 on the DTVP should be used as a cut-off point below which a child should receive visual-perceptual remediation. They also maintain that "a child's ability to learn to read is affected by his visual perceptual development" (1964, p. 493). To support these contentions, the authors conducted a study in a laboratory school classroom at UCLA. They report:

A group of 25 children between the ages of 4½ and 6½ were to be exposed to reading material but not forced to use it. All who used it were to be given training in word attack skills, phonics, observation of configuration, and use of contextual clues. The Frostig test was administered in July, 1962, and eight of the children were found to have visual perceptual quotients of 90 or below. It was predicted that these eight children would not attempt to learn to read because of their difficulties. This prediction proved to be highly accurate. In October, 1962, the children were rated for reading achievement. None of the children with a visual perceptual quotient below 90 had begun to read; of the two children with a perceptual quotient of 90, one had learned to read very well, while the other had not. Only one of the children with a PQ above 90 showed reading difficulties.   (p. 495)

The authors simply cannot use the obtained data to support their contention. Such support would require a carefully controlled study accounting for the fact that the observed differences were not a function of intellectual level, some other variable, or teacher expectancy. The validity data reported in the manual for the DTVP do not support the authors' contention that the test measures five operationally defined perceptual skills.

Summary

The DTVP is a group-administered test designed to assess what the author has defined as five relatively independent components of visual perception. Data about the reliability of the scale obviously indicate that the five areas are not consistently assessed, while factor-analytic studies have pretty well dismissed the notion that the five areas are independently assessed.

Individual subtests of the DTVP lack the necessary reliability and validity to be used in diagnostic prescriptive teaching. We simply cannot put a great deal of faith in the accuracy (freedom from error) of the scores a child earns on the DTVP subtests.

In its composite form, as reflected by the perceptual quotient, the DTVP is a relatively reliable measure for theoretical and research purposes. The total test provides a global score indicative of overall visual-perceptual skill development. Performance on the DTVP must be interpreted with considerable caution.

MEMORY FOR DESIGNS TEST

The Memory for Designs Test (Graham & Kendall, 1960) assesses the ability of persons over 8 years old to copy geometric designs from memory. The express purpose of the test is to provide an instrument to use in research on organic impairment and to use as an adjunct test in a battery of tests administered to persons suspected to be brain injured. The Memory for Designs Test is administered by asking a person to copy fifteen geometric designs, each of which is individually exposed for a period of 5 seconds and then withdrawn. Administration time usually requires about 10 minutes.

Scores

Individual designs are scored in terms of the number and kinds of errors in the subject's drawing. The total score, the sum of scores for individual drawings, is used to judge the person's performance. Scores for each of the fifteen drawings are assigned on a four-point scale, described by the authors as follows.

0 A score of 0 is assigned to a satisfactory reproduction or to an omitted design.

1 A score of 1 is assigned when more than two easily identifiable errors are made but the general configuration of the design is retained.

2 A score of 2 is given when the general configuration of the design has been lost.

3 A score of 3 is given when the design is reversed or rotated.

According to the authors, the weight given to different types of errors was assigned on an empirical basis. Because rotation errors were observed to be more prevalent in brain-injured subjects, such errors are penalized more heavily. The assignment of a score of 0 for omitted designs is based on the observation that about as many brain-injured as non-brain-injured persons omit designs.

In addition to the raw score, a difference score is obtained for performance on the Memory for Designs Test. The difference score statistically controls for the effects of chronological age and vocabulary level. Older individuals and those of higher intellectual level are expected to make fewer errors on the Memory for Designs Test.

Raw scores are interpreted in such a way that for adults a score of 12 or greater is seen as indicative of "brain damage," a score of 5 to 11 is interpreted as "borderline" performance, and a raw score of 0 to 4 is interpreted as "normal" performance.

To obtain difference scores, values are assigned to both chronological age and vocabulary level (as assessed by the Vocabulary section of the Stanford-Binet or the Wechsler scales), and the score for Vocabulary level is subtracted from the score for chronological age. The difference score is used to ascertain the presence or absence of brain injury.

Norms

The norms for the Memory for Designs Test are based on eight groups of persons who participated in research on the test. The subjects were obtained from various clinics and hospitals in the St. Louis area. Some subjects took the test as part of a psychological examination or under the guise that it was a part of a routine medical examination. Others were informed that they were participating in research. To be included in the normative sample, subjects had to have had formal schooling to at least a third-grade level and a vocabulary equivalent to a Stanford-Binet IQ of at least 70; they had to complete at least eleven of the fifteen designs; and they had to demonstrate that they had no marked motor incoordination nor uncorrected defect in near vision. For child subjects, the educational restriction was dropped, but the child had to have an IQ of at least 70 on the Stanford-Binet or Wechsler-Bellevue scale.[2]

It is quite difficult to get a handle on the actual normative sample for the Memory for Designs Test. Those who participated in the standardization included persons with a variety of brain disorders including more than fifteen different classifications of both acute and chronic conditions, persons with idiopathic epilepsy and various forms of psychosis, and a "normal" group of persons. The test was normed on a total of 535 normal persons, 47 subjects who had idiopathic epilepsy, and 243 who suffered some form of brain injury. Subjects ranged in age from 8 to 70 years.

Reliability

Three kinds of reliability are reported in the Memory for Designs manual. Interscorer reliability, obtained by the two authors independently scoring 140 protocols, is reported as .99. Split-half reliabilities for the performance of the same 140 subjects is reported to be .92.

Test-retest reliabilities on readministrations within 24 hours to select groups of subjects are reported in Table 15.1. Reliability indexes are in the .80s with the exception of the group with low vocabulary scores. The average Memory for Designs score for all groups was 1.89 lower on the retest than on the original test. The authors attribute this improvement in performance to a practice effect.

Validity

Validity data consist primarily of criterion validity scores showing that brain-injured individuals earn lower scores on the test than do non-brain-injured persons. The test does differentiate between the groups, and the scores on the test do demonstrate little correlation with either age or intelligence. Just because the test differentiates between groups does not mean that it measures what it says it measures.

---

2. The Wechsler-Bellevue is an adult test.

Table **15.1**   Index of Reliability on the Memory for Designs Test, and Difference in Mean Raw Scores on Test and Immediate Retest for Various Samples

SAMPLE	N	RELIABILITY	MEAN DIFF.
Control children	(32)	.81	.41
Test score 8	22		−.41
Test score 8	10		1.60
Control adults	(45)	.85	2.22
Test score 8	17		1.82
Test score 8	28		2.46
Brain-disordered	(27)	.88	3.30
Special adult	(98)		
Mental deficiency diagnosis or low vocabulary	34	.72	2.32
Questionable diagnosis	41	.90	1.66
Over 60 years, mixed diagnosis	23	.86	1.44
TOTAL	202	.89	1.89

SOURCE: Reprinted with permission of author and publisher from: Graham, F. K., and Kendall, B. S. Memory for Designs Test: revised general manual. *Perceptual and Motor Skills*, 1960, 11, 147–188. (Monograph Supplement 2-VII.)

Summary

The Memory for Designs Test was originally constructed for the purpose of identifying brain-injured persons. Scores obtained on the device are reasonably reliable compared to those obtained on other perceptual-motor devices, and the test does discriminate between groups of brain-injured and non-brain-injured persons. The user of the test must, however, be cautious because it is very easy to make errors in logic. The test uses a criterion-group approach. A person who performs *like* a brain-injured person is not necessarily brain-injured. The Memory for Designs Test assesses skill in copying designs from memory; it does *not* assess brain injury. The diagnosis of an individual as brain-injured on the basis of relative difficulty in copying designs is quite clearly and simply an inference. As long as test results are viewed in this manner, there is little problem. To view the results as factual indicators of the extent of brain injury is simply inappropriate.

√   VMI

DEVELOPMENTAL TEST OF VISUAL-MOTOR INTEGRATION   *2 - 15*

The Developmental Test of Visual-Motor Integration (VMI) (Beery & Buktenica, 1967) is a group-administered test designed to assess visual perception and motor coordination in children ages 2 to 15. The test consists of a series of twenty-four geometric designs of increasing difficulty to be copied with a pencil on paper. The test can be administered by a classroom teacher and usually takes about 15 minutes. Scoring is relatively easy as the designs are scored pass-fail, and individual protocols can be scored in a few minutes.

Scores

The manual for the VMI includes one page of scoring information for each of the twenty-four designs. The child's reproduction of each design is scored pass-fail, and criteria for successful performance are clearly articulated. A raw score for the total test is obtained by adding the number of correct reproductions up to three consecutive failures. Normative tables provided in the manual allow the examiner to convert the total raw score to a developmental age equivalent.

Norms

Although normative data for transforming raw scores to developmental age equivalents are provided in the VMI manual, there are no data about the sample on whom the test was standardized. Information about the standardization of the VMI is included in a separate monograph entitled *Visual-Motor Integration* (Beery, 1967). Beery reports that three samples, a middle-class suburban group, a rural group, and a lower-middle-class urban group, made up the standardization group. A total of 1,039 children participated in the normative sample; all were from Illinois. Although the number of boys and girls who participated in standardization is reported, there are no specific data about the demographic characteristics of the sample.

Reliability

Three kinds of reliability are reported for the VMI: interscorer reliability, test-retest reliability, and internal consistency. Beery reports that interscorer reliability was established by means of analysis of variance of raw scores for ten subjects selected at random from classes for the mentally retarded. The reliability coefficient for the ratings of three judges was .98.

Two-week test-retest reliability for 171 children was .83 for boys and .87 for girls. Studies by investigators other than the author reported reliabilities ranging from .80 to .85.

Internal consistency for the scale on the suburban sample is reported to be .93.

Validity

Selection of items for the VMI was on the basis of expert opinion. The authors present a number of indicators of validity. The scale is an age scale, and a correlation of .89 between chronological age and scores on the test is cited as evidence for validity.

A correlation of the VMI with the Frostig DTVP of .80 was reported, while correlations of scores on the VMI with scores on subtests of the 1961 edition of the Illinois Test of Psycholinguistic Abilities ranged from .20 to .81. In some cases performance on the VMI was more highly correlated with performance on auditory subtests than with performance on visual-motor subtests.

Summary

The VMI is designed to assess the integration of visual and motor skills by asking the child to copy geometric designs. As is the case with other such tests, the behavior sampling is limited, although the twenty-four items on the VMI certainly provide a larger sample of behavior than is provided by the nine items on the Bender Visual Motor Gestalt Test or the fifteen items on the Memory for Designs Test. The VMI has relatively high reliability in comparison to other measures of perceptual-motor skills. Validity is, however, questionable.

PURDUE PERCEPTUAL-MOTOR SURVEY

The Purdue Perceptual-Motor Survey (PPMS) (Roach & Kephart, 1966) was developed "to assess qualitatively the perceptual-motor abilities of children in the early grades" (p. 2). The survey, which consists of eleven subtests designed to measure some aspect of perceptual-motor development, includes twenty-two scorable items. The authors of the survey state that "the survey was not designed for diagnosis, per se, but to allow the clinician to observe perceptual-motor behavior in a series of behavioral performances" (p. 11).

Criteria used to include items in the PPMS are described by the authors in the test manual. Each item had to

(1) tap some perceptual-motor area; (2) be easy to administer and require a minimum of special equipment; (3) be representative of behavior familiar to all children; (4) have scoring criteria simple enough and clear enough that a minimum amount of training would be necessary for administration; and (5) not be over-structured so that it elicits a learned response. (p. 11)

Most items in the survey were chosen to be used with second, third, and fourth graders. The normative data are on children between 6 and 10 years of age. Items on the PPMS are grouped into five areas: Balance and Posture, Body Image and Differentiation, Perceptual-Motor Match, Ocular Control, and Form Perception. Each area samples certain behaviors.

Balance and Posture   Two activities, walking a balance beam and jumping, are used to assess balance and postural flexibility. The items are not precisely scored; rather, the examiner makes an effort to identify the extent to which children have "a general balance problem." The tasks assess the extent to which children use both sides of their bodies in a bilateral activity, shift from one side to the other in a smooth, well-coordinated fashion, and demonstrate rhythmic and coordinated control.

Body Image and Differentiation   Five tasks are used to assess body image and differentiation. These include (1) Identification of Body Parts, (2) Imitation of Movement, (3) Obstacle Course, (4) Kraus-Weber, and (5) Angels in the Snow. In general, the tasks assess the extent to which children have knowledge of their body parts, can imitate movement, can avoid obstacles, have good physical strength, and can move their bodies as directed.

Perceptual-Motor Match   The match between perceptual information and motor response is assessed by two activities in which children are asked to draw several geometric forms on a chalkboard and to engage in rhythmic writing. Chalkboard activities include (1) drawing a circle, (2) drawing two circles simultaneously, one with each hand, (3) drawing a lateral line, and (4) drawing two straight vertical lines simultaneously. In the rhythmic writing task children reproduce on paper eight patterns drawn on the chalkboard by the examiner. They must reproduce the patterns accurately, with a free rhythmic flow, and must make certain "perceptual-motor adjustments" in doing so.

Ocular Control   The ability of children to establish and maintain contact with a visual target is assessed by means of four tasks requiring them to maintain eye contact with a penlight. The examiner evaluates the extent to which children are able to move their eyes (as opposed to the entire head) smoothly in following the movements of a flashlight. Ocular control for both eyes and for each eye individually is assessed. In addition, convergence of the eyes in focusing on objects is evaluated.

Form Perception   The extent to which children demonstrate adequate form perception and can reproduce geometric designs is assessed by asking them to copy seven simple geometric forms: circle, cross, square, triangle, horizontal diamond, vertical diamond, and divided rectangle.

Scores

Scoring for the PPMS is subjective and largely qualitative. While numbers are assigned as scores, they are used to designate the quality of a child's perceptual-motor behaviors. The record form for the PPMS includes a series of check lists for each task. The check lists enable the examiner to take note of the specific difficulties a child experiences on each of the tasks.

The authors of the PPMS stress the fact that the survey is not a test but a device for designating problem areas. They state that "the probable level of measurement is ordinal" (p. 13).[3]

Norms

The PPMS was standardized on fifty children at each of the first four grades. Only children known to be free of motor defect who had not been referred to an agency for evaluation of their academic achievement were included in the normative sample. By administering the Wide Range Achievement Test, the authors established the fact that all children studied were achieving at or above grade level. They report that

every child that participated in the study from the normative group was achieving at least within his assigned grade level. . . . Since the data were collected in midyear, this meant that children were achieving at various levels at or above grade placement. For example, some third graders were achieving at grade three, zero month, in spelling, while others were achieving at a much higher level. In all, the range of achievement was known to be varied. (p. 14)

The reader of the manual is led to believe that all children earned scores on the WRAT no lower than the lower limit of their grade level (for example, no lower than 3.0). In the next sentence of the manual, however, the authors report that "it was assumed that intelligence, like achievement, was randomly distributed in the normative sample" (p. 14). The authors do not report data about the actual range of achievement and intelligence of children in the normative sample.

The authors do report the sex and socioeconomic status of children in the normative sample, but these data are reported only in the validity section of the manual. One needs to refer to validity tables to identify the numbers of children representing each specific socioeconomic group.

Reliability

The authors report a test-retest reliability of the PPMS of .95. They state that this coefficient was based on the performance of thirty children

---

3. *Ordinal* refers to rank order as discussed in Chapter 4.

selected randomly from the normative sample and that the test-retest interval was one week.

Validity

To establish validity for the PPMS, the authors compared the performance of children in the normative sample to that of a clinic sample of ninety-seven nonachievers matched for grade level and age with the normative group. The items of the scale were validated by demonstrating that the nonclinic children performed at a significantly higher level than the clinic children on all but two items of the scale.

Additional validity studies were performed to illustrate that performance on items on the survey increases with higher grade level and with higher socioeconomic status. Performances on only two items increased significantly with grade level, while means for the six socioeconomic groups were in the order 5, 4, 1, 2, 3, 6. Thus, the authors' own research failed to support their contentions about grade and socioeconomic status. The authors do not demonstrate that the survey measures what it says it measures.

Summary

The Purdue Perceptual-Motor Survey is designed to provide qualitative information regarding the extent to which children demonstrate adequately developed perceptual-motor skills. Because standardization was limited, the survey cannot be used for the purpose of making normative comparisons. Although good test-retest reliability has been demonstrated, validity of the scale is questionable. Individual teachers must judge whether they are willing to accept the authors' contention that the development of adequate perceptual-motor skills is a necessary prerequisite to the acquisition of academic skills. Such a claim is, to date, without support.

SUMMARY

Educational personnel typically assess perceptual-motor skills for one of three reasons: prevention, remediation, and differential diagnosis. The use of perceptual-motor tests to identify children who demonstrate perceptual-motor difficulties is based on the assumption that without special perceptual-motor training, these children will experience academic difficulties. They are used for remedial purposes to try to ascertain whether perceptual-motor difficulties are causing academic difficulties and must therefore be remediated. Third, perceptual-motor tests are used diagnostically to identify brain injury and emotional difficulties.

The most commonly used perceptual-motor tests were reviewed in this chapter. It was demonstrated that most currently used perceptual-motor tests lack the necessary reliability to be used in making important instructional decisions. Likewise, they lack demonstrated validity; we simply cannot say with much certainty that the tests measure what they purport to measure.

The practice of perceptual-motor assessment is linked directly to perceptual-motor training or remediation. There is a tremendous lack of empirical evidence to support the claim that specific perceptual-motor training facilitates the acquisition of academic skills or improves the chances of academic success. Perceptual-motor training will improve *perceptual-motor* functioning. When the purpose of perceptual-motor assessment is to identify specific important perceptual and motor behaviors that children have not yet mastered, some of the devices reviewed in this chapter may provide useful information; performance on individual items will indicate the extent to which specific skills (for example, walking along a straight line) have been mastered. There is no support for the use of perceptual-motor tests in planning programs designed to facilitate academic learning or remediate academic difficulties.

STUDY QUESTIONS

1. Homer, age 6-3, takes two visual-perceptual tests, the Developmental Test of Visual Perception (DTVP) and the Developmental Test of Visual-Motor Integration (VMI). On the DTVP he earns a developmental age of 5-6, and on the VMI he earns a developmental age of 7-4. Give two different explanations for the discrepancy between the scores.

2. Original measures of perceptual-motor characteristics were shown to discriminate between brain-injured and non-brain-injured adults. Identify at least two major problems in the current use of these tests to diagnose brain injury in school-age children.

3. Brairdale School decides to implement a preschool screening program to identify children with perceptual-motor problems. The decision is made to evaluate all 4-year-olds in the community with the Memory for Designs Test, the Developmental Test of Visual Perception, and the Purdue Perceptual-Motor Survey. You are on the team charged with implementation of this screening project. Would you object to the proposed screening, and if so, why?

4. Identify at least three major problems in current perceptual-motor assessment practices.

5. A local school district in Boston, Massachusetts, uses the DTVP to screen kindergarten youngsters for potential perceptual-motor problems. To whom are these children being compared?

ADDITIONAL READING

Buros, O. K. (ed.). *Seventh mental measurements yearbook.* Highland Park, NJ: Gryphon Press, 1972. (Reviews of sensory-motor tests, pp. 863–888).

Yates, A. J. The validity of some psychological tests of brain damage. *Psychological Bulletin*, 1954, *51*, 359–379.

Chapter 16

Assessment of Sensory Acuity

The *first* thing to check when a child is having academic or social difficulties is whether that child is receiving environmental information adequately and properly. In efforts to identify reasons why children experience difficulties, we too often overlook the obvious in search of the subtle. Vision and hearing difficulties do interfere with the educational progress of a significant number of schoolchildren. The teacher's role in assessment of sensory acuity is twofold. First, the teacher must be aware of behaviors that may indicate sensory difficulties and thus must have at least an embryonic knowledge of the kinds of sensory difficulties children experience. Second, the teacher must know the instructional implications of sensory difficulties. Informed communication with vision and hearing specialists is the most effective way to gain such information. The teacher must have basic knowledge about procedures used to assess sensory acuity in order to comprehend and use data from specialists. This chapter, therefore, differs from previous chapters. It provides basic knowledge about the kinds of vision and hearing difficulties pupils experience as well as an overview of procedures and devices used to assess sensory acuity.

VISUAL DIFFICULTIES

There are three ways in which vision may be limited: visual acuity may be limited; the field of vision may be restricted; or color vision may be imperfect. Visual acuity refers to the clarity or sharpness with which a person sees. You probably have heard it said that a keen-sighted person has "perfect" vision — 20/20 in both eyes.[1] The person might more accurately be described as demonstrating "normal" vision; the numbers 20/20 simply indicate that the person is able to see a standard-sized object from a standard number of feet away. This method of measuring visual acuity is derived from the use of the Snellen Wall Chart. A person is described as having 20/20 vision who at 20 feet is able to distinguish letters an average person can distinguish at 20 feet. A rating of 20/200 means that the person

---

1. It is also said that hindsight is always 20/20.

can distinguish letters at 20 feet that the average person can distinguish at 200 feet. Conversely, 20/10 vision means the person is able to distinguish letters at 20 feet that the average person can only distinguish at 10 feet. The former demonstrates limited vision, while the latter demonstrates better than average distant visual acuity.

The field of vision may be restricted in two ways. A person may demonstrate normal central visual acuity with a restricted peripheral field; this is usually referred to as *tunnel vision*. Or a person may have a *scotoma*, a spot without vision. If the spot occurs in the middle of the eye, it may result in central vision impairment.

Color vision is determined by the discrimination of three qualities of color: hue, saturation, and brightness. The essential difference between colorblind and normal persons is that hues that appear different to normal persons look the same to a colorblind person. Colorblind persons frequently do not know they are colorblind unless they have been tested and told so. They see the same things that other individuals see, and they usually have learned to call them by the same color names. Colorblindness is not an all-or-nothing thing. Most colorblindness is partial; the person has difficulty distinguishing certain colors, usually red and green. Total colorblindness is extremely rare. Colorblindness is an inherited trait found in about one out of twelve males and one out of two hundred females. There is no cure for colorblindness, and the condition is not usually regarded as a handicap.

Few people are totally blind; many have at least light perception and some light projection, either of which helps for mobility. Blindness, for legal purposes, is defined as

central visual acuity of 20/200 or less in the better eye, with correcting glasses, or central visual acuity of more than 20/200 if there is a field defect in which the peripheral field has contracted to such an extent that the widest diameter of visual field subtends an angular distance no greater than 20 degrees. (Hurlin, 1962, p. 8)

Blindness may be either congenital or acquired. Congenital blindness or blindness acquired prior to age 5 has the most serious educational implications.

It has been said that more people are blinded by definition (the legal definition cited above) than by any other cause (Greenwood, 1949). According to Barraga (1976, p. 13)[2]

---

2. Quotations from Barraga's *Visual handicaps and learning: A developmental approach* used in this discussion are copyright 1976 by Wadsworth Publishing Company, Inc., and reprinted by their permission.

the term *visually handicapped* is being used widely at present to denote the total group of children who have impairments in the structure or functioning of the visual sense organ — the eye — irrespective of the nature and extent of the impairment. This term has gained acceptance because the impairment causes a limitation that, even with the best possible correction, interferes with incidental or normal learning through the sense of vision (Taylor, 1973, p. 156).

When we deal with children, we are concerned primarily with visual handicaps that require special educational provisions. Barraga differentiates among three categories of visual handicaps; these are as follows.

Blind. This term [is] used to refer to children who have only light perception without projection, or those who are totally without the sense of vision (Faye, 1970). . . . Educationally, the blind child is one who learns through braille and related media without the use of vision (Halliday, 1970), although perception of light may be present and useful in orientation and movement.

Low Vision. Children who have limitations in distance vision but are able to see objects and materials when they are within a few inches or at a maximum of a few feet away are another subgroup. Most low-vision children will be able to use their vision for many school learning activities, a few for visual reading perhaps, whereas others may need to use tactual materials and possibly even braille to supplement printed and other visual materials. . . . Under no circumstances should low-vision children be referred to as "blind."

Visually Limited. This term refers to children who in some way are limited in their use of vision under average circumstances. They may have difficulty seeing learning materials without special lighting, or they may be unable to see distant objects unless the objects are moving, or they may need to wear prescriptive lenses or use optical aids and special materials to function visually. Visually limited children will be considered for all educational purposes and under all circumstances as seeing children. (1976, p. 14)

Estimates of the number of school-age children who experience visual difficulties range from 5 to 33 percent (U.S. Public Health Service, 1971). Obviously, estimates differ as a function of the definition used and the screening devices employed.

Teachers must be consistently on the lookout for signs of visual difficulty. When children complain of frequent headaches, dizziness, sensitivity to light, or blurred vision, efforts must be made to evaluate the extent to which they are seeing properly. Obvious signs of possible visual difficulty include crossed eyes; turned-out eyes; red, swollen, or encrusted eyelids; constant rapid movement of the eyes; watery eyes or discharges; and haziness in the pupils. These, too, should receive special attention in the form of referral for vision screening (U.S. Public Health Service, 1971).

Certain behaviors indicate possible visual difficulties. According to the

U.S. Public Health Service (1971), behaviors indicative of potential visual difficulties include holding books unusually close to or far from the eyes while reading; frequent blinking, squinting, or rubbing of the eyes; abnormal head tilting or turning; inattention in blackboard lessons; poor alignment in written work; unusual choice of colors in artwork; confusion of certain letters of the alphabet in reading (o's and a's, e's and c's, b's and h's, n's and r's); inability or reluctance to participate in games requiring distance vision or visual accuracy; and irritability when doing close work.

VISION TESTING IN THE SCHOOLS

Most schools now have vision screening programs, but the effectiveness of these programs is varied. Two fundamentally different kinds of tests are used: those that screen only central visual acuity at a distance and those that assess both central visual acuity and a number of other visual capabilities.

THE BASIC TEST

The standard Snellen Wall Chart is the most commonly used screening test to assess visual acuity. The test consists simply of a wall chart of standard-sized letters that a child is asked to read at a distance of 20 feet. The test provides limited information about vision, assessing only central visual acuity at a distance of 20 feet. Specific difficulties may be encountered in using the test with some school-age children. First, children may be unable to read the letters or to discriminate between letters like F and P. Second, children can often memorize the letters ahead of time. Third, the letters of the alphabet differ in legibility and lend themselves to guessing. The practical criterion for referral using this test is acuity of 20/40 or less in either eye for children in kindergarten through third grade, and 20/30 or less in either eye for those who are older (National Society for the Prevention of Blindness, 1961).

An adaptation of the Snellen Wall Chart, the Snellen E Test, is the most commonly used test with preschool children and those who are unable to read. The letter E is presented with its arms facing in one of four directions and the person being tested is asked either to name the direction, to point, or to hold up a letter E to match the stimulus. Again, this test assesses only central visual acuity.

MORE COMPREHENSIVE TESTS

Several tests assess more aspects of vision than central visual acuity. The Massachusetts Vision Test, introduced in 1940, assesses (1) visual acuity using the Snellen E, (2) *accommodative ability* (the automatic adjustment of the eyes for seeing at different distances) using a plus lens, and (3) muscle imbalance.

Whereas the basic screening tests measure only visual acuity from a distance, the Keystone Telebinocular assesses fourteen different visual skills. The instrument measures the visual functioning of each eye separately and the functioning of both eyes together. In taking this test, students sit in front of a telebinocular instrument, view three-dimensional test slides, and tell the examiner what they see. Visual functioning is assessed at both near point (16 inches) and far point (20 inches); the distances are produced optically, and children remain seated in front of the instrument throughout testing.

Several alternative tests may be administered using the Keystone Telebinocular: a screening test, a comprehensive test battery, the Keystone Plus-Lens Test, the Keystone Primary Skills Test, and the Keystone Periometer Test. Skills tested in the screening test are as follows:

FAR POINT	NEAR POINT
Simultaneous perception	Fusion
Fusion	Vertical eye posture
Color and depth perception	Usable vision
Usable vision	

Skills tested in the comprehensive test battery are as follows:

FAR POINT	NEAR POINT
Simultaneous perception	Fusion
Fusion	Vertical eye posture
Vertical and lateral eye posture	Usable vision of each eye and
Depth perception	both eyes together
Color discrimination	
Usable vision of each eye and both eyes together	

The Bausch and Lomb Orthorater is another instrument used for a more comprehensive assessment of visual functioning. The device assesses farsightedness, muscle balance at both near and far points, and visual acuity using the Snellen E. Like the Keystone Telebinocular, it is a relatively expensive instrument.

The Titmus Vision Tester, illustrated in Figure 16.1, is increasingly used for screening in public school settings. The device is used to assess both acuity and *phoria* (the tendency of the visual axis to turn in or out, up or down) at far and near points. In addition, slides are available to assess preschool children.

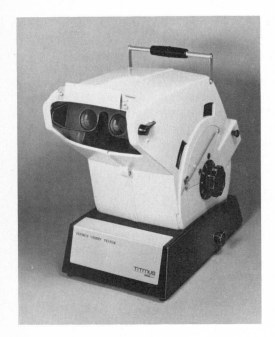

Figure **16.1**   A Titmus Vision Tester. (Courtesy Titmus Optical)

In selecting devices to screen visual functioning, it is imperative that the practitioner select devices that are diagnostically accurate, that is, devices that identify individuals who do indeed have visual difficulties. Error in the direction of overreferral to ophthalmologists and optometrists is better than missing anyone who has vision difficulties. Comparative studies of screening devices are difficult to locate. Studies summarized in bulletins published by the National Society for Prevention of Blindness (1961) and by the United States Public Health Service (1971) indicate that the Snellen Wall Chart continues to be a relatively effective screening test.

ASSESSMENT OF COLOR VISION

As we have indicated earlier, colorblindness is not usually an educationally handicapping condition. Nevertheless, it is important that color vision be assessed, primarily so that colorblind children and their parents can know that the children have this condition.

Colorblindness is a stable trait, and one we ought to be able to assess with considerable reliability and validity. However, current devices used to assess color vision are not as reliable and valid as would be expected. Adam, Doran, and Modan (1967) state that "it has repeatedly been stressed by experts in the field of color vision (e.g., Franceschetti, 1928; Wright, 1947, Waardenburg et al., 1963) that an accurate diagnosis of color vision can be attained only by the use of an anomaloscope" (p. 297). An *anomaloscope* is a scientific instrument that requires that a person indicate if two simultaneously presented light spots are of approximately equal brightness and if they are the same color. Salvia and Ysseldyke (1972) investigated the validity of measures of colorblindness as compared to the anomaloscope with mentally retarded boys. Validities were low; the tests misdiagnosed from 7 to 30 percent of the boys.

If measures of colorblindness are used with students, we recommend that at least two different tests be given. If a student is identified as colorblind on both tests, there is a strong likelihood that the student is colorblind.

A description of the tests most commonly used to assess color vision follows.

FARNSWORTH DICHOTOMOUS TEST FOR COLOR BLINDNESS

The Farnsworth Dichotomous Test for Color Blindness (Farnsworth, 1947) consists of fifteen colored caps that the student is asked to order with respect to a reference cap so that each cap is more like the preceding cap than any other. Diagnosis is made by plotting the order of the caps selected on a response sheet.

AO H-R-R PSEUDOISOCHROMATIC PLATES

The AO H-R-R Pseudoisochromatic Plates (Hardy, Rand, & Rittler, 1957) consist of twenty plates. Each plate is divided into four quadrants with background patterns and color (gray) identical for each quadrant and for each plate. In one or two of the quadrants, a symbol may appear, with no more than two symbols per plate. Subjects are asked to state what they see and where they see it.

DVORINE PSEUDO-ISOCHROMATIC PLATES

The Dvorine Psuedo-isochromatic Plates (Dvorine, 1953) consist of fourteen number plates and seven trail plates with multicolor dots and a number (or trail) embedded in a contrasting color. Subjects are asked to read the number or trace the trail with a fine brush.

ISHIHARA COLOR BLIND TEST

The Ishihara Color Blind Test (Ishihara, 1970) consists of fourteen plates similar in composition to those in the Dvorine Test. There are seven number plates and seven trail plates. Subjects are asked to name the number or trace the trail with a fine brush.

ASSESSMENT OF HEARING DIFFICULTIES[3]

The early detection of hearing difficulties is imperative so that appropriate remedial or compensatory procedures can be instituted. Children with hearing problems characteristically fail to pay attention, give wrong answers to simple questions, hear better when watching the teacher's face, and ask frequently to have words or sentences repeated. Also, children with impaired hearing may function below their educational potential, be withdrawn, or be a behavioral problem. Further, children who have frequent earaches, frequent colds or other upper respiratory infections, or draining ears may also have a concomitant hearing problem. Children who fail to articulate clearly and who demonstrate other speech and language problems, as well as children who fail to discriminate between words with similar vowels but different consonants, may also have impaired hearing (Duffy, 1964).

Children with one or more of the symptoms listed above should be referred for a hearing test. Depending on the school system, this test will be given by a school nurse, speech therapist, hearing therapist, or trained technician. These professionals have received training for efficiently and accurately testing the hearing of children and can ascertain the extent to which the child's hearing sensitivity is within normal limits. If a hearing loss is detected, the child is then referred to an ear doctor (*otologist* or *otolaryngologist*) for an otological evaluation or to a specialist in hearing evaluation and rehabilitation (*audiologist*) for a complete audiological evaluation. The otologist and audiologist can supply the appropriate remediation and rehabilitation.

The assessment of hearing difficulties is an exacting procedure that requires understanding several basic concepts. As a prerequisite to a discussion of the assessment of hearing, the anatomy and physiology of the peripheral auditory system will be briefly described. This description will, it is hoped, provide a greater insight into assessment procedures.

The peripheral auditory system can be described as being divided into

---

3. This section was specially written for this volume by Dr. Tom Frank, Assistant Professor of Speech Pathology and Audiology, College of Education, The Pennsylvania State University.

three parts: the external, middle, and inner ear. Each part makes a specific contribution to the hearing process. The external ear gathers sound from the environment and funnels it to the middle ear. The middle ear transmits and amplifies the sound and directs it to the inner ear. The inner ear analyzes the sound and initiates a neural response.

The sensation of hearing can be initiated in two ways. One is called *air conduction*; the other, *bone conduction*. These two modes of hearing serve as the basis for *pure-tone audiometry* — that is, hearing assessment employing pure tones as the test stimulus. When a sound passes through the complete peripheral mechanism (external, middle, and inner ear), the sound is said to have been heard by *air conduction*. When sound is introduced by mechanically vibrating the skull, the sound waves will bypass the external and middle ear and stimulate the inner ear. In this way, the sound is said to have been heard by *bone conduction*. Thus, air-conduction hearing depends on the function of the external, middle, and inner ear and neural pathways beyond; bone-conduction hearing depends on the function of the inner ear and beyond. It is important to recognize that bone-conduction hearing represents the true (organic) sensitivity of the inner ear.

If a child has a hearing loss due to a wax (*cerumen*) buildup in the external auditory canal or fluid in the middle ear (*serous otitis*), bone-conduction hearing will be normal because the inner ear is not affected. However, hearing by air conduction will be abnormal because the dysfunction is due to a pathology in the external ear or middle ear or both. This type of hearing loss (normal bone-conduction with abnormal air-conduction hearing sensitivity) is known as a *conductive hearing loss* because the pathology affects the sound-conducting mechanisms (the external and middle ear).

If a child has a hearing loss due to a dysfunction of the inner ear, the bone-conduction as well as the air-conduction hearing will be abnormal. In fact, the bone-conducted tone and the air-conducted tone will be heard at the same level (except in cases of a severe or profound hearing loss where bone-conducted responses cannot be obtained because of the bone-conduction output limits of the audiometer). This type of hearing loss (abnormal bone- and air-conduction hearing sensitivity usually occurring at the same level) is known as a *sensorineural hearing loss*.

A hearing loss can also be a combined conductive and sensorineural hearing loss. This type of hearing loss (abnormal bone-conduction and even more abnormal air-conduction hearing sensitivity) is known as a *mixed hearing loss*. For example, a mixed hearing loss could arise from fluid in the middle ear and hair-cell dysfunction in the inner ear.

The main purpose of hearing assessment in a school situation is the identification of children with hearing problems. Experience has indicated that teachers may not identify a child with a hearing loss and that teachers may identify a child with normal hearing as having a hearing disorder. Thus, every child should have a hearing evaluation.

The identification of children with hearing problems and subsequent provisions for medical, surgical, audiological, educational, and related services fall within the realm of a hearing conservation program. The vast majority of schools have hearing conservation programs; in fact, most states have laws requiring hearing testing. Hearing conservation programs generally include regularly scheduled auditory screening tests, auditory-threshold tests for those who fail the screening test, and medical (otological) examination and treatment.

There are several auditory screening tests that can be used for hearing assessment. These tests can be divided into two types, group or individual. It should be kept in mind that the purpose of a screening test is to identify if the child's hearing sensitivity is normal or abnormal.

Group hearing screening tests such as the Fading-Numbers Test (Dahl, 1949), the Massachusetts Hearing Test (Johnston, 1948), and the Pulse-Tone Group Test (Reger and Newby, 1947) have lost popularity because of their low validity and reliability compared with individual screening tests. For the most part, screening tests in hearing conservation programs are performed on an individual basis. The assumption (probably a valid one) is that the additional time required to screen a large number of children on an individual basis will be more effective in identifying children with a hearing problem than will a group screening procedure.

Hearing ability is assessed with an electronic instrument called an *audiometer*. There are many types of audiometers that can be used for hearing assessment. The type most commonly used in school settings is a portable unit known as a *pure-tone audiometer*. A photograph of a pure-tone audiometer is shown in Figure 16.2.

The pure-tone audiometer consists of an audio oscillator that generates pure tones of different frequencies (125, 250, 500, 750, 1,000, 1,500, 2,000, 3,000, 4,000, 6,000, and 8,000 Hz) covering the major portion of the auditory range (16 to 16,000 Hz). The term *Hertz* (Hz), after a German physicist, Heinrich Hertz, has been adapted to describe the frequency that defines the number of cycles per second of a sound. Frequency can also be described by the subjective impression it creates known as pitch. Within the audible range, as frequency increases so does the pitch. For example, a 125-Hz pure tone has a frequency of 125 cycles per second and is considered to be a low pitch compared with an 8,000-Hz tone, which is a high pitch.

The pure-tone audiometer also contains an amplifier and an attenuator system that can be adjusted in discrete steps to increase or decrease the intensity of a pure tone. Intensity can be described by a measurement unit known as a *decibel (dB)*. A decibel does not have a fixed absolute value; rather, it is simply a ratio relating the proportion of one value to another. In hearing assessment the decibel scale is referenced to a normal hearing

Figure **16.2**   A portable pure-tone audiometer. Sitting on top of the audiometer are the earphones and the bone vibrator. The dial to the left is the hearing-level dial, which controls the intensity of the pure tone. The dial to the right controls the frequency of the pure tone. The output switch is in the top middle of the audiometer and can be manipulated to direct the pure tone to the right or left earphone or to the bone vibrator. The interrupter switch is the black bar in the bottom middle of the audiometer. When this bar is depressed, a pure tone is presented. (Courtesy of Beltone Electronics Corporation)

level (*HL*). Since the ear does not have the same hearing sensitivity at each frequency, the audiometer is internally calibrated. As a result, 0 dB HL on the audiometer dial represents normal hearing sensitivity for each pure tone frequency. The hearing level can usually be varied from −10 dB HL for all frequencies to a maximum of 110 dB HL in the middle frequencies.

The physical intensity of a sound creates the subjective reaction known as *loudness*. The relation between intensity and loudness is that as intensity increases loudness increases. For example, a 1,000-Hz tone at 60 dB HL will be louder compared with a 1,000-Hz tone of 40 dB HL.

The pure-tone audiometer is provided with a silent switch that is used to

introduce or interrupt the pure tone. The output of the pure-tone audiometer can be routed to a right or left earphone, or to a bone-conduction
vibrator.

The American National Standards Institute has issued a detailed
standard for the specifications of audiometers (ANSI, S3.6, 1969). Pure-
tone audiometers manufactured in the United States after 1970 conform to
these standards. Thus, in general, American-made pure-tone audiometers
are very similar except for the location of the external dials and switches.

In an individual screening test, the earphones of an audiometer are
placed over the child's ears. The audiometer transmits pure tones, and the
child is asked to raise a hand when the tone is heard. Because earphones
are employed, the test tones stimulate the entire peripheral auditory system
(external, middle, and inner ear) so that the child's air-conduction hearing
is being tested.

The most definitive work on identification audiometry was compiled by
Darley (1961). It was suggested that hearing be screened at a hearing level
of 20 dB at 500, 1,000, 2,000, and 6,000 Hz and at a hearing level of 30 dB
at 4,000 Hz. That is, the hearing-level dial of the audiometer, which
regulates the intensity of the pure tone, should be placed on 20 dB; the
frequency dial should be adjusted to 500, 1,000, 2,000, and 6,000 Hz
respectively; and a tone should be presented. At 4,000 Hz the hearing-
level dial should be adjusted to 30 dB. This procedure is carried out for
each ear. Needless to say, hearing testing should be carried out in a very
quiet environment so that external noise does not mask perception of a
tone.

A screening level of 20 dB HL, however, may not be realistic unless
testing is done in a sound-treated environment, which most schools are not
likely to have. Thus, more casual criteria are to screen hearing at 25 dB HL
at 500, 1,000, 2,000, and 6,000 Hz and 30 dB HL at 4,000 Hz. If a child
fails to hear a tone in one or both ears, a second screening is usually
performed. The child who fails the second screening is referred for a
pure-tone threshold test.

In the *pure-tone threshold test* the child's hearing sensitivity is obtained as a
function of frequency. The purpose of this test is to find the hearing level
at which the child just barely hears the tone for each frequency that is
tested. The hearing level at which the child barely hears the tone is known
as the child's *threshold of auditory sensitivity*. Because in this test earphones
are again employed, the obtained thresholds are indicative of the child's
air-conduction hearing sensitivity. Bone-conduction hearing should not be
assessed in a school setting because of the many variables of this mode of
testing. Rather, the child's bone-conduction sensitivity should be assessed
by an audiologist or otologist who uses a sound-treated environment and
more refined and elaborate equipment and procedures.

The pure-tone threshold test should always be done in a very quiet environment. The frequencies tested are usually 1,000, 2,000, 4,000, 6,000, 1,000 (recheck), 500, and 250 Hz (listed in the test sequence). One ear is tested completely before the other is tested. Initially, the tone (at each frequency) is presented at a normally adequate intensity, usually 40 dB HL, so that the child can respond. The tester then decreases the intensity of the tone in ten-dB steps, noting a response at each decrement, until the child does not respond. The intensity of the tone is then increased in five-dB steps until a response is noted. The tone is then decreased and increased in this bracketing manner until the threshold is found.

The results of the pure-tone threshold test are usually plotted on a graph called an *audiogram*. An audiogram is shown in Figure 16.3. Frequency in Hertz (Hz) is plotted along the top of the audiogram at intervals from 125 to 8,000 Hz. Approximately half-octave intervals of 750, 1,500, 3,000, and 6,000 Hz are also denoted. Hearing level in decibels (dB) is plotted along the side of the graph from −10 to 110 dB in ten-dB steps. Symbols are plotted on the audiogram that depict the thresholds for each ear as a function of frequency and intensity. Each audiogram should contain an audiogram legend to define the meaning of the symbols. For example, an "O" indicates an air-conduction threshold for the right ear, and an "X" indicates an air-conduction threshold for the left ear. Also, it is common practice to depict thresholds for the right ear with red markings and for the left ear with blue markings. The American Speech and Hearing Association has issued guidelines for audiometric symbols (1974).

Figure 16.3 indicates that the sensitivity of air-conduction hearing is 30 dB HL for the right ear and 35 dB HL for the left ear from 250 to 8,000 Hz. The child whose audiogram this is could just barely hear the pure tone at (that is, her threshold was at) 30 dB HL for the right ear and 35 dB HL for the left ear.

The criteria for failing the pure-tone threshold test are the same as for the screening test: if the child's hearing level is 25 dB HL or more at any one of the frequencies 500, 1,000, 2,000, and 6,000 Hz or 30 dB HL or more at 4,000 Hz in one or both ears, the child has failed the pure-tone threshold test. The patient's hearing sensitivity shown on the audiogram in Figure 16.3 would be classified as a failure in each ear. Children who fail the pure-tone threshold test should be referred to an audiologist or to an otologist for further testing.

The actual diagnosis of a hearing problem in reference to the type of hearing loss (conductive, sensorineural, or mixed) and the severity must be completed by an audiologist or an otologist. Both audiologists and otologists are skilled in the administration and interpretation of various audiometric tests. Often the audiologist and otologist work as a team, since each has a particular area of expertise. For example, the otologist is

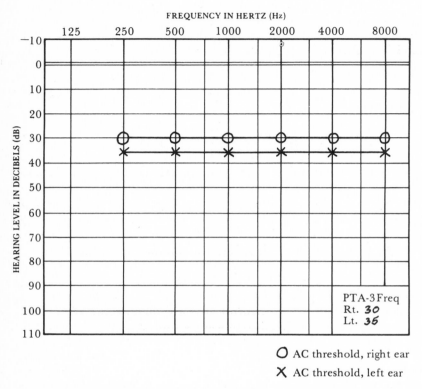

Figure 16.3 An audiogram showing a sensitivity of air-conduction hearing of 30 dB HL for the right ear and 35 dB HL for the left ear from 250 to 8,000 Hz

trained from a medical standpoint and has expertise in the physical examination of the ear. If the child has a conductive or a mixed hearing loss, the otologist can usually provide the appropriate medical-surgical treatment. The audiologist is trained from an academic and paramedical standpoint and has expertise in the area of hearing assessment and rehabilitation. If a child has an educationally significant hearing loss due to a noncorrectable conductive or mixed hearing loss or a sensorineural hearing loss, the audiologist can usually provide rehabilitation by prescribing the appropriate hearing aid. Also, the audiologist can make suggestions to teachers, hearing therapists, and speech therapists concerning the child's hearing ability in different environmental situations. Further, the audiologist has expertise in testing the hearing of nonverbal children and those who are, in general, difficult to test.

The most common type of hearing loss in school-age children is a conductive hearing loss. Remember that with a conductive loss the bone-conduction hearing sensitivity (true organic inner-ear hearing) is normal and that the air-conduction hearing sensitivity is abnormal. The pathology creating the hearing loss is located in the external ear, in the middle ear, or in both areas. The most common pathologies of the external ear are due to impacted wax and infection of the external auditory canal. The most common pathology of the middle ear in school-age children is due to a collection of fluid in the middle ear known as *serous otitis media.* The fluid usually forms when the middle ear does not receive proper aeration because of Eustachian tube dysfunction or hypertrophied adenoids obstructing the Eustachian tube. Serous otitis media is initially treated with decongestants and antihistamines. If the fluid remains after a month of medical treatment, it is usually removed surgically, and small tubes are placed in the *tympanic membrane* (ear drum) to ventilate the middle-ear space. The surgical procedure is called a *myringotomy and tubal insertion.* It should be noted that following the appropriate treatment for conductive hearing losses, the hearing can be restored to normal. In some cases, however, a conductive loss cannot be treated; and if the hearing loss is educationally significant ($\geq$25 dB), a hearing aid should be considered.

The causes of sensorineural hearing loss are far too numerous to describe in this chapter. Usually, a significant sensorineural hearing loss will be detected before a child enters school. However, subtle hearing losses (abnormal hearing in one ear, abnormal high-frequency hearing, mild hearing losses) that are educationally significant are usually identified in kindergarten or first grade. A sensorineural hearing loss will not respond to medical-surgical treatment. In the vast majority of cases, a hearing aid will be extremely beneficial.

A mixed hearing loss is due to a pathology that causes a conductive and a sensorineural loss. The otologist can usually alleviate the conductive part of the hearing loss. However, in some cases the conductive pathology cannot be corrected, and if the hearing loss is educationally significant, the use of a hearing aid is warranted.

The severity of a hearing loss is usually measured on the basis of the average air-conduction hearing sensitivity (threshold) for 500, 1,000, and 2,000 Hz. These frequencies are known as the *speech frequencies* because the vast majority of English speech sounds are contained in this frequency range. The decibel average for these three frequencies serves to predict the threshold for understanding speech. A scale of hearing impairment that shows the relations between the hearing threshold level and the probable handicap and needs has been devised by Goodman and Chasin (1976) (see Table 16.1). It should be noted that a child with a hearing loss of 25 dB HL or more has an educationally significant hearing loss.

Table **16.1**   Scale of Hearing Impairment, Descriptive Term of Hearing Loss, and Relations Between the Hearing Threshold Level and Probable Handicap and Needs

HEARING LEVEL IN dB[a]	DESCRIPTIVE TERM OF HEARING LOSS	PROBABLE HANDICAP AND NEEDS
−10 to 26 dB[b]	Normal limit	*No significant handicap for most children.* Some at upper limits may have difficulty in sustained attention and may benefit from a hearing aid.
27 to 40 dB	Mild	*Slight handicap for some but significant handicap for many children.* Difficulty hearing faint speech and speech at a distance; needs preferential seating; may benefit from lip-reading instruction; benefits from the use of a hearing aid.
41 to 55 dB	Moderate	*Significant handicap.* Understands conversational speech at a distance of 3 to 5 feet; needs a hearing aid, auditory training, lip reading, speech correction, and preferential seating.
56 to 70 dB	Moderate to severe	*Marked handicap.* Conversation must be loud to be understood; difficulty in groups and classroom discussions even with a hearing aid; same needs as child with significant handicap; may be in a special class for the hearing impaired and integrated into a regular class.
71 to 90 dB	Severe	*Severe handicap.* May hear a loud voice 1 foot from the ear; may identify environment noises; same needs as child with significant handicap; may enter a regular class at a later time.
More than 90 dB	Profound	*Extreme handicap.* May hear some loud sounds; probably does not rely on hearing as a primary communication channel; needs a special class or school for the deaf; some of these children may be integrated into regular high schools.

[a] Average hearing levels for 500, 1,000, and 2,000 Hz (re: ANSI 1969 standards for pure-tone audiometers).

[b] Some children with hearing levels within a normal limit are not free from otologic abnormalities, but these abnormalities are not necessarily educationally handicapping.

SOURCE: Reprinted, with slight adaptations, from Gellis, S., and Kagan, Benjamin: *Current Pediatric Therapy,* 6, © 1976 by the W. B. Saunders Co., Phila.

A student with hearing difficulties should receive special assistance from the classroom teacher. Often a child with hearing difficulties can be given preferential seating close to the teacher so the opportunity to hear the teacher's voice (and to lipread) will be at a maximum. Of course, if the teacher moves around the room, the benefits of preferential seating will be lost.

In some children the hearing problem may be intermittent: on some days these children will have normal hearing, and on other days they will demonstrate a hearing loss. The teacher must be able to cope with these children and not become discouraged with their up-and-down hearing. Such children often pass the hearing screening because they are tested on a day when their hearing is good. If the teacher suspects a hearing loss, arrangements should be made to test such children on days when they demonstrate poor hearing.

Far too often a teacher has children with hearing problems in class and does not know the cause or severity of the problem. Sometimes these children may become educationally retarded because the teacher did not know how to handle them. The teacher should not be afraid to discuss the classroom management of these children with the attending speech therapist, hearing therapist, audiologist, or otologist.

SUMMARY

Vision and hearing difficulties can have a significant effect on the performance of children in educational environments. This chapter has provided a basic overview of the kinds of vision and hearing difficulties children experience and of the procedures used to assess sensory acuity. Screening tests of both visual and auditory acuity must be individually administered. Individually administered screening tests that are appropriate and reasonably effective have been reviewed. The actual diagnosis of sensory difficulties must be completed by specialists: ophthalmologists, optometrists, audiologists, and otologists.

STUDY QUESTIONS

1. Identify several characteristics (behaviors) a child might demonstrate that would make you question whether that child is seeing adequately.

2. Identify several characteristics (behaviors) that might make you question whether a child is hearing adequately.

Chapter 17
Assessment of Language

The study of language involves many specialties: linguistics, psycholinguistics, sociology, learning theory, speech and speech pathology, and education, among others. There are more theories of language and its development than there are specialties; the theories range from those that posit that language is a function of and/or develops by means of biogenetic substrates activated by the environment (Chomsky, 1965; Lenneburg, 1967) to those that view language and its development as the exclusive function of learning and experience through the operation of reinforcement contingencies (Skinner, 1957). All theories adequately explain some aspects of language development and performance; probably no theory adequately explains all aspects.

A complete delineation of formal and informal assessment of language is far beyond the scope of this chapter. Schools usually employ individuals with extensive preparation in language and language dysfunction, such as speech or language therapists. However, other school personnel need an understanding of what language is and how it is assessed.

LANGUAGE: A WORKING DEFINITION

For the purposes of this discussion, *language* will be restricted to meaningful verbal communication. As shown in Figure 17.1, *language* is typically defined as consisting of vocabulary,[1] grammar, and phonation. Each of these three components of language can be assessed at three levels: *imitation* (for example, repeating what is said), *comprehension* (for example, understanding what is said), and *production* (for example, spontaneous speech).

VOCABULARY

Vocabulary refers to the words understood and produced by a person. Vocabulary is most often considered to be listening and speaking vocabulary, but it can also be reading and writing vocabulary.

---

1. Vocabulary is part of *semantics* (the meaning of a communication); however, semantics are typically not considered in school language assessments.

COMPONENTS

	Vocabulary	Grammar	Phonation
Imitation			
Comprehension	Listening Reading	Listening Reading	Discrimination
Production	Speaking Writing	Speaking Writing	Articulation

(left vertical label: WAYS OF MEASURING LANGUAGE)

Figure **17.1** Components of language assessment

Measures of vocabulary are typically norm-referenced devices. Several measures of a child's knowledge of word meanings are available and discussed elsewhere in this book. These are listed in Table 17.1. In individually administered tests, two different kinds of behaviors are used to assess the meanings of words. These are typically classified as measures of receptive and of expressive vocabulary. Individually administered devices are typically of two kinds: picture vocabulary tests, which require children to demonstrate comprehension of words by identifying the picture that most closely represents the meaning of a word read by an examiner; and expressive vocabulary measures, which require children to produce definitions of words. In the first instance, children give evidence of knowledge of word meaning simply by pointing to pictures; in the second, they must actually produce definitions.

Group-administered devices are likewise diverse. Vocabulary is assessed by asking children to associate words with pictures, to identify synonyms and antonyms, and to select which of several words best fits a definition. A note of caution is important. Most vocabulary tests are designed *not* to assess vocabulary as a component of language but to assess intellectual capability by measuring how well children have learned the meanings of words.

GRAMMAR

Grammar refers to the order and interrelationship of words that give meaning to a communication. For example, the group of words, "mountain the hiked in up they the sunshine," is meaningless, even though each word is meaningful.

Tests of grammatic competence have only recently received serious attention. To a certain extent, listening and reading comprehension tests

Table **17.1**   Tests Discussed Elsewhere in This Book That Provide Information About a Child's Vocabulary

Boehm Test of Basic Concepts	Iowa Tests of Basic Skills
California Achievement Test	Lee-Clark Reading Readiness Test
Cognitive Abilities Test	McCarthy Scales of Children's
Criterion Reading	Abilities
Culture Fair Intelligence Tests	Metropolitan Achievement Test
Diagnosis: An Instructional Aid:	Metropolitan Readiness Tests
Reading	Peabody Individual Achievement
Diagnostic Reading Scales	Test
Durrell Analysis of Reading Diffi-	Peabody Picture Vocabulary Test
culty	Pictorial Test of Intelligence
Fountain Valley Teacher Support	Primary Mental Abilities Test
System in Reading	Short Form Test of Academic
Full-Range Picture Vocabulary Test	Aptitude
Gates-MacGinitie Reading Tests	Silent Reading Diagnostic Tests
Gates-McKillop Reading Diagnostic	Stanford Achievement Test
Tests	Stanford-Binet Intelligence Scale
Gilmore Oral Reading Test	Stanford Diagnostic Reading Test
Gray Oral Reading Test	Tests of Basic Experiences
Henmon-Nelson Tests of Mental	Wechsler Intelligence Scale for
Ability	Children—Revised

assess grammatic competence, although they are not specifically intended to do so. Several standardized tests assess standard American English usage; Table 17.2 contains a list of such tests that were previously discussed. However, a word of caution is again necessary. Reading and listening comprehension tests may not present adequate samples of various linguistic forms (for example, negatives and passives). Also, vocabulary levels are typically manipulated on such tests so that failure (or poor performance) may be attributable to either lack of knowledge of vocabulary or lack of competence in grammar or both. Moreover, many of the tests do not allow the user to determine if poor performance is attributable to grammatical error or vocabulary.

PHONOLOGY

Phonology refers to sounds and their composites (words and sentences) and their relationship to articulation and acoustic reception. The forty-four speech sounds in American English can be combined into a practically

Table **17.2**   Tests Discussed Elsewhere in This Book That Provide Information
About a Child's Grammatic Competence

California Achievement Test	Gilmore Oral Reading Test
Criterion Reading	Gray Oral Reading Test
Diagnosis: An Instructional Aid: Reading	Iowa Tests of Basic Skills
	Metropolitan Achievement Test
Diagnostic Reading Scales	Peabody Individual Achievement Test
Durrell Analysis of Reading Difficulty	
	Silent Reading Diagnostic Tests
Fountain Valley Teacher Support System in Reading	Stanford Achievement Test
	Stanford Diagnostic Reading Test
Gates-MacGinitie Reading Tests	Woodcock Reading Mastery Tests

infinite number of permutations. School personnel are usually concerned
less with the imitation of these sounds than with their comprehension and
production, individually and in combination.

The comprehension of individual speech sounds can be either a discrimination or association task. Basically, we want to know if a child can
"hear" the difference between sounds (*discriminate*) and, in written language, can associate letters with sounds. The latter can be assessed by some
tests and subtests previously reviewed. The discrimination of speech
sounds can also be assessed by some previously reviewed tests and subtests.
These are listed in Table 17.3. The production of speech sounds is called
articulation. Formal evaluations of articulation are usually conducted by
speech therapists, although teachers often screen and refer children with
potential articulation problems. Articulation skills are developmental;

Table **17.3**   Tests Discussed Elsewhere in This Book That Provide Information
About Phonation Skills Such as Auditory Discrimination, Letter-Sound
Associations, and Sound Blends

California Achievement Test	Gates-McKillop Reading Diagnostic Tests
Criterion Reading	
Diagnosis: An Instructional Aid: Reading	Iowa Tests of Basic Skills
	Metropolitan Achievement Test
Diagnostic Reading Scales	Silent Reading Diagnostic Tests
Durrell Analysis of Reading Difficulty	Stanford Achievement Test
	Stanford Diagnostic Reading Test

some sounds are correctly produced at an earlier age than are others. The assessment of articulation should be criterion-referenced; the child either does or does not correctly articulate each sound. However, although there are absolute standards for articulation, these must be tempered by a knowledge of the developmental nature of articulation. Tests of articulation are vehicles for eliciting sound production. Although articulation can be tested by having a child imitate phonemes, it is often assessed through the production of words or sentences.

TECHNICAL CONSIDERATIONS IN THE ASSESSMENT OF LANGUAGE

Three facts are especially important in the assessment of language. The first is that there is some controversy about the nature of language development. Many have argued that the ability to comprehend language typically exceeds the ability to produce language (Taylor & Swinney, 1972). Others have argued that this is not the case (Bloom, 1974; Fernald, 1972). Since there is some disagreement in this area, estimates of any child's language development and performance should explicitly indicate *how* those estimates were made, that is, whether production or comprehension or both were measured.

The second fact to be considered is that language is environmentally determined. This is both obvious and subtle. Syrian children learn Arabic; Italian children learn Italian; and children in the United States learn American English. However, within many countries, and certainly within the United States, there are several forms or dialects of the basic language as well as of other standard languages. It is helpful to think of Walter Cronkite (or most major television newspeople) as speaking standard American English. Cronkite's articulation, the meanings of his vocabulary, and the grammar by which his words gain meaning are all readily understood by a majority of U.S. citizens. The *New York Times* is considered by many to be the standard for written American prose. However, there are discernible subgroups within the United States who speak or write quite differently; these groups may use different phonetics, have different meanings for words that sound the same as words in standard American English, and have different grammars. The point that must not be overlooked, however, is that these dialects are not wrong, pathological, or inferior. Rather, they represent languages used by minority language communities; the languages are different, but they are not inferior in terms of either complexity or utility.

Because of the necessity to consider the language community in which a child developed, the normative sample of language tests presents somewhat different requirements. Since standard American English is not the language used by all children in the United States, a representative sample of all children — and languages and dialects used — in the United States is neither required nor desirable. What are required are separate norms for each of the various language communities, of which standard American English should be one. Because of the special normative requirements in language assessment, the tests listed in Tables 17.1, 17.2, and 17.3 must be viewed with caution. These tests were not designed to assess language performance in the linguistic sense. Their normative samples are typically heterogeneous. Consequently, scores on these devices do not necessarily reflect comparisons to speakers of standard American English. As a final caution, children should never be diagnosed as having a language dysfunction unless they are dysfunctional in their primary language or dialect; yet children who do not have a language dysfunction may have a deficit in standard American English that can restrict both academic progress and economic mobility. Thus, the standard language should be taught, not because it is inherently superior but because it provides the child with greater access to the public culture.

The third major consideration is that it is difficult to determine the point at which a test ceases to measure primarily language competence and begins to assess intellectual competence. Language and intelligence are closely related, as previously discussed in Chapter 12. The ability to define words in isolation or to interpret long difficult passages is considered intelligent behavior. Unfortunately, there is no agreement about where language competence ends and intellectual competence begins. This point was previously made in the section dealing with reading comprehension. In assessing language performance we need to consider carefully the extent to which we really may be assessing intellectual competence.

LANGUAGE TESTS

ANALYSIS OF SPONTANEOUS LANGUAGE

The analysis of spontaneously produced language samples is becoming increasingly popular. A fairly large consecutive sample, from fifty to one hundred sentences, of oral language — either spontaneous or prompted by stimulus materials — can be recorded, accurately transcribed, and then analyzed in terms of vocabulary, grammar, and phonation. A fairly large sample of spontaneous or prompted written language can also be collected and the vocabulary and grammar analyzed. Such language samples provide considerable insight into a child's production of language. These techniques are methods of systematic observation and have the merits and limitations as well as the requirements of observation systems in general.

GOLDMAN-FRISTOE TEST OF ARTICULATION

The Goldman-Fristoe Test of Articulation (GFTA) (Goldman and Fristoe, 1972) is an individually administered, criterion-referenced device intended to assess competence in the articulation of consonant sounds in simple and complex contexts. It is as much a vehicle for eliciting particular sounds as a test. Eleven common consonant blends and all single-consonant sounds except *zh* are elicited. The tester listens for the particular consonants (more than one per word are evaluated) and rates the correctness of the production. The device may also be used to assess vowels and diphthongs. Teachers may administer the device provided they score only the *number* of errors. If the types of errors are to be categorized, a speech or language therapist should administer the device. The test is divided into three parts.

Sounds-in-Words   This subtest contains thirty-five pictures of familiar objects that elicit forty-four responses, either names of the pictures or questions pertaining to the pictures. The responses elicit all single-consonant sounds except *zh*; medial *h, w, wh,* and *y*; and final voiced *th*.

Sounds-in-Sentences   This subtest is intended to elicit content-controlled spontaneous speech in which the consonants most likely to be defectively articulated are produced. The format of the subtest requires the examiner to read two stories aloud. The stories are illustrated by either four or five pictures. After each story is read, children are asked to recount the major events of the story in their own words; the pictures are used for prompting.

Stimulability   This subtest is used with children who make articulation errors. The consonants that are misarticulated are re-examined by a three-phase procedure. First, the examiner asks the child to watch and listen carefully while the consonant is pronounced in a syllable. If the child pronounces the consonant correctly, he or she is again asked to watch and listen carefully while the consonant is used in a word. If the child correctly pronounces it in a word, he or she is again asked to listen and watch carefully while the sound is used in a sentence. This subtest is intended to provide clinical information about how easily the child can correct misarticulated sounds with stimulation. This clinical information is used to estimate the child's response to therapy.

Scores

While percentile ranks (based on the National Speech and Hearing Survey conducted by Hyll in 1971) are available for the Sounds-in-Words subtest, the test is most appropriately used as a criterion-referenced device. Several types of articulation errors and interpretations are provided.

Reliability

Three types of reliability are reported, using the percent-agreement method.[2] The raters used to estimate reliability were experienced speech clinicians. Test-retest reliability (one-week interval) for each phoneme was high. For Sounds-in-Sentences, the median reliability was 94 percent; for Sounds-in-Words, the median reliability for the phonemes was 95 percent. Interrater reliability (different clinicians rating the same speech samples) for the presence of error in the articulation of each sound was also computed. The median agreement was 92 percent for the presence of an error and 88 percent for the classification of the type of error. Finally, intrarater reliability was estimated by having six clinicians rescore the responses of four children. Median agreement for the number of errors and for the types of errors was 91 percent.

Validity

The validity of the GFTA rests on its content validity.

Summary

The GFTA is an individually administered, criterion-referenced device intended to assess the production of consonants in simple and complex contexts. The reliability and validity of the device appear to be excellent.

AUDITORY DISCRIMINATION TEST   5-8 yrs old

One of the more popular devices intended solely to assess auditory discrimination was developed by Wepman. The Auditory Discrimination Test (ADT) (Wepman, 1958) is an individually administered, norm-referenced device intended to assess the auditory discrimination skills of children between the ages of 5 and 8. The ADT is available in two forms, which were equated through an unspecified procedure. Each form contains forty pairs of words. Thirty of these word pairs consist of words that differ from each other in only one phoneme; ten consist of identical words. In the different-word pairs, the location of the differing phonemes varies

---

2. Number of agreements divided by number of agreements plus disagreements.

among initial, medial, and final positions. The administration of the device is simple; the examiner reads each word pair, and the child indicates if the two words are the same or different.

Scores

Scores are based on the child's performance on the different-word pairs. *The Manual of Administration, Scoring, and Interpretation of the Auditory Discrimination Test* (Wepman, 1973) contains tables with which raw scores can be converted to a five-point rating scale. The scale appears to be based on percentile ranks. (Wepman says the scale is based on cumulative frequencies, but the highest score and the lowest score represent only 15 percent.) Scores earned by the bottom 15 percent of the standardization group are said to be inadequate. If a child responds correctly to ten or fewer items, the test is termed invalid. If a child responds incorrectly to four or more same-word pairs, the test is also considered invalid.

Norms

Neither the number of children in the norm group nor their characteristics are mentioned.

Reliability

Wepman reports two test-retest stability coefficients greater than .90 and an alternate-form reliability estimate of .92. The sample used to estimate reliabilities is not described.

Validity

Eight studies are reported to establish the validity of the ADT. One cross-sectional study demonstrated that the mean raw scores increased slightly, but significantly, with age. Two longitudinal studies showed the same trend. From the studies summarized in the manual, the ADT appears to be related to academic achievement and articulation problems. The data presented do not establish the validity of the rating scores; in one study reported (an attempt to establish predictive validity), the mean reading score for second-grade children whose auditory perception was rated as inadequate was 2.8.

Summary

The ADT is a device intended to assess the auditory discrimination of children between 5 and 8. The sounds to be discriminated appear to represent an adequate sample of behavior for a screening device. The reliability of the Auditory Discrimination Test is adequate, but the norms are inadequately described.

NORTHWESTERN SYNTAX SCREENING TEST

One of the devices more commonly used to assess grammatic competence is the Northwestern Syntax Screening Test (NSST) (Lee, 1969). It is an individually administered device intended to screen children who may have grammatic deficiencies. The device consists of two parts. Part 1 contains twenty pairs of items intended to assess the comprehension of sentences containing various grammatic structures and forms (subject-verb agreement, gender, voice, negatives, interrogatives, and so on). Each pair uses a plate containing four drawings; for each sentence read by the examiner, there are three distracters and a correct picture. The examiner reads the sentence, and the child points to the correct drawing. Part 2 also contains twenty pairs of items intended to assess the child's production of sentences containing various grammatic structures. Each pair of sentences uses a plate containing two drawings. The examiner reads the two sentences depicted by the drawings, then points to one of the pictures and asks, "What is this picture?" The child is supposed to repeat the sentence read by the examiner. Both verbatim responses and responses that use the same grammatic structure and contain no other grammatic errors are credited.

Scores

The numbers correct on each part are converted to percentile ranges (ninetieth, seventy-fifth, fiftieth, twenty-fifth, and tenth). A score below the tenth percentile is specified for follow-up.

Norms

The NSST was standardized on 242 children between the ages of 3 years and 7 years, 11 months. The number of children in each age group varies from 13 (at 3-0 to 3-5) to 62 (at 5-6 to 5-11). The children in the sample came from upper- and middle-class midwestern homes where standard American English was spoken.

Reliability

No reliability data accompany the test.

Validity

The NSST can claim content validity, although the number of items measuring the various grammatic forms is quite limited. Although the NSST is a screening device, no data are presented to indicate the proportions of false positives and false negatives that can be expected. No data are reported to indicate the relationship between performance on the NSST and spontaneous speech samples.

Summary

The NSST is a screening device intended to assess children's competence in the comprehension and production of various grammatic forms. The sample of test items appears quite restricted. The size of some of the norm groups is small, and no reliability data are presented in the test manual. The NSST should be considered experimental.

ILLINOIS TEST OF PSYCHOLINGUISTIC ABILITIES   2-4 to   10-3

The revised edition of the Illinois Test of Psycholinguistic Abilities (ITPA) (Kirk, McCarthy, & Kirk, 1968) is an individually administered, norm-referenced device that can be used with children between the ages of 2 years, 4 months, and 10 years, 3 months. It was designed to assess relative ability in understanding, processing, and producing both verbal and non-verbal communications. The theory underlying the development of the ITPA is an adaptation of Osgood's (1957a, 1957b) psycholinguistic communication model. The ITPA contains ten regularly administered subtests and two supplementary tests. Each subtest is designed to minimize the demands of any factor other than that being measured. For example, the two subtests designed to assess understanding (auditory reception and visual reception) minimize response demands for the child by requiring only yes-no or pointing responses. Two levels of processing are assessed. The representational level requires some form of mediation; at the automatic level, "the individual's habits of functioning are less voluntary but highly organized and integrated" (Paraskevopoulos & Kirk, 1969, p. 14). At the representational level, both auditory association and visual association are measured. At the automatic level, closure (auditory, visual, and grammatic) and sequential memory (auditory and visual) are measured. Production is measured by testing both verbal expression and manual expression. The behaviors sampled by each subtest of the ITPA follow.

Auditory Reception (AR)   This subtest assesses vocabulary through a series of yes-no questions such as "Do witches cackle?" The grammatical form of the question remains constant; adjectives are used only at the upper level of the scale. The child responds by nodding or saying yes or no.

Visual Reception (VR)   This is a multiple-choice test assessing memory for visually presented, categorically related stimuli. A child is shown a stimulus (for example, a picture of a German shepherd dog). The examiner then removes the stimulus, shows a card with four pictures, and instructs the child to point to the one that was on the stimulus card. The correct response would be another breed of dog (for example, Chihuahua). A pointing response is all that is required.

Auditory Association (AA)   This subtest assesses skill in completing verbal analogies. The stimuli and the child's response are oral. "Brother is a boy. Sister is a _____?" is an example of the kind of stimulus question asked.

Visual Association (VA)   This subtest assesses skill in completing visual analogies. The stimuli are visual, the directions are oral, and the child's responses are manual (pointing). For example, the child is shown a picture of a tennis ball, a tennis racket, and a baseball, along with a blank; the examiner asks the child to select a picture from a multiple-choice array to fill the blank and complete the analogy.

The Verbal Expression (VE)   This subtest requires that the child describe familiar objects orally. The child is shown an object, like a button, and asked to tell the examiner all about it. Scoring is based primarily on quantity of verbal expression.

Manual Expression (ME)   This subtest assesses understanding of the use of various objects. The child must show how to use a pictured object (for example, a camera) by pretending to use it (that is, the child must pretend to hold a camera to one eye, look through a range finder, make various adjustments, and release the shutter).

Grammatic Closure (GC)   This subtest requires the child to supply the correct grammatical form of a word to complete a sentence. It uses pictures and oral statements read by the examiner. For example, the examiner shows the child a drawing such as that depicted in Figure 17.2 and says, "Here is one die; here are two _____." The child is expected to say "dice."

Auditory Closure (AC)   This supplementary test requires completing words with one or more missing syllables. The examiner asks the child to listen and tell what the examiner is talking about. An incomplete word is then spoken ("- olli - op," for instance), and the child is expected to say the entire word (*lollipop*).

Sound Blending (SB)   This is also a supplementary test. The examiner says a word but pauses for one-half second between syllables ("type - wri - ter"). The child must synthesize the sounds into a word.

Visual Closure (VC)   This subtest requires recognition of a familiar object when only part of the object is shown. The child is shown four line-drawing scenes; each scene contains several examples of familiar things, like a dog, which vary in their degree of completeness. The child must find as many as possible of the partially visible things in 30 seconds. Thus, if

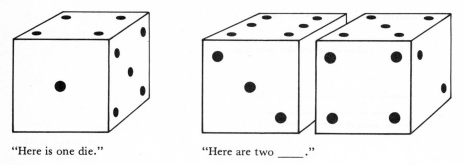

"Here is one die."   "Here are two _____."

Figure **17.2** An example of the format used in the Grammatic Closure subtest of the Illinois Test of Psycholinguistic Abilities

only the dog's tail is visible from behind a box, the child must indicate that there is a dog behind the box.

Auditory Sequential Memory (ASM)   This subtest requires the child to reproduce orally, in correct order, a sequence of digits presented orally at half-second intervals.

Visual Sequential Memory (VSM)   This subtest requires the child to reproduce a sequence of meaningless designs. The examiner exposes a card containing a sequence of two or more designs; the child is given a group of chips, each containing one design. The child must put the chips in order from memory.

Scores

The number of correct responses for each subtest and the total number of correct responses on the entire test may be converted to various kinds of scores. Raw scores can be transformed to scaled scores (SS) with a mean of 36 and a standard deviation of 6. The composite SS is based on the sum of raw-score points; the subtests are not equally weighted since raw-score variances differ. This means that some subtests count for more than other subtests in the total score.

Psycholinguistic ages (PLAs) are available for each subtest and for the total (composite) score. The PLAs were obtained by plotting a graph of mean CAs for the eight age groups and the mean raw scores for those eight groups. The means were then connected and intermediate values were interpolated. Paraskevopoulos and Kirk (1969) present data to demonstrate that the "standard deviation of PLA vary from test to test and from age to age" (p. 91). Thus, PLAs for different subtests are not comparable.

Psycholinguistic quotients (PLQs) are ratio scores (100 PLA/CA). Since PLQs are ratio scores, the unequal standard deviations that do not allow PLAs to be compared also do not allow PLQs to be compared. Moreover, the authors state that "since the standardization sample was comprised of average children, *deviation* PLQs could not be computed without questionable extrapolations" (Paraskevopoulos & Kirk, 1969, p. 80). Fourteen pages later the authors state that the composite scaled score, "in contrast to the PLQ, is essentially comparable in nature to a *deviation* intelligence quotient" (Paraskevopoulos & Kirk, 1969, p. 94). The composite scaled score is based on the same sample as the PLQ, a sample the authors state is too restricted for use in computing deviation scores without making questionable assumptions.

The technical manual also provides a percentage score that is interpretable as a percentile rank for average deviations. An *average deviation* is obtained by subtracting the mean of a particular child's scaled scores from each one of that child's scaled scores; the absolute differences are summed (+ and − signs are ignored), and the sum is divided by the number of scores. The percentage of children in the norming sample whose average deviation was equal to or greater than particular average deviations is shown in a table.

Norms

The ITPA was standardized on a narrowly defined group of children. Although the test was designed as a diagnostic device "for use with children encountering learning difficulties" (Paraskevopoulos & Kirk, 1969, p. 51), the normative procedures systematically excluded children who were having difficulty in school. The populations for the norm groups were "only those children demonstrating average intellectual functioning, average school achievement, average characteristics of personal-social adjustment, sensory-motor integrity, and coming from predominantly English-speaking families" (Paraskevopoulos & Kirk, 1969, pp. 51–52). It is not clear whether English-speaking means the same as standard-English-speaking. The norm sample consisted of 962 children between the ages of 2-7 and 10-1 residing in Bloomington, Illinois; Danville, Illinois; Decatur, Illinois; Madison, Wisconsin; and Urbana, Illinois. These communities were selected because of "practical requirements of accessibility and because of suitability to the requirements of being middle-class communities" (Paraskevopoulos & Kirk, 1969, p. 57). Children of school age were selected by sampling "middle-range" schools — schools judged by school administrators to be predominantly middle-class. Classes of normal children within the schools were sampled. The preschool sample was obtained by testing the younger siblings of the school sample and by referrals "made mostly by mothers of preschool siblings" (Paraskevopoulos & Kirk, 1969, pp. 55–56).

The normative group contains about 4 percent black children, which may be explained by the fact that schools with more than 10 percent black children enrolled were excluded from the sample. Some attempt is made to demonstrate that the five *communities* from which the sample was drawn are representative of the entire U.S. population (1960 census) in terms of median family income, education, and occupation of residents. However, since no attempt was made to select a sample representative of the community as a whole, such comparisons are misleading. The occupations of the fathers of the children actually selected are presented and do correspond to the 1960 census. Information about the intelligence of the norm group, as measured by the 1960 Stanford-Binet, indicates that the sample is severely restricted; the standard deviation of IQs is only 8.

Reliability

The technical manual accompanying the ITPA contains a most adequate description of the reliability data. Internal-consistency estimates (primarily KR-20) for each of the eight age groups are presented by age and subtest. Column 1 of Table 17.4 contains the lowest and highest estimates. Of the ninety-six coefficients (twelve subtests at eight ages), only nine equal or exceed .90; only at ages 5-7 through 6-1 does the composite reliability fall below .90.

Test-retest reliability with a five-to-six-month interval was computed for three age levels; 4-year-olds ($n = 71$), 6-year-olds ($n = 55$), and 8-year-olds ($n = 72$). These reliability estimates are presented in column 2 of Table 17.4. Test-retest reliabilities were considerably lower than the internal-consistency estimates. No subtest estimate exceeded .86. The 4-year-old sample also had a mean gain of twenty-five raw-score points over the interval; the 6-year-old group, twenty-seven raw-score points; and the 8-year-old sample, seventeen raw-score points.

The technical manual contains SEMs for raw scores, PLAs (in months), and scaled scores. Median reliability estimates for the differences between scores, based on internal-consistency estimates of reliability, are also presented. A table of median SEMs of scaled-score differences is provided. Evidence of excellent interscorer reliability for the Verbal Expression subtest is demonstrated. The technical manual presents all the reliability information necessary to evaluate ITPA scores.

Validity

The absence of validity data is striking. It is left to the consumer to determine content validity. Bateman's 1965 survey of research done with the experimental edition of the ITPA is cited in the Examiner's Manual. No estimates of validity with other language measures for the revised edition are presented. No evidence of predictive validity with school

Table **17.4**   Ranges of Reliability Estimates for Subtests of the ITPA

SUBTESTS	INTERNAL-CONSISTENCY[a]	TEST-RETEST[a]
AR	.84–.91	.36–.56
VR	.73–.87	.21–.36
AA	.74–.85	.62–.71
VA	.75–.82	.32–.57
VE	.51–.79	.45–.49
ME	.77–.83	.40–.51
GC	.60–.74	.49–.72
VC	.49–.70	.57–.68
ASM	.74–.90	.61–.86
VSM	.51–.96	.12–.50
AC	.45–.84	.36–.52
SB	.78–.91	.30–.63
Composite	.87–.93	.70–.83

[a] Not corrected for restriction in intelligence range.

achievement or teacher ratings for the revised edition is presented. Correlations provided indicate that the ITPA is very highly correlated with CA ($r = .96$), moderately correlated with intelligence, and slightly correlated with social class. Most distressing, however, is the lack of substantiation for the use of ITPA profiles as an indication of pathology. Paraskevopoulos and Kirk state that "the larger the average deviation of individual scores from a child's mean score, the most discrepant the child's growth, and the more likely it is that the child will have learning disabilities" (1969, p. 142). The authors provide no data to support this conclusion. Rather, they compare the average deviations of mentally retarded and normal children. Almost all definitions of learning disability *exclude* retarded children. Moreover, the reasoning behind such an argument, even if the authors demonstrated that learning-disabled children exhibited more dispersion in their scores than normal children did, is clearly fallacious: Learning-disabled children have wide dispersions; John has a wide dispersion; therefore, John has a learning disability. The argument contains an undistributed middle term.

Summary

The ITPA is an exciting instrument designed to assess several language functions. The norms appear inadequate; the validity is unestablished; and the reliability of the subtests is adequate only for experimental work.

SUMMARY

Language consists of vocabulary, grammar, and phonology. These three components are typically measured by assessing a child's comprehension or production of them. Language assessment presents three problems: (1) the controversy over the sequence in which language develops, (2) the necessity for separate norm samples for each different language group in the United States, and (3) the confusion between linguistic and intellectual competence.

STUDY QUESTIONS

1. Identify and explain three components of language.

2. Compare and contrast the requirements for adequate normative samples for language tests with the requirements for tests in other domains.

3. A school district in Austin, Texas, decides to screen preschool bilingual children using the ITPA, the NSST, and the Goldman-Fristoe. The parents of the bilingual children in the district protest the use of these tests with their children. To what extent is the protest justified? How might the school district defend its position? Consider specifically the norms, reliability, and validity of *each* of the three tests.

ADDITIONAL READING

Hammill, D., & Larsen, S. The effectiveness of psycholinguistic training. *Exceptional Children*, 1974, *41*, 5–14.

Irwin, J. V., & Marge, M. (eds.). *Principles of childhood language disorders.* Englewood Cliffs, NJ: Prentice-Hall, 1972. (Chapters 1 and 2.)

Kirk, S. A., & Kirk, W. *Psycholinguistic learning disabilities.* Urbana: University of Illinois Press, 1971.

Lenneberg, E. H. On explaining language. *Science*, 1969, *164*, 635–643.

Meyers, C. E., Sundstrom, P. E., & Yoshida, R. Y. The school psychologist and assessment in special education. *School Psychology Monographs*, *2*, 1974.

Minskoff, E. H. Research on psycholinguistic training: Critique and guidelines. *Exceptional Children*, 1975, *42*, 136–144. (Also the response by Newcomer, Larsen, & Hammill, 144–148.)

Schiefelbusch, R. L., Copeland, R. H., & Smith, J. O. (eds.). *Language and mental retardation: Empirical and conceptual considerations.* New York: Holt, Rinehart and Winston, 1967. (Chapters 8, 9, 10.)

Ysseldyke, J. E., & Sabatino, D. A. Identification of statistically significant differences between subtest scaled scores and psycholinguistic ages on the ITPA. *Psychology in the Schools,* 1972, *9*, 309–313.

Chapter 18

Assessment of Adaptive Behavior and Personality

This chapter differs from the other chapters that have dealt with tests of particular domains of behaviors. The differences in this chapter reflect differences in the constructs being measured and the methods of measuring them. Adequate personality development and social competence are nebulous concepts, ill-defined and subjectively measured. In essence, we are no longer dealing with behaviors but with interpretations of behaviors. In a very real sense, the methods and measurements discussed in this chapter assess conformity to theoretical or societal expectations. Behavior is evaluated in terms of the degree to which it is disturbing — either to the individual exhibiting the behavior or to people who come in contact with that individual.

Tests of personality, social-emotional behavior, and social maturity use items from several other domains of measurement (reading and writing, motor development, perceptual-motor integration, and so on). However, in the assessment of personality, social-emotional behavior, and social maturity, relative levels of skill development are *not* assessed. What is assessed is how those skills are typically used and how that use is interpreted. In social-emotional assessment, we do not look at the level of oral vocabulary; we look at how a person uses words. For instance, a person might use words in an "aggressive" manner — swearing, threatening, and so on. We do not look at drawings to assess the completeness of a human figure or the integration of circles and squares; we interpret drawings as indicative of underlying feelings and emotions.

Two frames of reference exist for evaluating whether a behavior is conforming. Is it deemed acceptable in the majority or public culture? Is it deemed acceptable in a minority or private culture? Social tolerance for particular behaviors depends on the particular behavior, the context in which the behavior is exhibited, the status of the individual exhibiting the behavior, and the orientation (and indeed presence) of an observer. It is hard to think of any behavior that is universally considered unacceptable. In various societies suicide is acceptable, homosexuality is openly practiced and condoned, aggressive language is expected. Within the majority culture of the United States, the same behaviors are interpreted differently, depending on the circumstances: total disrobing is an appropriate behavior before taking a bath; it is generally not considered appropriate behavior before being baptized. In wartime, taking a human life is sanctioned and even rewarded if the victim is an enemy soldier; in peacetime, the circumstances determine whether taking another's life is considered murder, manslaughter, or self-defense. Thus, the context and the circumstances determine in large part the evaluation of behavior.

Who exhibits a behavior also determines the interpretation of the behavior. It is widely recognized that for the same behavior a rich person may be labeled eccentric while a poor person is labeled insane. Some behaviors are simply overlooked if a person is old enough or has sufficient social status. For example, biting one's fingernails is considered self-abusive behavior on the AAMD Adaptive Behavior Scale; yet if the President of the United States bit his fingernails, he would be considered merely nervous. The research literature is replete with examples of how the extraneous characteristics of people influence evaluations of their performances.

Finally, for a behavior to be considered unacceptable someone must witness either the behavior or the results of the behavior. Thus, if a person runs naked through the business district of a large city at 4:13 A.M. and no one witnesses the event, then no one is disturbed by it, and the behavior will not be evaluated as unacceptable.

In recent years, there has been an increase in the use of behavioral rating scales as an alternative to both personality and social-maturity assessment. With this type of device, an observer indicates the presence (and sometimes the frequency of occurence) or absence of particular behaviors. The behaviors selected for rating are often determined on an a priori or empirical basis to be unacceptable in the majority or public culture. Such scales often provide norms that estimate the frequency of occurrence of each behavior in persons of various demographic characteristics. Such devices represent a compromise between social-adequacy scales, which give a summary score with norm-referenced interpretative data, and personality measures, which impute to the behaviors an underlying, hypothetical cause.

While the use of behavioral rating scales has been increasing, the use of personality tests in the schools is on the decline. The use of measures of social competence is also on the decline. However, there is renewed interest in them for two reasons. The individual items on such scales are being used as criterion-referenced items in educational planning, and recent court decisions have made mandatory the assessment of a student's adaptive behavior before that student can be placed in a class for the mentally retarded.

The remainder of this chapter is divided into two parts: the assessment of adaptive behavior and the assessment of personality. In the assessment of adaptive behavior, four commonly used devices are reviewed. In the assessment of personality, an overview is presented rather than a review of devices.

TESTS OF ADAPTIVE BEHAVIOR

The four devices reviewed in the pages that follow are used most often with handicapped children.

VINELAND SOCIAL MATURITY SCALE

The Vineland Social Maturity Scale (VSMS) (Doll, 1953) is perhaps the most widely known and widely used device for the assessment of social competence. In 1953, Doll published *Measurement of Social Competence: A Manual for the Vineland Social Maturity Scale*. This work is a model of what a technical manual should contain. The 664-page manual contains a detailed rationale and description of the scale as well as the necessary descriptions of norms, reliability, validity, administration and scoring, and applications. Where possible, Doll interweaves the rich research history of the scale with the explanations of its construction.

The administration of the device is unlike that of any other device discussed thus far in this book. The VSMS is *not* administered to the person being assessed. Rather, an interview procedure is used whereby an interviewer asks questions of a third person, or respondent, who is very familiar with the person being assessed. The examiner must be skilled in the general techniques of conducting clinical interviews. The *respondent* (the person being interviewed) must be well acquainted with the subject of the interview. The interviewer must be skillful in eliciting, integrating, and evaluating the respondent's observations of the subject. Based on the information provided by the respondent, the interviewer's task is to determine whether the subject *habitually and customarily* performs certain acts; it is not to determine if the subject *can* perform these acts.

Doll defined social competence as "a functional composite of human traits which subserves social usefulness as reflected in self-sufficiency and in service to others" (1953, p. 2). The VSMS assesses eight aspects of social competence. Although the 117 behaviors rated on the VSMS are clustered into eight areas, these eight areas are not subtests. The VSMS is an age scale similar in construction to the earlier editions of the Binet intelligence scales; different items appear at different age levels. The VSMS assesses social competence from birth through 30 years of age. Consequently, the items show remarkable variation—from "balances head" through "performs responsible routine chores" to "advances general welfare." Because of the tremendous age span and the complexities of social maturity, the behaviors sampled by the VSMS are difficult to characterize. Representative types of items in each of the eight clusters follow.

Self-Help General   The items under this general heading assess general self-help activities such as sitting and standing unsupported, avoiding simple hazards, and using the toilet unassisted.

Self-Help Eating   The items under this heading assess an individual's increasing responsibility in eating. Included are such skills as drinking from a cup with assistance, using a spoon to eat, discriminating edible from inedible objects, getting a drink unaided, and being completely self-sufficient at the dinner table.

Self-Help Dressing   The items under this heading measure an individual's responsibility in dress and personal hygiene. Included are such skills as putting on a coat, buttoning, washing, and dressing completely by oneself.

Locomotion   The items under this heading include walking, going about the house and yard, going about town, and going to near and distant places unattended.

Occupation   The items under this heading measure an individual's increasing orientation to gainful employment. At younger ages, occupation items assess occupying oneself while unattended, using vehicular toys, and doing routine chores. At older ages, items include being employed or continuing one's education, performing skilled work, engaging in beneficial recreation, and performing expert work.

Communication   Items under this heading assess command of increasingly demanding forms of communication. At very young ages, an individual is expected to demonstrate the rudiments of language (imitation of sounds, comprehension of instructions, speaking in complete sentences). At older ages, an individual is expected to read and write, use the telephone, use the mails, and enjoy reading.

Self-Direction   The items in this category deal with the use of money (for example, is trusted with money, makes minor purchases, buys for others) and assuming responsibility for oneself (for example, goes out in the daytime or at night unsupervised, looks after one's own health).

§ *Socialization* Items grouped in this category assess interpersonal relationships, including for early ages behaviors like playing increasingly difficult games, and at the adult level rather more imposing behaviors like contributing to the social welfare, inspiring confidence, and promoting the general welfare.

Scoring Procedures and Scores

The task of the interviewer is to determine if the subject of the interview *habitually and customarily* performs the act or skill assessed by an item. A subject who does is given a passing score on the item. A passing score (F+) is also given if the subject formerly performed a particular act or skill but has since outgrown the behavior or is now not allowed to perform that act because of circumstances unrelated to it. This is quite similar to another type of passing performance (NO+) — no opportunity but the ability to perform the act. Scores of plus-minus are awarded to emerging behaviors; plus-minus scores are counted as half-plus (that is, two plus-minus scores equal one plus). Items are scored as minus and not credited under several conditions. F− scores are awarded when the subject formerly performed the act but is no longer capable of doing so because of some impairment, such as senility or a physical handicap. NO− scores are awarded when a subject is restrained from participating in an activity because that subject gets into trouble; for example, certain adolescents may have no opportunity to go out at night unsupervised because when they do, they steal cars. Finally, a failing score is given if the subject usually does not perform the act. One other score, no information (NI), is awarded when the respondent cannot or does not provide adequate enough information for the interviewer to score the item.

The number of passing scores is summed and converted to a social age (SA), which is interpreted like any other age score. A ratio social quotient (SQ) can also be obtained ($100 \times SA/CA = SQ$). As in the case of age scores in general, the standard deviations of SAs and SQs vary at different chronological ages. Doll (1953) has tabled the means and standard deviations for SAs and SQs at each age.

Norms

A total of 620 white subjects, 10 males and 10 females at each age level from birth to 30 years of age, make up the norm sample. All subjects in the norm group were selected from the greater Vineland, New Jersey, area in 1935. Thus, the norms are over forty years old. Children with educational or mental retardation were excluded, as were children with physical handicaps. According to Doll, the normative data "show normal middle-class sampling without inclusion of marked extremes" (1953, p. 356).

Reliability

No internal-consistency estimates of reliability are provided in the manual. Doll does present a considerable amount of stability (test-retest) data. Two hundred fifty subjects from the norm sample were retested (1.7- to 1.9-year interval); SAs were grouped in one-year intervals, and the resulting test-retest correlation was .98. For the same sample, SQs were grouped in ten-point intervals, and the resulting test-retest correlation was .57. Since the stability estimate of the SQs should not be affected as much by CA, they are probably a better estimate.

Doll also reports inter-interviewer and inter-respondent correlations. For a sample of 123 feeble-minded subjects, he had the following retest data: 12 subjects had the same interviewer and the same respondent; 68 subjects had the same interviewer but different respondents; 19 subjects had different interviewers and the same respondent; and 25 subjects had different interviewers and different respondents. When the four conditions were pooled, the test-retest correlation was .92 for SA.

Validity

The validity of the VSMS rests on content analysis and correlations of ratings of social competence made by persons familiar with the subject, and social ages derived from the VSMS. These correlations tend to be quite substantial — over .80 typically. One of the major difficulties with the content of the VSMS is its age. The majority of items are as representative of social competence today as they were in the 1930s. However, the placement of the items in the scale may well be incorrect today. For example, using the telephone is placed at the 10.3-year level and going about town unattended is placed at the 9.4-year level. Our intuition tells us that children use the telephone at an earlier age now but that they may not go about town unattended until a later age.

Summary

The VSMS is a venerable instrument used to assess social competence. We believe it is badly in need of revision and updating. The item placement may no longer be appropriate, and the sample is very restricted.

CAIN-LEVINE SOCIAL COMPETENCY SCALE

The Cain-Levine Social Competency Scale (Cain, Levine, & Elzey, 1963) is a device intended to assess the independence of trainable mentally retarded children between the ages of 5 years and 13 years, 11 months. The scale is administered in a structured interview with someone who is very familiar with the subject; the subject is not interviewed. The interviewer introduces each item with a general question about the subject's behavior in a particular area and then probes the respondent's answers. The forty-four items that make up the scale are grouped into four subscales: Self-help, Initiative, Social Skills, and Communication.

Self-help   This subscale contains fourteen items "designed to estimate the child's manipulative ability, or motor skills" (Cain et al., 1963, p. 2). More points are awarded when it is reported that the subject performs the task adequately. Skills assessed include dressing, washing, eating, and helping with simple chores around the house.

Initiative   This subscale contains ten items designed to assess the extent to which the subject initiates activities or is self-directed. Skills assessed include dressing, toileting, completing tasks, hanging up clothes, and offering assistance.

Social Skills   This subscale contains ten items designed to ascertain the extent to which the subject maintains or engages in interpersonal relationships. Typical items are table setting, answering the telephone, and playing with and helping others.

Communication   This subscale contains ten items intended to ascertain the degree to which the subject's wants are communicated. Individual items range from the use of oral language and clarity of speech to delivery of messages and relating objects to actions.

Scoring Procedures and Scores

Thirty-eight items are rated on a four-point scale, while six items are rated on a five-point scale. For each item, a score of 1 represents the lowest level, or the absence, of behavior. For example, the item assessing question answering on the Communication subscale is scored 1 if the subject does not respond to questions, while it is scored 4 if the subject answers questions with a complete sentence. In those cases where the subject is not permitted by parents or guardians to participate in an activity or to demonstrate a skill, the subject receives a score of 1.

Raw scores on the forty-four items are summed. Since boys typically earn somewhat lower scores than girls earn, a constant (the magnitude of which depends on the age of the subject) is added to the total score earned by boys. Each subscale and the total raw scores can be converted to percentile ranks. Five age tables are provided for this purpose: 5-0 to 5-11, 6-0 to 7-11, 8-0 to 9-11, 10-0 to 11-11, and 12-0 to 13-11.

Norms

The Cain-Levine was standardized on 414 males and 302 females between the ages of 5-0 and 13-11. "The children aged 8-0 and older were enrolled in city and county public school programs in the state of California. The names of children aged 5-0 through 7-11 years were obtained from public school districts and from parent associations" (Cain et al., 1963, p. 8). IQ data from various sources are presented in the technical manual to demonstrate that the sample is "trainable." IQs ranged from 25 through 59. At the 5-0 to 5-11 age level, there is a large difference in mean IQs between boys ($\bar{X} = 30.09$) and girls ($\bar{X} = 45.50$). After age 8-0, the mean IQs stabilize in the low to mid 40s. Data provided by the test authors indicate that the occupational levels of the parents or guardians in the Cain-Levine sample tend to be biased toward overrepresentation of lower-class families. However, this difference may accurately reflect the frequency of mental retardation in the different social classes (see Farber, 1968).

Reliability

For the total score, odd-even internal consistencies, based on the standardization sample, range from .75 to .91. Internal consistencies for individual subtests tend to be lower, ranging from .55 to .95. Test-retest reliability estimates over a three-week interval for thirty-five children are quite high. Total raw-score stability is reported as .98, while three of the four subtests have stability coefficients that exceed .90. However, stability coefficients were apparently computed across ages.

Validity

The validity of the Cain-Levine rests on item selection and the correlation between social competence and MA and CA. Item selection was based on an examination of "all major curriculum guides developed for the trainable mentally retarded by public schools and institutions," "consultations with professional personnel," "discussions with parents," and "careful examination of existing scales and evaluational instruments" (Cain et al., 1963, p. 7). The scale correlates reasonably well (between .4 and .5) with CA and not very well with IQ (between .09 and .30).

Summary

The Cain-Levine is an interview-based device designed to assess social competence in self-help, initiative, social skills, and communication. The device is sufficiently reliable for screening purposes and appears to have adequate validity, although the normative sample was limited to children residing in California.

AAMD ADAPTIVE BEHAVIOR SCALE

The American Association on Mental Deficiency (AAMD) Adaptive Behavior Scale (Nihira, Foster, Shellhaas, & Leland, 1969) is intended to measure the behavior of three types of handicapped persons: retarded, disturbed, and developmentally disabled. Specifically, the scale is designed to provide a description "of the way an individual maintains his or her personal independence in daily living or of how he or she meets the social expectations of his or her environment" (Nihira et al., 1974, p. 5).

As is the case with other measures of social competence, the scale is administered to a third person who is asked about the subject's performance. The scale consists of two parts. Part 1 contains sixty-six items that rate skill use in ten domains. For each item there are several statements. Some items require that the respondent check the one statement that best describes the subject; other items require that all statements applying to the subject be checked. Item are grouped into areas, and areas are grouped into domains.

Part 1 consists of items grouped into ten domains that are described as follows.

Independent Functioning   In this domain skills are measured in eight areas: (1) Four items relate to eating — from use of utensils to table manners. (2) Two items deal with toilet use. (3) Five items deal with cleanliness and range from bathing to menstruation. (4) Posture and clothing items are clustered under the more general area of Appearance. (5) A separate area is used to assess care of clothing. (6) The area of Dressing and Undressing is measured by three items. (7) Two items (Sense of Direction and Use of Public Transportation) deal with travel. (8) The last area (Independent Functioning) is assessed by two items: Telephone Use and a miscellaneous item.

Physical Development   In this domain skills are measured in two areas: (1) Sensory Function (vision and hearing), and (2) Motor Development (balance, ambulation, motor control, and so on).

Economic Activity   In this domain skills are measured in two areas: (1) Money Handling (knowledge of money and budgeting), and (2) Shopping.

Language Development   In this domain skills are measured in three areas: (1) Expression is assessed by five items (Prelinguistic Communication, Articulation, Word Usage, Use of Complete and Progressively More Complex Sentences, and Writing). (2) Comprehension is assessed by two items: Understanding Complex Statements and Reading. (3) Social language development is assessed by Conversational and Miscellaneous Language Skills.

Numbers and Time   In this domain skills are assessed by items dealing with the understanding and use of numbers and time.

Domestic Activity   In this domain skills are measured in three areas: (1) Cleaning, (2) Food and Serving, and (3) Miscellaneous.

Vocational Activity   In this domain skills are assessed by three items related to performing complex jobs safely and reliably.

Self-direction   This domain consists of three areas: (1) In Initiative, two items (Initiation of Activities and Passivity) are included. (2) In Perseverance, two items (Attention and Persistence) are assessed. (3) In Leisure Time, several items assess what subjects do in their free time.

Responsibility   In this domain skills are measured by two items: Care of Personal Belongings and General Responsibility.

Socialization   In this domain seven items sample both appropriate and inappropriate behaviors. For inappropriate behaviors points are subtracted.

Part 2 consists of forty-four items grouped into fourteen domains. All items in part 2 are scored in the same way. The respondent rates all statements in each item that apply to the subject as a 1 (occasionally) or a 2 (frequently). A description of the domains assessed in part 2 follows.

Violent and Destructive Behavior   This domain consists of five items assessing personal and property damage as well as temper tantrums.

Antisocial Behavior   This domain consists of six items assessing teasing, bossing, disruptive behavior, and inconsiderate behavior.

Rebellious Behavior   This domain consists of six items assessing disobedience and insubordination.

Untrustworthy Behavior   This domain contains two items, Lying and Stealing.

Withdrawal   This domain contains three items, Inactivity, Withdrawal, and Shyness.

Stereotyped Behavior and Odd Mannerisms   This domain contains the two items described by the domain title.

Inappropriate Interpersonal Manners   This domain has one item.

Unacceptable Vocal Habits   This domain contains one item.

Unacceptable or Eccentric Habits   This domain contains four items.

Self-abusive Behavior   This domain contains one item.

Hyperactive Tendencies   This domain is also one item.

Sexually Aberrant Behavior   This domain contains four items dealing with masturbation, homosexuality, and socially unacceptable behaviors, such as rape.

Psychological Disturbance   This domain contains seven items that explore possible emotional disturbance.

Uses Medication   Use of medication for the control of hyperactivity, seizures, and so on is considered by the scale authors to be maladaptive.

Two aspects of the statements contained in each item on both parts are especially noteworthy. First, many statements are not only overly value-laden but also unnecessarily subjective. For example, hugging "too intensely" in public is viewed as unacceptable sexual behavior. One wonders to whom the hugging is too intense. The huggee or the observer? Second, the scale lacks proportion. For example, rape carries as much weight as being overly seductive in appearance. Similarly, attempted suicide is given the same number of points as acting sick after an illness.

Scores

Raw scores for each domain are summed. Tables in the manual accompanying the scale allow the examiner to convert raw scores to deciles only, although the tables are labeled *percentile ranks*. In part 1, the higher the decile rank, the better the development of the person. However, in part 2, the higher the decile rank, the more *maladaptive* is the person's behavior.

Norms

Deciles are based on evaluations by unspecified individuals of approximately 4,000 institutionalized persons in eleven age groups from a 3-year-old group to a 50-to-69-year-old group. The number of persons in each age group ranges from 528 at 10 to 12 years to 97 at age 3. Mean IQs (tests unspecified) for each age group range from 28 at age 3 to 45.8 at age 16 to 18.

Reliability

Only interrater reliability is considered in the manual. Pearson product-moment correlation coefficients were used to estimate interrater agreement by attendants for 133 institutionalized subjects. For part 1, the mean reliability estimates ranged from .71 (Self-Direction) to .92 (Independent Functioning). For part 2, the reliability estimates ranged from .37 (Unacceptable Vocal Habits) to .77 (Uses Medication).

Validity

Results of two factor-analytic studies conducted by one of the scale's authors with the previous edition of the scale are discussed. Three factors were found and were labeled *personal independence, social maladaption*, and *personal maladaption*. The results of two other studies are also mentioned briefly; these studies showed there was some correspondence between "clinical" judgment by undefined persons and ratings derived from the scale.

No evidence of content validity is presented. Examiners must judge for themselves the validity and appropriateness of the particular items.

Summary

The AAMD Adaptive Behavior Scale is a recent attempt to quantify adaptive behavior. Although expressly designed for use with various groups of handicapped persons, it is standardized only on institutionalized retardates. Estimates of interrater reliability are so low that some domains can be considered accurate enough only for screening purposes; some domains have such low interrater reliability that they are not even adequate for experimental work. Very limited validity data are presented for the previous edition of the scale. At its present stage of development, the scale does not appear adequate for making important educational decisions about individuals.

AAMD ADAPTIVE BEHAVIOR SCALE
PUBLIC SCHOOL VERSION (1974 REVISION)

A separate manual for the 1974 revision of the AAMD Adaptive Behavior Scale was prepared for use in public schools by Lambert, Windmiller, Cole, and Figueroa (1975). Those domains, areas, and items "which do not pertain to school and . . . which cannot necessarily be observed in school" were deleted (Lambert et al., 1975, p. iii). In part 1, domain 6 (Domestic

Activity) was deleted, while in part 2 domain 10 (Self-Abusive Behavior) and domain 12 (Sexually Aberrant Behavior) were omitted. Part 1 of the revision contains fifty-six items, as compared to sixty-six in the institutional version; part 2 contains thirty-nine items, as compared to forty-four in the institutional version. Teachers are the preferred respondents on the school version of the scale.

Scores and Norms

The school version was standardized on 2,600 California children in six age groups (7-3 through 13-2). It was standardized by type of educational placement (regular classes, special classes for the educable mentally retarded (EMR), special classes for the trainable mentally retarded, special classes for the educationally handicapped, and resource-room programs for the educationally handicapped); by sex; and by ethnic status (white, black, Spanish, and other). Data concerning socioeconomic status and residence (urban, suburban, rural) are also presented.

Three sets of percentile norm tables are provided. The examiner can compare the student being assessed to other students by (1) age and educational placement; (2) age, educational placement, and sex; and (3) age, educational placement, and ethnic status. The number of students to whom the student is compared varies considerably, from 239 to 4. A substantial proportion of the norm comparisons are based on a sample of less than 50.

Reliability

The authors state on page 51 of the manual: "We did not conduct reliability studies with the public school version. . . ."

Validity

Not only do the authors not know how reliable teacher judgments of adaptive behavior are, they do not know whether teacher judgments correspond to parent judgments. Lambert et al. report that the necessary data have been collected and will be analyzed at a later time.

The major validation activities appear to us to be contradictory to the purpose of the scale. On page xi, Lambert et al. discuss the background and need for a standardized measure of adaptive behavior:

Clearly, some measure of a child's ability to engage in social activities and to perform everyday tasks of daily living was needed — some measure of his adaptive behavior. . . . Assessment of adaptive behavior relies heavily on the community's judgment about an individual's degree of independence. . . .

To validate the scale, only EMR children were compared to children in regular classes. Significant correlations were interpreted as an indication of the scale's validity. However, on page 9, Lambert et al. state that to qualify for placement in a program for the educable mentally retarded

each pupil's measure of intellectual functioning was to have been at least two standard deviations below the norm for his age, and he was to have been experiencing difficulties in achieving basic skills at a level expected for his ability in a regular school program. Though a measure of adaptive behavior was not a mandatory part of the assessment battery on which a placement decision was based, many school psychologists . . . included observations and assessment of social functioning.

Therefore, a scale to measure a child's ability to perform everyday living tasks and meet the community's judgment of independence has been validated against low IQ and school failure. Adaptive behavior was not a mandatory part of the assessment process to determine EMR placement.

Summary

The school version of the AAMD Adaptive Behavior Scale contains no items that are not found in the institutional instrument from which it was derived. However, it contains several items less. The norms appear representative of California, but the number of children in some groups is too limited to provide stable percentile interpretations. Although the avowed purpose of the instrument is to aid in placement and program-planning decisions, the reliability and validity of the scale are not adequate for these purposes.

AN OVERVIEW OF PERSONALITY ASSESSMENT

Personality tests have been developed within the framework of "dynamic" psychology, including psychoanalysis and phenomenology. Various theorists hold that there are internal causes of behavior and that the identification of these causes will facilitate both an understanding of behavior and behavior change. In some cases, test authors design instruments to assess specific personality types, traits, or characteristics, such as aggression, withdrawal, dominance, paranoia, cyclothymia, and hysteria. Other test authors set out to identify needs, such as the need for affiliation and the need for nurturance, that allegedly motivate behavior.

Personality measures are usually constructed in one of two ways: a criterion-group approach or a factor-analytic approach.

The *criterion-group approach* is characterized by efforts to differentiate among certain groups of persons in the same way that tests of brain injury attempt to differentiate between brain-injured and non-brain-injured individuals. Thus, a test author might wish to develop a test to differentiate among hypochondriacs, hysterics, manic-depressives, and paranoid schizophrenics. Items are chosen that the author believes may distinguish personality types, and they are then administered to individuals who have been previously diagnosed as hypochondriacs, and so on. If the items adequately discriminate among known groups, they are included in the scale. The scale is then applied to individuals who have not yet been classified, under the presumption that if the test can distinguish previously identified *groups* of individuals it can distinguish among unclassified *individuals*. An individual who responds like members of a criterion group is said to exhibit a "personality" characteristic of the criterion group.

The *factor-analytic approach* to personality test construction is a statistical procedure for developing tests. Items believed to assess personality are administered to many persons, and scores are then factor-analyzed to identify clusters of intercorrelated items. These clusters of items are examined for common features and then named. Items that do not fit into clusters are disregarded.

METHODS OF MEASURING PERSONALITY

Walker (1973) provided a comprehensive guide to personality measures available for use with children. In it she identified five categories of measurement: attitude scales, measures of general personality and emotional development, measures of interests or preferences, measures of behavioral traits, and measures of self-concept. We have categorized the most commonly used personality tests according to Walker's system. These tests are listed in Table 18.1.

Walker also indentified several different kinds of measurement techniques, originally described by Lindzey (1959), that are used to assess personality. A description of these techniques follows.

Projective Techniques

Projective personality assessment is accomplished by showing ambiguous stimuli such as pictures of inkblots, and then asking children to describe what they see. Projective techniques also include interpretations of drawings, word associations, sentence completion, choosing pictures that fit moods, and creative expression (puppetry, doll-play tasks, and so on). Theoretically, projective techniques allow children to assign their own thoughts, feelings, needs, and motives to ambiguous, essentially neutral stimuli. Children theoretically project aspects of their personalities in their responses.

Table **18.1** Commonly Used Measures of Personality, Interests, and Traits

---

GENERAL PERSONALITY AND EMOTIONAL DEVELOPMENT

Bender Visual Motor Gestalt Test (Bender, 1938)
Blacky Pictures (Blum, 1967)
California Psychological Inventory (Gough, 1969)
California Test of Personality (Thorpe, Clark, & Tiegs, 1953)
Children's Apperception Test (Bellak & Bellak, 1965)
Draw-a-Person (Urban, 1963)
Early School Personality Questionnaire (Coan & Cattell, 1970)
Edwards Personal Preference Schedule (Edwards, 1959)
Edwards Personality Inventory (Edwards, 1966)
Eysenck Personality Inventory (Eysenck & Eysenck, 1969)
Family Relations Test (Bene & Anthony, 1957)
Holtzman Inkblot Technique (Holtzman, 1966)
House-Tree-Person (Buck & Jolles, 1966)
Human Figures Drawing Test (Koppitz, 1968)
Jr.-Sr. High School Personality Questionnaire (Cattell, Coan, & Belloff, 1969)
Minnesota Multiphasic Personality Inventory (Hathaway & McKinley, 1967)
Rorschach Inkblot Technique (Rorschach, 1966)
School Apperception Method (Solomon & Starr, 1968)
Sixteen Personality Factor Questionnaire (Cattell, Eber, & Tatsuoka, 1970)
Thematic Apperception Test (Murray, 1943)

INTERESTS OR PREFERENCES

A Book About Me (Jay, 1955)
Kuder Personal Preference Record (Kuder, 1954)
School Interest Inventory (Cottle, 1966)
School Motivation Analysis Test (Sweney, Cattell, & Krug, 1970)

PERSONALITY OR BEHAVIOR TRAITS

Burks' Behavior Rating Scale (Burks, 1969)
Devereux Adolescent Behavior Rating Scale (Spivack, Spotts, & Haimes, 1967)
Devereux Child Behavior Rating Scale (Spivack & Spotts, 1966)
Devereux Elementary School Behavior Rating Scale (Spivack & Swift, 1967)
Peterson-Quay Problem Behavior Checklist (Quay & Peterson, 1967)
Pupil Behavior Inventory (Vinter, Sarri, Vorwaller, & Schafer, 1966)
Walker Problem Behavior Identification Checklist (Walker, 1970)

SELF-CONCEPT

Piers-Harris Children's Self-Concept Scale (Piers & Harris, 1969)
Tennessee Self Concept Scale (Fitts, 1965)

Rating Scales

There are several types of rating scales; generally they require that a parent, teacher, peer, or "significant other" in a child's environment rate the extent to which that child demonstrates certain undesirable behaviors. Most rating scales are check lists designed to identify whether the child demonstrates certain behaviors believed to indicate some underlying pathology. Other rating scales require, in addition, that the rater estimate the frequency with which these behaviors are exhibited.

Self-report Measures

The self-report is a very common technique in personality assessment. It is used more frequently with adults than with children, however. Individuals being assessed are asked to reveal common behaviors in which they engage or to identify inner feelings. The devices used with children routinely ask them to identify feelings by checking happy or sad faces on a response form.

Situational Measures

According to Walker, "situational measures refer to a wide range of situations, ranging from highly structured to almost totally unstructured, that are designed to reveal to the tester something about an individual's personality" (1973, p. 31). Peer-acceptance scales and sociometric techniques are situational measures.

Observational Procedures

Most observational procedures used to assess personality or emotional characteristics are systematic. "Direct observation is the only procedure that allows one to observe the behavior as it occurs in the natural situation, thus reducing the chance of making incorrect assumptions" (Walker, 1973, p. 26).

Whatever technique is employed, it is only a vehicle for eliciting responses that are believed to represent a person's "true" inner state — feelings, drives, and so on. Responses are seldom interpreted at face value but are more often believed to be symbolic or representative. Consequently, the skill of the examiner is far more important than the device or vehicle for eliciting a person's responses.

TECHNICAL CHARACTERISTICS
Scores

The particular kinds of scores obtained for personality measures vary with the kind of measure used. Scoring systems range from elaborate multifactor systems with profiles to nonquantifiable interpretive information. Entire books and manuals have been written to describe scoring and interpretation procedures (for example, Exner, 1966; Hutt, 1960; Piotrowski, 1957). Some devices include very little information about scoring and interpretation.

Norms

Most personality assessment devices have inadequate norms. Walker states that "very few instruments have adequate standardization norms that are representative for a wide range of children of varying ethnic groups, intelligence levels, and socioeconomic backgrounds" (1973, p. 37).

Reliability

Many authors of personality measures do not report evidence of the reliability of their tests. When reliability data are reported, the reliabilities are generally too low to warrant use of the tests in making important educational decisions about individual children.

Validity

Definition of traits, characteristics, needs, and behaviors assessed by personality measures is not a common practice among test authors. Moreover, any effort to describe the specific behaviors sampled by the myriad of personality devices would be pointless, since the interpretation of the behaviors is of primary interest. Yet the absence of operational definitions creates a situation in which it is difficult to determine just what a test is designed to measure. Given this fact, it is impossible to assess how well the test measures what it purports to measure. According to Walker:

Underlying these inadequate socioemotional measures for young children is an inadequate and immature socioemotional developmental theory. No one theory to date satisfactorily describes the socioemotional aspects of man's development. More specifically, no theory is advanced enough to guide the development of a socioemotional measurement technology for young children. (1973, p. 40)

THE DECLINE OF PERSONALITY ASSESSMENT

During the last fifteen to twenty years, there has been a shift in emphasis in psychology from "dynamic" psychology to a more objective study of behavior. There is an increased emphasis on the study of observable, operationally defined behaviors and de-emphasis of unobservable thoughts, motives, drives, and traits that supposedly cause behavior. Most personality tests were originally designed to enable psychologists to get at those hidden aspects that supposedly cause persons to act in certain ways.

Along with a shift in theoretical orientation, there has developed an increased concern for accountability. Psychologists have been called on repeatedly to defend their activities and have had considerable difficulty defending the practice of personality assessment, both in terms of the psychometric adequacy of the devices used and the educational relevance of the information provided by those devices. Psychologists today operate at nearly polar extremes. There are those who routinely administer personality tests as parts of larger assessment batteries, believing that by using the tests they will be able to pinpoint pathology. Others openly reject the use of personality tests, believing that the devices are psychometrically inadequate and educationally irrelevant. They rely instead on interviewing and both formal and informal observation to gather information about interpersonal functioning.

Along with a shift in orientation and an increased skepticism about the adequacy of personality devices and the relevance of information obtained, we have witnessed an increased concern for the privacy of the individual. Not long ago, congressional hearings debated the extent to which personality assessment constituted invasion of privacy. Schools are now required by law to gain informed consent from parents before assessing children and may only maintain and disseminate *verified* information about a child. It has been increasingly difficult to convince parents that personality assessment *should* take place, and there is no way to verify the information gathered by personality tests.

SUMMARY

In the assessment of adaptive behavior and personality, the *interpretation* of a person's behavior is of primary concern. Both adaptive behavior and personality cut across more traditional domains such as perception and language. Indeed, behaviors sampled by the tests and procedures discussed in this chapter may be the same as those discussed in earlier chapters; the interpretations of these behaviors are couched in different terms, however, since the purpose of assessment is no longer the mastery of skills and facts.

In the evaluation of adaptive behavior, the primary purpose of assessment is to ascertain the extent to which an individual conforms to societal expectations. Assessment of infants and preschool children relies heavily on the normal course of maturation and development, while the assessment of school-age children, adolescents, and adults is more dependent on society's customs and mores. Thus, for older individuals, appropriate adaptive behavior is determined by several factors: the social tolerance for particular behaviors, the context within which behaviors are demonstrated, the status of the individual exhibiting the behavior, and the theoretical orientation of the person assessing the behavior. The various measures of adaptive behavior usually rely on the observations of a person who is familiar with the subject of the assessment and who describes to the interviewer performing the assessment the typical patterns of behavior of the subject.

The assessment of personality takes different forms depending on the theoretical context in which the particular test or method was developed. Most often, the aim of methods of assessing personality is to discover the underlying causes of behavior. The hypothetical causes vary with the theoretical orientation of the test authors. Five methods of assessing personality were discussed: projective techniques, rating scales, self-report measures, situational measures, and observational procedures. All of these techniques are best considered as ways of eliciting responses, which the examiner then interprets.

STUDY QUESTIONS

1. How does assessment of adaptive behavior differ from assessment of academic achievement?

2. Select any personality test and review:
   a. The kinds of behaviors sampled
   b. The adequacy of the norms
   c. The evidence of reliability
   d. The evidence of validity

3. For what reasons might personality tests be used in public school settings?

4. In order to justify classifying a student as mentally retarded, a certain school district is required to demonstrate that the student exhibits maladaptive social behavior. How might the school demonstrate that the student's behavior is maladaptive?

5. How might one validate a test of aggression?

6. Identify three major techniques for personality assessment.

ADDITIONAL READING

Anastasi, A. *Psychological testing.* New York: Macmillan, 1976. (Part 5: Personality tests, pp. 493–616.)

Buros, O. K. (ed.). *Seventh mental measurements yearbook.* Highland Park, NJ: Gryphon Press, 1972. (Reviews of personality tests, pp. 69–464.)

Buros, O. K. (ed.). *Personality tests and reviews*. Highland Park, NJ: Gryphon Press, 1970.

Cronbach, L. J. *Essentials of psychological testing*. Englewood Cliffs, NJ: Prentice-Hall, 1970. (Chapter 15: General problems in studying personality.)

Doll, E. A. *Measurement of social competence*. Educational Test Bureau, 1953.

Walker, D. K. *Socioemotional measures for preschool and kindergarten children*. San Francisco: Jossey-Bass, 1973.

Chapter 19
School Readiness

The format of this chapter differs from that of previous chapters for two reasons. First, in each of the preceding chapters tests of a particular domain were reviewed, but no particular domain of items can properly be called "readiness" items. Second, the uses to which readiness tests are put are different from the uses of the tests previously discussed.

The chapter is divided into three major sections. The first deals with a general description of readiness and includes the types of test items used to assess it. The second section deals with particular problems in the technical characteristics (norms and validity) and uses of readiness tests. The third section contains reviews of six tests of school readiness.

GENERAL CONSIDERATIONS

Readiness is usually considered essential for initial entry into school, although the concept of readiness can be appropriately applied at all levels of instruction. For example, to be ready for algebra instruction, the student must have mastered the more basic mathematical concepts and operations. Readiness for higher-level academic instruction is usually conceptualized as mastery of prerequisite material. Readiness for school entry is a more complex topic. Readiness for the first grade or even kindergarten is a generalized readiness and refers to both academic and social readiness. Academic readiness is most often thought of in terms of reading readiness but properly includes readiness for *all* academic instruction. We must also consider, however, a child's readiness for the social milieu of school. In school, children must follow the directions of an adult other than their parent or guardian, must enter into cooperative ventures with their peers, must not present a physical threat to themselves or others, must have mastered many self-help skills such as toileting, and so on.

Readiness for school entry is further complicated because there are two different orientations toward the topic. The first, a *skill orientation*, was implicit in the foregoing discussion. It holds that readiness involves the skill development and knowledge prerequisite to *beginning* instruction. Academic and social instruction is viewed as a program of sequential skills and knowledge that is built on previously mastered skills and knowledge.

From this perspective, skills learned in school build on skills learned at home. The second orientation, a *process orientation*, is further removed from direct instruction. Here readiness is viewed in terms of underlying processes (intelligence, discrimination, and so on) that are believed necessary to the acquisition of skills and knowledge. If the processes are mature or developed, the child is ready to learn, to acquire skills.[1]

Traditionally, formal readiness assessment has dealt with academic-process testing. For the most part, the tests have been norm-referenced and the abilities that are thought to underlie all, or at least most, academic skills are the most typically tested. Thus, intelligence or learning aptitude, which is believed to underlie all school subjects, is often a component of a readiness assessment. Indeed, intelligence tests were developed to predict school success and are often validated against achievement tests or teacher ratings. Entry into formal school programs is often predicated upon a mental age of 6 or more years. Intellectual readiness can be assessed by any of the better tests discussed in Chapters 13 and 14. Perceptual-motor development is also thought to underlie school achievement and particularly reading (see Chapter 15). Readiness tests often contain many items or subtests that are appropriately termed perceptual-motor. Although these items and tests are usually less predictive of school achievement than are intelligence tests, many people feel they are an important component of readiness. Language development (see Chapter 17) is obviously important for school success. Children must be fluent in the idiomatic English of their peers; they must also understand and use standard (formal) English.

The assessment of school readiness is not a unique kind of measurement. What makes a test a readiness test is *not* what the test measures or how the measuring is done; three distinctive features make a test a readiness test. First, readiness tests are typically administered before school entry or during kindergarten. Second, the tests are used to predict initial school success and to select those children who perform poorly — and thus are thought not to be ready for regular school experiences — for participation in remedial or compensatory educational programs or delayed school entry. Third, these tests often contain the word *readiness* in the test name.

TECHNICAL CONSIDERATIONS

School readiness is a deceptively simple concept. Knowledge of a child's readiness can provide the teacher with invaluable information that may insure that the child enters an instructional sequence at an appropriate level, or it can provide the teacher with a destructive self-fulfilling

---

1. See Chapter 22, Diagnostic-Prescriptive Teaching: Two Models (pp. 445–449).

prophecy that may actually hamper a child's development. Since decisions made on the basis of readiness tests are so important, the validity of the tests is crucial.

The purposes of readiness tests are

1. To predict who is not ready for formal entry into academic instruction

2. To predict who will profit from either remedial or compensatory educational programs in which readiness skills or processes are developed

It is apparent from these two purposes that the academic development of many children must be followed and documented. When the same children are followed and their progress recorded, the data are called *longitudinal*. Readiness data *must* be longitudinal in both standardization and validation. Specifically, to validate a readiness test, a large number of children must be tested before they enter school and then retested after a specific period of time in school — generally one year. Only in this way can we determine if children with poor scores on the readiness test will perform poorly during actual schooling.

If readiness tests do indeed accurately identify which children will do poorly in school, the educator is faced with a choice of whether to admit a child to the regular school program or take another action. If the child is admitted to the regular school program, the only justification for the test having been administered is that it gives the teacher sufficient information to take steps to overcome the deficits in the child's readiness. Such a use for readiness tests is not justified when one views readiness as physiological maturation. However, if readiness is viewed as depending on skills or processes susceptible to environmental manipulation, there is some justification.

If the child is not admitted to the regular school program, the educator can choose either to delay entry into the regular program, or to provide remedial or compensatory preschool or kindergarten programs. Either of these alternatives should be considered only in light of research data indicating that readiness tests are effective predictors of differential programming. In essence, aptitude-treatment interaction research is required to validate these uses. As an illustration of how this research might be accomplished, let us assume that a school district chooses to delay school entry for children who score poorly on a readiness test. To validate this action, it would be necessary to administer the test to a large number of children before admission to school and then divide the children randomly into two groups, admitting one group to school and delaying the entry of the other for, say, one year. After *both* groups had completed their first year of regular schooling (kindergarten or first grade), the groups would be compared on some measure of school success. Two of several possible outcomes are presented in Figure 19.1. In part a, no matter what their

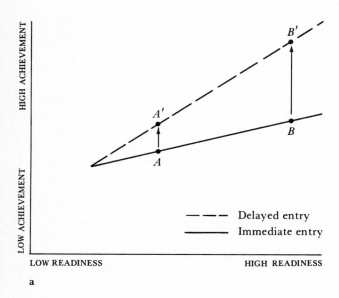

a

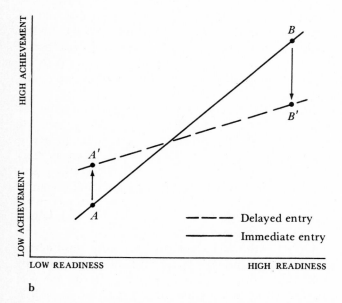

b

Figure **19.1**   Possible interactions between readiness and delayed school entry

readiness score, children perform better if their school entry is delayed. A child scoring fairly low on readiness would earn a performance score at point A if entered immediately into school but at point A′ if allowed to wait before entering; similarly, a child with high readiness would earn a higher performance score (B′ as compared to B) with delayed entry. In short, there is no *differential* advantage afforded by delaying children who score poorly on the readiness test. In part b, by contrast, there is a significant aptitude-by-treatment interaction: children who score poorly on the readiness test perform better in school (at A′rather than A) when their entry is delayed; but children who score well on the readiness test perform better in school (at B rather than B′) when they are immediately enrolled. The same type of research could be used to evaluate compensatory or remedial programs when placement decisions are based on readiness tests.

From the foregoing discussion, it is apparent that the validation of readiness tests is not a simple or convenient task. Validation takes a minimum of one or two years. It must take place in a variety of schools where distinctive features of the curriculum are carefully noted. It is possible that a particular readiness test may predict well who would profit from one type of remedial or compensatory program but not who would profit from another program. Similarly, the predictive validity may vary according to curriculum; one test may predict well a student's progress in one reading program but not predict that student's progress in another program.

Standardization sample norms are generally gathered for four groups; beginning kindergarten (September), middle kindergarten (January), end of kindergarten (June), and beginning first grade. Children tested for the norm group should also be retested at the end of first grade to determine predictive validity. In the area of readiness, perhaps more than any other, local longitudinal norms are very important.

Although the foregoing discussion has stressed norms and predictive validity, reliability should not be overlooked. As can be recalled from Chapter 6, reliability has a definite effect on validity. An unreliable test must have poor predictive validity. Finally, readiness is an area where tests *are* routinely used to make important educational decisions about individual children. Consequently, readiness tests must meet the highest technical standards.

SPECIFIC TESTS OF SCHOOL READINESS

DENVER DEVELOPMENTAL SCREENING TEST

The Denver Developmental Screening Test (DDST) (Frankenburg, Dodds, & Fandal, 1970) is an individually administered, norm-referenced, multiple-skill device designed for the early identification of children with developmental and behavioral problems. It is intended for use with children from birth to 6 years of age. No special training is needed to administer the screening test, which requires approximately 20 minutes to give, score, and interpret.

One hundred five skills are clustered into four general developmental areas that must be administered in the order in which they are discussed here. The first area is *personal-social development*. It contains twenty-three items. These can be clustered into three subareas: responding to another person (for example, smiling), playing (playing pat-a-cake, joining in interactive games), and self-care (dressing, washing, feeding). The second area, *fine motor development*, contains thirty items. These assess grasping and manipulation, building towers of various heights with blocks, drawing (for example, scribbling, drawing a person), and copying increasingly difficult geometric designs. The third area is *language development*. The twenty-one items in this area assess the ability of younger children to produce and imitate sounds and require older children to demonstrate factual knowledge (for example, parts of the body and composition of familiar objects) as well as command of more traditional measures of language development such as vocabulary and syntax. The thirty-one items in the fourth area, *gross motor development*, can be classified as requiring body control (for example, lifting the head, rolling over), mobility (getting to an object, walking), coordination (kicking a ball, riding a tricycle), and balance (jumping, balancing on one foot).

Scores

All items are presented on the scoring sheet in the format shown in Figure 19.2. Across the top and bottom of the scoring sheet are age lines. Each skill is enclosed in a rectangle with four discernible points along one of the horizontal sides. Vertical extensions of the four points intercept the age lines. For skill 1 in Figure 19.2, the vertical that goes from point A to the top age line intercepts the age line at about 2-1. This indicates that 25 percent of the children in the norm sample could perform skill 1 by the time they were about 2 years, 1 month old. Point B is the point at which 50 percent of the norm group could perform a skill. As shown in Figure 19.2, 50 percent of the children could perform skill 2 by age 3-4. Point C is the age at which 75 percent succeeded; 75 percent of the children could perform skill 4 by age 2-8. Point D is the age at which 90 percent successfully performed the skill. In Figure 19.2, 90 percent of the children in the norm group could perform skill 5 by age 4-1.

There is no formal basal rule for the scoring of the DDST.[2] Ceilings are

---

2. A *basal age* is the age at which a child performs all tasks correctly and below which the tester can assume that all items will be passed. A *basal rule* states the number of items a child must pass before a basal age can be assumed.

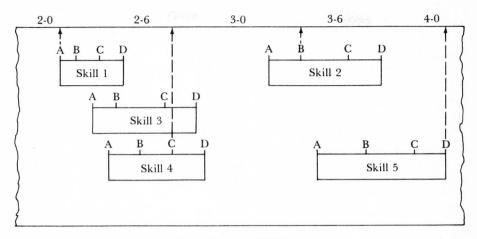

Figure **19.2**   Sample scoring sheet for the DDST

not important since the purpose of the test is to determine developmental lags, not level of functioning. The examiner should administer all test items through which the child's age line passes, and testing in each area should not be terminated until the child passes three items and fails three items.

Each item may be scored "pass," "fail," "passed by report," "refusal," or "no opportunity." Passed and failed items are observed directly by the examiner. Items passed by report (skills such as washing and drying the hands) are items that are difficult or time-consuming to administer but that can be observed reliably by the child's parents. If a parent reports that the child performs the particular task, the item is scored as a pass. Refusals are items to which the child *will not* respond whether the items are administered by the examiner or by the parents. If the examiner feels that the child *cannot* perform the task, the item is scored as failed. No-opportunity scores indicate that the child has not had the chance to learn the skill; such items are not included in the interpretation of the results.

Two types of scores are used. The first score is called a *delay*. A delay is scored if the child fails an item that is passed by 90 percent of the children who are younger; thus, a delay is an item that is failed and lies to the left of the age-line vertical. The second score is the interpretation of the results as either abnormal or normal. An *abnormal result* is scored (1) when the child has two delays in each of two sections or (2) when the child has two delays in one section, one delay in another section, and has not passed any items through which the age-line vertical passes.

Norms

The DDST was standardized on 543 boys and 493 girls from 2 weeks through 6-4 years of age who (we presume, although the test is not clear on this point) lived in Denver, Colorado. Children with serious, known handicaps or difficult births were excluded. The standardization sample approximated the 1960 census in terms of racial-ethnic composition, although there is a small but consistent overrepresentation of higher occupational levels for fathers. This bias may be the result of subject-finding techniques that relied on referrals.

The number of children in the sample at various ages is limited and is not evenly distributed. The number of children (in one-month intervals) from 1 month to 14 months ranges from thirty-six to forty-three, while the total number of children between 5 and 6 years of age is forty-seven.

Reliability

The authors report stability data (one-week interval) for the performance of twenty children who ranged in age from 2 months to 5 years, 6 months, and who were tested by the same examiner. For each of the twenty children, there was at least 90 percent agreement[3] on the pass-fail decisions on the items administered. However, no data on the reliability of delays or the final decision (normal-abnormal) are presented.

Interrater agreement was also evaluated during the standardization of the DDST, since it was important to know if two different examiners would elicit the same performances and score them in the same way. Using the percentage-agreement method, interrater reliability ranged from 80 to 95 percent agreement.

Validity

The authors never formally discuss the validity of the DDST. They could claim content validity by their method of item selection. They surveyed several intelligence and developmental tests from which they selected their items. The authors then present data (in the reliability section) demonstrating a strong positive relationship between the DDST and either the Stanford-Binet or the revised Bayley Infant Scales.

The DDST is a screening device. Implicit in its very name is the assumption that there is follow-up evaluation for children determined to be abnormal on the test. Two examples of follow-up evaluations are very briefly presented in the manual, but no systematic effort to determine false positives or false negatives[4] is made. Consequently, there is no way of knowing

---

3. Number of agreements divided by number of agreements plus disagreements.
4. A *false positive* is a child who is diagnosed as abnormal but on subsequent evaluation it is determined that the child is normal. A *false negative* is a child who is diagnosed as normal, but on subsequent evaluation it is determined that the child is abnormal.

whether the test identifies abnormal children, how many abnormal children it fails to identify, or how many normal children it identifies as abnormal.

Summary

The Denver Developmental Screening Test is a quickly administered and scored device that assesses a child's development in four general areas: personal-social, fine-motor, language, and gross-motor. The device is intended to provide a gross estimate of delayed development and must be followed by a more intensive evaluation. The test's reliability is adequate for a screening device, although the norms are questionable. Validity data are altogether lacking.

BOEHM TEST OF BASIC CONCEPTS

The Boehm Test of Basic Concepts (BTBC) (Boehm, 1971) is a group-administered, norm-referenced device that measures abstract concepts occurring frequently in preschool and primary curricula. The BTBC is intended to identify both the children who have not mastered the tested concepts and the concepts that the teacher should systematically teach to the class. The test is available in two forms (A and B), which are assumed to be roughly equivalent. Each form contains two levels of twenty-five concepts each; the first level (booklet 1) contains simpler concepts than the second level (booklet 2).

All concepts are tested in a similar format. The child is shown a set of pictures; the teacher reads a statement illustrated by one of the pictures. The child marks the picture that is most appropriate to the statement read by the teacher. (For example, "Mark the one where the boy is *next to* the horse.") The fifty concepts all deal with relative relationships. They can be categorized into four groups: (1) space (for example, next to, nearest), (2) quantity (few, not first or last), (3) time (after, beginning), and (4) miscellaneous (different, alike). Approximately 15 to 20 minutes are required for the administration of the test.

Scores

Two scores are provided for either form of the BTBC. Raw scores obtained on either form A or form B are converted to percentiles using the same table, since Boehm feels the two tests are equivalent. The conversion tables are entered with the child's raw score, grade placement (kindergarten, 1, 2, or 3), and socioeconomic level (presumably of the child rather than of the class). Separate norm tables are provided for mid-year and beginning-year administrations. Separate tables are provided for each form of the test for the percentage of children passing each concept. These tables are entered by the concept, by the child's grade in school, and by socioeconomic level. Since each concept is judged to be important in and of itself, these latter tables are judged to be especially helpful because they provide the teacher with some indication of the grade appropriateness of the concept.

Norms

Boehm considers her test to be most useful as a criterion-referenced device. Consequently, she states that "it was considered unnecessary to select standardization samples representative of . . . the nation as a whole" (Boehm, 1971, p. 19). Form A was standardized on children enrolled in kindergarten through grade 3 in sixteen U.S. cities. The volunteer sample was tested in either mid November to late February for mid-year norms or in September to October for beginning-year norms. Although separate norms are provided for low, middle, and high socioeconomic levels, no description is provided of how pupils were categorized. A description of the method of sampling different socioeconomic levels was not provided either. Boehm indirectly hints at the methods she used, however. "*As with the standardization of Form A* [emphasis added], the sample of each grade was subdivided by socioeconomic level, based upon the judgements of the local school administrators" (Boehm, 1971, p. 19). Form B was not standardized but was constructed in such a way as to be equivalent in difficulty to form A. Correlations between the two forms (one day to one week) are generally too low for the two forms to be considered equivalent, although they do have comparable means and standard deviations.

Reliability

Reliability was established by common norm-referenced procedures. Eighteen split-half reliability coefficients corrected by the Spearman-Brown formula are reported by grade and socioeconomic level for forms A and B. Form A is generally more reliable than form B. Reliabilities from both forms range from .12 to .94; the median coefficient is .81. Standard deviations range from .9 to 8.4; the median is 5.25. The standard errors of measurement (in raw-score points) range from 0.9 to 3.4; the median SEM is 2.15.

Validity

Boehm relies solely on content validity, but she does not present evidence to document the frequency of the fifty concepts in educational materials or curricula. Nonetheless, the fifty words have intuitive appeal as important concepts for children to have mastered before they begin their formal educations.

Summary

The BTBC is a norm-referenced, group-administered device intended to identify a child's mastery of fifty key concepts. The norms are inadequate, but this is not a major disadvantage, since the test is most effectively used to obtain information about a child's knowledge of each concept. Form A at the kindergarten level, where the test is perhaps most appropriately used, has marginal reliabilities (.86, .90, and .85) for the three socioeconomic levels.

LEE-CLARK READING READINESS TEST

The Lee-Clark Reading Readiness Test (LCRRT) (Lee & Clark, 1962) is a group-administered, norm-referenced, multiple-skill device designed to predict which children in a classroom are ready for reading instruction and which children need a "special developmental program" or a "full year of maturation and pre-reading preparation" (Lee & Clark, 1962, p. 2). The test is appropriately used with children finishing kindergarten or children entering first grade.

The LCRRT is divided into four subtests. The letter-matching test consists of two columns of twelve letters each. The child is required to draw a line to connect the same letters in the two columns. Practice items are administered before the start of this 2-minute test. The second subtest, a letter-discrimination task, consists of a four- by twelve-letter matrix. Each row of letters contains three letters that are the same and one that is different. The child is required to draw a line through the letter "that is not the same as the other letters" (Lee & Clark, 1962, p. 13). The letters vary in size but not in print style. After four practice items are administered, the child has 2 minutes to complete the twelve test items. The third subtest, an untimed picture vocabulary test, consists of twenty sets of pictures; the sets range from two stimulus pictures to five stimulus pictures. The child must mark the picture that matches the description read by the teacher. Two practice items are administered. The fourth subtest is an untimed letter and word recognition test using a match-to-sample format. The stimulus, which can vary from a single letter to a seven-letter English word, is separated by a dotted vertical line from four response options. The child must mark the letter or word in the response options that is the same as the stimulus. One practice item is administered before testing.

The LCRRT requires approximately 14 minutes to administer. The test may be given in two sittings, in which case subtests 1 and 2 should be administered first. Group size should probably not exceed six to eight children without someone to aid the tester.

Scores

Raw scores from each of the first three subtests and the total raw score (four subtests) may be converted to grade equivalents and classification scores. The classification scores (high, high average, low average, low) appear to be simple transformations, with high average and low average divided at the median. Insufficient data are presented in the test manual to determine at what point in the distribution (for example, quartile or standard deviation) high and high average or low and low average are separated.

Norms

The LCRRT was standardized on over 1,000 children of unknown age, sex, or demographic characteristics. The children in the norm sample were either at the end of kindergarten or entering first grade. The performances of the children in the 1962 sample were equated, through an unspecified procedure, with the performances of the children in the 1951 norm sample.

Reliability

Four split-half reliability coefficients, based on the total raw score and corrected by the Spearman-Brown formula, are presented in the LCRRT manual; the two coefficients for unspecified kindergarten samples were .96, while the coefficient for an unspecified first-grade sample was .87. The split-half reliability based on one combined group was also .96. Thus, the reliability of the total test for kindergarten children appears most acceptable. Standard errors of measurement in both raw scores and grade equivalents for these four groups are also presented. The test authors provide reliability coefficients for the subtests; we believe these are too low for individual decisions (that is, .56 to .88).

Validity

Lee and Clark report predictive validity coefficients (one- and two-year intervals) for the LCRRT and Lee-Clark reading tests that range from .42 to .56. They also report the results of studies done in Portland, Oregon, with the LCRRT. The readiness test was administered after two months of school, and teacher ratings were made in January, April, and May. The LCRRT correlated from .37 to .74 with teacher ratings of a child's ability to read. The Lee-Clark Reading test was also administered three times to these children. Correlations between the reading readiness test and the reading achievement test ranged from .25 to .70.

The readiness ratings (high, high average, low average, low) are of particular concern. The validity of these ratings is based on the performances of 177 children of unknown demographic characteristics who were enrolled in an undescribed reading program. These children were given the LCRRT during the first month of first grade and then given the Lee-Clark Reading Test (Primer) in April or May. Of the children who were rated as having low readiness, 22 percent were successful (according to Lee and Clark), while 15 percent of the children who were rated as having high readiness were unsuccessful. Two-thirds of the children rated high average and half of the children rated low average were successful readers in first grade. Using Lee and Clark's data, more than 28 percent of the children were incorrectly predicted for success or lack of success. From the predictive validity coefficients and the classification data, it is apparent that the LCRRT lacks the validity necessary to use the test to make educational decisions for children.

Summary

The LCRRT is a reliable test with norms of unknown appropriateness. The data presented by the authors do not demonstrate that the test has adequate predictive validity.

PRESCHOOL INVENTORY

The Preschool Inventory Revised Edition (Caldwell, 1970) is an individually administered, untimed device designed to assess the various skills deemed necessary for the school achievement of children 3 to 6 years of age. The first form of the device was known as the Preschool Achievement Test. After the first revision, it was known as the Preschool Inventory. The revised edition of the Preschool Inventory contains sixty-four items that can be administered in less than 15 minutes by anyone familiar with the device. The inventory assesses a child's knowledge of a variety of personal facts (such as name, age, and body parts), of social roles (mother,[5] teacher, and so on), of number concepts, of colors, and of geometric designs. The inventory also assesses whether a child follows instructions and copies various geometric forms.

Scores

In the initial versions of the test, the author sampled items as though a criterion-referenced device were being developed. Subsequent revisions have followed more traditional norm-referenced psychometrics. It is difficult to consider the current revision as a criterion-referenced device for several reasons. First, many items tap multiple behaviors; for example, given the response blank with a circle, square, and triangle, the child is requested to color the circle yellow. Second, the items were selected on the basis of their correlations with total score and not on relative educational importance. Percentile ranks are provided for five age ranges: 3-0 to 3-11, 4-0 to 4-5, 4-6 to 4-11, 5-0 to 5-5, and 5-6 to 6-5.

---

5. Curiously, if a child responds to the question "What does a mother do?" with "Has babies," the response is not correct.

Norms

National norms are based solely on the performance of 1,531 children attending Head Start classes. Only the performance of children who were tested in English were included. No formal sampling plan is discussed. The ethnic and sex compositions of the norm sample for each of the five age ranges are presented. The age samples are about equally divided between boys and girls and are predominantly black (68.2 percent). Regional norms are based on the responses of at least 100 children, but in such cases neither sex nor ethnic breakdown is provided. In addition, specialized norms are provided separately for 246 4-year-old children in Louisville, Kentucky; for 133 children in Phoenix, Arizona; and for 317 children in North Carolina. Thus, the normative sample can, at best, be considered circumscribed and voluntary.

Reliability

Two estimates of internal consistency, based on the performance of the standardization sample, are provided for each age group: KR-20 coefficients range from .86 to .92; split-half reliabilities (corrected by the Spearman-Brown formula) range from .84 to .93. Raw-score SEMs are also presented.

Validity

The initial form of the device, the Preschool Achievement Test, could lay some claim to content validity by the procedures used to select items. The author drew on her personal observations of deficits exhibited by disadvantaged preschool children, on the observations of others who had worked with disadvantaged children, and on inspections of various kindergarten curricula. In subsequent revisions, the total number of items was reduced from 161 to 64. The deletion of items may have reduced the scope of the Inventory. Yet if the test user is interested in the behaviors sampled, there is still ample claim to content validity.

Empirical validity is generally lacking. Stanford-Binet IQs were available for 1,476 children in the standardization sample; the correlation between the inventory and the Binet ranged from .39 (at 3 years) to .65 (at 5 years). In discussing the North Carolina norms, the author noted that in that sample the Inventory did not distinguish between children from high socioeconomic backgrounds and children from low socioeconomic backgrounds.

Summary

The Preschool Inventory is a quickly administered device that can give a teacher a list of accomplishments for a pupil. The estimated reliability of the device is adequate for screening purposes, but the norms limit the interpretation of percentiles.

TESTS OF BASIC EXPERIENCES

The Tests of Basic Experiences (TOBE) (Moss, 1972) are a set of group tests designed to assess the "richness of conceptual background" (Moss, 1972, p. 6) of children in preschool, kindergarten, and first grade. The tests are designed to assess "how well a child's experiences have prepared him for his introduction to many of the scholastic activities he will encounter" (Moss, 1972, p. 6). The author is careful to point out that group size should never exceed the size of a typical class and that proctors should be present in the ratio of one for every six to ten children tested.

The TOBE has two levels, neither of which requires reading: level K (preschool and kindergarten) and level L (kindergarten and first grade). The battery consists of four tests: language, mathematics, science, and social studies. There is also a General Concepts Test, which is a composite of items from each of the other tests. Administration time is approximately 25 minutes for each of the separate tests and for the composite.

The TOBE Mathematics Test measures "a child's mastery of fundamental mathematics concepts, terms associated with them, and his (her) ability to see relationships between objects and quantitative terms" (p. 7) ("Mark the empty one," "Mark the oldest girl," and so on).

The TOBE Language Test assesses basic concepts of "vocabulary, sentence structure, verb tense, sound-symbol relationship, and letter recognition" (p. 7). The language test also includes a novel section in which the child must derive meaning from a nonsense word by its context in the sentence ("He threw a pog. Mark the pog"; "Mark the one whose name begins with the same letter as *book*"; and so on). The TOBE Science Test is designed to assess the extent of a youngster's early experiences with "animals, humans, plants, machinery, weather and other phenomena" ("Mark the one with feathers," "Mark the vegetable," "Mark the one that can't burn"). The Social Studies Test, on the other hand, assesses how well a child recognizes and understands concepts of social groups (family, friends, community), social roles (jobs), social customs, rules of safety, and human emotions ("Mark the girl who is ready for a party," "Mark the best place to save money"). The General Concepts Test is composed of items from each of the other four areas.

Scores

Scoring of the TOBE is objective. A scoring key is included in the test manual, and each item is simply scored correct or incorrect. Raw scores (the number correct) may be transformed to percentile ranks, stanines, and standard scores. A class evaluation record is used to show for each child those concepts correctly identified, percentile ranks, and standard scores. The teacher may sum the columns for each concept to find the number of children in the class who correctly identified the concept. Thus, information is obtained about both individual and group knowledge of specific concepts.

Norms

The TOBE was standardized on 10,300 pupils attending a variety of public and private prekindergartens, kindergartens, first grades, and second grades. The standardization was completed in 422 classes in 145 schools in 44 cities stratified on the basis of geographic region and community size. No effort was made to stratify on the basis of race, sex, or socioeconomic status; the author states that it can be assumed that minority groups are represented insofar as they were attending the public and private schools of the areas sampled.

Reliability

Data about both internal-consistency and test-retest reliability are presented in the test manual. For level K, the number of prekindergarten children assessed with each test ranged from 685 to 714, while reliability coefficients ranged from .79 to .84. Kindergarten samples for level K ranged in size from 2,588 to 2,640, while internal-consistency coefficients ranged from .82 to .85. For level L, the number of kindergarten children assessed with each subtest ranged from 1,498 to 1,510, while internal-consistency coefficients ranged from .72 to .81. First-grade samples for level L ranged from 1,701 to 1,722; reliability coefficients from .78 to .82.

Test-retest reliabilities over a 6-week interval were computed for 5,497 children in kindergarten and first grade. The median test-retest reliability for level K administered to kindergarten children was .87; for level L administered to kindergarten children, .70; and for level L administered to first-grade children, .74. The General Concepts test-retest reliability was .78.

Validity

The TOBE was originally published in 1970 and revised in 1972. The original manual included data about content validity. After the TOBE was constructed, seventeen kindergarten and seventeen first-grade teachers were asked to participate in a content-validity study. They were sent the TOBE items and asked to place them in one of the four test areas or in a "would not use" category. Only 60 percent of the teachers returned the items. Tables in the manual indicate the percentage of agreement between teacher placement and test placement of items. Agreement ranged from 66 percent agreement on science items to 55 percent agreement on social studies items. The author does not indicate the extent to which changes, if any, were made on the basis of the data received from teachers.

The revised manual includes data on predictive validity. Correlations between scores on the TOBE level K in the fall and teachers' grades in May ranged from .21 to .36; on level L, correlations ranged from .19 to .38. Concurrent validity, as assessed by the relationship between scores on level L and teacher grades, both gathered in May, ranged from .23 to .49.

A second study investigated the relationship between teacher *ratings* of achievement in March and scores previously earned on the TOBE in November by "representative" samples of classes. The correlations ranged from .27 to .58, and it is stated in the manual that the median coefficient of .48 is high enough to consider the TOBE as a useful predictor of achievement.

A third study investigated the relationship between scores on the TOBE level L and scores on achievement and readiness measures. Eight first-grade classes in Catholic schools took the Metropolitan Readiness Test in the fall and the TOBE in the spring. Correlations ranged from .50 to .59. Another group of eight classes from the same diocese took the TOBE in the fall and the California Achievement Test in the spring. The author of the TOBE states that the test can be used to predict achievement but that it should not be used to determine readiness.

Finally, the TOBE correlated with the Preschool Inventory at about .66.

Summary

The Tests of Basic Experiences are a series of group-administered devices designed to assess pupil skill development in several areas. There are two levels of the test, one for use in preschool and kindergarten, the other for use in kindergarten and first grade. Separate tests assess development in language, mathematics, science, and social studies. A separate global scale assesses general concept development.

While the TOBE was standardized on many children, one cannot ascertain from the data in the test manual how representative the sample is. Reliability of the scale is adequate for such short tests, while additional validity data are needed.

METROPOLITAN READINESS TESTS

The 1976 revision of the Metropolitan Readiness Tests (MRT) (Nurss & McGauvran, 1976a, 1976b)[6] is a norm-referenced, group-administered,

---

6. Harcourt Brace Jovanovich was in the process of preparing various technical reports on the 1976 revision of the Metropolitan Readiness Tests at the time this review was written. The technical information used in this review comes from the teachers' manuals (Nurss & McGauvran, 1976a, 1976b), which are part of the specimen sets for each level.

multiple-skill battery intended to assess several important skills needed for early school success. The 1976 revision is the fourth in the series, which began in 1933 and was subsequently revised in 1949 and 1964. The tests are untimed, but typically require a total of approximately 80 to 90 minutes' administration time spread over several sessions. The child responds directly on the record form, which may be scored by hand or machine. The directions to the teacher for administering the tests are very clear and well organized. The directions to the children are also clear. A practice test is provided that should be administered several days before the MRT is given. Key concepts and skills (place keeping, making rows, and so on) are taught and practiced. The test authors are very sensitive to the difficulties involved in testing young children, and they stress small groups, proctors, and testing in several sessions; moreover, they provide multiple cues and checks to insure that the children do not lose their places.

The MRT consists of two levels. Level 1 is intended for use with children in the beginning or middle of kindergarten. Level 2 is intended for use with children at the end of kindergarten and the beginning of first grade. The two levels differ somewhat in content in order to reflect different levels of skill development. Two forms (P and Q) are available at each level. All tests, except copying, which is an optional test, employ a multiple-choice format.

Level 1 contains six regularly administered subtests; a description of each follows.

Auditory Memory   This subtest has twelve items. Each consists of four pictures of familiar objects. The teacher reads three or four nouns, and the child marks the response that contains the same sequence of nouns.

Rhyming   This subtest has thirteen items. Each item consists of four pictures, each representing a familiar word. The teacher names each picture in the response array and then reads a fifth word that rhymes with one of the four. The child marks the picture that has the name rhyming with the fifth word read by the teacher.

Letter Recognition   This subtest has eleven items. The child is shown four letters (both upper and lower case). The teacher names one of the letters, and the child marks it.

Visual Matching   This subtest has fourteen items using a match-to-sample format. Individual items consist of single letters, multiple letters, or nonsense symbols.

School Language and Listening   This subtest has fifteen items. The teacher reads a sentence, and the child marks the one picture in the response array that describes what the teacher read. The sentences require the child to comprehend prepositions, verb forms (tense and voice), and conjunctions as well as to draw inferences and separate relevant and irrelevant information.

Quantitative Language   This subtest has eleven items. The child is required to complete matrices, know cardinal and ordinal numbers, perform simple arithmetic operations, comprehend quantitative words such as *more*, and visually rearrange disjointed parts to form a familiar object.

Level 2 consists of eight subtests; a description of each follows.

Beginning Consonants   This subtest has thirteen items. The child is shown pictures of four familiar objects that the teacher names. The teacher then says a fifth word. The child must select the one word in the response array that begins with the same sound.

Sound-Letter Correspondence   This subtest has sixteen items. The child is shown a five-item array: a picture of a familiar object named by the teacher and four letters (or double letters, such as *gl*). The child marks the letter or letters with the same sound as the initial sound of the word read by the teacher.

Visual Matching   This subtest has ten items. The format is the same as that used at level 1, but the items are more difficult; that is, there are more elements in each item and greater similarity among the distractors (the incorrect response options).

Finding Patterns   This subtest has sixteen items. The child is presented with a stimulus and four response options. Stimuli and responses may be letters, numbers, or nonsense symbols. One of the response options contains the sequence presented in the stimulus item. See Figure 19.3 for an example of such an item.

School Language   This subtest has nine items. The teacher reads a passage, and the child selects the one picture of three that best represents what the teacher has read. The language demands, while more complex, are similar to those of the School Language and Listening subtest in level 1.

Listening   This subtest has nine items also. The teacher reads a passage, and the child selects the one picture of four that best represents what the teacher has read. The child must comprehend or infer the meaning of complex sentences with a considerable amount of distracting information.

Stimulus   Response options

Figure **19.3**   An example of a test item from the Finding Patterns subtest of the MRT

Quantitative Concepts   This subtest has nine items that are similar to, but more difficult than, those tested in Quantitative Language in level 1.

Quantitative Operations   In this subtest the child must demonstrate comprehension of cardinal and ordinal numbers, set meaning, single and double digits, simple arithmetic operations (addition, subtraction, and multiplication), and multiple operations (addition and then subtraction).

Scores

Raw scores can be converted to three types of derived scores: percentile ranks, stanines, and performance ratings. *Performance ratings* are ratings based on stanine intervals: a low rating consists of scores from the first three stanines, an average rating consists of scores from the middle three stanines (4, 5, 6) and a high rating consists of scores from the three highest stanines (7, 8, 9).

For level 1, beginning-of-kindergarten and middle-of-kindergarten norm tables for each form for various scores are available. Raw scores on each subtest may be converted to performance ratings. Letter Recognition and Visual Matching can be combined into a composite termed Visual Skill Area; School Language and Listening and Quantitative Language can be combined into a composite termed Language Skill Area. Each raw-score composite total can also be transformed into stanines or performance ratings. Finally, the raw scores for each of the six subtests may be summed; the total raw score, termed Prereading Skills, may be converted to both stanines and percentile ranks.

For level 2, two sets of norm tables are available for each form for various scores: end of kindergarten and beginning of first grade. No norm-referenced scores or interpretations can be made for individual subtests. The eight subtests can be combined into five different composite scores: Beginning Consonants and Sound-Letter Correspondence into a composite termed Auditory Skill Area; Visual Matching and Finding Patterns into Visual Skill Area; School Language and Listening into Language Skill Area; Quantitative Concepts and Quantitative Operations into Quantitative Skill Area; and the Auditory, Visual, and Language Skill areas into Prereading Skills. Performance ratings and stanines are available for each subarea (for example, Visual Skill Area). Percentile ranks and stanines are available for the Prereading-Skills composite.

Norms

The procedures used to develop the norms for both levels of the MRT were essentially the same. Data from the National Center for Educational Statistics were used as a basis for a stratified random sampling plan. Six levels of school population and five levels of socioeconomic status (estimated by the median years of schooling of the adult population in the district) formed the thirty strata. In addition, data were obtained from parochial schools, very small schools (enrollments less than 300), and large urban districts (enrollments greater than 100,000).[7] A total of more than 66,000 children participated in the standardization program for each level; approximately 50,000 children were used in developing the norm groups for each level. Sex, geographic, and ethnic data, as well as data indicating prior educational experience, are presented for each level. "Data from each school district were weighted so that the number of pupils in each stratum . . . [was proportional] . . . to the number of pupils in the U.S. population enrolled in school systems with similar characteristics" (Nurss & McGauvran, 1976a, p. 23). The norms appear representative; however, midyear norms for level 1 are interpolated. The two forms were statistically equated, and then the two levels were equated. The derived scores are based on smoothed curves of these equated data.

Reliability

Split-half reliability estimates (corrected by the Spearman-Brown formula), KR-20 estimates of internal consistency, and alternate-form reliability estimates are provided for each level. As shown in Table 19.1, the Prereading composites are sufficiently reliable to make educational decisions for children. The subtests in level 1 and the area scores in level 2 are generally not reliable enough for such decisions.

Validity

The validity of the MRT must rest on how well it samples behaviors necessary for school success and whether it predicts later school achievement. The content validity of the MRT was established by "an analysis of the beginning reading process and an extensive review of the reading research literature"; and "a sequential list of the skills necessary for beginning

---

7. No information is presented to indicate whether all the districts that were sampled agreed to participate.

Table **19.1** Ranges of Reliability Estimates for MRT, by Level, Type of Score, Form, and Method of Estimation

	FORM P		ALTERNATE FORM	FORM Q	
	SPLIT-HALF	KR-20		SPLIT-HALF	KR-20
Level 1					
Subtests	.73–.88	.67–.88	.58–.81	.70–.90	.71–.90
Prereading					
composite	.93	.92	.85	.95	.95
Level 2					
Area scores	.72–.93	.72–.92	.67–.86	.73–.92	.68–.91
Prereading					
composite	.94	.93	.87	.94	.93

reading was then prepared" (Nurss & McGauvran, 1976b, p. 25). Finally, test items to measure these skills were developed. The test items were constructed in such a way that their content was judged (presumably by the authors) "to be familiar to all kindergarten and Grade 1 pupils regardless of their sex, ethnic background, urban/rural residence, socioeconomic status, or geographic region" (Nurss & McGauvran, 1976a, p. 22). Minority-group consultants also screened test items, and those with possible ethnic bias were deleted. In addition the auditory items in level 2 were screened to guarantee that the sounds were "equally familiar to pupils who speak Spanish and to those who speak standard American English or a non-standard dialect" (Nurss & McGauvran, 1976a, p. 22). A major difficulty, however, is the limited number of items assessing various domains of the MRT. The authors are sensitive to this limitation and carefully caution test users:

The MRT does not provide in-depth diagnostic information about pupil strengths and weaknesses since each of the tests and skill areas contains a relatively small number of items. Scores should be viewed as suggestive of possible strengths and weaknesses subject to verification by other means suggested earlier.   (Nurss & McGauvran, 1976a, p. 16)

Predictive validity for both levels was established by correlating MRT scores obtained in the fall with achievement scores from the Metropolitan Achievement tests obtained in the spring. The prereading composite had a correlation of approximately .70 with both total reading and total math achievement scores for both levels. Level 2 was also used to predict Stanford Achievement Test (1973 edition) scores obtained *two* years later. The prereading composite was moderately to highly correlated with achievement: total reading, .69; total math, .65; total auditory, .68; basic battery, .75; and total battery, .78.

Summary

The MRT is a norm-referenced multiple-skill, group-administered device designed to assess a child's readiness for reading and other areas of school achievement. The device appears to be adequately normed and to have adequate reliability and substantial validity for a screening device. The MRT's major limitation is a relatively limited behavior sample. With judicial use, the 1976 revision of the MRT can provide very useful screening information.

SUMMARY

Readiness is a construct used to explain why some people succeed in a sequence of instruction and others fail. There are two different perspectives on readiness that determine how it is assessed. First, it can be viewed as the presence of the behavior, skills, and knowledge that are prerequisites to the mastery of skills or information to be taught. Second, readiness may be viewed as the presence of certain processes (intelligence, discrimination, and so on) that are believed to underlie the acquisition of the behavior or information to be taught.

While readiness tests contain items that assess competence in several domains, these tests are used exclusively to predict a person's success or failure in an instructional sequence or program. Therefore, certain technical characteristics, such as predictive criterion-related validity, are extremely important. Moreover, since readiness tests are routinely used to make individual placement decisions, these tests must conform to the highest standards of technical excellence. Several devices, both general and specific (reading readiness tests, for example) were reviewed in this chapter.

STUDY QUESTIONS

1. Differentiate between a *process orientation* and a *skill orientation* toward readiness.

2. In Chapter 2 we stated that a fundamental assumption in assessment was that only present behavior can be observed; any statement about future performance is an inference. Discuss the use of readiness measures in light of this assumption.

3. In the validity of readiness tests, what considerations are important?

ADDITIONAL READING

Buros, O. K. (ed). *Seventh mental measurements yearbook.* Highland Park, NJ: Gryphon Press, 1972. (Reviews of readiness tests, pp. 1148–1194.)

Stott, L. H., & Ball, R. S. Infant and preschool mental tests: Review and evaluation. *Monographs of the Society for Research in Child Development*, 1965, *30* (3, Serial No. 101).

Part 4

Applying Assessment Information

Assessment information is intended to be meaningful. Part 1 of this book described assessment as the process of collecting data for the purpose of making decisions about students enrolled in both regular and special educational settings. Part 2 introduced the technical considerations necessary for adequate understanding of test data. Part 3 was a description of the educationally relevant domains in which assessment data are collected and a critical review of the most commonly used tests.

At this point readers should have a basic understanding of the reasons for assessing children, of the technical characteristics necessary for adequate collection of data, of the kinds of data collected, and of the strengths and weaknesses of commonly used assessment devices.

Part 4 describes the application of assessment information to the making of decisions about children. It describes both where testing can and has gone wrong, and how it can be tremendously effective. Chapter 20 describes current misconceptions in profiling and provides training in the appropriate interpretation of assessment information. Chapter 21 is a description of legal and ethical principles that guide the collection, maintenance, and dissemination of assessment data. Chapter 22 is a primer on the interpretation and use of assessment information. The needs of various recipients of test data are described, and competing philosophies of interpretation and use of assessment data are discussed. Chapter 23 describes common abuses in assessment, but it also describes the potential of appropriate assessment to help us make better decisions about the students we are charged with serving.

Chapter 20
Profiles of Children's Performances

Teachers and psychologists are often interested in the relative levels of mastery that one child demonstrates in several areas. Such information is frequently used in classifying a child as exceptional and in planning educational programs. To ascertain if a child is more adept in one area than in another, the scores on various tests must be converted into comparable units of measurement. Standard scores are most easily used in profile analysis; therefore, testers usually convert all test scores to the same standard scores (for example, T-scores). When two or more scores for the same child are converted to the same units of measurement and plotted on one graph, that graph is called a *profile*. A profile is simply a graphic representation of a child's performance, expressed in comparable units of measurement, in several areas or on several tests. Relative differences in performances by the same child are known as *intraindividual differences*; a profile can also be a graphic representation of intraindividual differences.

In most educational settings, the assumption is made that abilities and skills develop at a consistent rate. To illustrate, consider any test with several subtests such as one of the Wechsler intelligence scales. If the standardization sample's average score on each subtest, expressed in standard scores, is plotted on a profile, the profile is flat; all scores are the mean, and the means are the same, since they have been converted to standard scores. However, when a profile is plotted for an individual member of the norming group, it is not perfectly flat, since the subtests on which the profile is based are not perfectly correlated. Members of the standardization sample can be expected to be ordered differently on different subtests. It should, therefore, be apparent that children in general cannot be expected to achieve exactly the same transformed scores on several subtests. Nonetheless, the relative flatness of a child's profile is thought to have considerable diagnostic meaning.

In interpreting a profile, one score is often assumed as a reference point to which all other scores are compared. Three "scores" are most commonly used as reference points: chronological age (CA), mental age (MA), and current grade placement (GP). GP can be used as a reference point in making achievement comparisons. Moreover, the grade in which a child is placed can be measured without error, and it is highly related to what a child is actually taught in school. CA is sometimes used as a reference point, particularly in profiles of motor skills. A child's MA is usually *believed* to be the most appropriate reference point to which to compare psychological and educational test scores because the development of the abilities measured by these tests is more closely related to intellectual development than to chronological age. There are three limitations to the use of MA as a reference point. First, MA and CA are highly related ($r = .9$); about 80 percent of the variance in MA scores is attributable to the variation in CA. Thus, MA is not too different from CA as a reference point. Second, CA can be measured with perfect reliability while MA cannot. Thus, when MA is used as a reference point, some measurement error is introduced. Third, MAs are often interpolated scores. Children can earn MAs of 7-3, for example, when no 7-year, 3-month-old, children are included in the sample.

The relationship between intelligence (MA or IQ) and other psychological and educational test scores is extremely important in educational diagnosis and pupil classification. The behaviors sampled by intelligence tests are thought to represent the psychological construct of intelligence. Consequently, rather than interpreting the behaviors sampled by intelligence tests simply as behaviors, there is a propensity to interpret scores derived from intelligence tests as cognitive levels or as potential. Such as interpretation can set unreal expectations. If a child of 6 earns an MA of 10, one is apt to believe the child is capable of achieving at a 10-year level. Such an expectation assumes that the child has had an adequate opportunity to learn skills at the 10-year level. Because of the graded nature of academic work, this assumption is seldom valid. We do not find the use of "potential" appealing; to use intelligence test results in such a way requires, at the very least, a recognition that such tests differ widely in the behaviors sampled. The *only* acceptable way to use potential is to couch it in terms of the particular test used — "intelligence, as inferred from the performance on the _____ test."

When MA is used as a reference point in interpretation of a child's profile, the assumption is implicitly made that MA represents potential and that differences between MA and other measures represent *over*attainment or *under*attainment. Comparable scores on intellectual measures and other measures in a profile are interpreted as "working up to one's potential"; the expectation is for a flat profile.

Flat profiles, on which all the scores occur within 1.6 standard deviations of the mean (the median 90 percent), are typically considered normal. Educators expect children with above-average intelligence to perform better than average in their academic work. If their achievement is not also above average, it is often a source of concern. Educators also expect the converse: children with relatively low scores on intelligence tests are expected to perform below average. If a child's achievement is commensurate with low measured intelligence, educators tend to be satisfied with a poor performance; intelligence is used to justify a child's poor performance. Apparently, many educators believe that a child who has not learned the skills and information assessed by intelligence tests cannot learn academic skills and information. There is sufficient evidence to demonstrate that such a belief is insupportable. In fact, we would argue that the purpose of basic education is to break the relationship between intelligence and achievement.

THE USES OF PROFILES

CLASSIFICATION

A main use of profiles is in classifying individuals as exceptional. Flat profiles of individuals whose functioning measures significantly below average in both intelligence and adaptive behavior are used to confirm diagnoses of mental retardation. Flat profiles of individuals who function significantly above average in intellectual and academic areas are used to confirm a label of *gifted*. Profiles in which wide discrepancies occur may also have diagnostic meaning. A child who has a significant discrepancy between measured intelligence and both measured achievement *and* perceptual or language functioning, or both, may have a learning disability. A definition of children with special learning disabilities formulated by the National Advisory Committee on Handicapped Children in their annual report to Congress in 1968 illustrates the interrelationship of "deficits" (meaningful differences) in achievement and in psychological processes:

Children with special learning disabilities exhibit a disorder in one or more of the basic psychological processes involved in understanding or using spoken or written languages. These may be manifested in disorders of listening, thinking, talking, reading, writing, spelling, or arithmetic. They include conditions which have been referred to as perceptual handicaps, brain injury, minimal brain dysfunction, dyslexia, developmental aphasia, etc. They do not include learning problems which are due primarily to visual, hearing, or motor handicaps, to mental retardation, emotional disturbance, or to environmental disadvantage. (p. 4)

Operationalization of this definition has involved a search for deficits, as is illustrated by Bateman's definition of children with learning disabilities as those who

manifest an educationally significant discrepancy between their estimated intellectual potential and actual level of performance related to basic disorders in the learning processes, which may or may not be accompanied by demonstrable central nervous system dysfunction, and which are not secondary to generalized mental retardation, educational or cultural deprivation, severe emotional disturbance, or sensory loss. (1965, p. 220)

A significant discrepancy between normal MA and reading age is often required for eligibility for remedial reading programs. A significant discrepancy between MA and achievement age for a child with a superior IQ (for example, IQ 130) is reason for not considering the child gifted. Thus, profiles and evaluations of intraindividual differences are at the heart of many diagnostic practices.

More esoteric uses of profile analyses include the possible diagnosis of neuropsychiatric disorders. Wide discrepancies in an individual's profile of abilities are often interpreted as an indication or even a demonstration of some underlying pathology. Individuals who are brain-injured, psychotic, neurotic, or educationally handicapped often exhibit large intraindividual differences on a profile; such differences are referred to as *scatter*. The difficulty is that persons who are brain-injured, disturbed, or disadvantaged sometimes do not exhibit scatter while normal individuals occasionally do exhibit scatter. Thus, while profile scatter may distinguish groups of individuals, it does not typically distinguish individuals (Dunn, 1968; Yates, 1954). In 1960 Cronbach wrote, "This type of analysis is no longer depended upon because empirical checks show that pattern analysis has little validity" (p. 192). If a child exhibits scatter, it is *not* safe to assume that there is some underlying pathology.

The Wechsler scales are a convenient example. Each subtest yields a separate score, so that the scales lend themselves readily to profile analysis. Simplistic interpretations of Wechsler profiles abound. If the verbal IQ is higher than the performance IQ, a child would by some be considered brain-injured; if the performance IQ is higher than the verbal IQ, the child may be considered to be disadvantaged, to have a language handicap, or to be disturbed. The research reported by Ralph Reitan (1966) illustrates the complexities in such interpretations. Using the Wechsler-Bellevue Intelligence Scale, Reitan has found that subjects with lesions of the left hemisphere perform poorly on the verbal subtests, patients with lesions of the right hemisphere perform poorly on the performance subtests, and persons with diffuse brain injury may or may not demonstrate discrepancies between verbal and performance scores.

While we believe that it is possible to make complex interpretations of underlying pathology in a pupil's profile, we also believe that there are four virtually insurmountable obstacles to such an interpretation by school personnel. First, school personnel typically lack the training and experience necessary to interpret appropriately intraindividual differences as indicative of underlying pathology. Second, although some tests used in the schools can separate groups of persons with various pathologies, the tests cannot separate *individuals* accurately (see Chapter 15). Third, the psychometric instruments useful in identifying pathology (for example, Halstead's Index; Halstead, 1947) are not used in the schools. Fourth, the battery of tests used to identify pathology is often much longer than the batteries typically employed by school personnel. For example, Reitan (1966), who has had some success in predicting the location and extent of brain injury, used a test battery that required one to two days to administer.

PROGRAM PLANNING

Profiles of achievement tests may be useful to teachers in program planning. If a child shows relatively poor achievement in one or two academic areas, the teacher may wish to provide additional instruction in those areas. To do so requires that the teacher have a clear understanding of exactly what content the achievement tests measure as well as the relationship of that content to the school's curriculum. Use of achievement-test profiles to plan instruction also requires that the teacher go far beyond the summary score that describes a child's relative performance. The child's test performance must be further analyzed to determine which skills the child has not mastered. Some tests, such as the Stanford Achievement Test, provide this information in addition to summary scores. Finally, a child's relatively high achievement in one or two academic areas may indicate a special interest or skill that the teacher can capitalize on in instruction.

PREREQUISITES TO THE INTERPRETATION OF PROFILES

The construction of any profile follows the same procedure: (1) converting all scores to the same units of measurement, and (2) plotting the scores on a graph that is scaled in the units of measurement to which the raw scores were converted. The proper analysis and interpretation of a child's profile require far more than intuition. Profile analysis entails three steps. The *first* step is to ascertain that there are reliable differences; only then may the attribution of those differences be hypothesized. If there are reliable differences in the profile, the *second* step is to examine the norm groups on which the tests are standardized: the first possible explanation of reliable profile differences that should be entertained is a difference in the norming samples. The *third* step is to interpret the profile differences that are at once reliable and *not* due to differences in the norming sample.

Hypothetical data are used to illustrate the prerequisites of profile analysis.

Martha, a 6-year, 11-month-old, child, earns a raw score of 119 on the Pictorial Test of Intelligence; this corresponds to an MA of 8-1. She makes ten errors on the Bender Visual Motor Gestalt Test according to the Koppitz scoring procedures; this corresponds approximately to a developmental age (DA) of 5-8. The three obtained ages (CA, MA, DA) are plotted with solid lines in the profile in Figure 20.1.

RELIABILITY

Before interpreting the meaning of differences in a child's profile, we must establish that the differences are reliable. In Chapter 6 we stated that a test score is the sum of a true score and some amount of error. Consequently, in Martha's case, she could have been lucky on the PTI and obtained a score somewhat higher than her true score. She could have been unlucky on the Bender and obtained a score somewhat lower than her true score. Thus, Martha's profile of true abilities may be considerably flatter than her profile of obtained abilities. In fact, this is always the case when test scores are less than completely reliable. Martha's profile of estimated true scores can be only partially plotted (broken line) in Figure 20.1, since the Bender manual does not provide adequate reliability information. If we wish to compare her PTI score and her Bender score to her CA, we have to construct confidence intervals for the two test scores. As explained in Chapter 6, we select the level of confidence (for example, 95 percent), find the z-scores of the normal curve between which that level of confidence is found (for example, 1.96), multiply the standard error of measurement by that z-score, and add and subtract that product from the estimated true score. In Martha's case, her CA falls within a 95 percent confidence interval for her MA (Figure 20.2).

Since insufficient data on the reliability of the Bender are presented in the test manual, we cannot generate a confidence interval to determine if Martha's DA differs significantly from her CA. For the same reason, Martha's MA and DA cannot be compared. However, several characteristics of difference scores are sufficiently important to repeat. Since the tests or subtests that make up a child's profile are typically correlated, difference scores are usually less reliable than the scores on which the differences are based. The reliability of difference scores is a function of the reliability of each test *and* the intercorrelation between the tests.

STANDARDIZATION-SAMPLE DIFFERENCES

Before differences between test scores can be interpreted as real, possible differences in standardization samples must also be considered. The differences in Martha's scores on the PTI and on the Bender may, in part, be

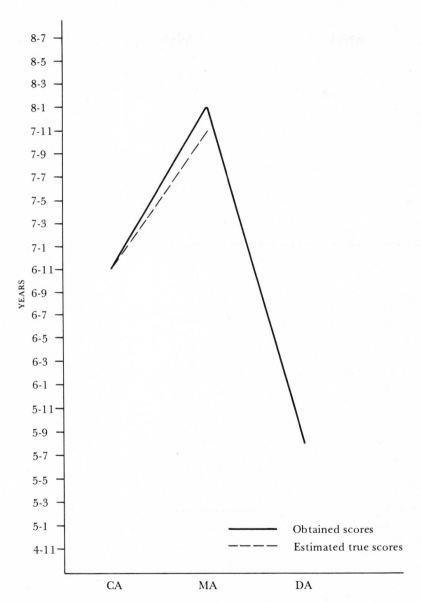

Figure **20.1** Martha's profile: chronological age, mental age (PTI), and developmental age (Bender)

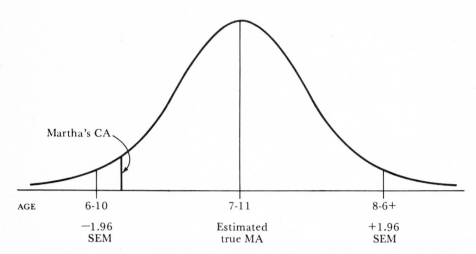

Figure **20.2**   Martha's CA falls inside a 95 percent confidence interval for her
MA

attributable to the fact that the two tests were standardized on different
samples. Any systematic difference in the standardization groups may be
reflected in the transformed scores.

For example, assume that test A was standardized on a sample of disadvantaged preschool children and test B was standardized on a group of
advantaged children attending an experimental preschool at a local university. A child who is in reality average on the skills or abilities measured by
the two tests is likely to perform above the mean on test A (since it was
standardized on children presumed to be below average) and below the
mean on test B (since it was standardized on children presumed to be above
average). The child's scores would appear to be discrepant simply because
the norms on which the two test scores are based are discrepant. Similarly,
any discrepancy in Martha's scores on the Bender and on the PTI could be
attributed to differences in the samples on which the two tests were
normed, provided that the Bender sample was more skilled than the PTI
sample.

In practice, it is difficult to determine if differences in standardization
samples are large enough to produce major discrepancies in a pupil's
profile. Norm-sample differences can combine with random fluctuation to
produce what appear to be significant discrepancies. Generally, the better
the test norms, the less likely are discrepancies attributable to norm differences. In Martha's case, the PTI is a well-normed test but the Bender is
not. In this instance, discrepant norm groups could be partially responsible for the differences in scores.

In some cases, it can be assumed that the difference in test scores is not a function of measurement error and probably not the result of norm differences — or definitely not, for tests normed on the same population. In these cases, differences in the skills or abilities measured (the behaviors sampled) should be used to explain differences in scores. Indeed, such an orientation is the thrust of Part 3 of this text. In the example of Martha, the PTI and the Bender represent different behavior samples. Martha may not copy geometric designs as well as she associates spoken words with pictures, discriminates geometric designs, has mastered simple number and size concepts, has acquired general information, or recalls geometric designs.

Finally, the data presented for Martha do *not* constitute proof of some underlying pathology. From this information, one must not presume that she has a learning disability, brain injury, psychopathology, or motor deficit.

DETAILED EXAMPLES OF PROFILE ANALYSIS

This section contains two examples of profile analyses. The procedures are complex, but they are extremely important. In each example, all necessary computations are demonstrated. Possible interpretations are also presented. The first example, Charles, is an adolescent who demonstrates a relatively flat profile of subaverage accomplishment. The second example, Julie, is a preschooler who demonstrates sharp discrepancies in her profile.

CHARLES

Charles is a hypothetical tenth-grade boy who is 15-6 years of age. He was tested on the revised Wechsler Intelligence Scale for Children (WISC–R) and on the Peabody Individual Achievement Test (PIAT). The analysis of Charles's profiles on these two tests is made in four parts: (1) an analysis of the WISC–R, (2) an analysis of the PIAT, (3) an analysis of the interrelationship of the WISC–R and PIAT, and (4) a summary interpretation.

Charles's Performance on the WISC–R

Charles earned a verbal IQ (VIQ) of 72, a performance IQ (PIQ) of 74, and a full-scale IQ (FSIQ) of 71. Table 20.1 contains his scores on each subtest and scale of the WISC–R and the estimated reliability of each subtest and scale. In Table 20.2, the results of the computation of Charles's estimated true scores on each scale (that is, VIQ, PIQ, FSIQ) and standard errors of measurement for each scale are presented. Confidence intervals of 95

Table **20.1**   Summary of Charles's Performance on the WISC–R

SUBTEST	SUBTEST RELIABILITY[a]	SCALED SCORE[b] AND IQS[c]
Information	.90	5
Similarities	.74	4
Arithmetic	.80	8
Vocabulary	.90	5
Comprehension	.72	5
VIQ	.94	72
Picture Completion	.68	8
Picture Arrangement	.73	3
Block Design	.85	7
Object Assembly	.68	6
Coding	.80	6
PIQ	.90	74
Full-scale IQ	.95	71

[a] Estimated from internal consistency.
[b] Mean = 10; standard deviation = 3.
[c] Mean = 100; standard deviation = 15.
SOURCE: Reliability data are from D. Wechsler, Manual for the Wechsler Intelligence Scale for Children–Revised (New York: Psychological Corporation, 1974), p. 28. Reproduced by permission. Copyright © 1974 by The Psychological Corporation, New York, N.Y. All rights reserved.

Table **20.2**   Estimated True Scores, SEMs, and 95 Percent Confidence Interval for Charles's WISC–R Scores

	VIQ	PIQ	FSIQ
$\bar{x}$	100	100	100
S	15	15	15
r_{xx}	.94	.90	.95
Obtained score	72	74	71
Estimated true score[a]	74	77	72
SEM($S\sqrt{1 - r_{xx}}$)	3.67	4.74	3.35
1.96 SEM	7.19	9.29	6.57
95% confidence interval	67–81	67–86	66–79

[a] The estimated true score is equal to: $\bar{x} + (r_{xx})$ (obtained score $- \bar{x}$).

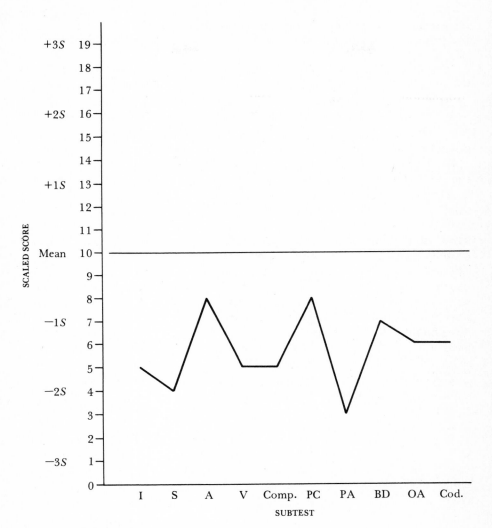

Figure **20.3**   Charles's WISC–R profile

percent for each score are also presented. Charles's estimated true verbal
IQ (from 67 to 81), performance IQ (from 67 to 86), and full-scale IQ
(from 66 to 79) are all significantly subaverage. In many school districts
Charles's IQ would qualify him for placement in a class for the educable
mentally retarded; his estimated true FSIQ is almost 2 standard deviations
below the mean.

Charles's profile on the subtests of the WISC–R is presented in Figure
20.3. The profile appears uneven. There are areas of relatively high

performance — Arithmetic (A) and Picture Completion (PC) — and there are areas of poor performance — Similarities (S) and Picture Arrangement (PA).

To ascertain if these profile differences are reliable, a number of statistics were computed for the differences among the subtests. Using the correlations (r) among the subtests and the estimated reliability of the subtests that were presented in various tables in the WISC–R manual, the reliability of the difference (r_{dif}) between each pair of subtests was computed using equation 6.6.

For example, the intercorrelation between the Similarities subtest and the Arithmetic subtest for 15-year, 6-month-old, persons was reported by Wechsler (1974) to be .46. For this age group, the reliability of the Similarities subtest was estimated to be .74, while the reliability of the Arithmetic subtest was estimated at .80. As shown in Table 20.3, by substituting into equation 6.7, the reliability of the difference between these two subtests is estimated to be .57.

The standard deviation of the difference (S_{dif}) among subtests was computed using equation 6.9. For example, the standard deviation of each scale score is 3 on the WISC–R; therefore, the variance (the standard deviation squared) is 9. The correlation between the Similarities and Arithmetic subtests is .46. As shown in Table 20.4, by substituting into equation 6.9, the standard deviation of the difference between the Arithmetic and Similarities subtests is 3.12.

The standard error of measurement for the difference (SEM_{dif}) among subtests was computed using equation 6.4. As shown in Table 20.5, the standard error of measurement of the difference between the Arithmetic and Similarities subtests is 2.03.

To test differences among the ten major subtests of the WISC–R requires forty-five comparisons. Table 20.6 contains the intercorrelations (r) among the ten subtests. It also contains the reliability of the difference (r_{dif}) between each pair of subtests, the standard deviation of the difference (S_{dif}) between each pair of subtests, and the standard error of measurement of the difference (SEM_{dif}) between each pair of subtests.[1]

The last step in ascertaining if any of the differences are reliable is to construct a confidence interval for the difference. As shown in Chapter 6, to construct a confidence interval for a difference score, one uses the obtained difference plus and minus the standard error of measurement of the difference. Thus, a 95 percent confidence interval would encompass the range *from* the difference less the product of 1.96 and the standard error of measurement of the difference *to* the difference plus the product

---

1. All calculations performed to eight decimal places, then rounded to the nearest hundredth.

Table **20.3**   Calculating the Reliability of the Difference Between the Similarities and Arithmetic Subtests of the WISC-R

Equation 6.7: $r_{\text{dif}} = \dfrac{\frac{1}{2}(r_{11} + r_{22}) - r_{12}}{1 - r_{12}}$

$r_{\text{dif}} = \dfrac{\frac{1}{2}(.74 + .80) - .46}{1 - .46}$

$r_{\text{dif}} = \dfrac{\frac{1}{2}(1.54) - .46}{.54} = \dfrac{.77 - .46}{.54}$

$r_{\text{dif}} = \dfrac{.31}{.54}$

$r_{\text{dif}} = .57$

Table **20.4**   Calculating the Standard Deviation of the Difference Between the Similarities and Arithmetic Subtests of the WISC-R

Equation 6.8: $S_{\text{dif}} = \sqrt{S_1{}^2 + S_2{}^2 - 2r_{12}S_1S_2}$

$= \sqrt{9 + 9 - (2)(.46)(3)(3)}$

$= \sqrt{18 - 8.28}$

$= \sqrt{9.72}$

$= 3.12$

Table **20.5**   Calculating the Standard Error of Measurement of the Difference Between the Similarities and Arithmetic Subtests of the WISC-R

Equation 6.9: $\text{SEM}_{\text{dif}} = S_{\text{dif}}\sqrt{1 - r_{\text{dif}}}$

$= 3.12\sqrt{1 - .57}$

$= 3.12\sqrt{.43}$

$= 2.03$

Table **20.6**   Data for Estimating the Significance of a Difference Between WISC–R Subtests for 15½-Year-Olds: Intercorrelation (r), Reliability of Difference (r_{dif}), Standard Deviation of Difference (S_{dif}), Standard Error of Measurement for a Difference (SEM_{dif})

SUBTEST	I	S	A	V	COMP.	PC	PA	BD	OA
Information									
Similarities									
r	.63								
r_{dif}	.51								
S_{dif}	2.58								
SEM_{dif}	1.81								
Arithmetic									
r	.46	.46							
r_{dif}	.72	.57							
S_{dif}	3.12	3.12							
SEM_{dif}	1.64	2.03							
Vocabulary									
r	.74	.67	.51						
r_{dif}	.62	.45	.69						
S_{dif}	2.16	2.44	2.97						
SEM_{dif}	1.34	1.80	1.64						
Comprehension									
r	.52	.58	.40	.66					
r_{dif}	.60	.36	.60	.44					
S_{dif}	2.94	2.75	3.29	2.47					
SEM_{dif}	1.85	2.20	2.08	1.85					
Picture Completion									
r	.40	.46	.35	.39	.42				
r_{dif}	.65	.46	.60	.66	.48				
S_{dif}	3.29	3.12	3.42	3.31	3.23				
SEM_{dif}	1.94	2.28	2.16	1.94	2.32				
Picture Arrangement									
r	.28	.40	.23	.33	.33	.42			
r_{dif}	.74	.56	.69	.72	.59	.49			
S_{dif}	3.60	3.29	3.72	3.47	3.47	3.23			
SEM_{dif}	1.82	2.18	2.06	1.82	2.22	2.30			
Block Desgin									
r	.38	.44	.42	.40	.42	.54	.43		
r_{dif}	.80	.63	.70	.79	.63	.63			
S_{dif}	3.34	3.17	3.23	3.29	3.23	2.88	3.20		
SEM_{dif}	1.50	1.92	1.77	1.50	1.97	2.06	1.94		
Object Assembly									
r	.31	.34	.16	.26	.32	.38	.33	.60	
r_{dif}	.70	.56	.69	.72	.56	.56	.41		
S_{dif}	3.52	3.45	3.89	3.65	3.50	3.34	3.47	2.68	
SEM_{dif}	1.94	2.28	2.16	1.94	2.32	2.40	2.30	2.06	
Coding									
r	.21	.31	.30	.34	.28	.16	.17	.38	.23
r_{dif}	.81	.67	.71	.77	.67	.69	.72	.72	.66
S_{dif}	3.77	3.52	3.55	3.45	3.60	3.89	3.86	3.34	3.72
SEM_{dif}	1.64	2.03	1.90	1.64	2.08	2.16	2.06	1.77	2.16

SOURCE: Intercorrelation (r) data are from D. Wechsler, Manual for the Wechsler Intelligence Scale for Children–Revised (New York: Psychological Corporation, 1974), p. 45. Reproduced by permission. Copyright © 1974 by The Psychological Corporation, New York, N.Y. All rights reserved.

of 1.96 and the standard error of measurement of the difference. In practice it is simpler to divide the obtained difference by the standard error of measurement of the difference. If the quotient *exceeds* 1.96, the difference falls *outside* the interval, and one would conclude that there is a real difference. If any of the differences are significant, it is useful to compute the estimated true difference as an aid in interpretation. Table 20.7 contains the obtained differences and the quotients for each difference between each of Charles's scores on the WISC–R. It can be seen from the values in Table 20.7 that only one value equals or exceeds 1.96. Charles's performance in Arithmetic is reliably greater than his performance in Similarities. All other differences between any two scaled scores in Charles's profile are not reliable. Charles may be better at solving arithmetic problems than at noting similarities among things. On the other hand, the one difference may well be chance fluctuation also, since we would expect *two* to *three* of the forty-five comparisons to exceed 1.96 on the basis of chance alone. Only one of the differences between any two scaled scores in Charles's profile is reliable. Although his profile appears uneven in Figure 20.3, the differences are best interpreted as chance variations.

Charles's Performance on the PIAT

Charles's performance on the PIAT is summarized in Table 20.8. His total performance of 192 items passed was equivalent to a standard score (mean = 100; standard deviation = 15) of 69. This is clearly a subaverage performance. He earned standard scores of 84 in Mathematics, 85 in Reading Recognition, 65 in Reading Comprehension, and 69 in both Spelling and General Information. A profile of Charles's subtest scores is presented in Figure 20.4.

The reliability of the PIAT total score is .92. Using equation 6.5, Charles's estimated true total score on the PIAT is 71. A 95 percent confidence interval for this score ranges from 63 to 80. We can be more than 95 percent confident that Charles's achievement is more than one standard deviation below the mean; it is clearly subaverage.

To ascertain if the differences in Charles's PIAT profile are reliable, the same procedures as were used with his WISC–R profile can be followed. The PIAT manual contains correlation and reliability data for the eighth and twelfth grades. Twelfth-grade data were used. Table 20.9 contains the correlations (r) among subtests, the estimated reliabilities of the differences (r_{dif}) between each pair of subtests, the standard deviation of the difference (S_{dif}) between each pair of standard scores, and the standard error of measurement of the difference (SEM_{dif}) between each pair of scores. Table 20.10 contains the obtained differences and the quotients of the differences divided by the appropriate standard errors of measurement. None of the quotients exceeds 1.96; none of the differences fall

Table **20.7** Obtained Differences and Quotients (Obtained Differences Divided by the SEM of the Differences) for Evaluating the Probability of the Differences in Charles's Profile on the WISC–R

SUBTEST (SCORE)	I(5)	S	A	V	COMP.	PC	PA	BD	OA
Similarities (4)									
Obtained difference	1								
Quotient	0.55								
Arithmetic (8)									
Obtained difference	3	4							
Quotient	1.83	1.97							
Vocabulary (5)									
Obtained difference	0	1	3						
Quotient	0.00	0.56	1.83						
Comprehension (5)									
Obtained difference	0	1	3	0					
Quotient	0.00	0.45	1.44	0.00					
Picture Completion (8)									
Obtained difference	3	4	0	3	3				
Quotient	1.55	1.75	0.00	1.55	1.29				
Picture Arrangement (4)									
Obtained difference	1	0	4	1	1	4			
Quotient	0.55	0.00	1.94	0.55	0.45	1.74			
Block Design (7)									
Obtained difference	2	3	1	2	2	1	3		
Quotient	1.33	1.56	0.56	1.33	1.02	0.49	1.55		
Object Assembly (6)									
Obtained difference	1	2	2	1	1	2	2	1	
Quotient	0.52	0.88	0.93	0.52	0.43	0.83	0.87	0.49	
Coding (6)									
Obtained difference	1	2	2	1	1	2	2	1	0
Quotient	0.61	0.99	1.05	0.61	0.48	0.93	0.97	0.56	0.00

Table **20.8** Summary of Charles's PIAT Performance

	RELIABILITY[a]	STANDARD SCORE[b]
Mathematics	.84	84
Reading Recognition	.86	85
Reading Comprehension	.63	65
Spelling	.75	69
General Information	.73	69
Total	.92	69

[a] Test-retest based on twelfth graders.
[b] Mean = 100; standard deviation =15.
SOURCE: Reliability data are from L. M. Dunn & F. C. Markwardt, *Manual for the Peabody Individual Achievement Test* (Circle Pines, Minn.: American Guidance Service, 1970), p. 44. Used by permission of American Guidance Service, Inc.

outside of a 95 percent confidence interval. The analysis of Charles's PIAT subtest profile reveals only random fluctuation.

Relationship of WISC-R and PIAT

The WISC-R and PIAT are often used together by psychologists and diagnosticians. Differences of these tests may be used to classify a child's performance, as previously discussed. To compare Charles's intelligence as estimated by the WISC-R and his achievement as estimated by the PIAT is most difficult, since the tests were normed on different samples. Moreover, as is often the case, no correlations between the devices (and subtests) could be found. Even though diagnosticians need these correlations to estimate the reliability of the differences among scores, they often compare tests scores without these data. To compare the subtests on the WISC-R and the subtests on the PIAT, the scores have to be transformed to comparable units. The WISC-R scaled scores can be transformed to standard scores with a mean of 100 and a standard deviation of 15 so that they are in the same units as the PIAT subtests. The PIAT scores can be transformed to standard scores with a mean of 10 and a standard deviation of 3 so that they are in the same units as the WISC-R scaled scores. Subtests from both tests can be transformed to a third standard score (*T*-scores, for example).

However, since the profiles for each test reveal primarily random fluctuations, only the total-test standard scores will be compared. They have the same means and standard deviations. The correlation between the

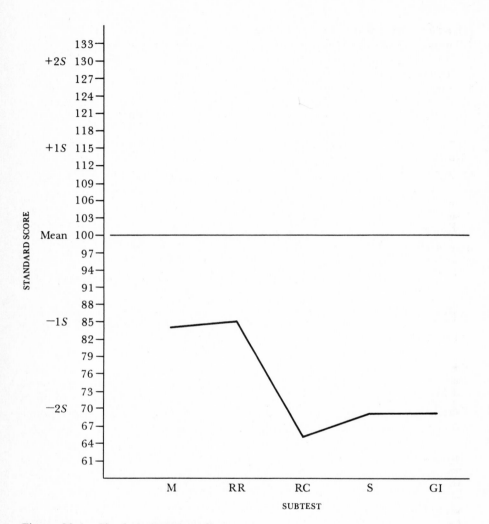

Figure **20.4**   Charles's PIAT profile

WISC–R FSIQ and the PIAT total score is unknown. Presumably, however, it exceeds zero. If it is *assumed* that the correlation between the tests is
.60, which is a value often found for the relationship between intelligence
and achievement tests, the reliability of the difference between the tests can
be *very crudely* estimated by the same procedures used to analyze previous
differences. As shown in Table 20.11, the obtained difference is 2, and the
estimated SEM of the difference is 8.48. The quotient (obtained difference

Table **20.9**   Data Necessary for the Computation of the Reliability of
Differences on the PIAT: Correlation Between Subtests (r), Reliability of
Differences (r_{dif}), Standard Deviation of Differences (S_{dif}), and Standard Error
of Measurement of Differences (SEM_{dif})

	MATHE-MATICS	READING RECOG-NITION	READING COMPRE-HENSION	SPELLING
READING **RECOGNITION**				
r	.59			
r_{dif}	.63			
S_{dif}	13.58			
SEM_{dif}	8.22			
READING **COMPREHENSION**				
r	.53	.73		
r_{dif}	.44	.06		
S_{dif}	14.54	11.02		
SEM_{dif}	10.92	10.71		
SPELLING				
r	.35	.53	.35	
r_{dif}	.68	.59	.52	
S_{dif}	17.10	14.54	17.10	
SEM_{dif}	9.60	9.37	11.81	
GENERAL **INFORMATION**				
r	.54	.57	.57	.24
r_{dif}	.53	.52	.26	.66
S_{dif}	14.39	13.91	13.91	18.49
SEM_{dif}	9.84	9.60	12.00	10.82

SOURCE: Intercorrelation (r) data are from L. M. Dunn & F. C. Markwardt, *Manual for the
Peabody Individual Achievement Test* (Circle Pines, Minn.: American Guidance Service, 1970),
p. 46. Used by permission of American Guidance Service, Inc.

over estimated SEM of the difference) does not exceed 1.96. The difference falls within a 95 percent confidence interval; therefore, the difference
may be assumed to reflect only chance fluctuation, unless differences in
norms are sufficient to hide a true difference.

Summary

Charles is a 15-year, 6-month-old, boy in the tenth grade. His performances on both the WISC–R and PIAT are very poor; we are 95 percent

Table **20.10**   Summary of Obtained and Differences Quotients (Obtained Differences Divided by SEM of the Difference) for Evaluating the Probability of the Differences in Charles's Profile on PIAT

SUBTEST (SCORE)	MATHE- MATICS (84)	READING RECOG- NITION (85)	READING COMPRE- HENSION (65)	SPELLING (69)
READING RECOGNITION (85)				
Obtained difference	1			
Quotient	1.34			
READING COMPREHENSION (65)				
Obtained difference	19	20		
Quotient	1.74	1.87		
SPELLING (69)				
Obtained difference	15	16	4	
Quotient	1.56	1.71	0.34	
GENERAL INFORMATION (69)				
Obtained difference	15	16	4	0
Quotient	1.52	1.67	0.33	0.00

Table **20.11**   Estimating Reliability of Difference Between WISC–R FSIQ and PIAT Total

	WISC–R	PIAT	DIFFERENCE
Obtained score	71	69	2
Reliability	.95	.92	—
Correlation between tests (guessed)			.60
Estimated reliability of difference			.84
Estimated S of difference			13.42
Estimated SEM of difference			8.48
Quotient (obtained difference / SEM_{dif})			.24

confident that his true IQ as estimated from the WISC–R is between 66 and 79 and that his true achievement as estimated from the PIAT is between 63 and 80. Both measures indicate that Charles is functioning at least 1 standard deviation below the population mean and perhaps more than 2 standard deviations below the mean. An analysis of Charles's performances on the various subtests reveals that his was essentially an even performance. *If* the two devices were appropriately administered and *if* the results are valid, Charles is functioning in the educable mentally retarded range. Of course, much more information is required before such a diagnosis could be made.

Searching for intraindividual differences in Charles's profile has been an involved, complicated procedure. Many test manuals provide the tester with tables containing the standard error of measurement of various differences; both the WISC–R and PIAT have such tables in the manual.[2]

The hypothetical data used in Charles's profile are noteworthy for two reasons. First, even wide discrepancies between scores (for example, PIAT Reading Recognition and Reading Comprehension) cannot be assumed to be real. Difference scores are so unreliable that a twenty-point difference (1.5 standard deviations) occurred by chance. Second, constructing a profile is far simpler than interpreting a profile. Simplistic and unsophisticated profile analyses that appear in so many textbooks on diagnostic-prescriptive teaching (for example, Bangs, 1968; Bush & Waugh, 1976; Kirk & Kirk, 1971; Lerner, 1976) are likely to be interpretations more of error than of real differences. The differences identified in these procedures are found by happenstance rather than logic and empirical evidence. These procedures lead to unnecessary and time-consuming training for deficits that probably do not exist and to the selection of methods and materials aimed at matching individual learning styles that appear to exist only because of chance fluctuation.

JULIE

Julie is a hypothetical 4-year, 6-month-old, girl who is attending kindergarten. She was tested on the Illinois Test of Psycholinguistic Abilities (ITPA). She earned 149 points, which corresponds to a psycholinguistic age (PLA) of 5-0, which is slightly higher than one would expect based on her CA of 4-6. Julie's raw scores were converted to scale scores (mean = 36; standard deviation = 6) and appear in Table 20.12 together with the estimated reliabilities of the subtests and her estimated true scaled scores. Julie's scaled scores are profiled in Figure 20.5. Her mean scaled score was 36.7, which approximates the standardization-sample mean.

Kirk, McCarthy, and Kirk (1968, p. 96) consider a discrepancy of 10 scaled-score points from a child's mean scaled score to be a substantial discrepancy "indicative of a discrepant function." Julie's score of 47 on the Visual Closure subtest, according to the test authors, may be a strength, while her scores on the Verbal Expression (SS = 24) and Grammatic Closure (SS = 27) subtests may indicate weaknesses. Julie's profile is

---

2. Neither manual explains how the SEMs are calculated; the reader does not know whether an approximate procedure or an exact procedure has been used.

Table **20.12**   ITPA Scaled Scores, Reliability Estimates, and Estimated True
Scores for Julie

SUBTEST	SCALED SCORE[a]	RELIABILITY	ESTIMATED TRUE SCORE
Auditory Reception	36	.89	36
Visual Reception	44	.86	43
Auditory Association	28	.85	29
Visual Association	45	.82	43
Verbal Expression	24	.76	27
Manual Expression	40	.83	39
Grammatic Closure	27	.69	30
Visual Closure	47	.59	42
Auditory Sequential Memory	40	.83	39
Visual Sequential Memory	36	.74	36

[a] Mean = 36; standard deviation = 6.

SOURCE: Reliabilities are from J. Paraskevopoulos & S. Kirk, *The development and psychometric characteristics of the Revised Illinois Test of Psycholinguistic Abilities* (Urbana: University of Illinois Press, 1969), p. 102. Copyright © 1969 by the Board of Trustees of the University of Illinois. Used by permission.

extremely uneven. Her estimated true scores are within 1 standard deviation of the mean only for Auditory Reception, Manual Expression, and both Auditory and Visual Sequential Memory. The Visual subtest scores for Reception, Association, and Closure are high, while her scores on Auditory Association, Verbal Expression, and Grammatic Closure are low.

To ascertain if these profile differences are reliable, the procedures followed earlier in the chapter were used. The ITPA manual contains subtest intercorrelations and internal-consistency reliability estimates, which allow the computation of the needed statistics. Table 20.13 contains the correlations (r) among subtests, the estimated reliabilities of the differences (r_{dif}) between each pair of subtests, the standard deviation of the difference (S_{dif}) between each pair of standard scores, and the standard error of measurement of the difference (SEM_{dif}) between each pair of scores. Table 20.14 contains the obtained differences and the quotients of the obtained differences divided by the appropriate standard errors of measurement. Several of the quotients equal or exceed 1.96; consequently, several differences fall *outside* a 95 percent confidence interval and may be considered reliable or true differences.

In Table 20.15, Julie's scaled scores have been reordered from highest to lowest and reliable differences indicated by inserting estimated true differ-

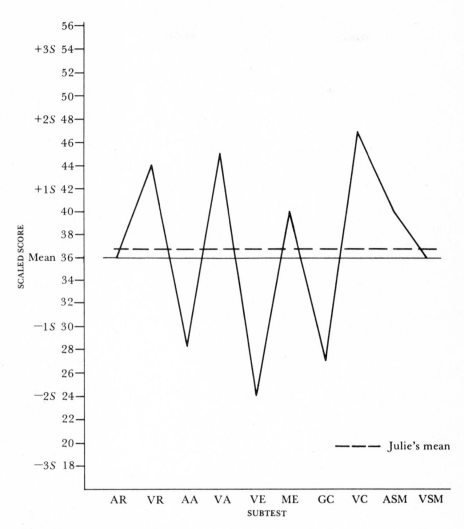

Figure **20.5** Julie's ITPA profile

ences.[3] Her scores on Visual Closure (VC), Visual Association (VA) and Visual Reception (VR), Auditory Sequential Memory (ASM) and Manual Expression (ME) do not differ among themselves. Her three highest scores (VC, VA, VR) are greater than her scores on Auditory Reception (AR), Visual Sequential Memory (VSM), Auditory Association (AA), Grammatic

---

3. These were computed using equation 6.8.

Table **20.13**   Data for Estimating the Significance of a Difference Between ITPA Subtests: Correlation (r), Reliability of Difference (r_{dif}), Standard Deviation of Difference (S_{dif}), and Standard Error of Measurement of Difference (SEM_{dif})

	AR	VR	AA	VA	VE	ME	GC	VC	ASM
VR									
r	.32								
r_{dif}	.82								
S_{dif}	7.00								
SEM_{dif}	3.00								
AA									
r	.48	.34							
r_{dif}	.75	.78							
S_{dif}	6.12	6.89							
SEM_{dif}	3.06	3.23							
VA									
r	.32	.28	.36						
r_{dif}	.79	.78	.74						
S_{dif}	7.00	7.20	6.79						
SEM_{dif}	3.23	3.39	3.45						
VE									
r	.19	.06	.36	.23					
r_{dif}	.78	.80	.70	.73					
S_{dif}	7.64	8.23	6.79	7.45					
SEM_{dif}	3.55	3.70	3.75	3.89					
ME									
r	.07	−.08	.16	.16	.42				
r_{dif}	.85	.86	.81	.79	.65				
S_{dif}	8.18	8.82	7.78	7.78	6.46				
SEM_{dif}	3.17	3.34	3.39	3.55	3.84				
GC									
r	.43	.23	.46	.20	.28	.08			
r_{dif}	.63	.71	.57	.69	.62	.74			
S_{dif}	6.41	7.45	6.24	7.59	7.20	8.14			
SEM_{dif}	3.89	4.02	4.07	4.20	4.45	4.16			
VC									
r	.21	.34	.36	.39	.21	.12	.15		
r_{dif}	.67	.58	.56	.52	.59	.67	.58		
S_{dif}	7.54	6.89	6.79	6.63	7.54	7.96	7.82		
SEM_{dif}	4.33	4.45	4.49	4.61	4.84	4.57	5.09		
ASM									
r	.01	−.02	.20	.04	.12	.17	−.03	.07	
r_{dif}	.86	.85	.80	.82	.77	.80	.77	.69	
S_{dif}	8.44	8.57	7.59	8.31	7.96	7.73	8.61	8.18	
SEM_{dif}	3.17	3.34	3.39	3.55	3.84	3.50	4.16	4.57	
VSM									
r	.26	.24	.26	.27	.00	.08	.07	.24	.08
r_{dif}	.75	.74	.72	.70	.75	.77	.69	.56	.77
S_{dif}	7.30	7.40	7.30	7.25	8.49	8.14	8.18	7.40	8.14
SEM_{dif}	3.65	3.79	3.84	3.98	4.24	3.93	4.53	4.91	3.93

SOURCE: Intercorrelation (r) data are from J. Paraskevopoulos & S. Kirk, *The development and psychometric characteristics of the Revised Illinois Test of Psycholinguistic Abilities* (Urbana: University of Illinois Press, 1969), p. 204. Copyright © 1969 by the Board of Trustees of the University of Illinois. Used by permission.

Table **20.14** Obtained Differences and Quotients (Obtained Differences Divided by SEM of the Difference) for Evaluating the Differences in Julie's ITPA Profile

SUBTEST (SCORE)	AR (36)	VR	AA	VA	VE	ME	GC	VC	ASM
VR (44)									
Obtained difference	8								
Quotient	2.67								
AA (28)									
Obtained difference	8	16							
Quotient	2.61	4.95							
VA (45)									
Obtained difference	9	1	17						
Quotient	2.77	.29	4.93						
VE (24)									
Obtained difference	12	20	4	21					
Quotient	3.38	5.41	1.07	5.40					
ME (40)									
Obtained difference	4	4	12	5	16				
Quotient	1.26	1.20	3.54	1.41	4.17				
GC (27)									
Obtained difference	9	17	1	18	3	13			
Quotient	2.31	4.23	0.25	4.29	0.67	3.12			
VC (47)									
Obtained difference	11	3	19	2	23	7	20		
Quotient	2.54	0.67	4.23	0.43	4.75	1.53	3.93		
ASM (40)									
Obtained difference	4	4	12	5	16	0	13	7	
Quotient	1.26	1.20	3.54	1.41	4.17	0.00	3.12	1.53	
VSM (36)									
Obtained difference	0	8	8	9	12	4	9	11	4
Quotient	0	2.11	2.08	2.26	2.83	1.02	1.99	2.24	1.02

Table **20.15**   Reordered ITPA Subtests (Highest to Lowest) with Estimated
True Differences Indicated Where Reliable Differences Were Found

	(47) VC	(45) VA	(44) VR	(40) ASM	(40) ME	(36) AR	(36) VSM	(28) AA	(27) GC	(24) VE
VA										
VR										
ASM										
ME										
AR	7.37	7.11	6.56							
VSM	6.16	6.30	5.92							
AA	10.64	12.58	12.48	9.60	9.72	6.00	5.76			
GC	11.60	12.42	12.07	10.01	9.62	5.67	6.21			
VE	13.57	15.33	16.00	12.32	10.40	9.36	9.00			

Closure (GC), and Verbal Expression (VE). Her scores on Auditory Sequential Memory (ASM), Manual Expression (ME), Auditory Reception
(AR), and Visual Sequential Memory (VSM) also do not differ among
themselves. Her scores on these four subtests (ASM, ME, AR, VSM) are
higher than her scores on Auditory Association (AA), Grammatic Closure
(GC), and Verbal Expression (VE). These latter three scores (AA, GC, VE)
do not differ among themselves.

Since the subtests were all normed on the same sample, the differences in
subtests should not be attributed to norm differences. The subtests do
differ in the behaviors sampled. Julie can find familiar objects that are
hidden (VC), can perform meaningful visual analogies (VA), and can
remember categories and find members of those categories that are visually
presented (VR) so well that these skills might be considered strengths. Her
performances on the sequential memory tasks (VSM, ASM) and her skills
in demonstrating the uses of common objects (ME) and in receptive vocabulary (AR) are about average in comparison both to her performances on
other subtests and to the norm sample. Her performances in completing
verbal analogies (AA), producing examples of standard American English
syntax (GC), and describing the physical and utilitarian characteristics of
familiar objects (VE) were so poor that they may indicate a weakness.

With the exception of the sequential memory subtests, the verbal subtests
tend to be lower: in reception, auditory is lower than visual; in association,
auditory is lower than visual; in expression, verbal is lower than manual;
and in closure, grammatic is lower than visual. We cannot conclude that
Julie has a generalized auditory problem, because her Auditory Sequential
Memory and Auditory Reception are both average. Although verbal areas
(AA, VE, and GC) are below average, the estimated true scores for these

subtests are within 1.5 standard deviations of the mean. Moreover, we cannot conclude that Julie has a generalized visual strength, because Visual Sequential Memory is average. Estimated true scores for Visual Closure, Visual Association, and Visual Reception are all greater than 1 standard deviation above the mean but not greater than 1.5 standard deviations. Thus, *all* of Julie's scores are in the median 90 percent of scores, even though there are reliable differences among scores.

Without qualitative information obtained during testing and without a great deal more information in general, it is impossible to conclude much more. Certainly, there is insufficient information to consider her ITPA performance indicative of pathology. It is likewise inappropriate to speculate about a "cause" or a "cure" of her irregular profile. Julie simply is currently better at some things than at others.

SUMMARY

Constructing and analyzing profiles are common practice, especially in special education. The proper analysis of a profile takes a surprising amount of time and often yields relatively little useful information. In the analysis of profiles, attention must be given to the reliability of differences, the differences in norms, and the differences in the behaviors sampled.

More than anything else discussed in this chapter, it is important to remember that an irregular profile does *not* constitute proof of anything but uneven skill development. The psychological meaning of uneven skill development depends on an abundance of other information. An uneven profile may support other evidence of pathology, or, at least, it may not contradict a tentative diagnosis. It proves nothing.

STUDY QUESTIONS

1. The definition of learning disabilities formulated by the National Advisory Committee on Handicapped Children specifies that learning-disabled children demonstrate a disorder in one or more of the basic psychological processes. Identify some major difficulties in identifying process deficits.

2. Identify two ways in which profiles might be used in planning educational programs for children.

3. Before one can interpret disorders or deficits in psychological processes, what three alternative explanations should be ruled out?

PROBLEMS

1. Harley is a 15½-year-old boy who earns the following scaled scores on the WISC–R:

Information	14	Picture Completion	9
Similarities	16	Picture Arrangement	14
Arithmetic	8	Block Design	8
Vocabulary	15	Object Assembly	7
Comprehension	13	Coding	6

    a. On graph paper, draw Harley's WISC–R profile.

    b. Using the data provided in Table 20.6, locate any reliable differences between Harley's subtest scores.

    c. Estimate the true difference for each reliable difference.

    d. How would you characterize Harley's verbal skills?

ANSWERS

1. (b) and (c)

	S	A	V	C	PC	PA	BD	OA	C
I		4.32			3.25		4.8	4.9	6.48
S		4.56			3.22		5.04	5.04	6.70
A			4.83	3.00		4.14			
V					3.96		5.53	5.76	6.93
C							3.15	3.36	4.69
PC						2.45			
PA							3.78	3.92	5.76
BD									
OA									

(d) Harley's verbal skills as measured by Information, Similarities, Vocabulary, Comprehension, and Picture Completion are superior to the nonverbal skills measured by Picture Completion, Block Design, Object Assembly, and Coding.

ADDITIONAL READING

Cronbach, L. J. *Essentials of psychological testing.* Englewood Cliffs, NJ: Prentice-Hall, 1970. (Chapter 11: Ability profiles in guidance.)

Chapter 21

Pupil Records: Collection, Maintenance, and Dissemination

Policies and standards for the collection, maintenance, and dissemination of information about children must balance two sometimes conflicting needs. Parents and children have a basic right to privacy; schools need to collect and use information about children (and sometimes parents) in order to plan appropriate educational programs. Schools and parents have a common goal, to promote the welfare of children. In theory schools and parents should agree on what constitutes and promotes a child's welfare, and in practice schools and parents generally do work cooperatively.

On the other hand, there have been situations where cooperation has been absent or schools have operated *against* the best interests and basic rights of children and parents. School personnel have flagrantly disregarded the rights to privacy of parents and children. Educationally irrelevant information about the personal lives of parents as well as subjective, impressionistic, unverified information about parents and children have been amassed by the schools. Parents and children have been denied access to pupil records, and therefore they have effectively been denied the opportunity to challenge, correct, or supplement those records. At the same time, schools have on occasion irresponsibly released pupil information to public and private agencies that had no legitimate need for or right to the information. Worse yet, parents and children were often not even informed that the information had been accumulated or released.

Abuses in the collection, maintenance, and dissemination of pupil information were of sufficient magnitude that the Russell Sage Foundation convened a conference in 1969 to deal with the problem. Professors of education, school administrators, sociologists, psychologists, professors of law, and a juvenile court judge participated in the conference to develop voluntary guidelines for the proper collection, maintenance, and dissemination of pupil data. Since 1969, the guidelines that were developed at the Russell Sage Conference have been widely accepted and implemented.

In 1974, many of the recommended guidelines became federal law when the Family Educational Rights and Privacy Act (PL 93-380, commonly called the Buckley amendment) was enacted. The basic provisions of the act are quite simple. Any educational agency that accepts federal money (preschools, elementary and secondary schools, community colleges, and colleges and universities) must give parents the opportunity to inspect, challenge, and correct their children's records. (Students aged 18 or older are given the same rights in regard to their own records.) Also, educational agencies must not release identifiable data without the parents' written consent. Violators of the provisions of the Family Educational Rights and Privacy Act are subject to punishment; no federal funds are given to agencies found to be in violation of the law.

The remainder of this chapter deals with specific issues and principles in the collection, maintenance, and dissemination of pupil information. The issues raised by and the recommendations of the Russell Sage Foundation Conference Guidelines (hereafter referred to as RSFCG) are drawn on. The Buckley amendment is considered as it applies.

COLLECTION OF PUPIL INFORMATION

Schools collect massive amounts of information about individual pupils as well as their parents. As we said in Chapter 1, information can be put to several legitimate educational uses: research and program evaluations, screening and placement decisions, individual program planning, and pupil guidance. A considerable amount of data must be collected if a school system is to function effectively in delivering educational services to children and in reporting the results of its educational programs to the various community, state, and federal agencies to which it may be responsible.

CLASSES OF INFORMATION

The RSFCG delineated three classes of information that schools typically collect. The first class of information (category A) includes the basic, minimum information schools need to collect in order to operate an educational program. Category-A data include identifying information (the child's and parents' name and address, the student's age, and so forth) as well as the student's educational progress (grades completed, achievement evaluations, attendance).

Category-B data are test results and other verified information useful to the school in planning a student's educational program or maintaining a student "safely" in school. Some of the data that pertain to maintaining a student safely in school can be considered absolutely necessary. For example, available records of medical and pharmacological information about severe allergic reactions such as a sensitivity to bee stings; special diets for children with certain chronic diseases such as diabetes; and unusual medical conditions such as hemophilia may mean the difference between life and death. Other category-B data may not be absolutely necessary, but they are nonetheless clearly important in providing an appropriate educational program for a student. Intelligence test data are clearly relevant if the school places a student in a special program for the mentally retarded. Certain types of aptitude or ability data may be necessary if the school district attempts to differentiate instruction on the basis of differences in abilities. Systematic observations, counselor ratings, and various standardized test scores may be useful in cases where a student has problems that are thought to "interfere" with school progress. Certain types of information about a family's background may be important in selecting and interpreting tests used for guidance and placement or in individualizing instruction.

Category-C data include information that may be *potentially* useful. When we are gathering information, we often do not know if a particular bit of information is important or should be followed up. Category C can be considered as the "place" where unevaluated but potentially useful information is stored until it can be considered category-B information or until it is removed from the student's records.

CONSENT

According to the RSFCG, no data should be collected without the consent of parents or their agents. The RSFCG accept the notion of representational consent for the collection of category-A information and certain types of category-B data (for example, intelligence or aptitude tests). *Representational consent* means that consent to collect data is given by appropriately elected officials such as the state legislature.

The RSFCG recommend that individual informed consent be obtained for the collection of information *not* directly relevant and essential to the education of particular children. Individual informed consent should be obtained in writing prior to the collection of category-C data. Informed consent means that the parent (or pupil) is "reasonably competent to understand the nature and consequences of his decision" (RSFCG, 1969, p. 17). Individual consent usually should be required for the collection of family information (religion, income, occupation, and so on), personality data, and other noneducational information.

The collection of research data requires individual informed consent of parents. Various professional groups, such as the American Psychological Association, consider the collection of data without informed consent to be unethical; according to the Buckley amendment, it is *illegal* to experiment with children without prior informed consent. Typically, informed consent for research-related data collection requires that the pupil or parents understand: (1) the purpose and procedures involved in the investigations, (2) any risks involved in participation in the research, (3) the fact that all participants will remain anonymous, and (4) the option given any participant to withdraw from the research at any time.

VERIFICATION

During the collection of information, some distinctions must be made in terms of the quality of the information. Verification is a key concept. *Verifying information* means to ascertain or confirm the information's truth, accuracy, or correctness. Depending on the type of information, verification may take several forms. For observations or ratings, verification means confirmation by another individual. For standardized test data, verification can be equated with reliable and valid assessment.

Information that is not verified cannot be considered category-A or category-B data. Unverified information can be collected, but every attempt should be made to verify such information before it is retained. For example, serious misconduct or extremely withdrawn behavior is of direct concern to the schools. Initial reports of such behavior by a teacher or counselor are typically based upon unverified observations. The unverified information provides hints, hypotheses, and starting points for diagnosis. However, if the data are not confirmable, they should not be collected and must not be retained. Similarly, data from unreliable tests (for example, the Illinois Test of Psycholinguistic Abilities or the Developmental Test of Visual Perception) should, we believe, be considered unverified information unless other data are presented to confirm the results.

MAINTENANCE OF PUPIL INFORMATION

Keeping test results and other information, once they are collected, should be governed by three principles. First of all, the information should be retained only as long as there is a continuing need for it. In any event, only category-A and category-B data, that is, verified data of clear educational value, should be retained. A pupil's school records should be periodically examined, and information that is no longer educationally relevant or no longer accurate should be removed. Natural transition points (for example, promotion from elementary school to junior high) should always be used to remove material from students' files.

The second major principle in the maintenance of pupil information is that parents have the right to inspect, challenge, and supplement student records. The Russell Sage Foundation Conference Guidelines recommended that "formal procedures should be established whereby a student or his parents might challenge the validity of any information contained in Categories 'A' or 'B' " (p. 23). This recommendation presupposes that parents have access to the data.

Parents of exceptional children have had the right to inspect, challenge, and supplement their children's school records for some time. The landmark right to education case (*Pennsylvania Association for Retarded Children* v. *Commonwealth of Pennsylvania*) not only won the guarantee of a free, public, appropriate educational program for *all* retarded children in Pennsylvania but it also guaranteed parents the right to inspect and challenge the contents of their children's school records. The consent agreement that terminated this suit, in addition to guaranteeing the right to education of all mentally retarded children in Pennsylvania, specified the right of parents to a due-process hearing:

The notice of the due process hearing shall inform the parent or guardian of his right . . . to examine before the hearing his child's school records including any tests or reports upon which the proposed action may be based, of his right to present evidence of his own.   (71-42, sec. 2f)

In Pennsylvania, the right to education and the right to a due-process hearing before changes in educational placement have been extended to all exceptional individuals, including the gifted. After 1972, several other right-to-education suits were brought against state departments of education.

Parents of all children won the right to inspect, challenge, and supplement their children's school records in 1974. The Buckley amendment brought the force of federal law to the RSFCG recommendations and the various right-to-education cases. No educational agencies receiving federal support may prevent parents (or persons 18 years of age or older) from (1) inspecting all official files and data related to their children or themselves, (2) challenging the content of such files, and (3) correcting or deleting inaccurate, misleading, or inappropriate information contained in the records.

The third major principle in the maintenance of pupil records is that the records should be protected from snoopers, both inside and outside the school system. In the past, secretaries, custodians, and even other students have had access, at least potentially, to pupil records. "Curious" teachers and administrators, who had no legitimate educational interest, had access. Individuals outside the schools, such as credit bureaus, have often found it easy to obtain information about former or current students. To make sure that only individuals with a legitimate need have access to the information contained in a pupil's records, the RSFCG recommend that pupil records be kept under lock and key. Adequate security mechanisms are necessary to insure that the information in a pupil's records is not available to unauthorized personnel.

DISSEMINATION OF PUPIL INFORMATION

Both access to information by officials and dissemination of information to individuals and agencies outside the school need to be considered. In both cases, the guiding principles are (1) the protection of pupils' and parents' rights of privacy and (2) the legitimate need to know of the person or agency to whom the information is disseminated.

ACCESS WITHIN THE SCHOOLS

The Russell Sage Foundation Conference recommended that category-A and category-B data may be released within the school district to school officials with a legitimate educational interest. Those desiring access to pupil records should sign a form stating why they need to inspect the records; a list of people who have had access to their child's files and the reasons why access was sought should be available to parents (RSFCG, 1969). The provisions of the Buckley amendment correspond to the Russell Sage Foundation Guidelines:

All persons, agencies, or organizations desiring access to the records of a student shall be required to sign a written form which shall be kept permanently with the file of the student, but only for inspection by the parents or student, indicating specifically the legitimate educational or other interest that each person, agency, or organization has in seeking this information. (Sec. 438, 4A)

When a pupil transfers from one school district to another, a pupil's records are also transferred. The Buckley amendment is very specific here as to the conditions of transfer. When a pupil's file is transferred to another school or school system in which the pupil plans to enroll, the school must (1) notify the pupil's parents that the records have been transferred, (2) send the parents a copy of the transferred records if the parents so desire, and (3) provide the parents with an opportunity to challenge the content of the transferred data.

ACCESS TO INDIVIDUALS AND AGENCIES OUTSIDE THE SCHOOLS

School personnel collect information about pupils enrolled in the school system for educationally relevant purposes. There is an implicit agreement between the schools and parents that the *only* justification for collecting and keeping any pupil data is educational relevance. However, because the schools have so much information about pupils, they are often asked for pupil data by potential employers, credit agencies, insurance companies, police, the armed services, the courts, and various social agencies. To divulge information to any of these sources is a violation of this implicit trust, unless the pupil (if over 18) or the parents request that the information be released.

First, we must recognize the fact that the courts and various administrative agencies have the power to subpoena pupil records from schools. In such cases, the Buckley amendment requires that the parents be notified that the records will be turned over in compliance with the subpoena.

Except in the case of the subpoena of records or their transfer to another school district, the RSFCG recommend that no school personnel release *any* pupil information without the written consent of the parents. The Buckley amendment takes a similar position when it states that no educational agency may release pupil information unless "there is written consent from the student's parents specifying records to be released, the reasons for such release, and to whom, and with a copy of the records to be released to the student's parents and the student if desired by the parents" (Sec. 438, b2A). While the Buckley amendment lists exceptions, such as applications for financial aid, the thrust of the law and of the Russell Sage Foundation Guidelines is to control the dissemination of personal pupil information.

SUMMARY

Schools are entrusted with the lives of children. Every day decisions are made that are intended to be in the children's best interests. These decisions are based on both objective information and professional interpretation of that information. The schools must exercise their power over the lives of children very carefully. When school personnel collect data, they must make sure that the data are educationally relevant; their authority does not include the power to snoop and pry needlessly. The schools need latitude in deciding what information is educationally relevant, but the parents must have the right to check and halt the school's attempts to collect some types of information. Parents' informed consent to the collection of information about their children is basic to the family's right to privacy.

The schools should periodically examine all pupil records and destroy all information that is not of immediate or long-term utility or that has not been verified. The information that is to be kept must be guarded. Parents, and students over 18, must be given the opportunity to examine records, to correct or delete information, and to supplement the data contained in files.

Sometimes information is gathered the release of which could be damaging or embarrassing to children and their families. Schools must not release data to outside agencies except under subpoena or with the written consent of parents or a pupil who is over 18. As in all areas of testing and data maintenance, common sense and common decency are required.

STUDY QUESTIONS

1. What principles should guide the collection of information from pupils and their parents?

2. What kinds of information should be kept in a pupil's cumulative folder? What principles should guide the keeping of this information?

3. Under what circumstances should information contained in pupils' records be disseminated to those outside the school building?

ADDITIONAL READING

Anastasi, A. *Psychological testing*. New York: Macmillan, 1976. (Chapter 3: Social and ethical implications of testing, pp. 45–66.)

Goslin, D. A. *Guidelines for the collection, maintenance and dissemination of pupil records*. Troy, NY: Russell Sage Foundation, 1969.

Goslin, D. A. Privacy regulations analyzed. *Insight: The council for exceptional children government report*, 1976, *8*, 3–4.

Chapter 22

Interpretation and Communication of Assessment Information

Assessment information is of little use unless the results are interpreted and communicated in such a way that they have an impact on educational decisions made for and by students. Assessment information is communicated to different audiences, and those audiences have different, although not necessarily mutually exclusive, needs.

THE NEEDS OF ADMINISTRATORS

Administrators use assessment information in making several different kinds of educational decisions. They need to support placement decisions for individual students, to evaluate their educational progress and to appraise the effectiveness of specific curricula and programs. Administrators typically need scores from norm-referenced devices.

Most states require that before students are placed in special education classes they receive individual psychoeducational evaluations that include assessments of intelligence, of academic achievement, and of personality. Administrators need the scores and interpretations from norm-referenced tests to document their placement decisions.

To ascertain the relative effectiveness of various curricula and alternative educational programs, administrators usually need to assess the progress students are making. This is typically done by evaluating achievement with norm-referenced devices. Obviously, criterion-referenced procedures *could* be used to look at mastery of subject-matter content, but such procedures require more time and considerably more individualization.

Administrators are often responsible for the selection of tests to be used in school systems. In selecting tests, they need know how accurately specific tests sample the behaviors they wish to assess. They also need to know the technical characteristics and technical adequacy of the specific tests they use.

THE NEEDS OF TEACHERS

Teachers typically want and need to know specifically what to do instructionally for students. They usually do not receive that information. Teachers have long expressed concern that mere knowledge of the extent to which a student deviates from normal is of little help in their efforts to devise an appropriate educational program for that student. They repeatedly ask for specific information about a student's skill-development strengths and weaknesses and for effective strategies to move students from where they are to where teachers want them to be. To examine the needs of teachers more closely, we must look at alternative diagnostic-intervention strategies.

Assessment, especially for teachers, is closely linked to intervention. The combination of diagnostic assessment practices with intervention practices forms one unit — a diagnostic-intervention process — and encourages us to seek direct relationships between the activities that occur in both components.

FOUR COMPONENTS OF THE DIAGNOSTIC-INTERVENTION PROCESS

The analysis of diagnostic-intervention activities provided by Cromwell, Blashfield, and Strauss (1975) helps clarify the nature of this process. Cromwell et al. define four components of the diagnostic-intervention process; they label them A, B, C, and D. Component A is historical etiological information, and B consists of currently assessable characteristics. The usefulness of this information for educational planning and programming is determined by the extent to which C, treatments or interventions, leads to D, identifiable outcomes. The diagnostic or assessment component consists of historical information and information about current characteristics (A and B); the intervention component consists of treatment and prognosis (C and D). According to Cromwell, Blashfield, and Strauss,

Diagnostic constructs that include C and D data (ACD, BCD, and ABCD) have clearly defined intervention procedures and prognostic statements. They are typically the most useful and valid diagnostic constructs. Diagnostic constructs that involve D without C (AD, BD, and ABD) have outcome predictions, positive or negative, independent of any known treatment for the condition. They are also valid diagnostic constructs but are useful only for prognoses. . . . AC, BC, or ABC constructs are invalid diagnostic constructs because they refer to currently used intervention procedures that have no known effect or outcome. Constructs developed from AB alone or CD alone are valid non-diagnostic constructs, which may be important for scientific understanding. AB constructs would describe relationships between historical and current observations, such as the relation of child rearing to current behavior. CD constructs describe intervention procedures associated with positive or negative outcomes, independent of the kind of diagnosis presented. (1975, p. 11)

Diagnostic-prescriptive teaching is a currently fashionable phrase for attempts to design instructional programs for students based on test performances. With the heightened awareness about learning disabilities, we have recently seen a dramatic increase in efforts to develop instructional programs for children based on their performance on batteries of tests. We need to look at the assumptions underlying diagnostic-prescriptive teaching to understand better the information teachers need.

DIAGNOSTIC-PRESCRIPTIVE TEACHING: TWO MODELS

Characteristically, the steps in diagnostic-prescriptive teaching[1] include identification of students who are experiencing learning difficulties, diagnostic delineation of their strengths and weaknesses, and prescriptive intervention (specification of goals, methods, strategies, materials, and so on) in light of these strengths and weaknesses. Effective diagnostic-prescriptive teaching requires that four critical assumptions be met:

1. Students enter a teaching situation with strengths and weaknesses.

2. These strengths and weaknesses are causally related to the acquisition of academic skills.

3. These strengths and weaknesses can be reliably and validly assessed.

4. There are well-identified links between students' strengths and weaknesses and the relative effectiveness of instruction.

The extent to which the assumptions underlying diagnostic-prescriptive teaching are met depends on how the educators involved view what they are assessing. Previous statements about diagnostic-prescriptive teaching have failed to make a clear distinction between two fundamentally different theoretical models: the *ability-training model* and the *task-analysis model*. Certain investigators (Bannatyne, 1968, 1969; Bateman, 1967a, 1967b; Frostig, 1967; Johnson & Myklebust, 1967; Kirk, McCarthy, & Kirk, 1968; and McCarthy, 1972) have advocated an *ability-training model*, in which the primary purpose of diagnosis is to identify *ability*, or process, strengths and weaknesses in order to prescribe interventions designed to remediate ability weaknesses. Within the ability-training model, the primary concern in

---

1. The description in this section is adapted from an earlier report: J. E. Ysseldyke & J. Salvia, Diagnostic-prescriptive teaching: Two models, *Exceptional Children*, 1974, *41*, 181–185. Copyright 1974 by The Council for Exceptional Children. Reproduced by permission.

diagnosis is the identification of perceptual, psychomotor, cognitive, or psycholinguistic ability deficits that are presumed to cause inadequate skill development. Treatments or interventions are either compensatory or remedial. Interventions are designed to remediate or compensate for psychomotor, cognitive, perceptual, or psycholinguistic deficits.

The *task-analysis model*, which has been espoused and demonstrated by Bijou (1970), Gold (1968), Mann (1970, 1971a, 1971b), and Resnick, Wang, and Kaplan (1973), advocates task analysis of complex instructional goals and intervention designed to teach specific *skills* that are components of the complex goals. When children fail academically, there is in the task-analysis model no effort to identify weaknesses in cognitive, perceptual-motor, or psycholinguistic abilities. Rather, complex skills are task-analyzed, broken down into the subskills that must be mastered before the student can be expected to master the more complex skill. Mastery of complex skills (like successful solution of problems in long division) is viewed as dependent on mastery of component skills (like successful solution of multiplication problems). The task analyst attempts to identify specific *skill-development* weaknesses, and to design interventions directed to remediation of those skill-development weaknesses.

Let us examine the extent to which each of the two models meets the assumptions underlying diagnostic-prescriptive teaching.

Strengths and Weaknesses

The first assumption in diagnostic-prescriptive teaching — that children enter a teaching situation with strengths and weaknesses — is accepted by adherents of both models, although it may be interpreted differently by the two groups. Essentially, the primary point of contention is what those strengths and weaknesses represent.

Within the task-analysis model, emphasis is placed on observed interindividual and intraindividual differences in skill development. Assessment of strengths and weaknesses within this model is typically restricted to evaluation of the student's position on skill continua. Emphasis is placed on the current level of skill development, the next skill to be mastered, and the behavioral components of that next skill.

On the other hand, adherents of the ability-training approach not only observe interindividual and intraindividual differences in skill development, but go beyond observable behaviors and attempt to identify the processes or abilities that *cause* observed differences. Psychoeducational evaluation is employed in an effort to identify strengths and weaknesses in perceptual, cognitive, psycholinguistic, and psychomotor abilities, functions, capacities, or processes.

Both groups recognize interindividual and intraindividual differences in skill development. However, adherents of the task-analysis model do *not* go beyond observed skill differences to infer ability differences. In fact, they reject the use of ability or process profiles (for example, ITPA profiles) to infer underlying deficits, while those who advocate ability training rely most heavily on ability profiles to prescribe differential instruction.

Relevance to Instruction

Those who engage in diagnostic-prescriptive teaching assume that what they assess is relevant to the acquisition of academic skills. Task analysts (1) evaluate the extent to which children demonstrate specific skills (using criterion-referenced measurement), (2) task-analyze the component behaviors necessary to successful completion of academic tasks, and (3) prescribe educational programs to teach specific component skills and their integration. Since the behaviors assessed are components of terminal skills (the skills a student must demonstrate in order to show that the instructional goal has been mastered), they are, to the task analyst, obviously relevant.

Proponents of the ability-training approach go an additional step. They hypothesize that certain adequately developed abilities or processes are prerequisites to the attainment of academic skills and cite as support for their contentions moderate to high correlations between performance on ability measures and performance on academic measures. Because performance on auditory-perceptual, visual-perceptual, psycholinguistic, psychomotor, and other ability measures is correlated with academic achievement, the abilities or processes are presumed to be causative. There is, however, no empirical support for the contention that perceptual, psycholinguistic, or motor training or remediation is a prerequisite to the attainment of academic skills (Mann, 1971a, 1971b; Ysseldyke, 1973, 1976). In fact, numerous studies (Bijou, 1970; Cohen, 1969; Gold, 1968) demonstrate that instructional situations can be manipulated to teach various skills without the additional step of ability remediation.

Reliable and Valid Assessment

The third assumption implicit in diagnostic-prescriptive teaching is that there are reliable and valid measurement devices that may be used to assess strengths and weaknesses. Throughout this book we have surveyed the reliabilities of norm-referenced diagnostic devices designed to assess specific skills and norm-referenced devices designed to assess processes or abilities believed to be necessary to the acquisition of those skills. We have seen that the vast majority of norm-referenced ability measures lack the necessary reliability and validity to be used in designing educational programs for children. A variety of hypothetical constructs that have not been reliably and validly assessed and that are of questionable relevance to instruction have been used to explain children's academic failures. Ability trainers see children as demonstrating "figure-ground difficulties," "visual-motor difficulties," and "visual sequential memory deficits" on the basis of their performances on ability measures with limited reliability. They typically assume that a child who performs differently from a "normal" child on a specific measure is in need of specialized instruction to alleviate or ameliorate the difference, a difference that in many cases may be simply an artifact of the special measurement device employed.

Diagnostic-prescriptive teaching within the task-analysis model requires assessment of observable skills and behaviors. High interrater reliability is necessary and characteristically is demonstrated rather than assumed (Bijou, Peterson, Harris, Allen, & Johnson, 1969; Kazdin, 1973). In addition, the model requires content validity. Task analysts do not have to demonstrate that their measurement devices reliably and validly assess some hypothetical construct; rather, they need only demonstrate that at least two people can agree on a description of the behavior to be assessed.

Diagnostic-Prescriptive Links

 The fourth assumption is that diagnostic information is useful in teaching children — that there are well-identified links between observed strengths and weaknesses and the relative effectiveness of different instructional interventions.

Adherents of the task-analysis approach maintain that norm-referenced instruments do not provide the teacher of handicapped children with sufficient information to plan appropriate instructional strategies, methods, materials, or techniques. Assessment within the task-analysis approach is, for this reason, typically limited to assessment of skill development. The purpose of assessment is placement of a student within an a priori sequence of instruction. The emphasis characteristically is on assessment of entry skills, component skills, and terminal behaviors.

Advocates of ability training contend that children who earn high scores on specific diagnostic devices profit more from one type of instruction, while children who earn low scores on the same devices profit more from a different type of instruction. Proponents of the ability-training approach will have to support their contentions with results from research on aptitude-treatment interaction (Reynolds & Balow, 1972). To date, there is little support for the claim that appropriate instructional interventions can be prescribed on the basis of an individual's performances on aptitude measures (Ysseldyke, 1973).

To date, educators have demonstrated a considerable amount of faith in diagnostic-prescriptive teaching — faith that is differently warranted depending on one's orientation. In this chapter we have delineated two fundamentally different theoretical approaches to diagnostic-prescriptive teaching. The task-analysis model is in the notation of Cromwell et al. (see p. 444) a BCD model: identification of hypothetical constructs presumed to cause academic difficulties is considered unnecessary; instead, the focus is on assessment of children's current characteristics (usually skills) and on prescription of specific interventions based on a child's current level of academic skill development. The model is a test-teach-test model, and one in which specific treatments have empirically demonstrated outcomes. The primary assumption in the task-analysis model is that academic success or failure is due to an interaction between the characteristics of an academic task and the extent of a child's mastery of the skills that are prerequisite to successful completion of that task. The task-analysis model meets the assumptions that underlie diagnostic-prescriptive teaching and as a BCD model is valid.

The ability-training model is an ABC model: an attempt is made to identify those process or ability deficiencies that presumably *cause* academic difficulties. The ability deficiencies are test-identified constructs ("figure-ground difficulties," "form-perception difficulties," and so on), and interventions are designed to alleviate or ameliorate these underlying causes of academic difficulty. Yet, to date, there is little evidence that we are able to assess ability strengths and weaknesses reliably and validly. There is even less empirical evidence to support the contention that specific interventions or treatments (C) lead to desirable academic outcomes (D). The ability-training model fails to meet the assumptions listed earlier. As an ABC model the model is invalid; according to Cromwell et al., "AC, BC, or ABC constructs are invalid diagnostic constructs because they refer to currently used intervention procedures that have no known outcome" (p. 11).

Teachers need specific information about pupil skill development and about what to do instructionally for a pupil. Teachers' needs can best be met by straightforward skill assessment. Teachers and diagnostic specialists need to examine repeatedly the relationship between the behaviors assessed by tests and the kinds of behaviors that they need information about or that they seek to predict. To interpret test information intelligently and in a way that will be of service to children, teachers need more than scores; they need information about the behaviors a child did and did not demonstrate in an assessment setting. Such assessments are obtained most readily by means of criterion-referenced assessment or item analysis of norm-referenced tests.

THE NEEDS OF PARENTS

Parents typically ask straightforward questions about the performances of their children on tests.[2] They want to know what a test says about their

---

2. Portions of the material in this section were taken directly from or adapted from Test Service Bulletin #54, The Psychological Corporation, 1959.

child. Questions such as "Is she profiting from schooling?" and "Is he doing as well as could be expected?" and "Will she be all right?" and "Will he graduate?" and "What can I do to help?" are not uncommon.

Several questions immediately come to the forefront when we consider communication of test results to parents and interpretation of those results so that they have meaning for parents. What about test results? Do they belong in the category of secrets, to be seen only by professional eyes and mentioned only in whispers? Or is their proper function best served when they become common knowledge in the school and its community? (In some towns, names and scores have been listed in the newspaper, much like the results of an athletic contest.) What content should be communicated? How should that content be communicated? What should I say when parents want to know their child's "IQ"? Should test profiles be sent home with students?

The Psychological Corporation Test Service Bulletin No. 54 identifies two commandments that provide a sound basis for communicating to parents the information obtained from testing. The two commandments are absolutely interdependent — without the second the first is empty, and without the first the second is pointless. The first commandment is: *Parents have the right to know whatever the school knows about the abilities, the performance, and the problems of their children*. And the second commandment is: *The school has the obligation to see that it communicates understandable and usable knowledge*.

Whether the school communicates with parents by written report or individual conference, it must make sure it gives *real* information — not just the illusion of information often conveyed by bare numbers or canned interpretations. Moreover, the information must be presented in terms that parents can understand and use.

Few educators would dispute the first commandment. Parents have the final responsibility for the upbringing and education of their children. This responsibility requires access to all available information bearing on educational and vocational decisions to be made for and by the child. The school is the agent to which parents have delegated part of the educational process — but the responsibility has been delegated, not abdicated. Thoughtful parents do not take these responsibilities and rights lightly.

The parents' right to know, then, we regard as indisputable. But to know what? Suppose that, as a result of careful testings, the school knows that Sally has mastered social studies and general science better than many others in her ninth-grade class but that few do as poorly as she in math. In English usage she stands about in the middle, but her reading is barely up to the lower level of the students who successfully complete college preparatory work in her high school. The best prediction that can be made of her probable scores on the College Boards three years hence is that they will fall in the range that would make her eligible for a two-year community college but not for a university. She grasps mechanical concepts better than most boys and far better than most girls. Looking over her test results and her records, her teacher recognizes that neatness and good work habits have earned Sally grades that are somewhat better than would be expected from her test scores.

All of these are things Sally's parents should know. Will they know them if they are simply given numbers — Sally's IQ, percentiles for two reading scores based on one set of norms, percentiles for several aptitude tests based on another set of norms, and grade-placement figures on an achievement battery?

Telling people things they don't understand[3] doesn't increase knowledge, at least not correct and usable knowledge. Transmitting genuine knowledge requires attention to *content, language,* and *audience.*

To begin with, if we want to transmit content, we must know what we are trying to get across. We need to know if there is evidence that the test results deserve any consideration at all. We also need to know the margins and probabilities of error in predictions based on the tests. If we do not know *both* what the scores mean and how much confidence we can place in them, we are in trouble at the start — neither our own use of the information nor our transmission of it to others will be very good.

Content — what we are going to say — and *language* — how we are going to put it — are inseparable when we try to tell somebody something. In giving information about test results, we need to think about the general content and language to use and also about the specific terms to use.

As noted earlier, the content we communicate and the language we use in reporting test results depends on who is receiving the information. If we are reporting to parents, we must pay special attention to the kinds of information they can understand. No single procedure is appropriate for every parent. The same information reported to different sets of parents may have radically different results. Telling the Cartwrights, for example, the test scores their daughter earned may serve to enhance their understanding of how much she has been profiting from school. Communication of the same information to the Falks may create in them unrealistic expectations about their daughter's performance. Similarly, communication of the same information to the Wycliffes may provide them with discussion material for their next Saturday evening bridge game. Counselors and teachers have no sure way of knowing what kind of parents they will be dealing with.

Specific terms used in expressing test results vary considerably in the

---

3. Obviously, there are some parents who *do* understand scores and to whom communication of this information is helpful. In most cases, however, it is not.

problems they pose. Consider, for example, the different kinds of numbers in which test results may be reported.

IQs should rarely if ever be reported as such to students or to their parents, because an IQ is likely to be seen as a fixed characteristic, as something more than a test score. People see it, too often, as a final conclusion about the individual rather than as a piece of information useful in further thinking and planning. Few things interfere more with real understanding than indiscriminate reporting of IQs to parents.

Grade-placement scores or standard scores of various kinds are less likely to cause trouble than IQ scores are. Still, they may substitute an illusion of communication for real communication. Without extensive explanations, grade scores have no more meaning to most parents than raw scores do. Grade placements seem so simple and straightforward that serious misunderstandings may result from their use. A seventh-grade pupil with grade-placement scores of 10.0 for reading and 8.5 for arithmetic does not necessarily rank higher in reading than in arithmetic when compared to the other seventh graders. Both scores may be at the ninety-fifth percentile for that particular class — arithmetic progress much more than reading progress tends to depend on what has been taught and thus to spread over a narrower range in any one class.

Percentiles probably are the safest and most informative numbers to use *provided* (1) it is made clear that they refer not to percentage of questions answered correctly but to percentage of people whose performance the student has equaled or surpassed, and (2) a description of the people with whom the student is being compared is provided. The second point — providing a definite description of the comparison or norm groups — is especially important in making the meaning of test results clear.

It may be unnecessary to use scores in reporting test results to parents. The most important thing to note is that a satisfactory report combines two kinds of information:

1. The student's test results

2. Information about the test or battery and the relationship of the student's performance to the performance of others who have taken the same test

The audience of parents to whom test-based information is to be transmitted includes an enormous range and variety of minds and emotions. Some are ready and able to absorb what teachers have to say. Reaching others may be as hopeless as reaching TV watchers with an AM radio broadcast. Still others may hear what is said, but invest the message with their own special needs, ideas, and predilections.

People who communicate test-based information to parents are in a position of both power and responsibility. Those reporting the results of achievement tests must understand the reasons for selecting a particular test battery for use in their school, the behaviors sampled by the test, and the purpose of giving the test. When reporting the results of an intelligence test, teachers and counselors must also be aware of research results and information in the test's manual about its usefulness. The knowledge of teachers and counselors and their ability to interpret the usefulness of tests is on the line. Parents do not blame test authors for publication of incorrect or misleading information — they *do* become upset with teachers and counselors who give them incorrect or misleading information.

Teachers, counselors, administrators, and school psychologists are exposed to judgment when telling parents about the abilities, skills and performances of their children. The parents have a right to know. They also have a right to be informed in terms that they can understand, absorb, and find useful.

THE NEEDS OF CHILDREN

In many cases it is highly desirable to communicate assessment results directly to children. To the extent that a child is believed capable of understanding the information, that child should be informed of the results of assessment and of the implications of those results. The two commandments discussed earlier about communication of test results to parents are equally important for children.

1. Children have the right to know whatever the school knows about their abilities, performance, and problems.

2. The school has the obligation to see that it communicates understandable and usable knowledge.

School personnel need first to ascertain how capable a particular child is of understanding the results of an assessment. School personnel must, whenever it is deemed appropriate, communicate assessment results in such a way that the child can understand and use the results. As is the case when communicating information to parents, it is imperative when communicating information to children to pay attention to content and language. We must know what it is we are trying to get across and we must know how to communicate effectively. Telling children scores (age scores, grade scores, or IQs) that they earned on tests probably will not provide them with useful information. Once again, assessment results are best communicated as percentiles.

Those who communicate assessment results to children are obligated to insure that children properly understand the results and their implications. Failure to communicate accurately is worse than failure to communicate at all.

SUMMARY

Assessment information is of little use unless it is interpreted and communicated so that it facilitates decision making. Different audiences have different kinds of needs for assessment data. These needs must be recognized, and both the assessment procedures used and the way in which information is interpreted and communicated must reflect these different needs.

This chapter has reviewed the specific needs of administrators, teachers, parents, and children with emphasis on the kinds of information to be collected and communicated for use in decision making by each group.

STUDY QUESTIONS

1. Under what conditions should parents be told their child's score on an intelligence test, and how should they be told?

2. Describe the four components of diagnostic-intervention activities delineated by Cromwell et al.

3. Differentiate between the ability-training and task-analysis approaches to diagnostic-prescriptive teaching.

4. One assumption underlying diagnostic-prescriptive teaching is that learner strengths and weaknesses are causally related to academic success. How do those who advocate an ability-training approach apply this assumption in practice? To what extent is there support for the activities they engage in?

5. How do the needs of administrators in regard to assessment information differ from the needs of teachers? What are the practical implications of these differing needs?

ADDITIONAL READING

Anderson, R. C., & Faust, G. W. *Educational psychology: The science of instruction and learning.* New York: Dodd, Mead, 1973. (Task analysis, pp. 57–84.)

Bijou, S. W. What psychology has to offer education — now. *Journal of Applied Behavior Analysis*, 1970, *3*, 65–71.

Bijou, S. W., & Peterson, R. F. Functional analysis in the assessment of children. In P. McReynolds (ed.), *Advances in psychological assessment* (vol. 2). Palo Alto, CA: Science and Behavior Books, 1971, pp. 63–78.

Cartwright, G. P., Cartwright, C. A., & Ysseldyke, J. E. Two decision models: Identification and diagnostic teaching of handicapped children in the regular classroom. *Psychology in the Schools,* 1973, *10,* 4-11.

Gronlund, N. E. *Measurement and evaluation in teaching.* New York: Macmillan, 1976.

Mann, L. Psychometric phrenology and the new faculty psychology: The case against ability assessment and training. *Journal of Special Education,* 1971, *5,* 3-14.

Sattler, J. *Assessment of children's intelligence.* Philadelphia: W. B. Saunders, 1974. (Chapter 24: Synthesis of test findings, pp. 349–366. Chapter 25: Report writing, pp. 368–400.)

Ysseldyke, J. Diagnostic-prescriptive teaching: The search of aptitude-treatment interactions. In L. Mann & D. Sabatino (eds.), *The first review of special education.* Philadelphia: JSE Press, 1973.

Ysseldyke, J. E., & Salvia, J. A. Diagnostic-prescriptive teaching: Two models. *Exceptional Children,* 1974, *41,* 181–185.

Chapter 23
Summary and Synthesis

Few practices in modern education and psychology have received as much criticism as have testing and decision making based on test scores. Few practices are so deserving of criticism; a poor test in the hands of an unskilled examiner is a lethal weapon. Even with good tests, testers and decision makers can fail to take into account the history and current life circumstances of the person being tested; even adequate testing devices are no guarantee that testers will correctly interpret test results or that they will consider the social and political consequences of their interpretations.

The assessment of intelligence provides a convenient example. Kamin (1975, p. 317) stated that "social science instruments are not neutral. The concepts they are embedded in, the aspects of reality they enable us to see, all have social and political consequences." Protests were touched off in the black community by Arthur Jensen's (1969) paper in the *Harvard Educational Review*, which posited a genetic basis for IQ differences between Blacks and Whites, and Richard Herrnstein's (1971) paper in the *Atlantic Monthly*, which posited a possible genetic basis for social-class IQ differences. These protests can be interpreted in three ways. First, they could be based on a misconception about the nature of intelligence tests. Intelligence has often been thought to reflect "capacity to learn," but Cleary, Humphreys, Kendrick, and Wesman point out that it should not be considered to be learning capability: "Items in all psychological and educational tests measure acquired behavior. The measures of even the simplest sensory and motor functions require a background of learning in order for the examinee to understand directions and make responses" (1975, pp. 20–21). Second, the protests may have arisen from the social ramifications of these papers. Propositions asserting racial or class inferiority are an affront to the personal worth of black and poor citizens. No one wishes to be considered unintelligent or be considered part of a group that is thought to be intellectually inferior. Third, the protests were also in response to the political ramifications that might be touched off by such papers. The issue raised by these papers is whether intelligence is a mutable trait. If intelligence is viewed as being predominantly under genetic control, then political policy would take one form: neglect (benign or otherwise) of those who score low on IQ tests. When intelligence is viewed as being primarily under environmental control, then political action takes a different form: advocacy of social programs designed to foster intellectual development and to enhance intellectual functioning.[1] Kamin (1975, p. 317) writes of the political and social abuses of intelligence testing in the United States during the first third of this century: "Since its introduction to America, the intelligence test has been used more or less consciously as an instrument of oppression against the underprivileged — the poor, the foreign born, and racial minorities." He demonstrates the sensational nature of intelligence-test data with the citations appearing in Figure 23.1.

Bersoff (1973, p. 982) describes the current status of intelligence testing in the following way:

Now IQ testing is outlawed in San Francisco, personnel selection tests are declared illegal unless directly relevant to employment, group intelligence measures are banned in the New York City schools, a whole profession which has distinguished itself from psychiatry primarily because its practitioners can test has been declared moribund, and school psychologists in Boston have been declared incompetent. In the last 10 years, what was once a silk purse has been transformed into a sow's ear.

The abuses of intelligence testing have caught the public's eye primarily because of the social and political consequences. However, the problems in intellectual assessment stem from technical inadequacy (that is, inadequate norms and lack of validity), imprecise definition of the trait being measured, and overzealous and incorrect interpretations of test results. Because intelligence tests are among the best tests available, it is ironic that most of the testing abuses that have aroused public ire have involved them. If other types of tests carried the obvious political and social ramifications that intelligence tests carry, and if they were exposed to the same degree of scrutiny by an aroused public, the outcry would be deafening. What goes wrong in the testing of intelligence goes wrong to a greater degree in every other kind of norm-referenced assessment.

According to Peterson (1968, p. 32), "The only legitimate reason for spending time . . . in assessment is to generate propositions which are useful in forming decisions of benefit to the persons under study." In Chapter 2, several purposes of testing were delineated. For each purpose, test information is intended to facilitate an educational decision. Too often, however, the tests used have no relevance to the decision they are intended to facilitate. Too often, the tests used are technically inadequate. Too often, the child tested differs systematically from the children in the

---

1. The absurdity of an either-or position is demonstrated by the genetic concept of *norm of reaction* (Gottesman, 1963). The relative contributions of genetics and environments are inseparable.

Figure **23.1**   Quotations that illustrate the use of tests to oppress people (cited in Kamin, 1975)

Their [Mexican and Indian children's] dullness seems to be racial, or at least inherent in the family stocks from which they come. The fact that one meets this type with such extraordinary frequency among Indians, Mexicans and negroes suggests quite forcibly that the whole question of racial differences in mental traits will have to be taken up anew . . . there will be discovered enormously significant racial differences which cannot be wiped out by any scheme of mental culture.

   Children of this group should be segregated in special classes . . . they cannot master abstractions, but they can often be made efficient workers. . . . There is no possibility at present of convincing society that they should not be allowed to reproduce . . . they constitute a grave problem because of their unusually prolific breeding. (Terman, 1916, p. 6)

Now the fact is, *that workman* may have a ten year intelligence while you have a twenty. To demand for him a home as you enjoy is as absurd as it would be to insist that every laborer should receive a graduate fellowship. How can there be such a thing as social equality with this wide range of mental capacity?

   . . . The man of intelligence has spent his money wisely, has saved until he has enough to provide for his needs in case of sickness, while the man of low intelligence, no matter how much money he would have earned, would have spent much of it foolishly. . . . During the past year, the coal miners in certain parts of the country have earned more money than the operators and yet today when the mines shut down for a time, those people are the first to suffer. They did not save anything, although their whole life has taught them that mining is an irregular thing and that . . . they should save. . . .   (Goddard, 1920, p. 8)

Never should such a diagnosis [of feeblemindedness] be made on the IQ alone. . . . We must inquire further into the subject's economic history. What is his occupation; his pay. . . . We must learn what we can about his immediate family. What is the economic status or occupation of the parents? . . . When . . . this information has been collected . . . the psychologist may be of great value in getting the subject into the most suitable place in society. . . . (Yerkes, 1923, p. 8)

Goddard reported that, based upon his examination of the "great mass of average immigrants," 83% of Jews, 80% of Hungarians, 79% of Italians, and 87% of Russians were "feebleminded" (Goddard, 1913). (Kamin, 1975, p. 319)

The fact that the immigrants are illiterate or unable to understand the English language is not an obstacle. . . . "Beta" [an intelligence test] . . . is entirely objective. . . . We . . . strenuously object to immigration from Italy . . . Russia . . . Poland . . . Greece . . . Turkey. The Slavic and Latin countries show a marked contrast in intelligence with the Western and northern European group. . . . We shall degenerate to the level of the Slav and Latin races. . . .   (Sweeney, to the House Committee, January 24, 1923, pp. 589–594)

Figure **23.1**   (Continued)

The immigration from [Poland and Russia] consists largely of the Hebrew elements. . . . Some of their labor unions are among the most radical in the whole country. . . . The recent Army tests show . . . these classes rank far below average intelligence. . . . See "A study of American Intelligence" by Carl C. Brigham. . . . Col. Robert M. Yerkes . . . vouches for this book, and he speaks in the highest terms of Prof. Carl C. Brigham.   (Kinnicutt, to the Senate Committee, February 20, 1923, pp. 80–81)

The country at large has been greatly impressed by . . . the Army intelligence tests . . . carefully analyzed by . . . Yerkes . . . (and Brigham). The experts . . . believe . . . the tests give as accurate a measure of intelligence as is possible. . . . The questions were selected with a view to measuring innate ability. . . . Had mental tests been in operation . . . over 6,000,000 aliens now living in this country . . . would never have been admitted. . . .   (Grant, to the Senate Committee, January 10, 1924, p. 837)

That part of the law which has to do with the nonquota immigrants should be modified. . . . All mental testing upon children of Spanish-American descent has shown that the average intelligence of this group is even lower than the average intelligence of the Portuguese and Negro children . . . in this study. Yet Mexicans are flowing into the country. . . .
   From Canada we are getting . . . the less intelligent of the working-class people. . . . The increase in the number of French Canadians is alarming. Whole New England villages and towns are filled with them. The average intelligence of the French Canadian group in our data approaches the level of the average Negro intelligence.
   I have seen gatherings of the foreign-born in which narrow and sloping foreheads were the rule. . . . In every face there was something wrong — lips thick, mouth coarse . . . chin poorly formed . . . sugar-loaf heads . . . goose-bill noses . . . a set of skew-molds discarded by the Creator. . . .   Immigration officials . . . report vast troubles in extracting the truth from certain brunette nationalities. (Hirsch, 1926, p. 28)

---

norming sample. Too often, the test selected inadequately samples the behaviors that are supposed to be assessed.
   When one considers the abuses that have occurred in psychoeducational assessment, it is easy to lose sight of the fact that the intentions of the testing establishment (testers and decision makers who use test data) are benevolent. The abuses that have occurred are the result of ignorance and overzealousness. The most crucial uses and consequently the most serious abuses of tests are those that involve decisions about individual children: screening, placement, program planning, and the evaluation of individual

<u>pupil progress</u>. Inappropriate testing for these purposes can result in wasted time, wasted money, and, more importantly, inappropriate classification and labeling and inappropriate educational programs.

SCREENING

SCREENING AND DIAGNOSIS

Screening is part of the two-phase operation of screening and diagnosis. The purpose of screening is to find potential deviance; those who are potentially deviant receive further diagnosis. Children identified during the individual diagnostic phase receive some additional service, such as remediation or segregation. For example, the school nurse may screen for visual acuity and recommend to the parents of all children who demonstrate an acuity problem that they consult an ophthalmologist or an optometrist who can diagnose the child's problem and prescribe corrective lenses if indicated. Children who are identified during the screening process and subsequently diagnosed as having a problem receive a treatment that ameliorates the condition. This is an appropriate school screening procedure for three reasons. First, screening is followed by diagnosis. Second, the problem isolated by the screening procedure is relevant to the educational progress of children because children are presumed to require adequate visual acuity to make satisfactory progress in school. Third, a treatment (for example, corrective lenses) that ameliorates or remediates the problem follows diagnosis.

Sensory screening programs contrast sharply with other screening programs. In many instances schools conduct screening programs for "problems" that do not exist in any absolute sense or for which there are no validated remedial or ameliorative programs. Most of the deviance with which the schools deal is behavioral in nature; it is also relative in nature. Deviance is defined in terms of relative standing in a distribution (a statistical definition), not in terms of some absolute level or standard of performance. Consequently, such school-defined exceptional conditions as mild mental retardation and learning disabilities are inferred from performances that are *relatively* inferior to the performances of other children. For example, if mental retardation were defined as an IQ in the lowest 3 percent of the population, there would always be mentally retarded individuals because there would always be a lowest 3 percent of the population. If a magic pill were invented that could raise the true IQ of all children by 100 points, there would still be a bottom 3 percent. To say that a child with a true IQ of 130 or 140 is mentally handicapped seems ridiculous, but that would be the case. When the American Association on Mental Deficiency lowered the cutoff for subaverage general intellectual functioning from one standard deviation below the mean to two standard deviations below the mean, they effectively reduced the prevalence of mental retardation in the schools by more than 50 percent. Any time that norm-referenced assessment is used to identify relative deviance, some deviants will always be found by definition. Society and its agents can arbitrarily determine just how many deviants there will be. To the extent that schools attempt to separate and order children, relative deviance is iatrogenic.[2]

PROBLEMS IN SCREENING

All too often when screening programs identify deviant children, three serious errors occur. First, screening procedures and tests may fail to identify truly deviant children. This is a serious error because if a child with a problem is missed during screening, the problem will go untreated. Errors in decision making during screening should occur only in the direction of identifying normal children as deviant (false positives). *None* of the tests intended as screening devices reviewed in this text established the proportions of false positives and false negatives. Consequently, the most important bit of information for any screening test is missing. Second, there may be failure to follow up screening with individual diagnosis. Screening devices and procedures are only rough approximations. Failure to follow up a screening program with valid individual assessment is unforgivable. Any errors in screening (except false negatives) can be corrected during individual diagnosis. Third, children may be identified as deviant, but the school district may have no validated program that can ameliorate or remediate the deviance. The research literature is replete with examples of programs that had intuitive appeal but were ineffectual.

PLACEMENT

Errors in placement decisions are the most serious errors that can be made. A child who is incorrectly placed in a special education program will suffer needless labeling and may receive an inappropriate education until re-evaluation takes place. Testing errors in the placement process can be divided into three types: the wrong test, the wrong interpretation, and dumb mistakes.

---

2. An *iatrogenic* condition occurs when a treatment produces pathology. For example, the prolonged administration of oxygen to premature infants caused retrolentalfibroplasia (RLF). RLF was an iatrogenic condition.

[handwritten: inadeq test / ad. test — wrong purpose / wrong child for norms of test]

① THE WRONG TEST

There are three ways that a wrong test may be used. First, a technically inadequate device may be selected. Second, a technically adequate device may be used for the wrong purpose, that is, for a purpose it was not designed for. Third, a technically adequate device may be used with the wrong child, a child whose characteristics differ greatly from the group on whom the test was standardized.

Poor Tests

Using a technically inadequate test is using the wrong test, and many tests are technically inadequate. Part II of this text stressed the psychometric characteristics of good tests. However, it contained little that has not been common knowledge for more than twenty years. In 1966 a joint committee of the American Psychological Association, the American Educational Research Association, and the National Council on Measurement in Education published *Standards for Educational and Psychological Tests and Manuals* (revised and reprinted in 1974 under the title *Standards for Educational and Psychological Tests*). This manual identifies the essential and desirable features of adequate tests. It specifies the information about test administration, standardization, reliability, and validity that must be included in adequate test manuals. Yet in reading the manuals for the vast majority of tests, one is led to conclude that test authors are unaware of what constitutes an adequate test. In far too many cases the information provided by the test authors themselves is damning. In a few cases the information provided by test authors demonstrates great sensitivity toward and understanding of assessment; unfortunately, these authors are exceptions.

In Chapter 2 we indicated that one of the assumptions underlying psychoeducational assessment was that the examiner is a trained professional skilled in the establishment of rapport, in administration, in scoring, and in interpretation of tests. We must question the skill of the examiner when technically inadequate tests are used for any purpose. We cannot understand how any examiner can select a norm-referenced device to aid in placement decisions when the authors of that device do not even describe the normative sample for the test (see Table 23.1 for a list of norm-referenced devices that have clearly inadequate descriptions of their standardization samples). We cannot understand how any examiner can use a norm-referenced device as an aid in placement decisions when the test authors present no information regarding reliability — or so little information that a standard error of measurement cannot be computed (see Table 23.2) — or when measurement error accounts for more than half of the total variance in test scores. We cannot understand how an examiner can use a device as an aid in placement decisions when the test

Table **23.1**   Tests with Norms That Are Inadequately Constructed or Described

---

Arthur Adaptation of the Leiter International Performance Scale (13)[a]
Bender Visual Motor Gestalt Test (15)
California Achievement Test (9)
Culture Fair Intelligence Tests (14)
Cognitive Abilities Test (14)
Developmental Test of Visual-Motor Integration (15)[b]
Developmental Test of Visual Perception (15)
Diagnostic Reading Scales (10)[b]
Durrell Analysis of Reading Difficulty (10)[b]
Full-Range Picture Vocabulary Test (13)[b]
Gates-MacGinitie Reading Tests (9)[b]
Gates-McKillop Reading Diagnostic Tests (10)[b]
Gilmore Oral Reading Test (10)
Goodenough-Harris Drawing Test (14)
Gray Oral Reading Test (10)
Henmon-Nelson Tests of Mental Ability (14)
Illinois Test of Psycholinguistic Abilities (17)
Memory for Designs Test (15)
Metropolitan Achievement Test (9)
Peabody Picture Vocabulary Test (13)
Primary Mental Abilities Test (14)
Purdue Perceptual-Motor Survey (15)
Quick Test (13)
Silent Reading Diagnostic Tests (10)
Slosson Intelligence Test (13)
Stanford-Binet Intelligence Scale (13)
Wide Range Achievement Test (9)

---

[a] Numbers in parentheses refer to the chapter in which the test is described.
[b] These tests include norms in their manuals but include *no* data about the group on whom the test was standarized.

authors present either inadequate evidence or no evidence regarding the validity of the measure (see Table 23.3).

Some people argue that the use of an inadequate device is better than the use of no test at all. The rationale given for the use of inadequate tests is that the children need help now. For example, Lerner (1976, p. 87) states that "the child with a learning disability, however, cannot wait until we have diagnostic tools that are without fault. . . . Formal tests can be useful in obtaining information that helps formulate a diagnosis when the tests are

Table **23.2**   Tests with Inadequate Reliability or Incomplete Reliability Data[a]

Arthur Adaptation of the Leiter International Performance Scale (13)[b]
Durrell Analysis of Reading Difficulty (10)
Full-Range Picture Vocabulary Test (13)
Developmental Test of Visual Perception (15)
Gates-McKillop Reading Diagnostic Tests (10)
Gilmore Oral Reading Test (10)
Gray Oral Reading Test (10)
Illinois Test of Psycholinguistic Abilities (17)
Primary Mental Abilities Test (14)
Quick Test (13)
Stanford-Binet Intelligence Scale (13)

[a] Nearly all socioemotional measures, as discussed in Chapter 18, have limited reliability.
[b] Numbers in parentheses refer to the chapter in which the test is described.

wisely used." The zeal to help a child is not justification for using technically inadequate tests. Tests with inadequate norms must not be used to rank children in comparison to unspecified populations. An unreliable test measures *error,* not the skill it purports to measure. A test without validity does not measure what its authors say it measures. Surely children must not be labeled, segregated, or treated differently on the basis of either measurement errors or their performances on norm-referenced tests that do not allow adequate norm-referenced interpretations. If poor tests are used to diagnose a condition, the diagnosis may be incorrect. A normal child may be recommended for special educational treatment. We do not fit a child who has normal vision with corrective lenses. Proponents of the use of inadequate tests seem to assume that a diagnosed child will be placed in a program that will help — or at least not harm — that child. This assumption should not be made a priori and in the absence of empirical evidence. It is an empirical question and, in many cases, has been settled as such. Many programs that were believed helpful to handicapped children have been demonstrated to produce no beneficial results (see Guskin & Spicker, 1968).

The Wrong Purposes

Using a technically adequate test for the wrong purposes is using the wrong test. For example, the Peabody Picture Vocabulary Test is a measure of receptive vocabulary and is explicitly described as such by its author. Yet because it provides an IQ, it is widely used as a measure of global intelligence. Clearly, a measure of one aspect of intellectual development (receptive vocabulary) cannot be used as a comprehensive measure of intelli-

Table **23.3**   Tests Having Questionable Validity[a]

Bender Visual Motor Gestalt Test (15)[b]
California Achievement Test (9)[c]
Developmental Test of Visual-Motor Integration (15)[c]
Developmental Test of Visual Perception (15)
Durrell Analysis of Reading Difficulty[b] (10)[c]
Full-Range Picture Vocabulary Test (13)[c]
Gates-MacGinitie Reading Tests (10)
Gates-McKillop Reading Diagnostic Tests (10)[c]
Gilmore Oral Reading Test (10)[c]
Gray Oral Reading Test (10)[c]
Henmon-Nelson Tests of Mental Ability (13)
Illinois Test of Psycholinguistic Abilities (17)
Metropolitan Achievement Test (9)[c]
Purdue Perceptual-Motor Survey (15)
Stanford-Binet Intelligence Scale (13)[c]
Wide Range Achievement Test (9)

---

[a] As discussed in Chapter 18, validity is extremely limited for nearly all socioemotional tests.
[b] Numbers in parentheses refer to the chapter in which the test is described.
[c] No validity data are included in the manuals for these tests.

gence. Another example of using an adequate test for inappropriate purposes is using an achievement test that is good in itself but does not reflect the content of the school's curriculum. The test may be technically adequate in all respects, but decisions about children's academic progress are not valid; progress through the school's curriculum is not being measured.

The Wrong Child

Using an adequate test with the wrong child is using the wrong test. Testing children who are not comparable to those in the test's norm group is this kind of error. Examiners often administer tests to children who are younger or older than the children in the standardization sample. For example, the Pictorial Test of Intelligence is a technically adequate test for children with chronological ages of 3 through 8. It is not appropriate to administer the test to a child who is 12 years old but who has a mental age of 6 years. The norm sample does not include 12-year-old children; the norms for the test were developed by CA, not by MA. Age-inappropriate devices are commonly, although erroneously, used with severely and profoundly retarded persons. More blatant errors have received some notoriety. Tests such as the Stanford-Binet Intelligence Scale have been used with children whose primary language is not English. Several lawsuits have been filed (for example, *Diana* v. *Board of Education*) on behalf of Spanish-speaking children, who rightfully claim that such practices are discriminatory. The logic of using a highly verbal test of intelligence with a child who is not fluent in the language of the test is faulty. Similarly, the use of tests with verbal directions (for example, WISC–R Performance scale) with deaf children is a widespread but unjustifiable practice. Such practices violate the assumption that the children tested have comparable acculturation to those in the norm group. When adequate tests are so conspicuously misused, we must again question the assumption that the examiner is a skilled professional.

THE WRONG INTERPRETATION

Testing can also go wrong in the misinterpretation of test scores. Even a good test provides only limited information. A good norm-referenced test, properly administered, scored, and interpreted can rank students only in terms of their current relative level of performance of certain behaviors. That rank is a very limited piece of information. Although many test and textbook authors claim otherwise, a good norm-referenced test cannot explain why a student has performed in a particular way or obtained a particular score. A good criterion-referenced device, properly administered, scored, and interpreted, can show the teacher only what skills and knowledge a student has acquired. It cannot explain why a student has acquired those skills and concepts or has not acquired other skills and concepts. In Chapter 2 we noted an important assumption: only present behavior is observed. When a student is tested, the only thing that can be observed is the student's performance of a limited number of tasks. Teachers cannot observe performances that are not tested or the reasons *why* a student performed in a certain way. As Wittrock (1970, p. 10) has noted, "The student's scores on standardized tests of interests, abilities, and achievement . . . do not enable us to make rigorous inferences about what the students have learned nor about the role of environments and intellectual processes in producing the learning."

Although the cause of a student's performance is often inferred, it is not observed. Teachers cannot observe mental retardation or giftedness on an intelligence test; they only infer these from an observed performance or classify the performance as indicative of mental retardation or giftedness. They cannot observe a student's performance on the ITPA Auditory Sequential Memory subtest and "see" a deficit in auditory sequential memory. Similarly, teachers cannot observe a student's performance on the Bender Visual Motor Gestalt Test and "see" a perceptual disorder that will interfere with school learning. They *may* observe difficulty in copying geometric designs. This difficulty *may* be indicative of a perceptual disorder; it *may* be indicative of a motor problem or of some other problem, such as failure to understand the instructions. Errors in copying geometric designs *may* be associated with a student's lack of academic success: in the case of a child who has not yet entered school, this is only a prediction; in the case of a student enrolled in school, it is a hypothesis. Deviant drawings are correlated with various disorders and with school success; they are not necessarily *causative* of success. Correlation is a necessary condition for causality, but it is an insufficient condition. To go beyond observable data and infer that unobservable difficulties will cause or are causing academic problems is an error in interpretation.

Similarly, errors in interpretation are often logical errors. Certain psychometric devices discriminate among diagnostic groups (that is, brain-injured and non-brain-injured adults). Simply because a child's performance on a test is similar to the typical performance of members of a particular group does *not* mean that the child belongs in that group. If Norman makes the kinds of errors that are typically made by persons who are brain-injured, one cannot classify him as brain-injured on that basis alone.

DUMB MISTAKES

Sometimes "little" things go wrong in testing that result in big errors. We have called these *dumb mistakes* because every tester should know that they are errors.

The Name's the Same

Several tests may purport to measure the same domain (intelligence for example), but this does not mean they do measure the same domain. As was shown in Part 3, there is great variation among tests in the behaviors sampled and the accuracy of measurement in the same domain.

The Score's the Same

Scores called by the same name are not interchangeable. Not only do the behaviors and the norms differ, the scores have different standard deviations, so that scores with the same numerical value (for example, IQ = 115) correspond to different percentile ranks. In some states IQ ranges for mental retardation appear in the school code. Thus, it is possible that a student would have to earn a higher IQ to get *out* of a special class than to get into one in the first place, since either deviation IQs or ratio IQs may be used regardless of their standard deviations.[3]

---

3. For example, if a state mandated an IQ of 80 as the maximum for placement in an EMR class, that limit would be a z-score of -1.33 on the WISC-R and of $-.80$ on the Slosson.

Six Binets a Day

Some school districts ask their personnel to administer too many tests. Assessment and testing are not synonymous. A fleet-footed psychologist may be physically capable of administering six individual intelligence tests a day but cannot perform six *assessments* per day. The assessor must understand the child's background and current status to select an appropriate assessment procedure; that takes time. The assessor must establish rapport; that takes time. The assessor must interpret the child's performance; that takes time. Relatively simple cases may be completed in 2 or 3 hours. Difficult cases may take more than 40 hours to assess.

4 + 4 = 10

Clerical errors do occur in scoring. The tester may use the wrong table in the test manual to convert raw scores to derived scores. The tester may subtract incorrectly and obtain the wrong CA. The tester may add incorrectly and get the wrong raw score. In a testing course, we recently had a student who made two addition errors in a case study. The net result was that the child being tested received an MA 2 years greater than earned and a reading achievement age 1.5 years less than earned. The child "demonstrated" a 4-year discrepancy because the tester added incorrectly.

PROGRAM PLANNING

Abuses involving placement decisions have received the most attention from educators, psychologists, and the courts. Recently, the use of standardized tests for program planning has also come under attack. If we use tests in planning the educational programs of individual pupils the data obtained from testing must provide information either about *what* to teach or about *how* to teach.

WHAT TO TEACH

What to teach a child requires knowledge of two things: first, what the child is to know at the end of the instructional sequence (the terminal learning objective), and second, what the child knows before the instructional sequence is begun. The difference between what is known before instruction and what should be known after instruction is *what to teach*.

Some achievement tests are very useful in helping a teacher determine what to teach: diagnostic achievement tests, criterion-referenced achievement tests, and those norm-referenced achievement tests that provide information about which instructional objectives the pupil has met in addition to summary scores of relative standing. These tests give teachers information that is directly relevant to teaching — what skills the pupil currently possesses. If teachers know what they want to teach (that is, the *terminal objective*), they will have the necessary information about what to teach.

Other types of tests provide far more limited information about what to teach. In essence, they provide a starting place for further assessment. Most group-administered achievement tests are not designed to provide the teacher with an itemized list of skills children have mastered. When teachers receive only grade equivalents (or some other score that summarizes relative standing), no detailed information about what to teach is provided. The number of items on such tests is usually quite restricted when compared to the number of items of interest. Moreover, the child's test responses are often not available to the teacher. Sometimes when machine scoring is used, long delays in receiving the test results make what might be useful information obsolete.

Tests other than achievement tests may also provide some information about what to teach. Technically adequate perceptual, perceptual-motor, language, and social-competence devices can all provide information about relative levels of development. If teachers have instructional objectives in these domains, they are provided with a starting place for further assessment. With more refined information about the skills a child currently demonstrates in these areas, teachers can help the child acquire more skills. However, from such a perspective, these skills are objectives in themselves.

HOW TO TEACH

How to teach implies such things as method of presentation, pacing, drill or repetitive practice, and organization of content. Implicit in the notion that test results are helpful in providing information about how to teach *must* be the realization that we are talking about only a modification (not a rewriting) of the basic principles of learning. Thus, for example, the principles of reinforcement are thought to apply to all animals, including humans. However, while the principles may apply to all individuals, various parameters may change because of individual differences. When we modify how we teach a student based on that student's test performance, we assume that the test and some parameter of learning are correlated.

Inferences about how to teach a student that are based on test scores are always generalizations. Some of these generalizations have their bases in empirical learning research, while others have no empirical support whatsoever. In the best of circumstances, when there is a research base, great care must be exercised to guarantee that the generalization applies to the individual. For example, a student may be legally blind but still able to learn visually. Students may have uncorrected visual impairments (for example, biocular vision) and still learn to read. Using test information to plan educational programs requires great sensitivity and judgment.

To a limited degree scores from intelligence tests also provide some information about how to teach. For example, students with low IQs (that is, mentally retarded persons) often need more practice during learning because overlearning facilitates their retention in several ways (Zeaman & House, 1963; Belmont, 1966). However, there is no precise relationship between the number of additional trials a student requires (that is, the amount of overlearning) and intelligence. Low IQ provides a hint that the teacher should be alert to the possibility that additional practice may be required.

Since the 1960s, there has been increased interest in other domains that are believed to underlie the acquisition of academic skills.

Some people believe that certain perceptual, perceptual-motor, and psycholinguistic abilities are necessary to the acquisition of academic skills. There are as many processes as there are test names. (There are also as many process disorders as there are tests that name processes.) A student who earns a low score on tests intended to assess a particular process is often said to have a deficit in that area. Some educators attempt to ameliorate the deficit by training the process. Individuals who espouse such an ability-training approach believe that certain processes or abilities must be trained and developed either before or concurrently with academic instruction. Some test authors reinforce these notions with references to remedial programs in the test manuals. For example, Kirk, McCarthy, and Kirk hint at the necessity of process remediation in the manual accompanying the Illinois Test of Psycholinguistic Abilities: "The remedial method recommended for this boy utilized a program which would help ameliorate his basic auditory deficiencies and at the same time teach him to read. This included special exercises to improve sound blending ability, auditory closure, and auditory memory" (1968, p. 100). The manual accompanying the Developmental Test of Visual Perception discusses a training project "conducted to assess methods of alleviating difficulties caused by faulty visual perception. . . . Upon training . . . all the children in the trained group received a retest score of 90 or above" (Frostig et al., 1964, pp. 495–496). Not only are process remediation and training recommended, but Frostig et al. go so far as to use scores on the Developmental Test of Visual Perception to preclude particular methods of instruction: "A score of 90 on the DTVP is regarded as one below which children are unlikely to learn to read, especially if taught mainly by visual methods" (1964, p. 496). The implication is quite clear. Children should not be taught to read by visual methods if they score below 90 on the DTVP.

The theory behind such assertions, the assumptions that underlie such assertions, and the efficacy of remedial procedures based on such assertions have been criticized in detail elsewhere (Mann, 1971; Ysseldyke, 1973; Ysseldyke & Salvia, 1974). One point, however, is relevant in terms of the focus of this text. The measures used to identify fractional processes tend to be poorly constructed devices with questionable norms, questionable reliability, and questionable validity.

ASSESSMENT OF INDIVIDUAL PROGRESS

The evaluation of a student's progress through a sequence of instruction presents special problems. Individualized instruction presumes that teachers try to match teaching strategies, materials, and so on, to individual students. The perceived effectiveness of teaching hinges on pupil progress. In one sense, evaluating progress is not difficult: if the teaching objectives are clearly specified and adequately measured, progress can then be evaluated in terms of the number and types of learning objectives met. Unfortunately, some teachers try to use norm-referenced screening devices for individual evaluation, although such tests do not have the necessary content validity for this purpose. Norm-referenced achievement tests sample too few behaviors to represent an individual student's progress accurately. More important, norm-referenced devices are constructed in such a way that they do not sample objectives that are usually met by all students; such items do not discriminate and are deleted. Another major limitation in the use of norm-referenced devices to assess individual pupil progress is that gain scores (difference scores) are used to assess progress. As can be recalled from Chapter 6, difference scores tend to be very unreliable.

Pupil progress should be assessed by criterion-referenced devices or systematic observation. Either procedure needs demonstrated reliability. The essential condition for assessing individual progress is to ascertain the extent to which a student is meeting the learning objectives that have been established. Norm-referenced tests usually cannot do this; nonetheless, assessment of pupil progress with norm-referenced devices remains a common practice.

PROGRAM EVALUATION

Program evaluation differs from the assessment of individual pupil progress because the purpose of evaluating a program is to assess its effectiveness with a *group* of pupils. In this area, norm-referenced assessment holds certain advantages: readily available tests with a variety of transformed scores, test items that have often been edited by experts and field tested, and known estimates of reliability. However, care must be exercised to insure that the program content is reflected in the test content. Criterion-referenced devices or systematic observations are more desirable, if economically feasible.

TESTING AND EDUCATIONAL DECISION MAKING: CONCLUSIONS

Until very recently norm-referenced assessment dominated the scene in special and remedial education. Tests were designed to predict success in the educational system, identifying those who were expected to achieve and supporting the rejection of those who were expected to fail. Reynolds (1975) calls attention to changes in special education that are dictating changes in assessment practices. In discussing court decisions that have mandated that the educational system provide an individually appropriate education for each child, he states:

We are in a zero-demission era; consequently schools require a decision orientation other than simple prediction; they need one that is oriented to individual rather than institutional payoff. In today's context the measurement technologies ought to become integral parts of instruction designed to make a *difference in* the lives of children and not just a *prediction about* their lives. (p. 15)[4]

There are several ways of gathering the data we need to support the educational decisions we are called upon to make. Technically adequate norm-referenced devices have certain advantages over other assessment practices when we must make screening or placement decisions. Norm-referenced devices provide objective measurement, a method of comparing the performance of a particular student to the performance of similar students and require no test-construction time of the user. They provide the teacher or diagnostic specialist with content created by and evaluated by experts in an already usable format. When appropriately administered, scored, and interpreted, norm-referenced devices can serve to protect children from haphazard and capricious decision making. Historically, tests were constructed to compensate for the inadequacies of observation and decision making based on subjective feelings about a student. Norm-referenced assessment adds a perspective to the making of placement decisions, a perspective that allows educators to say that a child with an IQ

---

4. *Zero-demission* and *zero-rejection* are synonyms referring to a situation in which no students are excluded from educational programs.

of 90 in a school district where the average IQ is 120 is normal — even though that child differs from the other children in the district.

Norm-referenced tests do have a place in educational decision making, provided they are used appropriately for the purposes for which they were designed. Two major difficulties confront both regular and special education: (1) the use of technically adequate devices for purposes other than those for which they were developed, and (2) the use of technically inadequate devices for any purpose. Reynolds (1975) describes the issue well:

> Although there are legitimate and important uses for norm-referenced tests and institutionally-oriented decisions, it is argued . . . that they have been vastly overemphasized at levels of relatively early education where the orientation most properly should be to individual payoff. (p. 25)

Criterion-referenced assessment, observation, and diagnostic teaching are the preferred techniques to use when deciding appropriate educational interventions for individual students or when evaluating the extent to which they have profited from instruction. Criterion-referenced devices may be selected from commercially available systems, or they may be teacher constructed. Teacher-constructed tests are developed by constructing items that assess the extent to which specific instructional objectives have been attained. Gronlund (1968, 1976) has written several texts on teacher-constructed tests. As Hofmeister (1975) states, "Criterion-referenced testing can reach its full potential only when it is so integrated into the day-by-day functioning of the classroom that it cannot easily be separated out as a 'testing' activity" (pp. 77–78).

Observation is an essential element of all classroom practices and, similarly, of all assessment practices. *Observation* is a generic term that can be applied to a range of activities from relatively informal observation of an individual to systematic counting of an individual's behaviors. Entire manuscripts have been written on observation (Boehm & Weinberg, 1977; Cartwright & Cartwright, 1974; Weinberg & Wood, 1975), and these outline the variety of systematic procedures that are used to observe students. Systematic observation is an integral component in the implementation of behavior modification in school settings. Kazdin (1973) has developed in detail the assessment strategies (frequency counting, duration counting, and interval recording) used when behavior-modification techniques are used in school settings. Observation is both an integral part of other assessment procedures and a separate alternative to them.

Diagnostic teaching is not a new concept; it is a practice in which any effective teacher engages. Simply put, the concept refers to the practice of systematic trial and evaluation of a variety of instructional strategies (including materials, methods of presentation, and methods of feedback) with individual students as part of their everyday educational program. Other assessment procedures can be used and are used within diagnostic teaching. Teaching strategies are modified according to whether specified techniques used in particular educational settings result in success or failure for the student.

Assessment is an integral part of the educational process and is engaged in for many educational purposes. The main question in obtaining assessment information is not, How can we use tests? Rather, the fundamental question is, How can we obtain the information necessary to make certain educational decisions? The recent and significant revisions in public policy relating to the education of handicapped children are reflected in the intent and provisions of Public Law 94-142, the Education for All Handicapped Children Act of 1975. PL 94-142 mandates zero exclusion within educational settings, appropriate educational programming for all handicapped children, placement of all children in "least restrictive environments," assurance of extensive identification procedures, and maintenance of individual educational plans for all handicapped children. Assessment data are used in making important decisions to implement the law. The different decisions require different kinds of information. Many of the convictions expressed in this book now have the force of law.

We have presented detailed information about tests in an effort to facilitate their intelligent use. We have attempted to be objective and yet critical in our review of contemporary assessment practices and devices. Used appropriately, tests can and do provide extremely useful information to facilitate decision making; used inappropriately, tests are worthless. As professionals, we must constantly be aware of the fact that our first responsibility is to children and that test-based decisions directly and significantly affect them.

ADDITIONAL READING

American Psychological Association. *Ethical standards of psychologists.* Washington, DC: American Psychological Association, 1963.

American Psychological Association, American Educational Research Association, & National Council on Measurement in Education. *Standards for educational and psychological tests.* Washington, DC: American Psychological Association, 1974. (The use of tests, pp. 56–73.)

Anastasi, A. Psychological tests: Uses and abuses. *Teachers College Record,* 1961, *62*, 389–393.

Bersoff, D. N. Silk purses into sows' ears: The decline of psychological testing and a suggestion for its redemption. *American Psychologist,* 1973, *28*, 892–899.

Block, J. H. Criterion-referenced measurements: Potential. *School Review,* 1971, 289–298.

Ebel, R. L. Criterion-referenced measurements: Limitations. *School Review,* 1971, 282–289.

Hobbs, N. *Issues in the classification of children* (vols. 1 and 2). San Francisco: Jossey-Bass, 1975.

McClelland, D. Testing for competence rather than for intelligence. *American Psychologist,* 1973, 1–14.

Meyers, C. E., Sundstrom, P. E., & Yoshida, R. Y. The school psychologist and assessment in special education. *School Psychology Monograph,* 1974, *2*.

Reynolds, M., & Hively, W. *Domain-referenced testing in special education.* Minneapolis: Leadership Training Institute/Special Education, 1975.

References

Adam, A., Doran, D., & Modan, R. Frequencies of protan and deutan alleles in some Israeli communities and a note on the selection relaxation hypothesis. *American Journal of Physical Anthropology,* 1967, *26*, 297–306.

American National Standards Institute. *Specifications for Audiometers.* ANSI S3.6, 1969. American National Standards Institute, Inc., New York, 1970.

American Psychological Association, American Educational Research Association, & National Council on Measurement in Education. *Standards for Educational and Psychological Tests.* Washington, DC: American Psychological Association, 1974.

American Speech and Hearing Association. Guidelines for audiometric symbols. *American Speech and Hearing Association Journal,* 1974, *16*, 260–263.

Ammons, R. B., & Ammons, H. S. *The Full Range Picture Vocabulary Test.* New Orleans: R. B. Ammons, 1948.

Ammons, R. B. & Ammons, C. H. The Quick Test (QT): Provisional Manual. *Psychological Reports,* 1962, *11*, 111–161.

Anderson, R. *Kuhlmann-Anderson Intelligence Tests* (7th ed.) Princeton: Educational Testing Service, 1963.

Arthur, G. *The Arthur Adaptation of the Leiter International Performance Scale.* Chicago, IL: C.H. Stoelting, 1950.

Bangs, T. E. *Language and learning disabilities of the pre-academic child.* New York: Appleton-Century-Crofts, 1968.

Bannatyne, A. Diagnostic and remedial techniques for use with dyslexic children. *Academic Therapy Quarterly,* 1968, *3*, 213–224.

Bannatyne, A. Diagnosing learning disabilities and writing remedial prescriptions. *Journal of Learning Disabilities,* 1969, *1*, 242–249.

Barraga, N. *Visual handicaps and learning: A developmental approach.* Belmont, CA: Wadsworth, 1976.

Bateman, B. An educator's view of a diagnostic approach to learning disorders. In J. Hellmuth (ed.), *Learning Disorders* (vol. 1). Seattle: Special Child Publications, 1965.

Bateman, B. Implication of a learning disability approach for teaching educable retardates. *Mental Retardation,* 1967, *5*, 23–25. (a)

Bateman, B. Three approaches to diagnosis and educational planning for children with learning disabilities. *Academic Therapy Quarterly,* 1967, *3*, 11–16. (b)

Beatty, L. S., Madden, R., & Gardner, E. F. *Stanford Diagnostic Mathematics Test.* New York: Harcourt Brace Jovanovich, in press.

Beery, K. E. *Visual-motor integration*. Chicago: Follett, 1967.

Beery, K. E., & Buktenica, N. *Developmental Test of Visual-Motor Integration*. Chicago: Follett, 1967.

Bellak, L., & Bellak, S. *Children's Apperception Test*. Larchmont, NY: C.P.S., 1965.

Belmont, J. M. Long-term memory in mental retardation. In N. R. Ellis (ed.), *International review of research in mental retardation* (vol. 1). New York: Academic Press, 1966.

Bender, L. *A visual motor Gestalt test and its clinical use*. New York: American Orthopsychiatric Association Research Monograph, 1938, No. 3.

Bene, E., & Anthony, J. *Family Relations Test; An objective technique for exploring emotional attitudes in children*. Windsor, Berks, England: NFER Publishing, 1957.

Bersoff, D. Silk purses into sows' ears: The decline of psychological testing and a suggestion for its redemption. *American Psychologist*, 1973, *10*, 892–899.

Bijou, S. W. What psychology has to offer education — Now. *Journal of Applied Behavior Analysis*, 1970, *3*, 65–71.

Bijou, S. W., Peterson, R. F., Harris, F. R., Allen, K. E., & Johnson, M. S. Methodology for experimental studies of young children in natural settings. *Psychological Record*, 1969, *19*, 177–210.

Bloom, B. (ed.). *Taxonomy of educational objectives: The classification of educational goals*. Handbook 1. *Cognitive domain*. New York: McKay, 1956.

Bloom, B., Hastings, J., & Madaus, G. *Handbook of formative and summative evaluation of student learning*. New York: McGraw-Hill, 1971.

Bloom, L. Talking, understanding and thinking. In R. Schiefelbusch and L. Lloyd (eds.), *Language perspectives, acquisition, retardation and intervention*. Baltimore: University Park Press, 1974, 193–296.

Blum, G. *Blacky Pictures: A technique for the exploration of personality dynamics*. Ann Arbor: Psychodynamic Instruments, 1967.

Boehm, A. E. *Boehm Test of Basic Concepts Manual*. New York: Psychological Corporation, 1971.

Boehm, A., & Weinberg, R. A. *The classroom observer: A guide for developing observation skills*. New York: Teachers College Press, 1977.

Bond, G. L., Balow, B., & Hoyt, C. *Silent Reading Diagnostic Tests*. Ardmore, PA: Meredith Corporation, 1970.

Bradbury, R. *Fahrenheit 451*. New York: Ballantine Books, 1953.

Buck, J., & Jolles, I. *House-Tree-Person*. Los Angeles: Western Psychological Services, 1966.

Burgemeister, B. B., Blum, L. H., & Lorge, I. *Columbia Mental Maturity Scale* (3rd ed.). New York: Harcourt Brace Jovanovich, 1972.

Burks, H. *Burks' Behavior Rating Scales*. El Monte, CA: Arden Press, 1969.

Buros, O. K. (ed.). *The nineteen-thirty-eight mental measurements yearbook.* New Brunswick, NJ: Rutgers University Press, 1938.

Buros, O. K. (ed.). *The nineteen-forty mental measurements yearbook.* Highland Park, NJ: Mental Measurements Yearbook, 1941.

Buros, O. K. (ed.). *The third mental measurements yearbook.* New Brunswick, NJ: Rutgers University Press, 1949.

Buros, O. K. (ed.). *The fourth mental measurements yearbook.* Highland Park, NJ: Gryphon Press, 1953.

Buros, O. K. (ed.). *The fifth mental measurements yearbook.* Highland Park, NJ: Gryphon Press, 1959.

Buros, O. K. (ed.). *Tests in print.* Highland Park, NJ: Gryphon Press, 1961.

Buros, O. K. (ed.). *The sixth mental measurements yearbook.* Highland Park, NJ: Gryphon Press, 1965.

Buros, O. K. (ed.). *The seventh mental measurements yearbook* (2 vols.). Highland Park, NJ: Gryphon Press, 1972.

Burt, C. Class differences in general intelligence: III. *British Journal of Statistical Psychology*, 1959, *12*, 15–33.

Bush, W. J., & Waugh, K. W. *Diagnosing learning disabilities.* Columbus, OH: Merrill, 1976.

Cain, L., Levine, S., & Elzey, F. *Manual for the Cain-Levine Social Competency Scale.* Palo Alto: Consulting Psychologists Press, 1963.

Caldwell, B. *Preschool Inventory Revised Edition.* Princeton, NJ: Educational Testing Service, 1970.

Caldwell, B. *Preschool Inventory Revised Edition — 1970: Handbook.* Princeton, NJ: Educational Testing Service, 1970.

Campbell, D., & Fiske, D. Convergent and discriminant validation by the multitrait-multimethod matrix. *Psychological Bulletin*, 1959, *56*, 81–105.

Cartwright, C., & Cartwright, G. P. *Developing observation skills.* New York: McGraw-Hill, 1974.

Cassel, R. *Child Behavior Rating Scale.* Los Angeles: Western Psychological Services, 1962.

Cattell, R. B. *Culture Fair Intelligence Test: Scale 1.* Champaign, IL: Institute for Personality and Ability Testing, 1950.

Cattell, R. B. *Handbook for the Culture Fair Intelligence Test: Scale 1.* Champaign, IL: Institute for Personality and Ability Testing, 1962.

Cattell, R. B. *Measuring intelligence with the Culture Fair Tests: Manual for scales 2 and 3.* Champaign, IL: Institute for Personality and Ability Testing, 1973. (a)

Cattell, R. B. *Technical Supplement for the Culture Fair Intelligence Tests scales 2 and 3.* Champaign, IL: Institute for Personality and Ability Testing, 1973. (b)

Cattell, R. B., & Cattell, A. K. S. *Culture Fair Intelligence Test: Scale 2.* Champaign, IL: Institute for Personality and Ability Testing, 1960. (a)

Cattell, R. B., & Cattell, A. K. S. *Handbook for the individual or group Culture Fair Intelligence Test: Scale 2.* Champaign, IL: Institute for Personality and Ability Testing, 1960. (b)

Cattell, R. B., & Cattell, A. K. S. *Culture Fair Intelligence Test: Scale 3.* Champaign, IL: Institute for Personality and Ability Testing, 1963.

Cattell, R., Coan, R., & Belloff, H. *Jr.-Sr. High School Personality Questionnaire,* Indianapolis: Bobbs-Merrill, 1969.

Cattell, R., Eber, H., & Tatsuoka, M. *Sixteen Personality Factor Questionnaire.* Champaign, IL: Institute for Personality and Ability Testing, 1970.

Chomsky, N. *Aspects of the theory of syntax.* Cambridge, MA: MIT Press, 1965.

Cleary, T. A., Humphreys, L. G., Kendrick, S. A., & Wesman, A. Educational uses of tests with disadvantaged students. *American Psychologist,* 1975, *30*, 15–41.

Coan, R., & Cattell, R. *Early School Personality Questionnaire.* Champaign, IL: Institute for Personality and Ability Testing, 1970.

Cohen, S. A. Studies in visual perception and reading in disadvantaged children. *Journal of Learning Disabilities,* 1969, *2*, 498–507.

Coleman, J., Campbell, E., Hobson, C., McPartland, J., Mood, A., Weinfeld, F., & York, R. *Equality of educational opportunity.* Washington, DC: National Center for Educational Statistics (F.S. 5.238:38001), 1966.

Connolly, A., Nachtman, W., & Pritchett, E. *Manual for the Key Math Diagnostic Arithmetic Test.* Circle Pines, MN: American Guidance Service, 1971.

Cottle, W. *School Interest Inventory.* Boston: Houghton Mifflin, 1966.

Cromwell, R. L., Blashfield, R. K., & Strauss, J. S. Criteria for classification systems. In N. Hobbs (ed.), *Issues in the classification of children* (vol. 1). San Francisco: Jossey-Bass, 1975.

Cronbach, L. Coefficient alpha and the internal structure of tests. *Psychometrika,* 1951, *16*, 297–334.

Cronbach, L. *Essentials of psychological testing.* New York: Harper, 1960.

Dahl, L. A. *Public school audiometry: Principles and methods.* Danville, IL: Interstate Press, 1949.

Darley, F. L. (ed.). Identification audiometry. *Journal of Speech and Hearing Disorders,* 1961, Monograph Supplement Number 9.

Davis, W. Q. *A study of test score comparability among five widely used reading survey tests.* Unpublished doctoral dissertation, Southern Illinois University, 1968.

Diana v. *Board of Education.* Civil Actions No. C-70-37 (N.C. Cal. 1970).

Dingman, H. & Tarjan, G. Mental retardation and the normal distribution curve. *American Journal of Mental Deficiency,* 1960, *64*, 991–994.

Doll, E. *Measurement of social competence: A manual for the Vineland Social Maturity Scale.* Princeton: Educational Testing Service, 1953.

Doll, E. *Vineland Social Maturity Scale.* Circle Pines, MN: American Guidance Service, 1965. (Originally published 1953.)

Down, A. L. Observations on an ethnic classification of idiots. In R. Vollman (ed.), *Down's Syndrome (Mongolism), a reference bibliography.* Washington, DC: United States Department of Health, Education and Welfare, 1969. (The paper by Down that appears in this collection was originally published in 1866.)

Duffy, J. *Report 5: Hearing problems of school-age children.* In *Maico Audiological Library Series I.* Minneapolis: Maico Electronics, 1964.

Dunn, L. M. *Peabody Picture Vocabulary Test.* Circle Pines, MN: American Guidance Service, 1965.

Dunn, L. M. Minimal brain dysfunction: A dilemma for educators. In H. C. Haywood (ed.), *Brain damage in school age children.* Washington, DC: Council for Exceptional Children, 1968.

Dunn, L. M., & Markwardt, F. C. *Peabody Individual Achievement Test.* Circle Pines, MN: American Guidance Service, 1970.

Durost, W. N., Bixler, H. H., Wrightstone, J. W., Prescott, G. A., & Balow, I. H. *Metropolitan Achievement Test.* New York: Harcourt Brace Jovanovich, 1971.

Durrell, D. D. *Durrell Analysis of Reading Difficulty.* New York: Harcourt Brace Jovanovich, 1955.

Dvorine, I. *Dvorine Pseudo-Isochromatic Plates* (2nd ed.). Baltimore: Waverly Press, 1953.

Edwards, A. *Edwards Personal Preference Schedule.* New York: Psychological Corporation, 1959.

Edwards, A. *Edwards Personality Inventory.* Chicago: Science Research Associates, 1966.

Ekwall, E. E. *Locating and correcting reading difficulties.* Columbus, OH: Merrill, 1970.

Exner, J. E. *Workbook in the Rorschach technique.* Springfield, IL.: C.C. Thomas, 1967.

Eysenck, H., & Eysenck, S. *Eysenck Personality Inventory.* San Diego: Educational and Industrial Testing Service, 1969.

Family Educational Rights and Privacy Act. PL 93-380.

Farber, B. *Mental retardation: Its social context and social consequences.* Boston: Houghton Mifflin, 1968.

Farnsworth, D. *The Farnsworth Dichotomous Test for Color Blindness.* New York: Psychological Corporation, 1947.

Faye, E. *The low vision patient.* New York: Grune and Stratton, 1970.

Fernald, C. Control of grammar in imitation, comprehension, and production, problems of replication. *Journal of Verbal Learning and Verbal Behavior,* 1972, *11*, 606–613.

Finch, F. *Kuhlmann-Finch Tests.* Circle Pines, MN: American Guidance Service, 1951.

Fitts, W. *Tennessee Self Concept Inventory.* Nashville: Counselor Recordings and Tests, 1965.

Frankenburg, W. K., Dodds, J. B., & Fandal, A. W. *Denver Developmental Screening Test.* Denver: Ladoca Project and Publishing Foundation, 1970.

French, J. L. *Pictorial Test of Intelligence.* Boston: Houghton Mifflin, 1964.

Frostig, M. Testing as a basis for educational therapy. *Journal of Special Education,* 1967, *2*, 15–34.

Frostig, M., Lefever, W., & Whittlesey, J. *Administration and scoring manual: Marianne Frostig Developmental Test of Visual Perception.* Palo Alto: Consulting Psychologists Press, 1966.

Frostig, M., Maslow, P., Lefever, D. W., & Whittlesey, J. R. *The Marianne Frostig Developmental Test of Visual Perception: 1963 standardization.* Palo Alto: Consulting Psychologists Press, 1964.

Gates, A. I., & MacGinitie, W. H. *Gates-MacGinitie Reading Tests.* New York: Teachers College Press, 1972.

Gates, A. I., & McKillop, A. S. *Gates-McKillop Reading Diagnostic Tests.* New York: Teachers College Press, 1962.

Gerweck, S., & Ysseldyke, J. E. Limitations of current psychological practices for the intellectual assessment of the hearing impaired: A response to the Levine survey. *Volta Review,* 1974, *77,* 243–248.

Ghiselli, E. *Theory of Psychological Measurement.* New York: McGraw-Hill, 1964.

Gilmore, J. V. & Gilmore, E. C. *Gilmore Oral Reading Test.* New York: Harcourt Brace Jovanovich, 1968.

Ginzberg, E., & Bray, D. W. *The Uneducated.* New York: Columbia University Press, 1953.

Gold, M. W. The acquisition of a complex assembly task by retarded adolescents. Urbana: University of Illinois, Children's Research Center, 1968. (Mimeographed)

Goldman, R., & Fristoe, M. *Goldman-Fristoe Test of Articulation.* Circle Pines, MN: American Guidance Service, 1972.

Goldstein, K. Die lokalisation in her grosshirnrinde. *Handb. Norm. Pathol. Physiologie.* Berlin: J. Springer, 1927.

Goldstein, K. The modifications of behavior consequent to cerebral lesions. *Psychiatric Quarterly,* 1963, *10,* 586–610.

Goldstein, K. *The organism.* New York: American Book, 1939.

Goodman, A. C., & Chasin, W. D. Hearing problems. In S. S. Gellis and B. M. Kagan (eds.), *Current Pediatric Therapy 6,* Philadelphia: W. B. Saunders, 1976.

Goslin, D. *Guidelines for the collection, maintenance, and dissemination of pupil records.* Troy, NY: Russell Sage Foundation, 1970.

Gottesman, I. Genetic aspects of intelligent behavior. In N. Ellis (ed.), *Handbook of mental deficiency.* New York: McGraw-Hill, 1963.

Gottesman, I. Biogenics of race and class. In M. Deutsch, I. Katz, & A. Jensen (eds.), *Social class, race, and psychological development.* New York: Holt, Rinehart and Winston, 1968.

Gough, H. *California Psychological Inventory,* Palo Alto: Consulting Psychologists Press, 1969.

Graham, F., & Kendall, B. S. Memory for Designs Test: Revised general manual. *Perceptual and Motor Skills,* 1960, *11*, 147–188.

Gray, W. S. & Robinson, H. M. *Gray Oral Reading Test.* Indianapolis: Bobbs-Merrill, 1967.

Greenwood, L. Shots in the dark. Cited by I. Schloss, Implication of altering the definition of blindness. In American Foundation for the Blind *Research Bulletin 3,* 1963.

Gronlund, N. *Constructing achievement tests.* Englewood Cliffs, NJ: Prentice-Hall, 1968.

Gronlund, N. *Measurement and evaluation in teaching* (3rd ed.). New York: Macmillan, 1976.

Guidelines for audiometric symbols. *American Speech and Hearing Association Journal,* 1974, *16*, 260–264.

Guilford, J. *The nature of human intelligence.* New York: McGraw-Hill, 1967.

Guskin, S., & Spicker, H. Educational research in mental retardation. In N. Ellis (ed.), *International review of research in mental retardation* (vol. 3). New York: Academic Press, 1968.

Guzaitis, J., Carlin, J. A., & Juda, S. *Diagnosis: An instructional aid (mathematics).* Chicago: Science Research Associates, 1972.

Hackett, M. G. *Criterion reading: Individualized learning management system.* Westminster, MD: Random House, 1971.

Hallahan, D. P. & Cruickshank, W. M. *Psychoeducational foundations of learning disabilities.* Englewood Cliffs, NJ: Prentice-Hall, 1973.

Halliday, C. *The visually impaired child — growth, learning, development — infancy to school age.* Louisville, KY: American Printing House for the Blind, 1970.

Halstead, W. C. *Brain and intelligence.* Chicago: University of Chicago Press, 1947.

Hammill, D., & Wiederholt, J. L. Review of the Frostig Visual Perception Test and the related training program. In L. Mann & D. A. Sabatino (eds.). *The first review of special education* (vol. 1). Philadelphia: Journal of Special Education Press, Grune and Stratton, 1973, 33–48.

Hardy, L. H., Rand, G., & Rittler, M. C. *AO H-R-R Pseudoisochromatic Plates.* Buffalo: American Optical Company, Instrument Division, 1957.

Harris, D. *Children's drawings as measures of intellectual maturity.* New York: Harcourt Brace Jovanovich, 1963.

Hathaway, S., & McKinley, J. *Minnesota Multiphasic Personality Inventory.* New York: Psychological Corporation, 1967.

Herrnstein, R. IQ. *Atlantic Monthly,* 1971, *43*, 228.

Hieronymus, A. N., & Lindquist, E. F. *Iowa Tests of Basic Skills: The teachers guide for the levels edition.* Boston: Houghton Mifflin, 1971.

Hieronymus, A. N., & Lindquist, E. F. *Iowa Tests of Basic Skills: Manual for administrators, supervisors, and counselors.* Boston: Houghton Mifflin, 1974.

Hiskey, M. *Hiskey-Nebraska Test of Learning Aptitude.* Lincoln, NB: Union College Press, 1966.

Hofmeister, A. Integrating criterion-referenced testing and instruction. In W. Hively & M. Reynolds (eds.), *Domain-referenced testing in special education.* Minneapolis: Leadership Training Institute/Special Education, University of Minnesota, 1975, pp. 77–88.

Holtzman, W. *Holtzman Inkblot Technique.* New York: Psychological Corporation, 1966.

Horn, J. *Crystallized and fluid intelligence: A factor analytic study of the structure among primary mental abilities.* Unpublished doctoral dissertation, University of Illinois, 1965.

Hurlin, R. G. Estimated prevalance of blindness in the U.S. — 1960. *Sight Saving Review,* 1962, *32*, 4–12.

Ishihara, S. *Ishihara Color Blind Test Book (Children).* Tokyo: Kanehara Shuppan, 1970.

Jastak, J. F., & Jastak, S. R. *Manual: The Wide Range Achievement Test.* Wilmington, DE: Guidance Associates, 1965.

Jay. E. *A book about me.* Chicago: Science Research Associates, 1955.

Jensen, A. R. How much can we boost IQ and scholastic achievement? *Harvard Educational Review,* 1969, *39*, 1–123.

Johnson, D., & Myklebust, H. *Learning disabilities: Educational principles and practices.* New York: Grune and Stratton, 1967.

Johnston, P. W. The Massachusetts Hearing Test. *Journal of the Acoustical Society,* 1948, *20*, 697–703.

Johnston, P. W. An efficient group screening test. *Journal of Speech and Hearing Disorders,* 1952, *17*, 8–12.

Kamin, L. J. *The science and politics of I.Q.* Hillsdale, NJ: Lawrence Erlbaum Associates, 1974.

Kamin, L. J. Social and legal consequences of IQ tests as classification instruments: Some warnings from our past. *Journal of School Psychology,* 1975, *13*, 317–323.

Kappauf, W. E. Studying the relationship of task performance to the variables of chronological age, mental age, and IQ. In N. Ellis (ed.), *International review of research in mental retardation* (vol. 6). New York: Academic Press, 1973.

Karlsen, B., Madden, R., & Gardner, E. F. *Stanford Diagnostic Reading Test.* New York: Harcourt Brace Jovanovich, 1977.

Kazdin, A. E. The effects of vicarious reinforcement in the classroom. *Journal of Applied Behavior Analysis,* 1973, *6*, 71–78.

Kirk, S. A., & Kirk, W. D. *Psycholinguistic learning disabilities: Diagnosis and remediation.* Urbana: University of Illinois Press, 1971.

Kirk, S., McCarthy, J., & Kirk, W. *Illinois Test of Psycholinguistic Abilities.* Urbana: University of Illinois Press, 1968.

Koppitz, E. *Human Figures Drawing Test.* New York: Grune and Stratton, 1968.

Koppitz, E. M. *The Bender Gestalt Test for Young Children.* New York: Grune and Stratton, 1963.

Koppitz, E. M. *The Bender Gestalt Test for Young Children: Volume II: Research and application, 1963–1973.* New York: Grune and Stratton, 1975.

Kuder, R. *Kuder Personal Preference Record.* Chicago: Science Research Associates, 1954.

Kuhlmann, R., & Anderson, R. G. *Kuhlmann-Anderson Test.* Princeton, NJ: Personnel Press, 1963.

Lambert, N., Windmiller, M., Cole, L., & Figueroa, R. *Manual for AAMD Adaptive Behavior Scale Public School Version (1974 revision).* Washington, DC: The Association, 1975.

Lamke, T., Nelson, M., & French, J. *Henmon-Nelson Tests of Mental Ability, 1973 revision.* Boston: Houghton Mifflin, 1973.

Lee, L. *Northwestern Syntax Screening Test.* Evanston, IL: Northwestern University Press, 1969.

Lee, J., & Clark, W. *Manual: Lee-Clark Reading Readiness Test.* Monterey, CA: California Test Bureau, 1962.

Lenneberg, E. *Biological foundations of language.* New York: Wiley, 1967.

Lerner, J. *Children with learning disabilities.* Boston: Houghton Mifflin, 1976.

Levine, E. Psychological tests and practices with the deaf: A survey of the state of the art. *The Volta Review,* 1974, *76*, 298–319.

Lindzey, G. On the classification of projective techniques. *Psychological Bulletin,* 1959, *56*, 158–168.

Madden, R., Gardner, E. R., Rudman, H. C., Karlsen, B., & Merwin, J. C. *Stanford Achievement Test.* New York: Harcourt Brace Jovanovich, 1973

Mann, L. Are we fractionating too much? *Academic Therapy,* 1970, *5*, 85–91.

Mann, L. Perceptual training: Misdirections and redirections. *American Journal of Orthopsychiatry,* 1970, *40*, 30–38.

Mann, L. Perceptual training revisited: The training of nothing at all. *Rehabilitation Literature,* 1971, *32*, 322–335. (a)

Mann, L. Psychometric phrenology and the new faculty psychology: The case against ability assessment and training. *Journal of Special Education,* 1971, *5*, 3–14. (b)

McCarthy, D. *Manual for the McCarthy Scales of Children's Abilities.* New York: Psychological Corporation, 1972.

Meeker, M. *The structure of intellect.* Columbus, OH: Merrill, 1969.

Mercer, J. The myth of 3% prevalence. In R. Eyman, C. E. Meyers, & G. Tarjan (eds.), *Sociobehavioral studies in mental retardation.* AAMD. Monograph, 1973.

Merriam, G. & C. *Webster's new collegiate dictionary.* Cambridge, MA: Riverside Press, 1953.

Miller, L. C., Loewenfeld, R., Lindner, R., & Turner, J. Reliability of Koppitz' scoring system for the Bender Gestalt. *Journal of Clinical Psychology,* 1963, *19*, 2111.

Mischel, W. Sex typing and socialization. In J. M. Tanner (ed.), *Carmichael's manual of child psychology.* New York: Wiley, 1970.

Moss, M. H. *Test of Basic Experiences.* Monterey, CA: CTB/McGraw-Hill, 1972.

Mueller, M. *A comparison of the empirical validity of six tests of ability with young educable retardates.* Nashville: Institute on Mental Retardation and Intellectual Development, IMRID Behavioral Science Monograph No. 1, 1965.

Murray, H. *Thematic Apperception Test.* Cambridge, MA: Harvard University Press, 1943.

National Advisory Committee on Handicapped Children. *Special education for handicapped children.* First Annual Report. Washington, DC: U.S. Department of Health, Education and Welfare, January 31, 1968.

National Society for the Prevention of Blindness. *Vision screening in schools.* Publication 257. New York: The Society, 1961.

Nelson, M., & French, J. *Henmon-Nelson Tests of Mental Ability: Primary Form 1.* Boston: Houghton Mifflin, 1974.

Newland, T. E. *Manual for the Blind Learning Aptitude Test: Experimental edition.* Urbana, IL: T. Ernest Newland, 1969.

Newland, T. E. Psychological assessment of exceptional children and youth. In W. Cruickshank (ed.), *Psychology of exceptional children and youth.* Englewood Cliffs, NJ: Prentice-Hall, 1971.

Nihira, K., Foster, R., Shellhaas, M., & Leland, H. *Adaptive Behavior Scales.* Washington, DC: American Association on Mental Deficiency, 1969.

Nunnally, J. *Psychometric theory.* New York: McGraw-Hill, 1967.

Nurss, J. R. & McGauvran, M. E. *Metropolitan readiness tests, teacher's manual, Part II: Interpretation and use of test results (level I).* New York: Harcourt Brace Jovanovich, 1976. (a)

Nurss, J. R. & McGauvran, M. E. *Metropolitan readiness tests, teacher's manual, Part II:*

Interpretation and use of test results (level II). New York: Harcourt Brace Jovanovich, 1976. (b)

O'Neill, J., & Oyer, H. *Applied audiometry.* New York: Dodd, Mead, 1966.

Osgood, C. E. Motivational dynamics of language behavior. In M. R. Jones (ed.), *Nebraska symposium on motivation.* Lincoln, NB: University of Nebraska Press, 1957, 348–424. Cited by Paraskevopoulos & Kirk, 1969. (a)

Osgood, C. E. A behavioristic analysis of perception and language as cognitive phenomena. In *Contemporary approaches to cognition.* Cambridge, MA: Harvard University Press, 1957, 75–118. Cited by Paraskevopoulos & Kirk, 1969. (b)

Otis, A. S., & Lennon, R. T. *Otis-Lennon Mental Ability Test: Technical Handbook.* New York: Harcourt, Brace and World, 1969.

Paraskevopoulos, J. N., & Kirk, S. A. *The development and psychometric characteristics of the Revised Illinois Test of Psycholinguistic Abilities.* Urbana: University of Illinois Press, 1969.

Pennsylvania Association for Retarded Children v. *Commonwealth of Pennsylvania,* 334 F. Supp. 1257 (E.D. Pa. 1971).

Peterson, D. R. *The clinical study of social behavior.* New York: Appleton-Century-Crofts, 1968.

Piers, E., & Harris, D. *The Piers-Harris Children's Self Concept Scale.* Nashville: Counselor Recordings and Tests, 1969.

Piotrowski, Z. *Perceptanalysis.* New York: Macmillan, 1957.

Psychological Corporation. *Test Service Bulletin #54: On telling parents about test results.* New York: Psychological Corporation, 1959.

Quay, H. C. Special education: Assumptions, techniques, and evaluative criteria. *Exceptional Children,* 1973, *40,* 165–170.

Quay, H. C., & Peterson, D. R. *Manual for the Behavior Problem Checklist.* Unpublished manuscript, University of Illinois, 1967.

Reger, S. N., & Newby, H. A. A group pure-tone hearing test. *Journal of Speech and Hearing Disorders,* 1947, *12,* 61–66.

Reitan, R. A research program on the psychological effects of brain lesions in human beings. In N. Ellis (ed.), *International review of research in mental retardation* (vol. 1). New York: Academic Press, 1966.

Resnick, L. B., Wang, M. C., & Kaplan, J. Task analysis in curriculum design: A hierarchically sequenced introductory mathematics curriculum. *Journal of Applied Behavior Analysis,* 1973, *6,* 679–710.

Reynolds, M. Trends in special education: Implications for measurement. In W. Hively & M. Reynolds (eds.), *Domain-referenced testing in special education.* Minneapolis: Leadership Training Institute/Special Education, University of Minnesota, 1975.

Reynolds, M. C., & Balow, B. Categories and variables in special education. *Exceptional Children,* 1972, *38,* 357–366.

Roach, E. F., & Kephart, N. C. *The Purdue Perceptual-Motor Survey.* Columbus, OH: Merrill, 1966.

Roberts, J. *Intellectual development of children by demographic and socioeconomic factors.* Washington, DC: DHEW No. (HSM) 72-1012, 1971.

Robinson, N., & Robinson, H. *The mentally retarded child.* New York: McGraw-Hill, 1976.

Rorschach, H. *Rorschach Ink Blot Test.* New York: Grune and Stratton, 1966.

Rubin, S. A re-evaluation of figure-ground pathology in brain-damaged children. *American Journal of Mental Deficiency,* 1969, *74*, 111–115.

Salvia, J., & Ysseldyke, J. E. Criterion validity of four tests for red-green color blindness. *American Journal of Mental Deficiency,* 1972, *76*, 418–422.

Salvia, J., Ysseldyke, J., & Lee, M. 1972 revision of the Stanford-Binet: A farewell to the mental age. *Psychology in the Schools,* 1975, *12*, 421–422.

Sattler, J. M. Analysis of functions of the 1960 Stanford-Binet Intelligence Scale, Form L-M. *Journal of Clinical Psychology,* 1965, *21*, 173–179.

Sattler, J. M. *Assessment of children's intelligence: revised reprint.* Philadelphia: W.B. Saunders, 1974.

Schaie, K. W., & Roberts, J. *School achievement of children by demographic and socioeconomic factors.* Washington DC: DHEW No. (HSM) 72-1011, 1971.

Shub, A. N., Carlin, J. A., Friedman, R. L., Kaplan, J. M., & Katien, J. C. *Diagnosis: An Instructional Aid (Reading).* Chicago: Science Research Associates, 1973.

Sitlington, P. L. Validity of the Peabody Individual Achievement Test with educable mentally retarded adolescents. Unpublished master's thesis, University of Hawaii, 1970.

Skinner, B. *Verbal behavior.* New York: Appleton-Century-Crofts, 1957.

Slosson, R. L. *Slosson Intelligence Test.* East Aurora, NY: Slosson Educational Publications, 1971.

Slosson, R. L. *Slosson Intelligence Test (SIT) for children and adults.* East Aurora, NY: Slosson Educational Publications, 1963.

Solomon, I. & Starr, B. *School Apperception Method.* New York: Springer, 1968.

Spache, G. D. *Diagnostic Reading Scales.* Monterey, CA: CTB/McGraw-Hill, 1963.

Spivack, G., & Spotts, J. *Devereux Child Behavior Rating Scale.* Devon, PA: Devereux Foundation Press, 1966.

Spivack, G., Spotts, J., & Haimes, P. *Devereux Adolescent Behavior Rating Scale.* Devon, PA: Devereux Foundation Press, 1967.

Spivack, G., & Swift, M. *Devereux Elementary School Behavior Rating Scale.* Devon, PA: Devereux Foundation Press, 1967.

Stevens, S. S. Mathematics, measurement, and psychophysics. In S. S. Stevens (ed.), *Handbook of experimental psychology.* New York: Wiley, 1951.

Sullivan, E. T., Clark, W. W., & Tiegs, E. W. *Short Form Test of Academic Aptitude.* Monterey, CA: CTB/McGraw-Hill, 1970.

Sweney, A., Cattell, R., & Krug, S. *School Motivation Analysis Test.* Champaign, IL: Institute for Personality and Ability Testing, 1970.

Tanner, J. M. Biological bases of development. In J. M. Tanner (ed.), *Carmichael's manual of child psychology.* New York: Wiley, 1970.

Taylor, O., & Swinney, D. The onset of language. In V. Irwin & M. Marge (eds.), *Principles of childhood language disabilities.* Englewood Cliffs, NJ: Prentice-Hall, 1972.

Terman, L., & Merrill, M. *Stanford-Binet Intelligence Scale, 1972 norms edition.* Boston: Houghton Mifflin, 1973.

Thorndike, R., & Hagen, E. *Cognitive Abilities Test.* Boston: Houghton Mifflin, 1971.

Thorndike, R., & Hagen, E. *Measurement and evaluation in psychology and education.* New York: Wiley, 1961.

Thorndike, R., & Hagen, E. *Technical manual: Cognitive Abilities Test.* Boston: Houghton Mifflin, 1974.

Thorpe, L., Clark, W., & Tiegs, E. *California Test of Personality.* Monterey, CA: California Test Bureau, 1953.

Thurstone, L. L. *A factorial study of perception.* Chicago: University of Chicago Press, 1944.

Thurstone, L., & Thurstone, T. *Primary Mental Abilities Test.* Chicago: Science Research Associates, 1965.

Tiegs, E. W., & Clarke, W. W. *California Achievement Test.* Monterey, CA: CTB/McGraw-Hill, 1970.

United States Department of Health, Education and Welfare, Public Health Service. *Vision screening of children.* PHS Document #2042. Washington, DC: United States Public Health Service, 1971.

Urban, W. *Draw-a-Person.* Los Angeles: Western Psychological Services, 1963.

Valett, R. E. A clinical profile for the Stanford-Binet. *Journal of School Psychology,* 1964, *2*, 49–54.

Vinter, R., Sarri, R., Vorwaller, D., & Schafer, E. *Pupil Behavior Inventory.* Ann Arbor: Campus Publishers, 1966.

Walker, D. K. *Socioemotional measures for preschool and kindergarten children.* San Francisco: Jossey-Bass, 1973.

Walker, H. *Walker Problem Behavior Identification Checklist.* Los Angeles: Western Psychological Services, 1970.

Wechsler, D. *Manual for the Wechsler Adult Intelligence Scale.* New York: Psychological Corporation, 1955.

Wechsler, D. *Manual for the Wechsler Preschool and Primary Scale of Intelligence.* New York: Psychological Corporation, 1967.

Wechsler, D. *Manual for the Wechsler Intelligence Scale for Children — Revised.* New York: Psychological Corporation, 1974.

Weinberg, R., & Wood, R. *Observation of pupils and teachers in mainstream and special education settings: Alternative strategies.* Minneapolis: Leadership Training Institute/Special Education, University of Minnesota, 1975.

Wepman, J. M. *Auditory Discrimination Test.* Chicago: Language Research Associates, 1958.

Werner, H., & Strauss, A. A. Pathology of figure-background relation in the child. *Journal of Abnormal and Social Psychology,* 1941, *36*, 236–248.

Wiley, J. A psychology of auditory impairment. In W. Cruickshank (ed.), *Psychology of exceptional children and youth.* Englewood Cliffs, NJ: Prentice-Hall, 1971.

Wittrock, M. C. The evaluation of instruction: Cause-and-effect relations in naturalistic data. In M. C. Wittrock & D. E. Wiley (eds.), *The evaluation of instruction.* New York: Holt, Rinehart and Winston, 1970.

Woodcock, R. W. *Woodcock Reading Mastery Tests.* Circle Pines, MN: American Guidance Service, 1973.

Yates, A. J. The validity of some psychological tests of brain damage. *Psychological Bulletin,* 1954, *51*, 359–379.

Ysseldyke, J. E. Diagnostic-prescriptive teaching: The search for aptitude-treatment interactions. In L. Mann & D. A. Sabatino (eds.), *The first review of special education.* Philadelphia: JSE Press, Grune and Stratton, 1973.

Ysseldyke, J. E. Process remediation with secondary learning disabled children. In L. Goodman & L. Mann (eds.), *Learning disabilities in the secondary school: Title III curricula development for secondary learning disabilities.* King of Prussia, PA: Montgomery County Intermediate Unit and the Pennsylvania Department of Education, 1975.

Ysseldyke, J. E., & Salvia, J. Diagnostic-prescriptive teaching: Two models. *Exceptional Children,* 1974, *41*, 181–186.

Zeaman, D., & House, B. J. The role of attention in retardate discrimination learning. In N. R. Ellis (ed.), *Handbook of mental deficiency.* New York: McGraw-Hill, 1963.

Zweig, R. L., & Associates. *Fountain Valley Teacher Support System in Reading.* Huntington Beach, CA: Richard L. Zweig Associates, 1971.

Appendixes

SOURCE FOR APPENDIX 1: Data are taken from table XXVIII of Fisher and Yates: *Statistical Tables for Biological, Agricultural and Medical Research,* 6th edition, published by Longman Group Ltd., London (previously published by Oliver and Boyd, Edinburgh), and are used by permission of the authors and publishers. Presentation of data used in the present volume is from *Statistics: An Intuitive Approach,* Third Edition, by G. H. Weinberg and J. A. Schumaker. Copyright © 1962, 1969, 1974 by Wadsworth Publishing Company, Inc. Reprinted by permission of the publisher, Brooks/Cole Publishing Company, Monterey, California.

APPENDIX 1   SQUARE ROOTS

n	$\sqrt{n}$	$\sqrt{10n}$	n	$\sqrt{n}$	$\sqrt{10n}$
1.00	1.00000	3.16228	1.50	1.22474	3.87298
1.01	1.00499	3.17805	1.51	1.22882	3.88587
1.02	1.00995	3.19374	1.52	1.23288	3.89872
1.03	1.01489	3.20936	1.53	1.23693	3.91152
1.04	1.01980	3.22490	1.54	1.24097	3.92428
1.05	1.02470	3.24037	1.55	1.24499	3.93700
1.06	1.02956	3.25576	1.56	1.24900	3.94968
1.07	1.03441	3.27109	1.57	1.25300	3.96232
1.08	1.03923	3.28634	1.58	1.25698	3.97492
1.09	1.04403	3.30151	1.59	1.26095	3.98748
1.10	1.04881	3.31662	1.60	1.26491	4.00000
1.11	1.05357	3.33167	1.61	1.26886	4.01248
1.12	1.05830	3.34664	1.62	1.27279	4.02492
1.13	1.06301	3.36155	1.63	1.27671	4.03733
1.14	1.06771	3.37639	1.64	1.28062	4.04969
1.15	1.07238	3.39116	1.65	1.28452	4.06202
1.16	1.07703	3.40588	1.66	1.28841	4.07431
1.17	1.08167	3.42053	1.67	1.29228	4.08656
1.18	1.08628	3.43511	1.68	1.29615	4.09878
1.19	1.09087	3.44964	1.69	1.30000	4.11096
1.20	1.09545	3.46410	1.70	1.30384	4.12311
1.21	1.10000	3.47851	1.71	1.30767	4.13521
1.22	1.10454	3.49285	1.72	1.31149	4.14729
1.23	1.10905	3.50714	1.73	1.31529	4.15933
1.24	1.11355	3.52136	1.74	1.31909	4.17133
1.25	1.11803	3.53553	1.75	1.32288	4.18330
1.26	1.12250	3.54965	1.76	1.32665	4.19524
1.27	1.12694	3.56371	1.77	1.33041	4.20714
1.28	1.13137	3.57771	1.78	1.33417	4.21900
1.29	1.13578	3.59166	1.79	1.33791	4.23084
1.30	1.14018	3.60555	1.80	1.34164	4.24264
1.31	1.14455	3.61939	1.81	1.34536	4.25441
1.32	1.14891	3.63318	1.82	1.34907	4.26615
1.33	1.15326	3.64692	1.83	1.35277	4.27785
1.34	1.15758	3.66060	1.84	1.35647	4.28952
1.35	1.16190	3.67423	1.85	1.36015	4.30116
1.36	1.16619	3.68782	1.86	1.36382	4.31277
1.37	1.17047	3.70135	1.87	1.36748	4.32435
1.38	1.17473	3.71484	1.88	1.37113	4.33590
1.39	1.17898	3.72827	1.89	1.37477	4.34741
1.40	1.18322	3.74166	1.90	1.37840	4.35890
1.41	1.18743	3.75500	1.91	1.38203	4.37035
1.42	1.19164	3.76829	1.92	1.38564	4.38178
1.43	1.19583	3.78153	1.93	1.38924	4.39318
1.44	1.20000	3.79473	1.94	1.39284	4.40454
1.45	1.20416	3.80789	1.95	1.39642	4.41588
1.46	1.20830	3.82099	1.96	1.40000	4.42719
1.47	1.21244	3.83406	1.97	1.40357	4.43847
1.48	1.21655	3.84708	1.98	1.40712	4.44972
1.49	1.22066	3.86005	1.99	1.41067	4.46094

(Cont.)

Appendix 1   *(Cont.)*

n	$\sqrt{n}$	$\sqrt{10n}$	n	$\sqrt{n}$	$\sqrt{10n}$
2.00	1.41421	4.47214	2.50	1.58114	5.00000
2.01	1.41774	4.48330	2.51	1.58430	5.00999
2.02	1.42127	4.49444	2.52	1.58745	5.01996
2.03	1.42478	4.50555	2.53	1.59060	5.02991
2.04	1.42829	4.51664	2.54	1.59374	5.03984
2.05	1.43178	4.52769	2.55	1.59687	5.04975
2.06	1.43527	4.53872	2.56	1.60000	5.05964
2.07	1.43875	4.54973	2.57	1.60312	5.06952
2.08	1.44222	4.56070	2.58	1.60624	5.07937
2.09	1.44568	4.57165	2.59	1.60935	5.08920
2.10	1.44914	4.58258	2.60	1.61245	5.09902
2.11	1.45258	4.59347	2.61	1.61555	5.10882
2.12	1.45602	4.60435	2.62	1.61864	5.11859
2.13	1.45945	4.61519	2.63	1.62173	5.12835
2.14	1.46287	4.62601	2.64	1.62481	5.13809
2.15	1.46629	4.63681	2.65	1.62788	5.14782
2.16	1.46969	4.64758	2.66	1.63095	5.15752
2.17	1.47309	4.65833	2.67	1.63401	5.16720
2.18	1.47648	4.66905	2.68	1.63707	5.17687
2.19	1.47986	4.67974	2.69	1.64012	5.18652
2.20	1.48324	4.69042	2.70	1.64317	5.19615
2.21	1.48661	4.70106	2.71	1.64621	5.20577
2.22	1.48997	4.71169	2.72	1.64924	5.21536
2.23	1.49332	4.72229	2.73	1.65227	5.22494
2.24	1.49666	4.73286	2.74	1.65529	5.23450
2.25	1.50000	4.74342	2.75	1.65831	5.24404
2.26	1.50333	4.75395	2.76	1.66132	5.25357
2.27	1.50665	4.76445	2.77	1.66433	5.26308
2.28	1.50997	4.77493	2.78	1.66733	5.27257
2.29	1.51327	4.78539	2.79	1.67033	5.28205
2.30	1.51658	4.79583	2.80	1.67332	5.29150
2.31	1.51987	4.80625	2.81	1.67631	5.30094
2.32	1.52315	4.81664	2.82	1.67929	5.31037
2.33	1.52643	4.82701	2.83	1.68226	5.31977
2.34	1.52971	4.83735	2.84	1.68523	5.32917
2.35	1.53297	4.84768	2.85	1.68819	5.33854
2.36	1.53623	4.85798	2.86	1.69115	5.34790
2.37	1.53948	4.86826	2.87	1.69411	5.35724
2.38	1.54272	4.87852	2.88	1.69706	5.36656
2.39	1.54596	4.88876	2.89	1.70000	5.37587
2.40	1.54919	4.89898	2.90	1.70294	5.38516
2.41	1.55242	4.90918	2.91	1.70587	5.39444
2.42	1.55563	4.91935	2.92	1.70880	5.40370
2.43	1.55885	4.92950	2.93	1.71172	5.41295
2.44	1.56205	4.93964	2.94	1.71464	5.42218
2.45	1.56525	4.94975	2.95	1.71756	5.43139
2.46	1.56844	4.95984	2.96	1.72047	5.44059
2.47	1.57162	4.96991	2.97	1.72337	5.44977
2.48	1.57480	4.97996	2.98	1.72627	5.45894
2.49	1.57797	4.98999	2.99	1.72916	5.46809

(Cont.)

Appendix 1   (*Cont.*)

n	$\sqrt{n}$	$\sqrt{10n}$	n	$\sqrt{n}$	$\sqrt{10n}$
3.00	1.73205	5.47723	3.50	1.87083	5.91608
3.01	1.73494	5.48635	3.51	1.87350	5.92453
3.02	1.73781	5.49545	3.52	1.87617	5.93296
3.03	1.74069	5.50454	3.53	1.87883	5.94138
3.04	1.74356	5.51362	3.54	1.88149	5.94979
3.05	1.74642	5.52268	3.55	1.88414	5.95819
3.06	1.74929	5.53173	3.56	1.88680	5.96657
3.07	1.75214	5.54076	3.57	1.88944	5.97495
3.08	1.75499	5.54977	3.58	1.89209	5.98331
3.09	1.75784	5.55878	3.59	1.89473	5.99166
3.10	1.76068	5.56776	3.60	1.89737	6.00000
3.11	1.76352	5.57674	3.61	1.90000	6.00833
3.12	1.76635	5.58570	3.62	1.90263	6.01664
3.13	1.76918	5.59464	3.63	1.90526	6.02495
3.14	1.77200	5.60357	3.64	1.90788	6.03324
3.15	1.77482	5.61249	3.65	1.91050	6.04152
3.16	1.77764	5.62139	3.66	1.91311	6.04979
3.17	1.78045	5.63028	3.67	1.91572	6.05805
3.18	1.78326	5.63915	3.68	1.91833	6.06630
3.19	1.78606	5.64801	3.69	1.92094	6.07454
3.20	1.78885	5.65685	3.70	1.92354	6.08276
3.21	1.79165	5.66569	3.71	1.92614	6.09098
3.22	1.79444	5.67450	3.72	1.92873	6.09918
3.23	1.79722	5.68331	3.73	1.93132	6.10737
3.24	1.80000	5.69210	3.74	1.93391	6.11555
3.25	1.80278	5.70088	3.75	1.93649	6.12372
3.26	1.80555	5.70964	3.76	1.93907	6.13188
3.27	1.80831	5.71839	3.77	1.94165	6.14003
3.28	1.81108	5.72713	3.78	1.94422	6.14817
3.29	1.81384	5.73585	3.79	1.94679	6.15630
3.30	1.81659	5.74456	3.80	1.94936	6.16441
3.31	1.81934	5.75326	3.81	1.95192	6.17252
3.32	1.82209	5.76194	3.82	1.95448	6.18061
3.33	1.82483	5.77062	3.83	1.95704	6.18870
3.34	1.82757	5.77927	3.84	1.95959	6.19677
3.35	1.83030	5.78792	3.85	1.96214	6.20484
3.36	1.83303	5.79655	3.86	1.96469	6.21289
3.37	1.83576	5.80517	3.87	1.96723	6.22093
3.38	1.83848	5.81378	3.88	1.96977	6.22896
3.39	1.84120	5.82237	3.89	1.97231	6.23699
3.40	1.84391	5.83095	3.90	1.97484	6.24500
3.41	1.84662	5.83952	3.91	1.97737	6.25300
3.42	1.84932	5.84808	3.92	1.97990	6.26099
3.43	1.85203	5.85662	3.93	1.98242	6.26897
3.44	1.85472	5.86515	3.94	1.98494	6.27694
3.45	1.85742	5.87367	3.95	1.98746	6.28490
3.46	1.86011	5.88218	3.96	1.98997	6.29285
3.47	1.86279	5.89067	3.97	1.99249	6.30079
3.48	1.86548	5.89915	3.98	1.99499	6.30872
3.49	1.86815	5.90762	3.99	1.99750	6.31664

(*Cont.*)

Appendix 1   (*Cont.*)

n	$\sqrt{n}$	$\sqrt{10n}$	n	$\sqrt{n}$	$\sqrt{10n}$
4.00	2.00000	6.32456	4.50	2.12132	6.70820
4.01	2.00250	6.33246	4.51	2.12368	6.71565
4.02	2.00499	6.34035	4.52	2.12603	6.72309
4.03	2.00749	6.34823	4.53	2.12838	6.73053
4.04	2.00998	6.35610	4.54	2.13073	6.73795
4.05	2.01246	6.36396	4.55	2.13307	6.74537
4.06	2.01494	6.37181	4.56	2.13542	6.75278
4.07	2.01742	6.37966	4.57	2.13776	6.76018
4.08	2.01990	6.38749	4.58	2.14009	6.76757
4.09	2.02237	6.39531	4.59	2.14243	6.77495
4.10	2.02485	6.40312	4.60	2.14476	6.78233
4.11	2.02731	6.41093	4.61	2.14709	6.78970
4.12	2.02978	6.41872	4.62	2.14942	6.79706
4.13	2.03224	6.42651	4.63	2.15174	6.80441
4.14	2.03470	6.43428	4.64	2.15407	6.81175
4.15	2.03715	6.44205	4.65	2.15639	6.81909
4.16	2.03961	6.44981	4.66	2.15870	6.82642
4.17	2.04206	6.45755	4.67	2.16102	6.83374
4.18	2.04450	6.46529	4.68	2.16333	6.84105
4.19	2.04695	6.47302	4.69	2.16564	6.84836
4.20	2.04939	6.48074	4.70	2.16795	6.85565
4.21	2.05183	6.48845	4.71	2.17025	6.86294
4.22	2.05426	6.49615	4.72	2.17256	6.87023
4.23	2.05670	6.50384	4.73	2.17486	6.87750
4.24	2.05913	6.51153	4.74	2.17715	6.88477
4.25	2.06155	6.51920	4.75	2.17945	6.89202
4.26	2.06398	6.52687	4.76	2.18174	6.89928
4.27	2.06640	6.53452	4.77	2.18403	6.90652
4.28	2.06882	6.54217	4.78	2.18632	6.91375
4.29	2.07123	6.54981	4.79	2.18861	6.92098
4.30	2.07364	6.55744	4.80	2.19089	6.92820
4.31	2.07605	6.56506	4.81	2.19317	6.93542
4.32	2.07846	6.57267	4.82	2.19545	6.94262
4.33	2.08087	6.58027	4.83	2.19773	6.94982
4.34	2.08327	6.58787	4.84	2.20000	6.95701
4.35	2.08567	6.59545	4.85	2.20227	6.96419
4.36	2.08806	6.60303	4.86	2.20454	6.97137
4.37	2.09045	6.61060	4.87	2.20681	6.97854
4.38	2.09284	6.61816	4.88	2.20907	6.98570
4.39	2.09523	6.62571	4.89	2.21133	6.99285
4.40	2.09762	6.63325	4.90	2.21359	7.00000
4.41	2.10000	6.64078	4.91	2.21585	7.00714
4.42	2.10238	6.64831	4.92	2.21811	7.01427
4.43	2.10476	6.65582	4.93	2.22036	7.02140
4.44	2.10713	6.66333	4.94	2.22261	7.02851
4.45	2.10950	6.67083	4.95	2.22486	7.03562
4.46	2.11187	6.67832	4.96	2.22711	7.04273
4.47	2.11424	6.68581	4.97	2.22935	7.04982
4.48	2.11660	6.69328	4.98	2.23159	7.05691
4.49	2.11896	6.70075	4.99	2.23383	7.06399

(*Cont.*)

Appendix 1   (*Cont.*)

n	$\sqrt{n}$	$\sqrt{10n}$	n	$\sqrt{n}$	$\sqrt{10n}$
5.00	2.23607	7.07107	5.50	2.34521	7.41620
5.01	2.23830	7.07814	5.51	2.34734	7.42294
5.02	2.24054	7.08520	5.52	2.34947	7.42967
5.03	2.24277	7.09225	5.53	2.35160	7.43640
5.04	2.24499	7.09930	5.54	2.35372	7.44312
5.05	2.24722	7.10634	5.55	2.35584	7.44983
5.06	2.24944	7.11337	5.56	2.35797	7.45654
5.07	2.25167	7.12039	5.57	2.36008	7.46324
5.08	2.25389	7.12741	5.58	2.36220	7.46994
5.09	2.25610	7.13442	5.59	2.36432	7.47663
5.10	2.25832	7.14143	5.60	2.36643	7.48331
5.11	2.26053	7.14843	5.61	2.36854	7.48999
5.12	2.26274	7.15542	5.62	2.37065	7.49667
5.13	2.26495	7.16240	5.63	2.37276	7.50333
5.14	2.26716	7.16938	5.64	2.37487	7.50999
5.15	2.26936	7.17635	5.65	2.37697	7.51665
5.16	2.27156	7.18331	5.66	2.37908	7.52330
5.17	2.27376	7.19027	5.67	2.38118	7.52994
5.18	2.27596	7.19722	5.68	2.38328	7.53658
5.19	2.27816	7.20417	5.69	2.38537	7.54321
5.20	2.28035	7.21110	5.70	2.38747	7.54983
5.21	2.28254	7.21803	5.71	2.38956	7.55645
5.22	2.28473	7.22496	5.72	2.39165	7.56307
5.23	2.28692	7.23187	5.73	2.39374	7.56968
5.24	2.28910	7.23878	5.74	2.39583	7.57628
5.25	2.29129	7.24569	5.75	2.39792	7.58288
5.26	2.29347	7.25259	5.76	2.40000	7.58947
5.27	2.29565	7.25948	5.77	2.40208	7.59605
5.28	2.29783	7.26636	5.78	2.40416	7.60263
5.29	2.30000	7.27324	5.79	2.40624	7.60920
5.30	2.30217	7.28011	5.80	2.40832	7.61577
5.31	2.30434	7.28697	5.81	2.41039	7.62234
5.32	2.30651	7.29383	5.82	2.41247	7.62889
5.33	2.30868	7.30068	5.83	2.41454	7.63544
5.34	2.31084	7.30753	5.84	2.41661	7.64199
5.35	2.31301	7.31437	5.85	2.41868	7.64853
5.36	2.31517	7.32120	5.86	2.42074	7.65506
5.37	2.31733	7.32803	5.87	2.42281	7.66159
5.38	2.31948	7.33485	5.88	2.42487	7.66812
5.39	2.32164	7.34166	5.89	2.42693	7.67463
5.40	2.32379	7.34847	5.90	2.42899	7.68115
5.41	2.32594	7.35527	5.91	2.43105	7.68765
5.42	2.32809	7.36206	5.92	2.43311	7.69415
5.43	2.33024	7.36885	5.93	2.43516	7.70065
5.44	2.33238	7.37564	5.94	2.43721	7.70714
5.45	2.33452	7.38241	5.95	2.43926	7.71362
5.46	2.33666	7.38918	5.96	2.44131	7.72010
5.47	2.33880	7.39594	5.97	2.44336	7.72658
5.48	2.34094	7.40270	5.98	2.44540	7.73305
5.49	2.34307	7.40945	5.99	2.44745	7.73951

(*Cont.*)

Appendix 1   *(Cont.)*

n	$\sqrt{n}$	$\sqrt{10n}$	n	$\sqrt{n}$	$\sqrt{10n}$
6.00	2.44949	7.74597	6.50	2.54951	8.06226
6.01	2.45153	7.75242	6.51	2.55147	8.06846
6.02	2.45357	7.75887	6.52	2.55343	8.07465
6.03	2.45561	7.76531	6.53	2.55539	8.08084
6.04	2.45764	7.77174	6.54	2.55734	8.08703
6.05	2.45967	7.77817	6.55	2.55930	8.09321
6.06	2.46171	7.78460	6.56	2.56125	8.09938
6.07	2.46374	7.79102	6.57	2.56320	8.10555
6.08	2.46577	7.79744	6.58	2.56515	8.11172
6.09	2.46779	7.80385	6.59	2.56710	8.11788
6.10	2.46982	7.81025	6.60	2.56905	8.12404
6.11	2.47184	7.81665	6.61	2.57099	8.13019
6.12	2.47386	7.82304	6.62	2.57294	8.13634
6.13	2.47588	7.82943	6.63	2.57488	8.14248
6.14	2.47790	7.83582	6.64	2.57682	8.14862
6.15	2.47992	7.84219	6.65	2.57876	8.15475
6.16	2.48193	7.84857	6.66	2.58070	8.16088
6.17	2.48395	7.85493	6.67	2.58263	8.16701
6.18	2.48596	7.86130	6.68	2.58457	8.17313
6.19	2.48797	7.86766	6.69	2.58650	8.17924
6.20	2.48998	7.87401	6.70	2.58844	8.18535
6.21	2.49199	7.88036	6.71	2.59037	8.19146
6.22	2.49399	7.88670	6.72	2.59230	8.19756
6.23	2.49600	7.89303	6.73	2.59422	8.20366
6.24	2.49800	7.89937	6.74	2.59615	8.20975
6.25	2.50000	7.90569	6.75	2.59808	8.21584
6.26	2.50200	7.91202	6.76	2.60000	8.22192
6.27	2.50400	7.91833	6.77	2.60192	8.22800
6.28	2.50599	7.92465	6.78	2.60384	8.23408
6.29	2.50799	7.93095	6.79	2.60576	8.24015
6.30	2.50998	7.93725	6.80	2.60768	8.24621
6.31	2.51197	7.94355	6.81	2.60960	8.25227
6.32	2.51396	7.94984	6.82	2.61151	8.25833
6.33	2.51595	7.95613	6.83	2.61343	8.26438
6.34	2.51794	7.96241	6.84	2.61534	8.27043
6.35	2.51992	7.96869	6.85	2.61725	8.27647
6.36	2.52190	7.97496	6.86	2.61916	8.28251
6.37	2.52389	7.98123	6.87	2.62107	8.28855
6.38	2.52587	7.98749	6.88	2.62298	8.29458
6.39	2.52784	7.99375	6.89	2.62488	8.30060
6.40	2.52982	8.00000	6.90	2.62679	8.30662
6.41	2.53180	8.00625	6.91	2.62869	8.31264
6.42	2.53377	8.01249	6.92	2.63059	8.31865
6.43	2.53574	8.01873	6.93	2.63249	8.32466
6.44	2.53772	8.02496	6.94	2.63439	8.33067
6.45	2.53969	8.03119	6.95	2.63629	8.33667
6.46	2.54165	8.03741	6.96	2.63818	8.34266
6.47	2.54362	8.04363	6.97	2.64008	8.34865
6.48	2.54558	8.04984	6.98	2.64197	8.35464
6.49	2.54755	8.05605	6.99	2.64386	8.36062

(Cont.)

Appendix 1   *(Cont.)*

n	$\sqrt{n}$	$\sqrt{10n}$	n	$\sqrt{n}$	$\sqrt{10n}$
7.00	2.64575	8.36660	7.50	2.73861	8.66025
7.01	2.64764	8.37257	7.51	2.74044	8.66603
7.02	2.64953	8.37854	7.52	2.74226	8.67179
7.03	2.65141	8.38451	7.53	2.74408	8.67756
7.04	2.65330	8.39047	7.54	2.74591	8.68332
7.05	2.65518	8.39643	7.55	2.74773	8.68907
7.06	2.65707	8.40238	7.56	2.74955	8.69483
7.07	2.65895	8.40833	7.57	2.75136	8.70057
7.08	2.66083	8.41427	7.58	2.75318	8.70632
7.09	2.66271	8.42021	7.59	2.75500	8.71206
7.10	2.66458	8.42615	7.60	2.75681	8.71780
7.11	2.66646	8.43208	7.61	2.75862	8.72353
7.12	2.66833	8.43801	7.62	2.76043	8.72926
7.13	2.67021	8.44393	7.63	2.76225	8.73499
7.14	2.67208	8.44985	7.64	2.76405	8.74071
7.15	2.67395	8.45577	7.65	2.76586	8.74643
7.16	2.67582	8.46168	7.66	2.76767	8.75214
7.17	2.67769	8.46759	7.67	2.76948	8.75785
7.18	2.67955	8.47349	7.68	2.77128	8.76356
7.19	2.68142	8.47939	7.69	2.77308	8.76926
7.20	2.68328	8.48528	7.70	2.77489	8.77496
7.21	2.68514	8.49117	7.71	2.77669	8.78066
7.22	2.68701	8.49806	7.72	2.77849	8.78635
7.23	2.68887	8.50294	7.73	2.78029	8.79204
7.24	2.69072	8.50882	7.74	2.78209	8.79773
7.25	2.69258	8.51469	7.75	2.78388	8.80341
7.26	2.69444	8.52056	7.76	2.78568	8.80909
7.27	2.69629	8.52643	7.77	2.78747	8.81476
7.28	2.69815	8.53229	7.78	2.78927	8.82043
7.29	2.70000	8.53815	7.79	2.79106	8.82610
7.30	2.70185	8.54400	7.80	2.79285	8.83176
7.31	2.70370	8.54985	7.81	2.79464	8.83742
7.32	2.70555	8.55570	7.82	2.79643	8.84308
7.33	2.70740	8.56154	7.83	2.79821	8.84873
7.34	2.70924	8.56738	7.84	2.80000	8.85438
7.35	2.71109	8.57321	7.85	2.80179	8.86002
7.36	2.71293	8.57904	7.86	2.80357	8.86566
7.37	2.71477	8.58487	7.87	2.80535	8.87130
7.38	2.71662	8.59069	7.88	2.80713	8.87694
7.39	2.71846	8.59651	7.89	2.80891	8.88257
7.40	2.72029	8.60233	7.90	2.81069	8.88819
7.41	2.72213	8.60814	7.91	2.81247	8.89382
7.42	2.72397	8.61394	7.92	2.81425	8.89944
7.43	2.72580	8.61974	7.93	2.81603	8.90505
7.44	2.72764	8.62554	7.94	2.81780	8.91067
7.45	2.72947	8.63134	7.95	2.81957	8.91628
7.46	2.73130	8.63713	7.96	2.82135	8.92188
7.47	2.73313	8.64292	7.97	2.82312	8.92749
7.48	2.73496	8.64870	7.98	2.82489	8.93308
7.49	2.73679	8.65448	7.99	2.82666	8.93868

(Cont.)

Appendix 1   (*Cont.*)

n	$\sqrt{n}$	$\sqrt{10n}$	n	$\sqrt{n}$	$\sqrt{10n}$
8.00	2.82843	8.94427	8.50	2.91548	9.21954
8.01	2.83019	8.94986	8.51	2.91719	9.22497
8.02	2.83196	8.95545	8.52	2.91890	9.23038
8.03	2.83373	8.96103	8.53	2.92062	9.23580
8.04	2.83549	8.96660	8.54	2.92233	9.24121
8.05	2.83725	8.97218	8.55	2.92404	9.24662
8.06	2.83901	8.97775	8.56	2.92575	9.25203
8.07	2.84077	8.98332	8.57	2.92746	9.25743
8.08	2.84253	8.98888	8.58	2.92916	9.26283
8.09	2.84429	8.99444	8.59	2.93087	9.26823
8.10	2.84605	9.00000	8.60	2.93258	9.27362
8.11	2.84781	9.00555	8.61	2.93428	9.27901
8.12	2.84956	9.01110	8.62	2.93598	9.28440
8.13	2.85132	9.01665	8.63	2.93769	9.28978
8.14	2.85307	9.02219	8.64	2.93939	9.29516
8.15	2.85482	9.02274	8.65	2.94109	9.30054
8.16	2.85657	9.03327	8.66	2.94279	9.30591
8.17	2.85832	9.03881	8.67	2.94449	9.31128
8.18	2.86007	9.04434	8.68	2.94618	9.31665
8.19	2.86182	9.04986	8.69	2.94788	9.32202
8.20	2.86356	9.05539	8.70	2.94958	9.32738
8.21	2.86531	9.06091	8.71	2.95127	9.33274
8.22	2.86705	9.06642	8.72	2.95296	9.33809
8.23	2.86880	9.07193	8.73	2.95466	9.34345
8.24	2.87054	9.07744	8.74	2.95635	9.34880
8.25	2.87228	9.08295	8.75	2.95804	9.35414
8.26	2.87402	9.08845	8.76	2.95973	9.35949
8.27	2.87576	9.09395	8.77	2.96142	9.36483
8.28	2.87750	9.09945	8.78	2.96311	9.37017
8.29	2.87924	9.10494	8.79	2.96479	9.37550
8.30	2.88097	9.11043	8.80	2.96648	9.38083
8.31	2.88271	9.11592	8.81	2.96816	9.38616
8.32	2.88444	9.12140	8.82	2.96985	9.39149
8.33	2.88617	9.12688	8.83	2.97153	9.39681
8.34	2.88791	9.13236	8.84	2.97321	9.40213
8.35	2.88964	9.13783	8.85	2.97489	9.40744
8.36	2.89137	9.14330	8.86	2.97658	9.41276
8.37	2.89310	9.14877	8.87	2.97825	9.41807
8.38	2.89482	9.15423	8.88	2.97993	9.42338
8.39	2.89655	9.15969	8.89	2.98161	9.42868
8.40	2.89828	9.16515	8.90	2.98329	9.43398
8.41	2.90000	9.17061	8.91	2.98496	9.43928
8.42	2.90172	9.17606	8.92	2.98664	9.44458
8.42	2.90345	9.18150	8.93	2.98831	9.44987
8.44	2.90517	9.18695	8.94	2.98998	9.45516
8.45	2.90689	9.19239	8.95	2.99166	9.46044
8.46	2.90861	9.19783	8.96	2.99333	9.46573
8.47	2.91033	9.20326	8.97	2.99500	9.47101
8.48	2.91204	9.20869	8.98	2.99666	9.47629
8.49	2.91376	9.21412	8.99	2.99833	9.48156

(*Cont.*)

Appendix 1   *(Cont.)*

n	$\sqrt{n}$	$\sqrt{10n}$	n	$\sqrt{n}$	$\sqrt{10n}$
9.00	3.00000	9.48683	9.50	3.08221	9.74679
9.01	3.00167	9.49210	9.51	3.08383	9.75192
9.02	3.00333	9.49737	9.52	3.08545	9.75705
9.03	3.00500	9.50263	9.53	3.08707	9.76217
9.04	3.00666	9.50789	9.54	3.08869	9.76729
9.05	3.00832	9.51315	9.55	3.09031	9.77241
9.06	3.00998	9.51840	9.56	3.09192	9.77753
9.07	3.01164	9.52365	9.57	3.09354	9.78264
9.08	3.01330	9.52890	9.58	3.09516	9.78775
9.09	3.01496	9.53415	9.59	3.09677	9.79285
9.10	3.01662	9.53939	9.60	3.09839	9.79796
9.11	3.01828	9.54463	9.61	3.10000	9.80306
9.12	3.01993	9.54987	9.62	3.10161	9.80816
9.13	3.02159	9.55510	9.63	3.10322	9.81326
9.14	3.02324	9.56033	9.64	3.10483	9.81835
9.15	3.02490	9.56556	9.65	3.10644	9.82344
9.16	3.02655	9.57079	9.66	3.10805	9.82853
9.17	3.02820	9.57601	9.67	3.10966	9.83362
9.18	3.02985	9.58123	9.68	3.11127	9.83870
9.19	3.03150	9.58645	9.69	3.11288	9.84378
9.20	3.03315	9.59166	9.70	3.11448	9.84886
9.21	3.03480	9.59687	9.71	3.11609	9.85393
9.22	3.03645	9.60208	9.72	3.11769	9.85901
9.23	3.03809	9.60729	9.73	3.11929	9.86408
9.24	3.03974	9.61249	9.74	3.12090	9.86914
9.25	3.04138	9.61769	9.75	3.12250	9.87421
9.26	3.04302	9.62289	9.76	3.12410	9.87927
9.27	3.04467	9.62808	9.77	3.12570	9.88433
9.28	3.04631	9.63328	9.78	3.12730	9.88939
9.29	3.04795	9.63846	9.79	3.12890	9.89444
9.30	3.04959	9.64365	9.80	3.13050	9.89949
9.31	3.05123	9.64883	9.81	3.13209	9.90454
9.32	3.05287	9.65401	9.82	3.13369	9.90959
9.33	3.05450	9.65919	9.83	3.13528	9.91464
9.34	3.05614	9.66437	9.84	3.13688	9.91968
9.35	3.05778	9.66954	9.85	3.13847	9.92472
9.36	3.05941	9.67471	9.86	3.14006	9.92975
9.37	3.06105	9.67988	9.87	3.14166	9.93479
9.38	3.06268	9.68504	9.88	3.14325	9.93982
9.39	3.06431	9.69020	9.89	3.14484	9.94485
9.40	3.06594	9.69536	9.90	3.14643	9.94987
9.41	3.06757	9.70052	9.91	3.14802	9.95490
9.42	3.06920	9.70567	9.92	3.14960	9.95992
9.43	3.07083	9.71082	9.93	3.15119	9.96494
9.44	3.07246	9.71597	9.94	3.15278	9.96995
9.45	3.07409	9.72111	9.95	3.15436	9.97497
9.46	3.07571	9.72625	9.96	3.15555	9.97998
9.47	3.07734	9.73139	9.97	3.15753	9.98499
9.48	3.07896	9.73653	9.98	3.15911	9.98999
9.49	3.08058	9.74166	9.99	3.16070	9.99500
			10.00	3.16228	10.0000

APPENDIX 2   AREAS OF THE NORMAL CURVE

Area equals the proportion of cases between the z-score and the mean; extreme area equals .5000 less the proportion of cases between the z-score and the mean.

z	.00	.01	.02	.03	.04	.05	.06	.07	.08	.09
0.0	.0000	.0040	.0080	.0120	.0160	.0199	.0239	.0279	.0319	.0359
0.1	.0398	.0438	.0478	.0517	.0557	.0596	.0636	.0675	.0714	.0753
0.2	.0793	.0832	.0871	.0910	.0948	.0987	.1026	.1064	.1103	.1141
0.3	.1179	.1217	.1255	.1293	.1331	.1368	.1406	.1443	.1480	.1517
0.4	.1554	.1591	.1628	.1664	.1700	.1736	.1772	.1808	.1844	.1879
0.5	.1915	.1950	.1985	.2019	.2054	.2088	.2123	.2157	.2190	.2224
0.6	.2257	.2291	.2324	.2357	.2389	.2422	.2454	.2486	.2517	.2549
0.7	.2580	.2611	.2642	.2673	.2704	.2734	.2764	.2794	.2823	.2852
0.8	.2881	.2910	.2939	.2967	.2995	.3023	.3051	.3078	.3106	.3133
0.9	.3159	.3186	.3212	.3238	.3264	.3289	.3315	.3340	.3365	.3389
1.0	.3413	.3438	.3461	.3485	.3508	.3531	.3554	.3577	.3599	.3621
1.1	.3643	.3665	.3686	.3708	.3729	.3749	.3770	.3790	.3810	.3830
1.2	.3849	.3869	.3888	.3907	.3925	.3944	.3962	.3980	.3997	.4015
1.3	.4032	.4049	.4066	.4082	.4099	.4115	.4131	.4147	.4162	.4177
1.4	.4192	.4207	.4222	.4236	.4251	.4265	.4279	.4292	.4306	.4319
1.5	.4332	.4345	.4357	.4370	.4382	.4394	.4406	.4418	.4429	.4441
1.6	.4452	.4463	.4474	.4484	.4495	.4505	.4515	.4525	.4535	.4545
1.7	.4554	.4564	.4573	.4582	.4591	.4599	.4608	.4616	.4625	.4633
1.8	.4641	.4649	.4656	.4664	.4671	.4678	.4686	.4693	.4699	.4706
1.9	.4713	.4719	.4726	.4732	.4738	.4744	.4750	.4756	.4761	.4767
2.0	.4772	.4778	.4783	.4788	.4793	.4798	.4803	.4808	.4812	.4817
2.1	.4821	.4826	.4830	.4834	.4838	.4842	.4846	.4850	.4854	.4857
2.2	.4861	.4864	.4868	.4871	.4875	.4878	.4881	.4884	.4887	.4890
2.3	.4893	.4896	.4898	.4901	.4904	.4906	.4909	.4911	.4913	.4916
2.4	.4918	.4920	.4922	.4925	.4927	.4929	.4931	.4932	.4934	.4936
2.5	.4938	.4940	.4941	.4943	.4945	.4946	.4948	.4949	.4951	.4952
2.6	.4953	.4955	.4956	.4957	.4959	.4960	.4961	.4962	.4963	.4964
2.7	.4965	.4966	.4967	.4968	.4969	.4970	.4971	.4972	.4973	.4974
2.8	.4974	.4975	.4976	.4977	.4977	.4978	.4979	.4979	4980	.4981
2.9	.4981	.4982	.4982	.4983	.4984	.4984	.4985	.4985	.4986	.4986
3.0	.4987	.4987	.4987	.4988	.4988	.4989	.4989	.4989	.4990	.4990

SOURCE: Data for Appendix 2 are taken from table VIII$_4$ of Fisher and Yates: *Statistical Tables for Biological, Agricultural and Medical Research*, 6th edition, published by Longman Group Ltd., London (previously published by Oliver and Boyd, Edinburgh), and are used by permission of the authors and publishers. Presentation of data used in the present volume is from *Statistics: An Intuitive Approach,* Third Edition, by G. H. Weinberg and J. A. Schumaker. Copyright © 1962, 1969, 1974 by Wadsworth Publishing Company, Inc. Reprinted by permission of the publisher, Brooks/Cole Publishing Company, Monterey, California.

APPENDIX 3   PERCENTILE RANKS FOR z-SCORES OF NORMAL CURVES

z	AREA[a]	z	AREA[a]	z	AREA[a]
−4.0	.000	−1.0	.159	2.0	.977
−3.9	.000	−0.9	.184	2.1	.982
−3.8	.000	−0.8	.212	2.2	.986
−3.7	.000	−0.7	.242	2.3	.989
−3.6	.000	−0.6	.274	2.4	.992
−3.5	.000	−0.5	.308	2.5	.994
−3.4	.000	−0.4	.345	2.6	.995
−3.3	.001	−0.3	.382	2.7	.996
−3.2	.001	−0.2	.421	2.8	.997
−3.1	.001	−0.1	.460	2.9	.998
−3.0	.001	0.0	.500	3.0	.999
−2.9	.002	0.1	.540	3.1	.999
−2.8	.003	0.2	.579	3.2	.999
−2.7	.004	0.3	.618	3.3	.999
−2.6	.005	0.4	.655	3.4	1.000
−2.5	.006	0.5	.692	3.5	1.000
−2.4	.008	0.6	.726	3.6	1.000
−2.3	.011	0.7	.758	3.7	1.000
−2.2	.014	0.8	.788	3.8	1.000
−2.1	.018	0.9	.816	3.9	1.000
−2.0	.023	1.0	.841	4.0	1.000
−1.9	.029	1.1	.864		
−1.8	.036	1.2	.885		
−1.7	.045	1.3	.903		
−1.6	.055	1.4	.919		
−1.5	.067	1.5	.933		
−1.4	.081	1.6	.945		
−1.3	.097	1.7	.955		
−1.2	.115	1.8	.964		
−1.1	.136	1.9	.971		

[a] Move decimal two places to the right for the percentile rank. Values are rounded to three places.

SOURCE: Adapted from table VIII$_4$ of Fisher and Yates: *Statistical Tables for Biological, Agricultural and Medical Research*, 6th edition, published by Longman Group Ltd., London (previously published by Oliver and Boyd, Edinburgh), by permission of the authors and publishers. Presentation of data used in the present volume is from *Statistics: An Intuitive Approach*, Third Edition, by G. H. Weinberg and J. A. Schumaker. Copyright © 1962, 1969, 1974 by Wadsworth Publishing Company, Inc. Reprinted by permission of the publisher, Brooks/Cole Publishing Company, Monterey, California.

APPENDIX 4   LIST OF EQUATIONS USED IN THE TEXT

LOCATION IN TEXT	TERM DEFINED	EQUATION
(4.1)	Mean	$\bar{X} = \dfrac{\Sigma X}{N}$
(4.2)	Variance	$S^2 = \dfrac{\Sigma(X - \bar{X})^2}{N}$ or $S^2 = \dfrac{\Sigma X^2}{N} - \left(\dfrac{\Sigma X}{N}\right)^2$
p. 52	Pearson product-moment correlation coefficient, where X and Y are scores on two tests	$r = \dfrac{N\Sigma XY - (\Sigma X)(\Sigma Y)}{\sqrt{N\Sigma X^2 - (\Sigma X)^2}\ \sqrt{N\Sigma Y^2 - (\Sigma Y)^2}}$ or $r = \dfrac{\Sigma Z_x Z_y}{n}$
p. 65	Percentile rank for a particular score	%ile = percent of people scoring below the score $+ \frac{1}{2}$ percent of people obtaining the score
(5.1)	z-score	$z = \dfrac{X - \bar{X}}{S}$
(5.2)	Any standard score	$SS = \bar{X}_{ss} + (S_{ss})(z)$
(6.2)	Coefficient alpha	$r_{aa} = \dfrac{k}{k - 1}\left(1 - \dfrac{\Sigma S^2_{\text{items}}}{S^2_{\text{test}}}\right)$
(6.3)	Spearman-Brown correction for test length	$r_{xx} = \dfrac{2r_{(1/2)(1/2)}}{1 + r_{(1/2)(1/2)}}$
(6.4)	Standard error of measurement	$SEM = S\sqrt{1 - r_{xx}}$

APPENDIX 4 *(Cont.)*

LOCATION IN TEXT	TERM DEFINED	EQUATION
(6.5)	Estimated true score	$X' = \bar{X} + (r_{xx})(X - \bar{X})$
(6.6)	Lower and upper limits of a confidence interval, where z-score determines level of confidence	Lower limit $= X' - (z)(\text{SEM})$ Upper limit $= X' + (z)(\text{SEM})$
(6.7)	Reliability of a difference	$r_{xx(\text{dif})} = \dfrac{\frac{1}{2}(r_{aa} + r_{bb}) - r_{ab}}{1 - r_{ab}}$
(6.8)	Standard deviation of a difference	$S_{\text{dif}} = \sqrt{S_a{}^2 + S_b{}^2 - 2r_{ab}S_a S_b}$
(6.9)	Standard error of measurement of a difference	$\text{SEM}_{\text{dif}} = \sqrt{S_a{}^2 + S_b{}^2 - 2r_{ab}S_a S_b} \times \sqrt{1 - \dfrac{\frac{1}{2}(r_{aa} + r_{bb}) - r_{ab}}{1 - r_{ab}}}$
(6.10)	Estimated true difference	$d' = (\text{obtained difference})(r_{xx(\text{dif})})$

APPENDIX 5   LIST OF PUBLISHERS

Individuals wishing to purchase test specimen kits or secure additional test materials can write the test publisher. The following is a list of the publishers whose tests are reviewed in this book.

American Association on Mental Deficiency, 5201 Connecticut Ave. N.W., Washington, DC 20015

American Guidance Service, Inc., Publishers Bldg., Circle Pines, MN 55014

American Printing House for the Blind, 1839 Frankfort Ave., Louisville, KY 40206

American Psychological Association, Inc., 1200 17th St. N.W., Washington, DC 20036

Arden Press, P.O. Box 804, El Monte, CA 91734

Bausch & Lomb, Inc., Rochester, NY 14602

Bobbs-Merrill Co., Inc., 4300 West 62nd St., Indianapolis, IN 46268

California Test Bureau/McGraw-Hill, Del Monte Research Park, Monterey, CA 93940

Campus Publishers, 711 North University Ave., Ann Arbor, MI 48108

Consulting Psychologists Press, Inc., 577 College Ave., Palo Alto, CA 94306

Counselor Recordings and Tests, Box 6184, Acklen Station, Nashville, TN 37212

The Devereux Foundation Press, Devon, PA 19333

Educational and Industrial Testing Service, P.O. Box 7234, San Diego, CA 92107

Educational Testing Service, Princeton, NJ 08540

Follett Educational Corp., 1010 West Washington Blvd., Chicago, IL 60607

Gallaudet College Book Store, Kendall Green, Washington, DC 20002

Grune & Stratton, Inc., 757 Third Ave., New York, NY 10017

Harcourt Brace Jovanovich, Inc., 757 Third Ave., New York, NY 10017

Harvard University Press, 79 Garden St., Cambridge, MA 02138

Marshall S. Hiskey, 5040 Baldwin, Lincoln, NB 68508

Houghton Mifflin Company, Test Editorial Offices, P.O. Box 1970, Iowa City, IA 52240

Institute for Personality and Ability Testing, 1602 Coronado Drive, Champaign, IL 61820

Ladoca Project and Publishing Foundation, Inc., East 51st Ave. and Lincoln St., Denver, CO 80216

Language Research Associates, 950 E. 59th St., Chicago, IL 60621

Charles E. Merrill Publishing Co., 1300 Alum Creek Drive, Columbus, OH 43216

T. Ernest Newland, 702 South Race St., Urbana, IL 61801

Appendix 5   (*Cont.*)

NFER Publishing Company Ltd., 2 Jennings Bldgs., Thames Ave., Windsor, Berks. SL4 1QS, England

Personnel Press, Inc., 20 Nassau St., Princeton, NJ 08540

Psychodynamics Instruments, Ann Arbor, MI 48108

The Psychological Corporation, Division of Harcourt Brace Jovanovich, 304 East 45th St., New York, NY 10017

Psychologists and Educators Press, 419 Pendik, Jacksonville, IL 62650

Random House, Inc., 201 East 50th St., New York, NY 10022

Russell Sage Foundation, 230 Park Ave., New York, NY 10017

Science Research Associates, Inc., 250 East Erie St., Chicago, IL 60611

Slosson Educational Publications, 140 Pine St., East Aurora, NY 14052

Stoelting Co., 424 North Homan Ave., Chicago, IL 60624

Teachers College Press, 502 West 121st St., New York, NY 10027

The University of Illinois Press, Urbana, IL 61801

Western Psychological Services, 12031 Wilshire Blvd., Los Angeles, CA 90025

Richard L. Zweig Associates, Inc., 20800 Beach Blvd., Huntington Beach, CA 92648

Index of Names

Subject Index